T0321968

Handbook of Research on Advanced Data Mining Techniques and Applications for Business Intelligence

Shrawan Kumar Trivedi
BML Munjal University, India

Shubhamoy Dey
Indian Institute of Management Indore, India

Anil Kumar
BML Munjal University, India

Tapan Kumar Panda
Jindal Global Business School, India

A volume in the Advances in Business
Information Systems and Analytics (ABISA)
Book Series

www.igi-global.com

Published in the United States of America by
  IGI Global
  Business Science Reference (an imprint of IGI Global)
  701 E. Chocolate Avenue
  Hershey PA, USA 17033
  Tel: 717-533-8845
  Fax: 717-533-8661
  E-mail: cust@igi-global.com
  Web site: http://www.igi-global.com

Library of Congress Cataloging-in-Publication Data

Names: Trivedi, Shrawan Kumar, 1985- editor.
Title: Handbook of research on advanced data mining techniques and
  applications for business intelligence / Shrawan Kumar Trivedi, Shubhamoy
  Dey, Anil Kumar, and Tapan Kumar Panda, editors.
Description: Hershey, PA : Business Science Reference, [2017]
Identifiers: LCCN 2016052414| ISBN 9781522520313 (hardcover) | ISBN
  9781522520320 (ebook)
Subjects: LCSH: Business intelligence--Data processing. | Data mining. | Big
  data.
Classification: LCC HD38.7 .H3624 2017 | DDC 658.4/7202856312--dc23 LC record available at https://lccn.loc.
gov/2016052414

This book is published in the IGI Global book series Advances in Business Information Systems and Analytics (ABISA) (ISSN: 2327-3275; eISSN: 2327-3283)

British Cataloguing in Publication Data
A Cataloguing in Publication record for this book is available from the British Library.

For electronic access to this publication, please contact: eresources@igi-global.com.

Advances in Business Information Systems and Analytics (ABISA) Book Series

Madjid Tavana
La Salle University, USA

ISSN:2327-3275
EISSN:2327-3283

MISSION

The successful development and management of information systems and business analytics is crucial to the success of an organization. New technological developments and methods for data analysis have allowed organizations to not only improve their processes and allow for greater productivity, but have also provided businesses with a venue through which to cut costs, plan for the future, and maintain competitive advantage in the information age.

The **Advances in Business Information Systems and Analytics (ABISA) Book Series** aims to present diverse and timely research in the development, deployment, and management of business information systems and business analytics for continued organizational development and improved business value.

COVERAGE

- Decision Support Systems
- Legal information systems
- Business Intelligence
- Data Analytics
- Business Process Management
- Business Information Security
- Management information systems
- Data Management
- Strategic Information Systems
- Statistics

IGI Global is currently accepting manuscripts for publication within this series. To submit a proposal for a volume in this series, please contact our Acquisition Editors at Acquisitions@igi-global.com or visit: http://www.igi-global.com/publish/.

Titles in this Series

For a list of additional titles in this series, please visit: www.igi-global.com

Business Analytics and Cyber Security Management in Organizations
Rajagopal (EGADE Business School, Tecnologico de Monterrey, Mexico City, Mexico & Boston University, USA)
and Ramesh Behl (International Management Institute, Bhubaneswar, India)
Business Science Reference • copyright 2017 • 346pp • H/C (ISBN: 9781522509028) • US $215.00 (our price)

Handbook of Research on Intelligent Techniques and Modeling Applications in Marketing Analytics
Anil Kumar (BML Munjal University, India) Manoj Kumar Dash (ABV-Indian Institute of Information Technology and Management, India) Shrawan Kumar Trivedi (BML Munjal University, India) and Tapan Kumar Panda
(BML Munjal University, India)
Business Science Reference • copyright 2017 • 428pp • H/C (ISBN: 9781522509974) • US $275.00 (our price)

Applied Big Data Analytics in Operations Management
Manish Kumar (Indian Institute of Information Technology, Allahabad, India)
Business Science Reference • copyright 2017 • 251pp • H/C (ISBN: 9781522508861) • US $160.00 (our price)

Eye-Tracking Technology Applications in Educational Research
Christopher Was (Kent State University, USA) Frank Sansosti (Kent State University, USA) and Bradley Morris
(Kent State University, USA)
Information Science Reference • copyright 2017 • 370pp • H/C (ISBN: 9781522510055) • US $205.00 (our price)

Strategic IT Governance and Alignment in Business Settings
Steven De Haes (Antwerp Management School, University of Antwerp, Belgium) and Wim Van Grembergen
(Antwerp Management School, University of Antwerp, Belgium)
Business Science Reference • copyright 2017 • 298pp • H/C (ISBN: 9781522508618) • US $195.00 (our price)

Organizational Productivity and Performance Measurements Using Predictive Modeling and Analytics
Madjid Tavana (La Salle University, USA) Kathryn Szabat (La Salle University, USA) and Kartikeya Puranam
(La Salle University, USA)
Business Science Reference • copyright 2017 • 400pp • H/C (ISBN: 9781522506546) • US $205.00 (our price)

Data Envelopment Analysis and Effective Performance Assessment
Farhad Hossein Zadeh Lotfi (Islamic Azad University, Iran) Seyed Esmaeil Najafi (Islamic Azad University, Iran)
and Hamed Nozari (Islamic Azad University, Iran)
Business Science Reference • copyright 2017 • 365pp • H/C (ISBN: 9781522505969) • US $160.00 (our price)

www.igi-global.com

701 E. Chocolate Ave., Hershey, PA 17033
Order online at www.igi-global.com or call 717-533-8845 x100
To place a standing order for titles released in this series, contact: cust@igi-global.com
Mon-Fri 8:00 am - 5:00 pm (est) or fax 24 hours a day 717-533-8661

Editorial Advisory Board

List of Contributors

Table of Contents

Section 1
Business Intelligence With Data Mining: Process and Applications

    A. Sheik Abdullah, Thiagarajar College of Engineering, India
    S. Selvakumar, G. K. M. College of Engineering and Technology, India
    A. M. Abirami, Thiagarajar College of Engineering, India

    Hirak Dasgupta, Symbiosis Institute of Management Studies, India

    A. Sheik Abdullah, Thiagarajar College of Engineering, India
    R. Suganya, Thiagarajar College of Engineering, India
    S. Selvakumar, G. K. M. College of Engineering and Technology, India
    S. Rajaram, Thiagarajar College of Engineering, India

    Raghvendra Kumar, LNCT College, India
    Prasant Kumar Pattnaik, KIIT University, India
    Priyanka Pandey, LNCT College, India

    Masoumeh Zareapoor, Shanghai Jiao Tong University, China
    Pourya Shamsolmoali, CMCC, Italy
    M. Afshar Alam, Jamia Hamdard University, India

Section 3
Big Data Analytics: Its Methods and Applications

Section 4
Advanced Data Analytics: Decision Models and Business Applications

Detailed Table of Contents

Section 1
Business Intelligence With Data Mining: Process and Applications

Data analytics mainly deals with the science of examining and investigating raw data to derive useful patterns and inference. Data analytics has been deployed in many of the industries to make decisions at proper levels. It focuses upon the assumption and evaluation of the method with the intention of deriving a conclusion at various levels. Various types of data analytical techniques such as predictive analytics, prescriptive analytics, descriptive analytics, text analytics, and social media analytics are used by industrial organizations, educational institutions and by government associations. This context mainly focuses towards the illustration of contextual examples for various types of analytical techniques and its applications.

In the age of information, the world abounds with data. In order to obtain an intelligent appreciation of current developments, we need to absorb and interpret substantial amounts of data. The amount of data collected has grown at a phenomenal rate over the past few years. The computer age has given us both the power to rapidly process, summarize and analyse data and the encouragement to produce and store more data. The aim of data mining is to make sense of large amounts of mostly unsupervised data, in some domain. Data Mining is used to discover the patterns and relationships in data, with an emphasis on large observational data bases. This chapter aims to compare the approaches and conclude that Statisticians and Data miners can profit by studying each other's methods by using the combination of methods judiciously. The chapter also attempts to discuss data cleaning techniques involved in data mining.

Chapter 3

A. Sheik Abdullah, Thiagarajar College of Engineering, India
R. Suganya, Thiagarajar College of Engineering, India
S. Selvakumar, G. K. M. College of Engineering and Technology, India
S. Rajaram, Thiagarajar College of Engineering, India

Classification is considered to be the one of the data analysis technique which can be used over many applications. Classification model predicts categorical continuous class labels. Clustering mainly deals with grouping of variables based upon similar characteristics. Classification models are experienced by comparing the predicted values to that of the known target values in a set of test data. Data classification has many applications in business modeling, marketing analysis, credit risk analysis; biomedical engineering and drug retort modeling. The extension of data analysis and classification makes the insight into big data with an exploration to processing and managing large data sets. This chapter deals with various techniques, methodologies that correspond to the classification problem in data analysis process and its methodological impacts to big data.

Chapter 4

Raghvendra Kumar, LNCT College, India
Prasant Kumar Pattnaik, KIIT University, India
Priyanka Pandey, LNCT College, India

This chapter used privacy preservation techniques (Data Modification) to ensure Privacy. Privacy preservation is another important issue. A picture, where number of clients owning their clustered databases (Iris Database) wish to run a data mining algorithm on the union of their databases, without revealing any unnecessary information and requires the privacy of the privileged information. There are numbers of efficient protocols are required for privacy preserving in data mining. This chapter presented various privacy preserving protocols that are used for security in clustered databases. The Xln(X) protocol and the secure sum protocol are used in mutual computing, which can defend privacy efficiently. Its focuses on the data modification techniques, where it has been modified our distributed database and after that sanded that modified data set to the client admin for secure data communication with zero percentage of data leakage and also reduce the communication and computation complexity.

Chapter 5

Masoumeh Zareapoor, Shanghai Jiao Tong University, China
Pourya Shamsolmoali, CMCC, Italy
M. Afshar Alam, Jamia Hamdard University, India

The fraud detection method requires a holistic approach where the objective is to correctly classify the transactions as legitimate or fraudulent. The existing methods give importance to detect all fraudulent transactions since it results in money loss. For this most of the time, they have to compromise on some genuine transactions. Thus, the major issue that the credit card fraud detection systems face today is that a significant percentage of transactions labelled as fraudulent are in fact legitimate. These "false alarms" delay the transactions and creates inconvenience and dissatisfaction to the customer. Thus, the objective of this research is to develop an intelligent data mining based fraud detection system for secure online payment transaction system. The performance evaluation of the proposed model is done on real credit card dataset and it is found that the proposed model has high fraud detection rate and less false alarm rate than other state-of-the-art classifiers.

Chapter 6

Gebeyehu Belay Gebremeskel, Chongqing University, China
Chai Yi, Chongqing University, China
Zhongshi He, Chongqing University, China

Data Mining (DM) is a rapidly expanding field in many disciplines, and it is greatly inspiring to analyze massive data types, which includes geospatial, image and other forms of data sets. Such the fast growths of data characterized as high volume, velocity, variety, variability, value and others that collected and generated from various sources that are too complex and big to capturing, storing, and analyzing and challenging to traditional tools. The SDM is, therefore, the process of searching and discovering valuable information and knowledge in large volumes of spatial data, which draws basic principles from concepts in databases, machine learning, statistics, pattern recognition and 'soft' computing. Using DM techniques enables a more efficient use of the data warehouse. It is thus becoming an emerging research field in Geosciences because of the increasing amount of data, which lead to new promising applications. The integral SDM in which we focused in this chapter is the inference to geospatial and GIS data.

Section 2
Social Media Analytics With Sentiment Analysis: Business Applications and Methods

Chapter 7

Amir Manzoor, Bahria University, Pakistan

Over the last decade, social media use has gained much attention of scholarly researchers. One specific reason of this interest is the use of social media for communication; a trend that is gaining tremendous popularity. Every social media platform has developed its own set of application programming interface (API). Through these APIs, the data available on a particular social media platform can be accessed. However, the data available is limited and it is difficult to ascertain the possible conclusions that can be drawn about society on the basis of this data. This chapter explores the ways social researchers and scientists can use social media data to support their research and analysis.

Chapter 8

T. K. Das, VIT University, India

Business organizations have been adopting different strategies to impress upon their customers and attract them towards their products and services. On the other hand, the opinions of the customers gathered through customer feedbacks have been a great source of information for companies to evolve business intelligence to rightly place their products and services to meet the ever-changing customer requirements. In this work, we present a new approach to integrate customers' opinions into the traditional data warehouse model. We have taken Twitter as the data source for this experiment. First, we have built a system which can be used for opinion analysis on a product or a service. The second process is to model the opinion table so obtained as a dimensional table and to integrate it with a central data warehouse schema so that reports can be generated on demand. Furthermore, we have shown how business intelligence can be elicited from online product reviews by using computational intelligence technique like rough set base data analysis.

Chapter 9

A. M. Abirami, Thiagarajar College of Engineering, India
A. Sheik Abdullah, Thiagarajar College of Engineering, India
A. Askarunisa, KLN College of Information Technology, India
S. Selvakumar, G. K. M. College of Engineering and Technology, India
C. Mahalakshmi, Thiagarajar College of Engineering, India

It requires sophisticated streaming of big data processing to process the billions of daily social conversations across millions of sources. Dataset needs information extraction from them and it requires contextual semantic sentiment modeling to capture the intelligence through the complexity of online social discussions. Sentiment analysis is one of the techniques to capture the intelligence from Social Networks based on the user generated content. There are more and more researches evolving about sentiment classification. Aspect extraction is the core task involved in aspect based sentiment analysis. The proposed modeling uses Latent Semantic Analysis technique for aspect extraction and evaluates senti-scores of various products under study.

Chapter 10

Vinod Kumar Mishra, Bipin Tripathi Kumaon Institute of Technology, India
Himanshu Tiruwa, Bipin Tripathi Kumaon Institute of Technology, India

Sentiment analysis is a part of computational linguistics concerned with extracting sentiment and emotion from text. It is also considered as a task of natural language processing and data mining. Sentiment analysis mainly concentrate on identifying whether a given text is subjective or objective and if it is subjective, then whether it is negative, positive or neutral. This chapter provide an overview of aspect based sentiment analysis with current and future trend of research on aspect based sentiment analysis. This chapter also provide a aspect based sentiment analysis of online customer reviews of Nokia 6600. To perform aspect based classification we are using lexical approach on eclipse platform which classify the review as a positive, negative or neutral on the basis of features of product. The Sentiwordnet is used as a lexical resource to calculate the overall sentiment score of each sentence, pos tagger is used for part of speech tagging, frequency based method is used for extraction of the aspects/features and used negation handling for improving the accuracy of the system.

Chapter 11

Karteek Ramalinga Ponnuru, BML Munjal University, India
Rashik Gupta, BML Munjal University, India
Shrawan Kumar Trivedi, BML Munjal University, India

Firms are turning their eye towards social media analytics to get to know what people are really talking about their firm or their product. With the huge amount of buzz being created online about anything and everything social media has become 'the' platform of the day to understand what public on a whole are talking about a particular product and the process of converting all the talking into valuable information is called Sentiment Analysis. Sentiment Analysis is a process of identifying and categorizing a piece of text into positive or negative so as to understand the sentiment of the users. This chapter would take the reader through basic sentiment classifiers like building word clouds, commonality clouds, dendrograms and comparison clouds to advanced algorithms like K Nearest Neighbour, Naïve Biased Algorithm and Support Vector Machine.

Chapter 12

Sanjiva Shankar Dubey, BIMTECH Greater Noida, India
Arunesh Sharan, AS Consulting, India

This chapter will focus on the transformative effect Business Intelligence (BI) brings to an organization decision making, enhancing its performance, reducing overall cost of operations and improving its competitive posture. This chapter will enunciate the key principles and practices to bridge the gap between organization requirements vs. capabilities of any BI tool(s) by proposing a framework of organizational factors such as user's role, their analytical needs, access preferences and technical /analytical literacy etc. Evaluation methodology to select best BI tools properly aligned to the organization infrastructure will also be discussed. Softer issues and organizational change for successful implementation of BI will be further explained.

Chapter 13

Amir Manzoor, Bahria University, Pakistan

Over the last decade, social media platforms have become a very popular channel of communication. This popularity has sparked an increasing interest among researchers to investigate the social media communication. Many studies have been done that collected the publicly available social media communication data to unearth significant patterns. However, one significant concern raised over such practice is the privacy of the individual's social media communication data. As such it is important that specific ethical guidelines are in place for future researches on social media sites. This chapter explores various ethical issues related to researches related to social networking sites. The chapter also provides a set of ethical guidelines that future researches on social media sites can use to address various ethical issues.

Section 3
Big Data Analytics: Its Methods and Applications

Chapter 14

Keerthi Suneetha, SVEC, India

With the arrival of technology and rising amount of data (Big Data) there is a need towards implementation of effective analytical techniques (Big Data Analytics) in health sector which provides stakeholders with new insights that have the potential to advance personalized care to improve patient outcomes and avoid unnecessary costs. This chapter covers how to evaluate this big volume of data for unknown and useful facts, associations, patterns, trends which can give birth to new line of handling of diseases and provide high quality healthcare at lower cost to all citizens. This chapter gives a wide insight of introduction to Big Data Analytics in health domain, processing steps of BDA, Challenges and Future scope of research in healthcare.

Chapter 15

This chapter elaborates on mining techniques useful in big data analysis. Specifically, it will elaborate on how to use association rule mining, self organizing maps, word cloud, sentiment extraction, network analysis, classification, and clustering for marketing intelligence. The application of these would be on decisions related to market segmentation, targeting and positioning, trend analysis, sales, stock markets and word of mouth. The chapter is divided in two sections of data collection and cleaning where we elaborate on how twitter data can be extracted and mined for marketing decision making. Second part discusses various techniques that can be used in big data analysis for mining content and interaction network.

Chapter 16

Big data analytics in recent years had developed lightning fast applications that deal with predictive analysis of huge volumes of data in domains of finance, health, weather, travel, marketing and more. Business analysts take their decisions using the statistical analysis of the available data pulled in from social media, user surveys, blogs and internet resources. Customer sentiment has to be taken into account for designing, launching and pricing a product to be inducted into the market and the emotions of the consumers changes and is influenced by several tangible and intangible factors. The possibility of using Big data analytics to present data in a quickly viewable format giving different perspectives of the same data is appreciated in the field of finance and health, where the advent of decision support system is possible in all aspects of their working. Cognitive computing and artificial intelligence are making big data analytical algorithms to think more on their own, leading to come out with Big data agents with their own functionalities.

Chapter 17

For any forward-looking perspective, organizational information which is typically historical, incomplete and most of the time inaccurate, needs to be enriched with external information. However, traditional systems and approaches are slow, inflexible and cannot handle new volume and complexity of information.

Big data, an evolving term, basically refers to voluminous amount of structured, semi-structured or unstructured information in the form of data with a potential to be mined for 'best in class information'. Primarily, big data can be categorized by 3V's: volume, variety and velocity. Recent hype around big data concepts predicts that it will help companies to improve operations and makes faster and intelligent decisions. Considering the complexities in realms of supply chain, in this study, an attempt has been made to highlight the problems in storing data in any business, especially under Indian scenario where logistics arena is most unstructured and complicated. Conclusion may be significant to any strategic decision maker / manager working with distribution and logistics.

Section 4
Advanced Data Analytics: Decision Models and Business Applications

Chapter 18

G. Sreedhar, Rashtriya Sanskrit Vidyapeetha (Deemed University), India
A. Anandaraja Chari, Rayalaseema University, India

Web Data Mining is the application of data mining techniques to extract useful knowledge from web data like contents of web, hyperlinks of documents and web usage logs. There is also a strong requirement of techniques to help in business decision in e-commerce. Web Data Mining can be broadly divided into three categories: Web content mining, Web structure mining and Web usage mining. Web content data are content availed to users to satisfy their required information. Web structure data represents linkage and relationship of web pages to others. Web usage data involves log data collected by web server and application server which is the main source of data. The growth of WWW and technologies has made business functions to be executed fast and easier. As large amount of transactions are performed through e-commerce sites and the huge amount of data is stored, valuable knowledge can be obtained by applying the Web Mining techniques.

Chapter 19

Hanna Sawicka, Poznan University of Technology, Poland

This chapter presents the concept of stochastic multiple criteria decision making (MCDM) method to solve complex ranking decision problems. This approach is composed of three main areas of research, i.e. classical MCDM, probability theory and classification method. The most important steps of the idea are characterized and specific features of the applied methods are briefly presented. The application of Electre III combined with probability theory, and Promethee II combined with Bayes classifier are described in details. Two case studies of stochastic multiple criteria decision making are presented. The first one shows the distribution system of electrotechnical products, composed of 24 distribution centers (DC), while the core business of the second one is the production and warehousing of pharmaceutical products. Based on the application of presented stochastic MCDM method, different ways of improvements of these complex systems are proposed and the final i.e. the best paths of changes are recommended.

The problem analyzes a supply chain comprised of two front-runner retailers and one supplier. The retailers' offer customers delay in payments to settle the accounts against the purchases which is received by the supplier. The market demand of the retailer depends on time, retail price and a credit period offered to the customers with that of the other retailer. The supplier gives items with same wholesale price and credit period to the retailers. The joint and independent decisions are analyzed and validated numerically.

This chapter expresses efficiency of fuzzy goal programming for multiobjective aggregate production planning in fuzzy stochastic environment. The parameters of the objectives are taken as normally distributed fuzzy random variables and the chance constraints involve joint Cauchy distributed fuzzy random variables. In model formulation process the fuzzy chance constrained programming model is converted into its equivalent fuzzy programming using probabilistic technique, α-cut of fuzzy numbers and taking expectation of parameters of the objectives. Defuzzification technique of fuzzy numbers is used to find multiobjective linear programming model. Membership function of each objective is constructed depending on their optimal values. Afterwards a weighted fuzzy goal programming model is developed to achieve the highest degree of each of the membership goals to the extent possible by minimizing group regrets in a multiobjective decision making context. To explore the potentiality of the proposed approach, production planning of a health drinks manufacturing company has been considered.

Cloud computing has been a major focus of business organizations around the world. Many applications are getting migrated to the cloud and many new applications are being developed to run on the cloud. There are already more than 100 cloud service providers in the market offering various cloud services. As the number of cloud services and providers is increasing in the market, it is very important to select the right provider and service for deploying an application. This paper focuses on recommendation of cloud services by ranking them with the help of opinion mining of users' reviews and multi-attribute decision making models (TOPSIS and FMADM were applied separately) in tandem on both quantitative and qualitative data. Surprisingly, both TOPSIS and FMADM yielded the same rankings for the cloud services.

Preface

The complete work of this book is divided into four sections. The first section titled "Business Intelligence with Data Mining: Process and Applications" includes all the chapters related to business Analytics with data mining and its applications. The second section titled "Social Media Analytics with Sentiment Analysis: Business Applications and Methods" contains all the chapters related to social media analytics techniques and its applications of business intelligence. In the third section titled "Big Data Analytics: Its Methods and Applications" covers all the chapters related to big data processes and its applications. The last section includes the chapters related to advance decision models for business analytics titled as "Advance Data Analytics: Decision Models and Business Applications". The brief description of each section as follows:

The first section of this book is "Business Intelligence With Data Mining: Process and Applications" where the chapters related to data mining methods and its applications have been discussed. The first chapter of this section authored by A. Sheik Abdullah, S. Selvakumar, and A. M. Abirami, explains about data analytics where they explain Data analytics mainly deals with the science of examining and investigating raw data to derive useful patterns and inference. Data analytics has been deployed in many of the industries to make decisions at proper levels. It focuses upon the assumption and evaluation of the method with the intention of deriving a conclusion at various levels. Various types of data analytical techniques such as predictive analytics, prescriptive analytics, descriptive analytics, text analytics, and social media analytics are used by industrial organizations, educational institutions and by government associations. This context mainly focuses towards the illustration of contextual examples for various types of analytical techniques and its applications. In the second chapter, Hirak Dasgupta aims to compare the approaches and conclude that statisticians and data miners can profit by studying each other's methods by using the combination of methods judiciously. The chapter also attempts to discuss data cleaning techniques involved in data mining. The third chapter of this section authored by A. Sheik Abdullah, R. Suganya, S. Selvakumar, and S. Rajaram, deals with various techniques, methodologies that correspond to the classification problem in data analysis process and its methodological impacts to big data. The fourth chapter written by Raghvendra Kumar, Prasant Kumar Pattnaik and Priyanka Pandey, presented various privacy preserving protocols that are used for security in clustered databases. The Xln(X) protocol and the secure sum protocol are used in mutual computing, which can defend privacy efficiently. Its focuses on the data modification techniques, where it has been modified our distributed database and after that sanded that modified data set to the client admin for secure data communication with zero percentage of data leakage and also reduce the communication and computation complexity. The fifth chapter of this section authored by Masoumeh Zareapoor, Pourya Shamsolmoali and M. Afshar Alam, shows the performance of new credit card fraud detection technique which is based on, firstly balancing the transaction records, and then applies the proposed algorithm to detect the fraudulent transactions. At the end, we conduct a series of experiments to evaluate the effectiveness of our proposed techniques. In *the chapter six* authored by Belay Gebremeskel, Yi Chai, and Zhongshi He, incorporates tremendous novel ideas and methodologies as the integral of spatial data mining (SDM), which is highly pertinent and serve as a single inference material for researchers, experts, and other users.

The second section of this book is "Social Media Analytics With Sentiment Analysis: Business Applications and Methods" where the chapters related to social media analytics methods and related applications have been discussed. In Chapter 7 authored by Amir Manzoor, explores the ways social researchers and scientists can use social media data to support their research and analysis. Chapter 8 written by T. K. Das, presents a new approach to integrate customers' opinions into the traditional data warehouse model. He has taken Twitter as the data source for this experiment where at first, a system which can be used for opinion analysis on a product or a service has been built. The second process is to model the opinion table so obtained as a dimensional table and to integrate it with a central data warehouse schema so that reports can be generated on demand. Furthermore, he has shown how business intelligence can be elicited from online product reviews by using computational intelligence technique like rough set base data analysis. Chapter 9 authored by A. M. Abirami, A. Sheik Abdullah, A. Askarunisa, S. Selvakumar, and C. Mahalakshmi proposes a modeling technique that uses latent semantic analysis (LSA) technique for aspect extraction and evaluates senti-scores of various products under study. In Chapter 10, Vinod Kumar Mishra, and Himanshu Tiruwa provide an overview of aspect based sentiment analysis with current and future trend of research on aspect based sentiment analysis. This chapter also provides an aspect based sentiment analysis of online customer reviews of Nokia 6600. To perform aspect based classification they are using lexical approach on eclipse platform which classify the review as a positive, negative or neutral on the basis of features of product. The senti-word net is used as a lexical resource to calculate the overall sentiment score of each sentence, pos tagger is used for part of speech tagging, frequency based method is used for extraction of the aspects/features and used negation handling for improving the accuracy of the system. Chapter 11 written by Ponnuru Ramalinga Karteek, Rashik Gupta, and Shrawan Kumar Trivedi, take the reader through basic sentiment classifiers like building word clouds, commonality clouds, dendrograms and comparison clouds to advanced algorithms like K Nearest Neighbour, Naïve Biased Algorithm and Support Vector Machine. In Chapter 12, Sanjiva Shankar Dubey and Arunesh Sharan enunciate the key principles and practices to bridge the gap between organization requirements vs. capabilities of any BI tool(s) by proposing a framework of organizational factors such as user's role, their analytical needs, access preferences and technical / analytical literacy etc. Chapter 13 authored by Amir Manzoor explores various ethical issues related to researches related to social networking sites. This chapter also provides a set of ethical guidelines that future researches on social media sites can use to address various ethical issues.

The third section of this book is "Big Data Analytics: Its Methods and Applications" where the chapters related to Big data analytics methods and their applications have been discussed. In this section, Chapter 14, written by K. Suneetha, covers how to evaluate this big volume of data for unknown and useful facts, associations, patterns, trends which can give birth to new line of handling of diseases and provide high quality healthcare at lower cost to all citizens. This chapter gives a wide insight of introduction to Big Data Analytics in health domain, processing steps of BDA, Challenges and Future scope of research in healthcare. Chapter 15 authored by Khadija Ali Vakeel elaborates on mining techniques useful in big data analysis. Specifically, it will elaborate on how to use association rule mining, self-organizing maps, word cloud, sentiment extraction, network analysis, classification, and clustering for marketing intelligence. The application of these would be on decisions related to market segmentation, targeting and positioning, trend analysis, sales, stock markets and word of mouth. The chapter is divided in two sections of data collection and cleaning where we elaborate on how twitter data can be extracted and mined for marketing decision making. Second part discusses various techniques that can be used in big data analysis for content and interaction network. In Chapter 16, Balamurugan Balusamy, Priya Jha, Tamizh Arasi, and Malathi Velu discuss the Big data analytics in recent years had developed lightning fast applications that deal with predictive analysis of huge volumes of data in domains of finance, health, weather, travel, marketing and more. Business analysts take their decisions using the statistical analysis of the available data pulled in from social media, user surveys, blogs and internet resources. Customer sentiment has to be taken into account for designing, launching and pricing a product to be inducted into the market and the emotions of the consumers' changes and is influenced by several tangible and intangible factors. The possibility of using big data analytics to present data in a quickly viewable format giving different perspective of the same data is appreciated in the field of finance and health, where the advent of decision support system is possible in all aspects of their working. Cognitive computing and artificial intelligence are making big data analytical algorithms to think more on their own, leading to come out with big data agents with their own functionalities. In Chapter 17, Supriyo Roy and Kaushik Kumar, explore the usefulness of applying big data concepts in these emerging areas of logistics are explored with different dimensions. Conclusion of this paper may seem to be significant to any strategic decision maker / manager working with specific field of distribution and logistics.

The last section of this book is "Advanced Data Analytics: Decision Models and Business Applications" where the chapters related to advance data analytics techniques and their applications have been discussed. Chapter 18, written by G. Sreedhar and A. A. Chari, considers the important element of Page load time of a website for assessing the performance of some well-known online Business websites through statistical tools. Also this research work considers the optimum design aspect of Business websites leading to improvement and betterment of online business process. Chapter 19, written by Hanna Sawicka, presents the concept of stochastic multiple criteria decision making (MCDM) method to solve complex ranking decision problems. This approach is composed of three main areas of research, i.e. classical MCDM, probability theory and classification method. The most important steps of the idea are characterized and specific features of the applied methods are briefly presented. The application of Electre III combined with probability theory, and Promethee II combined with Bayes classifier are described in details. Two case studies of stochastic multiple criteria decision making are presented. The first one shows the distribution system of electro-technical products, composed of 24 distribution centers (DC), while the core business of the second one is the production and warehousing of pharmaceutical products. Based on the application of presented stochastic MCDM method, different ways of improvements of these complex systems are proposed and the final i.e. the best paths of changes are recommended. In Chapter 20, Nita H. Shah discusses the problem that analyzes a supply chain comprised of two front-runner retailers and one supplier. The retailers' offer customers delay in payments to settle the accounts against the purchases which is received by the supplier. The market demand of the retailer depends on time, retail price and a credit period offered to the customers with that of the other retailer. The supplier gives items with same wholesale price and credit period to the retailers. The joint and independent decisions are analyzed and validated numerically. Chapter 21, written by Animesh Biswas and Arnab Kumar De, expresses efficiency of fuzzy goal programming technique for multi-objective aggregate production planning in fuzzy stochastic environment. The parameters of the objectives are taken as normally distributed fuzzy random variables and the chance constraints involve joint Cauchy distributed fuzzy random variables. In model formulation process the fuzzy chance constrained programming model is converted into its equivalent fuzzy programming form using the concepts of probabilistic technique, α-cut of fuzzy numbers and taking expectation of parameters of the objectives. De-fuzzification technique of fuzzy numbers is used to find multi-objective linear programming model. Membership function of each objective is constructed depending on their optimal values. Afterwards a weighted fuzzy goal programming model is developed to achieve the highest degree of each of the membership goals to the extent possible by minimizing group regrets in a multi-objective decision making context. To explore the potentiality of the proposed approach, production planning of a health drinks manufacturing company has been considered. Chapter 22, written by Timmaraju Srimanyu, Vadlamani Ravi, and G. R. Gangadharan, focuses on recommendation of cloud services by ranking them with the help of opinion mining of users' reviews and multi-attribute decision making models (TOPSIS and FMADM were applied separately) in tandem on both quantitative and qualitative data. Surprisingly, both TOPSIS and FMADM yielded the same rankings for the cloud services.

Acknowledgment

The editors would like to acknowledge the help of all the people involved in this project and, more specifically, to the authors and reviewers that took part in the review process. Without their support, this book would not have become a reality.

We would like to thank each one of the authors for their contributions. The editors wish to acknowledge the valuable contributions of the reviewers regarding the improvement of quality, coherence, and content presentation of chapters. Most of the authors also served as referees; we highly appreciate their double task.

We are grateful to all members of IGI publishing house for their assistance and timely motivation in producing this volume.

We hope the readers will share our excitement with this important scientific contribution the body of knowledge about various applications of Handbook of Research on Advanced Data Mining Techniques and Applications for Business Intelligence.

Shrawan Kumar Trivedi
BML Munjal University, India

Shubhamoy Dey
Indian Institute of Management Indore, India

Anil Kumar
BML Munjal University, India

Tapan Kumar Panda
Jindal Global Business School, India

Section 1
Business Intelligence With Data Mining:
Process and Applications

Chapter 1
An Introduction to Data Analytics:
Its Types and Its Applications

A. Sheik Abdullah
Thiagarajar College of Engineering, India

S. Selvakumar
G. K. M. College of Engineering and Technology, India

A. M. Abirami
Thiagarajar College of Engineering, India

ABSTRACT

Data analytics mainly deals with the science of examining and investigating raw data to derive useful patterns and inference. Data analytics has been deployed in many of the industries to make decisions at proper levels. It focuses upon the assumption and evaluation of the method with the intention of deriving a conclusion at various levels. Various types of data analytical techniques such as predictive analytics, prescriptive analytics, descriptive analytics, text analytics, and social media analytics are used by industrial organizations, educational institutions and by government associations. This context mainly focuses towards the illustration of contextual examples for various types of analytical techniques and its applications.

INTRODUCTION: DATA ANALYTICS

Data analytics is the knowledge of investigating raw data with the intention of deriving solution for a specified problem analysis. Nowadays analytics has been used by many corporate, industries and institutions for making exact decision at various levels. The mechanism of drawing solutions during analysis of large datasets with the intention of determining hidden patterns and its relationship. Analytics differs from mining with the mechanism of determining the new patterns, scope, techniques and its purpose.

DOI: 10.4018/978-1-5225-2031-3.ch001

ANALYTICS PROCESS MODEL

The Mechanism of analytics has been used variantly with machine learning, data science and knowledge discovery. The process model initially starts with the data source which is in raw form of representation. The data needed for analysis has to be selected with accordance to the problem need for data interpretation. The identified data may contain various missing fields, irrelevant data items. This has to be resolved and cleaned. Then the data has to be transformed accordingly to the necessary format for evaluation and this can be made by the data standardization techniques such as min-max normalization, Z-score normalization and normalization by decimal scaling. As an outcome the final evaluated pattern provides the visualized data representation of the data which can be fed up for evaluation and interpretation. The workflow of the process model is depicted in Figure 1.

ANALYTIC REQUIREMENTS

The Analytical model should actually solve the chosen problem in which it has to be developed. In order to achieve or to solve the defined problem it should be properly defined. The model to be developed must have predictive capabilities in order to determine the patterns and interpretations from the observed data. Then the model should resemble an interpretable power and it should be justifiable in nature. Even though the model is to be interpretable it should adhere to its statistical performance. The efficiency in collecting the data, processing, analyzing it also plays a role in the requirement of the analytical requirements.

Figure 1. Analytics process model

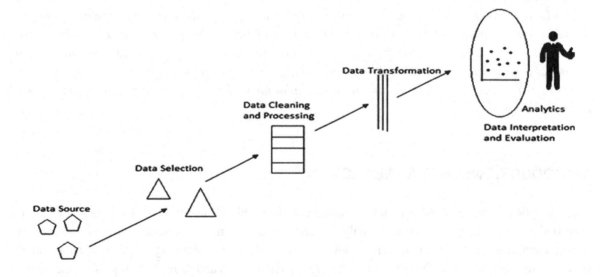

TYPES OF ANALYTICS

Predictive Analytics

Predictive analytics mainly deals with the mechanism of predicting or observing the target value of measure. The value of measure signifies the performance of the analytical model which is being developed. There by the nature of the developed model can be ascertained with the measured value. Hence the term predictive analytics if often said to be supervised learning because the target variable will be known in prior with accordance to the definition of the tuple of record (T. Hastie, R. Tibshirani, & Friedman, 2001). There are various sorts of algorithms used in predicting the nature of a data or a real world problem, such as:

1. Linear regression
2. Logistic regression
3. Support vector machines
4. Neural network
5. Decision trees
6. Ensemble methods such as boosting and bagging

Let us discuss about one of the techniques in predictive analytics such as linear Regression.

Linear Regression

The working of simple linear regression involves a response variable and a predictor variable. In simple straight line linear regression, it involves a single predictor variable but in case of logistic regression it involves more than one predictor variable (Jiawei Han, Micheline Kamber & Jian Pei, 2011). The straight line regression is represented in the Equation 1 as follows:

$$Y = W_0 + W_1(x) \tag{1}$$

The co-efficient W_0 and W_1 are referred to as the weights of the predictive function. Consider let D be the dataset which contains the values for predictor and response variable X and Y, which is represented of the form:

$$\{x_1, y_1\}, \{x_2, y_2\} \dots\dots\dots\dots\dots\dots \{x_D, y_D\}$$

The regression co-efficient can be determined using linear regression as give in Equation 2 as follows:

$$W_1 = \frac{\left(\sum (x_i = \bar{x}) \cdot (y_i - \bar{y})\right)}{\left(\sum (x_i = \bar{x})^2\right)} \tag{2}$$

$\bar{x}$ is the mean value of $x_1, x_2 \dots\dots\dots x_D$
$\bar{y}$ is the mean value of $y_1, y_2 \dots\dots\dots y_D$

From the determined value of W1 the value of W0 can be obtained. There by if any predictor variable has to be identified its response value can be determined.

Descriptive Analytics

Descriptive analytics mainly deals with the intention of describing the patterns of a customer behavior. In predictive analytics the label (target) which will be known in advance but in descriptive analytics there will be no such target measure or a target variable (Srikant. R & Agarwal. R, 1995). This technique is also referred to as unsupervised learning because the target variable is not known to influence the learning phenomenon (Bart Baesens, 2014). There are about various techniques that deals with descriptive analytics such as:

1.   Association rule mining
2.   Sequence rule mining
3.   Data clustering

Let us discuss about one of the techniques in Descriptive analytics such as sequence rule mining.

Sequence Rule Mining

The mechanism of sequence rule mining is to determine the maximum sequences among the set of all sequence that has been determined from the given transactional data. It must possess a certain degree of support and confidence level. Considering the market based analysis of a transactional data the number of maximal sequences determined for the item set signifies the frequency level of that sequence among all the items. Consider the following example of transactional data which contains the sequence of the items purchased, the session time of purchase, and the items as depicted in Table 1.

Table 1. Sequence rule for a transactional dataset

Session Time	Sequence of Item Purchased	Items Purchased
1.1	1	A1
1.1	2	A4
1.1	3	A3
1.1	4	A2
1.2	1	A3
1.2	2	A1
1.2	3	A4
1.3	1	A2
1.3	2	A4
1.4	1	A1
1.4	2	A2
1.4	3	A3

Table 1 can be represented in the form of sequence rule as follows:

```
Session time:
1.1: A1 A4 A3 A2
1.2: A3 A1 A4
1.3: A2 A4
1.4: A1 A2 A3
```

The support for sequence rule mining can be determined by identifying that the consequent can appear at the subsequent phase of the sequence. One another step is that the consequent appears after the antecedent of the sequence. For the above example consider the sequence from A1->A3 the resultant value for the support becomes 2/4 = 50% and form the second step 1/4 =25% respectively.

Text Analytics

Text analysis is also known as text mining. Text analysis involves in extracting structured information from the collection of documents. Generally, it is performed using Natural Language Processing (NLP) techniques. It includes sub processes like pre-processing, Part-of-Speech (PoS) tagging, feature extraction, classification and so on.

Text pre-processing includes removal of stop words, stemming, etc. Usually the words like 'a' an', the' do not convey any meaning. The words which are of type articles, prepositions, and pronouns are removed. Stemming is the process of removing derived words to their word stem, base or root form. For example, the words 'construction', 'constructing', are reduced to 'construct'. There are many stemming algorithms available. The Porter Stemming algorithm (or 'Porter stemmer') is a process for removing the commoner morphological and in flexional endings from words in English. Its main use is as part of a term normalization process that is usually done when setting up Information Retrieval systems.

In PoS tagging, the sentences in the data set collection are tokenized using the PoS tagger. During this process, a part of speech such as noun, verb, adverb, adjective, conjunctions, negations and the like are assigned to every word in the sentences. For example, "Place is very good" is tagged as shown in Table 2.

There are many free PoS taggers available. Python library functions, Stanford NLP tools are readily available to do PoS tagging.

Table 2. PoS tagging of sentence

Word	PoS Tagging	Meaning
Place	/NN	Noun
is	/VB	Verb
very	/RB	Adverb
good	/JJ	Adjective

BagOfWords (BOW)

BagOfWords (BoW) is usually adopted to represent the text documents. It is named as Term Document matrix. The cell value in the matrix depicts the occurrences of a term in the particular document. In Boolean model, the cell value takes '0' if the term is absent or '1' if it is present. In Term Frequency (TF) model, the cell value takes the number of occurrences of a term (term frequency) in the particular document. In order to give importance to rarely occurring term in the document collection, Term Frequency - Inverse Document Frequency (TF-IDF) is used.

Latent Semantic Indexing (LSI)

Latent semantic indexing (LSI) is an *indexing* and retrieval method that uses a mathematical technique called singular value decomposition (SVD) to identify patterns in the relationships between the terms and concepts contained in an unstructured collection of text. LSI understands the patterns among words in an intelligent way. It considers documents that have many words in common to be semantically close, and ones with few words in common to be semantically distant. This enables the document classification more or less similar to human being action.

Latent Dirichlet Allocation

Latent Dirichlet allocation is a way of automatically discovering topics from the sentences. It is used for topic modeling or feature extraction in text documents. It is the best technique used for document classification.

Social Media Analytics

Writing in social media to express one's views becomes common now-a-days. The enormous growth of social media through online reviews, discussions, blogs, micro-blogs, twitter, etc on the Web, enable individuals and organizations to make decisions using these content. In the same way, there has been an increase in attention on social media as a source of research data in areas such as decision making, recommender systems, etc. The power of social media is described by (Jagadeesh Kumar, 2014) and it can be effectively used to influence public opinion or research behavior. Social media analysis can be defined as the analysis of user generated content written in the common or public discussion forums, blogs and other social media networking sites to make or improve business decisions.

Social media has its foot print in almost all types of industries like tourism, healthcare, and so on. (Ting, 2014) analyzed blogs and showed the necessity of travel blogs for sharing of experience among people. (Zeng, 2014) suggested and demonstrated the impact of social media analytics to the economic contribution of tourism industry and thereby to the country. His work also justified that the user generated content in social media web sites are perceived as recommendations from like-minded friends mostly by the younger generations of this century. (Jacobsen, 2014) made a study on Mallorca (Spain) tourism using the destination-specific surveys and showed how visual content and types of content creators make differences in the holiday decision-making.

Social media analysis adds value to improve health care through patient engagement by increasing access to information and ability to receive the information in real-time. It provides opportunities for patients to share their experiences with others. It enables health care industry to improve their service quality.

Much of social media text research has been undertaken in marketing and retail sector to improve customer satisfaction, recommend new products and so on. Social media, as a data source, contains valuable consumer insights and enable business intelligence. Social media text analysis helps the business to take marketing decisions based on the most discussed topics in the social media. It also enables them drill into the data to see what is causing the dissatisfaction among users. It provides multi-dimensional insight of a brand and its features, promotions, shoppers, consumers, and influencers. It delivers trend analysis, behavior tracking, and overall understanding.

The sentiment analysis framework identifies the key discussion concepts from the user reviews or comments. Feature based or aspect level sentiment analysis is to classify sentiment with respect to specific aspects of the entities. For example, the sentence "The camera's picture quality is good, but its battery life is short" evaluates two aspects, picture quality and battery life, of camera (entity). The sentiment on camera's picture quality is positive, but the sentiment on its battery life is negative. The picture quality and battery life of camera are the opinion targets. The user generated data provides a higher degree of accuracy about what exactly the user feels about a particular place. Feature based analysis recommends the feature of a particular product whether it is positive or negative. This information can be used to improve business outcomes and ensure a very high level of user satisfaction.

Survival Analytics

Survival analytics is one of the categories of statistics which mainly deals with the happening of an event with respect to time. It provides the justification of the reliability of the event in accordance with time. For example, predicting the behavior of market based analysis, web catalog visits by customer and so on. The techniques that deals with the survival analysis measurements are;

1. Kaplan-Meier plot
2. Propositional hazards
3. Tree structured survival models
4. Parametric model

Case Study

The following case study deals with the explanation of the development of a decision tree for the weather dataset. The manual step by step process for the weather numeric dataset has been solved with respect to that of the results in rapid miner tool.

In accordance with the weather dataset with numeric attributes as shown in Table 3, the attribute temperature and humidity are numerical. Therefore, an efficient classification algorithm must have the capability to be dealt with numerical data rather than categorical. The decision tree classification algorithm resolves this problem by making binary split among the range of the attribute values. Let us consider the attribute humidity the values of the attributes are sorted in ascending order as in Table 4.

Discretization among the numeric attribute values involves the partitioning of the values by adopting the strategy of breakpoints i.e halfway between the either side of the data values by ensuring the split is made in accordance with the majority of the class values on one side and remaining in the other. Therefore, when applying this in the above values we get 9 sort of breakpoints between them such as in Table 5.

7

Table 3. Dataset description

S no	Outlook	Temperature	Humidity	Wind	Play
1	Sunny	85	85	False	No
2	Sunny	80	90	True	No
3	Overcast	83	86	False	Yes
4	Rain	70	96	False	Yes
5	Rain	68	80	False	Yes
6	Rain	65	70	True	No
7	Overcast	64	65	True	Yes
8	Sunny	72	95	False	No
9	Sunny	69	70	False	Yes
10	Rainy	75	80	False	Yes
11	Sunny	75	70	True	Yes
12	Overcast	72	90	True	Yes
13	Overcast	81	75	False	Yes
14	Rainy	71	91	True	No

Table 4. Ordering level 1

65 Yes	70 No Yes Yes	75 Yes	80 Yes Yes	85 No	86 Yes	90 No Yes	91 No	95 No	96 yes

Table 5. Ordering level 2

Yes	No Yes Yes	Yes	Yes Yes	No	Yes	No Yes	No	No	Yes

The values obtained by considering the halfway split among the values are 67.5, 72.5, 82.5, 85.5, 88, 90.5, and 95.5. While considering the halfway split if the instances with same values fall into the different class label then the split at those points cannot be considered as in Table 6.

In this partition, if the preceding class values is of same then there occurs no problem in merging those partitions which belongs to same classes as in Table 7.

If the adjacent partition consists of the same sort of the majority of a particular class label then they can be merged together without affecting the rule. Therefore, the final discretization as in Table 8 is:

The split value for the attribute Humidity is:

Humidity: ≤ 82.5 (Yes)

> 82.5 and ≤ 95.5 (No)

> 95.5 (Yes)

Table 6. Ordering level 3

Yes	No Yes Yes	Yes Yes Yes	No	Yes	No Yes	No No	Yes

Table 7. Ordering level 4

Yes No Yes Yes Yes Yes Yes	No	Yes No Yes No No	Yes

Table 8. Ordering level 5

Yes No Yes Yes Yes Yes Yes	No Yes No Yes No No	Yes

The split at the point 95.5 makes the partition to fall most of the labels to fall in one split and only one yes tuple in the other split thereby it won't be considered to be as a binary split while adapting the halfway binary split among the class labels. Hence the split value 82.5 is considered to be as the breakpoint among the class labels of yes and no tuples.

The attribute temperature is also found to be numeric, therefore while adopting the same procedure we get the following result as in Table 9.

While choosing breakpoints i.e halfway binary split the values are found to be 64.5, 66.5, 70.5, 72, 77.5, 80.5 and 84. Here, in this partition if the first and the second split are removed then the majority of the class label is found to be Yes therefore the split at those point can be removed. Accordingly, if there are number of occurrences of the same values of the labels then the split at those points can be removed without causing any problems for errors. The resultant partition is shown in Table 10 as follows,

If the adjacent partitions in the split seems to have same sort of majority in their class label values, then they can be merged together. Hence the resultant partition is shown in Table 11 as follows:

At this point, the split value for the attribute temperature is found to be 77.5

i.e ≤ 77.5 (Yes)

> 77.5 (No)

Table 9. Ordering level 6

Yes	No	Yes Yes Yes	No No	Yes Yes Yes	No	Yes Yes	No

Table 10. Ordering level 7

Yes No Yes Yes Yes	No No Yes Yes Yes	No Yes Yes No

Table 11. Ordering level 8

Yes No Yes Yes Yes No No Yes Yes Yes	No Yes Yes No

The resultant values produced by the splitting criterion method with numerical dataset are similar to that of the categorical attribute values. Hence for any sort of real world problem decision tree classification algorithm handles both categorical and numerical attributes in a similar way of generating decision trees.

An Example: Weather Dataset

Importing a dataset in rapid miner can be made in variety of formats such as csv, excel, xml, access, database, arff, xrff, spss, sparse, Dasylab, Url etc. The format that we are importing the dataset is of .csv format as described in Figure 2. The dataset contains four attributes and a class label play. The class label is of binominal which contains nine yes's and five no's tuple.

Open a new project in rapid miner as depicted in Figure 3 and then import read csv operator as in Figure 4. Each of the process that we are creating contains one of the operators of this type hence referred to be as the root operator. This operator provides a set of parameters that are of global relevance to the process like initialization of parameters.

After loading the csv file as in Figure 5 i.e., the weather dataset from the dataset folder which contains the weather dataset in csv format and select the type for the attribute that has been chosen for classification and select the class label option for the attribute that has to be fixed as label as in Figure 6 after all these steps are complete then click finish to end the import configuration wizard.

After the importing wizard is complete then click and drag the decision tree operator as in Figure 7 this operator learns decision tree for both of the numerical and categorical data. Decision tree classification method is considered to be one of the best classification techniques which can be easily understood. Each node in the decision tree is labeled with an attribute and the outcomes of the attribute is mapped to the next attribute with maximal gain values. The evaluation of the tree stops when the leaf node has been reached.

Figure 2. Dataset in csv format

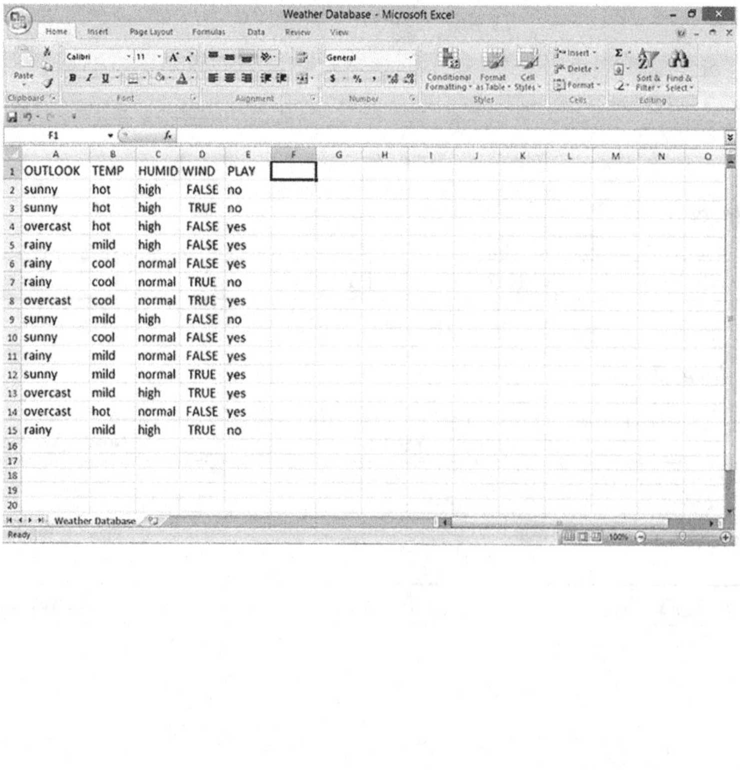

OUTLOOK	TEMP	HUMID	WIND	PLAY
sunny	hot	high	FALSE	no
sunny	hot	high	TRUE	no
overcast	hot	high	FALSE	yes
rainy	mild	high	FALSE	yes
rainy	cool	normal	FALSE	yes
rainy	cool	normal	TRUE	no
overcast	cool	normal	TRUE	yes
sunny	mild	high	FALSE	no
sunny	cool	normal	FALSE	yes
rainy	mild	normal	FALSE	yes
sunny	mild	normal	TRUE	yes
overcast	mild	high	TRUE	yes
overcast	hot	normal	FALSE	yes
rainy	mild	high	TRUE	no

Figure 3. Creating a new project

Figure 4. Importing csv operator

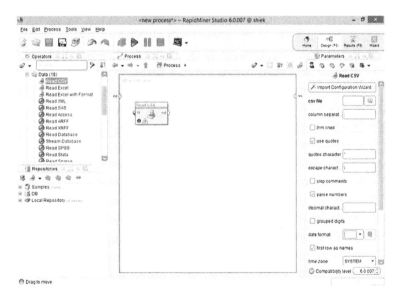

From the tree as in Figure 8 we can observe that the root node is selected to be outlook because it has the maximal gain value among all the attributes that are in accordance with the weather dataset. Hence from the distributions made by the attribute outlook the prediction has been made and the next attribute with maximal gain is chosen for the next level of classification and the final destination is reached when the maximal depth is reached.

Figure 5. Loading data into the operator

Figure 6. Selecting the label attribute

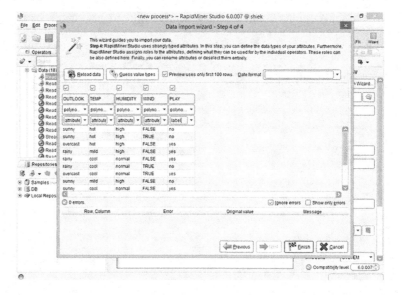

FUTURE SCOPE AND DIRECTIONS

This chapter mainly focuses towards methods available for analytics with an example illustration. Each type of analytics has its applications towards various fields mapping to real world scenarios. The future scope and enhancement can be made with accordance to the applicability to solve use cases concerned with the type of analytical requirement across various domains. Meanwhile, the nature of the environment, the type of data plays a significant role in the way of processing analytical procedures. However, each type of analytics has broad variance in analysis and determination of results. Proper and suitable analytical technique has to be selected and adhered for the type of the data and the environment that has been chosen.

Figure 7. Adding the decision tree operator

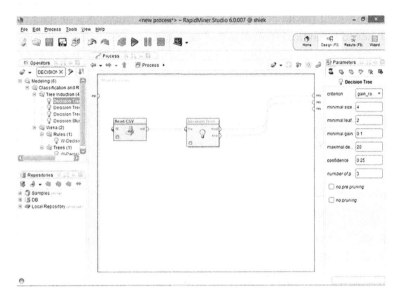

Figure 8. Generated decision tree

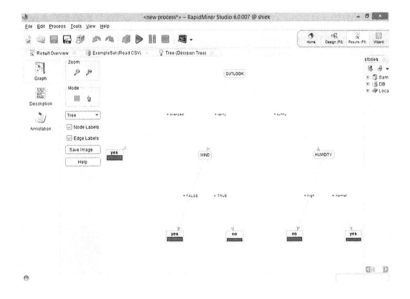

CONCLUSION

Analytics provides the way for determining the meaningful and undiscovered patterns with accordance to various types of data. It relies upon the factors such as statistics, Research, and in programming for the operations such as data optimization, prediction, classification and correlation analysis. The chapter provides a detailed framework about data analytics its types and its application. Each type of analytics can be applied towards various domain of expert. Predictive and survival analytics has been mostly deployed over medical informatics to predict the nature and behavior of specified disease. The impact of a specific disease and its risk factors can be greatly determined by the results interpreted by analytics. The data observed from social media contains various formats and types of data that can be analyzed as a whole using advanced analytical techniques. The inference and determination has to be observed to a great extent.

REFERENCES

Baesens, B. (2014). *Analytics in a big data world: The essential guide to data science and its applications*. Wiley.

Grivan, M., & Newman, M. E. J. (2002). Community structure in social and biological network. In *Proceedings of the National Academy of Sciences*.

Han, J., & Pei, M. K. A. J. (2011). Data Mining: Concepts and Techniques. In *Data Management Systems*. Morgan Kaufmann Publishers.

Hastie, Tibshirani, & Friedman. (2001). *Elements of Statistical learning: Data mining, inference, and prediction*. Springer-Verlag.

Jacobsen, , Jacobsen, & Munar. (2014). Motivations for sharing tourism experiences through social media. *Tourism Management*.

Srikant, R., & Agarwal, R. (1995). Mining generalized association rules. In *Proceedings of the International Conference on Very Large Databases*.

Ting, K.-C. T., Ting, P.-H., & Hsiao, P.-W. (2014). Why are bloggers willing to share their thoughts via travel blogs? *International Journal of Technology Management, 64*(1), 89. doi:10.1504/IJTM.2014.059237

Zeng, B. Z., & Gerritsen, R. (2014). *What do we know about social media in tourism? A review*. Tourism Management Perspectives.

Chapter 2
Data Mining and Statistics:
Tools for Decision Making in the Age of Big Data

Hirak Dasgupta
Symbiosis Institute of Management Studies, India

ABSTRACT

In the age of information, the world abounds with data. In order to obtain an intelligent appreciation of current developments, we need to absorb and interpret substantial amounts of data. The amount of data collected has grown at a phenomenal rate over the past few years. The computer age has given us both the power to rapidly process, summarize and analyse data and the encouragement to produce and store more data. The aim of data mining is to make sense of large amounts of mostly unsupervised data, in some domain. Data Mining is used to discover the patterns and relationships in data, with an emphasis on large observational data bases. This chapter aims to compare the approaches and conclude that Statisticians and Data miners can profit by studying each other's methods by using the combination of methods judiciously. The chapter also attempts to discuss data cleaning techniques involved in data mining.

INTRODUCTION

The fact that there has been a recent increase in the interest shown by many in the field of data mining or knowledge discovery or machine learning, has surprised many statisticians. Data mining attacks problems of descriptive data (i.e. effective summaries of data), identifies relationships among variables within a data set and uses a set of previously observed data to construct predictors of future observations. A well-established set of techniques for attacking all these problems have been developed by statisticians. Various algorithms and techniques such as: Statistics, Clustering, Regression, Decision trees, association rules, neural networks etc. are used for making predictions and also used in data mining.

Data mining, as it is practised at present, has evolved over nearly four decades, since the use of computers and accessories started being used for data collection and static data provision. Relational database management Systems (RDBMS) and Structured Query languages (SQL) were developed during the 80s

DOI: 10.4018/978-1-5225-2031-3.ch002

and 90s for providing dynamic data at the level of the record. Subsequently, online data processing and multi-dimensional databases and data warehouses came to be used (Cios et al., 2010).

The purpose of data mining is knowledge discovery. It extracts hidden information from large databases and hence is a powerful technology with a great potential for companies to focus on the analysis of the stored database (Adejuwon & Mosavi, 2010).

Both the techniques—Data mining and Statistic—use some common software packages by the software vendors (IBM, SAS, and many more). By strict definition "statistics" or statistical techniques are not data mining. They were being used long before the term data mining was coined to apply to business applications. However, statistical techniques are driven by the data and are used to discover patterns and build predictive models. And from the users' perspective you will be faced with a conscious choice when solving a "data mining" problem as to whether you wish to attack it with statistical methods or other data mining techniques. Today people have to deal with up to terabytes of data and have to make sense of it and glean the important patterns from it. Statistics can greatly help in this process by helping to answer several important questions about their data: what patterns are there in the database? What is the chance that an event will occur? Which patterns are significant? What is a high-level summary of the data that gives some idea of what is contained in the database? For these reasons, it is important to have some idea of how statistical techniques work and how they can be applied. Data miners should have a foundation of knowledge in Statistics. Data mining is an interdisciplinary field with contributions from statistics, artificial intelligence, and decision theory and so on (Yahia & El-Mukashfi El-Taher, 2010).

Data mining is not just an "umbrella" term coined for the purpose of making sense of data. The major distinguishing characteristic of data mining is that it is data driven, as opposed to other methods that are often model driven. In statistics, researchers frequently deal with the problem of finding the smallest data size that gives sufficiently confident estimates. In data mining we deal with the opposite problem, namely, data size is large and we are interested in building a data model that is small (not too complex) but still describes the data well (Cios et al., 2010).

In other words, the essential difference between data mining and the traditional data analysis (i.e. statistics) is that data mining is to mine information and discover knowledge on the premise of no clear assumption.

Some definitions on data mining given by different authors are as follows:

- "Data mining is the exploration and analysis of large quantities of data in order to discover meaningful patterns and rules" (Linoff & Berry, 2014).
- "Statistics with Scale and Speed" (Darryl Pregibon).
- "Data mining is the analysis of (often large) observational data sets to find unsuspected relationships and to summarize the data in novel ways that are both understandable and useful to the data owner" (Hand, Mannila, & Smyth, 2001).
- "Statistics is at the core of data mining - helping to distinguish between random noise and significant findings, and providing a theory for estimating probabilities of predictions, etc. However Data Mining is more than Statistics. Data mining covers the entire process of data analysis, including data cleaning and preparation and visualization of the results, and how to produce predictions in real-time, etc" (Gregory Piatetsky-Shapiro).

PREPARING DATA FOR ANALYSIS: HOW TO CLEAN UP DATA?

Data cleaning, also known as data cleansing or scrubbing, deals with detecting and removing errors and inconsistencies from data in order to improve the quality of data. Data quality problems are present in single data collections, such as files and databases, e.g., due to misspellings during data entry, missing information or other invalid data. After cleaning the data set will be consistent with other similar data sets in the system. Data cleaning is required to maintain the high quality of the data set. A high quality of a data set includes the following parameters:

1. **Validity:** The degree to which the measures conform to defined business rules or constraints.
2. **Accuracy:** The data was recorded correctly.
3. **Uniqueness:** Entities are recorded once.
4. **Completeness:** All relevant data was recorded.
5. **Consistency:** The data agrees with itself.
6. **Timeliness:** The data is kept up to date.
7. **Uniformity:** The degree to which a set data measures are specified using the same units of measure in all systems.

Data that is to be analyzed by data mining techniques can be incomplete (lacking attribute values or certain attributes of interest, or containing only aggregate data), noisy (containing errors, or outlier values which deviate from the expected), and inconsistent (e.g. containing discrepancies in the department codes used to categorize items). Incomplete, noisy and Inconsistent data are common properties of large, real world data bases. Incomplete data can occur for a number of reasons. Attributes of interest may not always be available, such as customer information for sales transaction data. Other data may not be included simply because it was not considered important at the time of entry. Relevant data may not be recorded due to misunderstanding, or because of equipment functions. Missing data, particularly for tuples with missing values for some attributes, may need to be inferred. Data can be noisy, having incorrect attribute values because of many reasons. There may be errors in data transmissions or technological limitations, such as limited buffer size for coordinating synchronized data transfer and consumption. Therefore, it's useful to run the data through some data cleaning techniques (Han, Kamber, & Pei, 2012).

Missing Values

Many tuples have no recorded value for several attributes such as customer income. The following methods are used to go about filling in the missing values for an attribute:

1. **Ignore the Tuple:** This is usually done when the class label is missing. This method is not very effective, unless the tuple contains several attributes with missing values. The method does not give good results when the percentage of missing values per attribute varies considerably.
2. **Fill in the Missing Values Manually:** This approach is time consuming and may not be feasible given a large data set with many missing values.
3. **Use a Global Constant to Fill in the Missing Value:** Replace all missing attribute values by the same constant, such as a label like "Unknown", or $-\infty$. If missing values are replaced by, say, "Unknown", then the mining program may mistakenly think that they form an interesting concept,

since they all have a value in common that of "Unknown". Therefore, this method is simple but it is not recommended.

4. Use the attribute mean to fill in the missing value.
5. Use the attribute mean for all samples belonging to the same class as the given tuple.
6. **Use the Most Probable Value to fill in the Missing Value:** This is determined with inference based tools using a Bayesian theorem or decision tree induction.

Methods 3 to 6 bias the data. The filled in value may not be correct. Method 6, however is a popular strategy. In comparison to the other methods, it uses the most information from the present data to predict missing values.

Noisy Data

Noise is a random error or variance in a measured variable. Given a numeric attribute, e.g., demand or sales, how can the data be smoothed to remove the noise? The important techniques are described briefly:

1. **Binning Method:** Binning methods "smooth" a sorted data value by consulting the "neighbourhood", or values around it. The sorted values are distributed into a number of 'buckets', or 'bins'. Because binning methods consult the neighbourhood of values, they perform local smoothing.
2. **Clustering:** Outliers may be detected by clustering, where similar values are organized into groups or \clusters".
3. **Regression Analysis:** *D*ata can be smoothed by fitting data to a function, such as with regression analysis. Linear regression involves finding the "best" line of fit between two variables, so that one variable can be used to predict the other. Multiple linear regression is a technique where there are two or more than two independent variables and one dependent variable. Using regression to find a mathematical equation to fit the data helps smooth out the noise.
4. **Combined Computer and Human Interaction:** Outliers may be identified through a combination of computer and human inspection. For example, an information-theoretic measure was used to help identify outlier patterns in a handwritten character data base for classification. The measure's value reflected the "surprise" content of the predicted character label with respect to the known label patterns.

Inconsistent Data

There may be inconsistencies in a data recorded for some transactions. Knowledge engineering tools may also be used to detect violation of known data constraints. For example, known functional dependencies between attributes can be used to find values contradicting the functional constraints.

Data cleaning is one of the most important issues of Data preparation. The other important issues in data preparation are:

•   **Data Integration:** Data integration combines data from multiple sources to form a coherent data store. Metadata, correlation analysis, data conflict detection, and the resolution of semantic heterogeneity contribute towards smooth data integration.

- **Data Transformation:** Data transformation routines conform the data into appropriate forms for mining. For example, attribute data may be normalized so as to fall between small ranges, such as 0 to 1.0.
- **Data Reduction:** Data reduction techniques include singular value decomposition (the driving element behind principal component analysis), wavelets, regression, log-linear models, histograms, clustering, sampling and the construction of index trees.

STATISTICS AND DATA MINING

Statistics is a branch of mathematics which deals with collection, organization, presentation, analyzing and interpretation of data. However, statistics is not as scary as mathematics for many students pursuing a degree on business administration or management because it is used by every individual for his/her day to day decision making, taking into consideration the risk and uncertainty in this age of little or scarce information. Therefore, it can be said that the data is critical for any decision making. More and better data will lead to better understanding of the data and hence result in better decision making by an individual or an organization.

The statistical techniques regression analysis, probability, Bayes' theorem, decision theory are a few examples which have been the stepping stone for the foundation of both-statistics and data mining.

The definition of data mining is (Han, Kamber, & Pei, 2012):

Data mining is a business process for exploring large amounts of data to discover meaningful patterns and rules.

The characteristics of Data mining can be explained with reference to the important parts of the above definition.

Data Mining is a Business Process

Data mining is a business process that interacts with other business processes. In particular, a process does not have a beginning and an end; it is on-going. The business strategy of any organization or business must include collecting data, analysing data for long term benefit and acting on the results.

At the same time, data mining readily fits with other strategies for understanding markets and customers. Market research, customer panels, and other techniques are compatible with data mining and more intensive data analysis. The key is to recognize the focus on customers and the commonality of data across the enterprise.

Data mining is not limited to business. Both the major parties during the U.S elections utilized data mining of potential voters. Examples of some current data mining products are:

- **IBM:** "Intelligent Miner"
- **Silicon Graphics:** "Mine Set"
- **SAS Corporation:** "SAS Enterprise Miner"
- **California Scientific Software:** "Brain Maker"

Large Amounts of Data

In the age of information, the world abounds with data. It is becoming the case that in order to obtain an intelligent appreciation of current developments, we need to absorb and interpret substantial amounts of data. The amount of data collected has grown at a phenomenal rate over the past few years. Gone are the days of manual analysis and interpretation of data because of the simple reason that manual analysis is slow, expensive and highly subjective. In fact, manual analysis is becoming more impractical these days as the data sets grow larger in size. There is a need to scale up human analysis capabilities to handle the large data sets that we can collect is both economic and scientific. Data collected and stored in data ware houses are used by businesses to gain competitive advantage, increase efficiency and provide valuable services to customers. The computer age has given us both the power to rapidly process, summarize and analyse data and the encouragement to produce and store more data. How much is a lot of data? The possible answers may be "all transactions for 10 million customers" or "terabytes of data".

Because computing power is readily available, a large amount of data is not a handicap; it is an advantage. Data mining lets the computers do what computers do best-dig through lots and lots of data. This, in turn, lets people do what people do best, which is set up the problem and understand the results.

Meaningful Patterns and Rules

The most important part of the definition of data mining is the part about meaningful patterns. The operational side of the business generates data, necessarily generating patterns at the same time. However, the goal of data mining is not to find just any patterns in data, but to find patterns that are useful for the business (Linoff & Berry, 2014).

Finding patterns can be of immense importance to a business. Patterns can serve routine business operations as well as it can mean targeting retention campaigns to customers who are most likely to leave. It can mean optimizing customer acquisition both for the short-term gains in customer numbers and for medium- and long term benefit in customer value.

These days' companies are busy developing business models centred on data mining. Most business houses/corporations have databases on the computer giving minute details of operations and transactions. Companies tend to aggregate data from different sources, bringing the data together to get a more complete picture.

Major Issues in Data Mining

Data mining is a dynamic and fast expanding field with great strengths. The major issues in data mining research are (Han, Kamber, & Pei, 2012):

1. **Mining Methodology:** Researchers have been vigorously developing new data mining methodologies. The various aspects of mining methodology are:
    a. **Mining Various New Kinds of Knowledge:** Data mining covers a wide spectrum of data analysis and knowledge discovery asks, from data characterization and discrimination to association and correlation analysis, classification, regression, clustering, sequence analysis and trend and evolution analysis. Due to the diversity of applications, new mining tasks continue to emerge, making data mining a dynamic and fast growing field.

b. **Mining Knowledge in Multidimensional Space:** When searching for knowledge in large data sets, we can explore the data in multidimensional space i.e. we can search for interesting patterns among combinations of dimensions (attributes) at varying levels of abstraction. Such mining is known as (exploratory) multidimensional data mining. In many cases, data can be aggregated or viewed as a multidimensional data cube. This can substantially enhance the power and flexibility of data mining.

c. **Data Mining - An Interdisciplinary effort:** The power of data mining can be substantially enhanced by integrating new methods from multiple disciplines. For e.g. bug mining- to mine data with natural language text or data mining method for information retrieval and natural language processing.

d. **Boosting the Power of Discovery in a Networked Environment:** Multiple sources of data are interconnected by the Internet. Semantic links across multiple data objects can be used to advantage in data mining. Knowledge derived in one set of objects can be used to boost the discovery of knowledge in a related or semantically linked set of objects.

e. **Handling Uncertainty, Noise, or Incompleteness of Data:** Data often contain noise, errors, exceptions or uncertainty, or are incomplete. Errors and noise may confuse the data mining process, leading to the derivation of erroneous patterns. Data cleaning, data pre-processing, outlier detection and removal, and uncertainty reasoning are examples of techniques that need to be integrated with the data mining process.

f. **Pattern Evaluation and Pattern Guided Mining:** Not all the patterns created by data mining process are interesting. Data mining techniques help in assessing the interestingness of discovered patterns based on subjective measures. These estimate the value of patterns with respect to a given user class based on user beliefs or expectations.

2. **User Interaction:** The user plays an important role in the data mining process.

a. **Interactive Mining:** The data mining process should be highly interactive. Thus, it is important to build flexible user interfaces and an exploratory mining environment, facilitating the user's interaction with the system. Interactive data mining should allow users to dramatically change and focus of a search, to refine mining requests based on returned results, and to drill, dice and pivot through the data and knowledge space interactively, dynamically exploring "cube space" while mining.

b. **Incorporation of Background Knowledge:** Background knowledge, constraints, rules and other information regarding the domain under study should be incorporated into the knowledge discovery process. Such knowledge can be said to be used for pattern evaluation as well as to guide the search toward interesting patterns.

c. **Ad Hoc Data mining and Data Mining Query Language:** Query languages such as SQL have played an important role in flexible searching because they allow users to pose ad hoc queries. Similarly, high level data mining query languages will give users the freedom to define ad hoc data mining tasks. Optimization of the processing of such flexible mining requests is another promising area of study.

d. **Presentation and Visualizing of Data Mining Results:** The data mining results should be presented vividly and flexibly so that the discovered knowledge can be easily understood and directly usable by humans. This is especially crucial if the data mining process is interactive.

3. **Efficiency and Scalability:** Efficiency and scalability are always considered when comparing data mining algorithms.

   a. **Efficiency and Scalability of Data Mining Algorithms:** Data mining algorithms must be efficient and scalable in order to effectively extract information from huge amounts of data in many data repositories or in dynamic data streams. Efficiency, scalability, performance, optimization and the ability to execute in real time are key criteria that derive the development of many new data mining algorithms.

   b. **Parallel, Distributed and Incremental Mining Algorithms:** These algorithms came into existence due to the humongous size of the data sets, the wide distribution of data, and the organizational complexity of some data mining methods. Such algorithms first partition the data into "pieces". Each piece is processed, in parallel, by searching for patterns. The parallel processes may interact with one another. The patterns from each partition are eventually merged. Cloud computing and Cluster computing, which are computers in a distributed and collaborative way to tackle very large scale computational tasks, are also active research themes in parallel data mining.

4. **Diversity of Database Types:** The wide diversity of data base types brings about challenges to data mining. These include:

   a. **Handling Complex Type of Data:** Diverse applications generate a wide spectrum of data types such as structured, semi structured and unstructured data, from stable data repositories to dynamic data streams, from simple data objects to temporal data, biological sequences, sensor data, hypertext data, multimedia data, social network data and many more. It is unrealistic to expect one data mining system to mine all kinds of data, given the diversity of data types and different goals of data mining. The construction of effective and efficient data mining tools are diverse applications remain a challenging and active area of research.

   b. **Mining Dynamic, Networked and Global Data Repositories:** Multiple sources of data are interconnected by the Internet and various kinds of networks forming gigantic, distributed and heterogeneous global information systems and networks. Mining such gigantic, interconnected information networks may help disclose many more patterns and knowledge in heterogeneous data sets than can be discovered from a small set of isolated data repositories.

5. **Data Mining and Society:**

   a. **Social Impacts of Data Mining:** With data mining penetrating our everyday lives, it is important to study the impact of data mining on society. How can we use datamining to the benefit of our society? How can we guard against its misuse? With the booming of the internet (i.e. ecommerce, social networks, blogs, etc.) the concerns about the personal privacy issue is being debated by one and all. People are afraid that their personal information is being collected and utilized in an unethical manner that is increasingly a potential cause of worry. Businesses collect information in many ways in order to understand the purchasing behaviour of their customers. In cases of acquisition, the personal information of customers owned by one company is sold to the other company.

   b. **Security:** A big issue especially when the businesses own the details of the customer e.g. PAN number, Aadhaar card number, mobile number, birthdays, family income, etc. It is a matter of great concern the way the information about the customers is being utilized by the companies.

    c.   **Privacy Preserving Data Mining:** The misuse of the information collected through data mining is a potential threat to the privacy of the customer. This information is being utilized by unethical people to exploit the vulnerable customer. The improper disclosure or use of data and the potential violation of individual privacy and data protection rights are areas of concern that need to be addressed. Also, the inaccuracy of the process of data mining may lead to inaccurate information about the customer which in turn will affect the decision making of the companies. The aim is to observe data sensitivity and preserve people's privacy while performing successful data mining.

Statistical Modelling

Rational procedures of decision making depend upon a well-founded scientific method, based on logic as well as empiricism. Phenomenological research emphasizes more on statistical approaches using empirical data whereas decision models use both statistical and mathematical models dealing with comparatively more highly controlled situations in an organization. Moreover, they are prescriptive in nature as against descriptive models (which are based on empiricism) of phenomenological research.

In this section those statistical models are discussed which lay the foundation for data mining. The techniques are:

- Tools for Descriptive/Summarizing data.
- Counting and probability techniques.
- Regression analysis (Linear, Discriminant, Logistic and cluster analysis).

Tools for Summarizing Data

There are two major ways of summarizing data:

1.   The first provides the graphical representation of the data i.e. with the help of histograms and the second provides the measures of central tendency and the amount of variation in the data. There are three measures of central tendency. These three measures will not be the same for distribution of values that are not symmetrical and, when different, they are useful for different purposes.
    a.   The mean is calculated by dividing the sum of all observations by the number of observations.
    b.   The median is obtained by finding the value below which 50 percent of the observations lie.
    c.   The mode is found by determining the most frequently appearing observation in the data. Data can have more than one mode.
2.   Variation or Dispersion measures how 'spread out' the data is. The popular measures of variation are standard deviation and variance. The variance is the square of the standard deviation.

Counting and Probability Techniques

Bayes classification methods are the most important probability techniques which have applications in data mining. Bayesian classifiers are statistical classifiers that can predict class membership probabilities such as probability that a given tuple belongs to a particular class. Bayesian classification is used on Bayes' theorem. Studies comparing classification algorithms have found a simple Bayesian Classier known as the naïve Bayesian classifier to be comparable in performance with decision tree and selected neural network classifiers. Bayesian classifiers have also exhibited high accuracy and speed when applied to large databases (Han, Kamber, & Pei, 2012).

Naïve Bayesian Classifiers assume that the effect of an attribute value on a given class is independent of the values of other attributes. This assumption is called class conditional independence. It is made to simplify the computations involved and, in this sense, is considered "naïve". When this assumption holds true, then the naïve Bayesian classifier is the most accurate in comparison with all other classifiers. In practice, however, dependencies can exist between variables. Bayesian belief networks specify joint conditional probability distributions. They allow class conditional independencies to be defined between subsets of variables. They provide a graphical model of causal relationships, on which learning can be performed. Trained Bayesian belief networks can be used for classification. Bayesian belief networks are also known as belief networks, Bayesian networks, and probabilistic networks.

A belief network is defined by two components- a directed acyclic graph and a set of conditional probability tables. Each node in the acyclic graph represents a random variable. The variables may be discrete or continuous valued. They may correspond to the actual attributes given in the data or to "hidden variables' believed to form a relationship e.g. in case of a medical data, a hidden variable may indicate a syndrome, representing a number of symptoms that, together characterize a specific disease. Each arc represents a probabilistic dependence. If an arc is drawn from a node X to node Y, then node X is a parent or immediate predecessor of Y, and Y is the descendant of X. Each variable is conditionally independent of its non-descendants in the graph, given its parents (Han, Kamber, & Pei, 2012).

Regression Analysis

Regression analysis is by far the most widely used and versatile dependence technique, applicable in every facet of business decision making. For example, regression analysis is the foundation for business forecasting models to model of a firms' performance in a market. Regression models are used to study how consumers make decisions or form impressions and attitudes. In statistics, prediction is usually synonymous with regression analysis. The objective of regression analysis is to predict a single dependent variable from the knowledge of one or more independent variables. When the problem involves a single independent variable, the technique is called simple regression. When the problem involves two or more independent variables it is called multiple regression. The basic idea is that a model is created that maps values from predictors in such a way that the lowest error occurs in making a prediction.

$Y = b0 + b1X1$ ....Simple regression equation

$Y = b0 + b1X1 + b2X2$ ....Multiple regression equation

where, b0 is the Y-intercept, b1, b2 are the regression coefficients, X1 and X2 are the variables.

In case of simple regression, the relationship between the two variables is plotted in a Scatter diagram with a straight line (regression line) passing through the scattered points. This straight line tends to minimize the error between the actual prediction value and the estimated values i.e. the point on the regression line. The objective is to obtain the smallest possible sum of squared errors as the measure of prediction accuracy. As researchers, we are always interested in improving our prediction. We are searching for one or more additional (independent) variables that might improve our prediction.

Although we have a number of independent variables, the question facing the researcher is-which one to choose? Here we can rely on the concept of association, represented by the coefficient of correlation. Two variables are said to be correlated if changes in one variable are associated with changes in the other variable. Therefore, coefficient of correlation is fundamental to regression analysis by describing the relationship between two variables.

We can select the "best" independent variable based on the correlation coefficient because the higher the correlation coefficient, the stronger the relationship and hence greater the predictive accuracy. In regression equation, we represent b0 as the intercept. The amount of change in the dependent variable due to the independent variable is represented by b1, also known as the regression coefficient. Using the method of least squares, we can estimate the values of b0 and b1such that the sum of squared errors of prediction is minimized. The prediction error, the difference between the actual and the predicted values of the dependent variable is termed as residual (e or ė) (Hair et. al., 2012).

Improvements in predicting the dependent variable are possible by adding independent variables and even transforming them to represent non- linear relations. To do so, we must make several assumptions about the relationships between the dependent and the independent variables that affect the statistical procedure (least squares) used for multiple regression. The basic issue is to know whether in the course of calculating the regression coefficients and predicting the dependent variable, the assumptions of regression analysis have been met. We must know whether the errors in prediction are as a result of the absence of a relationship between the variables or caused by some characteristics of the data not accommodated by the regression model. The assumptions to be examined include (Linoff & Berry, 2014):

1. Linearity of the phenomenon measured.
2. Constant variance of the error terms.
3. Independence of the error terms.
4. Normality of the error term distribution.

The assumptions underlying multiple regression analysis apply both to the individual variables (independent and dependent) and to the relationship as a whole. Once the variate has been derived, it acts collectively in predicting the dependent variable, which necessitates assessing the assumptions not only for the independent variables, but also for the variate. The principal measure of the prediction error for the variate is the residual- the difference between the observed and the predicted values for the dependent variable. Plotting the residuals versus the independent or the predicted values is the method of identifying assumption violations for the overall relationship (Hair et. al., 2012).

In logistic regression, the dependent variable assumes only two discrete values. For example, a bank might like to develop an estimated regression equation for predicting whether a person will be approved for a credit card. The dependent variable can be coded as y=1 if the bank approves the request for credit card and y=0 if the bank rejects the request for a credit card. Using logistic regression, we can estimate the probability that the bank will approve the request for a credit card given a particular set of values for the chosen independent variables.

Logistic regression and Discriminant analysis are the appropriate statistical techniques when the data involves a single categorical dependent variable and several metric independent variables. In many cases, the dependent variable consists of two groups or classifications, for example, male versus female, high versus low or good versus bad. In other instances, more than two groups are involved, such as low, medium and high classifications. Discriminant analysis and logistic regression are capable of handling either two groups or multiple (three or more) groups. The results of discriminant analysis and logistic regression can assist in profiling the intergroup characteristics of the subjects and in assigning them to their appropriate groups (Hair et. al., 2012).

Cluster Analysis/ Clustering

Identifying groups of individuals or objects that are similar to each other but different from individuals in other groups can be intellectually satisfying, profitable, or sometimes both. Using your customer base, you may be able to form clusters of customers who have similar buying habits or demographics. You can take advantage of these similarities to target offers to subgroups that are most likely to be receptive to them. Based on scores on psychological inventories, you can cluster patients into subgroups that have similar response patterns. This may help you in targeting appropriate treatment and studying typologies of diseases. By analyzing the mineral contents of excavated materials, you can study their origins and spread (Linoff & Berry, 2014).

Some business applications are:

- You need to identify people with similar patterns of past purchases so that you can tailor your marketing strategies.
- Suppose we have a database of the characteristics of lots of different people, and their credit rating e.g. how much they earn, whether they own their house, how old they are, etc. You want to be able to use this database to give a new person a credit rating. Intuitively, you want to give similar credit ratings to similar people.

A large number of techniques have been proposed for forming clusters from distance matrices. The most important types are hierarchical techniques, optimization techniques and mixture models.

Hierarchical Methods or Hierarchical Clustering

There are two major types of hierarchical techniques: divisive and agglomerative. Agglomerative hierarchical techniques are the more commonly used. The idea behind this set of techniques is to start with each cluster comprising of exactly one object and then progressively agglomerating (combining) the two nearest clusters until there is just one cluster left consisting of all the objects. An example of Agglomerative clustering can be clustering people by Age.

Nearness of clusters is based on a measure of distance between clusters. All agglomerative methods require as input a distance measure between all the objects that are to be clustered. This measure of distance between objects is mapped into a metric for the distance between clusters (sets of objects) metrics for the distance between two clusters. If we take the example of clustering people by Age, the distance between two people is simply the difference in their ages.

Hierarchical clustering method can be categorized into-agglomerative or divisive clustering. Agglomerative clustering method starts by letting each object form its own cluster and iteratively merges cluster into larger clusters, until all the objects are in a single cluster whereas divisive clustering involves placing all the objects in one cluster, which is the hierarchy's root. It then divides the root cluster into smaller sub-clusters.

Farthest Neighbor (Also Called Complete Linkage)

Here the distance between two clusters is defined as the distance between the farthest pair of objects with one object in the pair belonging to a distinct cluster. This method tends to produce clusters at the early stages that have objects that are within a narrow range of distances from each other. If we visualize them as objects in space the objects in such clusters would have a more spherical shape.

Group Average (Also Called Average Linkage)

Here the distance between two clusters is defined as the average distance between all possible pairs of objects with one object in each pair belonging to a distinct cluster.

When an algorithm uses the minimum distance to measure the distance between clusters, it is called as nearest neighbor clustering algorithm. If the clustering process is terminated when the distance between nearest clusters exceeds a user defined threshold, it is called as single linkage algorithm.

Automatic cluster detection is an undirected data mining technique of data mining that can be used to learn the structure of complex data. Directed data mining techniques can always measure their performance with respect to a target variable whereas undirected techniques have no such reference point.

Clustering does not answer any question directly, but studying clusters can lead to valuable insights. One important application of clustering is customer segmentation. Clusters of customers form naturally occurring customer segments of people whose similarities may include similar needs and interests.

Another important application of clustering is breaking complex data sets into simpler clusters to increase the chance of finding patterns that were drowned out in the original data. Automatic cluster detection is a form of modeling. Clusters are detected in training data and the rules governing the clusters are captured in a model, which can be used to score previously unclassified data. Scoring a dataset with a cluster model means assigning a cluster labels to each record or in case of soft clustering, assigning several scores indicating the probability of membership in various clusters. After cluster labels have been assigned, they often become input to directed data mining models (Linoff & Berry, 2014).

The K-means cluster detection algorithm creates clusters with boundaries that extend half way to the neighbouring clusters in all directions, even if the neighbor is very far away. In directions, where no neighbor exists, a K-means cluster goes on forever. Including a maximum cluster diameter in the cluster scoring model is therefore recommended so distant outliers are declared to be members of no cluster.

The cluster centroid or average cluster member provides one way of thinking about what cluster members have in common. The variables with large z-scores define major differences between a cluster and its neighbours and the population as a whole.

In the K-means clustering algorithm, the cluster centers can be used to define a Voronoi diagram, a diagram whose lines mark the points that are equidistant from the two nearest seeds. The result is that each region on a Voronoi diagram consists of all the points closest to one of the cluster centers, making Voronoi diagrams a good way to visualize the K-means clustering algorithm (Linoff & Berry, 2014).

K-means clustering is a scalable and powerful technique and can run on very large data sets. Managers can implement K-means clustering using SQL.The K-means algorithm has a number of variations including soft K-means, K-medians, K-medoids and K-modes. Each of these extends the usefulness of the technique to new domains. K-means and its close relatives are good, general purpose clustering tools, but there are situations when other cluster detection techniques are more appropriate (Linoff & Berry, 2014).

NEXT GEN TECHNIQUES

Decision Trees

Decision tree comprises of nodes and branches connecting the nodes. The nodes located at the bottom are known as leaves and indicate classes. The top of the node in the tree is called the root. Decision nodes include all the nodes except the leaves. The decision nodes specify the decision to be performed. All decision tree algorithms are based on Hunt's algorithm of concept learning which embodies a method used by humans when learning simple concepts i.e. finding key distinguishing features between two categories (Linoff & Berry, 2014).

Example of Business applications:

- Suppose your organization is using legacy software. Some influential stakeholders believe that by upgrading this software your organization can save millions, while others feel that staying with the legacy software is the safest option, even though it is not meeting the current company needs. The stakeholders supporting the upgrade of the software are further split into two factions: those that support buying the new software and those that support building the new software in-house. In the meeting room the stakeholders point out the negative risks for each option, thus adding to the confusion.

By exploring all possibilities and consequences, you can quantify the decisions and convince stakeholders. This is known as Decision Tree Analysis.

- Decision tree can help a mobile company to set up a predictive model to understand the 'Churn' among the post -paid mobile subscribers. Churn can be voluntary churn i.e. when the customer decides to leave or Involuntary Churn i.e. when the company tells customer to leave, usually because they have not been paying the bills.

Decision trees are grown using a recursive algorithm that evaluates all values of all inputs to find the split that causes the greatest increase in purity in the children. The same thing happens again inside each child. The process continues until no more splits can be found or some other limit is reached. The tree is then pruned to remove unstable branches. Several tests are used as splitting criteria, including the chi-square test for categorical targets and the F test for numeric targets. There are many different decision tree algorithms such as CART, CHAID, etc. (Linoff & Berry, 2014).

CART stands for Classification and Regression Trees and is a data exploration and prediction algorithm developed by Leo Breiman, Jerome Friedman, Richard Olshen and Charles Stone and is nicely detailed in their 1984 book "Classification and Regression Trees." In building the CART tree each predictor is picked based on how well it teases apart the records with different predictions. For instance, one measure that is used to determine whether a given split point for a give predictor is better than another is the entropy metric. The measure originated from the work done by Claude Shannon and Warren Weaver on information theory in 1949. They were concerned with how information could be efficiently communicated over telephone lines. Interestingly, their results also prove useful in creating decision trees (Linoff & Berry, 2014).

One of the great advantages of CART is that the algorithm has the validation of the model and the discovery of the optimally general model built deeply into the algorithm. The CART algorithm is relatively robust with respect to missing data. If the value is missing for a particular predictor in a particular record, that record will not be used in making the determination of the optimal split when the tree is being built. In effect CART will utilizes as much information as it has on hand in order to make the decision for picking the best possible split.

Another equally popular decision tree technology to CART is CHAID or Chi-Square Automatic Interaction Detector. CHAID is similar to CART in that it builds a decision tree but it differs in the way that it chooses its splits. Instead of the entropy or Gini metrics for choosing optimal splits the technique relies on the chi square test used in contingency tables to determine which categorical predictor is furthest from independence with the prediction values.

In a nutshell, decision trees possess certain advantages and disadvantages (Goyal & Rajan, 2012):

- They are computationally simple.
- They reveal relationships between the rules which are written from the tree.
- They generate very complex rules which are hard to prune.
- They require large amounts of memory to store.

Neural Networks

Neural network or Artificial Neural network derives its name from their historical development which started off with the premise that machines could be made to think if scientists found ways to mimic the structure and functioning of human brain on the computer. Artificial neural networks were created to simulate the working of biological neural networks using digital computers.

The inspiration for artificial neural networks is a biological model of how brains work. Although predating digital computers, the basic ideas have proven powerful. In biology, neurons fire after their inputs reach a certain threshold. The field has really taken off since the 1980s, when statisticians started to use them and understand them better (Linoff & Berry, 2014).

The neural network is a complete package for expert consulting services. Here the neural network is deployed by trusted experts who have a track record of success. Either the experts are able to explain the models or they are trusted that the models do work.

The neural network is a complete solution for fraud prediction (e.g. HNC's Falcon system for credit card fraud prediction and Advanced Software Applications Model MAX package for direct marketing). This allows the neural network to be carefully crafted for one particular application and once it has been proven successful it can be used over and over again without requiring a deep understanding of how it works.

Neural networks have a long history of application in other areas such as the military for the automated driving of an unmanned vehicle at 30 miles per hour on paved roads to biological simulations such as learning the correct pronunciation of English words from written text.

The most common network for predictive modeling is the multilayer perceptron. Radial basis function networks are also popular. Radial basis function (RBF) networks have been very useful in data mining tasks because of their many desirable characteristics. First, the time required to train RBF networks is much shorter than the time required for most other types of neural networks. Second, their topology is relatively simple to determine. Third, unlike most of the supervised learning neural network algorithms that find only a local optimum, the RBF's find a global optimum. Like other neural networks they are universal approximators, which means they can approximate any continuous function to any degree of accuracy, given a sufficient number of hidden layer neurons (Cios et al., 2010).

When designing the RBF network, before its training, the following key parameters must be determined:

1. Topology, i.e. determination of the number of hidden layer neurons (and their centers) and determination of the number of output neurons.
2. Selection of the similarity/ distance measures.
3. Determination of the hidden layer neuron radii.
4. Selection of the basis functions.
5. Neuron models used in the hidden and output layers.
6. After the selection of the parameters the confidence measures are used to calculate the confidence in the output of an RBF network on new unseen data.

Although RBF topology consists of only three layers, how many neurons should be used in a hidden layer, needs to be determined. The number of neurons in the input layer is defined by the dimensionality of the input vector, X. The input layer nodes are not neurons at all: they are just feeding the input vector into all hidden layer neurons (Cios et al., 2010).

The number of neurons in the output layer is determined by the number of categories present in the training data. For e.g. for three categories, we would have three output neurons.

The most complicated part of using a neural network is the preparation of input data. With neural networks, getting all the inputs to be numeric and in a small range, is of utmost importance i.e. to find good numeric representations for categorical data. Since neural networks are sensitive to data issues, therefore, extra attention is paid towards data transformations.

As compared to decision trees, neural networks are explained by weights and also comprises of complicated mathematical formula. Decision trees are popular because they can provide a list of rules. Unfortunately, making sense of this is beyond our human powers of comprehension. Overall neural networks are very powerful and can produce good models; they just can't tell us how they do it (Linoff & Berry, 2014).

Association Rules

Association rule mining, one of the most important techniques. The aim of association rules is to extract interesting correlations, frequent patterns, associations or casual structures among sets of items in the transaction databases or other data repositories. Due to good scalability characteristics of the association rules algorithms and ever growing size of the accumulated data, association rules are an essential data mining tool for extracting knowledge from data. The discovery of interesting associations provides a source of information often used by businesses for decision making. Some application areas of association rules are market-basket data analysis, cross marketing, catalog design, loss-leader analysis, clustering, data pre-processing, genomics, etc.

The areas of application of association rules include, but not limited to telecommunication networks, market and risk management, inventory control etc.

An association rule is an expression of $X \rightarrow Y$, where X is a set of items, and Y is a single item. Association rule methods are an initial data exploration approach that is often applied to extremely large data set. An example is grocery store market basket data. Work on more efficient algorithms continues. Association rules mining provides valuable information in assessing significant correlations. They have been applied to a variety of fields, to include medicine and medical insurance fraud detection. Business applications in addition to market basket analysis include warranty analysis. The most popular method is the a priori algorithm. A number of methods have been developed to efficiently identify market basket relationships.

Market basket data in its rawest form would be the transactional list of purchases by customer, indicating only the items purchased together (with their prices). This data is challenging because of a number of characteristics:

1.   A very large number of records (often millions of transactions per day).
2.   Sparseness (each market basket contains only a small portion of items carried).
3.   Heterogeneity (those with different tastes tend to purchase a specific subset of items).

The aim of market-basket analysis is to identify what products tend to be purchased together. Analyzing transaction-level data can identify purchase patterns, such as which frozen vegetables and side dishes are purchased with steak during barbecue season. This information can be used in determining where to place products in the store, as well as aid inventory management. Product presentations and staffing can be more intelligently planned for specific times of day, days of the week, or holidays. Another commercial application is electronic couponing, tailoring coupon face value and distribution timing using information obtained from market baskets. Data mining of market basket data has been demonstrated for a long time, and has been applied in a variety of applications.

Market-Basket analysis, one of the most intuitive applications of association rules, strives to analyze customer buying patterns by finding associations between items that customers put into their baskets. For example, one can discover that customers buy bread and milk together, and even some particular brands of milk are more often bought with certain brands of bread, e.g., multigrain bread and Amul milk. These and other more interesting (and previously unknown) rules can be used to maximize profits by helping to design successful marketing campaigns, and by customizing store layout. In case of the milk and bread example, the retailer may not offer discounts for both at the same time, but just for one; the milk can be put at the opposite end of the store with respect to bread, to increase the customer traffic so that customers may possibly buy more products.

In case of market basket analysis, we represent each product in a store as a Boolean variable, which represents whether an item is present or absent. Each customer's basket is represented as a Boolean vector, denoting which items are purchased. The vectors are analyzed to find which products are bought together (by different customers) i.e. associated with each other. These occurrences are represented in the form of association rules.

An example of association rule can be illustrated as follows in Table 1.

Association Rule

An implication expression of the form:

{X}→{Y}, where X and Y are item sets and (→means co-occurrence not Causality)

Table 1. Association rule example

Transaction ID	Items
1	Bread, Milk
2	Bread, Biscuit, Diaper, Eggs,
3	Milk, Diaper, Biscuit, Pepsi
4	Bread, Milk, Diaper, Biscuit
5	Bread, Milk, Diaper, Pepsi

Examples of Association Rules:

{Milk} → {Bread}

{Milk, Bread} → {Eggs, Pepsi}

{Diaper, Bread} → {Milk}

Rule Evaluation Metrics

- **Support(s):** Fraction of transactions that contain both X and Y
- **Confidence(c):** Measures how often items in Y appear in transactions that contain X

For example:

{Milk, Diaper} → {Biscuit}

$$S = \frac{\text{No of times }\left(\text{Milk, Diaper, Biscuit}\right)\text{ appears}}{\text{Total no. of Transactions}} = 2/5$$

$$C = \frac{\text{No of times }\left(\text{Milk, Diaper, Biscuit}\right)\text{ appears}}{\text{No. of times }\left(\text{Milk, Diaper}\right)\text{ appears}} = 2/3$$

Market basket analysis can be very useful to small businesses. However, specialty data mining software capable of supporting market basket analysis is expensive, and requires specialists who understand that software. While the software Poly Analyst is easy to use, it also involves additional investment, and the output is "black box" in the sense that it is difficult to see why particular products were grouped together.

Generating market basket groups through SQL queries provides a means to obtain association rule data without the need for additional software. The benefit of this method is not just saving the required investment for software acquisition and its training costs, but in the flexibility and accuracy of the results. The associations discovered between items through the SQL queries are more accurate, discovering the relationships that were not identified by the commercial software. This method provides users with a set of associations that are readily available for grouping based on any desired item. In this method, the relationships are known and controlled by users, and the number of sale transactions for paired items is available to the user, which is an advantage comparing to the commercial software output that does not describe the association rules.

REFERENCES

Adejuwon, A., & Mosavi, A. (2010). Domain Driven Data Mining-Application to Business. *International Journal of Computer Science*, *7*(4), 41-44.

Cios, K. J., Pedrycz, W., Swiniarski, R. W., & Kurgan, L. (2010). *Data Mining: A Knowledge Discovery Approach*. Springer Limited.

Goyal, M. & Rajan, V. (2012). Applications of Data Mining in Higher Education. *International Journal of Computer Science*, *9*(2), 113-120.

Hair, J., Black, W., Tatham, R. L., & Anderson, R. (2011). *Multivariate Data Analysis*. Pearson Education.

Han, J., Kamber, M., & Pei, J. (2012). Data Mining Concepts and Techniques (3rd ed.). Elsevier Inc.

Hand, D., Mannila, H., & Smyth, P. (2001). *Principles of Data Mining*. Cambridge, MA: The MIT Press.

Linoff, G., & Michael, B. (2014). *Data Mining Techniques*. Wiley Publishing Inc.

Yahia, M. E., & El-Mukashfi El-Taher, M. (2010). A New Approach for Evaluation of Data Mining Techniques. *IJCSI*, *7*(5), 181–186.

Chapter 3
Data Classification:
Its Techniques and Big Data

A. Sheik Abdullah
Thiagarajar College of Engineering, India

R. Suganya
Thiagarajar College of Engineering, India

S. Selvakumar
G. K. M. College of Engineering and Technology, India

S. Rajaram
Thiagarajar College of Engineering, India

ABSTRACT

Classification is considered to be the one of the data analysis technique which can be used over many applications. Classification model predicts categorical continuous class labels. Clustering mainly deals with grouping of variables based upon similar characteristics. Classification models are experienced by comparing the predicted values to that of the known target values in a set of test data. Data classification has many applications in business modeling, marketing analysis, credit risk analysis; biomedical engineering and drug retort modeling. The extension of data analysis and classification makes the insight into big data with an exploration to processing and managing large data sets. This chapter deals with various techniques, methodologies that correspond to the classification problem in data analysis process and its methodological impacts to big data.

INTRODUCTION

Data is an abstract concept from which information and knowledge are derived. Raw unprocessed data often moves and crosses stage by stage for its exact representation and processed form of representation. Data is a collection of facts which is the representation of values and measurements.

Meanwhile information is referred to as processed data. It reveals the content or message through direct or indirect form of representation. Hence it is in a meaningful form of representation which can be easily conveyed and understood by the users. It resolves uncertainty and ambiguity.

DOI: 10.4018/978-1-5225-2031-3.ch003

Qualities of Data

The quality signifies the characteristics of data which are specifically suited for the data analysis process. The following characteristics represent the quality of a good data:

1. Accurate
2. Represented numerically
3. Relationship
4. Signified for definite purpose
5. Completeness
6. Clearly Understandable

Types of Data Elements

At the start of every data analysis it is necessary to identify the type of data which can then be considered for analysis. The following represents the types of data elements which can be used up for the determination of the type of data.

Continuous Data

These are the type of data elements which are defined upon an interval scale. Examples include income of employees in an organization, sales of an enterprise and so on.

Categorical Data

These kinds of data elements are of three types:

1. **Ordinal Data:** The type of data elements which takes restricted set of values with meaningful ordering. Example includes the classification of age into young, middle age and old group.
2. **Nominal Data:** These are the type of data elements which takes restricted set of values with no any such meaningful ordering between them. Example includes profession of employees, marital status and so on.
3. **Binary Data:** These are the types of data elements that can take only two values. Examples include gender and employment status of an employee.

Data Standardization

Data standardization is the mechanism of normalizing the data to a defined specified range. It provides the mechanism of coding the data to a smaller specified range. The following are the data normalization procedures used up for scaling the given variable.

Min-Max Normalization

This type of normalization scales up the data into a smaller specified range most probably [0-1]. It is represented as:

$$X_{new} = \left(\frac{\left(X_{old} - \min\left(X_{old} \right) \right)}{\left(\max\left(X_{old} \right) - \min\left(X_{old} \right) \right)} \right) \cdot \left(new\,\max - new\,\min \right) + new\,\min \tag{1}$$

where the newmin and newmax are the newly specified minimum and maximum values respectively.

Z-Score Normalization

In this type of normalization, the mean value of the altered data values will be reduced to zero. It is represented by:

$$Z_{score} = \frac{\left(x_i - \mu \right)}{\sigma} \tag{2}$$

where, μ is the mean value and σ is the standard deviation.

Normalization by Decimal Scaling

This type of normalization transforms the data range into {-1 1}. It is represented by the formula,

$$X_{new} = X_{old} \div 10^N \tag{3}$$

Missing Data

In a dataset of records missing data can occur due to various reasons the information is incomplete, non-applicable, disclose of information and so on. But some of the analytical techniques in data mining deals directly with missing data values before taking the data for analyzing the results. The following are some of the methods to deal with missing data values (Little & Rubin, 2002):

- **Replace the Missing Value:** This provides the mechanism of replacing the field of missing value with an known value, one way is to determine the mean and then fill the tuple of record of missing value. In certain cases of dataset with large tuples of records then this case might be tedious.
- **Remain the Data Tuple for Analysis:** In some cases, the missing field of data might be meaningful. When considering those cases, they can be categorized into a separate category of class of record during analysis which then makes some exact predictive results.
- **Delete the Tuple of Record:** This is one of the straightforward opinion in which the data record gets removed during the analysis phase. If the missing field of record is removed at random phase, then the target analysis might not be meaningful for data prediction and interpretation.

Data Classification: An Introduction

Data mining algorithms are classified into three different learning approaches: supervised, unsupervised and semi-supervised. In supervised learning, the algorithms works with a set of examples whose labels are well-known. The labels can be small values (nominal) in the case of the classification task, or numerical values in the case of the regression task. In unsupervised learning, quite the reverse, the labels of the examples in the dataset are unidentified, and the algorithm usually aims at grouping examples according to the resemblance of their attribute values, characterizing a clustering job. At last semi-supervised learning is usually used when a small subset of labelled examples is offered, together with an massive number of unlabeled examples.

The classification task can be seen as a supervised method where every instance fit in to a class, which is specified by the value of a unique goal attribute or basically the class attribute. The goal attribute can take on definite values, each of them corresponding to a class. Each example consists of two parts, specifically a set of predictor attribute values and a goal attribute value. The former are used to predict the value at the last. The predictor attributes should be significant for predicting the class of an instance. In the classification task the set of examples being extracted is divided into two mutually exclusive and exhaustive sets, called the training set and the test set. The classification process is respectively divided into two phases:

1. **Training Phase:** In this phase, a classification model is built from the training set.
2. **Testing Phase:** In this phase, the model is evaluated on the test set.

In the training phase, the algorithm has right to use to the values of both predicator attributes and the goal attributes for all illustrations of the training set, and it utilizes that information to construct a classification model. This model represents classification information – basically, a relationship between predictor attribute values and classes – that permit the forecast of the class of an illustration given its predictor attribute values. For testing phase, the test set the class values of the examples is not exposed. In the testing phase, only once a prediction is made is the algorithm authorized to see the actual class of the just classified example. One of the key goals of a classification algorithm is to exploit the predictive accuracy obtained by the classification model when classifying examples in the test set unseen throughout training phase.

In some cases, such as lazy knowledge, the training phase is absent entirely, and the classification is performed straightly from the relationship of the training instances to the test example. The output of a classification algorithm may be presented for a test instance in one of the two ways:

1. **Discrete Tag:** In this case, a tag is returned for the test instance.
2. **Numbers Set:** In this case, a numbers set can be converted to a discrete label for a test instance, by selecting the class with the elevated set for that test instance.

Data Classification Technologies

In this segment, the different methods that are frequently used for data classification will be discussed. The most common methods used in data classification are decision trees, Support Vector Machine methods, Naive Bayesian method, instance-based method and neural networks. The classification among technologies is illustrated in Figure 1.

Figure 1. Data mining paradigms

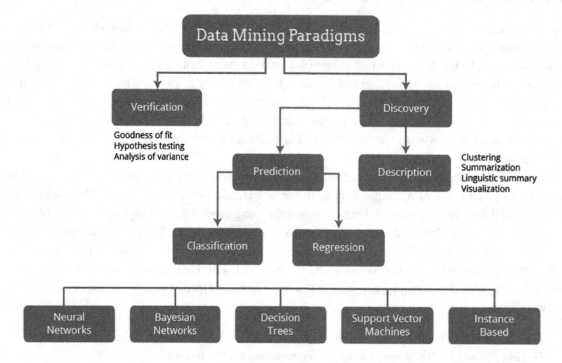

APPROACHES TO DATA CLASSIFICATION

Decision Trees

Decision tree learning is a process for resembling discrete-valued target functions, in which the learned function is represented by a decision tree. It generates a hierarchical partitioning of the data, which relates the different partitions at the leaf level to the different classes. Decision trees classify illustrations by sorting them down the tree from the root to a few leaf nodes, which provides the classification of the instances. Each node in the tree specifies a test of some attribute of the illustration, and each branch falling from that node corresponds to one of the possible values for this attribute. An occurrence is classified by starting at the root node of the tree, testing the attribute specified by this node, then shifting down the tree branch corresponding to the value of the attribute in the given example. This procedure is then repeated for the sub tree rooted at the new node (Breiman, Friedman, Olshen, & Stone, 1992).

The hierarchical partitioning at each level is created with the use of an inference split criterion. The inference split criterion may either use a condition on a single element or it may contain a condition on multiple elements. The former is referred to as a univariate split, while the last is referred to as a multivariate split (Brodley & Utgoff, n.d.). The objective is to pick the attribute that is most useful for classifying examples. The overall approach is to try to recursively split the training data so as to maximize the bias among the diverse classes over diverse nodes. The discrimination among the different classes is maximized, when the point of skew among the diverse classes in a given node is maximized. A measure such as gini-index or entropy is used in order to quantify this skew.

For example if $q1......qk$ is the fraction of the records belonging to the k different classes in a node N, then the gini-index G(N) of the node N is defined as follows:

$$G(N) = 1 - \sum_{i-1}^{k} qi^2 \tag{4}$$

The value of G(N) lies between 0 and 1-1/k. The lesser the significance of G(N), the superior the skew. In this cases where the classes are regularly balanced, the value is 1-1/k. The alternative measure is entropy E(N):

$$E(N) = -\sum_{i-1}^{k} qi \cdot \log(qi) \tag{5}$$

The value of the entropy lies between 0 and log(k). The value is log(k), when the records are perfectly balanced among the different classes. This matches to the scenario with maximum entropy. The smaller the entropy, the greater the skew in the data. Thus gini-index and entropy provide an effectual way to assess the quality of a node in terms of its level of discrimination between the different classes.

Algorithm Decision Trees

```
01: Begin
02:          for d=1 to number of training observations and its class values
03:              for a=1 to number of candidate attributes
04:                  Select a splitting criterion
05:              end for
06:          end for
07:          Create a node N_d
08:          if all observations in the training dataset have the same class
output
          value C, then
09:              return N_d as a leaf node labeled with C.
10:              if attribute list = {Ø}, then
11:                  return N_d as a leaf node labeled with majority class
output value.
12:                  Apply selected splitting criterion
13:                  Label node N_d with the splitting criterion attribute.
14:                  Remove the splitting criterion attribute from the at-
tribute list.
15:                  for each value i in the splitting criterion attribute.
16:                      D_i = no. of observations in training dataset satis-
fying attribute value i.
17:                      if D_i is empty then
18:                          attach a leaf node labeled with majority class output
value to node N_d.
19:                      else
20:                          attach the node returned by decision tree to node N_d.
```

```
21:                    end if
22:                 end for
23:                    return node N_d
24:                 end if
25:              end if
```

There are various specific decision-tree algorithms:

- **ID3:** Iterative Dichotomiser 3
- **C4.5:** Successor of ID3
- **CART:** Classification and Regression Tree
- **CHAID:** Chi-Squared Automatic Interaction Detector
- **MARS:** Extends decision trees to handle numerical data better

Support Vector Machines (SVM)

SVM was first introduced by Vapnik and has been very effective method for regression, classification and pattern recognition. It is measured a good classifier because of its high generalization recital without the necessitate to add a priori facts, even when the measurements of the input space is very high. The goal of SVM is to find the finest classification function to distinguish between parts of the two classes in the training data. SVM methods employ linear circumstances in order to split out the classes from one another. The design is to use a linear condition that separates the two classes from each other as well as possible. Consider the medical application, where the risk of ultrasound liver disease is related to diagnostic features from patients. SVM is used as a binary classifier to predict whether the patient is diagnosed with liver disease or not. In such a case, the split condition in the multivariate case may also be used as stand-alone condition for classification. This, a SVM classifier, may be considered a single level decision tree with a very carefully chosen multivariate split condition. The effectiveness of the approach depends only on a single separating hyper plane. It is difficult to define this separation.

Support Vector Machine is a supervised learning technique used for classification purpose. For supervised learning, a set of training data and category labels are available and the classifier is designed by exploiting this prior known information. The binary SVM classifier takes a set of input data and predicts each given input, in which of the two possible classes the data belongs to. The original data in a finite dimensional space is mapped into a higher dimension space to make the separation easier. The vector classified closer to the hyper plane is called support vectors. The distance between the support vector and the hyper plane is called the margin; the higher marginal value gives lower the error of the classifier. The separation among higher and lower dimensions is described in Figure 2.

Support vector machines are normally labelled for binary classification problems. Therefore, the class variable yi for the ith training instance Xi is assumed to be drawn from {-1, +1}. The most significant criterion, which is commonly used for SVM classification, is the maximum margin hyper plane. The metric for the concept of the "best" classification function can be recognized geometrically. For a linearly separable dataset, a linear classification role matches to a separating hyper plane f(X) that bypasses through the centre of the two classes, separating the two.

Figure 2. Dimensions for support vector machines

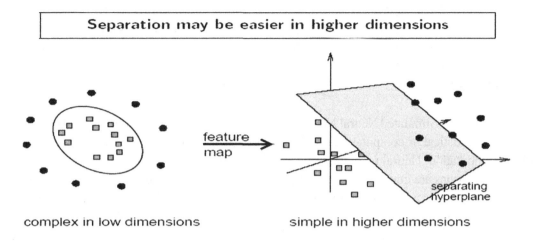

Once this function is determined, new data instance f(x, n) can be classified by simply testing the sign of the function f(xn); Xn fit in to the positive class if f(Xn)>0. Since there are a lot of such linear hyper plane, SVM assure that the best such function is established by maximizing the margin between the two classes. The separation among classes is described in Figure 3.

Naturally, the margin is stated as the amount of space, or partition between the two sets as defined by the hyper plane. Geometrically, the margin matches to the shortest distance between the closest data point to a point on the hyper plane. To make sure that the maximum margin hyper planes are actually established.

One of the initial disadvantages of SVM is its computational ineptitude. But this dilemma is being solved with immense success. One approach is to split a large optimization dilemma into a series of smaller dilemmas, where each dilemma only engages a couple of carefully chosen variables so that the

Figure 3. Marginal values in a hyper plane

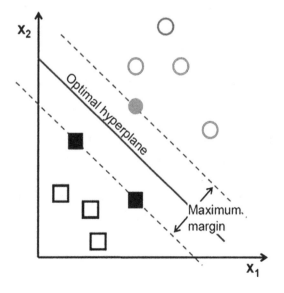

optimization can be ended powerfully. The process repeats until all the decomposed optimization problems are solved successfully. A more new approach used for SVM optimization problem is Sequential Minimal Optimization methods, which consider the problem of learning an SVM as that of finding an approximate minimum set of instances (Han, Kamber, & Pei, 2011).

Neural Network

A Neural Network or Simulated Neural Network (SNN) is an interconnected cluster of artificial neurons that employ a statistical or computational model for information processing based on a correlation approach to computation. Neural networks were modelled after the cognitive processes of the brain. In human brain, neurons are connected to one another via points, which are referred to as synapses. They are capable of predicting new observations from existing observations. This biological analogy is retained in an artificial neural network. The basic computation unit in an ANN consists of unified processing elements also called units, nodes, or neurons. These neurons can be arranged in different kinds of architecture by connections between them. The neurons within the network work together, in parallel, to produce an output task. Since the computation is achieved by the collective neurons, a neural network can still produce the output function still if a few number of the individual neurons are malfunctioning (the network is robust and fault tolerant).

In general, each neuron inside a neural network has an related activation number. In addition, each connection between neurons has a weight correlated with it. These quantities replicate their counterparts in the biological brain: firing rate of a neuron, and power of a synapse. The activation of a neuron depends on the activation of the other neurons and the weight of the edges that are related to it. The neurons within a neural network are regularly arranged in layers. The quantity of layers within the neural network, and the quantity of neurons within each layer normally matches the nature of the examined fact.

After the size has been decided, the network is usually then focused to training. Here, the network accepts a sample training input with its related classes. It then applies an iterative process on the input in order to fine-tune the weights of the network so that its future forecasts are best possible. After the training phase, the network is ready to perform forecasts in new sets of data (Hastie, Tibshirani, & Friedman, 2001).

Neural networks can frequently construct very accurate predictions. However, one of their greatest criticisms is the fact that they represent a "black-box" approach to investigate. They do not offer any insight into the underlying nature of the phenomena. The most basic architecture of the neural network is a perceptron, which holds a set of input nodes and an output node. The output unit receives a set of inputs from the input units. There are d different input units which are exactly equal to the dimensionality of the underlying data. The data is supposed to be numerical. Categorical data may need to be transformed to binary representations, and therefore the number of inputs may be larger. The output node is associated with a set of weights W, which are used in order to compute a function f(.) of its inputs. Each component of the weight vector is associated with a connection from the input unit to the output unit. The weights can be viewed as the analogue of the synaptic strengths in biological systems. In case of perceptron architecture, the input nodes do not carry out any computations. They simply pass on the input attribute forward. Computations are performed only at the output nodes in the basic perceptron architecture. The output node uses its weight vector along with the input attribute values in order to compute a function of the inputs. A typical function, which is computed at the output node, is the signed linear function:

$$Z_i=\sin\{W.X_i+b\} \tag{6}$$

The output is a predicted value of the binary class variable, which is assumed to be drawn from {-1, +1}. The notation b denotes the bias. Thus, for a vector Xi drawn from a dimensionality of d, the weight vector W should also contain d elements. Now consider a binary classification problem, in which all labels are drawn from (+1, -1}. We assume that the class label of Xi is denoted by yi. In that case, the sign of the predicted function zi yields the class label. The input layers with activation function are described in Figure 4.

In the case of single layer perceptron algorithms, the training process is easy to carry out by using a gradient descent approach. The major challenge in training multilayer networks is that it is no longer known for intermediate (hidden layer) nodes, what their "expected" output should be. This is only known for the final output node. Therefore, some type of "error feedback" is needed, in order to choose the changes in the weights at the intermediate nodes. The training process proceeds in two phases, one of which is in the forward direction, and the other is in the backward direction.

Data Classification using c4.5 Decision Tree Algorithm: A Case Study Example

The following example clearly depicts the creation of decision trees using c4.5 Decision Tree Algorithm using rapid miner studio. The following dataset in Table 1 corresponds to iris dataset with the class label contact lenses.

The Table 1 describes the contact lenses database which contains four attributes and a class labeled attribute. The class labeled attribute is defined with three sorts of distributions such as hard, soft and none. The distribution hard describes that the patients to be fitted with hard contact lenses and the soft defines the category of patients to be fitted with soft contact lenses and the category none defines that the patient doesn't have to be provided with contact lenses.

The attributes that are used up for the prediction are all of nominal. The attribute age has been provided with three distributions such as young, pre-presbyopic and presbyopic. The distribution young signifies the young age of the patients and presbyopic is a condition where the eye exhibits a diminished

Figure 4. Neural network model

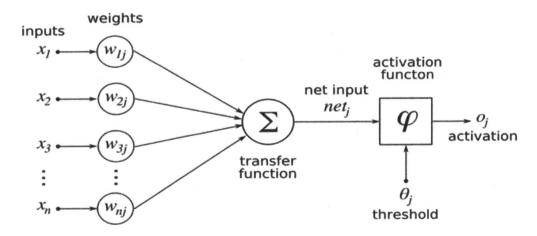

Table 1. The contact lenses database

Age	Spectacle-Prescrip	Astigmatism	Tear-Prod-Rate	Contact-Lenses
young	myope	no	reduced	none
young	myope	no	normal	soft
young	myope	yes	reduced	none
young	myope	yes	normal	hard
young	hypermetrope	no	reduced	none
young	hypermetrope	no	normal	soft
young	hypermetrope	yes	reduced	none
young	hypermetrope	yes	normal	hard
pre-presbyopic	myope	no	reduced	none
pre-presbyopic	myope	no	normal	soft
pre-presbyopic	myope	yes	reduced	none
pre-presbyopic	myope	yes	normal	hard
pre-presbyopic	hypermetrope	no	reduced	none
pre-presbyopic	hypermetrope	no	normal	soft
pre-presbyopic	hypermetrope	yes	reduced	none
pre-presbyopic	hypermetrope	yes	normal	none
presbyopic	myope	no	reduced	none
presbyopic	myope	no	normal	none
presbyopic	myope	yes	reduced	none
presbyopic	myope	yes	normal	hard
presbyopic	hypermetrope	no	reduced	none
presbyopic	hypermetrope	no	normal	soft
presbyopic	hypermetrope	yes	reduced	none
presbyopic	hypermetrope	yes	normal	none

ability to focus on near objects with age ranges between 40-50 and pre-presbyopic signifies the age ranges between 21-31 years.

The attribute spectacle-prescription has been provided with two distributions such as myope and hypermeterope. The distribution myope defines a person with myopia i.e an nearsighted person and the distribution hypermeterope defines a person with hyperopia i.e an farsighted person.

The attribute astigmatism is a type of refractive error of the eye. Refractive errors cause blurred vision and are the most common reason for using contact lenses or glasses. The attribute is provided with two distribution such as yes or no by which we can estimate whether the person is having blurred vision or not. The attribute tear production rate signifies whether the person is having normal or reduced level of tear in eyes. The process of loading the data into the tool is illustrated in Figure 5, Figure 6, Figure 7 and Figure 8.

The mechanism of loading the data and assigning the class label is illustrated in Figure 9 and Figure 10. The class label has to be assigned in order to make the operator under supervised learning paradigm.

Figure 5. Create a csv file which contains the contact-lenses dataset

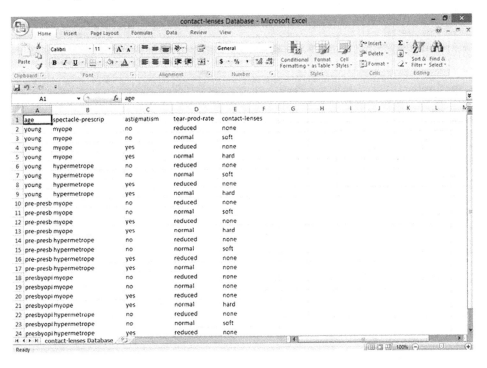

Figure 6. Create a new project in the rapid miner

Figure 7. Open the project

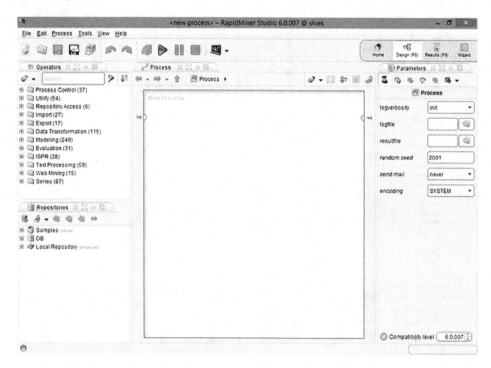

Figure 8. Click and drag the read csv operator

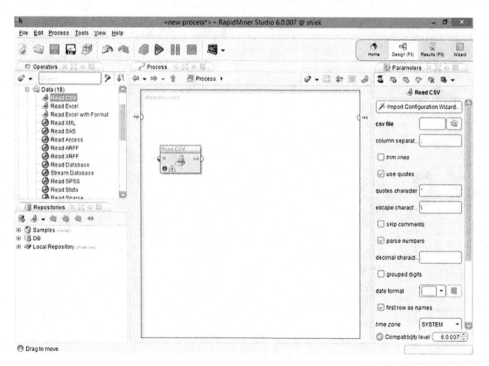

Figure 9. Import the csv file of the contact lenses dataset through the read csv operator

Figure 10. Finish the import configuration wizard

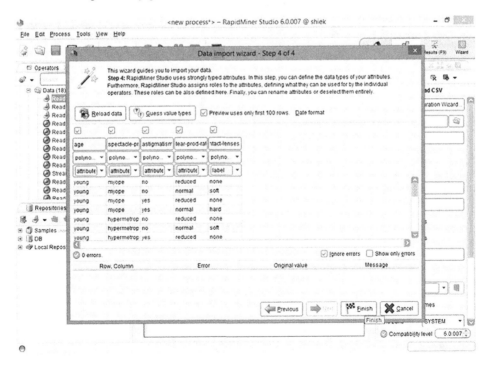

The mechanism of loading the decision tree operator is illustrated in Figure 11. Then save the project accordingly as given in Figure 12. Then click on save and run, as a result the final tree gets generated as in Figure 13.

EXPERIENCING THE ART OF BIG DATA

Each day, 2.5 quintillion bytes of data are produced. These data come from digital pictures, videos, posts to social media websites, intelligent sensors, purchase transaction records, cell phones GPS signals etc. This is known as Big Data. In small, the term Big Data applies to information that can't be processed or analyzed using traditional processes or tools. Increasingly, organizations nowadays are facing more and more Big Data challenges. They have access to prosperity of information, but they don't know how to acquire value out of it because it is sitting in its most raw form or in a semi structured or unstructured format; and as a result, they don't even recognize whether it's merit keeping. There is no doubt that Big Data and particularly what we do with it has the probable to become a powerful force for innovation and value creation.

Data now stream from daily life: from phones and credit cards and televisions and computers; from the infrastructure of smart cities; from sensor-equipped buildings, trains, buses, planes, bridges, and factories (Zikopoulos, Eaton, deRoos, Deutsch, & Lapis, 2012).

Figure 11. Import the decision tree operator next to read csv operator and connect the operators

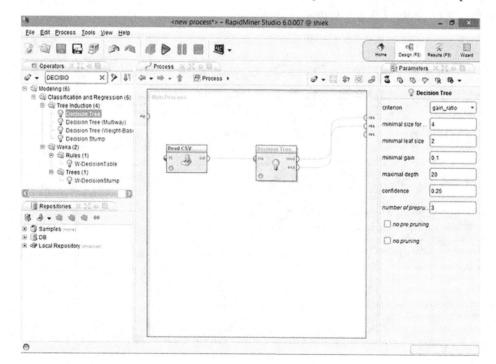

Figure 12. Save the project

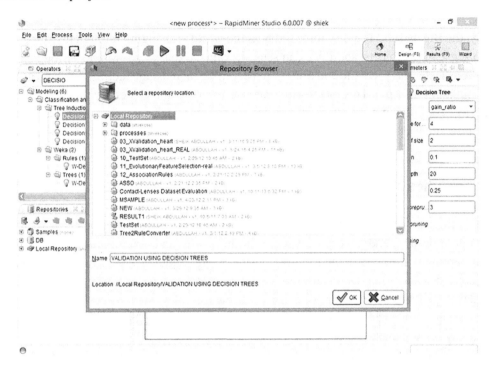

Figure 13. Tree creation using Decision tree classification algorithm

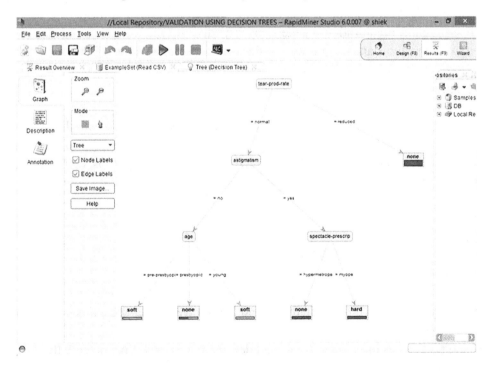

Big Data

Quite simply, the Big data era is in full force today as the world is changing through instrumentation, we are clever to sense more objects, and if we can sense it, we tend to try and store it. Through advances in communications technology, people and things are becoming increasingly connected –and not just some of the time, but all of the time. This intersecting rate is a escape train. Generally referred to as machine-to-machine (M2M), interconnectivity is responsible for double digit year over year data growth rates. Finally, because small integrated circuits are now so cheap, we are able to add intelligence to almost everything.

Big Data Analytics

This outline of big data analytics will help you to know big data analytics, the business worth it gets to many corporate industries and government sector in the world, and how organizations across diverse industries are applying it to tackle their unique business requirements. Every big data source has different characteristics, including the occurrence, volume, velocity, type, and veracity of the data. When big data is developed and stored, extra dimensions come into play, such as governance, security, and policies. Choosing a structural design and constructing an appropriate big data solution is challenging because so many issues have to be considered (Zicari, 2012).

Big data analytics is the procedure of gathering and analyzing large sets of data (called big data) to find out patterns and other useful information. Big data analytics can assist organizations to better appreciate the information contained within the data and will also help recognize the data that is most important to the business and future business decisions. For most organizations, big data analysis is a challenge. Consider the huge volume of data and the different unstructured formats of the data that is collected across the entire organization and the many ways diverse types of data can be joined, contrasted and analyzed to find patterns and other useful business information (Warden, 2011).

Importance of Big Data

The genuine problem is not acquiring large amounts of data. It's what you do with the data that counts. The optimistic vision is that organizations will be clever to take data from any source, harness applicable data and analyze it to find answers that enable the following (Zikopoulos, deRoos, Parasuraman, Deutsch, Corrigan, & Giles, 2013):

- Cost cutbacks
- Time cutbacks
- New product development and optimized offerings
- Smarter commerce decision making

For example, by combining unstructured data and high-powered analytics, it is possible to:

1. Determine root causes of failures, issues and defects in near-real time, potentially saving billions of dollars annually.
2. Optimize routes for many thousands of package delivery vehicles while they are on the road.

3. Generate retail coupons at the point of sale based on the customer's current and past purchases.
4. Recalculate entire risk portfolios in minutes.
5. Quickly identify customers who matter the most.
6. Use click stream analysis and data mining to detect fraudulent behavior.
7. Like conventional analytics and business intelligence solutions, big data mining and analytics helps expose hidden patterns, unidentified correlations, and other useful business information. However, big data tools can analyze elevated-volume, huge-velocity, and high-variety information benefits far better than conventional tools and RDBMS that struggle to capture, manage, and process big data within a reasonable elapsed time and at an acceptable total cost of ownership.

CONCLUSION

Data classification has its application towards various domains such as medical data analysis, sensor data analysis, weather data analysis and so on. The impact of ascertaining the segregation and manipulation of data records has to be considered. This chapter mainly deals with the qualities, types of data, classification techniques and the impact of big data. Data classification techniques can be applied over variety of data analysis task to determine the patterns and variations in the observed data. Meanwhile, the growth of data into a factor of big data analytics with its rapid types has to be considered during data classification. The combination of data optimization with classification makes the level of prediction to a good observed point.

REFERENCES

Breiman, L., Friedman, J., Olshen, R., & Stone, P. (1992). *Classification and regression trees.* Belmont, CA: Wadsworth International Group.

Brodley, C.E., & Utgoff, P.E. (n.d.). *Multivariate decision trees.* Academic Press.

Han, J., Kamber, M., & Pei, J. (2011). *Data Mining: Concepts and Techniques.* Morgan Kaufmann Publishers.

Hastie, T., Tibshirani, R., & Friedman, J. (2001). *Elements of Statistical learning: Datamining, Inference, and Prediction.* Springer. doi:10.1007/978-0-387-21606-5

Little, R. J. A., & Rubin, D. B. (2002). *Statistical analysis with missing data.* Wiley. doi:10.1002/9781119013563

Warden, P. (2011). *Big Data Glossary.* O'Reilly.

Zicari, R. (2012). *Big Data: Challenges and Opportunities.* Academic Press.

Zikopoulos, P., deRoos, D., Parasuraman, K., Deutsch, T., Corrigan, D., & Giles, J. (2013). *Harness the Power of Big Data.* McGraw -Hill.

Zikopoulos, P., Eaton, C., deRoos, D., Deutsch, T., & Lapis, G. (2012). *Understanding Big Data – Analytics for Enterprise Class Hadoop and Streaming Data.* McGraw-Hill.

Chapter 4
Secure Data Analysis in Clusters (Iris Database)

Raghvendra Kumar
LNCT College, India

Prasant Kumar Pattnaik
KIIT University, India

Priyanka Pandey
LNCT College, India

ABSTRACT

This chapter used privacy preservation techniques (Data Modification) to ensure Privacy. Privacy preservation is another important issue. A picture, where number of clients owning their clustered databases (Iris Database) wish to run a data mining algorithm on the union of their databases, without revealing any unnecessary information and requires the privacy of the privileged information. There are numbers of efficient protocols are required for privacy preserving in data mining. This chapter presented various privacy preserving protocols that are used for security in clustered databases. The Xln(X) protocol and the secure sum protocol are used in mutual computing, which can defend privacy efficiently. Its focuses on the data modification techniques, where it has been modified our distributed database and after that sanded that modified data set to the client admin for secure data communication with zero percentage of data leakage and also reduce the communication and computation complexity.

INTRODUCTION

In recent years, Agarwal et al. (1993) Agarwal, Imielinski, and Swamy (1993) and Srikant and Agarwal (1994) suggested data mining became a very interesting topic for the researcher due to its vast use in modern technology of computer science but due to its vast use it faces some serious challenges regarding data privacy and data privacy became an interesting topic. Many methods techniques and algorithms are already defined and presented for privacy preserving data mining. These privacy preserving techniques can be classified mainly in two approaches; the authors Agrawal and Srikant (2000) and Lindell and

DOI: 10.4018/978-1-5225-2031-3.ch004

Pinkas (2000) suggested Data modification and Secure Multi-party Computation approach. Data Mining suggested by Kantarcioglu and Clifto (2004) in last few decades has become very useful as the database are increasing day by day many people now connected with the computers by Han and Kamber (2006), so it becomes necessary for computer researchers to make the data so fast to access, also need to find right data. The term Data Mining emphasize on the fact of extracting the knowledge from large amount of data, so data mining is the process through which, we collect knowledgeable data from very large data suggested by Sheikh, Kumar, and Mishra (2010).

Now, the database is very large which consists so much information but what we want to find is the relevant data from large database or want to find some patterns which becomes very difficult with normal DBMS but with the use of data mining techniques we can find the hidden patterns and information from large database system. So, we can also term data mining as the knowledge mining, pattern extraction etc. But before applying data mining techniques we need to apply some processes which we known as pre-processing of data. Although data mining is one of the step involved in process of knowledge discovery, still it becomes more popular by name then that (Jangde, Chandel, & Mishra, 2011).

The data mining technique authored by Sugumar, Jayakumar, and Rengarajan (2012) can be used on Bio-Database (Iris database) for analyzing and acquiring different relations in the food condition of market or environmental conditions authored by Lakshmi and Rani (2012) and many more to find the relations which can tell the cause of any disease at very early stage so that proper precautions can be taken. Bio-Database is the collection of information of medical science by Muthulakshmi and Rani (2012), which contains information about patients, diseases and cause of diseases and many more things related to medical science but this database of Bio-Database contains very huge amount of data or the information which is not easy to analyze and also finding out some useful information from that is also very difficult. We use data mining techniques in order to get some useful information from this huge database. Medical science and market analysis is a field where large amount of data is gathered and collected from many sources now the challenge is to find the appropriate information and pattern from that data so that it can be used for further research to find some valuable results for the patients and customers but security is the major issue we should be very careful while sending data from one place to other otherwise it may create some harmful effects. In this chapter, work is mainly to provide privacy by Vaidya, Clifton, Kantarcioglu, and Patterson (2008) to such type of data so that the information remains safe while transferring data from one place to other. In this chapter, we are going to concentrate on finding the valuable information or patterns or relations between many things from large dataset which can be of any field and then security will be our major concern while transferring data from one environment to other environment for which we will use data modification techniques by Vaidya (2004), which will provide security to database and ensures secure transformation of valuable data.

SECURE ANALYSIS OF IRIS DATABASE USING THE WEKA TOOL

Data mining is the technique which is to be applied to large database to find useful patterns and information. In this chapter, we are going to take an iris database that is iris database which we treat as a centralized database. This centralized database is then divided into distributed databases for this we are going to use K means clustering techniques, in which one centralized data is divided different clusters and each cluster is distributed into different parts. After converting centralized database into distributed database, we now emphasize on security issues as while communicating data from one place to other we need to provide security to our database for that first we use decimal system that is first we convert the clustered data into decimal system due to which we provide one extra information to computers resulting in high speed performance. After converting this clustered database, we now need to find different useful patterns which are done by calculating support count, confidence like values of the clustered database which is done by using Association rule mining and Apriori algorithm of data mining. We will get different results from different clustered database, now what we need is to communicate this valuable data with the admin for which first we need privacy as there is possibilities that someone in between the communication of data may change the valuable data which will cause many hazards so in order to secure our communications from intruders, we will use data modification techniques. There are many data modification techniques which we can prefer for preserve our valuable database one of the techniques which we are using here in our chapter is data swapping technique. in this technique we keep the original data as it is but before sending the valuable data to admin, we put changes in one copy and use that copy for communication in this copy we swap the data between different attributes values or just for example we convert all 0 to 1 and at the same time all 1 to 0 then in addition we can use another data modification method which we known as noise addition data modification method in this after using first data modification method we will add some noise value to the data due to which intruder will have to work a lot in order to crack this valuable information and our data will be secure for communication. Now we will send this valuable copy to the admin where he will apply the same methods which we have applied on client side for our database. After receiving the copy and applying all the methods by admin head he will broadcast the analyzed results to all the distributed clients situated in distributed environment. When all the clients receive the broadcasted value or the relations from head admin they will follow all the relations as according to head admin and the process will end here. Now this process will get repeated every time when client who is situated in distributed environment need to send valuable data to admin head. So in this way clients will be able to send their valuable data to head admin and at the same time the head admin will get the proper data in which he was interested. So in this way our communication will be safe and we will be able to maintain the privacy of our valuable database.

Algorithm:

   Input: Taken Centralized database (Iris Database)

   Process: Data Modification and Data Analysis

   Output: Secure Data Analysis in distributed database environments

   Step1: Consider the centralized database (DB) (Iris Database)

   Step2: Converting the centralized database into the distributed database using the K means clustering techniques (DB=DB1+DB2...........+DBn)

   Step3: Taken the clustered database (DB1, DB2..........DBn)

   Step4: Converting the Words or Sentences into the ASCII code

   Step5: Converting ASCII code (Decimal Value) into the Binary Value

   Step6: Taken the Binary Value in the given database

   Step7: By using the K-Means clustering algorithm for calculating the mean and standard deviation with the help of weka tool.

   Step8: Now the cluster 1 to n sends their mean and standard dev to the sub cluster head.

   Step9: Now the sub cluster head decrypted and calculates the avg. value for data analysis by using the following formula

$$\text{Avg. mean value} = \sum_{i=1}^{n} \text{mean i} / N \; // \; N = \text{No of cluster}$$

$$\text{Avg. standard dev.} = \sum_{i=1}^{n} \text{Standard dev. i} / N \; // \; N = \text{No of cluster}$$

Step10: Now the sub cluster heads sends their avg. mean and standard dev. To cluster head

Step11: After that cluster head calculates their global mean and standard dev. By using the following formula

$$\text{Global mean value} = \sum_{i=1}^{n} \text{mean i} / N \; // \; N = \text{No of sub cluster head}$$

$$\text{Global standard dev.} = \sum_{i=1}^{n} \text{Standard dev. i} / N \; // \; N = \text{No of sub clusterhead}$$

Step12: Now the cluster head broadcast the analyzed value to all the sub cluster present in the clustered environment.

Step13: After that the sub cluster head sends their analyzed value to all the clusters present in it

Step14: Process end.

In the implementation work, we are taking the Iris centralized database that contains five attributes, then we divided the centralized database into the distributed database by applying the K means clustering techniques and then we implemented this work with the help of Weka tool for finding the mean and standard deviation. For implementation purpose consider a centralized iris database, which is shown in Table 1, for reducing the access time we convert the decimal values into the binary form. After that we conversion we divided the centralized database into the distributed database. After that we take the distributed cluster database of all sites and use the concept of data swapping for providing the high privacy to our distributed database.

After inserting distributed database into the weka tool, the table contains four number of attribute (sepal length, sepal width, petal length, petal width and class attribute), in this case we are not selecting any attribute in our database and then the snapshot is showing the single line weight from o to 10.

After inserting distributed database into the weka tool, the table contains four number of attribute (sepal length, sepal width, petal length, petal width and class attribute), in this case we areselecting all five attributes in our database, and then the snapshot is showing the single line weight from 0 to 10. Figure 1 shows after selecting all the Attributes. After inserting distributed database table6into the weka tool, the table contains four number of attribute (spell length, sepal width, petal length, petal width and class attribute), in this case we are selecting all attribute in our database, then we filter our database using the Association multi filter in weka tool then we get the running information (Figure 1) of the tool. That contains 10 instance and 5 attributes as well as relationship between the attributes.

Like that if, we insert distributed database into the weka tool, the table contains four number of attribute (spell length, sepal width, petal length, petal width and class attribute), in this case we are selecting all attribute in our database, then we filter our database using the Association multi filter in weka tool

Table 1. Centralized database (Iris Database)

S. No.	Sepal Length (cm)	Sepal Width(cm)	Petal Length(cm)	Petal Width (cm)	Class
1	5.1	3.5	1.4	0.2	1
2	4.9	3.0	1.4	0.2	1
3	4.7	3.2	1.3	0.2	1
4	4.6	3.1	1.5	0.2	1
5	5.0	3.6	1.4	0.2	1
6	5.4	3.9	1.7	0.4	1
7	4.6	3.4	1.4	0.3	1
8	5.0	3.4	1.5	0.2	1
9	4.4	2.9	1.4	0.2	1
10	4.9	3.1	1.5	0.1	1
11	5.4	3.7	1.5	0.2	1
12	4.8	3.4	1.6	0.2	1
13	4.8	3.0	1.4	0.1	1
14	4.3	3.0	1.1	0.1	1
15	5.8	4.0	1.2	0.2	1
16	5.7	4.4	1.5	0.4	1
17	5.4	3.9	1.3	0.4	1
18	5.1	3.5	1.4	0.3	1
19	5.7	3.8	1.7	0.3	1
20	5.1	3.8	1.5	0.3	1
21	5.4	3.4	1.7	0.2	1
22	5.1	3.7	1.5	0.4	1
23	4.6	3.6	1.0	0.2	1
24	5.1	3.3	1.7	0.5	1
25	4.8	3.4	1.9	0.2	1

then we get the running information (Figure 2) of the tool. That contains 10 instance and 5 attributes as well as relationship between the attributes.

Like that if we, insert distributed database into the weka tool, the table contains four number of attribute (spell length, sepal width, petal length, petal width and class attribute), in this case we are selecting all attribute in our database, then we filter our database using the Association multi filter in weka tool then we get the running information (Figure 3) of the tool. That contains 5 instance and 5 attributes as well as relationship between the attributes.

After running all the cluster distributed tables into the weka tool, we get the values of the means and standard deviation for the attribute pettle length. Now they consider the attribute pettle length as the locally frequent item sets. If we want that the attribute is globally frequent of not then we used the following calculation for all the clusters. For providing the high privacy to the our cluster database we used the concept of random number for the different cluster, for cluster 1, 2 and 3, random number are 3, 2 and 1 respectively.

Figure 1. Shows run time information of weka tool after insertion of table 6

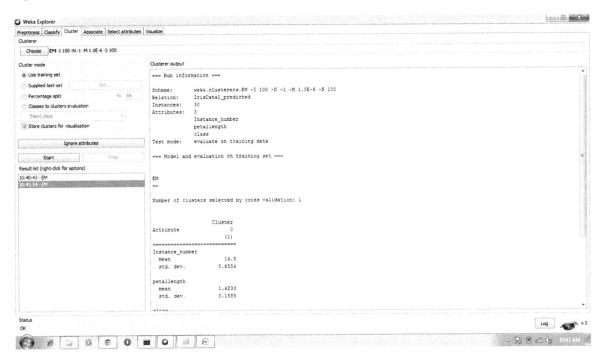

Figure 2. Shows mean and standard deviation of table 7

Figure 3. Shows mean and standard deviation of table 8

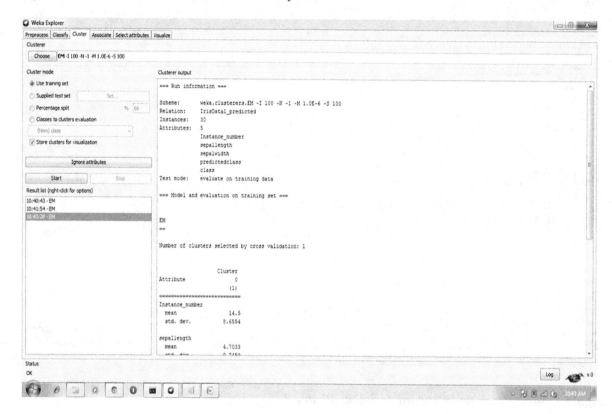

Calculation for the Clustered Database 1

- Select locally frequent item set pettle length whose mean and standard deviation are 1.4233 and 0.1585.
- Partial mean1= Local Mean1+ Random Number1= 1.4233+3=4.4233
- Partial Standard Deviation 1=Local Standard Deviation1 + Random Number1= 3+0.1585=3.1585

Calculation for the Clustered Database 2

- Select locally frequent item set pettle length whose mean and standard deviation are 0.2467 and 0.0991.
- Partial mean2= Local Mean2+ Random Number 2-Local Mean1=0.2467+2-4.4233=-2.1766
- Partial Standard Deviation 2= Local Standard Deviation2 + Random Number 2- Local Standard Deviation1= 0.0991+2-3.1585=-1.0594

Calculation for the Clustered Database 3

- Select locally frequent item set pettle length whose mean and standard deviation are 4.703 and 0.7460.
- Partial mean3= Local Mean3+ Random Number3 -Local Mean2=4.703+1-2.1766=3.5264

- Partial Standard Deviation 3= Local Standard Deviation3 + Random Number3- Local Standard Deviation2= 0.7460+1-1.0594=0.6866
- After calculation of partial mean and standard deviation, now we calculates the value of global mean and standard deviation:
  - Global mean= Partial Mean-($\sum$ Random Number)=3.5264-(3+2+1)=-2.4736
  - Global Standard Deviation= Partial Deviation - ($\sum$ Random Number) =0.6866-(3+2+1)=-5.3134

In the above calculation of the global mean and standard deviation for the data analysis, we found that the attribute pettle length is locally frequent item set but globally infrequent item because the value of mean and standard deviation is not above or equal to zero. So the cluster 3 broadcast that the attribute pettle length is globally infrequent item sets.

CONCLUSION

The difficulty of preserving privacy in association rule mining is when the database is divided into different number of clusters n (n>2) number of sites when no trusted party is considered. A replica which adopts a sign based to find the global association rules by preserving the privacy constraints. The replica capably finds global frequent item sets even when no clients can be treated as trusted and also used the data modification technique to preserve the privacy to individual datasets. The trusted party initiates the process and prepares the merged list. All the clients compute the partial supports and total supports for all the item sets in the merged list using the data modification technique and based on these results finally trusted party finds global frequent item sets. Further enhancement is to preserve the client dataset and reduce the communication and computation complexity from n^2 to n log (n) with zero percentage of data leakage.

REFERENCES

Agarwal, R. (1993). Mining association rules between sets of items in large database. In *Proc. of ACM SIGMOD'93*. ACM Press. doi:10.1145/170035.170072

Agarwal, R., Imielinski, T., & Swamy, A. (1993). Mining Association Rules between Sets of Items in Large Databases. In *Proceedings of the 1993 ACM SIGMOD International Conference on Management of Data*, (pp. 207-210). doi:10.1145/170035.170072

Agrawal, R., & Srikant, R. (2000). Privacy-Preserving Data Mining. In Proceedings of the 2000 ACM SIGMOD on Management of Data, (pp. 439-450). doi:10.1145/342009.335438

Han, J. (2006). *Data mining concepts and techniques*. San Francisco: Morgan Kaufmann.

Jangde, P., Chandel, G. S., & Mishra, D. K. (2011). Hybrid Technique for Secure Sum Protocol. *World of Computer Science and Information Technology Journal, 1*(5), 198-201.

Kantarcioglu, M., & Clifto, C. (2004). Privacy-Preserving distributed mining of association rules on horizontally partitioned data. *IEEE Transactions on Knowledge and Data Engineering Journal, 16*(9), 1026-1037.

Lindell, Y., & Pinkas, B. (2000). Privacy preserving data mining. In *Proceedings of 20th Annual International Cryptology Conference (CRYPTO)*.

Muthu Lakshmi, N. V. (2012). Privacy Preserving Association Rule Mining without Trusted Site for Horizontal Partitioned database. *International Journal of Data Mining & Knowledge Management Process, 2*, 17–29. doi:10.5121/ijdkp.2012.2202

Muthulakshmi, N. V., & Rani, S. K. (2012). Privacy Preserving Association Rule Mining in Horizontally Partitioned Databases Using Cryptography Techniques. *International Journal of Computer Science and Information Technologies, 3*(1), 3176 – 3182.

Sheikh, R., Kumar, B., & Mishra, D. (2010a). A Distributed k- Secure sum Protocol for Secure Multi Site Computations. *Journal of Computing, 2*, 239–243.

Sheikh, R., Kumar, B., & Mishra, D. (2010b). A modified Ck Secure sum protocol for multi party computataion. *Journal of Computing, 2*, 62–66.

Srikant, R., & Agarwal, R. (1994). Mining generalized association rules. In VLDB'95, (pp. 479-488).

Sugumar, Jayakumar, R., & Rengarajan, C. (2012). Design a Secure Multi Site Computation System for Privacy Preserving Data Mining. *International Journal of Computer Science and Telecommunications, 3*, 101–105.

Vaidya, Clifton, Kantarcioglu, & Patterson. (2008). Privacy preserving decision trees over vertically partitioned data. *ACM Transactions on Knowledge Discovery from Data, 2*(3), 14–41.

Vaidya, J. (2004). *Privacy preserving data mining over vertically partitioned data* (Ph.D. dissertation). Purdue University.

KEY TERMS AND DEFINITIONS

Clustering: Division of data into groups of similar objects is called Clustering. Certain fine details are lost by representing the data by fewer clusters but it achieves simplification. It models data by its clusters. Data modeling puts clustering in a historical perspective rooted in mathematics, statistics, and numerical analysis. According to machine learning perspective, clusters correspond to hidden patterns, the search for clusters is unsupervised learning, and the resulting system represents a data concept. From a practical perspective clustering plays an important role in data mining applications such as scientific data exploration, information retrieval and text mining, spatial database applications, Web analysis, CRM, marketing, medical diagnostics, computational biology, and many others.

Distributed Association Rule Mining (DARM): Distributed association rule mining technique for a vertical partitioned data set across several sites. Let I = {i1, i2, .in} be a set of items and T = {T1, T2... Tn} be a set of transactions where each T∪ I, i. A transaction Ti contains an item set X∪I only if I, X ∪T. An association rule associated is of the form X ∪Y(X ∪Y ∪ 0) with support S and confidence

C if S% of the transactions in T contains X∪Y and C% of transactions that contain X also contain Y. In a horizontally partitioned Data base, the transactions are distributed among n sites. Support (X ∪Y) = probc (X∪Y) /Total number of transaction the global support count of an item set is the union or product of all local support counts. Support g (X) = Support1(x) ∪Support2(x) ∪…∪Support n(x). Confidence (X ∪Y) = Support (X ∪Y) / Support(X). The global confidence of a rule can be expressed in terms of the global support. Confidence g (X ∪Y) = Support g (X ∪Y) / Support g(X). The aim of the distributed association rule mining is to discover all rules with global support and global confidence greater than the user specified minimum support and confidence. The subsequent steps, utilizing the secure sum and secure set union methods described earlier are used. The basis of the algorithm is the Apriori algorithm, which use the (k-1) sized frequent item sets to generate the k sized frequent item sets.

Distributed Database: In modern days, distributed database has become a vital area of information processing. It eradicates many of the short comings of the centralized database and fit more naturally in many organizations that follow decentralized structure. A distributed database is a group of data which logically belongs to the same system but is spread over the sites of a computer network. It may be stored in multiple computers located in the same physical location, or may be dispersed over a network of interconnected computers. A distributed database system consists of loosely coupled sites that share nonphysical components.

Privacy Preserving Association Rule Mining (PPARM): In clustered data is distributed in among site the number of site will be greater than two. And no site is consider as a trusted party all the party have their individual private data and no other party will able to know other party data. Privacy preserving association rule mining in clustered database mainly using three techniques Cryptography technique, Heuristic based technique and Reconstruction based technique.

Privacy Preserving Technique (PPT): Privacy preservation in data mining is an important concept, because when the data is transferred or communicated between different parties then it's compulsory to provide security to that data so that other parties do not know what data is communicated between original parties. Preserving in data mining means hiding output knowledge of data mining by using several methods when this output data is valuable and private. Mainly two techniques are used for this one is Input privacy in which data is manipulated by using different techniques and other one is the output privacy in which data is altered in order to hide the rules.

Chapter 5
Data Mining for Secure Online Payment Transaction

Masoumeh Zareapoor
Shanghai Jiao Tong University, China

Pourya Shamsolmoali
CMCC, Italy

M. Afshar Alam
Jamia Hamdard University, India

ABSTRACT

The fraud detection method requires a holistic approach where the objective is to correctly classify the transactions as legitimate or fraudulent. The existing methods give importance to detect all fraudulent transactions since it results in money loss. For this most of the time, they have to compromise on some genuine transactions. Thus, the major issue that the credit card fraud detection systems face today is that a significant percentage of transactions labelled as fraudulent are in fact legitimate. These "false alarms" delay the transactions and creates inconvenience and dissatisfaction to the customer. Thus, the objective of this research is to develop an intelligent data mining based fraud detection system for secure online payment transaction system. The performance evaluation of the proposed model is done on real credit card dataset and it is found that the proposed model has high fraud detection rate and less false alarm rate than other state-of-the-art classifiers.

INTRODUCTION

Electronic society make the life more convenient and easy, the use of online mode of payment in banking system is one of the most essential parts of our daily life. "Electronic payment system is a combination of commerce and technology". This idea which allows payment process to be performed across a computer network (electronically) is not a new thing. It has been proposed in 1980. But the electronic payment system officially started at the 1997 and until present an enormous number of different payment techniques developed by researchers. Many of these methods entered to the market but they were not so successful since the consumers didn't get satisfaction. An electronic payment system is conducted in "different electronic commerce categories such as Business to business, business to customer, customer

DOI: 10.4018/978-1-5225-2031-3.ch005

to business and customer to customer". To participate in the electronic payment system the "costumer and the merchant should access the internet" also in other side; their bank accounts (costumer and the merchant) should be at the banks which have connection to the internet. Electronic payment is "much powerful, convenient and portable". Among all variety of payment systems "credit card is more popular and become the most convenient and essential instrument" to conduct electronic payment due to the following features (Jithendra, 2011):

- They allow making purchase without carrying a lot of cash.
- They allow making purchases without being worry about local currency.
- They allow convenient ordering by email.
- They are simple and comfortable.

Credit cards are "convenient and flexible method of payment". Credit card is a small plastic card that can be used either in physical or virtual way (Ngai et al., 2011). In a physical way, "the cardholder (costumer) handover his/her card physically to a merchant for making a payment". While in virtual way, only some important and confidential information about a card such as "card number, expiration date and secure code" is required for making transactions, and there is no need to present the physical card. Usually "such purchases are normally done on the Internet or over the telephone". Credit cards are not the panacea that we might hope for, because by increasing the number of transactions which have been done through credit card, "the fraudsters' activities are also increased significantly". Among the all type of fraud, financial fraud is more dangerous and frightening, because it costs hundreds of millions of dollars per year in damages and hurts hundreds of millions of people. According to "publisher of payments industry newsletter", global credit card fraud cost $12.4 billion in 2015 (Bloomberg, 2015). Unfortunately, no one is completely safe from being defrauded. As the credit card is the easiest and popular method in payment industry, so "it is considered as a good place to make a fraud because in a short time fraudsters can earn lots of money". To commit the fraud, "in case of offline payment" which using credit card physically, fraudsters must steal the credit card itself to make fraudulent transactions, while in the case of "online payment "which can occur over phone or internet, fraudsters must steal card's information only (Ramanathan, 2012). Thus, "a secured banking system requires high speed authentication machines" that let legitimate transactions to pass easily, while detect the fraudulent transaction which attempt by others. The most popular and trusted technique in credit card fraud detection is Data mining technique, because "millions of transactions are handled every day and to process such a huge amount of data human assessing is inefficient". According to a survey in 2015, "the five best fraud detection companies" are listed in Table 1 (Top Credit Card Processors, 2015).

Table 1. Credit card fraud detection: best fraud detection services (July 2015)

Rank	Name of Company	Year Founded
1	Ethoca Limited	2003
2	Norse Corporation	2010
3	Facility Management Advisors	2009
4	MaxMind	2002
5	Kount	2007

CONTRIBUTIONS

The major contribution of this research is an intelligent data mining based fraud detection system named FraudMiner. The challenges are listed as follow:

- Credit card dataset is a strongly imbalanced data and hence general classifiers could not classify them into fraud and legal properly.
- Due to security reasons, banks do not provide the real dataset to the individual researchers.
- Banks are ready to give only anonymized data for research (the customer transaction data where the field names are changed so that the researcher would not get any idea of what it is).

Thus, the major considerations while developing FraudMiner was to develop a fraud detection system that can handle class imbalance as well as anonymized data. During the training phase, from the customer transaction data, the proposed system prepares two pattern databases namely legal pattern database and fraud pattern database. These databases are created by using frequent itemset mining. Then a matching algorithm that matches the incoming transaction of a particular customer with his/her legal as well as fraud patterns in the corresponding databases is used for classifying each incoming transaction. If "the incoming transaction is matching more to legal pattern than fraud pattern, then it is considered as legal and if it is matching more to the fraud pattern than the legitimate one it can be classified as fraud".

SECURITY ISSUES IN ONLINE PAYMENT

The "online payment transaction contain of four groups". The first group is costumer, the real person who is the legal owner of the card and makes a legitimate transaction. "Second group is the credit card issuer which is the costumer's bank (issuing bank)". "The third group is the merchant who sells goods or products to the costumer". "Finally the forth group is the merchant's bank here called as acquiring bank) where finally the transaction amount from customer's account transferred". Figure 1 gives an overview of a typical conventional online payment transaction in a retail store.

1. In step 1, costumer hand over his/her card to merchant for making transaction, then the merchant swipes the card through the reader of the Point Of-Sales (POS) terminal which has been provided to the merchant by the acquiring bank, and enters the transaction amount into the POS terminal as well.
2. In step 2, the transaction details, merchant details and credit card details (that is stored in the card) has been sent to the acquiring bank.
3. In step 3, "the acquiring bank sends the information to the issuing bank for verification. In fact, in this step they want to check whether the card has any sign of fraudulent transactions".
4. In step 4 the transaction authorization (or rejection) is sent to the acquiring bank.
5. In this step the notification of step 4 is passed back to the merchant.
6. In the last step if everything is fine (ie., the amount withdraws from the costumer account and deposit to merchant account) then the costumer can receive his/her goods and confirmed the legality of transactions with his/her signature.

Figure 1. A typical electronic payment system

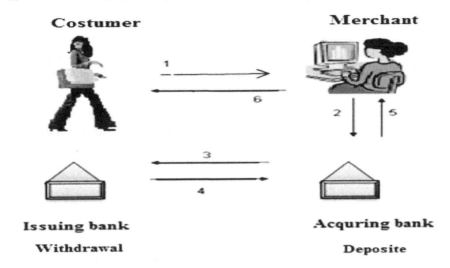

With increasing number of electronic shopping every day, credit card usage is also becoming more popular. Even you cannot only do shopping from your home, you can even get discount on the product that purchased through credit card (Jithendra, 2011). Credit card allows the customers to borrow money to pay for the product and goods they purchase. According to (Jithendra, 2011) customers and merchants both of them can get benefit from credit card payment systems, since cardholders enjoyed the convenience of credit card and "merchants also found that the costumers that using credit card for making transactions usually spends more than other costumers that they had to pay cash; the average of credit card users is about 126% more than if cash is used".

As the numbers of credit card transactions are increasing day by day, and the issuing procedure became complicated, so, "the banks started to sell the processing service to great companies such as, visa card, master card companies". This reduces the task of banks to issue credit card and also makes a greater growth for the payments systems. As more and more people choose the online shopping and paying their bills online, the rate of online financial fraud also increased. Fraud is the use of false representations to monetary gain. Since its detection is complex, there is not yet a fraud detection method that can detect the fraud in an efficient way. Thus, we can say "any business that involves money can be compromised by fraudulent acts", such as Insurance, Telecommunications (Farvaresh et al., 2011), and Credit Cards (Abdelhalim et al., 2009). According to (Ngai et al, 2011) among all areas of internet fraud, financial fraud is more significant and dangerous one since in the recent past, there has been an effort to develop methods to combat this type of financial fraud.

TYPE OF CREDIT CARD FRAUD

Credit card is more convenient to use than carry cash and is a big concern if not used carefully. The most important pitfall of credit card usage is credit card fraud. "As the number of cards increasing so, does the risk of fraud". Since "more cards have been issued for making more purchases, the fraud is likely to continue with new types of fraud". Due to different type of fraud credit card fraud is grouped into transaction fraud and application fraud. Transaction frauds occur when legitimate costumer's information are abused by criminals. Whereas application fraud occurs when fraudsters obtain a card from issuing financial institution/bank by using other people's information and keep using the cards with the stolen identity (Currently, banks deny issue of credit cards to people who have insufficient income or whose profile fit the profile of those likely to commit fraud). "Credit card frauds are defined in the following ways:

- Act of criminal deception mislead with internet by using the unauthorized credit card accounts or by getting sensitive information
- Unlawful or unauthorized use of account for personal gain
- Misrepresentation of account information to purchase goods

Diversity of Credit Card Fraud

It can be categorized in five groups (Phua, 2007) which are; lost or stolen cards, counterfeit credit card, card not present, identity-theft fraud, and mail & non-receipt fraud. The fraud statistics (Kim & Kim, 2002) provided "by federal trade commission, consumer centinel network" in 12th. July 2015 are shown in Figure 2. From the result (Figure 2) it obtains that lost and stolen cards represent 28% and a considerable proportion is for the counterfeit fraud, which is 46% of all fraud.

Figure 2. Credit card fraud statistics (July 2015)

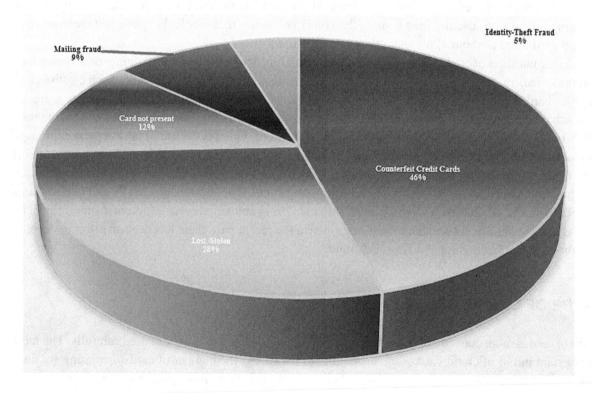

DATA MINING TECHNIQUES

"Data Mining is a family of machine learning techniques that automatically go through huge amount of data and can discover meaningful information which is hidden". Some of databases are very large, so it is inconvenient and sometimes impossible to manually discover the patterns from them. The data mining techniques is "the automatic discovery of valuable information from massive data". Tan et al. state that Data Mining technique is combination of "data analysis techniques" with "sophisticated algorithms" which can easily process the dataset. Hormozi et al. (2204) noted that data mining is a marketing technique that focuses on the most useful and valuable information in the database and allows managers to make a decision about their product. Fayyad et al. (1996) noted, data mining is the easiest tool to find the valuable patterns in databases to make a best decision. Generally, Data mining is a blend of different areas such as machine learning, artificial intelligence, visualization, statistics, and database research and pattern recognition (Manikas, 2008). These areas are much related to each other and "it is difficult to distinguish where each of these areas overlap". Figure 3 represents the above statement (data mining and the fields that influenced it).

Figure 3. Related fields of data mining

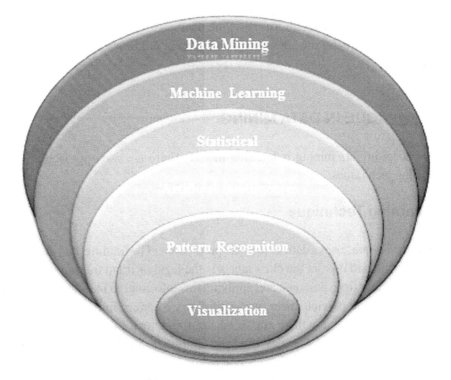

APPLICATIONS OF DATA MINING

Data mining techniques is used widely in different forms and is caused the enhancement of many applications. Data mining contains of the following steps:

1. **Data Cleaning**: The original data (raw data) are not clean and contain missing value or noise. We need to apply data cleaning techniques to the original data to remove these erroneous and create a new dataset that contain significant information.
2. **Data Selection**: In the previous step, we may not collect "all the relevant and important data". So, this step helps us to choose the most useful data for data mining technique.
3. **Data Transformation**: Even after cleaning the dataset, still it is not ready for mining, so we should transform them into forms that can be suitable for the mining process. For example, data may need to be converted into numeric values to be used in a neural network.
4. **Data Mining**: After cleaning and transformation steps, now the dataset is ready to use to extract the important patterns or desired information. Many mining techniques have been developed that can be used often based on the type of information we are seeking and the type of data that we have. Some of the techniques are association rule mining, fuzzy logic, clustering, neural networks, classification and genetic algorithms.
5. **Pattern Evaluation**: This step is to identify the truly interesting and relevant patterns "by visualization and removing redundant patterns from the database".
6. **Decisions**: At the end, we use the above acquired patterns & knowledge to make better decisions/ conclusions.

LEARNING TECHNIQUE IN DATA MINING

Another crucial concept in data mining is learning model. There are two approaches; supervised and unsupervised learning techniques.

Supervised Learning Technique

Supervised learning technique "uses a dataset to make predictions. The training data includes class label". For instance, in the credit card dataset the class labels is the legal or fraud transactions. The key idea in supervised model is learning from past data and applying this information to future cases. Any incoming transactions compare with the previous patterns; if it follows a pattern in the fraudulent transaction as is described by the trained model, it will be classified as a fraudulent. In contrast if the new transaction follows the legitimate pattern then will be classified as a legitimate. Supervised model requires the availability of class for each training sample which is not always given in a real world problem, so, we may face problem to use this method for such datasets. Another limitation of supervised learning models is that, "it cannot detect new frauds, because the behaviour of new fraud is unknown to the trained model and therefore the system cannot detect it". We can group the supervised technique into classification and regression. Neural networks and Support Vector Machines (SVMs) are the most popular applications of supervised techniques (Yu et al., 2010).

Unsupervised Learning

This method does not require class labels for model construction. It is constructed by using normal behaviour without using class labels, and then used to "detect outlier instances which deviate from the normal behaviour". Particularly unsupervised models can detect the new fraud types, since they are not limited to the pattern which we are created in training dataset. They often have a more exploration in compare to supervised models.

DATA MINING TECHNIQUES

The prediction and description in data mining are achieved by using the following tasks.

Classification

Classification is one of the most common learning models in the application of data mining that can "classify each record of data into one of the predefined classes" (Ngai et al., 2011). Most popular classification techniques are decision trees (Agrawal & Srikant, 1994), bayesian classifiers (Excell, 2012), support vector machine (Wu et al, 2007) and neural network (Aleskerov & Freisleben, 1997). Classification model in credit card fraud detection technique are mainly using credit card transactions for classifying them as legitimate or fraudulent.

Clustering

Clustering is the most common data mining approach which is based on unsupervised learning. It can categorize data into different groups according to their characteristics, then "each group is a cluster". Task of clustering technique is similar to the task of classification technique. Classification technique tries to separate data records into "a set of predefined classes" while in clustering method, "class labels are unknown (it is unavailable in dataset) and it is up to the clustering algorithm to find an acceptable class". Thus, the clustering method referred as "an unsupervised classification" (Ngai et al., 2011). The result of clustering defined as; "objects in one cluster have a high similarity, whereas being very dissimilar to the objects in the other clusters". Clustering is a useful method which can be used as an outlier detection tool to detect attributes that deviate from normal patterns. Recently, clustering techniques have been widely used in many real-world applications such as document clustering (Hanagandi et al., 1996) and credit card fraud detection. Most common clustering techniques are K-means (Cover & Hart, 1967) and self-organizing map (Zaslavsky & Strizhak, 2006).

Prediction

Prediction is very similar to classification method; it estimates the upcoming values based on the patterns of a dataset. The only difference is, in prediction the classes are not a discrete attribute but a continuous. There are two main types of predictions; predict unavailable data values or predict a class label for dataset. This method uses a large number of past values as predefined patterns to estimate probable future values. Logistic and neural networks models are the most commonly example of this method. Prediction techniques are mainly using in credit card fraud detection to predict any incoming transaction as legitimate or fraudulent.

Outlier Detection

Outlier detection occurs when any data element is grossly different or incompatible from the remaining dataset (Ngai et al., 2011). Outliers are "data elements that cannot be grouped in a given class or cluster". Outlier detection techniques are mainly using credit card transactions to detect any abnormality of data to classify them as legitimate or fraudulent.

Regression

This method is a statistical model which used to expose the relationship between one or more variables (Charniak, 1991). Many practical experiences used logistic regression as a standard (Qibei & Chunhua, 2011).

Visualization

Visualization is best technique to deliver complex patterns through the clear presentation of data (Hunt et al., 1998).

FRAUDMINER: THE PROPOSED FRAUD DETECTION MODEL

With the advent of communications techniques, e-commerce as well as online payment transactions are increasing rapidly. Along with this, financial frauds associated with these transactions are also growing which have resulted in loss of billions of dollars every year globally. Among the various financial frauds, credit card fraud is the most old, common and dangerous one due to its widespread usage because of the convenience it offers to the customer. According to Kount Company which is the top five fraud detection companies in the world, 40% of the total financial fraud is related to credit card (topcreditcardprocessors.com in the month of August 2015). Fraudster gets access to credit card information in many ways. According to a latest report by CBC News, smart phones are used to skim credit card data easily with a free Google application. However, fraud is becoming increasingly more complex and financial institutions are under increasing regulatory and compliance pressures.

In order to combat with these frauds, banks need more sophisticated techniques of fraud detection. The major problem for e-commerce business today is that fraudulent transactions appear more and more like legitimate ones (Liu et al., 2007) and a simple fraud detection method is not efficient to detect the frauds. Moreover, the credit card transaction dataset are "strongly imbalanced data and the legal and fraud transactions vary at least hundred times (Mukhanov, 2008) (In real dataset more than 98% of the transactions are legal while "only 2% or less" of them are fraud). Both Merchant's and card issuer's interests is to detect fraud as soon as possible. Otherwise costumer will lose their trust in both the card issuer and the merchant. A good banking system for electronic commerce must let genuine users to conduct their business easily, while flagging and detecting suspicious transaction attempts by others which are called as fraudster.

Even though fraud detection has a long history, not that much research has happened in this area. The reason is the unavailability of real world data on which researchers can perform experiments. Since this kind of dataset is sensitive, banks are reluctant to provide this data to researchers. Due to this difficulty in finding dataset, not many detection techniques have been developed and even fewer of literature are known to have been implemented in actual datasets. When any transaction is done, the fraud detection system generally starts to evaluate it, and classifies the new transaction to one of the classes: 'fraudulent' or 'legitimate'. Fraud detection is generally a data mining classification where "its objective is to correctly classify the transactions either legitimate or fraudulent".

AN OVERVIEW ON CREDIT CARD FRAUD DETECTION TECHNIQUES (CCFD)

As we explained in section 3, due to this dearth of real credit card transaction dataset, not that much research has been developed in this area, and even fewer are known to have been implemented in actual detection systems. Still we can find some successful application of various data mining techniques in fraud detection such as; outlier detection (Manikas, 2008), self-organizing maps (Zaslavsky & Streak, 2006), neural network (Dorronsoro et al., 1997), Bayesian classifier (Excell, 2012), support vector machine (Kim et al., 2002), artificial immune system (Mohammad & Zitar, 2011), fuzzy systems (Quah et al., 2008) genetic algorithm (Duman et al., 2011), and K-nearest neighbour (Cover & Hart, 1967).

We can refer that, detecting the frauds are "a complex computational task" and even the results show that there is no any detection system with confidence predicts the transactions to legitimate or fraudulent (Bolton & Hand, 2002).

As a consequence, one of the common approaches to fight fraud is create mechanisms that distinguish fraudulent from legitimate behaviours. Technically, these mechanisms can be created by using a data mining classification technique which making use of past customers records that already known as fraudulent and legitimate. However, applying classification techniques for fighting fraud always deal with a particular problem which we discussed them in next section. Because of this essential characteristic, the result of applying traditional and existence classification techniques, like decision trees or neural networks, are not enough for obtaining a good classifier. Most of credit card fraud detection techniques that reported in literature are based on detecting and avoiding of abnormal behaviour of real user/cardholder. Technically, these mechanisms can be created using a data mining technique by making use of a set of historical records of customer's transactions which already known as fraudulent and legitimate (the training set).

Supervised learning model in credit card fraud detection technique require accurate information of previous transactions (Legitimate & fraudulent transactions) in training dataset. In next step, the classifier is used to assign class labels to the testing dataset for which the class label is unknown. There are five main supervised learning techniques:

1. Naïve bayes
2. Decision trees
3. Neural networks
4. K-nearest neighbour (KNN)
5. Support vector machines (SVM)

While unsupervised learning model does not require class label for model construction. This model simply determines which observations are most dissimilar from the norm.

Yap et al. (2013), Potamitis (2013), and Bolton et al. (2013) in their research discussed that unsupervised learning method discover those objects that have unusual behaviours. The baseline of model is constructed without using the class labels. The model represents the "normal behaviour of real user, and is then used to detect objects which deviate from the normal behaviour of user". In fact, unsupervised learning methods can detect old and new fraud types since they do not require any information about previous fraudulent patterns, while supervised learning techniques can detect only known frauds. Unsupervised learning is often called 'cluster analysis' because it aims to group the data to develop classification labels automatically. A more sophisticated method that is used in many literatures is neural networks. The neural network technique can be used as supervised or unsupervised technique and "the output may contain one or several nodes". For multi-dimensional features neural network technique is one of the choices. The pitfall of this technique is, size of dataset for training, because neural network models require large amount of data in training part to obtain their maximum performance.

TECHNIQUES BASED ON DERIVED ATTRIBUTES

Some of the detection techniques usually calculate derived data attribute to model costumer's usual transaction behaviour, such as average of transaction amounts per week or typical currencies that costumer normally performs transactions in. This derived attribute technique needs sufficient information about normal behaviour of customers, and then any simple deviation from normal pattern should be considered as a suspicious transaction.

Rule Based Techniques

Some of detection techniques use some rules in their engine for better detection, for example they known some of the transactions as an essentially suspicious when:

- Multiple transactions on a single card but shipped to different addresses
- Multiple orders of the same item
- Multiple cards used using a single IP address
- Several transactions on a single card in a short time span.
- Rushed or overnight shipping

These patterns are coded as rules by human experts into a detection system that follows the expert system technique with static rules, or can be indicated of fraudulent behaviour in the system.

In earlier fraudsters were not aware of the fraud detection techniques in banking payment system, thus they didn't use any sophisticated strategies to make a fraudulent transaction and their transaction more likely lead to recognizable frauds. But recently the fraudsters are having very sophisticated methodology to perform mislead, which is not even recognized by human experts. Any fraud techniques after a while decrease in efficiency, then the fraudsters also trying to find out the new techniques for doing their job.

Provost (2002) in his research on the Bolton points out that there are several ways that the credit card fraud detection systems can be approached. These ways include the following:

Hand & Blunt (2001) provide an overview of some data-mining work which they have performed on credit card transaction data. They show a number of amazingly linear relationships between different aspects of the data in a number of diagrams and plots in their research work. For example, card spending diagram, that suddenly jumps or suddenly changes of slope (for example number of transactions or expenditure rate suddenly exceeding some threshold) should be picked up by a detection system.

All of these methods and hypothesis, can be combined or used separately, run in sequence or run in parallel, and be a base of very different technique. This means that a large number of theoretical credit card detection approaches are possible. But verification of the performance of these approaches and comparison between them is very difficult since the data sets are typically not available to other researchers to do research on.

Bolton and Hand (2002) and Kim and Kim (2002) proposed outlier detection techniques to detect abnormality in credit card transactions. Outlier detection technique is considered as an unsupervised technique, which does not require any knowledge of fraudulent or legitimate transactions in historical databases. These techniques only look for any deviation in the dataset. The advantage of this method is that they can detect any types of fraud. However, outlier detection can cause legitimate irregular behaviour to be classified as a fraud, thus causing inconveniences to the customer.

Ghosh and Reilly (1994) in their research work used neural network technique for detecting the credit card frauds that contains of a three layered feed forward network with only two training passes to achieve a reduction of 22% to 47% in total credit card fraud loses.

Aleskerov et al. (1997) developed a credit card fraud detection technique (CCFD) that is called CardWatch. Construction of this method is upon the neural network algorithm. This system can handle large amount of data therefore is an efficient method for large financial companies like, banks. But, this system is required to construct a separate neural network for each customer, so, there is need a very large network and higher amounts of resources to maintain.

Dorronsoro et al. (1997) developed credit card fraud detection technique based on neural network that is called Minerva. This system is embedded in credit card transaction servers to detect fraud transactions in real time. "It uses a novel nonlinear discriminate analysis which combines the multilayer perceptron of a neural network with Fisher's discriminate analysis method". Minerva does not require a large set of patterns because it acts only on previous pattern. The disadvantage of this method is that, determining a set of meaningful variable for detection is difficult and also obtaining effective datasets for training is not easy.

Syeda et al. (2002) proposed a "fast credit card fraud detection system (CCFD) by a parallel granular neural network which uses fuzzy neural networks for knowledge discovery". The importance of their research is mostly on optimizing the speed of the implemented algorithm.

Chiu and Tsai (2004) found that the problem of credit card transaction data is because of natural skewness of dataset. Generally, the ratio of fraud transactions to legal transactions in real credit card transaction datasets is extremely low (less than 3%). The proposed method used "web service techniques" to share their fraud transactions to a centralized data centre and then used a rule-based data mining technique to the dataset to detect credit card frauds.

The studies of combining data mining algorithms have increased in recent years and their results show outperforms the single algorithm methods.

MAIN CHALLENGES IN CREDIT CARD FRAUD DETECTION TECHNIQUES

We can group the main challenges in credit card fraud detection as follow:

- Unavailability of real world dataset
- Anonymised Data Set
- Unbalanced Data Set
- Size of the Data Set
- Overlapping dataset
- Different error costs
- Determining the appropriate evaluation parameters

Unavailability of Real Dataset

The most important issues associated with credit card fraud detection technique is unavailability of real world dataset, and it mentioned by many authors. Even though fraud detection has a long history, not that much research has happened in this area. The reason is unavailability of real world data, because banks are not ready to reveal their customer's sensitive information due to privacy reasons.

Anonymised Dataset

Due to privacy reasons, financial companies like banks, are not ready to provide their customer's information as it is to the researchers. They used to change the field names so that the researcher would not get any idea about actual fields. This anonymous nature of the dataset makes the research difficult as it makes the derived attribute concept impossible.

Unbalanced Dataset

Datasets are said to be balanced if there are approximately, as many positive instances as there are negative ones. In the other word, unbalanced distribution occurs when there is much more samples one instance to compare of another instance. In imbalanced datasets the detection model to know a little about the smaller instances classes, and much more about the larger classes and eventually, affecting in this way its predicting accuracy. The distribution of credit card transaction data is extremely skewed.

Tuo et al. (2004) stated that credit card transaction dataset is basically a "rare problem" since approximately for every million transactions, there are only hundred fraudulent transactions, hence using purely the accuracy measure for the detection system may not be appropriate. Maes et al. (1993), Aleskerov et al. (1997) and Dorronsoro et al. (1997) in their research have dealt with highly imbalanced dataset and noted that in their dataset "the fraudulent transactions are much fewer than legitimate transactions". Hassibi (2000) also remarked, out of 12 billion transactions which are processed, approximately 10 million transactions are fraudulent. This gives rise to the challenges of the selecting the appropriate evaluation function for the fraud detection technique. When the dataset is imbalance the standard classifiers like SVM, NB are often biased towards the large instances which are called majority class. These classifiers try to minimize the error rate regardless of data distribution. As mentioned in references highly imbalanced dataset hurts evaluation results. Most of the researcher in area of credit card fraud detection not considering skewed or imbalanced data and the issue of imbalance dataset is not studied widely.

TECHNIQUES TO HANDLE CLASS IMBALANCE

Oversampling

Oversampling tries to balance class distribution by replicating the minority instances to improve the performance of classifiers. State of art algorithm for oversampling problem is SMOTE (Syntactic minority over sampling). SMOTE generates synthetic minority instances to repeat the minority class (Ghosh & Liu, 2007). But SMOTE technique is dangerous since it blindly generalizes the minority classes regardless to the majority classes.

Under-Sampling

Under-sampling (Yap et al, 2013) tries to balance the dataset by eliminating and removing the majority (legitimate) instances. The major problem with this technique is that it may discard useful and important data for the induction process. The state of art algorithm for handling undersampling is "Tomek Links".

Size of Data

Millions of credit card transactions processed every day. To analysis such huge amounts of data requires considerable computing power. Phua et al. (2005) has provided a good analysis of credit card fraud detection, and stated that the datasets usually are in the range of million records, which require considerable computer power for analysis of dataset. It creates certain restrictions for the researchers.

Overlap Dataset

Another complicating factor in imbalanced dataset is that the classes may be overlapping. Overlapping means, when a legal transaction seems very similar to a fraud transaction or fraud transaction seems very similar to a legal transaction (Table 2). This is also a problem and creates difficulty in the analysis of credit card fraud, because it can lead to an incorrect model construction.

Table 2. Sample of overlapping problem

Custattr1	Hour	Amount	Zip	Field1	Field2	Field3	Field4	Indicator1	Indicator2	Flag1	Flag2	Flag3	Flag4	Flag5	Class
23461	0	12.95	852	3	0	-2753	24	0	0	1	1	1	0	1	1
23461	0	12.95	852	3	0	-2753	24	0	0	1	1	1	0	1	0

Different Error Costs

The cost of misclassifying a fraud transaction as legal is much higher than classifying a legal as fraud as it results in money loss. Therefore, most of the fraud detection techniques available today give preference for reducing the misclassification of fraud into legal. The misclassification of legitimate into fraudulent delays the transaction and results in customer dissatisfaction.

APPROPRIATE EVALUATION PARAMETERS

False-positive and false-negative rates are two common measures for the fraud detection techniques. They have an opposite relationship, in this way the false positive decrease and false negative increase for better performance. Many researches in this area have shown that, the accuracy is not appropriate parameters for imbalanced dataset, as with good accuracy all fraud transactions will be misclassified. The cost of misclassifying fraud transaction is higher than the cost of misclassifying legal transaction. So we must consider not only the precision which is correctly classifying instances, but also the sensibility which is correctly classify fraud instances of each costumer. Hand (2007) reported that, the most common measure for classification methods is misclassification rate and the area under the ROC curve. We could confirm from the prior research work that misclassification rate has been very common function for fraud detection methods. However, we could not find any application of the ROC curve to fraud detection in the literature. But in our work we found that error rate parameter when the class sizes are highly imbalanced is not a good choice, because, in such problems the good error rate can be attained by classifying all instances as a larger class. "For example let us assume our detection method correctly classifies 99% of the legitimate instances as legitimate and 99% of the fraudulent instances as fraudulent, so the false-negative and false-positive rate is 1%. The result sounds quite good". However, if the fraud class is 0.1% of all the instances, then 91% of those flagged as fraudulent are in fact legitimate instances.

UCSD-FICO DATA MINING CONTEST 2009 DATA SET

There are different types of credit card transaction datasets with different fraud properties, for example, number of fraudulent transaction, type of fraud and the distribution of fraud transactions among legal transactions. In order to evaluate our proposed model, UCSD-FICO data mining contest 2009 data set is used. The dataset is a real credit card transaction dataset and the objective was to detect fraudulent transactions. They provided two versions of the dataset - "easy" and "hard" versions and we have used the "hard" version for the evaluation of our model. Moreover, the fields of the dataset are anonymized so strongly that it is hard to derive any new field and thus the fraud detection methods depending on aggregation and derived attributes will not work efficiently on this data. The dataset contains 100,000 credit card transactions, and 20 features/attributes. The dataset was already labelled by bank (legitimate/ fraudulent). Figure 4 shows the structure of our dataset. The dataset is highly imbalanced; the number of fraudulent transaction is 2349 out of 100,000 transactions.

Figure 4. Structure of UCSD data mining contest 2009 dataset

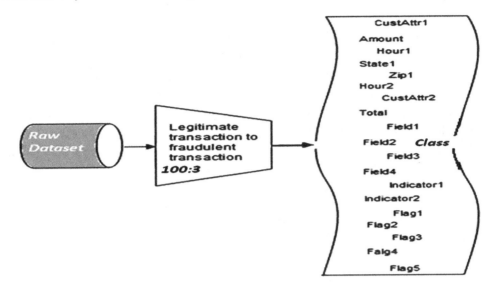

DATA PRE-PROCESSING

Dataset pre-processing is very important and vital theory in data mining technique. Pre-processing is to organize the original dataset, remove all irrelevant attributes, noises and simplifies the data. In order to address this issue, we include a pre-processing phase in our work. Pre-processing in this research mainly includes data cleaning, and reduction, since the unprocessed banking dataset isn't suitable for applying g data mining techniques directly. We used the hard version of the dataset that contains of two sub datasets, training & testing set. The training set is labelled as a 'legitimate', 'fraudulent' and the testing set is unlabelled. We have used only the labelled training dataset. "It contains 100,000 transactions of 73729 individual customers". The attributes contain of 20 fields including class label and are listed as; custAttr1, custAttr2, amount, hour1, state1, zip1,...., hour2, total, indicator1, indicator2, flag2, and Class. Fields custAttr1 and custAttr2 are found to be same for particular customer, as they are the card number and e-mail id of the customer. Both these fields are unique to a particular customer and thus we decided to keep only one. ie, custAttr1. The fields total and amount as well as hour1 and hour2 are found to be same for each customer and thus we removed total and hour2. Similarly, state1 and zip1 are also found to be representing the same information and thus we removed state1.

All other fields are anonymized and therefore we decided to keep them as it is. For evaluation of our model the following procedure is used. First, we removed the transactions corresponds to those customers who have only one transaction in dataset since it appears either in training or testing dataset only. Now the dataset has been reduced to 40918 transactions. Then we divided these 40918 transactions into two- training Set with 21000 transactions and testing set with 19918 transactions. Again from the training dataset we removed the transactions correspond to those customers who have only one transaction in the training dataset since it is hard to find a pattern from a single transaction. Now the training dataset has been reduced to 19165 transactions.

FRAUDMINER: PROPOSED FRAUD DETECTION MODEL

The proposed fraud detection model (FraudMiner) is outlined in Figure 5. The proposed model contain of two phases training & testing. During the training phase, legal transaction pattern and fraud transaction pattern of each customer is created from their legal transactions and fraud transactions respectively by using frequent itemset mining. Then during the testing phase, the matching algorithm detects to which pattern the incoming transaction matches more. In this way, if the new transaction that enter to our detection model is matching more with legal pattern of the particular customer then the algorithm returns '0' (ie, legal transaction) and if the incoming transaction is matching more with fraud pattern of that customer then the algorithm returns '1' (i.e., fraudulent transaction).

PATTERN DATABASE CONSTRUCTION USING FREQUENT ITEMSET MINING (TRAINING)

Frequent itemsets are set of items that occur simultaneously in as many transactions as the user defined minimum support. The metric support(X) is defined as the fraction of records of database D that contains the itemset X as a subset.

$$Support(X) = (count(X))/ (|D|)$$

Figure 5. Proposed credit card fraud detection model

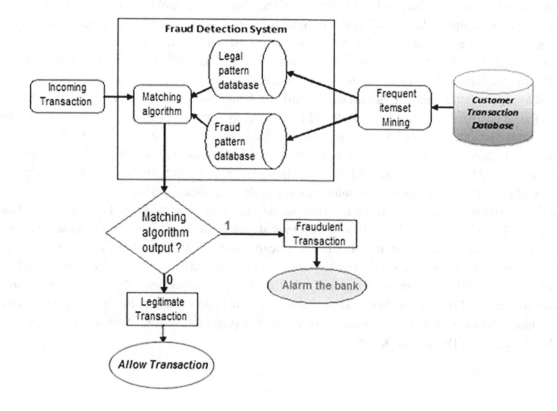

In credit card transaction data, the legal pattern of a customer is the set of attribute values specific to a customer when he does a legal transaction which shows the customer behaviour. It is found that the fraudsters are also behaving almost in the same manner as that of a customer. This means that fraudsters are intruding into customer accounts after learning their genuine behaviour only. Therefore, instead of finding a common pattern for fraudster behaviour it is more valid to identify fraud patterns for each customer. Thus, in this research we have constructed two patterns for each customer – legal pattern and fraud pattern. When frequent pattern mining is applied to credit card transaction data of a particular customer, it returns set of attributes showing same values in a group of transactions specified by the support. Generally, the frequent pattern mining algorithms like Apriori return many such groups and the longest group containing maximum number of attributes is selected as that particular customer's legal pattern. The training (Pattern Recognition) algorithm is given below:

Step 1: Separate each customer's transactions from the whole transaction database D.

Step 2: From each customer's transactions separate his/her legal and fraud transactions.

Step 3: Apply Apriori algorithm to the set of legal transactions of each customer. The Apriori algorithm returns a set of frequent itemsets. Take the largest frequent itemset as the legal pattern corresponds to that customer. Store these legal patterns in legal pattern database.

Step 4: Apply Apriori algorithm to the set of fraud transactions of each customer. The Apriori algorithm returns a set of frequent itemsets. Take the largest frequent itemset as the fraud pattern corresponds to that customer. Store these fraud patterns in fraud pattern database.

The training algorithm is given as below:

```
Begin
                Group the transactions of each customer together.
                Let there are 'n' groups corresponds to 'n' customers
                for i=1 to n do
                        Separate each group Gi into two different groups LGi
and FGi of legal and fraud                          transactions. Let
there are 'm' legal and 'k' fraud transactions
                        FIS= Apriori(LGi,S,m);  //Set of frequent itemset
                        LP=max(FIS); //Large Frequent Itemset
                        LPD(i)=LP;
                        FIS= Apriori(FGi,S,k);  //Set of frequent itemset
                        FP=max(FIS);  //Large Frequent Itemset
                        FPD(i)=FP;
        endfor
            return LPD & FPD;
End
```

FRAUD DETECTION USING MATCHING ALGORITHM (TESTING)

After finding the legal and fraud patterns for each customer, the fraud detection system traverses these fraud and legal pattern databases in order to detect frauds. These pattern databases are much smaller in size than original customer transaction databases as they contain only one record corresponds to a customer. This research proposes a matching algorithm which traverses the pattern databases for a match with the incoming transaction to detect fraud. If a closer match is found with legal pattern of the corresponding customer then the matching algorithm returns'0' giving a green signal to the bank for allowing the transaction. If a closer match is found with fraud pattern of the corresponding customer then the matching algorithm returns'1' giving an alarm to the bank for stopping the transaction. "The size of pattern databases are n x t where "n" is the number of customers and "t" is the number of attributes". The following steps are the matching algorithm process:

Step 1: Count the number of attributes in the incoming transaction matching with that of the legal pattern of the corresponding customer. Let it be lc.

Step 2: Count the number of attributes in the incoming transaction matching with that of the fraud pattern of the corresponding customer. Let it be fc.

Step 3: If fc=0 and lc is more than the user defined matching percentage then the incoming transaction is legal.

Step 4: If lc=0 and fc is more than the user defined matching percentage then the incoming transaction is fraud.

Step 5: If both fc and lc are greater than zero and fc>=lc then the incoming transaction is fraud else it is legal.

The testing algorithm is given as below:

```
Begin
        lc=0;//legal attribute match count
        fc=0;//fraud attribute match count
        for i=1 to n do
           if (LPD(i,1) = T(1)) then //First attribute
                            for j=2 to k do
                                if (LPD(i,j) is valid and LPD(i,j)=T(j))
then
                                            lc=lc+1;
                                endif
                            endfor
    endif
    endfor
          for i=1to n do
                if (FPD(i,1) = T(1)) then
                        for j=2 to k do
                                if (FPD(i,j)is valid and
FPD(i,j)=T(j)) then
```

```
                                        fc=fc+1;
                                        endif
                        endfor
            endif
  endfor
 if (fc=0) then  //no fraud pattern
          if((lc/no. of valid attributes in legal pattern)>=mp)then
                        return(1);//fraud transaction
          else return (0); //legal transaction
      endif
  elseif (lc=0) then //no legal pattern
                  if ((fc/no.of valid attributes in fraud pattern)>=mp)then
                        return(0); //legal transaction
                  else return (1); //fraud transaction
                  endif
  elseif (lc>0 && fc>0) then //both legal and fra
ud                                                                      patterns
are available
                  if(fc >=lc)  then return(1);//fraud transaction
          else return(0); //legal Transaction
                  endif
  endif
End
```

IMPLEMENTATION

All the meta-classification models and outputs were obtained using Matlab R2013. In addition to matlab, the open source data mining software "Weka [47] and Microsoft Excel are also used. Weka is open source software that was developed by the University of Waikato, in New Zealand; it contains a large set of data mining algorithms and is widely used in academia.

Training and Testing Dataset Creation

The following procedure is used for creating the new dataset for evaluating our model.

First, we removed the transactions corresponds to those customers who have only one transaction in dataset since it appears either in training or testing dataset only. Now the dataset has been reduced to 40918 transactions. Then we divided these 40918 transactions into two-training Set with 21000 transactions and testing set with 19918 transactions. Again from the training dataset we removed the transactions correspond to those customers who have only one transaction in the training dataset since it is hard to find a pattern from a single transaction. Now the training dataset has been reduced to 19165 transactions. From this dataset, we have randomly selected different groups of customers and their corresponding transactions in the training and testing dataset, to evaluate the performance of fraud miner with increasing number of transactions. The data distribution is shown in Table 3.

Table 3. Imbalanced Data

No. of Customer	Number of Transactions in Training Set			Number of Transactions in Testing Set		
	Legal	Fraud	Total	Legal	Fraud	Total
200	652	25	489	17	506	677
400	1226	48	1274	864	30	894
600	1716	64	1780	1244	48	1292
800	2169	71	2240	1612	57	1669
1000	26041	131	2735	2002	102	2104
1200	3056	157	3113	2604	144	2748
1400	3440	158	3598	3083	147	3230

Legal/Fraud Pattern Creation

From the training set (for each group) in Table 3, fraud and legal patterns are created for each customer by using the proposed training algorithm. We set the minimum support as 0.9 and selected the large itemset as the pattern. For example, the largest itemset is:

hour = 0
zip = 950
field1 = 3
field2 = 0
field3 = 2429
field4 = 14
indicator1 = 0
indicator2 = 0
flag1 = 0
flag2 = 0
flag3 = 0
flag4 = 0
flag5 = 1.

Then the corresponding pattern is as follows in Table 4:

Here, '9999' represent an invalid field because this field has different values in each transaction and hence it is not contributing to the pattern.

Table 4. Corresponding pattern

0	9999	950	3	0	2429	14	0	0	0	0	0	0	1

EVALUATION METRICS

In this work, fraudulent transaction is considered as positive class and legitimate transaction as negative class, hence the meaning of the terms TP, TN, FP and FN are defined as follows:

- TP refers to the number of fraudulent transactions which predicted as fraud
- TN refers to the number of legitimate transactions which predicted as legal
- FP refers to the number of legitimate transactions which predicted as fraud
- FN refers to the number of fraudulent transactions predicted as legal

At the end, the performance of the proposed method is evaluated in terms of five metrics as:

- Sensitivity
- Specificity
- False alarm rate
- Precision
- Balanced classification rate

In this work, we use frequent itemset mining technique in credit card transaction data, to create the legal pattern of a particular customer as well as a fraudulent pattern of same costumer if there is. Because from the obtained pattern is found that the fraudsters are also behaving almost in the same manner as that of a customer. This means that fraudsters are intruding into customer accounts after learning their genuine behaviour only. Therefore, instead of finding a common pattern for fraudster behaviour it is more valid to identify fraud patterns for each customer. Thus, in this research we have constructed two patterns for each customer – legal pattern and fraud pattern. When frequent pattern mining is applied to credit card transaction data of a particular customer, it returns set of attributes showing same values in a group of transactions specified by the support. Generally, the frequent pattern mining algorithms like Apriori (Agrawal & Srikant, 1994) return many such groups and the longest group containing maximum number of attributes is selected as that particular customer's legal pattern.

Figure 6. Performance comparison of classifiers on term of sensitivity

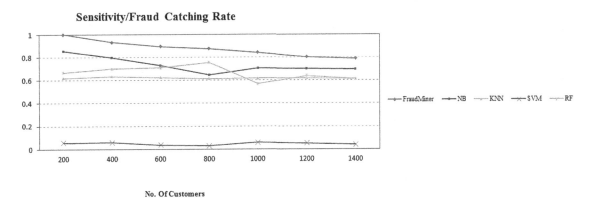

Figure 7. Performance comparison of classifiers on term of specificity

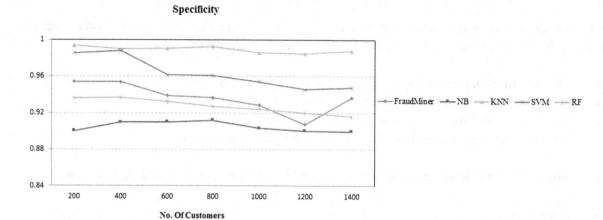

Figure 8. Performance comparison of classifiers on term of balanced classification rate

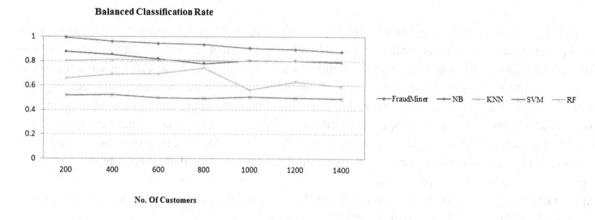

Figure 9. Performance comparison of classifiers on term of false alarm rate

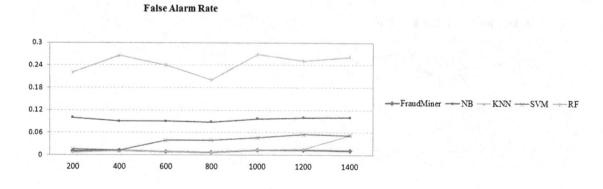

Figure 10. Performance comparison of classifiers on term of precision

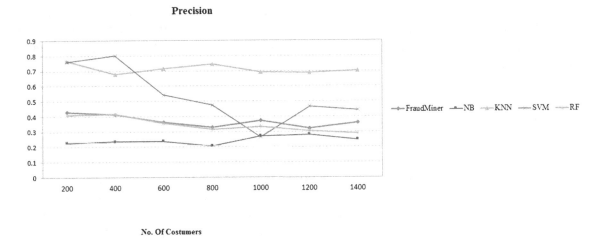

The performance evaluation of the proposed model is done to determine how well the proposed model performs in comparison to the other techniques. See Figure 6, Figure 7, Figure 8, Figure 9, and Figure 10. The state of the art classifiers which we used are (support vector machine (SVM), nearest neighbour (KNN), naïve bayes (NB) and random forest (RF). These are the base classifiers used in the credit card fraud detection models described in literature review. Among these classifiers Random Forest is used by the winner of the UCSD-FICO Data Mining Contest 2009. Before giving the data to the classifiers, we tried to apply SMOTE [20], (which is an oversampling technique to handle to class imbalance). But, the performance was degraded due to highly imbalancedness of the dataset. Hence we supplied the data directly to the classifiers. In Fraud detection, the most important measure is sensitivity or fraud detection rate, since the loss due to fraud depends on this metric. From the performance evaluation it is found that FraudMiner is having the Highest Fraud Detection Rate than other classifiers. The second important measure is, false alarm rate that it shows the customer dissatisfaction due to false alarm (legal transaction, but suspected as fraud). FraudMiner shows very less false alarm rate near to KNN. Performance of FraudMiner on other metrics like accuracy, precision & specificity is also equally good with that of KNN. "The balanced metrics-BC is used to show the competence of FraudMiner for handling imbalancedness problem and eventually FraudMiner showed decent performance according to this measure". It is found that our model could not recognize only those frauds, where there is no pattern difference between the legal and fraud transactions (overlapping). For instance, consider the following transactions in the test data set of Figure 11:

Figure 11. Example of overlapped data

custAttr1	amount	hour1	Zip1	field1	field2	field3	field4	indicator1	indicator2	flag1	flag2	flag3	flag4	flag5	class
123456789 0123867	12.95	9	432	3	0	5454	10	0	0	1	0	0	0	1	1
123456789 0123867	12.95	9	432	3	0	5454	10	0	0	1	0	0	0	1	0

In Figure 11, the attributes of both transactions are same, but one is legal, and other is fraud. Fraud-Miner could not recognize this fraud transaction because the pattern database contains only legal pattern for this customer and both the transactions are matching with that pattern. It is found that when both fraud and legal patterns for a customer is available in the pattern database, then FraudMiner shows 100% fraud detection capability.

CONCLUSION

We propose a fraud detection model whose performance is evaluated with an anonymized dataset and found that, the proposed model is having good performance since it is independent of attribute name. The second superiority of proposed model is, having ability to handle imbalanced dataset. It is incorporated in the model by creating two separate pattern databases for fraud & legal transactions. Both customer and fraudulent behaviours are found to be changing gradually over a short period of time; this may degrade the performance of fraud detection model. Therefore, the fraud detection model should be adaptive to these behavioural changes. These behavioural changes can be incorporated into the proposed model by updating the fraud & legal pattern databases. This can be done by running the proposed pattern recognition algorithm at fixed time points like once in 3 months or six months or once in every one lakh transactions. More over the proposed fraud detection method takes very less time to evaluate the algorithms, which is also an important parameter in real time applications; because the fraud detection is done by traversing the smaller pattern databases rather than the large transaction database.

REFERENCES

Abdelhalim & Traore. (2009). Identity Application Fraud Detection using Web. *International Journal of Computer and Network Security*, 31-44.

Agrawal, R., & Srikant, R. (1994). Fast algorithm for mining association rules in large databases. IBM Almaden Research Center.

Aleskerov, E., & Freisleben, B. (1997). CARD WATCH: a neural network based database mining system for credit card fraud detection. In *Proceedings of the computational intelligence for financial Engineering*.

Bloomberg. (2015). *How ATT Could Keep Crooks from Using Your Credit Card*. Retrieved from http://www.bloomberg.com/news/2015-06-26/how-at-t-could-keep-crooks-from-using-your-credit-card.html

Bolton, R. J., Hand, D. J., Provost, F., Breiman, L., Bolton, R. J., & Hand, D. J. (2002). Statistical fraud detection: A review. *Statistical Science*, *17*(3), 235–255. doi:10.1214/ss/1042727940

Charniak, E. (1991). Bayesians networks without tears. *Artificial Intelligence Magazine*, *12*(4), 49–63.

Chiu, C. C., & Tsai, C. Y. (2004). A Web services-based collaborative scheme for credit card fraud detection. In *e-Technology, E-Commerce and e-Service; IEEE International Conference on*.

Cover, T., & Hart, P. E. (1967). Nearest neighbour pattern classification. *IEEE Transactions on Information Theory*, *13*(1), 21–27. doi:10.1109/TIT.1967.1053964

Dorronsoro, Ginel, Sgnchez, & Cruz. (1997). Neural fraud detection in credit card operations. *IEEE Transactions on Neural Networks*, (8), 827-834.

Duman, E., & Ozcelik, M. H. (2011). Detecting credit card fraud by genetic algorithm and scatter search. *Expert Systems with Applications*, *38*(10), 13057–13063. doi:10.1016/j.eswa.2011.04.110

Excell D. (2012). Bayesian inference-the future of online fraud protection. *Computer Fraud & Security*, (2), 8-11.

Farvaresh, H., & Sepehri, M. (2011). A data mining framework for detecting subscription fraud in telecommunication. *Engineering Applications of Artificial Intelligence*, *24*(1), 182–194. doi:10.1016/j.engappai.2010.05.009

Fayyad, U., Shapiro, G. P., & Smyth, P. (1996). From data mining to knowledge discovery: An overview. Advances in Knowledge Discovery and Data Mining, 1–34.

Ghosh, S., & Reilly, D. L. (1994). Credit Card Fraud Detection with a Neural- Network.*Proceedings of the Twenty-Seventh Hawaii International Conference on System Science* (pp. 621-630). doi:10.1109/HICSS.1994.323314

Hanagandi, V., Dhar, A., & Buescher, K. (1996). Density-bascd clustering and radial basis function modeling togenerate credit card fraud scores. *Computational Intelligence for Financial Engineering, Proceedings of the IEEE/IAFE Conference on.*

Hand D. J. (2007). *Statistical techniques for fraud detection, prevention, and evaluation.* NATO advanced study institute on mining massive data sets for security.

Hand, D. J., & Blunt, G. (2001). *Prospecting for gems in credit card data. IMA Journal of Management Mathematics.*

Hassibi, K. (2000). Detecting payment card fraud with neural networks. Business Applications of Neural Networks, 141-157. doi:10.1142/9789812813312_0009

Hormozi, A. M., & Giles, S. (2004). Data Mining: A Competitive Weapon for Banking and Retail Industries.Information Systems Management, 62-71.

Hunt, J., Timmis, J., Cooke, D., Neal, M., & King, C. (1998). Development of an artificial immune system for real-world applications.Artificial Immune Systems and their Applications, 157–186.

Jithendra Dara Laxman Gundemoni. (2006). *Credit card security and E-payment Enquiry into credit card fraud in e-payment* (Master thesis). Lulea University of Technology.

Kim, M. J., & Kim, T. S. (2002). A Neural Classifier with Fraud Density Map for Effective Credit Card Fraud Detection.*Proceedings of the Third International Conference on Intelligent Data Engineering and Automated Learning.* doi:10.1007/3-540-45675-9_56

Maes, S., Tuyls, K., Vanschoenwinkel, B., & Manderick, B. (1993). Credit card fraud detection using Bayesian and neural networks. In *Proceedings of the First International NAISO Congress on Neuro Fuzzy Technologies.*

Manikas, K. (2008). *Outlier Detection in Online Gambling* (Master thesis). Department of Computer Science. University of Goteborg, Sweden.

Mohammad & Zitar. (2011). Application of genetic optimized artificial immune system and neural networks in spam detection. *Applied Soft Computing*, (11), 3827–3845.

Mukhanov, L. E. (2008). Using Bayesian belief networks for credit card fraud detection.*Proceeding of the IASTED International Conference on Artificial Intelligence and Applications*.

Ngai, E. W. T., Hu, Y., Wong, Y. H., Chen, Y., & Sun, X. (2011). The application of data mining techniques in financial fraud detection: A classification framework and an academic review of literature. *Decision Support Systems*, *50*(3), 559–569. doi:10.1016/j.dss.2010.08.006

Phua, C., Lee, V., Smith, K., & Gayler, R. (2005). A comprehensive survey of data mining based fraud detection research. *Artificial Intelligence Review*.

Phua, C. W. C. (2007). *Data Mining in Resilient Identity Crime Detection* (Doctoral thesis). Clayton School of Information Technology, Monash University.

Potamitis, G. (2013). *Design and Implementation of a Fraud Detection Expert System using Ontology-Based Techniques* (Masters Dissertation). Faculty of Engineering and Physical Sciences, Monash University.

Provost, F. (2002). Comment on: Statistical Fraud Detection—A review. *Statistical Science,* (17), 249-251.

Qibei, L., & Chunhua, J. (2011). Research on Credit Card Fraud Detection Model Based on Class Weighted Support Vector Machine. *Journal of Convergence Information Technology*, *6*(1), 62–68. doi:10.4156/jcit.vol6.issue1.8

Quah, J. T. S., & Sriganesh, M. (2008). Real-time credit card fraud detection using computational intelligence. *Expert Systems with Applications*, *35*(4), 1721–1732. doi:10.1016/j.eswa.2007.08.093

Ramanathan, V. (2012). *Adversarial face recognition and phishing detection using multi-layer data fusion* (Doctoral Dissertation). George Mason University.

Syeda, M., Zhang, Y. Q., & Pan, Y. (2002). Parallel Granular Neural Networks for Fast Credit Card Fraud Detection. *Proceedings of the IEEE International Conference*, (1), 572–577 doi:10.1109/FUZZ.2002.1005055

Top Credit Card Processors. (2015). *Rankings of Best Fraud Detection Companies*. Retrieved from http://www.topcreditcardprocessorsguide.com/rankings-of-best-fraud-detection-companies

Tuo, J., Ren, S., Liu, W., Li, X., Li, B., & Lei, L. (2004). Artificial immune system for fraud detection. *IEEE International Conference on Systems, Man and Cybernetics*, (2), 1407-1411. doi:10.1109/ICSMC.2004.1399827

Yap, B. W., Rani, K. A., Rahman, H. A. A., Fong, S., Khairudin, Z., & Abdullah, N. N. (2013). An application of oversampling, undersampling, bagging and boosting in handling imbalanced datasets. In *Proceedings of International Conference on Advanced Data and Information-Lecture Notes in Electrical Engineering*, (pp. 13-22).

Yu, L., Yue, W., Wang, S., & Lai, K. K. (2010). Support vector machine based multi agent ensemble learning for credit risk evaluation. *Expert Systems with Applications*, *37*(2), 1351–1360. doi:10.1016/j. eswa.2009.06.083

Zaslavsky V., A. Strizhak. (2006). Credit card fraud detection using self organizing maps. *Information & Security: An International Journal,* (18), 48-63.

Chapter 6

The Integral of Spatial Data Mining in the Era of Big Data:
Algorithms and Applications

Gebeyehu Belay Gebremeskel
Chongqing University, China

Chai Yi
Chongqing University, China

Zhongshi He
Chongqing University, China

ABSTRACT

Data Mining (DM) is a rapidly expanding field in many disciplines, and it is greatly inspiring to analyze massive data types, which includes geospatial, image and other forms of data sets. Such the fast growths of data characterized as high volume, velocity, variety, variability, value and others that collected and generated from various sources that are too complex and big to capturing, storing, and analyzing and challenging to traditional tools. The SDM is, therefore, the process of searching and discovering valuable information and knowledge in large volumes of spatial data, which draws basic principles from concepts in databases, machine learning, statistics, pattern recognition and 'soft' computing. Using DM techniques enables a more efficient use of the data warehouse. It is thus becoming an emerging research field in Geosciences because of the increasing amount of data, which lead to new promising applications. The integral SDM in which we focused in this chapter is the inference to geospatial and GIS data.

INTRODUCTION

Data Mining (DM) is a rapidly expanding field in many disciplines. It plays a significant role in human activities and has become an essential component in various areas and issues that employed to Knowledge Discovery (KD) process to analyzing large-scale data from different sources and perspectives (Martin et al., 2001; Krzysztof et al., 1996). It is greatly inspiring to analyze massive data types, which

DOI: 10.4018/978-1-5225-2031-3.ch006

includes geospatial, astronomic, climate, image and other forms of data sets. The fast growths of data are characterized as high volume, velocity, variety, variability, value and others, which can be collected and generated from various sources. The data includes, satellite, remote sensing, Geographic Positioning System (GPS), areal images, photographs, log files, social media, machines, video, textual, which are too complex and big to capturing, storing and analyzing, and challenging by traditional tools (Diansheng & Jeremy, 2009). These sources have strained the capabilities of classical relational Database Management Systems (DBMS) and spawned a host of new technologies, approaches, and platforms called "Big Data." Therefore, the potential values of geospatial data using DM techniques are great and are clearly established by a growing number of studies (Deepali, 2013; Ranga et al., 2012).

In the last two decades, the integrity of DM and Geographic Information Systems (GIS) was limited, and the actual spatial data analysis techniques suffer from the huge amount of complex data to process (Anselin, 1998). Indeed, earth observation data (acquired from optical, radar and hyperspectral sensors installed in terrestrial, airborne or space-borne platforms) is often heterogeneous, multi-scale, incomplete, and composed of diverse objects. However, the existing data analytics were traditional and doing very basic spatial analysis functionality, which confined to analysis that involves descriptive statistical displays, such as histograms and/or pie charts. Moreover, the complete DM process is a combination of many sub-processes, which includes data extraction and cleaning, feature selection, algorithm's design and other analytics of the spatial data (Zaragozi, et al., 2012). In many geospatial research works, the non-spatial data did not well addressed and synthesis by any of the various data analysis techniques. Based on these and other facts, we proposed an Integral Spatial DM (ISDM) to discuss and introduced a novel way of handling and analyzing geospatial and non-spatial data that allows flexibility to describe elements together to optimize spatially based decision-making process (Carlos et al., 2013; Xing et al., 2013).

In this chapter, we discussed the integral DM techniques and algorithms and its significance in GIS and spatial data analysis. The key intervention, and success of Spatial DM (SDM) are a clear business need that data analytics aligns with the Geo-referencing environment and IT strategies, which improve and optimize a spatial decision-making culture, a strong data infrastructure, the right analytical tools, and people skill in the use of spatial data analysis. It is thus becoming an emerging research field in Geosciences because of the increasing amount of data, which lead to being new promising applications (Gennady et al., 2006). Therefore, the need of DM in the domain of GIS is manifold advantages as to advance and automate spatial data search for hidden patterns in complex databases, offers great potential benefits of applying GIS-based decision-making. Recently, the task of integrating these two technologies has become critical, especially as various public and private sector organizations possessing large databases with thematic and geographically referenced data begin to realize the huge potential to gain valuable information and knowledge implicit. For example, to analyze Geo-referenced statistical data, searching for explanations of disease clusters, assessing the impact of changing land-use patterns on climate change and doing customer segmentation based on spatial location are mentioned among its applications (Luís et al., 2005).

This chapter research work is vitally essential to DM and GIS specialists, scientists and researchers by giving novel ideas and techniques of DM for GIS domain in which we focused the inference of geographic positioning or coordinating data that can include astronomical, satellite and spacecraft, and other forms of referenced image data. The DM algorithms are employed when analyzing spatial and related types of data on the use of spatial warehouses, data cubes, OLAP, and clustering methods. Therefore, the field of GIS is a well-identified domain of DM, which is complex due to the nature of spatial data types, relationships and correlation between features that an effectiveness of many algorithms depends on the proper processing of relationships with surrounding. The applications for mining spatial data are included generalization-based methods, clustering, spatial associations, approximation and aggregation, mining in image and raster databases, spatial classification and trend detection.

The chapter is organized as section 2 deals with spatial data type and structure of GIS in consideration of spatial database or data sources, features representations, exploration. In section 3, we discussed SDM tasks and techniques. Section 4 is about spatial data structure, and section 5 and 6 are about SDM models and algorithms respectively. In section 7 and 8, we discussed its applications trend predictions and challenges. Finally, we summarized in section 9, which followed by the acknowledgment and referenced articles lists. In general, in this chapter, we explore the use of DM techniques and algorithms to discover potentially interesting spatial data patterns in a Geoscience for the above type of applications.

SPATIAL DATA TYPE AND STRUCTURE IN GIS

Spatial data is data related to spacing, which includes image data that typically downloaded into GIS systems for knowledge processing purposes. The complexity, volume, variability and data collection and generation fast made it big, which cannot handle, analyze and interpret using traditional data analysis tools. The GIS data is optimized for establishing spatial relationships among objects, which can be produced rapidly from a variety of sources (Ahmad, 2008; Anselin, 1998). The number and size of the spatial database, for example, for Geo marketing, traffic control or environmental studies, medical diagnosis, weather predictions is fast growing, which result in an increasing need for SDM techniques and algorithms.

SDM and Temporal DM (TDM) are the two broad GIS data categories. They are fundamental databases of discovering interesting, useful, nontrivial pattern's information or knowledge from large-scale data, which related to space or geographical regions (Sumuthi et al., 2008; Gennady et al., 2006; Yu and Kang, 2004). DM techniques and algorithms provide advanced prediction capabilities for record-based data and then processing those using DM tools or software to convert it to record format or data patterns and models. Such as, segmentation algorithms of unsupervised and supervised classification methods, descriptive and predictive spatial models and algorithms for large time-series analysis are presented to assist experts in their knowledge discovery (Parimala et al., 2011). The use of high-resolution satellite images now enables the observation of small objects, while the use of very high temporal resolution images enables monitoring of changes in high frequency.

The great thing about geographically referenced data is that data sets structures that compiled from independent sources can be combined and will align, spatially in a coherent way. GIS data, in addition to representing things graphically, records attributes reflecting information that is critical to understanding what things are searching the resources can be as easy as doing a web search, for example, in Google or some such tool (Marlene et al., 2010; Karl and Ober, 2001). However, most data owner organizations or individuals are not always willing to provide their data, unless they know about apprehending information about the research or projects. In such case, depending on our research, demand, we can identify the most potential and willing resources. Because of these facts, most organizations did not put their data on the web, rather they keep it to their track of typically do not use Computer-Aided Drafting (CAD) tools to manage their data. Database tools such as GIS are better to deal with very large datasets, and they are deeper regarding being able to attach meaning to represent, and more flexible in accommodating real world coordinate systems (Hanan, 1995).

The referencing systems of the data sets are organizations of inferences to entities and phenomena and their attributes. For example, numeric references can reflect relative sequence and magnitude, absolute count or weight, or rational relationships, which need to determine whether arithmetic and algebraic logic apply. Date and time references are important to distinguish events that happened before or after some other point in time. It refers to manipulating with the logic that allows revealing the interval that elapsed between them. If time references are given in a dataset, the metadata should indicate the time zone. The text string is needed when the reference did not represent the coordination's of numeric spatial positions. Such as whereby two references that are equal are said to refer to the same quality. When evaluating data, it is crucial to make reference to a specific purpose. We know that all data are flawed. The question is: How will the flaws in the data impact the analysis that we intend to make? Once we have had a look at a dataset and its metadata, we may be able to evaluate whether it is fitting to or not.

Spatial Data Type and Sources

A spatial database stores a large amount of space-related data, such as maps, preprocessed remote sensing or medical imaging data, which has many features distinguishing them from relational databases. The data are collected in a huge amount from different sources. They carry topological and/or distance information, usually organized by sophisticated, multidimensional spatial indexing structures that addressed by spatial data access methods and often require spatial reasoning, geometric computation, and spatial knowledge representation techniques (Theresa & Frederick, 2010; Valliappa & Travis, 2009; Hanan, 1995). Therefore, SDM refers to the extraction of spatial relationships, or other interesting patterns not explicitly stored in spatial databases. It can be used for understanding spatial data and its relationships, constructing knowledge bases, reorganizing the databases and optimizing queries (Ravikumar & Gnanabaskaran, 2010).

The important thing is that merely knowing and search the data source is organizing the data well and put it properly and safely for various purposes. The applications are ranging from remote sensing and satellite telemetry systems to computer cartography, medical diagnosis, weather analysis and prediction and other types. Various national and international agencies are also providing spatial data in different dimensions. Most common data sources are satellite images, medical images, human body's protein structure and all those data that can be represented in the form of cuboids, polygon, cylinder, etc. (Ahmad, 2008).

Spatial data include geographic and computer-aided design data. GIS and RS data are being mapped and associated satellite raster information. Whereas, computer-aided design data are integrated circuit design, building designs, parallelepiped (or parallelogram in 2D), ellipsoid (or ellipse in 2D), and landmarks based representation, where landmarks are sampled boundary points (Yu & Kang, 2005). In the most spatial database research works, the 2D databases are not more efficient in storing, indexing and queuing of data based on spatial locations. Additionally, for 2D databases, applying standard index structures is challenging, such as B-trees or hash indices, to answer such a query efficiently (Hanan, 1995). However, the 2D data sets are essential to model features from a variety of scientific domains. Parallelepipeds (or parallelograms) that applied to regular shape and also ellipsoids or ellipses are appropriate for vortices, whereas, the landmarks are effective to model highly irregular shaped features such as defect structures in materials (Figure 1). The number of landmarks needed to represent a feature is a domain dependent. The framework supports elemental shapes such as lines and splines.

Figure 1. Spatial data sets representation sample model

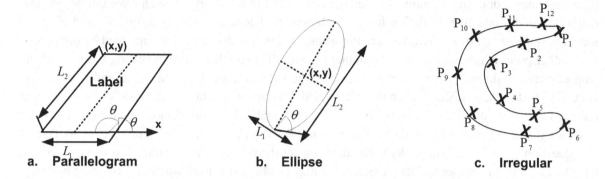

The data set represented as 'D' that consists of 'n' features extracted from $r > 1$ snapshots, taken at time steps $t_{1,...,}$ t_r $(t_1 < ... < t_r)$. For spatial data that involves multiple maps, one can arbitrarily assign a unique ID to each map. The n features are further categorized into l types, where it governs by the underlying domain. A feature's geometric properties are captured by their representation as mentioned above.

Shape-based representation framework supports three main distance measurements for two objects o_i and o_j in the same snapshots:

1. **Point:** It is the Euclidian distance between object centroids.
2. **Line:** It is the displacement distance between two line segments identified for the two involved objects respectively, such as an ellipse represented objects one can take the major axis as the identified line segment.
3. **Boundary:** It is the shortest pairwise distance between the landmarks of o_i and o_j.

The last two measurements take objects' geometric properties into account, and the framework also supports Hausdorff distance (Xing et al., 2013). Moreover, the spatial relationships of o_i and o_j have a T_o relationship if the distance between them is $\leq \varepsilon$, a user-specified parameter. If two objects o_i and o_j are neighbors, they will have a closed T_o relationship that can concern the above/below spatial relationship, which is called Spatial Object Association Pattern (SOAP).

SOAP characterized the close T_o or is above relationships among multiple object types. The framework supports the discovery of various SOAP types, namely Star, Clique, Sequence, and min-Link (Figure 2a, 2b, 2c, and 2d). These SOAP types can be abstracted as undirected graphs. In such graphs, a node corresponds to an object type, and an edge indicates a fulfilled close T_o or is above relationship between two object types. Star SOAPs (Figure 2a) have a center object-type, which is required to have a close T_o relationship with all the others in the same SOAP. Clique SOAPs shape (Figure 2b) requires that a close T_o relationship holds between every pair of the involved objects. Sequence SOAPs shape (Figure 2c) identify sets of objects that are spatially arranged in order and the two adjacent objects in a SOAP meet both the close T_o and is above criteria. The min-Link SOAPs shape (Figure 2d) are a parameterize SOAP type, where the value of a minimum-Link is user-specified. Informally, that a min-Link = 1 SOAP requires to every involved feature in at least l neighbors in the same SOAP.

Figure 2. Graphic representation of feature of spatial data relationships

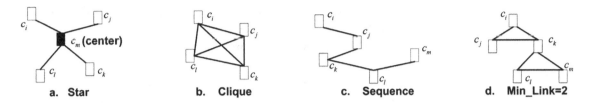

The graphic representation of spatial data features relationships of SOAP types (Figure 2) characterized as distance-based, topological, and directional types. The close T_o relationship is both distance and topology based, whereas, for the sequence, SOAPs is more appropriate to a directional type spatial relationship, which is essential to understand the different interacting behaviors in many scientific applications.

Spatial Data Representation and Formats

Spatial data references to observations and measurements related to real-world or imaginary entities and phenomena, which organized as tables, vector feature classes, and raster layers. This basic spatial data structure provides a predictable means of the Geoscience schema in which permits our tools to exchange information and to engage information in operations and to discover associations concerning information from different data sources (Hanan, 1995).

Tables

It is a tabulated format, which serves as a container for records about entities that can be distinguished by their attributes. There are various forms that include plain text, command delimited files, and other numeric types.

Vector Features

These represent spatial objects with data structures whose basic primitive are points, lines and polygons merely extend the range of data types and associated logic traditionally offered in tables. It allows precise representation of coordinates, and it's useful for analysis. The ISO standards for logical data types were extended to handle spatial data: defined by its coordinates 'points,' sequence of points connected with line 'lines' and sequence of connected chains 'polygon' and surfaces in the mid-1990s (Nada et al., 2008). Furthermore, Text Files By including numeric fields for X and Y coordinates can associate references to point entities in a text file. The fundamental operations to manipulate vector data are the distance, area (if it is a polygon), the length (if it is a chain or polygon), interface or union, a mutual position of two objects.

Raster Image

It is the type or structure of space model or format spatial data. It allows us to distinguish and form associations among different classes of discrete entities of raster images provide containers for representations of locations that identified by cells or pixels, which can be associated with attributes. The regular grid of cells contains a single value and its position defined by its indices on the grid. The resolution of the raster depends on its pixel size (Daniel et al., 2003). The smaller the pixel size is, the higher the resolution, but also the larger the data size of the spatial data model schema.

The geospatial is useful to consider how complexes of a feature class and raster can be organized to make data models that are coherent regarding the relationships among features and potentially also engaged with rasters. Higher-order data collections that operate this way thought of as Schema in the sense of their abstract organization, or as data models when they are implemented and used. An advantage of thinking of schema in this way is that toolkits may be developed inferences and perform experiments involving the constitution of elements and relationships among them. In many applications of reasoning, it is necessary to classify of entities having similar properties as if general rules might be applied to them. In GIS, we encounter categories of the qualitative sort, such as land use classification systems, and we also have categories in a spatial sense such as zip code boundaries or census tracts. In either case, the coarseness or fine-grain of our classification system will affect our ability to model certain phenomena and relationships. For example, that the pattern of population density is much different if we use a block-level in contrast to a tract-level aggregation. The same is true for land use classes. One classification system may distinguish five classes of housing according to lot-size, another may lump all housing and industrial uses into one class, called urban land. Given the choice of two data sets reflect observations of the same entities, the level of granularity in the referencing systems used will render one or the other less fit to use for a given purpose.

Spatial Feature Representation

Spatial data represented in graphic or non-graphics forms. The former includes maps, drawing, animations, and others either 2D or 3D that is achieved through the use of point, linear and areal symbols. Colors and patterns are also in use as visual variables. A map of 2-D is a spatial representation of reality, used for recording and conveying information about the spatial and semantic characteristics of the natural world and cultural phenomena. Geospatial mapping has been a popular mode of spatial representation and is still popularly used in practice because of their measurability, which results from the use of mathematical laws, intuitive view from symbolization and overview from generalization. Based on their contents, maps are usually classified as topographic maps (terrain surface and features on the surface with balance), thematic maps (the theme of natural phenomena) and spatial maps the hybrid of the two, for example, tourist maps. A topographic representation map is a type of qualitative map, whereas, the thematic map could be either quantitative or qualitative. Map scale, usage, the size of the area covered, color and others are also criteria of map classifications in which interesting to distinguish maps into real and virtual.

The spatial features representations are vitally significant to SDM techniques, which provide an access of image classification that enables to describe the visual appearance of a small patch topology extracted from a training set, clustered and quantized. The fixed set of representatives, the so-called visual words, are used for describing the features of an image that represent the absolute or relative frequencies of the occurring visual words called, which indicates different object categories. In some case, we might not have enough spatial information for the proper feature representations, in such case we need to use or apply objects natural scenes of similar orientation and spatial structure. Then after the object vectors will use for describing the image and representation of its features.

EXPLORING SPATIAL DATA MINING

SDM is the process of searching valuable and implicit knowledge from large-scale spatial data, which can be used for understanding Geospatial layout and environmental observation (Maike, 2008). It is an essential to discover relationships between spatial and non-spatial data constructing knowledge bases reorganizing databases and optimizing queries (Sumuthi et al., 2008). The challenge for SDM is the exploration of efficient mining techniques and algorithms due to massive and complexity of the spatial data sets, which is the question of how do we look at it and where the need to start learning how to use it. The key to exploring and understand the spatial data is to examine the attributes and features of each component towards the domain context or research issues (Parimala et al., 2011; Danhuai & Weihong, 2008; Daniel et al., 2008).

Understanding of geospatial data is essential to define a Geo-referencing (spatial) data and metadata sets. To have a meaningful insight about it, we need to have a conceptual model (Figure 3), which could refer to real-world entities and phenomena and these, in turn, may be represented by the traces of observations and measurements that have been gathered according to some method such as SDM tool. The geospatial data should be measured and observed to encode using regular, predictable and documented referencing systems. For example, the data that employed for many types of research or other academic works are collected and shared through open sources (sometimes by a certain protocols, or rules), which exists and re-used to represent concepts in our models. Therefore, before doing so, one must have an understanding of the purposes, and methods and referencing systems surrounding the production of a data set.

As it showed in Figure 3, the purposes/questions of the conceptual model and its concepts, know the behavior of the data what makes work worth doing. For example, what data and for which analysis, we

Figure 3. Conceptual spatial data modeling framework

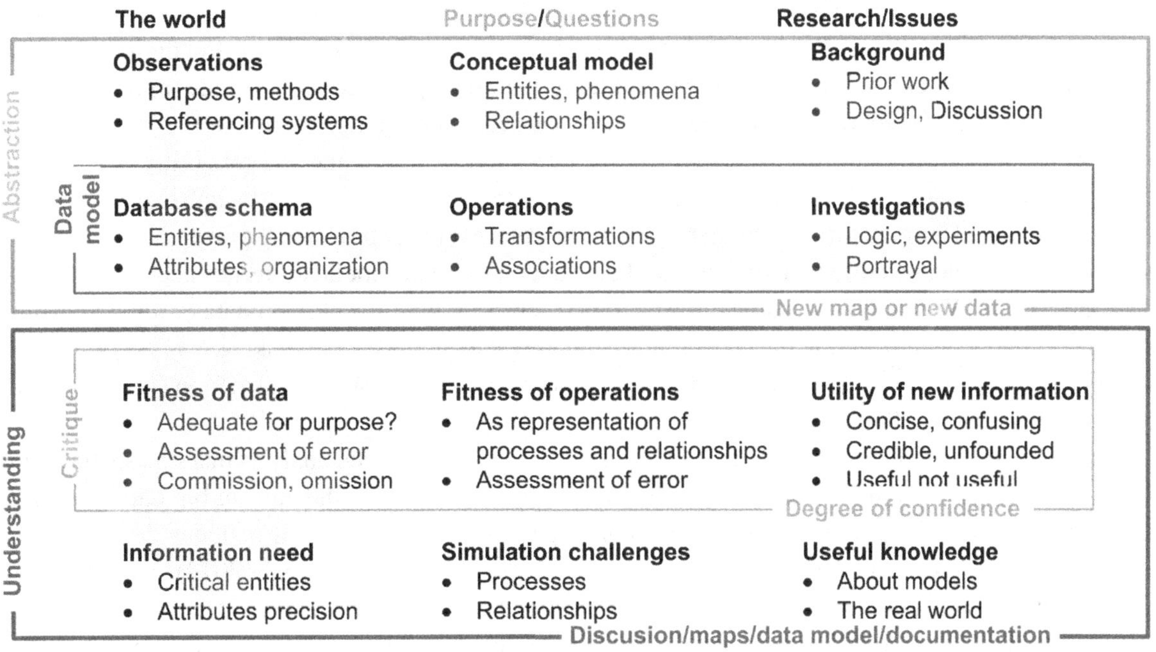

need data for this chapter of the integral SDM algorithms and applications, or data for city map, which is pertinent to define in advance why we need it. It is a step of clarifying the attributes of the entities, its intern relationships and the procedural steps of the investigations of SDM algorithms and applications. By having this understanding, the analyst will know what need to observe and measure about, which need a good deal of prior scholars about the processes, mining algorithms, and there are many existing data sets that represent the work in its sub contents (Carlos et al., 2013). Each of the data sets represents records of some observations and measurements that we made for some specific analysis. The more important question is whether on the available dataset is good enough to represent the model or the research in general. Metadata is the information about data. It revealed us as the need of many things that may be necessary for evaluating the fitness of the data for the given purpose. It is a sort of real-world entity's real data sets intended to represent, what were the methods used to discover, observe and measure these entities, which evolves, who collected the data and for what purpose, what time does the data represent. Moreover, the spatial referencing systems were used to record observations for the geometry of each feature, includes what is the spatial precision employed in these measurements, and others?

For extracting of patterns from spatial data, there is a need for various methods and techniques by which we can collect meaningful patterns of data from various samples. It should also note that several methods with different goals may be applied successively to achieve the desired result. Sometimes formal metadata documents do not exist in a data set, and we have to make inferences about the quality of the data according to such things that can be observed during the process of obtaining the data or by looking at it with GIS software.

Spatial Big Data and Its Era

Geospatial Data has always been big data, and, the key to big data is analytics. In a normal spatial data setup, the analysis is a set of a program, which operates on a structured data set. What sets apart Big Data analytics is the need to analyzes also unstructured and structured geospatial data streams in real time. Thus, big data analytics for geospatial data is available to allow users to analyze massive volumes of geospatial data. The GIS and RS data, including, aerial surveys using photography and digital cameras, sensor networks, radar, etc. have grown exponentially with data production crossing storage capacity. For instance, petabyte archives for remotely sensed Geo-data were being planned in the 1980s (Ranga et al., 2012), and growth has met expectations. The ever increasing volume and reliability of real-time sensor observations demanding advanced and scalable data exploration tools to visualize and to model the spatial enabled the content system. In the past, limited access to the processing power that makes high volume or high-velocity collection of geospatial data useful for many applications has been a bottleneck (Deepali, 2013). Workstations capable of fast geometric processing of vector geodata brought a revolution in GIS. Now big processing through cloud computing and analytics can make greater sense of data and deliver the promised value of imagery and all other types of geospatial information (Joaquín et al., 2010; Shuliang et al., 2009).

The era of spatial big DM algorithms and its applications to handle and analysis massive spatial data, which are large in its volume, variability, value, in which is the issue of the current big data analytics. The key is the need to look at all data in ensembles specific to applications. It includes data-intensive computing, middleware, analytics and scientific and social applications (Deepali, 2013). Since big data is not a data or data structure; it is the newly emerged and advanced data science to analysis and predicts such complex and multi-sources data. As in any typical big data application workflow, the SDM is used for filtering, transformation, extraction, and other pre-processing operations on geospatial data, including raster imagery. High-volume, high-velocity data coming in from multiple sources such as sensors, satellites, and location feeds from mobile devices, can be aggregated in the big DM processed to identify relevant high-value data (Fengli et al., 2011). The big data appliance is ideal for processing raw imagery and even applying specialized image processing like feature identification and tagging. It processed, transformed, high-value data can be accessed directly from the SDM integrated with other spatial data in a spatial database. Imagery analysis in the cloud has become a reality through web services on publicly available data as well as on proprietary commercial data and secured business and government data (Zaragozi et al., 2012).

Spatial Data Mining Tasks and Techniques

In many DM, research works the term tasks and techniques employed synonymy list of activates. However, the way uses, such a word, for example 'classification' and/or 'clustering'... as a task or techniques differ as the perception, experience and skills of the researchers and scientists (Yu & Kang, 2004). It is because a task in simple terms 'an activity that needs to accomplish within a defined period –classification' just to classify the given data or tasks accordingly without having a procedure and iterative process. A technique is a procedure to complete a given task (Joaquín et al., 2010). Like 'classification' as a technique performing steps and analysis to define a data model or pattern. Therefore, the interactions or relationship between a task and technique are influenced strongly by the user experience and knowledge. A knowledgeable user requires a wider range of facilities, and will normally expect to be provided with finer, more precise tools than a less knowledgeable user before he or she regards the design to be either efficient, accurate, or pleasurable (Karl and Ober, 2001; James et al., 1980)

SDM tasks and techniques are the activities of searching valuable information or knowledge implicit through the iterative process of KD. It consists of data selection, data cleaning, data transformation, pattern searching and finding presentation and interpretation and/or evaluation (Figure 4) (Gebeyehu et al., 2013).

Figure 4. Knowledge discovery iterative processes conceptual model

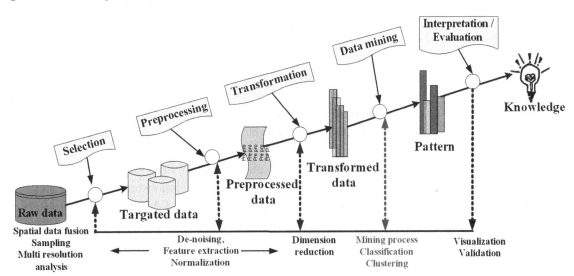

As it showed in Figure 4, the steps of DM are the process of exploration and analysis massive data to discover meaningful patterns and rules that can be discovered using DM depend on the tasks performed. The approach could be descriptive (which 'describe' the general properties of existing data) and predictive, (which try to make 'predictions' based on certain inferences drawn from the available data). Both the tasks provide excellent results in discovering the most repeated instances of variables for a given data set.

SDM Tasks

The tasks of SDM are very diverse and distinct as the nature of the data and issues. The analysis is important tasks of GIS in which allows spatial operations with data (network analysis or filtering of raster data), measuring functions (distance, direction between objects), statistical analyzes or terrain model explore (visibility analysis). The different tasks are needed various methods and techniques to define the patterns, and some of the major tasks what we selected for this work as follows (Diansheng & Jeremy, 2009).

Data Processing and Summarization

Data processing is the procedural tasks of data preparation for various applications including data analysis and summarization purposes (Joaquín et al., 2010). It can be classified as pre- and post-processing of data, which is essential to gain proper decision outcomes. Pre-processing data, since the fundamental of exploration and model or pattern developments, it is well studied by including an understanding of the domain contexts and problems. However, the preprocessing of spatial data has lagged behind. Hence, there is a need for preprocessing techniques for spatial data to deal with problems such as treatment of missing location information and imprecise location specifications, cleaning of spatial data, feature selection, and data transformation (Luís et al., 2005). Unique features of SDM from classical DM can be described as data input, attributes, relationship and interactions (Sanjay et al., 2001). Analyst or users may select, filter, aggregate, clean and/or transform data into a much more understandable form. Unwanted and useless portions may be extractor cut from the existing data, hence to improve the productivity and applicability of the data. It is a fundamental that to summarize and abstract the set of data. This results in a smaller set, which gives a general overview of the data, usually with aggregate information (Soriful et al., 2013).

The data inputs of SDM are more complex, which includes extended objects such as points, lines, and polygons according to their attributes (non-spatial and spatial attributes) (Baazaoui et al., 2007). Non-spatial attributes are used to characterize non-spatial features of objects, such as name, population, and the unemployment rate for a city. They are the same as the attributes used in the data inputs. Spatial attributes are used to define the spatial location and extent of objects that include information related to locations, e.g., longitude, latitude, elevation and shape (Martin et al., 2001). Relationships among non-spatial objects are explicit in data inputs, e.g., arithmetic relation, ordering, is an instance of, a subclass of, and membership. In contrast, relationships among spatial objects are often implicit, such as overlap, intersect, and behind. One possible way to deal with inferred spatial relationships is to materialize the relationships into traditional data input columns and then apply classical DM techniques (Sanjay et al., 2001). However, the materialization can result in loss of information. Another way to capture implicit spatial relationships is to develop models or techniques to incorporate spatial information into the spatial data mining process.

Prediction

SDM prediction concerned with the creation of models that are capable of producing spatial analysis that can be applied to unseen, future cases. The statistics-based predictive geospatial DM methods used in the likelihood ratio and conditional probability in which the prediction models and estimation procedures depend on the basic quantitative relationships of geospatial data sets (Diansheng & Jeremy, 2009). The approach gives spatial pattern or model based on previous history or patterns of data items. The values of specific attributes of the data can be calculated accurately with iterative methods and different samples of data. For example, in weather prediction system we classify satellite images into different classes by some common properties and patterns (Sanjay et al., 2001).

SDM based spatial data modeling is a key challenge in spatial classification problems that arise in geospatial domains. Markov random fields (MRF) are a popular model for incorporating spatial context into image segmentation and land-use classification problems. Fundamental predictions of inter-linked spatial data improve the overall spatial analysis accuracy that needs to be solved in a scientific prediction of geospatial positioning. It is a systematic approach to establishing the multi-variable gray theory in which linear dynamic special model using mutual pit data and the correlation degree analysis. For example, suppose that we want to predict the value of Y(s) given the data 'Y' is:

$$\widehat{Y}(s_0) = x^t(s_0)\beta + \Sigma_{(0,1,\ldots n)} \Sigma^{-1}(Y - X\beta) \tag{1}$$

where $\Sigma_{(0,1,\ldots n)}$ is the cross-covariance between s_0 and all observation sites $\{s_1, \ldots, s_n\}$. The computational difficulty is related to matrix factorization of large 'n'. The prediction is the well-known Kriging equation (Soriful et al., 2013). It is the optimal prediction based on the Gaussian likelihood. The task of making predictions at $n_{k0} \geq 1$ unobserved sites, all situated within block 'k'. The first step is to augment the data vector with an unobserved vector Y_{k0} at n_{k0} prediction locations s_0 such that the augmented vector $Y_k^a = (Y_{k0}^t, Y_k^t)^t$. By including Y_{k0} as unobserved data in the block composed likelihood and setting the derivative of l_{CL} (the specified location 'l' and 'Composited Likelihood') with respect to $Y_{k0} = 0$, we obtain the composite predictions $\widehat{Y}_{k0}$.

Regression

Statistical regression spatial modeling tasks have been compared on similar data sets to determine which of those modeling techniques works best. The models run in a non-spatial regression setup are assuming that the relative differences between these models will also hold in a spatial cross-validation regression setup (Sanjay et al., 2001). The various approaches, such as support vector regression have been determined as the best modeling technique when comparing the models' root mean squared prediction error in which it will serve as a benchmark technique against any further models that have to be completed (Maike, 2008).

For example, given a set of data items, regression identifies a dependency of some attribute values upon the values of other attributes in the same item and applies these values to other data items or records. The Spatial Auto Regression (SAR) model is an extension of the classical regression model for incorporating spatial dependence. In regression models, data records which appear in the training set must not appear in the test set during a cross-validation learning setup. On these approaches of sampling methods do not take spatial neighborhoods of data records into account, which may be rendered invalid when using non-spatial models of spatial data. It leads to over-fitting and underestimates the true prediction error of the regression model (Siddhi et al., 2012). Therefore, the core issue of the SDM regression tasks is to avoid having neighboring or the same samples in training and testing data subsets during a cross-validation approach. The modern spatial regression model adapted to accommodating spatial data. To keep standard regressions modeling techniques such as neural networks, support vector regression, bagging, regression trees and others are essential to optimize SDM performance and applications (Maike, 2008).

Classification

Spatial classification refers to deriving models that related to certain spatial inference characteristics by analyzing spatial objects, such as the areas of a region, which aimed to find the classification rules between spatial and non-spatial attributes of spatial data objects. It is the task of predefined categorical rules, determine to classify an object according to its attributes to which of these specific data item belongs. Thus, the task of SDM classification derives a function or model, which determines the class of an object, based on its attributes. A set of objects given at the training set. In it, every object is represented by a vector of attributes along with its groups. A classification function or model constructed by analyzing the relationship between the attributes and the classes of the objects in the sample set (Theresa & Frederick, 2010). That is, the rule classification method is a type of association rule where one of the variables (the class variable) must be considered as a consequence for any transactions (Zaragozi et al., 2012).

Classification is to build (automatically) a model that can classify a class of objects to predict the classification or missing attribute value of future objects (whose class may not be known). It is a two-step process. In the first process, based on the collection of training spatial data sets, a model is constructed to describe the characteristics of a set of data classes or concepts. Since data classes or concepts are predefined, this step is also known as supervised learning (i.e., which class the training sample belongs to be provided). In the second step, the model is used to predict the classes of future objects or data (Martin et al., 2001). Therefore, the goal spatial classification is to build a model for predicting classes in which it is built using a position of the training data and then tested for the remainder of the data 'testing data.' In the learning data, all the attributes are used to build the model, and the testing data used for one value are hidden. The extension of spatial attributes is to consider also the attribute of objects on a neighborhood path starting from the current object.

Trend Analysis

A trend is a temporal pattern in some time-series data. A spatial trend is defined as a pattern of change of a non-spatial attribute in the neighborhood of a spatial object (Luís et al., 2005). The set of data items identifies relationships between attributes and items such as the presence of one pattern implies the presence of another pattern. Therefore, spatial trends refer to the changes of non-spatial attributes when away given space object. Analyzing spatial trends on spatial data structure and spatial access methods need to use various approaches such as regression analysis.

Clustering

Clustering is an unsupervised learning process. Clustering is the process of grouping a set of physical or abstract objects into classes of similar objects. It is grouping a given a set of spatial data items that are similar. The group identification task assisted by spatial clustering algorithms has a wide range of applications as finding relevant information on increasingly large spatial databases have recently become a highly demanded task. For example, in a given set of satellite images, identify a subgroup of objects of patterns is essential. Its features can be color (colored, no colored), size, shape and image behavior, which helps to process and define classes for a set of objects (Nada et al., 2008, Krzysztof et al., 1996). The objects are so clustered that the intra-class similarities are maximized, and the interclass similarities are minimized. It has done based on some criteria defined on the attributes of the objects. Once the clusters are decided, the objects are labeled with their corresponding clusters. The common features of the object in a cluster are summarized to form the class description (Raymond & Jiawei, 1994).

In classification, which record belongs which class is predefined, while in clustering, there are no predefined classes. In clustering, objects are grouped together based on their similarities. Similarities between objects are defined by similarity functions, which similarity is usually, quantitatively specified as distance or other measures by corresponding domain experts. Thus, the spatial clustering analysis is to divide the objects of the spatial database into different meaningful sub-classes according to some characteristics; objects of the same sub-class have certain features with high similarity, which has obvious differences to characteristics of various subclasses. The advantages of using cluster analysis are: the structure which can be found directly from the data, does not require any background knowledge (Soriful et al., 2013).

Model Visualization

Visualization plays a very important role in understanding and demonstrating the desired task properly. Its techniques to assist conventional DM tasks that make more attract and interactive of considerable interest in the process of spatial data exploration. Visualization techniques may range from simple scatter plots and histogram plots over parallel coordinates to 3D data items (Carlos et al., 2013; Yu & Kang, 2005). In the use of visualization for SDM is the approach of choosing appropriate parameters for spatial data cleaning methods. On one hand, algorithm performance is improved through visualization. On the other hand, characteristics and properties of methods and features of data are visualized as feedbacks to the user. Therefore, it is an essential to visualize data quality, algorithm parameter selection, and measurement of noise removing methods on parameter sensitiveness (Nada et al., 2008).

SDM based spatial data or geospatial data visualization essential to gain meaningful insights and understanding to describe the real-world objects or phenomena with specific locations and associated statistical values or attributes. By considering just one statistical attribute at a time, we can interpret geospatial data sets as points in a 3D data space—that is, two geographical dimensions and a statistical dimension. Because real-world data set distributions are often non-uniform. Therefore, visualizing large geospatial data sets involves mapping the two geographical dimensions to screen coordinates and encoding the statistical value by color (Nagaprasad et al., 2010; Shuliang et al., 2009).

SDM Techniques

Various kinds of patterns can be discovered from databases and can be presented in different forms. Based on dynamic SDM techniques can be classified into descriptive and predictive formats (Anthony et al., 2009). The former concisely describes the behavior of data sets and presents interesting general properties of the data. Whereas the latter attempts to construct, models are tended to help predict the behavior of the new data sets.

Association Rules

Association rule mining techniques are discovering interesting associations between attributes contained in a database that primarily focused on the patterns and dependencies in data sets. When performing clustering methods on the data, we can find only characteristic rules, describing spatial objects according to their non-spatial attributes (Hongyan et al., 2009). In many situations, we want to discover spatial rules that associate one or more spatial objects with others. Spatial mining association rules work as the expression of the form $A => B[S, C]$. Where 'A' is a specific attribute-value association, and 'B' is a specific class attribute instance of the sets of spatial or non-spatial predicates of 'S' (support) is the probability of A and B appearing together in a transaction. 'C' is the confidence of the rule that the probability of B appearing in a transaction where A is present. Meaning that an event of type 'B' occurs at node 'n' with support 'S' and confidence 'C' given that antecedents 'A' all hold true. Every antecedent is defined as:

$$A_i = (B_i, D_i, T_i, N_i) \tag{2}$$

where A_i is true iff a certain type of event B_i occurred N_i times at a distance D_i from node n and T_i times units before B. $D_i, T_i,$ and N_i Usually donated interval, such as T_i = "*more than five minutes ago*", D_i = "*less than 20 meters away*", or N_i "*between one and five times*". For example, spatial association rules: is a (B, "school") A close to (B, "sports center") => close to (B, "park") [0.5%, 80%). This rule states that 80% of schools that are close to sports centers are also close to parks, and 0.5% of the data belongs to such a case. Based on these measures, the task of association rule mining is to find all association rules within the data set D_i that satisfy certain user-defined thresholds for minimum support and minimum confidence, denoted by $min-sup$ and $min-conf$ respectively (Zaragozi et al., 2012). The approach to finding such rules involves (i) all set of attribute values that satisfy $min-sup$ within D_i are found. Next, these sets are used to generate rules of the form $A => B[S, C]$ that satisfy $min-conf$.

Various kinds of spatial predicates can constitute a spatial association rule. For instance, distance information (such as close to and far away) topological relations (like intersect, overlap, and disjoint), and spatial orientations (like left off and west of) (Martin et al., 2001). The spatial association mining needs to evaluate multiple spatial relationships among a large number of spatial objects; the process could be quite costly. An interesting mining optimization or progressive refinement is adopted in the spatial association analysis that employed to mine large data sets roughly using a fast algorithm and then improves the quality of mining in a pruned data set using a more dynamic algorithm. For mining spatial associations related to the spatial predicate, we can first collect the candidates that pass the minimum support threshold by applying a certain rough spatial evaluation algorithm, for example, using a minimum bounding rectangle structure (which registers only two spatial points rather than a set of complex polygons). Then evaluating the relaxed spatial predicate, 'g' close to, which is a generalized 'c' close to covering a broader context that includes close to, touch, and intersect. If two spatial objects are closely located, their enclosing minimum bounding rectangles must be closely located, matching 'g' close to (Theresa & Frederick, 2010).

Clustering

Spatial clustering techniques have an important role in the class identification of records in a database, which is a fundamental DM technique that applied to databases whose records have attributes intrinsically related to some spatial semantics. It is a process of grouping a set of spatial objects to find appropriate classes of elements in a set of data. It is an interesting and fundamental approach to the process of KDD in unsupervised learning, which did not have a target field and the relationship between the data identified by a bottom-up approach. Clustering can also be described as a method for classifying data in an exclusive manner, where each data element belongs to exactly one subset or cluster (Daniel et al., 2003; Raymond & Jiawei, 1994). Clustering algorithms are useful in detecting underlying structure within the data. It is an essential to deal with the large-scale geospatial data sets by having different algorithms, namely K-mean clustering, Self-Organizing Mapping (SOP), partitioning, hierarchical, density-based and grid-based methods (Sumuthi et al., 2008).

K-means clustering is the most widely used methods as the algorithm (KMC). It can be formally described as a given set of 'm' data elements in 'D' comprising of 'n' attributes, and an integer 'k', determine a set of 'k' elements in D called centers, to minimize the distance from every element to its closest center." Each element is attached to its nearest center, thereby subdividing elements in D into k clusters. This approach of decomposing a data set into disjoint clusters is also known as "partition clustering." KMC first initializes a set of k cluster centers $G \in D, i = 1,...,k$. Cluster centers can be assigned, for instance, in a random fashion. Once the centers are initialized, the clustering algorithm assigns each of the remaining, unselected data elements to the center that it is most similar to, i.e. the center that is closest in value. $c\left(e_i\right)$ denotes the index of the center closest to a data element e_i, and then the goal of k-means clustering is to minimize the mean-squared distance between each e_i and its nearest cluster center $g_{c\left(e_i\right)}$. This distance or distortion error is provided as:

$$E_k = \sum_{i \in D} \left\| e_i - g_{c\left(e_i\right)} \right\|^2 \tag{3}$$

when all the data elements have been grouped, the position of each cluster center is recomputed based on the distances between the data elements within each cluster. The e_i, which is closest to all the elements within the cluster assigned to the new cluster center. Once all cluster centers have been recomputed in this fashion, the remaining e_i are reassigned to the emerge centers.

Self-Organizing Maps (SOM) (Diansheng & Jeremy, 2009) are used to organize unstructured data much like the k-means clustering approach. SOM-based algorithms can generate clusters from raw data. They can also produce lower dimensional projections of high-dimensional data. The SOM algorithm works on the principle of competitive learning, an adaptive process by which neurons in a neural network become more and more sensitive to different input categories. An SOM consists of a two-dimensional network of neurons arranged in a grid. Initially, each cell is assigned a reference vector (or reference value) in a random fashion. Every data element e_i from the input data set is assigned to the neuron with reference vector that best represents e_i. Locating the nearest reference vector in the SOM approach, is very similar to searching for the closest center in the k-means clustering approach.

The spatial data or SDM approaches are user defined distance thresholds that are termed spatial neighbors. These neighborhoods are then used to detect clusters, trends (Siddhi et al., 2012), which are the relative differences in non-spatial attributes values when defining spatial neighborhoods. In their approach, two elements e_i and e_j are considered spatial neighbors e_i and e_j lie within a distance threshold of each other, and if e_i's non-spatial attribute values do not differ from those of e_j by more than a user-defined similarity threshold. For spatial cluster detection, a new cluster C is created for an $e_i \in D$ that does not belong to any cluster. Then, for all elements $e_j \in D$ not part of any cluster, e_j is added to C if e_j is a spatial neighbor of e_i. The process is repeated for all elements in D belong to a cluster.

The clusters are then visualized to display both the spatial and the non-spatial attribute characteristics of the data set (Nagaprasad et al., 2010; Anselin, 1998). Spatial trends (increasing or decreasing) have also been discovered using the concept of spatial neighbors. A spatial trend tracks the change in one or more non-spatial attribute values when moving away from a certain specific location. To detect decreasing trends starting from a location e_i, e_i's neighbors are examined to find an e_j whose attribute values are lower than that of e_i. e_j is added to the current trend, then, e_j is examined in a similar fashion.

Decision Trees

Decision Trees performs classification by constructing a tree based on training instances with leaves having class labels. The tree is traversed for each test instance to find a leaf, and the class of the leaf is the predicted class. It is a directed knowledge discovery in the sense that there is a specific field whose value we want to predict (Ravikumar & Gnanabaskaran, 2010).

Neural Network

Neural Networks (NN) offer a mathematical model that attempts to mimic the human brain. The network is composed of a large number of highly interconnected processing elements (neurons) working in the parallel to solve a specific problem that learns by example. It has proven to be the most significant improvement in information extraction in spatial data analysis. The classification of geospatial data using NNs began appearing in geospatial literature in the past years. It represented as a layered set of interconnected processors. These processor nodes are frequently referred as neurnodes to indicate a relationship with the neurons of the brain. Each node has a weighted connection to several other nodes in adjacent layers. Individual nodes take the input received from connected nodes and use the weights jointly to compute output values (Nagaprasad et al., 2010). The performance NN on a differently trained spatial data set presented that shows how information from sequence and structure come together to improve the prediction accuracy of the network, which provides a reliable way of finding likely active sites.

Neural network SDM based KDD vitally essential to aid research towards robot learning through demonstration and imitation. The NN SDM techniques, such as differential ratio DM used to identify the salient trends within spatiotemporal data combined with a neural multilayer perceptron classifier. Among its tremendous advantages:

1. It is an independent statistical analysis tool in which no need specific variable definition. It allows the target classes to be defined by their distribution in the corresponding domain of each data source, which is essential to the integration of GIS and RS spatial data.
2. It is capable and dynamic computational mechanism able to acquire, represent, and compute a mapping from one multivariate space of information to another, given a set of data representing that mapping and NN models share various characteristics.
3. It is to identify internally a set of rules for matching input data to output conclusions for which NNs is composed of a set of nodes and the interconnected processing elements.
4. NN uses learning algorithms to model knowledge and save spatial knowledge in weighted connections, mimicking the function of a human brain. It is also capable to the models feedforward backpropagation ANN.

SPATIAL DATA MINING SYSTEMS

In the past, spatial database systems implemented for data management purposes in which focus on the development of spatial data structure and transaction processing and supporting spatially based decision-making process (Siddhi et al., 2012). The increasing integration of spatial database systems with GIS data streams and database technology led to a growing and demanding, dynamic and scalable data exploratory tools for which fertile to the emerge of DM in the GIS domain. The interests of business and organizations using spatial data for decision support have benefited terminology from parallel advances in knowledge discovery in large databases in the business world using concepts and techniques of DM systems. Therefore, SDM system is a subject-specific application of DM in GIS and remote-sensing spatial database analysis. It has its theoretical foundations in conventional DM and relies heavily on general DM techniques to handle the attribute component of spatial data (Gebeyehu et al., 2013). Moreover, the understanding of the principles and methods of DM is essential for users of SDM systems.

SDM system is an essential to extract interesting and useful spatial patterns and relationships within massive spatial data sets in which interoperability refers to the ability of intelligent SDM communicate and exchange spatial data, patterns, and others via the Internet (Daniel et al., 2008). It is the solution of handling and analysis spatial data in different locations. It is also playing an essential role in privacy and security and spatial data exploration efficiency. SDM system is important to extend spatial web standards and web-based DM. Such as PMML (Predictive Modeling Markup Language) support a novel SDM system concepts and models, which pertinent to implement the DM algorithms for SDM, enhance the interactivity between users and the system. It provides multiple exporting models to exhibit the results in an intuitive manner that convenient for analyzing and decision-making.

Spatial Data Structure

Spatial data structures are the implementation of spatial concepts to define the corresponding spatial data models. To valid the implementations of spatial concept, a spatial data structure must follow the property of spatial data models. Spatial data structures are concerned with the efficiency of the implementation, namely:

1.   Minimizing storage requirements to reduce the amount of space to hold the data.
2.   It is maximizing SDM performance to improve the processing speed of spatial or geometrical operations (Valliappa & Travis, 2009).

The representation of data internal to a computer system and its architecture are crucial factors to be considered in the design of spatial data structure. Spatial data structures are then built from the standard data structure to optimize the performance mining process or data explorations (Yu & Kang, 2004).

To advance the SDM performance and applications, spatial data structure vitally essential, which the data are organized based on space or geometry. Spatial data structures are also pertinent to intersection detection and collision detection that allow problems (queries) about the spatial relationships of objects to be solved. The spatial data consist of spatial objects made up of points, lines, regions, rectangles, surfaces, volumes, and even data of higher dimension, which includes time. The representation of spatial data is to separate it structurally from the non-spatial data while maintaining proper links between the two (Siddhi et al., 2012). The data needs of spatial operations are performed directly on the spatial data structures, which provide the freedom to choose a more appropriate spatial structure than the imposed non-spatial structure (such as a relational database) (Yu & Kang, 2005). Spatial data structures have manipulated spatial data that have been geometric coordinates of multiple points, namely the 'X', 'Y' and 'Z' and also the time components. These n-dimensional data of multi-attributes search require special access and indexing techniques, which includes quadrant tree, K-d-tree (k-dimensional), R-tree, grid files, and others (Theresa & Frederick, 2010).

R-Tree

The r-trees are an interesting access spatial data structure in which its variants are designed to organize a collection of arbitrary spatial objects (most two-dimensional rectangles) by representing them as d-dimensional rectangles that confer considerable advantages of spatial queries. It is the most common index structure for organizing spatial data, which can be used for shapes of multiple dimensions. The idea of an R-tree is to group nearby objects and enclose them inside yet another minimum bounding rectangle that included all objects in the database and then eventually leading to a root node. Each node in the tree corresponds to the smallest d-dimensional rectangle that encloses its son nodes. The leaf nodes contain pointers to the actual objects in the database, instead of sons. The objects are represented by the smallest aligned rectangle containing them (Manikandan & Srinivasan, 2013).

These trees are used to store rectangular regions (in the n-dimensional space) from a media object. A particular kind of R-trees is the bi-dimensional one that contains rectangular regions from a spatial database. Within R-trees, each leave contains either grouped object's entries (r, <RID>). Where 'r' is an n-dimensional region, and <RID> is an identifier of a media entity, (which can consist of, for example, a pointer to a page and an entry on that page). The root and the intermediary nodes of an R-tree contain entries that have the form (r, < pointer to page>), where the pointer refers a page from the secondary memory. Often the nodes correspond to disk pages and, thus, the parameters defining the tree are chosen so that a small number of nodes are visited during a spatial query. Note that the bounding rectangles corresponding to different nodes may overlap that an object may be spatially contained in several nodes, yet it is only associated with one node. It means that a spatial query may often require several nodes to be visited before ascertaining the presence or absence of a particular object.

Each R-tree has an associated order (whole number), may it be K. Each node, except for the leaves, contains a set with at most K-rectangles and, at least, $\lceil K/2 \rceil$ rectangles (possibly excluding the root). A rectangle can be simple or compound from many sub-rectangles. On the leaves, one can find simple rectangles while compound rectangles can be found on intermediary nodes. The insertion of a new the rectangle in an R-tree is performed as it follows: firstly, it is analyzed which of the roots associated rectangles need to be least extended (regarding the covered area) to incorporate the rectangle to be inserted. Then, if there is enough room, the new rectangle is inserted. Otherwise, the node will split, by respecting the principle of getting a minimum area of the two rectangles. The deletion of a node must ensure that the nodes will not be filled with the minimum of $\lceil K/2 \rceil$. It's guaranteed by re-distribution of the rectangles so that the minim area to be obtained.

K-d-Tree

The *k*-d tree is a multi-dimensional search binary in which every node from such a tree is a structure with two data fields called a k-dimensional pointer and label. On each level of this tree, the discrimination is performed on a single attribute. The partitioning of the search space according to various attributes is done alternately for each attribute from the n-dimensional space. Every node from the same level has the same discriminator (the partitioning attribute of the object space). For k = 1 one gets an ordinary search binary tree. For a given node 'P' of the k-d-tree, the discriminator is the level corresponds to the attribute, which is 'A', and the value of 'A' in' 'P' is KA(P), then all the descendants of the node 'P' can be partitioned into two sub-spaces. In the first one, the records with the values of the attribute 'A' lower than KA(P) can be found. Within the second one, the records that have the value of the attribute 'A' upper than KA(P) are distributed.

In the k-d- tree spatial data structure, relying on the binary subdivision. D-dimensional hyperspace is cyclically sub-divided along each of the d-dimensions. Each node has two children regardless of the dimensionality of the data. In a 2d tree, the plane is first divided into two at some value of 'X' and the next subdivision in each of the children is of some value of 'Y' and then back to 'X' and so on.

Quad-Tree

A quad-tree is a non-uniform subdivision of the area where an axis-aligned box region is split into four quadrants by two axis-aligned dividing lines. It is used to describe a class of hierarchical data structures, which are based on the principle of recursive decomposition space that consists in the data-driven partitioning of object space in several quadrants and to execute multi-key comparisons on each tree level. The differentiation of these spatial data structures is based on the data they represent, namely the rule of decomposition, and the resolution. Each node from such a tree partitions the object space in K-quadrants on the successive iterations. If the region is not homogenous, each quadrant is subdivided into sub-quadrants and so on. Therefore, the process is represented by a tree of 4, and the root node corresponds to the entire array.

It is a maximal block representation in which the blocks have standard sizes and positions. In principle, it is dividing and conquers the successive subdivision of an image array into quadrants, each of which in turn can be subdivided into another quadrant, and so on. The structure forms the tree with nodes representing heterogeneous areas and levels for homogenous areas with a single value. A quad-tree, in general, reduces considerably the space needed to represent a raster image. Each raster of the node represents a quadrant labeled in order North-West, North-East, South-West and South-East in the region represented by the node, which can be traced in various algorithms of the quadrant tree applications.

Grid Files

It is a popular and simple type of grid multi-dimensional tree structures in which similar to k-d-trees that the divides the n-dimensional object hyperspace in equal-sized groups. It is a space filling that each cell or voxel (volume pixel) has a list of objects, which intersects it. The uniform grid is used to determine which objects are near to another object by examining object lists of the cells the object overlaps (Figure 5). The points that belong to a cell can be interlinked into a dynamic list. The structure of this kind of grid is rigid, and its directory can be rare and large. Grid file performs better for retrievals that are based on partial or exact matches. The grid contains two parts: a directory (each entry point to a data bucket) and a set of linear scales (n simple vectors). These scales are used to identify the index of the grid directory, which refers to the respective group of data.

As it showed in Figure 5, the intersections for a given object are found by going through the object lists for all voxels containing the object, performing intersection tests against objects on those lists. The algorithms of the object interactions detections are shown in Figure 5.

Figure 5. Uniform grid files architecture

Grid files
- 3D array of cells (Voxwls) that tiles space
- Each cell points to all intersecting surfaces
- Intersection angle from cell to cell

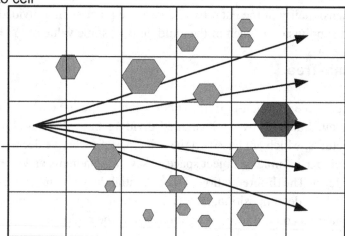

The algorithms for grid base object interaction mining described as:

1. **for** i = 1- **to** - n // n = the sample vectors
2. $\vec{v}_{\min}$ = voxel (min(bbox(objects(i))))
3. $\vec{v}_{\max}$ = voxel (max(bbox(object(i))))
4. **for** x = $v_{\min\,x}$ **to** x = $v_{\max\,x}$
5. **for** y = $v_{\min.y}$ **to** x = $v_{\max.y}$
6. **for** z = $v_{\min.z}$ **to** x = $v_{\max.z}$
7. **for** j = 1 **to** n_objects (voxel (x,y,z))
8. **if** (not tested (object(i), object(j)))
9. Intersect (object(i), object(j))

The uniform grid-based spatial data structure and mining performances are optimal as long as the objects are uniformly distributed. However, if the objects are non-uniformly distributed or clustered, the method we employed is changed into pairwise testing, with $O\left(n^2\right)$ performance.

B-Tree

The B-tree is the classic index structure used in pretty much all database products. It is not a spatial index. However, we mention it here since it would typically be used underlying a quadtree index, and also just to provide a base level to which the other indexes can be compared as it showed in Figure 6.

A B-tree is a generalized form of a binary tree. The key feature making it efficient for disk-based database usage is the ability to store more than one record per node, and to have 2 or more children per node. It makes the tree flatter than a binary tree would be. Finally, allowing each node to be partially empty for more efficient update operations, as records can be inserted and deleted from space, and only infrequently is there a need to split or combine nodes. Thus, the leaf node will contain copies of the records that in a simple B-tree would be stored at the higher levels of the trees. The sequential scans completed purely by reading the leaf nodes without the need to jump "upwards" to fetch a single missing record. The other optimization is to make the leaf nodes a linked list, again allowing a scan to proceed directly to the next leaf node, without having to go "upwards" via the common parent node.

Figure 6. B-tree based spatial quadtree index

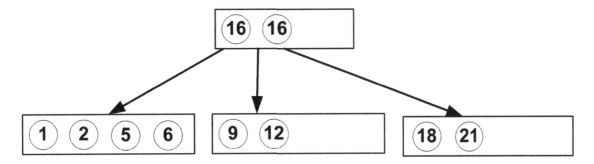

The spatial data structure in general, essential to SDM supported by spatial index structure to provide fast access and mining process to spatial data storage and manipulation. Clustering the spatial structure data is pertinent to avoid or reduce the challenges or problems in the process of a large amount of spatial data.

Spatial Data Mining Models

Spatial data models are formalizations of spatial concepts humans use to conceptualize space, which is necessary to manipulate symbols according to formal rules. The formalization of spatial concepts employs well understood mathematical findings to describe the meanings of the operations to be performed on spatial objects. The need for the view of geometry in a special data model is the independent of implementation aspects (Chris, 2006). The SDM models, therefore, differ in their powers and capabilities to guarantee the formalization of the spatial data. Their differences become apparent when users try to modify the geometry or want to verify its consistency.

Model Architecture

The SDM models, architecture is essential to describe the relationships between attributes and the target values in which an automatic configuration of the parameters used in the DM algorithms that supported or suggested to the user according to the data sets and the selected model. It is important to emphasize the application of prediction methods to spatial data sets require different partitioning schemes than simple random selection like in standard DM techniques (Danhuai & Weihong, 2008). Therefore, the spatial model architecture uses spatial block validation sets involving classification and regression, as shown in Figure 7.

Figure 7. Spatial modeling algorithms architectural view

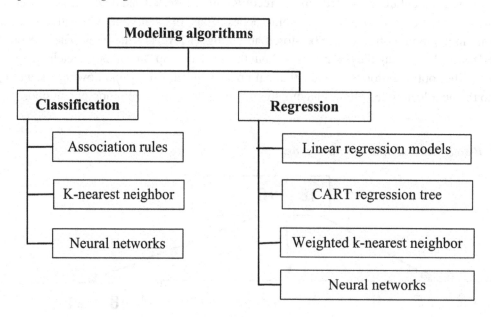

The model representation is an essential to users in which provide a choice access among the listed modules of multiple classifications and regression procedures (Figure 7). The users can also test learned prediction models on unseen (test) regions. All prediction results are graphically displayed, as well as the neural network (NN) learning process and the learned structures of NNs and regression trees (Maike, 2008).

Model Integration and Functionality

Spatial model integration and defined functionality are essential to improve prediction accuracy that implemented through different schemes. The integrated spatial model is important to drive attributes and to predict proper actions (Ahmad, 2008). The functionality of the model is, therefore, to preserve the benefits of an easy to design and use Windows-based Graphical User Interface (GUI), quick programming in analytical tools such as MATLAB and fast execution of programming languages namely C++ compiled code as appropriate for DM purposes. Support for the remote control of centralized spatial data architecture could access via LAN and World Wide Web or the Internet in a simple term.

The spatial modeling, integration and functionality provide an open interface that is easily extensible to include additional intelligent DM algorithms in which more advanced DM techniques are involved in the system (Gebeyehu et al., 2013). Furthermore, advanced distributed aspects of the spatial data can be implemented, namely simultaneous multi-user connections and real-time knowledge exchange among learning models in a distributed or parallel system (Maike, 2008).

Spatial Data Mining Algorithms

Spatial data are interrelated that distribution of one feature does not only depend on its characteristics but also related to other features in some degree. The hidden patterns of large databases revealed is essential to identify the association rule between dependent and independent variables (Hongyan et al., 2009; Krzysztof et al., 1996). GIS alone does not have algorithms to carry out such task (Deepak et al., 2013). Therefore, SDM algorithms deal with discovering the knowledge embedded in GIS vector data, which are stored in GIS shape files. These geospatial data structures stored as one geographic feature per shapefile like point feature layer, multipoint and polygon feature layers. The algorithm needs for the enhancement and deal with mining all vector types of map objects (Shuliang et al., 2009, Daniel et al., 2003).

The algorithm considered not only the non-spatial properties of the classified object, but also the non-spatial properties of its adjacent object. The object that satisfies any adjacency relation will be seen as an adjacent object (Manikandan, & Srinivasan, 2013).

Spatial Autoregressive Model

Spatial dependencies are modeled in the framework of regression analysis in which directly modeled in the regression equation. The dependent values y_i' are related to each other, i.e., then the regression equation can be modified as

$$y = \rho W y + X\beta + \varepsilon \tag{4}$$

where 'W' is the neighborhood relationship contiguity matrix and 'ρ' is a parameter that reflects the strength of spatial dependencies between the elements of the dependent variable. After the correction term $\rho W y$ is introduced, the components of the residual error vector ' ε ' are then assumed to be generated from independent and identical standard normal distributions. The spatial data input/output computational value is estimated by 'ρ' and 'β' that can be derived using maximum likelihood theory or Bayesian statistics. Bayesian approach using sample-based Markov Chain Monte Carlo (MCMC) methods can be found in (Raymond & Jiawei, 1994).

Gaussian Process Learning

The Gaussian process learning approaches of MRFs are widely used to model spatial homogeneity, which is important to classify modeling spatial heterogeneity. The statistical process is finding the optimal linear predictor naming kriging (the famous mining engineer) in which the same model to the Gaussian process regression model that underlying stochastic process. The linear predictor obtained by kriging is optimal in a least-square sense, whereas, the Gaussian process regression model corresponds to a simple or ordinary kriging model. Therefore, the conventional maximum likelihood classifier (MLC) typically models the class-conditional distribution of $p(\mathrm{x} \mid \mathrm{y})$ a multi-vitiate Gaussian distribution, which defined as:

$$p\left(x \mid y = y_i\right) \sim N\left(\mu_i, \Sigma_i\right) \tag{5}$$

where $X = \left(x_1, \mathrm{x}_2, ..., \mathrm{x}_d\right)^T$, the d-dimensional vector is represented spectral bands of a pixel in a hyperspectral image and $y \in \left\{y_1, y_2, ..., y_c\right\}$ is the LULC class label. The parameters for multi-variant Gaussians, $\theta_i = \left(\mu_i, \Sigma_i\right)$, are obtained by the maximum-likelihood estimation (MLE) that assumed to be constant over all possible locations. As (Marlene et al., 2010) discussed the assumption does not hold in general that the spatial heterogeneity can be modeled via non-parametric Gaussian process model in which the class-conditional distribution of the ith class is modeled as a function of spatial coordinates:

$$p\left(x(s) \mid \mathrm{y}_i\right) \sim N\left(\mu_i(s), \Sigma_i\right) \tag{6}$$

where $\mu_i\left(s^*\right) = \left(\mu_{i1}\left(s^*\right), \mu_{i2}\left(s^*\right), ..., \mu_{id}\left(s^*\right)\right)$. If the ' i ' iteration of the ith class omitted the equation notation can be simplified as each spectral band of 'X' is modeled as a random process indexed by a spatial coordinate $s = \left(s_1, \mathrm{s}_2\right)$ then the jth band of 'X,' x_j can be defined as:

$$x_j\left(s\right) \equiv f_j\left(s\right) + \varepsilon_j \tag{7}$$

where $f_j\left(s\right)$ a Gaussian is random process, and ε_j is an additive related Gaussian noise:

$$\varepsilon \sim N\left(0, \sigma_{ij}^2\right) \tag{8}$$

Given $f_j(s)$ then the class conditional distribution of x_j is defined as:

$$p\left(x_j(s) \mid f_j(s)\right) = N\left(f_j(s), \sigma_{\in j}^2\right)$$ (9)

If the Gaussian Process (GP) mean value is 0, the computational value of $f_j(s)$ is defined as:

$$f_j(s) \sim GP\left(0, \mathrm{k}_j\left(s_l, \mathrm{s}_m\right)\right)$$ (10)

where $\mathrm{k}_j\left(s_l, \mathrm{s}_m\right)$ is a spatial covariance function between locations s_l and s_m. The zero-mean prior assumption corresponds to the simple kriging model in spatial statistics, whereas, in practice, we can approximately satisfy the zero-mean assumption by normalizing given feature values. Therefore, the characteristic of a Gaussian random process is solely defined by a covariance function.

Markov Random Field Classifiers (MRFC)

Random spatial data variable's interdependency relationship is represented by an undirected graph (i.e., asymmetric neighborhood matrix or a Markov Random Field) (Anthony et al., 2009). The Markov property specifies that a variable depends only on the neighbors and is independent of all other variables. The spatial location prediction problem can be modeled by assuming the class label, $f_L(s_i)$ of different locations, s_i constitute an MRF in which the random variable $f_L(s_i)$ is independent of $f_L(s_j)$ if $W(s_i, \mathrm{s}_j) = 0$. The Bayesian rule can be used to predict $f_L(s_i)$ from feature value vector 'X' and neighborhood class label vector L_M as follows:

$$pr\left(l(s_i) \mid X, L \mid l(s_i)\right) = \frac{pr\left(X(s_i) \mid l(s_i), L \mid l(s_i)\right) pr\left(l(s_i) \mid L \mid l(s_i)\right)}{pr\left(X(s_i)\right)}$$ (11)

The solution procedure can estimate $pr\left(l(s_i) \mid L \mid l(s_i)\right)$ from the training data by examining the ratios of the frequencies of class labels to the total number of locations in the spatial framework. $pr\left(X(s_i) \mid l(s_i), L \mid l(s_i)\right)$ can be estimated using kernel functions from the observed values in the training data set. For reliable estimates, larger training data sets are needed. It is also significant for the Bayesian classifiers without spatial context to compute huge complex spatial data distribution. It accomplished by taking contiguous regions (windows) instead of sample points. An assumption on $pr\left(X(s_i) \mid l(s_i), L \mid l(s_i)\right)$ may be useful if large enough training data set is not available. A common assumption is the uniformity of influence from all neighbors of a location. Another familiar assumption is the independence between 'X' and L_N, hypothesizing that all interactions between neighbors are captured via the interaction in the class label variable. Many domains also use specific parametric probability distribution forms, leading to simpler solution procedures.

Mixture Models

Mixture models are widely used in clustering and semi-supervised learning. The Gaussian Mixture Model (GMM) based clustering consists of clustering and parameter estimation computational algorithms. Clustering algorithms towards SDM techniques are discussed previously. It is also an essential component to GMM as fitted to the training data that can use the model to predict labels for each cluster. The approach carried out using the maximum likelihood procedure as the discriminant function g(.) defined as:

$$g_i\left(x\right) = -\ln\left|\Sigma_i\right| - \left(x - \mu_i\right)^t \left|\Sigma_i\right|^{-1} \left(x - \mu_i\right) \tag{12}$$

Each pixel (feature vector) is assigned to a cluster label 'i' and $g_i(x)$ is maximum overall cluster labels. Therefore, the computational complexity of GMM model fitting depends on the number of iterations and time to compute the expectation (E) and maximization (M) steps. For example, if the size of the training data set size is N, and the number of components is M with the dimensionality 'd', the cost of E and M steps are O(NMD + NM) and O(2NMD) respectively at each iteration.

The parameter estimation based GMM is essential to solving the model parameter estimation problem by assuming the training data set D_j is generated by a finite GMM that consists of M components. If the labels for each of these components were known, then problem simply reduces to the usual parameter estimation problem, and we could have used maximum likelihood estimation in which the parameter estimation technique is based on the well-known expectation maximization algorithm (Raymond & Jiawei, 1994). Let us assume that each sample x_j comes from a super-population D_j, which is a mixture of a finite number (M) of clusters, $D_1, D_2,..., D_M$ in some proportions $\sigma_1, \sigma_2,..., \sigma_M$ respectively, where $\sum_{i=1}^{M} \sigma_i = 1$ and $\sigma_i \geq 0 \left(i = 1,..., M\right)$. The data D_j can be modeled $D = \left\{x_i\right\}_{i=1}^{n}$ as being generated independently from the following mixture density.

$$p\left(x_i \mid \Theta\right) = \sum_{j=1}^{M} \sigma_j p_j(x_i \mid \theta_j) \tag{13}$$

$$L\left(\Theta\right) = \sum_{i=1}^{n} \ln\left[\sum_{j=1}^{M} \sigma_j p_j\left(x_i \mid \theta_j\right)\right] \tag{14}$$

where $p_j\left(x_i \mid \theta_j\right)$ is the pdf corresponding to the mixture 'j' and parameterize by Θ_j, and $\Theta = \left(\sigma_1, \sigma_2,..., \sigma_M, \theta_1, \theta_2,..., \theta_M\right)$ denotes all unknown parameters associated with the M component mixture density.

Proximity Measurement

Proximity measurement is the algorithms of similarity (or distance) computations between two data objects, namely Euclidean, density based, and others (Xing et al., 2013; Valliappa and Travis, 2009). The Euclidean distance between points 'p' and 'q' is the length of the line segment connecting them as $\left(\overline{pq}\right)$. Subject to: $P = \left(p_1, p_2, ..., p_n\right)$ and $q = \left(q_1, q_2, ..., q_n\right)$ of the two points in Euclidean n-space, then the distance from p to q, or from 'q' to 'p' is given by:

$$d\left(p, q\right) = d\left(q, p\right) = \sqrt{\left(q_1 - p_1\right)^2 + \left(q_2 - p_2\right)^2 + ... + \left(q_n - p_n\right)^2} = \sqrt{\sum_{i=1}^{n} \left(q_i - p_i\right)^2} \qquad (15)$$

The position of a point in a Euclidean n-space is a Euclidean vector. So, p and q are Euclidean vectors, starting from the origin of space, and their tips indicate two points. The Euclidean norm, or Euclidean length, or magnitude of a vector measures the length of the vector is:

$$|p| = \sqrt{p_1^2 + p_2^2 + ... + p_n^2} = \sqrt{p.p} \qquad (16)$$

A vector can be described as a directed line segment from the origin of the Euclidean space (vector tail) to a point in that space (vector tip). If we consider that its length is the distance from its tail to its tip, it becomes clear that the Euclidean norm of a vector has been just a special case of Euclidean distance: the Euclidean distance between its tail and its tip. The distance between point's p and q may have a direction (e.g. from p to q), so it may be represented by another vector, given as:

$$q - p = \left(q_1 - p_1, q_2 - p_2, ..., q_n, p_n\right) \qquad (17)$$

In a three-dimensional space (n=3), this is an arrow from p to q, which can be regarded as the position of 'q' relative to 'p'. It may be called a displacement vector if p and q represent two positions of the same point at two successive instants of time. The distance between point's p and q may have a direction (e.g. from p to q), so it can be represented by another vector as:

$$\left\|q - p\right\| = \sqrt{\left(q - p, \left(q - p\right)\right)} \qquad (18)$$

or

$$\left\|q - p\right\| = \sqrt{|p|^2 + |q|^2 - 2p.q} \qquad (19)$$

SPATIAL DATA MINING APPLICATIONS

SDM is highly significant to automatic discovery of knowledge from a spatial database. DM techniques include discovering hidden associations between different data attributes, classification of data based on some samples, and clustering to identify intrinsic patterns. Effective with the geospatial database, spatial data can be materialized for inclusion in DM applications for which SDM capable of discovering the specific prospects with addresses located in a given issue or areas (neighborhoods, cities, or regions). The addresses are geocoded into longitude/latitude points and stored in a spatial geometry object supports the data at a specific location influenced by data in the neighborhood. For example, the value of a house is largely determined by the value of other houses in the neighborhood called the spatial correlations. The spatial analysis and mining feature in GIS spatial data are essential to exploit spatial correlation by using the location attributes of data items in several ways. It includes binning (discretizing) data into regions (such as categorizing data into northern, southern, eastern, and western regions). Materializing the influence of neighborhood (such as the number of customers within a two-mile radius of each store), and for identifying collocated data items (such as video rental stores and pizza restaurants) can be mentioned.

The legacy of DM in GIS is to perform spatial predicates and relationships for a set of spatial data using thematic layers. Each layer contains data about a specific kind of spatial data (that is, having a specific "theme"), for example, parks and recreation areas, or demographic income data. The spatial paradigm essential to define a preprocessing step before the application of DM techniques, or it could be used as an intermediate step in spatial mining, as shown in Figure 8.

Figure 8 shows that the integral of SDM. It is expected to have wide applications in GIS, which includes, Geo-marketing, remote sensing, image database exploration, medical imaging, navigation, traffic control, environmental studies, and many other areas where spatial data are used (Ranga et al., 2012; Tsung et al., 2010). A crucial challenge to SDM is the exploration of efficient mining techniques due to the huge amount of spatial data and the complexity of spatial data types and spatial access methods.

Figure 8. The conceptual paradigm model of the integral of spatial and DM

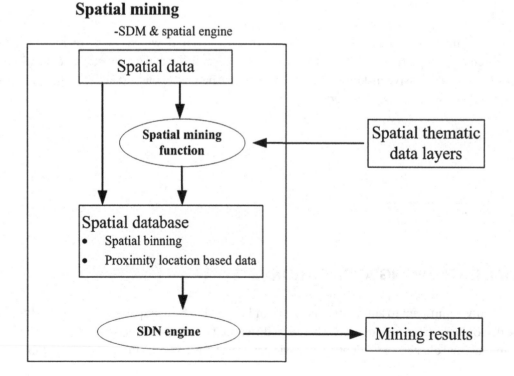

For the last two decades, Geographic Information Systems (GIS) have existed as the independent technology in which its method, traditions, and approaches to visualization and data analysis spatial data sets. However, it had a big gap or limitation on its very basic spatial analysis functionality. Many are confined to analysis that involves descriptive statistical displays (Deepak et al., 2013), such as histograms or pie charts that are inevitable DM in the field. DM offered great potential benefits for applying GIS-based, decision-making and gained as an integrated approach, which becomes critical essential to various public and private sector organizations possessing large databases with thematic and geographically referenced data begin to realize the huge potential of the information hidden there. Such as statistical offices requiring analysis or dissemination of Geo-referenced statistical data, public health services searching for explanations of disease clusters, environmental agencies assessing the impact of changing land-use patterns on climate change and Geo-marketing companies doing customer segmentation based on spatial location are few (Ravikumar & Gnanabaskaran, 2010; Chris, 2006).

SDM for the field of GIS and the geospatial database is an essential tool support efficient technique. For example, an operation of integrated commercial databases is pertinent to exploit spatial locations and characterizations as it showed in Figure 9.

As it showed in Figure 9, spatial index structures, such as R-trees are important to speed up the processing of spatial queries such as region queries or nearest neighbor queries. If the spatial objects are fairly complex, but also retrieving the neighbors of some object, this way is still very time-consuming. Therefore, when creating all neighborhood paths with a given source object, a very large number of neighbors operations have to be performed for which many spatial databases need to be dynamic and updates on objects such as geographic maps or proteins. In such approaches, materializing the relevant neighborhood graphs and avoiding access to the spatial objects themselves may be worthwhile. In addition to this, knowing the distance between the neighboring objects and their relational interactions vitally important and the data characteristics (distance, direction, and topological relations) are defined and properly stored in spatial databases, and the data exploration computational flow conceptualizes as in Figure 10.

The conceptual model visualizes the steps in Figure 10, the spatial data collected from various sources by having preprocessing, and transformation passed to the data engine for data modeling and further explorations. Spatial data, including an image, are typically downloaded into GIS systems for processing purposes, and the GIS data are optimized for establishing spatial relationships among objects (Fengli et al., 2011). Spatial data can be produced rapidly from a variety of sources and the use of spatial data to improve many human tasks. In fact, the current trend of interconnecting different data sources through

Figure 9. Spatial neighborhood based object index

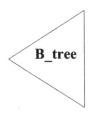

Object ID	Neighbor	Distance	Direction	Topology
o_1	o_2	y_1	Southwest	Disjoint
o_1	o_3	y_2	Northwest	Overlap
----	----	----	----	----

Figure 10. Conceptual modeling of SDM applications based on neighborhood object index

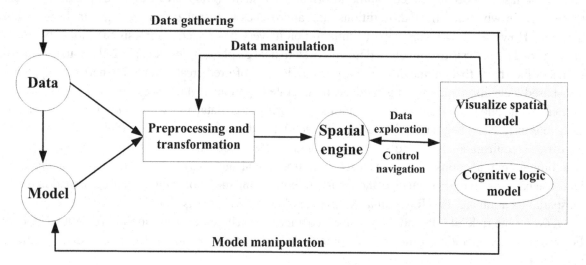

the Web will ultimately give rise to the Internet of Things where every source will have its own Uniform Resource Identifier, and geospatial data will become omnipresent. The metadata of the information or data is important whenever data are intended for serious use. In addition to being essential for understanding an individual data set, systematically structured metadata is also a key element of data infrastructures such as searchable catalogs of data, or automated systems for mapping and analysis (Martin et al., 2001).

Spatial Data Mining Trend Prediction and Challenges

Data mining is a promising an interdisciplinary field in which confluence statistics and computer science in advancing of machine learning, artificial intelligence, and others. It is a technology of spanning several disciplines, including, database systems, and information retrieval systems. DM has involved into an important and active area of research of theoretical challenges and practical applications associated with the problem. It is the process of discovering interesting and previously unknown knowledge from large-scale data in the real-world data sets, which is still a growing and highly demanding fields to explore massive data of business, science and engineering, namely, GIS geospatial data, astronomy and space data, etc. The trend of data mining prediction is the legacy of such fields but also due to the ever-growing data in its volumes, variability, complexity, data sensitivities and other many factors, DM has many potential challenges.

Spatial Data Mining Trends

Spatial mining is the process of searching and discovering valuable information and knowledge in large volumes of geospatial data. It draws basic principles from concepts in spatial ML, statistics, pattern recognition and 'soft' computing (Ravikumar & Gnanabaskaran, 2010). Using DM techniques enables a more efficient use of the spatial data warehouse or other repositories. It is thus becoming an emerging research field in Geoscience because of the increasing amount of data, which lead to new promising applications. For example, the use of images now enables the observation of small objects, while the use of high temporal resolution images enables monitoring of changes in high frequency.

Figure 11. Simple linear trend of spatial changes

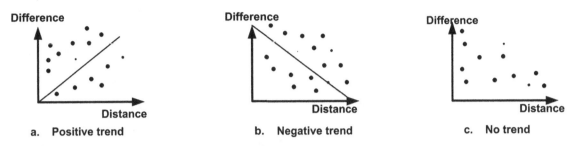

A spatial trend is a regular change of one or more non-spatial attributes when moving away from a given start object 'O'. For its trend analysis, the neighborhood paths are used starting from 'O' to model the movement. As it is shown in Figure 11, the regression model on the respective attribute values for the objects described the regularity of changes.

Spatial trend detection is a procedural processing from its original or starts objects to the change. Let say for some object 'O' is belonging to a given spatial database 'D' defined as $O \in D$. The analysis of the regular change is performed on some non-spatial attributes of the regression models. The independent variable (X) yields the distance between any databases objects of O_i. The dependent variable (Y) measures the difference between the values of non-spatial attributes of a given object (say $\{O_1, O_2, ..., O_n\}$. The sets of $X \ and \ Y$ containing one observation for each element of a subset 'S' of D. If the absolute value of the correlation coefficient of the two objects are found to be large enough, 'S' identifies a part of D, which showing a significant spatial trend for the specified attributes starting from O_1.

SPATIAL DATA MINING CHALLENGES AND FUTURE ISSUES

The actual spatial data analysis techniques suffer from the huge amount of complex data to process. Indeed, geospatial data have been often heterogeneous, multi-scale, incomplete, and composed of complex objects. Segmentation algorithms, unsupervised and supervised classification methods, descriptive and predictive spatial models and algorithms for large time series analysis will be presented to assist experts in their knowledge discovery. As the size of spatial data increases exponentially, the structure of data becomes more complex, which demanding DM techniques for successful analysis than other classic exploratory tools. SDM is pertinent to handle and analysis, such ever growing data and its complexity. However, this large size and the high dimensionality of spatial data is big potential challenges in which demanding the integration of mining tools and agents to introduce a system parallel processing and distribution of spatial data. DM is a legacy to innovate more dynamic and intelligent GIS data mining tools (Baazaoui et al., 2007).

SDM is a promising area in which many problems require in-depth study. Spatial data have characteristics of massive, non-linear, multi-scale and ambiguity, so extracting knowledge from a spatial database is more challenging (Tsung et al., 2010). The difficulties are very wide, including spatial data handling, exploration, and distributions. The actual spatial data analysis techniques suffer from the huge amount of complex data to process. Indeed, spatial data visualization and observation (acquired from optical, radar and hyperspectral sensors installed in terrestrial, airborne or space-borne platforms) is often heterogeneous, multi-scale, incomplete, and composed of complex objects. Segmentation algorithms, unsupervised and supervised classification methods, descriptive and predictive spatial models and algorithms for large time-series analysis will be presented to assist experts in their knowledge discovery (Parimala et al., 2011; Daniel et al., 2008).

The SDM algorithms are adopted from general DM algorithms and did not consider storage, processing of the spatial data and the spatial data itself characteristics. Spatial data are different from the data in the relational database and has their access methods; so traditional DM techniques are often unable to analyze complex spatial phenomena and objects. The efficiency of SDM techniques, standardization of SDM query language, less interaction of knowledge discovery systems, single approaches of spatial data exploration methods and tasks, integrating with other systems and others are the potential challenges SDM performances (Deepali, 2013).

CONCLUSION

SDM is becoming an integral part of the operations in science and engineering, especially earth science, astronomy, climatology, and other image data processing. Applications using discovery-driven techniques are also finding increased use. While many of the deployed applications, primarily employ predictive modeling techniques, application developers and end users alike are beginning to recognize the need to use additional techniques from the discovery-SDM repertory. In this book chapter, we are also investigating and introduce novel methodologies if the integral SDM in the field of GIS. It is the finding of useful associations and characteristics that may well exist implicitly in spatial databases, which provides an interesting spatial pattern and automated search knowledge implicit in spatial databases. The phenomenon is discussed in 8 subtopics, including its applications and challenges. SDM is an advanced and systematic process of capturing inherent associations among spatial and non-spatial data in the presence of concise data reality and conceptual frameworks to accommodate data semantics and enhanced performance. The legacy of DM is its scalability and adaptability tasks and techniques that can be applied to the nature of the data and geospatial behavior to retrieve a pattern from the data objects distribution in a particular data set, such as satellite imagery, GIS, medical image analysis, and others.

We also explored the potential of DM computational analysis for massive spatial data sets in which the tool implemented to extract interested and regularity knowledge from such large-scale spatial databases, and can be used to understand the spatial data and found the relationship between spatial data and non-spatial data in the real-world problems. DM in GIS is in its young stage, which is highly demanding for various applications that need to study in depth. Besides to develop and improve their theories and methods, SDM needs to learn and draw mature theoretical method for knowledge discovery, databases, robotics, and other techniques for which visualization and clear understanding for GIS as a science, including earth, space, and other dynamic fields. Therefore, DM is a promising tool for many fields to handle and explore their ever-growing data, and SDM in the field is now used on many issues and achieved great results. Thus, it can be predicted SDM would not only promote the development of spatial science and computer science, but also, for enhancing human ability to understand and transform the world, thus serve the human society better.

ACKNOWLEDGMENT

We are very thankful to the anonymous reviewers for their useful comments, and the works are supported by the National Natural Science Foundation (NNSF) of China under Grant 61374135, 61203321, 61203084.

REFERENCES

Ahmad Haris Abdul Halim. (2008). Integration between Location Based Service (LBS) and Online Analytical Processing (OLAP): Semantic Approach. *Journal of Information Systems, Research & Practices, 1*(1).

Anselin, L. (1998). Interactive techniques and exploratory spatial data analysis. Academic Press.

Lee, A. J. T., Chen, Y.-A., & Ip, W.-C. (2009). Mining frequent trajectory patterns in spatial–temporal databases. *Information Sciences, 179*(13), 2218–2231. doi:10.1016/j.ins.2009.02.016

Zghal, B. (2007). A Framework for Data Mining Based Multi-Agent: An Application to Spatial Data, World Academy of Science. *Engineering and Technology International Journal of Computer Information Science and Engineering, 1*(5), 202–206.

Valêncio et al. (2013). 3D Geovisualisation Techniques Applied to Spatial Data Mining. Springer-Verlag.

Bailey-Kellogg, C., Ramakrishnan, N., & Marathe, M. V. (2006). Spatial Data Mining to Support Pandemic preparedness. *SIGKDD Explorations, 8*(1), 80–82. doi:10.1145/1147234.1147246

Guo, D., & Cui, W. (2008). Mining moving objects trajectories in Location-based services for spatiotemporal database update, Geoinformatics and Joint Conference on GIS and Built Environment: Geo-Simulation and Virtual, GIS Environments. *Proceedings of the Society for Photo-Instrumentation Engineers, 7143*, 71432M. doi:10.1117/12.812625

Daniel, A., et al. (2008). Visual Data Mining in Large Geospatial Point Sets. *IEEE Computer Society*, 36-44.

Daniel, A. K., et al. (2003). PixelMaps: A New Visual Data Mining Approach for Analyzing Large Spatial Data Sets. *IEEE International Conference on Data Mining.*

Kaundinya, D. P., Balachandra, P., Ravindranath, N. H., & Ashok, V. (2013). A GIS (geographical information system)-based spatial data mining approach for optimal location and capacity planning of distributed biomass power generation facilities: A case study of Tumkur district, India. *Energy, 52*, 77–88. doi:10.1016/j.energy.2013.02.011

Deepali Kishor Jadhav. (2013). Big Data: The New Challenges in Data Mining. *International Journal of Innovative Research in Computer Science & Technology, 1*(2), 39-42.

Guo, D., & Mennis, J. (2009). Spatial data mining and geographic knowledge discovery—An introduction, Elsevier, Computers. *Environment and Urban Systems, 33*(6), 403–408. doi:10.1016/j.compenvurbsys.2009.11.001

Zhang, F. (2011). A GIS-based method for identifying the optimal location for a facility to convert forest biomass to biofuel, Elsevier. *Biomass and Bioenergy*, *35*, 3951–3961.

Gebremeskel, G. B. (2013). Data Mining Prospects in Mobile Social Networks. IGI Global.

Gennady Andrienko, et al. (2006). Mining spatiotemporal data. *J Intell Inf Syst.*, *27*, 187-190. doi: 10.1007/s10844-006-9949-3

Samet, H. (1995). *Spatial Data Structures*. Reading, MA: ACM Press.

Liu, H., Wang, X., He, J., Han, J., Xin, D., & Shao, Z. (2009). Top-down mining of frequent closed patterns from very high dimensional data, Elsevier. *Information Sciences*, *179*(7), 899–924. doi:10.1016/j.ins.2008.11.033

Pérez-Ortega, et al. (2010). Spatial Data Mining of a Population-Based Data Warehouse of Cancer in Mexico. *International Journal of Combinatorial Optimization Problems and Informatics*, *1*(1), 61-67.

Anders & Kochen. (2001). *Data mining for Automated GIS data Collection*. Wichmann Verlag Heidelberg.

Koperski, et al.. (1996). Spatial Data Mining: Progress and Challenge, Survey Paper.*SIGMOD Workshop on Research Issues on data Mining and Knowledge Discovery* (DMKD).

Teixeira, et al.. (2005). Online data mining services for dynamic spatial databases II: quality air location based services and sonification.*II International Conference and Exhibition on Geographic Information*.

Krause-Traudes, M. (2008). Spatial data mining for retail sales forecasting. *11th AGILE International Conference on Geographic Information Science*, (pp. 1-11).

Manikandan, G., & Srinivasan, S. (2013). An Efficient Algorithm for Mining Spatially Co-located Moving Objects. *American Journal of Applied Sciences*, *10*(3), 195–208. doi:10.3844/ajassp.2013.195.208

Marlene, D. (2010). Privacy Issues of Spatial Data Mining in Web Services. *International Journal of Engineering Science and Technology*, *2*(10), 5626–5636.

Martin Ester et al. (2001). *Algorithms and Applications for Spatial Data Mining, Geographic Data Mining, and Knowledge Discovery, Research Monographs in GIS*. Taylor and Francis.

Lavrac, N. (2008). Mining Spatio-temporal Data of Traffic Accidents and Spatial Pattern Visualization. *Metodološki Zvezda*, *5*(1), 45–63.

Nagaprasad, S. (2010). Spatial Data Mining Using Novel Neural Networks for Soil Image Classification and Processing. *International Journal of Engineering Science and Technology*, *2*(10), 5621–5625.

Parimala, M. (2011). A Survey on Density Based Clustering Algorithms for Mining Large Spatial Databases. *International Journal of Advanced Science and Technology*, *31*, 59–66.

Vatsavai, et al. (2012). *Spatiotemporal Data Mining in the Era of Big Spatial Data: Algorithms and Applications*. ACM.

Ravikumar, K., & Gnanabaskaran, A. (2010). ACO based spatial data mining for risk traffic analysis. *International Journal of Computational Intelligence Techniques*, *1*(1), 6-13.

Ng, R. T., & Han, J. (1994). Efficient and Effective Clustering Methods for Spatial Data Mining. *Proceedings of the 20th VLDB Conference*.

Chawla, et al. (2001). Modeling Spatial Dependencies for Mining Geospatial Data. *Proceedings of the 2001 SIAM International Conference on Data Mining*.

Wang, et al. (2009). Cloud Model-Based Spatial Data Mining. *Geographic Information Sciences, 9*(1-2), 60-70. DOI: 10.1080/10824000309480589

Rajan, et al. (2012). Efficient Utilization of DBMS Potential in Spatial Data Mining Applications – Neighborhood Relation Modeling Approach. *International Journal of Information and Communication Technology Research, 2*(5), 465-470.

Hoque, S. (2013). A Clustering Method for Seismic Zone Identification and Spatial Data Mining. *International Journal of Enhanced Research in Management and Computer Applications*, 2(9), 5–13.

Sumuthi, S. (2008). Spatial Data Mining: Techniques and its Applications. *Journal of Computer Applications*, 1(4), 28–30.

Beaubouef & Petry. (2010). Methods for handling imperfect spatial info. In R. Jeansoulin, . . . (Eds.), Fuzzy and Rough Set Approaches for Uncertainty in Spatial Data (pp. 103–129). Springer.

Chen, T.-H., & Chen, C.-W. (2010). Application of data mining to the spatial heterogeneity of foreclosed mortgages. *Expert Systems with Applications*, 37(2), 993–997. doi:10.1016/j.eswa.2009.05.076

Lakshmanan, V., & Smith, T. (2009). Data Mining Storm Attributes from Spatial Grids. *American Metrological Society*, 26, 2353–2365.

Su, et al. (2013). Uncertainty-aware visualization and proximity monitoring in urban excavation: a geospatial augmented reality approach. *Visualization in Engineering*, 1-13. Retrieved from http://www.viejournal.com/content/1/1/2

Qian & Zhang. (2005). *The Role of Visualization in Effective Data Cleaning*. ACM.

Qian & Zhang. (2004). *GraphZip: A Fast and Automatic Compression Method for Spatial Data Clustering*. ACM.

Zaragozi, B., Rabasa, A., Rodríguez-Sala, J. J., Navarro, J. T., Belda, A., & Ramón, A. (2012). Modeling farmland abandonment: A study combining GIS and data mining techniques. *Agriculture, Ecosystems & Environment*, 155, 124–132. doi:10.1016/j.agee.2012.03.019

ADDITIONAL READING

Rancic, D. (2008). Mobile Devices as Personal GIS Client Platforms. *International Journal of Computers*, 2(4), 470–478.

Chunchun, H. (2011). Traffic Flow Data Mining and Evaluation Based on Fuzzy Clustering Techniques. *International Journal of Fuzzy Systems*, 13(4), 344–349.

Pande, S. R. (2012). Data Clustering Using Data Mining Techniques. *International Journal of Advanced Research in Computer and Communication Engineering, 1*(8), 494–499.

KEYWORDS AND DEFINITIONS

Data Proximity: Proximity refers to co-occurrence between terms of language, which support the presence of two or more *terms* within a given set of data. Therefore, Data proximity is a data-driven approach to corpus semantics analysis in various data mining techniques, which discriminate the data based upon the idea that words occurring together or in similar contexts.

Geo-References: It is the process of assigning spatial coordinates to each pixel of the raster data, which is spatial in nature, but has no explicit geographic reference system.

GIS: It is also known as Geospatial information systems, or science is a piece of computer software and hardware systems that enable users to capture, store, manage and analyze geographically referenced data for the purpose of manipulation, viewing and analysis in whichever context and parameters the user desires or needs.

Mining Algorithms: It is a set of heuristics and computational methods to define the optimal parameters for creating the mining model from the spatial data that can be applied to the entire dataset to extract actionable patterns and detailed statistics.

RS: It is a software application that process remote sensing data, which specialized that capable of reading file formats that contain sensor image data, Georeferencing information such as satellite data and sensor metadata.

Spatial Big Data: It is big spatial data have been and continue to be, collected with global positioning systems, wearable devices and others ways, which innovate a dynamic and scalable phenomenon and technology to analysis big and complex spatial data to acquire new insights and knowledge, to support decision and policy making process.

Spatial Data Mining: The process of extracting knowledge implicit from large-scale Geo-referencing and image raster data sets, which is previously unknown and interesting information for the optimal decision-making process.

Spatial Database: It is a database to store and query data that represents objects defined in a geometric space, which includes points, lines, and polygons.

Spatial Relational Database: It is the data attributes recording based on their explicit locations and extension of spatial objects, which influenced and defined its spatial neighborhood (such as topological, distance and direction relations) that are used by spatial data mining algorithms.

Section 2
Social Media Analytics With Sentiment Analysis:
Business Applications and Methods

Chapter 7
Social Media as Mirror of Society

Amir Manzoor
Bahria University, Pakistan

ABSTRACT

Over the last decade, social media use has gained much attention of scholarly researchers. One specific reason of this interest is the use of social media for communication; a trend that is gaining tremendous popularity. Every social media platform has developed its own set of application programming interface (API). Through these APIs, the data available on a particular social media platform can be accessed. However, the data available is limited and it is difficult to ascertain the possible conclusions that can be drawn about society on the basis of this data. This chapter explores the ways social researchers and scientists can use social media data to support their research and analysis.

INTRODUCTION

Arguably the most famous headline in the newspaper's 150-year history, DEWEY DEFEATS TRUMAN is every publisher's nightmare on every election night. Like most newspapers, the Tribune, was lulled into a false sense of security by polls that repeatedly predicted a Dewey victory while under sampling the supporters of Truman (Mosteller & Doob, 1949). This event did not discredit polls and the way they are conducted. But this event emphasized the need to develop more sophisticated statistical techniques and higher standards that could provide more accurate and rigorous poll results. After almost 70 years, the use of online social media data as a tool to predict human behavior has brought us to a similar situation where many are questioning the validity of the predictions offered by the social media data analysts. The massive social media datasets combined with powerful computational techniques (such as machine learning, natural language processing, and network analysis) have provided huge opportunities to understand human behavior. Increasing amount of evidence suggest that many of the social media data analyses do not provide true representation of the real world (Tufekci, 2014; Cohen & Ruths, 2013).

Social researchers and analysts can use social media data for two important purposes. First, this data can help determine the information seeking behavior of public. This in turn can help determine

DOI: 10.4018/978-1-5225-2031-3.ch007

the public awareness and level of interest in certain topics and the sources of information they use to get information about these topics. Second, analysis of social media data can help reveal public opinion of and human behavior against specific events. Social media data can be benchmarked against other sources of data. However, social media researchers should be cautious while interpreting the results of their research or generalizing their findings. This is because the research methods used to analyze social media data are still developing and their best practices of use are still to be developed (Department for Work and Pensions, 2014).

The objective of this chapter is to look at social media role in social research and analysis by exploring in what ways social researchers and analysts can use the social media to support their research and analysis. The chapter would highlight issues involved in the study of human behavior through large scale social media datasets. These issues are not new to social science. However, the new kinds of data and entry of many new communities of researchers into the social science domain requires that these issues should be revisited and updated. The chapter also discusses various strategies that can be used to address these issues. After introduction, section two would discuss role of social media in social research. The section three would discuss various issues associated with use of social media data. Some strategies to deal with these issues would be provided in section four. Future research directions would be provided in section five. The chapter would be concluded in section six.

SOCIAL MEDIA AND SOCIAL RESEARCH

This section would provide a general overview of the use of social media data for social research. After providing a broad definition of social media, the chapter moves on to describe the usefulness for social science research of the data generated by the social media platforms. Though applications are still in nascent stages, the online social media holds promising potential to predict public opinion on different issues and the sources of information masses look for information about these topics. The chapter also compares social media with traditional social science research methods (such as sample surveys) to highlight their associated strengths and weaknesses.

Social Media: The Definition

Social media may be defined as websites or other internet based services where the content being communicated is created by the people who use the service. On social media sites there is no clear distinction between producer and consumer of the content (Bruns, 2008). Different social media sites distinguish the producers and consumer differently e.g. by awarding status based on the amount of content produced or by allowing everyone to create the same kind of content. Users can also decide the ways in which they would like to interact with social media sites. Some create content while other only consume but never create any content (Department for Work and Pensions, 2014).

Within this broad definition of social media, there are other sites as well. These sites can be differentiated from other social media sites on two aspects. First, the way in which these site manage the identities of their users and second their dedication to a specific theme or niche interest (Ellison, 2007). Besides, there are other sites whose purpose is not to facilitate communication among users but to serve as archives of large amounts of social data. One good example is Google (Department for Work and Pensions, 2014).

Use of Social Media

Social media consists of technologies that are either Internet-based or non-Internet based. Recently, the research community has started to focus their research on social media. This interest is driven by the rapid increase in social media use during this decade. In 2015, 65% of American adults used social networking sites, up from 7% in 2005 (Andrew Perrin, 2015). Emergence of many "mass appeal" social media websites (such as Facebook and Twitter) has driven much of this change. Due to ease of use and generic nature, these sites have attracted a large number of uses. The network effect created by this mass usage has helped promote further uptake of social media (Dutton, Blank, & Groselj, 2013). There is no guarantee that these popular social media sites will continue to grow. We have seen examples from the past where sites, such as MySpace.com, enjoyed significant usage but then disappeared quickly. However, it appears that current market leaders in online social media have learnt from the mistakes of their predecessors and are expected to be on the scene for some long time.

Social media researchers should consider this fact that use of social media is not even across population and particularly imbalanced across different age groups. The use of online social media sites is very common amongst the users aged 14-34. More than 80% of this user population also uses social network sites (Dutton, Blank, & Groselj, 2013). On the demographics side this imbalance is not very significant. Gender-wise, there exist differences in use of social media sites. For example, male users used business-oriented social media sites (such as LinkedIn) more frequently while women used sharing sites (such as Pinterest) (Acquisti & Gross, 2006). Some more recent studies have shown that this gender disparity in social media usage is diminishing and low income users constitute a larger portion of total Internet users (Office for National Statistics, 2012).

One of the important pattern with respect to the use of social media sites is in terms of which users actively creates online content, the frequency of their content creation, and what specific types of content they create. It appears that a small majority of users (12 % is responsible for creating majority of the content present on social media sites (Ortega, Gonzalez-Barahona, & Robles, 2008). 50% of social media users only visit the sites monthly (Dutton, Blank, & Groselj, 2013). Some users actively spend time online while others only go online for some specific reasons (White & Le Cornu, 2011). The social media research is still in nascent stages. Researchers need caution to draw any conclusions about the reasons why people may or may not prefer to develop content on social media sites. It is also important to understand the role of technological environment which is changing rapidly. However, it can be said that certain user attributes (such as age, education, and skill level) appear to influence the user choice of content creation on the social media (Hargittai & Walejko, 2008) and there is higher probability of highly educated users to create political content than social/entertainment content (Blank, 2013). People having extrovert orientation are found to spend more time on social media sites and over time we see changes in usage patterns of social media (Yasseri, Sumi, & Kertész, 2012). Due to restrictions on social media usage at workplace, many people connect only after work or weekends. However, this trend is changing as the mobile Internet access is becoming commonplace (Department for Work and Pensions, 2014). Given this, it can be said that inferences drawn from analysis of data from a random sample of social media users cannot be generalized for the population in many facets. Using such sample may create many issues. These issues are discussed below.

Social Media in Social Research: Application Areas

Currently, both academicians and practitioners are using social media as a tool of public relations management. Frequently, social media is being used as a debate platform to form opinions on many issues. The focus of this chapter is how the social media data can be utilized to aid social research and analysis. In this regard, there are two salient areas where social media data can help social researchers. The first is the use of social media to understand the thinking of public about some current topic and second is the use of social media to analyze public opinion or sentiment on specific issues. While these two applications can be performed using traditional surveys of the public the real utility of social media lies in its ability to improve on existing methods in some respect. In general, it can be argued that social media data is very useful in terms of quick delivery of results, the scale of data analysis, the cost at which the analysis can be performed. Social media analysis can also address one particular limitation of sample survey method i.e. access to sub-groups within the population.

Use of Social Media to Understand Important Issues

The knowledge of public thinking is an important pre-requisite to determine their opinion about a particular topic. This is an area where social media can add real value. Opinion polls suffer from one critical limitation. While the sponsors of these polls are interested in knowing the people opinion about a political topic, people themselves may not be interested in the topic. As such polls become meaningless in these situations because a majority of public may not be thinking about it before the poll. Asking open-ended questions may help address this issue to some extent but these questions often provide very vague and generalist answers and it is difficult to be certain people answers were based on their genuine thinking about these issues.

Therefore, social media provides many advantages when it comes to gain insight into currently significant issues since social media provides a forum to obtain voluntary comments and develop conversations. Analysis of social media data can help determine the public thinking of about a particular topic at any given time. A variety of indicators from social media are already being used frequently (e.g. trending topics on Twitter, traffic statistics, and search terms entered into Google) to know what people are thinking. Depending upon the usage rates, certain social media sites can openly claim to provide a representative view of public about a particular topic (Ripberger, 2011). Researchers have also started to use social media data to predict human behavior (Choi & Varian, 2012; Mestyán, Yasseri, & Kertész, 2013). The prediction of human behavior or the public opinion can also be used to identify key information sources that people not only use to get information about a topic but also to shape their opinion about that topic. This is something that traditional public surveys have struggled to determine correctly but at best can get vague answers. Social media site, such as Google, can inform researchers a clear picture of information landscape people are looking at for a particular issue. Social media sites, such as Facebook, can add another aspect in the bigger picture by providing information about topics people talking about and the sources of information they are counting on. This information the information landscape connected to a particular issue is important for an organization because they can come to know their own standing in people's eyes and they can also come to know the other organizations influencing the debate on particular issues. This information can help organizations in deciding how much investment they should make in traditional media to gain desired visibility.

Use of Social Media to Capture Public Opinion

Determining public opinion about specific topics can be advantageous. It can help academicians and practitioners to know the topics public thinking about and, more specifically, what they are thinking about it. In determining public opinion, traditional social research methods (such as surveys) are more developed but social media data can help us determine opinions of the group of social media users on a particular topic. However, this determination of opinion varies depending on the extent to which the particular social media platform is considered public. A wide variety of social characteristics of social media users (such as age and gender) can be used to construct more representative samples (Graham, Hale, & Gaffney, 2014). Techniques are being developed for automatically identifying such characteristics (e.g. by determining gender based on user's style of language). This automatic identification is helpful in cases where such characteristics are not actually available (Newman, Groom, Handelman, & Pennebaker, 2008). It is also possible to determine someone's political preferences by looking at who a person choose to connect to on Twitter (Golbeck & Hansen, 2014). It is the limitation of social media that non-internet users cannot be samples in a social media research. But traditional social research methods also suffer from same problem where the participant selection is generally biased towards those who are easily accessible. Besides potential bias in sampling, automatic detection of opinions expressed in messages is another methodological problem that can be corrected using techniques such as sentiment analysis (Feldman, 2013). This technique is based on constructing a list of words and attaching a sentiment score with each word. More complex techniques also look groupings of words and the grammar of text. However, these techniques are still developing and not able to offer a perfect analysis.

Despite these limitations, social media offers many possibilities. It can help us determine public opinion quickly so it is a better choice to determine public opinion on breaking news for example. For example a study found that feeling of outrage and hate following a murder case in London in 2013 were quickly softened as soon as the victim's family appealed for peace (Goodwin, 2013). The detection of such quick public emotions can be very difficult using traditional social research methods.

Sampling difficulties are not relevant in every case. Many a times, researcher finds it relevant simply knowing the opinion of social media users. Whether this opinion can be generalized to a larger population or not does not affect core value of this opinion. In addition, social media sites, such as Twitter, provide good coverage of certain social groupings (such as celebrities) and offer the promise of accessing and determining opinions of these specific groupings. It is also possible to combine social media data analysis with more traditional social research techniques. For example, researchers can use to spot sub populations of interest and then use traditional social research methods to obtain their opinion (Bartlett, Birdwell, & Littler, 2011).

Challenges of Using Social Media Data

This section builds on the discussion in the previous section and provide review of practical challenges involved with using social media data for social research. These challenges can be broadly divided into two categories: technical challenges, methodological challenges and legal/ethical challenges.

Technical Challenges

The first technical issue in the use of social media data is the significant computer skills. These skills are needed both to access to data and analyze this data. Currently there exist a large gap in demand/supply of these skills. Though off-the-shelf solutions are available that can help researchers in social data analytics but significant investment of time is required to gain mastery of the use of these software to obtain deep insight from the data. Organizations willing to do their own data analytics need to develop significant IT infrastructure and skilled IT team that is capable of collecting and analyzing large datasets. Due to decreasing costs of data storage, even small and medium sized enterprises can develop the required IT infrastructure.

Methodological Challenges

The first challenge is that social media, in general, allows access to information as it is being published. These sites, such as Twitter, do not allow access to the archive of their information. As such, a sense of urgency is needed on the behalf of researchers working on a research project to react very quickly to events and make sure they capture information as it is created (Gonzalez-Bailon & Wang, 2013).

The second challenge attributed to determining the extent to which the measured sentiment on social media can be attributed to real people. Due to the commercial value and significance of social media, many organizations are actively engaging with different communities on these sites. This engagement can be through fake social media accounts. Organizations create these fake accounts to broadcast messages and to artificially increase the number of friends or followers of certain individuals. As such, the landscape of social media can differ significantly from reality. Many famous personalities maintain professionally managed social media accounts to construct an image that they can use to have strategic influence on other users (Ruths & Pfeffer, 2014). This issue can be counteracted by using techniques to discover fake accounts. In fact, social media sites themselves are actively looking and blocking such accounts. Facebook recently amended its policy to allow only those user names that represent real persons (Furnas & Gaffney, 2012).

The third challenge is representation of human populations. The first issue in this regard is population bias. It is generally assumed in many social media research studies that a large sample can reduce the platform-specific noise (Armstrong, 2014). In fact this is not true. There can be significant population biases across different social media platforms (Mislove, Lehmann, Ahn, Onnela, & Rosenquist, 2011). For example, Instagram attracted adults aged 18 to 29 (Duggan & Brenner, 2013) while Pinterest's majority of users were high-income female users (Pinterest, 2013). According to Ruths and Pfeffer (2014), researchers seldom take measures to correct these sampling biases. The second issue is the platform-specific sampling problem. Social media data does not provide accurate representation of the overall platform's data because each social media platform provider applies their own algorithms and processes for sampling and filtering their data. These algorithms and processes are dynamic, proprietary, and undocumented (Ruths & Pfeffer, 2014). As such, developing reliable and reproducible studies of human behavior that correctly account for the biases is very difficult. There are many researchers that have special relationships with the social media platform providers. These researchers, also called "embedded researchers" (Ruths & Pfeffer, 2014) enjoy elevated access to platform-specific data and algorithms. As such we see a divide among the community of social media researchers. Irony of the fact is that despite a platform's inner workings, these embedded researchers reveal their data used to generate their findings.

The fourth challenge is representation of human behavior. The first challenge in this regard is human behavior and online platform design. Social platforms implicitly target and capture human behavior according to behavioral norms. These norms develop around and as a result of the specific platforms. One example is Twitter. The way users view Twitter as a platform for political discussion affects how representative political content will be. The social media platforms are temporal and change with shifts in population composition and current events. Therefore, challenge of accounting for platform-specific behavioral norms is complicated further (Ruths & Pfeffer, 2014). The second challenge is distortion of human behavior. The tools of online social platforms are not designed to represent social behavior or provide good data for research. As such, the way social media platform store and server data can destroy aspects of the human behavior of interest. For example, the search results reported by Google can include terms suggested by auto-complete and not the actual text typed by the user (Lazer, Kennedy, King, & Vespignani, 2014). These platform specific design feature can either obscure or lose important aspects of the underlying human behavior.

The fifth challenge is proxy population. Every social media research question defines a population of interest but these are proxy populations because human populations rarely self-label. The quantitative relation between the proxy and original populations studied, typically, is unknown and results in a serious bias that can produce substantially incorrect estimates (Cohen & Ruths, 2013).

The sixth challenge is incompatible data and methods. Since most social media platform prohibit retaining or sharing their dataset, researchers cannot develop canonical data sets for the evaluation and comparison of computational and statistical methods. There are no established practices of coding of research methods and therefore new methods are developed to analyze social data but these methods cannot directly compared to existing methods on a single data set.

Another challenge is that the fields of social media research tend to publish only successful studies when modeling or predicting a specific social phenomenon. With no failed studies available, it is difficult to assess the extent to which successful findings are the result of random chance. This issue has been observed when predicting political election outcomes with Twitter (Ioannidis, 2005; Ruths & Pfeffer, 2014)

We discussed earlier that social media users are not representative of the general public. Only a small proportion of total users post the majority of content and an automatic assessment of the opinions on social media sites is difficult. While there exist techniques to deal with each technical challenge discussed so far, the technique of benchmarking of social media measure can be used to address all the technical challenges associated with social media data. Benchmarking can be conducted in a variety of ways. First, researchers can compare two different topics of interest at the same time. Second, they can track the same topic over the period of time to track any changes in public opinion.

Legal and Ethical Challenges

There are many legal and ethical issues centered on access of social media data and the relationship of researchers both to the social media platform provider and the end users which actually contributed to the content.

First the researcher has many obligations towards the social media platform provider since it is the company that provides the platform and owns the data. Many large social media platform provider have summed up these obligations in specific terms of service. While the terms of service may vary in content, in general, the social media platform providers have no issue if the researchers use data publicly available on these platforms provided that this data is not made available for download somewhere else. Many large social media platform provider (such as Facebook and Twitter) have developed specific technical interfaces for the accessing of data (called Application Programming Interfaces or API) to both monitor and set limits on the data usage. Smaller social media platform provider are less likely to provide API access and their data is generally available for download by extracting from web pages through a process called scrapping. The process of scrapping involves repeatedly accessing a given website. A problem with this process is this data extraction from a large website can take long time. Another issue is that while the content is provided for free, it is also typically protected by various copyright and intellectual property laws and it is difficult to say definitively what is legal and what is not. Researchers can minimize these legal problems by adhering to the terms of service of platform provider, minimizing site server load, not using data for commercial purposes, and not making this data available for download anywhere else. Still a large amount of social media data still lie beyond the reach of scraping. One good example if Facebook where the researcher can only access data about mass number of Facebook users only for a limited set of data types. Facebook has recently started to do its own research. Hence, researchers using Facebook data may also be required to work with Facebook's own researchers (Department for Work and Pensions, 2014).

Researchers also have obligations towards the people who create the data on social media platforms. The legal landscape is still developing and it is more complicated given that the users of social media platforms come from across the geographic boundaries. That makes social media and social media data subject to overlapping legal regimes. Researchers using social media data need be cautious about data storage, data security, and presentation of results of data analysis in an anonymous / aggregate fashion (Sweeney, 2002).

Another ethical challenge is obtaining the traditional informed consent of participants. This is because there is a large number of participants and contacting them individually can be a daunting task. It may reasonable to assume that these users should be aware that the content they are creating can be made public and used for other purposes. In reality, very few users are aware of it and as such researchers should make sure that people whose data are utilized do not suffer any negative effects from this utilization. To do so, researchers should ensure that data are anonymized and stored securely, and that only aggregate level results are reported (Department for Work and Pensions, 2014).

STRATEGIES TO DEAL WITH SOCIAL MEDIA DATA CHALLENGES

It is important to understand that strategies provided here are not meant to work in every social media research. This is because of the creative and dynamic nature of social media research. Every social media researcher should look at these strategies as a checklist that covers major issues present in every social media research.

Data Collection

Platform-Specific Biases

Researchers should ensure that they have anticipated and informed the reader of all possible platform-specific factors that could produce incorrect estimates. These factors can include the type of data stored by the platform used in the study, the way the data was stored (Cohen & Ruths, 2013), the demographics of the users, user behavior specific to the social media platform used in the study. In an ideal case scenarios, these biases should be quantified (Pinterest, 2013).

Data-Specific Biases

If the researcher did not access directly the data maintained by social media platforms, there can be some explicit or implicit biases. If researcher used API or scraping technique to collect data, any associated explicit or implicit biases should be discussed (McPherson, Smith-Lovin, & Cook, 2001).

Proxy-Specific Biases

Most (if not all) social media studies make at least some use of proxy populations (Armstrong, 2014). This proxy may be used simply to define a group. Researchers should quantify the proxy population biases. Making reader aware of the sources of such biases would not only establish credibility of the researcher but also provide critical review of the work.

Methods

Correction for Non-Human Data

Researchers should use appropriate state-of-the-art methods to ensure the participants of their studies include authentic humans and do not include celebrities and organizations accounts.

Corrections for Platform and Proxy Population Biases

A more preferred high-level approach to account for biases is to make appropriate statistical corrections that are informed by platform and proxy population biases. It may not be possible to make such corrections e.g. due to lack of knowledge of the exact amount of bias or the complexity of the technique being used. In that case, a researcher can test the robustness of the findings by running the same analysis on a dataset in which the explicit biases have been introduced and/or removed. In case the findings are not significantly different, it means the findings are robust and can be accepted.

Corrections for Platform-Specific Algorithms

Social media researches on human behavior may focus on platform-specific or platform-independent phenomena but they must mention how the platform-specific algorithms may affect the results of the study. If the user behavior studies is general in nature, the researcher must show evidence that their findings are supported on other social media platform as well. If the researcher claims that the user behavior studied is platform-specific than he/she must show evidence that the research has addressed the possibility that the platform has changed its algorithms and site design over time. This, in turn, would require researcher to show evidence that results are reproducible over time. Researchers should note that declaring a particular user behavior platform-specific can make their research findings more limited and they wouldn't be able to make broad claims about the nature of the human behavior studied in their research. Any such findings will have limited generalizability and would be carefully evaluated within the context of the data and methods.

Comparison of Methods

In order definitely test whether a new method does outperform the existing methods, the researcher should analyze the same dataset with both new and existing methods. This testing is important if the research study claims to introduce a new research method.

Corrections for Overfitting Specific Data Sets and Multiple Hypothesis Testing

In order provide corrections for overfitting specific data sets and multiple hypothesis testing, researchers should consider providing comparison of new findings on two or more distinct datasets. The distinct datasets can be collected at different time periods, using different methods, or on different platforms. By performing similar analysis on multiple distinct datasets, a researcher can reduce the risk that the findings are the result of overfitting of data to a particular data set. Since negative or failed social media research studies are seldom published, such an analysis can establish that findings are not dependent on a particular method or time (Schoen et al., 2013).

Researchers should note that seldom they would find enough data for their research. However, they need to carefully evaluate their findings for any known biases that can substantially distort their findings and provide ambiguous generalizability. Every reasonable attempt should be made to remove such biases. Often, this problem can be addressed by scaling back the scope or reframing the central hypothesis of a study to address a more specific aspect of human behavior on a given platform. Researchers should understand that by making their readers aware of difficult-to-assess bias present in their research, they would create new research directions and advances the state of the field. This move would not only provide greater transparency but also contribute to substantial advances in the study of human behavior on and through social media platforms.

FUTURE RESEARCH DIRECTIONS

One particular area where further research is needed is analysis of a variety of further social media platforms that could provide useful insight. Future research can also consider benchmarking social media data to other existing sources of information such as (server logs of web pages). Future researchers can also analyze how traffic statistics change on individual pages. This analysis can serve as a useful further measure of what the public is currently thinking. It can then be benchmarked against the results from social media data analysis.

CONCLUSION

This chapter has shown how social media data could be used to help determine public and human behavior and, in particular, to explore the extent to which such data could act as a reliable source of public opinion and predictor of human behavior. In general, social data makes it possible to explore the extent to which people are thinking about a particular topic, and where they go for information on that topic. However, these public opinions and human behavior cannot be easily generalized to broader public opinion or behavior. Methods for analyzing their sentiment remain a work in progress. Nevertheless social media do provide an impression of how much a topic is being discussed, and the total spread of its awareness around people using social media. The biases and issues in social media data analysis will not affect all research in the same way. Well-reasoned judgment on the part researchers is needed. Many of the issues have well-known solutions. In some cases, the solutions are difficult to fit with practical realities or the existing solutions may be subject to biases of their own. The issues highlighted have different origins and specific solutions. But, they all require increased awareness of what is actually being analyzed when working with social media data.

REFERENCES

Acquisti, A., & Gross, R. (2006). Imagined communities: Awareness, information sharing, and privacy on the Facebook. In *International workshop on privacy enhancing technologies* (pp. 36–58). Springer. doi:10.1007/11957454_3

Armstrong, K. (2014). Big data: A revolution that will transform how we live, work, and think. *Information Communication and Society*, *17*(10), 1300–1302. doi:10.1080/1369118X.2014.923482

Bartlett, J., Birdwell, J., & Littler, M. (2011). The new face of digital populism. *Demos (Mexico City, Mexico)*.

Blank, G. (2013). Who creates content? Stratification and content creation on the Internet. *Information Communication and Society*, *16*(4), 590–612. doi:10.1080/1369118X.2013.777758

Bruns, A. (2008). *3.1. The Active Audience: Transforming Journalism from Gatekeeping to Gatewatching*. Academic Press.

Choi, H., & Varian, H. (2012). Predicting the present with Google Trends. *The Economic Record*, *88*(s1), 2–9. doi:10.1111/j.1475-4932.2012.00809.x

Cohen, R., & Ruths, D. (2013). Classifying Political Orientation on Twitter: It's Not Easy! In *Seventh International AAAI Conference on Weblogs and Social Media*. Retrieved from http://www.aaai.org/ocs/index.php/ICWSM/ICWSM13/paper/view/6128

Department for Work and Pensions. (2014, December 18). *Use of social media for research and analysis*. Retrieved July 5, 2016, from https://www.gov.uk/government/publications/use-of-social-media-for-research-and-analysis

Duggan, M., & Brenner, J. (2013, February 14). *The Demographics of Social Media Users — 2012*. Retrieved from http://www.pewinternet.org/2013/02/14/the-demographics-of-social-media-users-2012/

Dutton, W. H., Blank, G., & Groselj, D. (2013). *OxIS 2013 Report: Cultures of the Internet*. Oxford, UK: Oxford Internet Institute, University of Oxford.

Ellison, N. B. (2007). Social network sites: Definition, history, and scholarship. *Journal of Computer-Mediated Communication*, *13*(1), 210–230. doi:10.1111/j.1083-6101.2007.00393.x

Feldman, R. (2013). Techniques and applications for sentiment analysis. *Communications of the ACM*, *56*(4), 82–89. doi:10.1145/2436256.2436274

Furnas, A., & Gaffney, D. (2012, July 31). *Statistical Probability That Mitt Romney's New Twitter Followers Are Just Normal Users: 0%*. Retrieved July 6, 2016, from http://www.theatlantic.com/technology/archive/2012/07/statistical-probability-that-mitt-romneys-new-twitter-followers-are-just-normal-users-0/260539/

Golbeck, J., & Hansen, D. (2014). A method for computing political preference among Twitter followers. *Social Networks*, *36*, 177–184. doi:10.1016/j.socnet.2013.07.004

Gonzalez-Bailon, S., & Wang, N. (2013). The bridges and brokers of global campaigns in the context of social media. *SSRN Work. Pap.*

Goodwin, M. (2013, May 25). London attack: generations divided on feelings about Muslims after killing. *The Guardian*. Retrieved from https://www.theguardian.com/uk/2013/may/26/public-attitude-muslims-complex-positive

Graham, M., Hale, S. A., & Gaffney, D. (2014). Where in the world are you? Geolocation and language identification in Twitter. *The Professional Geographer*, *66*(4), 568–578. doi:10.1080/00330124.2014.907699

Hargittai, E., & Walejko, G. (2008). The Participation Divide: Content creation and sharing in the digital age 1. *Information Communication and Society*, *11*(2), 239–256. doi:10.1080/13691180801946150

Ioannidis, J. P. (2005). Why most published research findings are false. *PLoS Medicine*, *2*(8), e124. doi:10.1371/journal.pmed.0020124 PMID:16060722

Lazer, D., Kennedy, R., King, G., & Vespignani, A. (2014). The parable of Google flu: Traps in big data analysis. *Science*, *343*(6176), 1203–1205. doi:10.1126/science.1248506 PMID:24626916

McPherson, M., Smith-Lovin, L., & Cook, J. M. (2001). Birds of a Feather: Homophily in Social Networks. *Annual Review of Sociology*, *27*(1), 415–444. doi:10.1146/annurev.soc.27.1.415

Mestyán, M., Yasseri, T., & Kertész, J. (2013). Early prediction of movie box office success based on Wikipedia activity big data. *PLoS ONE*, *8*(8), e71226. doi:10.1371/journal.pone.0071226 PMID:23990938

Mislove, A., Lehmann, S., Ahn, Y.-Y., Onnela, J.-P., & Rosenquist, J. N. (2011). Understanding the Demographics of Twitter Users. In *Fifth International AAAI Conference on Weblogs and Social Media*. Retrieved from http://www.aaai.org/ocs/index.php/ICWSM/ICWSM11/paper/view/2816

Mosteller, F., & Doob, L. W. (1949). *The pre-election polls of 1948*. Social Science Research Council.

Newman, M. L., Groom, C. J., Handelman, L. D., & Pennebaker, J. W. (2008). Gender differences in language use: An analysis of 14,000 text samples. *Discourse Processes*, *45*(3), 211–236. doi:10.1080/01638530802073712

Office for National Statistics. (2012). *Internet Access - Households and Individuals - Office for National Statistics*. Retrieved July 5, 2016, from http://www.ons.gov.uk/peoplepopulationandcommunity/house-holdcharacteristics/homeinternetandsocialmediausage/bulletins/internetaccesshouseholdsandindividuals/2013-02-28

Ortega, F., Gonzalez-Barahona, J. M., & Robles, G. (2008). On the inequality of contributions to Wikipedia. In *Hawaii International Conference on System Sciences, Proceedings of the 41st Annual* (pp. 304–304). IEEE. doi:10.1109/HICSS.2008.333

Perrin, A. (2015, October 8). *Social Media Usage: 2005-2015*. Retrieved from http://www.pewinternet.org/2015/10/08/social-networking-usage-2005-2015/

Pinterest. (2013). *13 "Pinteresting" Facts About Pinterest Users* [INFOGRAPHIC]. Retrieved July 5, 2016, from https://www.pinterest.com/pin/234257618087475827/

Ripberger, J. T. (2011). Capturing curiosity: Using Internet search trends to measure public attentiveness. *Policy Studies Journal: The Journal of the Policy Studies Organization*, *39*(2), 239–259. doi:10.1111/j.1541-0072.2011.00406.x

Ruths, D., & Pfeffer, J. (2014). Social media for large studies of behavior. *Science*, *346*(6213), 1063–1064. doi:10.1126/science.346.6213.1063 PMID:25430759

Schoen, H., Gayo-Avello, D., Takis Metaxas, P., Mustafaraj, E., Strohmaier, M., & Gloor, P. (2013). The power of prediction with social media. *Internet Research*, *23*(5), 528–543. doi:10.1108/IntR-06-2013-0115

Sweeney, L. (2002). k-anonymity: A model for protecting privacy. *International Journal of Uncertainty, Fuzziness and Knowledge-based Systems*, *10*(5), 557–570. doi:10.1142/S0218488502001648

Tufekci, Z. (2014). Big Questions for Social Media Big Data: Representativeness, Validity and Other Methodological Pitfalls. In *Eighth International AAAI Conference on Weblogs and Social Media*. Retrieved from http://www.aaai.org/ocs/index.php/ICWSM/ICWSM14/paper/view/8062

White, D. S., & Le Cornu, A. (2011). Visitors and Residents: A new typology for online engagement. *First Monday*, *16*(9). doi:10.5210/fm.v16i9.3171

Yasseri, T., Sumi, R., & Kertész, J. (2012). Circadian patterns of wikipedia editorial activity: A demographic analysis. *PLoS ONE*, *7*(1), e30091. doi:10.1371/journal.pone.0030091 PMID:22272279

ADDITIONAL READING

Festinger, L., Back, K. W., & Schachter, S. (1950). *Social pressures in informal groups: A study of human factors in housing* (Vol. 3). Stanford University Press.

Heider, F. (2010). Attitudes and cognitive organization. *The Journal of Psychology*, *21*(1). doi:10.1080/00223980.1946.9917275

Russell, S. J., Norvig, P., Canny, J. F., Malik, J. M., & Edwards, D. D. (2003). *Artificial intelligence: a modern approach* (Vol. 2). Prentice hall Upper Saddle River.

KEY TERMS AND DEFINITIONS

Big Data: Refers to the large volume of data – both structured and unstructured – that a business deals with on a day-to-day basis.

Human Behavior: Refers to the array of every physical action and observable emotion associated with individuals, as well as the human race as a whole.

Population Bias: A type of bias which could influence the results of big data projects.

Privacy: Refers to the right to be let alone, or freedom from interference or intrusion.

Public Opinion: Refers to an aggregate of the individual views, attitudes, and beliefs about a particular topic.

Public Relations: A strategic communication process that builds mutually beneficial relationships between organizations and their publics.

Social Media: Social media refers to websites and applications that enable users to create and share content or to participate in social networking.

Social Media Platform: A software that helps brands engage their consumers across social media networks like Facebook.

Chapter 8
Business Intelligence through Opinion Mining

T. K. Das
VIT University, India

ABSTRACT

Business organizations have been adopting different strategies to impress upon their customers and attract them towards their products and services. On the other hand, the opinions of the customers gathered through customer feedbacks have been a great source of information for companies to evolve business intelligence to rightly place their products and services to meet the ever-changing customer requirements. In this work, we present a new approach to integrate customers' opinions into the traditional data warehouse model. We have taken Twitter as the data source for this experiment. First, we have built a system which can be used for opinion analysis on a product or a service. The second process is to model the opinion table so obtained as a dimensional table and to integrate it with a central data warehouse schema so that reports can be generated on demand. Furthermore, we have shown how business intelligence can be elicited from online product reviews by using computational intelligence technique like rough set base data analysis.

INTRODUCTION

Organizations spend a lot of money for conducting surveys on their products to get feedback, to know defects in the products and for future enhancements. Firstly, customer opinions help one to know how a particular product or service is perceived by the customers, reflecting customers' satisfaction and expectations that can be used to determine their current and future expectations (Das, Acharjya & Patra, 2014). Secondly, it can provide opportunity to improve one's products and services to satisfy customers and build loyalty. Third, they may be of help in understanding the product dimensions or attributes that are important to different customer segments, and even to discover new segments based on customers' liking/disliking of similar product attributes. Fourth, businesses gather essential information about the products and services offered by competitors to improve upon their products and services to remain competitive.

Companies do different types of surveys like product fulfillment survey, competitive products and market survey, brand equity survey, customer service survey, new-product acceptance survey, customer

DOI: 10.4018/978-1-5225-2031-3.ch008

trust and loyalty survey etc. for product enhancements (Das & Kumar, 2013). Such surveys demand lofty budget, manpower and time, though the report so generated may not be trustworthy

Therefore, the main objective of this work is to reduce expenditure on survey by using on-line social networks. On-line social networks (OSNs) such as Facebook, Google+, and Twitter provide lot of information which can be exploited for effective business. The objective is to analyze posts, tweets and other public discussions on products and elicit business intelligence. The results of analysis are depicted in the form of cumulative graphs, pie charts and tables to facilitate easy interpretation by the end-users. The purpose is to help businesses understand customer responses on their products and services. Reports generated through this process are unbiased and genuine as compared to other approaches to survey and analysis. The proposed method can yield solutions which is cost effective and time saving.

OPINION MINING

Opinion mining popularly known as sentiment analysis has been evolved as an interesting research area in recent years. Most research has focused on analyzing the content of either product review (Dave, Lawrence & Pennock (2003) or movie reviews(Pang et al, 2004). Furthermore sentiment analysis has been extended to other domains such as news, blogs and debates also. Sentiment analysis or opinion mining refers to the application of natural language processing, computational linguistics and text analytics to identify and extract subjective information implicit in source materials. It is an excellent means for handling many business intelligence tasks as it describes sentiment analysis as a process that categorizes a body of textual information to determine feelings, attitudes and emotions towards a particular issue or object. Generally speaking, sentiment analysis aims to determine the attitude of a speaker or a writer with respect to some topic or the overall contextual polarity of a document. The attitude may be one's judgment, assessment, sensitiveness or emotional state of the author when commenting about a subject. Opinion mining deals with detection and classification of sentiments in a text (Bifet & Frank, 2010). Sentiment analysis research achieves two things: i) identifying the polarity of the underlying subject in the text, and ii) determining the strength of the polarity (severity or intensity). Generally, the sentiment polarity is classified as positive, negative or neutral classes and the strength of polarity is expressed in numeric figures. Keywords like dazzling, brilliant, phenomenal, excellent, fantastic, spectacular, cool, awesome, thrilling obviously expresses a favorable context of the subject while keywords like terrible, awful, worst, horrible, stupid, waste express unfavorable sentiment. Sentiment elicitation is done at different levels focusing on either single words, phrases, complete sentences or a complete document by adopting techniques such as unigrams, bi- grams, N-Grams, and opinion words.

INTELLIGENT TECHNIQUES FOR OPINION MINING

One can use supervised techniques (Pang, Lee & Vaithyanathan, 2002), unsupervised techniques (Paltoglou & Thelwall, 2012) or a hybridization of them (Zhang et al, 2011) for opinion mining. Classification of sentiments generally done by supervised techniques by using machine learning approach. Pang et al (2002) first applied machine learning methods to perform sentiment analysis. In this approach, we build and train a sentiment classifier to determine positive, negative and neutral sentiments. This method is quite successfully applied to classification of sentences and documents. By this method, an inductive process learns about the characteristics of a class during a training phase, by observing the properties of a number of pre-classified documents and applies the acquired knowledge to determine the best classification for new, unseen documents, during testing. This has been studied by Pang et al. by using three different algorithms: Support Vector Machines (SVMs), Naive Bayes and Maximum Entropy classifiers (Scholz & Conrad, 2013), using a variety of features, such as unigrams and bi-grams, part-of-speech tags, binary and term frequency feature weights and others. Their best attained accuracy in a dataset consisting of movie reviews was attained using a SVM classifier with binary features. Tang et al (2008) also concluded that SVM performs better than other classifier for sentiment classification. Liu (2007) generated various classifiers on features like unigram and parts of speech (POS) based features. These classifiers are combined using several combination rules. It has been found that combined classifier outperforms individual classifier (Batista & Ratt, 2012). Lexicon based methods is based on function of opinion words in context (Ding, Liu & Yu, 2008). Opinion words are commonly used to express positive or negative sentiments e.g. fantastic and reckless. This approach generally uses a dictionary of opinion words to determine sentiment polarity (positive, negative or neutral).The dictionary is called the opinion lexicon. This approach of using the lexicon to determine the opinion orientation is called the lexicon based approach for sentiment analysis. Dictionary or lexicon-based sentiment analysis is typically based on lists of words with some sort of pre-determined emotional weight. Examples of such dictionaries include the General Inquirer (GI) dictionary and the Linguistic Inquiry and Word Count (LIWC) software.

A few attempts have been reported, which uses Genetic Algorithm to solve the opinion mining problem (Abbasi et al., 2008). They developed the Entropy Weighted Genetic Algorithm (EWGA) for opinion feature selection. The features and techniques result in the creation of a sentiment analysis approach geared towards classification of web discourse sentiments in multiple languages.

TWITTER AND TWITTER API

Twitter is an online social networking service that enables its users to send and read text-based messages of up to 140 characters, known as tweets. Twitter was created in March 2006 by Jack Dorsey. The online social media service rapidly gained worldwide popularity, generating over 340 million tweets daily and handling over 1.6 billion search queries per day. Since its launch, Twitter has become one of the ten most visited websites on the Internet, and has been described as "the SMS of the Internet". Unregistered users can read tweets, while registered users can post tweets through the website interface. Normally, there are two types of Twitter APIs in use:

1. REST API
2. Streaming API

The functions of these APIs are depicted in Figure 1 and Figure 2.

A dedicated HTTP connection has to be kept open while connecting to a streaming API. For example, consider a web application which accepts user requests, makes one or more requests to Twitter's API, and then displays the results as a response to the user's initial request. In this scenario, streaming APIs will not be able to establish a connection in response to a user request. However, the application can be connected by REST API to address this issue.

The HTTP handling process in this model is more complex than the first, but to have a real-time stream of tweet data makes the integration worthy for many applications.

Figure 1. REST API

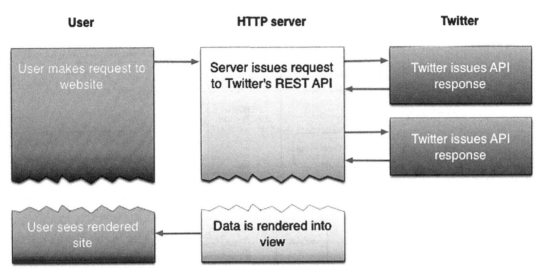

Figure 2. Streaming API

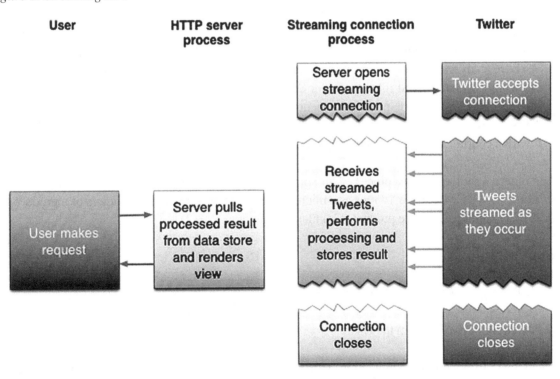

EXPERIMENTAL SET UP

In this work, we present a new approach to integrate customers' opinions into the traditional data ware-house model. Experiment is conducted in two major steps:

Figure 3. Sentiment analysis process

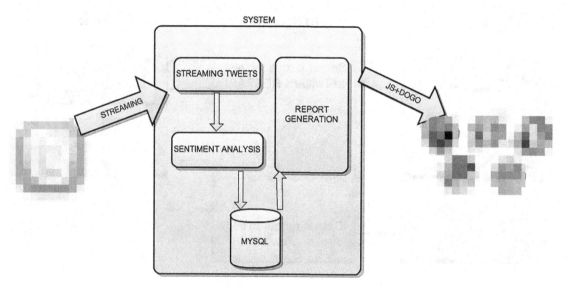

1. The first process relates to sentiment analysis. We have built a system which can be used for opinion analysis on a product or a service. The system processes the tweets by pulling data from tweeter posts, connecting to Alchemy API by REST call method and shows the result of sentiment analysis. We have analyzed opinions on the product Samsung Galaxy. The proposed system accesses public tweets by twitter API and filters them for Samsung Galaxy. The analysis is carried out to classify the sentiments as positive, negative or neutral and consolidates the results in an opinion table.
2. The second process is to model the opinion table so obtained as a dimensional table and to integrate it with a central data warehouse schema so that reports can be generated on demand.

See Figure 3 for the analysis process. Our approach of sentiment analysis is based on opinion words in the context. We have chosen Twitter as a micro-blogging platform where customers of a product can express their opinion about the product (Gokulakrishnan et al., 2012).

Methodology

The experiment consists of the following five steps:

Step 1: Getting keywords from the User

Users need to provide the application with keywords relating to the product for which analysis is being carried out. Based on the keywords relevant tweets are filtered out from the available tweets. For our experiment, we have considered tweets relating to the product Samsung Galaxy.

Step 2: Streaming public tweets from the Twitter

Initially, the application is registered with the Twitter for obtaining necessary credentials. After proving the required credential Twitter generates a unique token key and token secret access key, which needs to be embedded in the application for authentication. For this the user needs to authorize the application manually. Next, token secret key is generated which is saved for future use in the authentication process. The REST API returns the user with an XML file containing all the Tweets in XML format, which the user needs to parse after streaming for obtaining the content and other parameters of the tweet.

Step 3: Sentiment Analysis

In this phase each tweet is analyzed based on the keywords provided by the user in a given context. Based on the severity of the keywords used, the score is generated. For sentiment analysis, we have used Alchemy API which is a web service that analyzes unstructured content e.g. news articles, blogs, posts, e-mails, etc. Alchemy API is a text mining platform providing the most comprehensive set of semantic analysis capabilities in the natural language processing field. Alchemy API provides the ability to extract keyword-level sentiments (positive/negative/neutral). It uses a hybrid approach with natural language processing which incorporates both linguistic and statistical analysis techniques into a single unified system.

First of all, one has to register the application with Alchemy API to get the API access key. Next, a REST call is built by embedding credentials and tweets. After processing, REST response is received in XML file. Figure 4 represents an XML response containing the polarity of the sentiment (positive, negative or neutral) along with the severity (score).

Step 4: Storing in a Database

The tweets thus obtained and the scores of the sentiment analysis are stored in a database. The XML input source file is parsed to get the details of the tweets such as tweet id, time, username, type, score and tweet descriptions are stored in the database. Figure 5 shows a snapshot of the tweet detail table.

Step 5: Report Generation

Figure 4. An XML response

```
▼<results>
   <status>OK</status>
 ▶<usage>...</usage>
   <url/>
   <language>english</language>
 ▼<docSentiment>
     <type>positive</type>
     <score>0.348793</score>
   </docSentiment>
 </results>
```

Figure 5. Detailed Tweet table

	id	time	username	type	score	tweet
81	327120328675454976	1366826538000	JAPSG	positive	0.27838600	Samsung Galaxy S 4 Review: Gimme One Smartphone, with Everyth
82	327120335537311746	1366826540000	DanielRadFlo	neutral	0.00000000	RT @TechnoBuffalo: Ruggedized Galaxy S4 Will Be Announced in t
83	327120335872868352	1366826540000	brunourti	neutral	0.00000000	samsung galaxy s ??????? http
84	327120341711339520	1366826541000	michevirg	neutral	0.00000000	samsung galaxy 580 i5800 http://
85	327120354206158848	1366826544000	Ryaad_94_iv	positive	0.07209610	RT @AdopteUnLegging: Prise en main de la fonction photo du n
86	327120358668906496	1366826545000	buscaml	neutral	0.00000000	@TodoChileVentas Funda Carcasa Flip Cover Samsung Galaxy S3
87	327120363278450689	1366826548000	buscaml	neutral	0.00000000	@MfrizR Funda Carcasa Flip Cover Samsung Galaxy S3 I9300 + La
88	327120370039672832	1366826548000	Aman_Banka	neutral	0.00000000	Rumors - Water & Dust Proof Samsung Galaxy S4 in works, Launchi
89	327120370383601664	1366826548000	GSMinsider	neutral	0.00000000	Samsung Galaxy S Relay 4G Receiving Android 4.1.2 Jelly Bean
90	327120373265096704	1366826549000	terryris9	neutral	0.00000000	samsung galaxy tab gt p6800 htt

Different analysis is carried out by using the data from the tweet table. The results of analysis are presented to the end-user in the form of pie charts, cumulative graphs, and tables.

Figure 6 represents a generic preview of feedback obtained by the analysis. It categorizes the percentage of positive, negative and neutral tweets based on the number of tweets in each category.

Figure 7 shows the count of positive, negative and neutral tweets collected from the stream over a period of time. The X-axis indicates the time duration in seconds while the Y-axis indicates the count of the tweets.

Figure 6. Pie chart representation of Tweet polarity

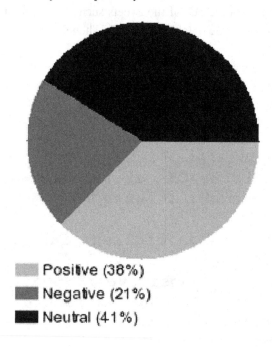

Positive (38%)
Negative (21%)
Neutral (41%)

Figure 7. Sentiments over time

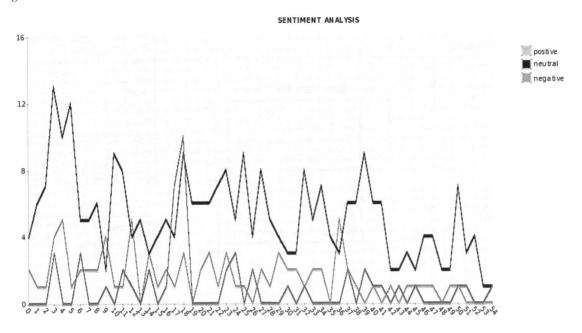

INTEGRATING OPINION WITH MULTI-DIMENSIONAL MODEL

Business intelligence is the process of extracting data from an OLAP database and then analyzing that data for information that can be used to make business decisions. For example, OLAP and business intelligence help to answer the following types of queries about business data:

- What is the overall opinion polarity about Samsung Galaxy yesterday?
- What is the sentiment score of a particular product over a period of one week?
- What percentage of tweets reported negative sentiments?

To facilitate such type of user queries, we propose the following multi dimensional model. A comparable model has been proposed by Yaakub et al (2011) to integrate sentiment polarity to customer analysis model. However, our approach is to pull out twitter data automatically, processing it for sentiment evaluation and integrating the obtained sentiment with the dimensional model.

Dimensional Model

Here we describe a multidimensional model to integrate product's characteristics and opinions on the products (or services). The objective is to model the opinions as a new dimensional table which would be loaded periodically. After loading of dimensional table, the associated workflow for loading fact table is started. This transfers the opinions to the fact table that contains other dimensions such as customers, products and time.

Figure 8 shows a star schema consisting of dimensions such as customer, product, opinion, time, and sentiment fact table.

Figure 8. Star schema of data warehouse

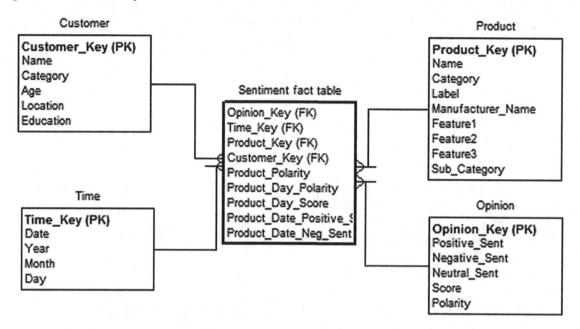

OLAP Cube Containing Opinions

Customer opinions are analyzed by OLAP and data cubes. A data cube is a data structure that aggregates the measures along the hierarchies of the dimensions that one requires to analyze. Many data cubes can be created to analyze the opinion in different hierarchies. Figure 9 shows a three-dimension data cube which contains product name, date and opinion polarity.

From this model, the count of tweets extracted on a particular day for a specific product can be reported, e.g. for product Samsung Galaxy on 25th March 2013, the number of tweets classified as positive, negative and neutral can be visualized. Similarly, detail reports about the opinions can be generated for other products of the company which are currently in the market along the time dimension. This research is an attempt to measure the sentiment which is purely qualitative and expressive. By using this architecture, the highly unstructured tweets are transferred to a fact table for measuring and summarizing.

BUSINESS INTELLIGENCE FROM ONLINE PRODUCT REVIEW

With the advent of e-commerce applications, more and more users interact via web 2.0 applications by posting their comments and going through other users' comments (Zhang, 2008). Before buying an expensive product, normally a buyer does an initial ground work that consists of collecting data about the product from friends, relatives, users of the product, and all other possible sources. Normally, the views of other users of a product leave a lasting impression in one's mind. But with the growth of online social networks (OSN) and popularization of review sites, forums, blogs and discussion groups, consumer's data is no more limited to the word of mouth. According to a survey, 81% of Internet users have done online search on a product at least once (Dang, Zhang & Chen, 2010). ; between 73-87%

Figure 9. Cube containing opinion dimension

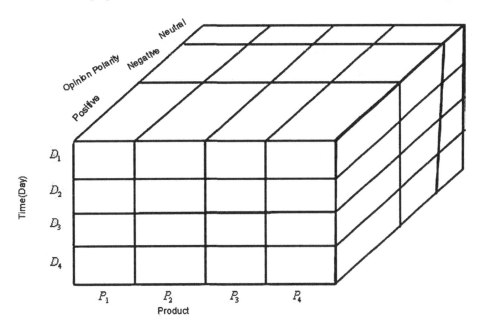

report that reviews had a significant influence on their purchase (Pang & Lee, 2008). Also it has been known from a survey that 3/4th of the buyers' purchasing decision is influenced by the reviews posted by other users. Thus, it is evident that the influence of online reviews makes a difference while taking a purchasing decision. Online postings are of two types, i) textual description about the product which consists of experience, feelings, sentiments, opinions, ii) collective summarization of overall satisfaction about the product's features and performance in the form of ratings. Ratings are provided in the scale of 1-5 or 1-10. Reviews play an important role in deciding the prospective buyer's purchasing orientation (Chung, Chen & Nunamaker, 2005). A product having reviews with higher star rankings has always been the preferred one as it builds confidence and motivates towards buying that product. In the other hand negative reviews, negative sentiments influence the buyer to refrain from buying a product. For a company, the impact of reviews goes a long way in building the market segment, growth in sales, customer retention and also creating new customer base (Zhu & Zhang, 2010).

FOUNDATIONS OF ROUGH COMPUTING

Rough set theory has been used as a tool to process uncertain and incomplete information. One of its strength is the attribute dependencies, their significance among inconsistent data. At the same time, it does not need any preliminary or additional information of the data. Therefore, it classifies imprecise, uncertain or incomplete information expressed in terms of data acquired from experience.

Rough Sets

In this section we recall the definitions of basic rough set theory developed by Pawlak (1991). Let U be a finite nonempty set called the universe. Suppose $R \subseteq (U \times U)$ is an equivalence relation on U. The equivalence relation R partitions the set U into disjoint subsets. Elements of same equivalence class are said to be indistinguishable. Equivalence classes induced by R are called elementary concepts. Every union of elementary concepts is called a definable set. The empty set is considered to be a definable set, thus all the definable sets form a Boolean algebra and (U, R) is called an approximation space. Given a target set X, we can characterize X by a pair of lower and upper approximations. We associate two subsets $\underline{R}X$ and $\overline{R}X$ called the R-lower and R-upper approximations of X respectively and are given by:

$$\underline{R}X = \cup\{Y \in U / R : Y \subseteq X\}$$

$$\overline{R}X = \cup\{Y \in U / R : Y \cap X \neq \phi\}$$

The R-boundary of X, $BN_R(X)$ is given by $BN_R(X) = \overline{R}X - \underline{R}X$. We say X is rough with respect to R if and only if $\overline{R}X \neq \underline{R}X$, equivalently $BN_R(X) \neq \phi$. X is said to be R-definable if and only if $\overline{R}X = \underline{R}X$ or $BN_R(X) = \phi$. So, a set is rough with respect to R if and only if it is not R-definable

Rough Set Based Rule Induction

Rough set theory has been applied successfully almost in all areas (Das, 2016). One of the application is decision rule extraction from attribute value table (Hu, 2012; Das, Acharjya & Patra, 2014). Also decision rules can be automatically extracted as performed from clinical data sets (Roy et al, 2012). Most of these methods are based on generation of discernibility matrices and reducts (Thangavel et al, 2005). As large volumes of data are available from the Internet and other digital storage media, automatic rule-induction methods are being increasingly used to extract decision rules from such data (Chung & Tseng, 2012). Examples of rule-induction methods include C4.5, RIPPER (Cohen, 1995), and CN2 (Clark & Niblett, 1989). Among these, association rule mining and rough-set theory are well-established and widely used methods for extracting decision rules from unstructured data sets. Rough set in hybridizing with Support Vector Machine (SVM) has been used for unstructured data analysis e.g. text classification (Chen & Liu, 2008) and emotion recognition from text (Teng et al., 2007).

Recently, many applications have been designed using reduct and classification algorithms based on rough sets (Roy, Viswanatham & Krishna, 2016).. A decision table may have more than one reducts. Anyone of the reduct can be used in stead of the original table for rule induction. A reduct is a minimal set of features that preserves the indiscernibility relation produced by a partition of the universal set. The rough set-based approach to inductive learning consists of two steps. The first step is to find multiple single covering sets for all training instances held in a decision table. By this, more than one covering set (reduct) would be found. The second step is to transform multiple sets of reducts to the corresponding sets of rules.

LEM2 (Learning from Examples Module) is a local algorithm based on rough set theory which is explained as follows:

1. Let s be a pair (a, v), the set of all tuples of attribute 'a' having value 'v'.
2. Let C be a concept and S be set of all s. Set S is minimal complex of C if and only if C depends on S and S is minimal.
3. Let I be the set of all attribute– value pairs. I is a local covering of C, if and only if:
   a. Each member of I is a minimal complex of C.
   b. $\bigcup\limits_{S \in I} [S] = B$
   c. I is minimal

For each concept C, LEM2 induces production rules by computing a local covering I.

A Numerical Illustration

In this section, we explain how LEM2 algorithm induces production rules from a decision table as shown in Table 1. The table has attributes such as references, publications, Ph.D. and a decision attribute "Grant". The attribute References may have values "excellent", "very good" or "good", Publications may be "yes" or "no", Ph.D. takes the values "yes" or "no". The task is to decide whether a research grant would be sanctioned to the candidate or not. We have used LEM2 algorithm for deriving rules from the domain of values of attributes which would be mapped to decision attribute "Grant".

Table 1. A decision table

Candidates	References	Publications	Ph.D	Grant(Decision)
1	Very Good	Yes	No	Yes
2	Excellent	Yes	Yes	Yes
3	Good	No	No	No
4	Good	Yes	No	No
5	Very Good	Yes	Yes	Yes
6	Good	No	Yes	No
7	Very Good	No	Yes	No

From the table:

[(References, Very Good)] = {1, 5, 7}, [(References, Excellent)] = {2}

[(References, Good)] = {3, 4, 6}, [(Publication, Yes)] = {1, 2, 4, 5 }

[(Publication, No)] = {3, 6, 7 }, [(Ph.D, No)] = {3, 4,6, 7}, [(Ph.D, Yes)] = {1, 2, 5}.

Let the concept C is the set {1, 2, 5}. Initially, the target T is equal to C.

The set $S(T)$ is {(References, Very Good), (References, Excellent), (Publication, yes), (Ph.D, no), (Ph.D, yes)}.

Table 2. Attribute Value Pairs

Attribute-value	Candidate set	Attribute-value	Candidate set
(References, Very Good)	{1, 5}	(Ph.D, yes)	{2, 5}
(References, Excellent)	{2}	(Ph.D, no)	{1}
(Publication, yes)	{1, 2, 5}		

Out of the above attribute-value pairs in Table 2, (Publication, yes) is the most relevant with respect to target T .

Furthermore, [(Publication, yes)] = {1, 2, 4, 5} $\not\subset$ {1, 2, 5}, so (Publication, yes) is not a minimal complex of C. The algorithm LEM2 looks for another attribute-value pair s. The following list shows remaining attribute-value pairs, relevant with T ,

(References, Very Good) - {1, 5}, (References, Excellent) - {2}, (Ph.D, no) - {1} and

(Ph.D, yes) - {2, 5}.

From the above, there is a tie between (References, Very Good) and (Ph.D, yes).

The attribute-value pair (References, Very Good) is selected because |(References, Very Good)| = 3 and |(Ph.D, yes)| = 4.

The first minimal complex T is equal to {(Publication, yes), (References, Very Good)} as [(Publication, yes)] $\cap$ [(References, Very Good)] = {1, 5}.

The set S describes examples {1, 5}, thus the target T is equal to the set consisting

of the remaining example {2}. The set $S(T)$ of all relevant attribute-value pairs is:

{(References, Excellent), (Publication, yes), (Ph.D, yes)}

(References, Excellent) – {2}, (Publication, yes) – {2}, (Ph.D, yes) – {2}.

From above, there is a tie between all three attribute-value pairs. The cardinality of the block of (References, Excellent) is minimal, hence this pair is selected. At the same time, {(References, Excellent)} is a minimal complex. Thus, the local covering of the concept C = {1, 2, 5} is the following set:

{{(Publication, yes), (References, Very Good)}, {(References, Excellent)}}

The corresponding production rules are

(Publication, yes) $\wedge$ (References, Very Good) => (Grant, yes)

and (References, Excellent) =>(Grant, yes).

The production rules for the concept {3, 4, 6, 7} may be induced by LEM2 in a similar way.

SYSTEM OVERVIEW

Here, we have presented various components of the proposed system, i.e. on-line review collection, attribute selection, decision table construction, rule induction and top-5 rules selection. The designed system has been formed for extracting decision rules by analyzing on-line customer reviews on a product or a service. For our experiment, we have gathered reviews on Samsung Galaxy S5 from the Samsung home page. The reviews are preprocessed and decision rules have been extracted by using rough set based LEM2 algorithm. Such rules are helpful for business analysts in understanding product dimensions, their attributes and inherent association among them. Figure 10 depicts the overall rule extraction process.

METHODOLOGY

The methodology for rule extraction is a five-step process which is explained below:

Step 1: Attribute Selection

A huge volume of textual data is posted on the Samsung portal on the product Samsung Galaxy S5 describing its features (attributes). Attribute selection refers to the process of selecting relevant and important attributes out of a large number of attributes such that further analysis can be carried out ef-

Figure 10. Rule extraction process

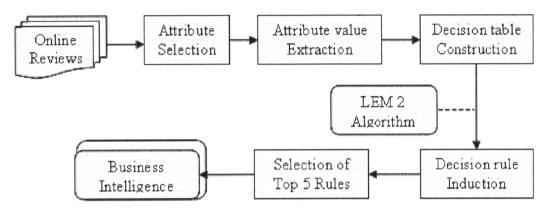

ficiently. We have considered four important attributes such as feature, performance, design and value for the Samsung Galaxy S5. Here is a sample review posted on the site.

"Amazing! I upgraded from the s3 and this phone is amazing. It is so much faster and better looking than my s3. Plus the screen a bit bigger and the resolution is better. I also love that it's water proof as well. Water proof testing was the first thing I did with the phone. The battery life is good as well. Overall I really like this phone and it looks durable for the next 2 months."

Step 2: Attribute Value Extraction

A review is associated with a "star" rating with values 1,2,3,4 and 5. A 5-star would mean excellent and a 1-star meaning poor. Each of the attributes feature, performance, design and value are rated out of 5 by the reviewer and the date of review posting is also recorded. Table.1 shows information about a couple of reviews and their overall rating.

Step 3: Decision Table Construction

Generally, the decision table consists of data of a particular problem. It records values eof conditional attributes and the accompanying decision attribute in a large number of samples. Attributes A1, A2, A3

Table 3. Attributes and their ratings

User	Date of Posting	Consumer Ratings				
		Feature	Performance	Design	Value	Star
boblannonuk	15/4/2014	5	4	4	5	*****
warajoker	14/8/2014	5	5	5	5	*****
Mano	14/8/2014	1	1	1	1	*
proudmom1981	9/8/2014	5	5	5	5	*****
RWilliams	6/8/2014	2	2	2	1	*
Wraith38	1/7/2014	2	5	5	3	***
Dav1979	17/6/2014	5	1	3	3	**

and A4 represent the feature, performance, design and value of the product respectively. The decision table is modeled based on the attributes (A1, A2, A3, A4) and decision attribute (A5). The star rating in the numerical form (1, 2, 3, 4, 5) represents the value of the decision attribute. For this specific problem, a decision table has been formulated which is represented in table 4. It would be further processed in subsequent steps for computing decision rules.

Step 4: Decision Rule Extraction

A decision rule is a logical implication of the form 'if...then' which belongs to entirely different domain. Typically a decision rule is of the form $(a_1 = v_1), (a_2 = v_2), ..., (a_n = v_n) \Rightarrow d$ where $a_1, a_2, .., a_n$ are the attributes and $v_1, v_2, ..., v_n$ are their corresponding values. Decision attribute d is the implication from the set of values of the attributes. For inducing decision rule from decision table, we have implemented Rough set theory algorithm LEM2 by using ROSE2 (Rough Set Data Explorer) software (available at http://idss.cs.put.poznan.pl/site/).

Step 5: Analysis and Discovering Business Intelligence

The output of the previous process is in the form of set of rules. The rules generated out of the data set are being analyzed in this step for discovering business intelligence. The analysis is to identify keywords in the textual reviews that give rise to a particular decision. Likely, for the decision classes 1, 2, 3, 4, 5; a set of keywords has been are identified which would be further analyzed for discovering business intelligence.

RESULTS AND DISCUSSION

Out of 1156 reviews posted in Samsung U.K. portal, we have randomly selected 82 useful reviews and thus a decision table is being constructed. The table has attributes A1, A2, A3, A4 and a decision attribute A5. All these attributes have range of values between 1 and 5.

Classes = {1, 2, 3, 4, 5}

Table 4. Decision table for product review

Review	A1	A2	A3	A4	A5(Decision)
1	5	4	4	5	5
2	5	5	5	5	5
3	1	1	1	1	1
4	5	5	5	5	5
5	2	2	2	1	1
6	2	5	5	3	3
7	5	1	3	3	2

The followings are the list of all the rules induced from the data set:

Rule 1. (A1 = 1) => (A5 = 1)
Rule 2. (A1 = 2) & (A3 = 2) => (A5 = 1)
Rule 3. (A1 = 3) & (A3 = 1) => (A5 = 1)
Rule 4. (A2 = 3) & (A3 = 2) => (A5 = 1)
Rule 5. (A1 = 3) & (A2 = 3) & (A4 = 3) => (A5 = 1)
Rule 6. (A2 = 1) & (A3 = 4) & (A4 = 2) => (A5 = 1)
Rule 7. (A1 in {3, 2}) & (A2 = 2) & (A4 = 3) => (A5 = 2)
Rule 8. (A1 = 5) & (A2 = 1) => (A5 = 2)
Rule 9. (A1 = 2) & (A2 = 3) => (A5 = 2)
Rule 10. (A2 = 2) & (A3 = 3) => (A5 = 2)
Rule 11. (A1 = 5) & (A4 = 1) => (A5 = 2)
Rule 12. (A1 = 4) & (A2 = 2) & (A4 = 3) => (A5 = 3)
Rule 13. (A1 = 2) & (A3 = 5) => (A5 = 3)
Rule 14. (A1 = 3) & (A4 = 2) => (A5 = 3)
Rule 15. (A2 = 3) & (A3 = 5) => (A5 = 3)
Rule 16. (A1 = 3) & (A3 = 2) => (A5 = 3)
Rule 17. (A2 = 5) & (A3 = 2) => (A5 = 3)
Rule 18. (A2 = 5) & (A3 = 4) & (A4 = 3) => (A5 = 3)
Rule 19. (A3 in {4, 3}) & (A4 = 4) => (A5 = 4)
Rule 20. (A1 = 4) & (A3 = 3) & (A4 in {3, 5}) => (A5 = 4)
Rule 21. (A1 = 5) & (A4 = 4) => (A5 = 4)
Rule 22. (A1 = 5) & (A3 = 4) & (A4 = 3) => (A5 = 4)
Rule 23. (A1 = 5) & (A2 = 5) & (A4 = 3) => (A5 = 4)
Rule 24. (A1 = 4) & (A2 = 4) => (A5 = 4)
Rule 25. (A2 = 5) & (A3 = 4) & (A4 = 5) => (A5 = 4)
Rule 26. (A1 = 4) & (A2 = 5) & (A3 = 5) & (A4 = 3) => (A5 = 4)
Rule 27. (A2 = 4) & (A4 = 5) => (A5 = 5)
Approximate rules
Rule 28. (A3 = 5) & (A4 = 5) => (A5 = 4) OR (A5 = 5)
Rule 29. (A1 = 2) & (A2 = 1) & (A4 = 1) => (A5 = 1) OR (A5 = 2)
Rule 30. (A1 = 4) & (A2 = 5) & (A3 = 5) & (A4 = 4) => (A5 = 3) OR (A5 = 4)

The above result shows that there are 27 rules and 3 approximate rules. All the rules are evaluated basing on the metrics support value and confidence value. Out of the above 30 rules, we have filtered top 5 rules based on the number of matches in the data set. Table 5.5 shows top 5 rules in decreasing order of frequency. From these rules many interesting association between the attributes is discovered.

In this phase we have grouped all the rules based on the decision attributes outcome. For example, from first six rules it is clear that the rating is 1 (A5=1). So the rules producing decision as 1(very low) are grouped. Rule 1 is the minimal decision rule. i.e. (A1 = 1) => (A5 = 1). This rule has a support of 57.89%. Other rules don't have the minimum support. Similarly for the ratings 2, 3, 4 and 5, the effective rule is being selected from the list.

Table 5. Top-5 rules

No.	Rules	Attributes	Match
1	(Design in {4, 3}) & (value = 4) => (Ranking = 4)	2	13
2	(Feature = 1) => (Ranking = 1)	1	11
3	(Design = 5) & (value = 5) => (Ranking = 4) OR (Ranking = 5);	2	10
4	(Feature = 4) & (performance = 4) => (Ranking = 4)	2	8
5	(Feature = 4) & (Design = 3) & (value in {3, 5}) => (Ranking = 4)	3	5

Discussion

Customer dissatisfaction on a product cannot be expressed through numerical ratings only (e.g., 1, 2, 3, etc.). For instance, if a customer has given poor rating '1' for feature, it is difficult to conclude which of the features were not liked by the customer. In our example, Galaxy S5 features include 16mp primary camera, 5.1 inch touch screen, 1920 x 1080 pixel resolution, Android 4.2 OS, 1.9 GHZ quad core processor, 2GB RAM, 16GB memory, 2800 mAh battery, heart rate sensor and many more. So, for an in-depth analysis, textual reviews have to be studied and related keywords can be picked up, e.g., a review with 5 star ranking is associated with the following comments:

- 'Back to the Smart phone on the market - The amazing just got better'
- "Love the water proof feature!"
- "I just got my new S5 and I love this phone. The processors are super fast and the resolution is by far the best of the Samsung phones"
- *The keywords like "amazing", "water proof", "fast processor" help the business intelligence system to capture the views of the customers more accurately.*

CONCLUSION

In this chapter, we have developed methods to discover business intelligence from unstructured text data. In phase-I, we have analyzed the twitter data and the extracted opinion is integrated with a data warehouse schema. The proposed model overcomes the drawbacks of traditional surveys of directly interviewing customers; instead the system gathers the required data from online social networks (OSN) such as Twitter, Facebook, MySpace, Blogs, and many other discussion forums where the users generally talk to their mates about the products. Such data help a product manufacturer/service provider to understand the public pulse and thereby improve their products/services.

In phase-II, we focused on online customer postings and derived decision rules from unstructured textual data by using rough set based rule induction LEM2 algorithm. Service providers/managers can have better insight to their products through these rules and can further analyze it along different dimensions. They can discover the knowledge as to what makes a customer give a higher star ranking feedback on a product. Our approach can help in analyzing customer reviews in an automatic manner, thus reducing the manual effort to a great extent in dealing with voluminous reviews. Our work can be further extended for different products and services by automatic acquisition of knowledge gained through business intelligence.

REFERENCES

Abbasi, A., Chen, H. & Salem, A. (2008). Sentiment Analysis in Multiple Languages: Feature Selection for Opinion Classification in Web Forums. *ACM Transactions on Information Systems*, *26*(3), 12:1-12:34.

Batista, L., & Ratt, S. (2012). A Multi-Classifier System for Sentiment Analysis and Opinion Mining. In *Proceedings of the IEEE/ACM International Conference on Advances in Social Networks Analysis and Mining*(pp. 96-100).

Bifet, A., & Frank, E. (2010). Sentiment knowledge discovery in Twitter streaming data. In *Proceedings of the13th International Conference on Discovery Science* (pp. 1–15), Canberra, Australia. Springer. doi:10.1007/978-3-642-16184-1_1

Chen, P., & Liu, S. (2008). Rough set-based SVM classifier for text categorization. In *Proceedings of the Fourth IEEE International Conference of Natural Computation*, (Vol. 2, pp. 153–157).

Chung, W., & Tseng, T. L. (2012). Discovering business intelligence from online product reviews: A rule-induction framework. *Expert Systems with Applications*, *39*(15), 11870–11879. doi:10.1016/j.eswa.2012.02.059

Chung, W., Chen, H., & Nunamaker, J. F. (2005). A visual framework for knowledge discovery on the web: An empirical study on business intelligence exploration. *Journal of Management Information Systems*, *21*(4), 57–84.

Clark, P., & Niblett, T. (1989). The CN2 induction algorithm. *Machine Learning*, *3*(4), 261–283. doi:10.1007/BF00116835

Cohen, W. (1995). Fast effective rule induction. In *Proceedings of the twelfth international conference on machine learning*(pp. 115–123). Lake Tahoe, CA: Morgan Kaufmann.

Dang, Y., Zhang, Y., & Chen, H. (2010). A lexicon-enhanced method for sentiment Classification: An experiment on online product reviews. *IEEE Intelligent Systems*, *25*(4), 46–53. doi:10.1109/MIS.2009.105

Das, T. K. (2016). Intelligent Techniques in Decision Making: A Survey. *Indian Journal of Science and Technology*, *9*(12), 1–6. doi:10.17485/ijst/2016/v9i12/86063

Das, T. K., & Kumar, P. M. (2013). BIG Data Analytics: A Framework for Unstructured Data Analysis. *IACSIT International Journal of Engineering and Technology*, *5*(1), 153–156.

Das, T. K., Acharjya, D. P., & Patra, M. R. (2014). Opinion Mining about a Product by Analyzing Public Tweets in Twitter. In Proceedings of the 2014 International Conference on Computer Communication and Informatics (pp. 1- 4), Coimbatore, India: IEEE Xplore.

Das, T. K., Acharjya, D. P., & Patra, M. R. (2014). Business Intelligence from Online Product Review - A Rough Set Based Rule Induction Approach. In *Proceedings of the 2014 International Conference on Contemporary Computing and Informatics* (pp.800-803). Mysore, India: IEEE Xplore.

Dave, K., Lawrence, S., & Pennock, D. M. (2003). Mining the peanut gallery: opinion extraction and semantic classification of product reviews. In *Proceedings of the International World Wide Web Conference* (pp. 519–528). doi:10.1109/ICCCI.2014.6921727

Ding, X., Liu, B., & Yu, P. S. (2008). A holistic lexicon-based approach to opinion mining. In*Proc. of the Intl. Conf. on Web search and web data mining, WSDM '08,* (pp. 231–240). doi:10.1145/1341531.1341561

Gokulakrishnan, B., Priyanthan, P., Ragavan, T., Prasath, N., & Perera, A. (2012). Opinion mining and sentiment analysis on a twitter data stream. In *Proceedings of the International Conference on Advances in ICT for Emerging Regions* (pp. 182-188). doi:10.1109/ICTer.2012.6423033

Hu, Z. (2012). *Decision Rule Induction for Service Sector Using Data Mining - A Rough Set Theory Approach* (M. S. Thesis). The University of Texas at El Paso.

Liu, B. (2007). *Web data mining: Exploring hyperlinks, contents, and usage data.* Berlin: Springer-Verlag.

Paltoglou, G., & Thelwall, M. (2012). Twitter, MySpace, Digg: Unsupervised Sentiment Analysis in Social Media. *ACM Transactions on Intelligent Systems and Technology, 3*(4), 66:1-66:19.

Pang, B., Lee, L., & Vaithyanathan, S. (2002). Thumbs up: Sentiment classification using machine learning techniques. In *Proceedings of the International Conference on Empirical Methods in Natural Language Processing* (pp. 79–86). doi:10.3115/1118693.1118704

Pang, B., & Lee, L. (2004). A sentimental education: sentiment analysis using subjectivity summarization based on minimum cuts. In *Proceedings of the Association for Computational Linguistics* (pp. 271–278).

Pang, B., & Lee, L. (2008). Opinion mining and sentiment analysis. *Foundations and Trends in Information Retrieval, 2*(1-2), 1–135. doi:10.1561/1500000011

Pawlak, Z. (1991). *Rough sets: Theoretical aspects of reasoning about data.* Dordrecht, The Netherlands: Kluwer Academic Publishers. doi:10.1007/978-94-011-3534-4

Roy, S. S., Gupta, A., Sinha, A., & Ramesh, R. (2012). Cancer data investigation using variable precision Rough set with flexible classification. In *Proceedings of the Second International Conference on Computational Science, Engineering and Information Technology* (pp. 472-475). ACM. doi:10.1145/2393216.2393295

Roy, S. S., Viswanatham, V. M., & Krishna, P. V. (2016). Spam detection using hybrid model of rough set and decorate ensemble. *International Journal of Computational Systems Engineering, 2*(3), 139–147. doi:10.1504/IJCSYSE.2016.079000

Scholz, T., & Conrad, S. (2013). Opinion Mining in Newspaper Articles by Entropy-based Word Connections. In *Proc. of the 2013 Conference on Empirical Methods in Natural Language Processing* (pp. 1828–1839).

Teng, Z., Ren, F., & Kuriowa, S. (2007). Emotion recognition from text based on the rough set theory and the support vector machines. In *Proceedings of 2007 international conference of the natural language processing and knowledge engineering* (pp. 36– 41). Beijing, China: IEEE Computer Society. doi:10.1109/NLPKE.2007.4368008

Thangavel, K., Jaganathan, P., Pethalakshmi, A., & Karnan, M. (2005). Effective classification with improved quick reduct for medical database using rough system. *Bioinformatics and Medical Engineering, 5*(1), 7–14.

Tumasjan, A., Sprenger, T., Sandner, P., & Welpe, I. (2010). Predicting elections with twitter: What 140 characters reveal about political sentiment. *Word Journal Of The International Linguistic Association, 280*(39), 178–185.

Yaakub, M. R., Li, Y., & Feng, Y. (2011). Integration of Opinion into Customer Analysis Model. In *Proceedings of the Eighth IEEE International Conference on e-Business Engineering*(pp. 90-95). doi:10.1109/ICEBE.2011.53

Zeng, L., Li, L., & Duan, L. (2012). Business intelligence in enterprise computing environment. *Information Technology and Management, Springer, 13*(4), 297–310. doi:10.1007/s10799-012-0123-z

Zhang, L., Ghosh, R., Dekhil, M., Hsu, M., & Liu, B. (2011). *Combining lexicon based and learning-based methods for twitter sentiment analysis.* Technical Report HPL-2011-89.

Zhang, Z. (2008). Weighing stars: Aggregating online product reviews for intelligent e-commerce applications. *IEEE Intelligent Systems, 23*(5), 42–49. doi:10.1109/MIS.2008.95

Zhu, F., & Zhang, X. M. (2010). Impact of online consumer reviews on sales: The moderating role of product and consumer characteristics. *Journal of Marketing, 74*(2), 133–148. doi:10.1509/jmkg.74.2.133

Chapter 9
Sentiment Analysis

A. M. Abirami
Thiagarajar College of Engineering, India

A. Askarunisa
KLN College of Information Technology, India

A. Sheik Abdullah
Thiagarajar College of Engineering, India

S. Selvakumar
G. K. M. College of Engineering and Technology, India

C. Mahalakshmi
Thiagarajar College of Engineering, India

ABSTRACT

It requires sophisticated streaming of big data processing to process the billions of daily social conversations across millions of sources. Dataset needs information extraction from them and it requires contextual semantic sentiment modeling to capture the intelligence through the complexity of online social discussions. Sentiment analysis is one of the techniques to capture the intelligence from Social Networks based on the user generated content. There are more and more researches evolving about sentiment classification. Aspect extraction is the core task involved in aspect based sentiment analysis. The proposed modeling uses Latent Semantic Analysis technique for aspect extraction and evaluates senti-scores of various products under study.

INTRODUCTION

Social media, as a data source, contains valuable consumer insights and enable business intelligence. Writing in social media to express one's views becomes common now-a-days. The power of social media is described by (Jagadeeshkumar, 2014) and it can be effectively used to influence public opinion or research behavior. Text analytics shows the necessity of analysis of blogs, the experiences shared among people. There has been an increase in attention on social media as a source of research data in areas such as decision making, recommender systems, etc. Social media analytics research has been undertaken in marketing, retail and similar other sectors to improve customer satisfaction, recommend new products and so on.

Opinions are central to almost all human activities and are key influencers of our behaviors. It becomes common nowadays to ask one's friends and family for opinions before buying any new product or

DOI: 10.4018/978-1-5225-2031-3.ch009

avail new service. For this reason, human beings always seek others opinions before making decisions. This is not only true for individuals but also true for organizations. An individual or organization may collect public opinions or views and use it for decision making. The beliefs and perceptions of reality, the choices made and the tradition upon how others view and evaluate the products form the basis for opinion mining or sentiment analysis.

Sentiment analysis is the field of study that analyzes people's opinions, sentiments, evaluations, appraisals, and emotions towards entities such as products, services, individuals, organizations, topics, issues, events, and their attributes. It extracts people's opinion about an entity. It identifies the attitude of a speaker or writer about some topic. In recent years, it has been witnessed that opinionated postings in social media have helped in business improvement, and have great impact on social and political systems. It deals with the analysis of emotions, opinions and facts in the sentences which are expressed by the people. It allows us to track attitudes and feelings of the people by analyzing blogs, comments, reviews and tweets about all the aspects (Bing Liu, 2010). The enormous growth of social media like online reviews, discussions, blogs, micro-blogs, twitter, etc on the web, enable individuals and organizations to make decisions using these content.

TYPES OF SENTIMENT ANALYSIS

Sentiment Analysis is one of the applications of Information Extraction (IE). It is defined as the automatic extraction of subjective content from digital text and predicting the subjectivity as positive or negative. The types are illustrated in Figure 1.

Figure 1. Sentiment analysis approach

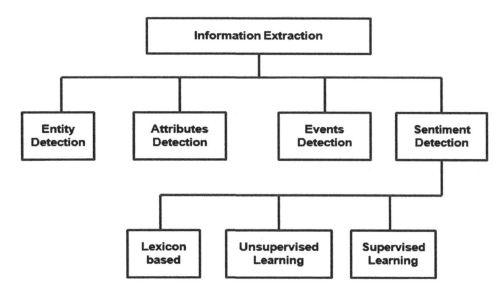

Sentiment analysis is performed at various levels as follows:

- Document level classification
- Sentence level classification
- Aspect or Feature level classification and Summarization
  ○ Named Entity Recognition
  ○ Feature level analysis

Document Level

The main task of this level is to classify whether positive or negative sentiment expressed in the whole document. For example, given a product review, the system determines whether the review expresses an overall positive or negative opinion about the product. This level of analysis applicable for single entity not for multiple entities

Sentence Level

The task of this level is to identify whether each sentence expresses positive, negative or neutral opinion. This is related to subjectivity analysis. All these sentence level sentiment classifications can be summarized to get overall opinion about the product.

Entity and Aspect Level

Both document level and sentence level analysis analyzes only the opinion expressed in the document or sentence. They do not find out what exactly people liked or not liked. Aspect level analysis is fine grained analysis. It is also known as feature level analysis. In aspect-based sentiment analysis, the system takes set of reviews (e.g. online consumer reviews from social media) as input for particular entity (e.g. Laptop, Mobile, Camera). The main task of this system is to identify the main aspects of entity and to extract opinion words about the aspect and calculate sentiment polarity of the aspect (positive, negative or neutral).

There are mainly three approaches in sentiment analysis. In lexicon based approach, lexicon dictionary is used for identifying the polarity of the text. In machine learning based approach, either the model is trained using pre-labeled dataset of positive, negative, or neutral content. Or unsupervised learning is used for sentiment classification.

SENTIMENT ANALYSIS METHODS AND TECHNIQUES

In text analytics, data pre-processing is the first step before actual analysis starts. Semi-structured text has to be converted into structured format. Data has to cleaned and irrelevant data needs to be removed so as to provide focus over the useful data. For example, unrelated reviews can be filtered from the data set collection. Stop words, punctuations, stemming can be done to get rich content.

Text analytics is to distil out structured information from unstructured or semi-structured text. For example, text analytics applications reap movie reviews from various blogs and review statements, highlight the best and worst parts of the movie and suggest a movie that meets the users' expectations. General Web search gives the set of pages related to keyword search however it cannot analyze the contents of web pages. There are many challenging tasks like understanding the human language, interpreting positive or negative comments, identifying sarcasm or emotions and so on. Text analytics include two major steps:

1. Text extraction engine that takes input documents and label them with annotations
2. Business analytics engine that analyzes further to perform knowledge discovery, decision making, business improvement and so on

The process of sentiment analysis is explained in Figure 2.

Information Retrieval (IR) Techniques

Information Retrieval (IR) techniques like vector space modeling can be used for this conversion. The free text is thus modeled into structured format. Different IR techniques for feature selection and classification of various datasets like movie reviews, etc. has been surveyed by (Vinodhini, 2012). SentiTFIDF model was proposed by (Kranti Ghag, 2014) which finds the senti-stop-word by using the proportional frequency of the words and by comparing the distribution of words among positive and negative documents in a movie dataset. Improved TF-IDF method was proposed by (Mingyong Liu, 2012) for text categorization, and showed 62% and 67% accuracy for 20newsgroup dataset by using Naïve Bayes and SVM classifiers. (Justin Martineau, 2009) proposed a general-purpose technique called DeltaTF-IDF, which gives weight and scores to words before classification. The accuracy of the sentiment analysis is measured by Support Vector Machines.

TF-IDF stands for Term Frequency-Inverse Document Frequency, and the tf-idf weight is a weight often used in information retrieval and text mining. This weight is a statistical measure used to evaluate how important a word is to a document in a collection or corpus. The importance increases proportionally to the number of times a word appears in the document but is offset by the frequency of the word in the corpus.

Figure 2. Sentiment analysis framework

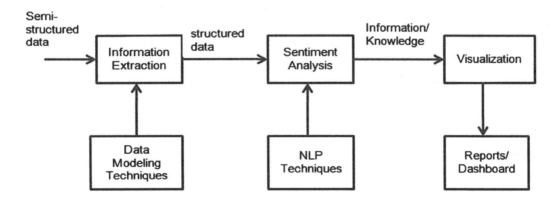

Latent Semantic Analysis (LSA)

LSA is a fully automatic mathematical or statistical technique for extracting and inferring relations of expected contextual usage of words in passages of discourse. It is not a traditional natural language processing or artificial intelligence program; it uses no humanly constructed dictionaries, knowledge bases, semantic networks, grammars, syntactic parsers, or morphologies, or the like, and takes as its input only raw text parsed into words defined as unique character strings and separated into meaningful passages or samples such as sentences or paragraphs. The first step is to represent the text as a matrix in which each row stands for a unique word and each column stands for a text passage or other context. Each cell contains the frequency with which the word of its row appears in the passage denoted by its column. Next, the cell entries are subject to a preliminary transformation, in which each cell frequency is weighted by a function that expresses both the word's importance in the particular passage and the degree to which the word type carries information in the domain of discourse in general. Next, LSA applies singular value decomposition (SVD) to the matrix. This is a form of factor analysis, or more properly the mathematical generalization of which factor analysis is a special case. In SVD, a rectangular matrix is decomposed into the product of three other matrices. One component matrix describes the original row entities as vectors of derived orthogonal factor values, another describes the original column entities in the same way, and the third is a diagonal matrix containing scaling values such that when the three components are matrix-multiplied, the original matrix is reconstructed.

Natural Language Processing (NLP) Techniques

Natural Language Processing (NLP) techniques have been applied to structured text. In this step, the sentences are tokenized using the PartOfSpeech (POS) tagger. During this process, a part of speech such as noun, verb, adverb, adjective, conjunctions, negations and the like are assigned to every word in the sentences. Bo Pang (2002) applied machine learning techniques for extracting subjective portions of document for sentiment classification. Arun Meena (2007) developed a framework for sentiment analysis for words or phrases in presence of conjuncts using word dependencies and dependency trees. Xiaowen Ding (2007) built Opinion Observer, a linguistic rule based system, which was able to detect the polarity of opinions context based and with the use of opinion aggregation function. Damien Poirier (2008) developed a model for opinion analysis on movie reviews using machine learning techniques and NLP techniques by building the dictionaries. There are many dictionaries available like General Inquirer (GI), Bing Liu's collection, and so on. The General Inquirer dictionary is further explained in next section. Table 1 shows PoS tagging of a simple sentence: "The camera is good but battery is poor".

Aspect Based Sentiment Analysis

There are three main approaches for aspect extraction:

- Frequent nouns and noun phrases
- Exploiting opinion and target relations
- Topic modeling

Table 1. PoS tagging of a sentence

Word	POS Tagger Label	Label Expansion	GI Mapped Category
The	*DT*	*Determiner*	
camera	*NN*	*Noun*	
is	*VBZ*	*Verb*	
good	*JJ*	*Adjective*	*Positiv, Pstv, Virtue, Eval, PosAff*
but	*CC*	*Coordinating conjunction*	*Conj Conj1*
battery	*NN*	*Noun*	
is	*VBZ*	*Verb*	
poor	*JJ*	*Adjective*	*Negativ, Ngtv, Week, Passive, Vice, NegAff*

Frequent Nouns and Noun Phrases

This method identifies the explicit expressions (ie., Noun and Noun phrases) from a set of reviews in a given domain. Noun and Noun phrases are identified by a PoS tagger and their frequency of occurrences is counted. More frequent terms are kept as aspects. This method is simple and effective. Popescu (2005) tried to remove non-aspects of entities. They used PMI measure to improve the precision of this method.

Using Opinion and Target Relations

Since opinions have targets, they are obliviously related. Their relationship can be exploited to extract aspects which are opinion targets because sentiment words are often known. Hu and Liu (2004) used this method for extracting infrequent aspects. In this method, the same sentiment word can be used to describe or modify different aspects.

Using Topic Model

Topic models represent a family of computer programs that extract *topics* from *texts*. A topic to the computer is a list of words that occur in statistically meaningful ways. A text can be an email, a blog post, a book chapter, a journal article, a diary entry – that is, any kind of unstructured text. Unstructured means that there are no computer-readable annotations that tell the computer the semantic meaning of the words in the text. The two main basic models, pLSA (Probabilistic Latent Semantic Analysis) and LDA (Latent Dirichlet allocation) can be used in features extraction from the text.

For example, consider the word "unpredictable", when it comes in movie review "The film is unpredictable", it becomes positive opinion. When it comes in software domain "Unpredictable program", it becomes negative opinion. In the first sentence, unpredictable is opinion word, the story is an implicit aspect. In the second sentence, unpredictable is opinion word, the program is an explicit aspect. Here the same word gives different polarity based on the context. More fine-grained aspect based approach needs to be used for context aware learning. Context-aware learning deals the problem of ambiguity by attempting to examine the opinion of the term in a given context.

Table 2. General inquirer category

GI Category	Details
Negative	Negative outlook
Hostile	Attitude or concern with hostility or aggressiveness
Pain	Suffering, lack of confidence, or commitment
Virtue	Assessment of moral approval or good fortune
Vice	Assessment of moral disapproval or misfortune
Negate	Reversal or negation including "dis", "in", and "un" words
NegAff	Denoting negative feelings and emotional rejection

Sentiment Dictionary

In general, the words like adjective, adverb or verb expresses the sentiment in the sentence. Based on the category determined by the General Inquirer (GI) for the sentimental word (positive, negative, strong, weak, pleasure, pain and feel), the senti-score is assigned for the word. Table 2 shows the sample categories of GI dictionary.

Using this categorization of dictionary, senti-score for each word is assigned. Simple positive adjective word is given the score +1, strong positive word is assigned the value +2, strong negative word is assigned the value -2 and so on. Consider an example with the words 'very good' or 'extremely good'. The senti-scores of these words 'very good' and 'extremely good' are assigned +2. Because, the word 'very' is categorized as "overst", 'good' as "positive" and 'extremely' as "strong" by General Inquirer. The category 'Overstated' indicates realms of speed, frequency, causality, size, etc by GI.

Analysis is done for conjuncts and negations used in the sentence by observing the position where they occur in the sentence or clause. The rules are applied and then senti-score is determined. For eg, 'not good' is assigned score -1, considering it as a negative word. Consider another example, "the roads are wide but they are not clean". PoS tagger identifies the presence of conjunct 'but'. The following rule is applied:

< conjunction = but >

< rule LC = positive, RC = negative, polarity = negative />

< rule LC = negative, RC = positive, polarity = positive />

< /conjunction >

This sentence may be assigned the score -1 due to the presence of conjunct 'but'. The blog writer expresses his feelings here.

There are many dictionaries like GI, LIWC, Wordnet, SentiWordNet available to determine the category of words. GI has more than 180 categories. Emotional and cognitive orientation words are categorized in a simple way. Based on the category of the word, different weights can be assigned along with the score, which improves the accuracy of sentiment classification.

SENTIMENT ANALYSIS AND BIG DATA

The development of Internet has strong influence in all types of industries like tourism, healthcare and any business. The availability of Internet has changed the way of accessing the information and sharing their experience among users. Social Networks sites contain huge and highly unstructured data like combination of text, smiley, images, videos and animations. Text from different sources is in various formats. This makes the extracting opinion from the user generated content more difficult.

Sentiment Analytics applications analyze feeds from social media data such as blogs, twitter, Facebook, etc. and help business get deep insights into how customer perceive their brand and products and what their competitors are doing to excite the market. This is achieved by extracting words from the messages posted in the social media that refer to positive or negative sentiments about a particular topic of interest. Sentiment analysis enables to recognize the use and impact of social media on different industries or Corporate by analyzing the users' feelings expressed in the form of free text, thereby gives the quality indicators of services or products related with them.

Textual analysis in social media applications has been providing a great esteemed level of sentiment analysis. The most admiring challenge for textual analysis most probably involves web visits, log data analysis, web server log for the client side validation. The following Figure 3 depicts the log analysis from server side data analysis.

SOCIAL SENTIMENT ANALYSIS: A BIG DATA PERSPECTIVE

Upon the leverage of sentiment analysis in a big data perspective various tools are available for extracting attitudes, emotions, and opinions. The metrics for defining the quality with big data includes feelings, opinions, re-tweets, replies, data conversation from time to time. With the usage of tools such as radian6, Google analytics the emotional and sentimental aspects from the big unstructured data can be extracted. The following are the data tools available for social sentiment analysis for big data.

Figure 3. Log file data analysis

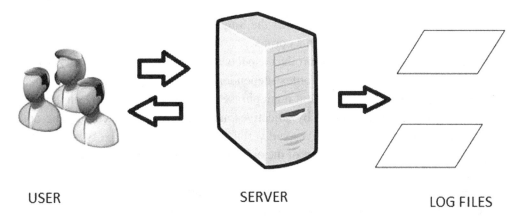

USER   SERVER   LOG FILES

- Hoot suite
- People browser
- Google analytics
- Tweetstats
- Page lever
- Social mention

In today's real world perspective sentiment analysis with an automated feature analysis has been used up for the better sentiment extraction. Moreover to rely upon proper data sentiment analysis tool such as synthesio, radian6 the lower level of accuracy level can be greatly estimated and defined in across manual sentiment experiments. Social networks refers to the set of nodes (users) connected by edges (relationship), with the intent of transformation of messages. Some of the examples of social media are:

- Data spread among illness with peoples.
- Users connected by web links.
- Transformation of messages among users.
- Transformation of messages among inters bank details.

In connectivity among social group of users the edges can be of weight based interaction, data exchange, emotional aspects. Hence sentiments, emotions among user interaction can be signified with interactions during specific periods. Social media networks among the group of users can be represented by means of sociograms.

CREATING SENTIMENT ANALYSIS MODELS

In the aspect based sentiment analysis, context dependent lexicon dictionary generation and aspect term polarity determination are considered as the main tasks. To build a context dependent sentiment lexicon dictionary, Latent Semantic Analysis (LSA) is applied on product reviews. The classification phase is carried out as follows: the opinion words related with the product aspect are drawn out using the dependency relations provided by Stanford Parser, then the polarity of the extracted words are combined to obtain overall aspect polarity. Latent Semantic Analysis is used to calculate the strength of the semantic association between words and classes. LSA uses the Singular Value Decomposition (SVD) to analyze the statistical relationships among words in a corpus.

Sentiment analysis model takes list of product aspects and opinion word associated with the aspect derived from the free text reviews. After context-dependent lexicon library generation, aspect-opinion pair is generated from reviews using frequent noun phrases and opinion exploiting method. The earlier studies show that opinions are expressed by adjectives and verbs in the sentences. The opinions are obtained by the extraction of those adjectives and verbs. The aspect opinion pairs are generated based on the opinion keywords. The nearest aspect of the opinion words are found and being analyzed to form the aspect-opinion pair.

Context aware learning deals the problem of ambiguity by attempting to examine the opinion of the term in a given context. After aspect opinion pair generation, the polarity of the opinion word is found using sentiment dictionary which contains positive, negative and neutral score for every opinion word. If the polarity of the opinion words is neutral, then those words are identified as a context terms or ambiguous term. The system collects context terms and stores them in a context dependent sentiment lexicon. The number of co-occurring context terms in positive and negative documents acts as an indicator for the ambiguous terms positive or negative charge. For example, consider the sentences - "long battery life with high picture quality" and "This program takes a long time to execute". In this example, "long", comes positive in the first sentence and used in camera domain and negative in the second sentence and used in the software domain. So the same word (long) has a different meaning in different domains. The word 'long' is context dependent word i.e. polarity of the word depends on the context. The co-occurrence of opinion and aspect is calculated by using TF-IDF. The polarity of the opinion word is retrieved from SentiWordnet and context-dependent lexicon dictionary. This score is used as prior sentiment score. Aspect classification and ranking is performed using LSA score and prior sentiment score.

UNSTRUCTURED BIG DATA IN SENTIMENT ANALYSIS

The term big data is coined by the words Velocity, Variety, Volume and Veracity. The available big data can be categorized into structured, unstructured and Semi-structured. A mixture of open source data projects are in progress with hadoop and big data environments. Most probably for sentiment analysis is Not only Structured Query Language (NoSQL) has been adopted for storage and retrieval of big data sets when compared to traditional data storage platforms. Various forms of NoSQL data models have been introduced such as MongoDB, Graph databases and so on. Moreover, schema less models are deployed in data model such as MongoDB in which both of the regular search and expression level searches for each of the sentences includes an particular value (Illku et al, 2015).

Large scale and real time analysis can be made for sentiment analysis using hadoop ecosystem tools. The entire system consists of a lexicon builder and a sentiment classifier which provides the capability of running large scale data using the map reduce framework. Hence it is possible to run more data in parallel when compared to traditional systems. Thereby with the map reduce framework it is possible to manage the data, its scalability, performance and data extraction.

In accordance with the data analysis models in sentiment analysis a specific sort of human intervention is required to analyze the historical patterns and tendencies. One specific fact is the structure of the sentiments which are more likely to be addressed, moreover traversing the structure of data is required in effective forms of sentiment analysis (Manisha Shinde-Pawar, 2015).

CASE STUDY

Online shopping sites like amazon, flipkart, snapdeal have to get review from consumer about the variety of services and products. Aspect based sentiment analysis and summarizing opinions from text about specific entities and their aspects can help consumers decide what to purchase and help business to monitor their reputation and understand the need of the market.

Five review dataset for different products like Canong3, Canon power shot, Noki6610, DVD, ipod are considered. Aspect term extraction methods have been evaluated mainly on customer reviews, often from the consumer electronics domain (Hu and Liu, 2004; Popescu and Etzioni, 2005; Ding et al., 2008).

Combined method of frequency based noun phrases and opinion exploiting is used to extract the aspects from the reviews and each sentence is manually annotated with aspect terms.

Table 3 shows the number of sentences of dataset and how many aspect term occurrences they contain. The third column ($n = 0$) shows that there are many sentences with no aspect terms. The fourth ($n=1$) and fifth ($n \geq 2$) columns show that most sentences contain exactly one aspect term occurrence.

Figure 4 explains sentiment classification for the aspect 'button' of the product DVD player. More negative words have been accumulated in the negative quadrant and very few words have been used in positive or very positive quadrants. It shows that this particular feature has some drawbacks felt by the consumers or users. Figure 5 shows the aspect ranking of the product DVD player. Among all the features, 'quality' of DVD player has secured better ranking. Aspect based sentiment classification with context awareness helps in aspect summarization too.

Table 3. Aspect term extraction from dataset

Dataset	Sentences containing n aspect term occurrences			
	Total number of Sentences	n=0	n=1	n ≥ 2
Cannong3	536	86	200	250
DVD	703	153	228	322
Nokia 6160	578	137	180	261
Ipod	799	13	368	418
Canon power shot	202	16	88	98

Figure 4. Aspect classification of DVD player

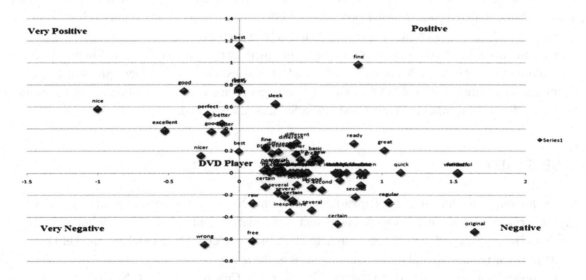

Figure 5. Aspect ranking for DVD player

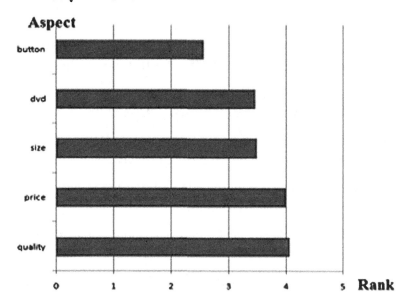

CONCLUSION

Aspect sentiment analysis has been done on various electronic products like DVD player based on consumer reviews. The study shows that the polarity of the ambiguous terms depends on the context. It means that the same word can act positive in one domain and negative in another domain. Normally those types of words are considered as neutral. The proposed methodology aspect based sentiment analysis for product reviews using context aware learning has improved the accuracy using LSA as LSA produces more relevant aspects. In future, the semantic web technologies can be used along with machine learning and natural language processing techniques to improve the context aware learning in sentiment analysis.

REFERENCES

Meena & Prabhakar, T.V. (2007). Sentence Level Sentiment Analysis in the Presence of Conjuncts Using Linguistic Analysis. *29th European Conference on Information Retrieval Research ECIR 2007*, (LNCS) (vol. 4425, pp. 573 – 580). Springer.

Liu, B. (2010). *Sentiment Analysis and Opinion Mining*. Morgan & Claypool Publishers.

Pang, B., Lee, L., & Vaithyanathan, S. (2002). Thumps up? Sentiment Classification using Machine Learning techniques. *Proceedings of Empirical Methods in Natural Language Processing EMNLP*, *10*, 79–86. doi:10.3115/1118693.1118704

Poirier, D., & C'ecile, B. (2008). Automating Opinion analysis in Film reviews: The case of statistic versus Linguistic approach. *Language Resources and Evaluation Conference*.

Hu, M., & Liu, B. (2004). Mining opinion features in customer reviews.*Proceedings of the 19th International Conference on Artificial Intelligence*, (pp. 755-760).

Jagadeesh Kumar, M. (2014). Expanding the boundaries of your research using social media: Stand-up and be counted. *IETE Technical Review*, *31*(4), 255–257. doi:10.1080/02564602.2014.944442

Martineau, J., & Finin, T. (2009). Delta TFIDF - an Improved Feature Space for Sentiment Analysis. *Third AAAI International Conference on Weblogs and Social Media.*

Ghag & Shah. (2014). SentiTFIDF – Sentiment Classification using Relative Term Frequency Inverse Document Frequency. *International Journal of Advanced Computer Science and Applications, 5*(2).

Liu & Yang. (2012). An improvement of TFIDF weighting in text categorization. International Proceedings of Computer Science and Information Technology, 47(9).

Popescu & Etzioni, O. (2005). Extracting product features and opinions from reviews.*Proceedings of the Conference on Human Language Technology and Empirical Methods in Natural Language Processing.*

Vinodhini & Chandrasekaran. (2012). Sentiment Analysis and Opinion Mining: A survey. *International Journal of Advanced Research in Computer Science and Software Engineering, 2*(6).

Ding & Liu. (2007). The Utility of Linguistic Rules in Opinion Mining.*Proceedings of the 30th Annual International ACM SIGIR Conference on Research and Development on Information Retrieval.*

Ha, Back, & Ahn. (2015). MapReduce Functions to Analyze Sentiment Information from Social Big Data. *International Journal of Distributed Sensor Networks.*

Shinde-Pawar. (2015). Formation of smart sentiment analysis technique for big data. *International Journal of Innovative Research in Computer and Communication Engineering.*

Chapter 10
Aspect–Based Sentiment Analysis of Online Product Reviews

Vinod Kumar Mishra
Bipin Tripathi Kumaon Institute of Technology, India

Himanshu Tiruwa
Bipin Tripathi Kumaon Institute of Technology, India

ABSTRACT

Sentiment analysis is a part of computational linguistics concerned with extracting sentiment and emotion from text. It is also considered as a task of natural language processing and data mining. Sentiment analysis mainly concentrate on identifying whether a given text is subjective or objective and if it is subjective, then whether it is negative, positive or neutral. This chapter provide an overview of aspect based sentiment analysis with current and future trend of research on aspect based sentiment analysis. This chapter also provide a aspect based sentiment analysis of online customer reviews of Nokia 6600. To perform aspect based classification we are using lexical approach on eclipse platform which classify the review as a positive, negative or neutral on the basis of features of product. The Sentiwordnet is used as a lexical resource to calculate the overall sentiment score of each sentence, pos tagger is used for part of speech tagging, frequency based method is used for extraction of the aspects/features and used negation handling for improving the accuracy of the system.

INTRODUCTION

Sentiment analysis is an area of text classification that starts in early of the last decade and has recently been receiving a lot of attention from the researchers and academicians. Sentiment analysis includes an analysis of data sets, such as online review, social media, blogs, and discussion groups, which contain opinions and opinion can be classify as positive, negative, or neutral. Opinion plays an important role in our information-collection behavior before taking a decision with applications in many fields, including recommender, customer intelligence, advertising systems and information retrieval.

DOI: 10.4018/978-1-5225-2031-3.ch010

Sentiment analysis can be also considered as the computational study of human opinions and sentiments, likes/dislikes, good\bad toward an entity such as products, services, organization, individual, issues, event, topics and their attributes. It is basically combination of natural language and data mining process that aims to extract user opinion and sentiment, expressed in positive, negative and neutral comments, by analyzing a large amount of unstructured user generated data. It is a task of automatically extracting the user opinion and sentiment from a plain text over the web. Sentiment analysis or opinion mining refers to the application of natural language processing, computational linguistics and text analysis to identify and extract subjective information from large amount of data.

Sentiment analysis also refers to identification and extraction of subjective information from text sources. It aims to determine the opinion of a person with respect to something in particular or the overall contextual polarity of a document. Sentiment analysis and its application in various disciplines; in information extraction, it is used to discard subjective information, in question-answering, it identifies opinion-oriented questions. Sentiment analysis is also used in the business intelligent and politics. Application areas of sentiment analysis are very vast and challenging. Sentiment analysis has focused on a great deal of attention as its very wide application in opinions detection, customer review summary, and other systems which is required to extract public opinions and sentiments. Some application areas of sentiment analysis are given in the next sub section.

APPLICATIONS OF SENTIMENT ANALYSIS

Sentiment occurs in almost all human activity because they describe the human behaviors. Whenever the human want to take a decision they want to know about others opinion. In real words, all business organization and all politicians want another opinion about their product and political condition even individual consumer also wants to know the opinion of the other user before purchasing any new product. In the past, whenever we want to take any decision we discuss it with our family member and friends for personel decisions and for taking any decision for an organizing we conducted the surveys. These traditional method are very time consuming and always does not give a good result.Application as a sub-component technology:Sentiment analysis plays an important role for enabling one technology for other system e.g. it cannot recommend those systems to be acquired with other if the systems contain more negative review. Detection of flame in the email and other type of communication is another use of sentiment classification. An online system, it helpful to take only the positive material in their system avoids all negative ads and content to be added to the online system and also helpful to the improve the online system and also helpful in the citation analysis, resulted increases the human computer interaction.

Application in Business and Government

Sentiment analysis is well suited in various intelligence applications. Business intelligence is one of the main application of sentiment analysis e.g. for any organization it is important to know what is the current position of their organization and for a businessman it is important to know the current position of their product and material in the market and due to the rapidly increase of web uses it is easy to analyze it with the help of user generated review and sentiment analysis is the best tool for it. Government intelligence is the another application in which we can analyze the user opinion on the new policy started by the government allowing the automatic analysis of the opinions that people submit about pending policy or government-regulation proposals.

In this chapter we provide an overview of aspect based sentiment analysis with current and future trend of research. We gave a prototype algorithm for aspect based sentiment analysis and for better understanding of the topic we provide an experimentation for the aspect based sentiment analysis in which we use sentiwordnet as a lexical resource to calculate the overall sentiment score of each sentence, pos tagger is used for part of speech tagging and frequency based method is used for extraction of the aspects/features. We also use negation handling for improving the accuracy of our system.

BACKGROUND

Now days the internet and web is used in every field of life. Due to the rise of internet and web its popularity among the peoples as a communication medium and business platform is increasing. People can very easily express their views on internet which generates very much amount of user data. Exponential growth of social networking has increased the amount of information generated over the internet on daily basis. The use of online shopping is also increasing as the vast amount of users is using internet to do shopping. The generated data of the views of customers is in unstructured form over the internet. The user generated content is the important source of extracting sentiment and opinions about the products. To extract the user opinion and sentiment from a large amount of data is very typical task. Many researchers have worked in this field of sentiment analysis in the last decade and still it's a very active research area. In last few years due to the rapid increase in the use of internet, plenty of work has been done in the field of sentiment analysis with special focus on aspect based sentiment analysis. Some important contributions are as follows:

- **Ghosh and Kar (2013)** has proposed a technique for sentence level sentiment classification of the online product review using the sentiwordnet a lexical resource. They semantically classify sentiment using rule based method and check the subjectivity and objectivity of an individual sentence and decided the semantic orientation using lexical resource.

- **Bhadane, et al. (2015)** gaves an overview of various type of method used for sentiment classification and techniques for measuring the opinions.

- **Varghese and Jayasree (2013)** has classified the unstructured user opinion text. They used sentiwordnet for classification, pos tagger for feature extraction, SVM classifier for quantitative classification and co reference resolution to resolve all the anaphora that appears in the opinion sentences. For the evaluation they checked the precision, recall and accuracy of a sentence and they achieved the 77.98% accuracy.

- **Chinsha and Shibily (2014)** have developed an aspect based opinion mining system for restaurant reviews, which automatically finds important aspects and opinions of a restaurant by analyzing the reviews. They used linguistic rule, sentiwordnet and two word phrases for sentiment detection with automatically extracted the aspect.

- **Singh, et al. (2013)** performed sentiment analysis using machine learning approach, unsupervised approach and two naive bayes approach and analytically showed that naive bayes approach gives better result in comparison to other two approaches. They also showed that semantic orientation approach achieved good result but it need to calculate lots of PMI values which is very time consuming while sentiwordnet approach achieved lowest accuracy but are easy to use and does not require any training data set.

- **Nithya and Maheswari (2014)** performed a sentiment analysis of unstructured reviews for polarity and subjectivity detection. They used naive bayes classifier for identifying the feature and check their polarity. For feature extraction they used the pos tagger and for finding the polarity of a sentence they used a SentiStrength a lexical based classifier.

- **Taylor, et al. (2014)** extended the work of Bing Liu's aspect-based opinion mining approach. Bing Liu's approach is mainly focused on the physical product. They purposed a new NLP based rule for aspect level sentiment analysis which helps users to digest the vast availability of opinions in an easy manner.

- **Suchdev, et al. (2014)** classified the sentiment of the tweets using machine learning techniques and to increase the accuracy they used the symbolic technique with machine learning. They also used knowledge based approach and using backtracking method to measured the slag word frequency count.

- **Abulaish, et al. (2009)** presented an opinion mining system to classify the opinion and product feature from reviews. They used the semantic and linguistic approach for classifying the feature and used the sentiwordnet for classifying the polarity. They refine the rule based method to achieve the good accuracy and generate the feature based summary.

- **Gautam and Yadav (2014)** proposed a set of machine learning techniques with semantic analysis for classifying product reviews based on twitter data. They classified a large amount of reviews by using twitter dataset which are already labeled. They used naïve byes technique to improve the accuracy over maximum entropy and SVM technique and shows that the accuracy has improved from 88.2% to 89.9%.

- **Jo and Oh (2011)** proposed two models to discover aspects and sentiment in reviews. There models assume that one sentence contains exactly one aspect, they split sentences not only by punctuations but also by conjunctions. They use a part of-speech tagger for more accurate negation detection to make each aspect clear, filter out words that are common across many senti-aspects by adding a background language model. They show that the senti-aspects found by aspect based sentiment unification model (ASUM) can be used to illustrate direct sentiments toward the same aspect, in the evaluation of sentiment classification.

MAIN FOCUS

Sentiment Analysis is basically process of identifying whether a given text is subjective or objective and if it is subjective, then classify whether it is negative, positive or neutral. Sentiment analysis is basically study in three levels: document level, sentence level and entity\aspect level. In document level we identify the whole document as a positive, negative or neutral, in sentence level we analyze a particular sentence as a positive, negative and neutral and in entity\aspect level, which is also known as feature level, we analyze the feature of a particular product or item. Aspects\features can be understood with an example of restaurant review in which we can extract the aspects like its food, service, location, charges etc which described whole restaurant easily. Aspect based opinion mining deals with the extraction of opinion aspects by applying various techniques. Aspects are either in hidden form in the text or itself appears in the text accordingly known as implicit and explicit aspects. Aspect level is very useful for taking fast decisions. In document and sentence level classification, each document/ sentence is classified as a single entity, a negative opinion document/sentence about an entity does not mean that the customer has negative opinions about all aspects of the entity. Likewise, a positive opinion document does not mean that the author is positive about everything. For effective and correct opinion about an entity, we need to classify the sentiment on the basis of different aspect of an entity.

Types of Opinions

The opinions can be categorizes as regular opinion and comparative opinion. A regular opinion is a simple opinion expressed in any document and it is mainly divided in two sub task namely direct opinion and indirect opinion. Direct opinion is expressed directly on an entity or entity aspect e.g. "the sound quality is great" describe directly the sound quality and give positive opinion. Indirect opinion is an opinion that is expressed indirectly on any product or document or aspect of product or document and based on its effects on some other entities e.g." after seeing the environment of restaurant my mood going worse" describe the bad environment of a restaurant which indirectly give the negative opinion. Most of the study focuses on direct opinion. Indirect opinion needs more analysis and complex task. Comparative opinion expresses a relation of similarities or differences between two or more entities and a preference of the opinion holder based on some shared aspects of the entities like nokia is better than micromax. Nokia is better shows two comparative opinions.

The opinions can be also classified on the basis of how they express in the text as explicit and implicit opinion. An explicit opinion is an opinionated statement that gives a regular or comparative opinion e.g. "nokia perform great" and "nokia is better than micromax". An implicit opinion is an objective statement that implies a regular or comparative opinion. Objective statement is the statements which cannot directly contain any opinion it only contain facts e.g. "The battery life of Nokia phones is longer than micromax phones".

Opinion and Target Relations

The opinions expressed in sentence have certain targets and they are clearly related to each other. Their relationships can be abused to find aspects, which are opinion targets, because opinion words are generally known for us e.g. "The battery is good". In this sentence the good is the opinion word and with the help of this it is easy to find an aspect of battery. This type of relation is also useful for finding the infrequent aspect. Several methods are used for better understanding of the relation between the opinion word and target e.g. dependency parsing and rule based method. The same opinion word can be used to classify or customize the different aspects. If a sentence does not have a frequent aspect but has some opinion words, the nearest noun/noun phrase to each opinion word is extracted. This method turns out to be very useful in practice even when it is applied alone. This is very useful relation in sentiment analysis because an aspect is rare to be important if nobody expresses any opinion or sentiment about it.

Aspect Level Classification

We can classify the sentiment at the aspect level, which we called aspect based sentiment analysis, it is also called feature based sentiment analysis. It covers both the entity and aspect to achieve the goal in aspect level; it discovers every quintuple in a given document. Aspect can be categories as an explicit aspect or implicit aspect. Explicit aspects are directly present in the document e.g. "the size of the phone is not good" it directly shows the feature of a particular domain. Explicit aspects are only noun and noun phrase. Implicit aspect are hidden aspect in the document e.g. "the phone is not fit in my pocket" this show the indirect aspect size and it indirectly shows the feature of a particular domain.

- **Aspect Extraction:** Aspect is basically the noun and noun phrase so first we use the pos tagger to extract all nouns and noun phrase then we apply different approach to extract the aspect. Some of these approaches are:
- **Frequency Based Approach:** In this approach to extract the aspect first we used a pos tagger to extract the noun and noun phrases and check their occurrence frequencies and only the frequent ones are kept. Frequent one can be decided on the basis of a threshold value of the frequency and frequency threshold can be decided experimentally. This method work well in the medium size corpus while in large size corpus they extract a large number of frequent noun and noun phrases as a product aspect which may be not a genuine aspect.
- **Propagation Approach:** In this method the opinion lexicon expansion and target extraction tasks iteratively based on propagation using the dependency relations between the opinion word and target (aspect/feature). In this process initially we require only seed opinion lexicon and using the seed opinion lexicon we extracted new opinion words and targets for further target and opinion word extraction. This method adopts a rule based strategy, it follow a dependency rules to extract the opinion words and targets (aspect/feature) The propagation ends until no more new opinion words or targets can be identified.
- **Aspect Ranking Based Approach:** In aspect rankling approach, we arrange all aspects in the decreasing order of their frequency of occurrence and take only highest frequent aspect. The basic idea for aspect ranking is that, those aspects which most frequently talked and consider in the review has higher importance in the analysis and subsequently considered as high ranking aspect. We can also maintain a list of opinion words which are generally used to modify a particular feature to compute feature relevance. Relevant features are generally modified by various opinion words.
- **Other Approaches:** In 2007 a language model for aspect extraction came into existence and in this model it is assumed that the important aspect are used more often in the review in the same year and it is used as a syntactic pattern learned via pattern mining to extract the aspect. In 2008 author used a supervised technique to extract the aspect they treated target extraction as a topic co reference resolution problem. The key of their approach is use of cluster opinions, sharing the same target together. Another approach to extract aspect is the use of topic modeling. Topic modeling is to model the generations of a document set and mine the implied topics in the documents.

Opinion Aspect Pruning

During the extraction some incorrect opinion target and word are extracted so opinion aspect pruning is remove the noise beside the genuine target and opinion word, this is not essential only desirable. Currently no effective method for pruning is available. There are two types of noise occuring during the aspect extraction, one is the ordinary nouns that are not targets but are extracted as targets due to parsing errors and second is names of other competing products on which the reviewers also expressed opinions. The problem of extraction of incorrect opinion target can be avoided by doing pruning based on clauses and pruning of other products and dealers. In pruning based on clauses method the sentence contains only one target unless there are any conjunction like "and" and "or". If the sentence does not contain any conjunction and contain two aspects then we remove one of them. Filter non-aspect based on frequency and which is less frequent are removed and in pruning of other products and dealers method is used when comparing one aspect of a review product with the other.

Popular Techniques/Approaches for Sentiment Analysis

Machine learning approach, lexical based approach and hybrid approach are most popular approach/ techniques for sentiment analysis.

Machine Learning Approach

This approach basically works on machine learning algorithm to classify the sentiment analysis and uses the syntactic and linguistic feature (Medhat et al., 2014). In this approach there is a set of training records and each record is defined by a class and the classification model is exhibit one of the class label. This approach can be further classified as supervised learning approach and unsupervised learning approach. Supervised learning approach depends on the existing training data set and in supervised learning we need a labeled training and test data set for classification. Test and training data are usually product review. The major disadvantages of supervised machine learning approach is use of large labeled data for training which is very time consuming as well as this is also very difficult to create this large amount of labeled data. Unsupervised learning approach does not use the labeled data set and obviously the collection of unlabelled data is easier in comparison to the labeled data.

Lexicon-Based Approach

Lexicon based approach used a lexical resource for the classification process. In this approach we use the opinion lexicons and they are the collection of positive and negative opinion word express in the document. These are also called opinion phrase and idioms and together are called opinion lexicon. This approach is further classified as manual approach or automatic approaches. Dictionary based and corpus based approach are widely used automatic approaches. In dictionary based approach first we manually select the small set of opinion words and then these word are search for its synonyms and antonyms from WordNet or other corpa and repeat the process until no new opinion word are found and last manually check the error. Disadvantage of this approach is the inability to find opinion words with domain and context specific orientations. Corpus-based approach depends on syntactic pattern in which one set of opinion word is used to find the other opinion word in the large corpus. It also overcomes with the problem of finding opinion words with context specific orientations.

Features for Sentiment Analysis

Feature selection is the very essential task for the sentiment analysis in data driven approach. To convert a sentence in a feature vector is very important step for sentiment analysis.

Term Presence and Term Frequency

Term frequency is very essential part in the text classification and information retrieval task. Term presence is more important than term frequency for a sentiment analysis task. For indicating the occurrence of word we used a binary-valued feature vector, 1 for occurring and value 0 for not occurring, but for numerous sentences it countered as we seen many more frequent occurring sentence contain less information than the rare occurring sentence or word.

Term Position

Word appearing elsewhere contain less sentiment and weightage than the word contain in certain position. This is similar than information retrieval. In the review, the word contains negative sentiment throughout but the presence of positive word at the starting of the review play a very important role for determines the sentiment. Thus the sentence appearing in the first and last in sentence has more weightage than it appear elsewhere.

N-Gram Features

N-grams are able to capture the context up to some degree and are mostly applied to natural language processing task. Generally N-gram are of three types 1-unigram 2-bigram 3-trigram. In the movie review unigram perform better than bigram but doing some changes bigram and trigram give better performance.

Part of Speech

In most of the NLP task, part of speech information is most commonly used. They provide a raw form of word sense disambiguation; this is the most important reason of using part of speech. Pos tagger will be used for part of speech and with the help of part of speech we can extract all noun, adjective and adverb from a text document. Adjective and adverb are basically the opinion word and noun and noun phrases are feature and aspect of given product review. There is a strong correlation between the adjective and subjective. It achieved an accuracy of around 82.8% in movie review domains using only adjectives in movie review domains.

Topic-Oriented Features

Phrases and bag-of-words are broadly used as features. But in different domain a specific phrase value carry a small relation with whole text sentiment. Analyze the text which feat those aspects and which represent whole text is a challenging task in the sentiment analysis. With the use of phrases and bag-of–word will cannot differentiate the locally and globally meant of text in review and all of which are used in affluence in many converse domain.

Prototype Algorithm for Aspect Based Sentiment Analysis

Input: Labeled Data Set
Output: Positive and negative polarity of a particular feature in the data set

Step 1: Pre-processing the review
- a. Remove unwanted text
- b. Remove stop words
- c. Stemming

Step 2: Find the feature \Aspects and opinion words
- a. Find noun, adjective, adverb and verb using pos tagger
- b. Noun\Noun phrases = Aspect\Feature
- c. Adjectives = opinion words

Step 3: Apply frequency based method for finding feature\aspect
- a. Check the frequency of noun in the review data set
- b. Take the most frequent noun as feature\aspect
- c. Ignore unfrequented nouns

Step 4: Check the polarity of the opinion word with respect to feature using sentiwordnet

Step 5: Match the words with review dataset
- a. If (positive polarity score > negative polarity score)
- b. Print ("the feature is positive")
- c. If (positive polarity score < negative polarity score)
- d. Print ("the feature is negative")

Step 6: Apply negation handling.
- a. Input – Negation word file which contain all negative words
- b. If (opinion word found in the sentence)
- c. If (opinion word is positive)
  - i. If (negation word found in the sentence)
  - ii. Print (polarity of a sentence should be negative)
  - iii. Else
  - iv. Print (polarity of a sentence should be positive)

End
- a. If (opinion word found in the sentence)
  - i. If (opinion word is negative)
  - ii. If (negation word found in the sentence)
  - iii. Print (polarity of a sentence should be positive)
  - iv. Else
  - v. Print (polarity of a sentence should be negative)

Detail Description of Terminology used in Algorithms

Review Sentence Tagging

A POS tagger parses a string of words and tags each word with its part of speech. The use of Stanford pos tagger for POS tagging is beneficial because of its good performance. It helps to tag the texts of the reviews without any need for training data. This tagger used by splitting text into sentences and to produce the part-of-speech tag for each word (whether the word is a noun, verb, adjective, etc) e.g. of pos tag sentence of the sentence ....this is really big step with quality of camera.... is..... this/DT is/ VBZ really/RB big/JJ step/NN with/IN quality/NN of/DT camera/NN.

Aspect Extraction

The process of aspect extraction is described in following steps:

Step 1: From all tag sentences by pos tagger we collect all nouns and find the unique noun among the nouns.

Step 2: Retrieved the entire frequent nouns and ignore the unfrequented nouns. Then set the threshold value for frequent nouns and extract all nouns as an aspect/feature which is above the threshold value.

Sentiment Classification using Sentiwordnet

As we know sentiwordnet is an open lexical resource for sentiment classification in which all the score of the opinion word are store in the positive and negative way in the synset term. Each score are from 0.0 to 1.0 and there sum is 1.0 for each synset. To calculate the score of each sentence with the help of these score we calculate the score of all sentences which consist an aspect term and finally combine the score and if the positive score is grater then negative score then we consider the polarity of a feature is positive otherwise negative.

Negation Handling

Negation handling is an important task in the sentiment analysis. Without the explicit use of any negative word, negation can be expressed in different ways. In the sentence "i do not like this move" the negation handling can be done by reverse the polarity of all words appearing after negative word which is 'do not' in this sentence but it cannot work in the sentences like "I do not like the movie but I like the action". Therefore for negation handling we need to consider also the scope of negation as well. So in this case the thing that can be done is to change polarity of all words appearing after a negation word till another negation word appears. But still there can be problems, for example, in the sentence "Not only did I like the acting, but also the direction", the polarity is not reversed after "not" due to the presence of "only". So this type of combinations of "not" with other words e.g. "only" has to be kept in mind while designing the algorithm.

Performance Measuring Parameters

The performance of aspect based sentiment analysis (Figure 1) can be measured as the precision, recall and accuracy which are defined as follows:

$$\text{Precision} = \frac{TP}{TP + FP} \tag{1}$$

$$\text{Recall} = \frac{TP}{TP + FN} \tag{2}$$

$$\text{Accuracy} = \frac{TP + TN}{TP + FN + FP + FN} \tag{3}$$

Where:

- TP is true positive. True positive means predict the sentence positive and it also really positive
- TN is true negative. True negative means predict the sentence negative and it also really negative
- FP is false positive. False positive means predict the sentence positive but it is not actually positive it is either negative or neutral
- FN is false negative. False negative means predict the sentence negative but it is not negative actually it is either positive or neutral.

Experimentation

We collected the reviews for the product (Mobile Nokia 6600) from the internet domain and we generated the data set from those reviews. Table 1 shows the data set for the product reviews of Nokia 6600. It contains number of total sentences from reviews and number of positive and negative sentences in the reviews. This is obtained after the process of finding the subjectivity of the sentences and splitting the sentence into positive and negative sentences.

We calculated the positive score, negative score and polarity of each aspect of products using sentiwordnet. The Table 2 shows the positive score, negative score and the polarity of the features.

Figure 1. Graphical representation of aspect based sentiment analysis

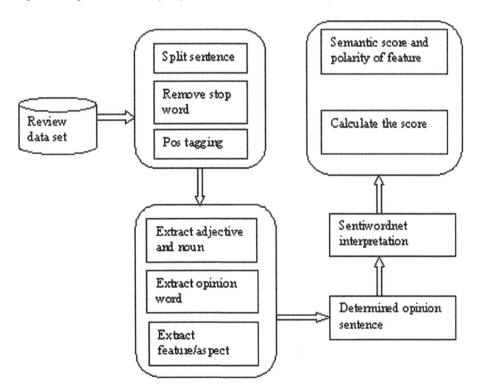

Table 1. Data set for Nokia 6600

Nokia 6600	Total Sentence	Positive Sentence	Negative Sentence
	546	250	118

Table 2. Scores and polarity of aspects/features

Aspect/Feature	Positive Score	Negative Score	Polarity
Battery	0.08	0.02	Positive
Feature	0.11	0.28	Negative
Nokia	0.12	0.18	Negative
Phone	0.02	0.05	Negative
Quality	0.00	0.00	Neutral
Radio	0.00	0.00	Neutral
Service	0.00	0.00	Neutral
Use	0.00	0.00	Neutral

From the Table 2 it is clear that the polarity of the product is negative on the basis of average scores of the aspects. To check the accuracy we calculate the precision and recall. For this task we firstly categorised the true positive, true negative, false positive and false negative from the review sentences then calculated the precision, recall and accuracy from the Equations 1, 2 and 3.

Table 3 shows the scores of the precision, recall and accuracy of the aspects.

Basic Requirement for Experimentation

This experimentation has done on eclipse or Netbean platform which have a development interface for java programs. We use a Stanford parsing tool for finding adjective and noun/noun phrase and an open lexical resource sentiwordnet for obtaining the positive or negative scores of all opinion words in the

Table 3. Precision, recall and accuracy of the aspects

Aspect/Feature	Precision	Recall	Accuracy
Battery	1.0000000	0.80000000	0.8000000
Feature	0.9736842	0.75510204	0.7400000
Nokia	0.9846154	0.76190480	0.7529412
Phone	0.9891892	0.72332020	0.7176471
Quality	0.9900498	0.73431736	0.7289377
Radio	0.9907407	0.74564460	0.7343174
Service	0.9911111	0.74581940	0.7408638
Use	0.9919028	0.72700300	0.7227139

Figure 2. Accuracy of aspects

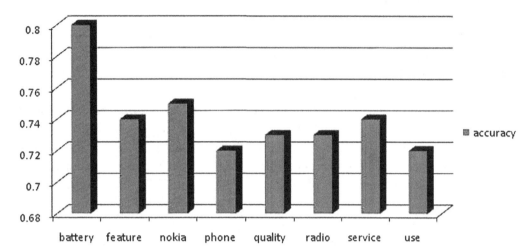

form of synset terms. We also use the list of all positive and negative words which is very useful for splitting the review data in the positive and negative reviews.

After calculating the accuracies of each aspect (Figure 2), we calculate the average accuracy for the product by applying the following formula:

$$\text{Average accuracy} = \frac{\sum_{n=1}^{n} score\,of\,Aspects}{total\,no\,of\,aspects} \tag{4}$$

The final accuracy of the aspects of the product Nokia 6600 is calculated as 74%.

FUTURE AND CURRENT TRENDS

Sentiment analysis is basically a classification task in three different levels: aspect level, document level, and sentence level. Sentiment analysis mainly concentrate on identifying whether a given text is subjective or objective and if it is subjective, then whether it is negative positive or neutral. Sentiment analysis is also considered as a subfield of computational linguistics concerned with extracting sentiment and emotion from text. The data set is the main issue in sentiment analysis and the main source of the data set is product review. Sentiment analysis is not important for only product, review it is also used in many other fields like the stock market, politics etc. The major challenges and scope for the researcher in the sentiment analysis are as follows.

Comparative Sentence Identification

Comparative sentence means where the comparison between two object is done e.g. "product a is better than product b" it completely change the polarity of a sentence. To clearly understand these comparative sentence, a well effective sequential information, modelling and structure are needed. Product review are mainly contain subjective information but comparative sentence contain both subjective and objective items. Thus to identify the comparative sentence is very difficult task because only few indicator will help to identify such sentence and those indicator also present in the sentence which are not comparative.

Leveraging Domain-Dependency

Almost all sentiment analysis and opinion mining research the domain dependency is an important issue. All approaches perform differently in different domain e.g. any approach can perform well in the product domain but may be not suitable for the politics feedback analysis. The one major and obvious reason is the difference in vocabularies across different domains. So designing the domain dependent model is also a very challenging task. Lots of work can be done in this field. In 2006 a reasearcher build a domain dependent classifier using a machine learning technique. In 2009 they build a query-specific subjective lexicon to improve the result but it also exploit some domain independent feature. Yang et al. (2006) propose a set of domain in dependent features and performed in the movie and product domain. There are several avenues open for the research in this field using the machine learning techniques that achieves good accuracy.

Association of Different Opinion

A document contains much opinionated information about many different topics in a single document. In this situation separation of opinionated information from factual information and look for opinion–topic associations in the documents need a very effective approach. To finding the association between the topic and corresponding opinion, various techniques can be used. Some of these techniques are: Natural language processing (NLP) techniques (like POSTagging and Syntactic Parsing) are used to identify opinion words and syntactic relation between the sentiment expression and subjective terms. Pos tagger is helpful to identify the opinion word as they identify all noun, adjective, verbs in the given piece of a document and the adjective is considered as a opinion word, Proximity-based techniques used to find the topic-association in textual document for example it say the proximity of the query terms to the opinionated sentences in the document helps to find that level of opinion–topic association necessary for opinion finding task. They just check the occurrence opinionated word around the query word.

Challenges in Natural Language Processing (NLP)

It is not forget that sentiment analysis is a NLP problem. It touches every aspect of NLP, e.g., negation handling, coreference resolution and word sense disambiguation, which combines more difficulties, since these are not solved problems in NLP. However, it is also useful to understand that sentiment analysis is a highly restricted NLP problem because the system does not need to fully understand the semantics of each sentence or document but only needs to understand some aspects of it, i.e., positive or negative sentiments and their target entities or topics. In this sense, sentiment analysis offers a great platform for NLP researchers to make tangible progresses on all fronts of NLP with the potential of making a huge practical impact.

Contextual Polarity of Words

An accurate polarity identification of a opinion word is still need a deep analysis. We cannot assign a polarity with respect to the prior polarity of a word. A polarity of a word is also affected by its surrounded word for example if the word "good" show the positive polarity the word "not good" it show the negative polarity because it contains a negation word. The new polarity define by its context is called contextual polarity the context can be defined by the negation or by other ways. In 2003, Yi et al. used a lexicon and manually developed high-quality patterns to classify contextual polarity. Popescu and Etzioni (2005) use a relaxation labelling of an unsupervised classification technique to recognize the contextual polarity of words. They use the bootstrapping approach to classify the polarity of tuples. Negations (only not) has also taken into account when identifying contextual polarities

CONCLUSION

In this chapter first we provide an overview of sentiment analysis with special emphasis on aspect based sentiment analysis. A prototype algorithm has introduced for aspect based sentiment analysis and a case study has carried out for better understanding of aspect based sentiment analysis. For the aspect based sentiment analysis we have used the sentiwordnet 3.0 and for implementation of proposed system we used java programming language on eclipse platform. For the simulation and analysis of the system we used mobile (Nokia-6600) review data. The pos tagger, which does not need of trained data, has been used to tag the sentences. To remove the stop word and unwanted data, we pre-process the data and not using stemming because it put the distortion in review data. We checked the subjectivity of the sentence using the list of positive and negative word and used frequency based method for aspect extraction in which we checked the frequency of noun which is considered as aspect and take most frequent noun as a product aspect. We used sentiwordnet for semantic analysis of data and calculate the final score for classifying the polarity of each aspect/feature in terms of positive and negative. By using these techniques we obtain a good result in terms of precision, recall and accuracy. These techniques are very easy to use with respect to supervised machine learning techniques because it cannot need any training and testing data. This technique is also taking less time for computation in large data set because it cannot need to train a data. This system extract only the explicit features therefore in order to upgrade the system in future, we plan to develop some extraction technique which also extract the implicit feature of a product. The other possible extension of this system is hybrid approach i.e. by combining the sentiwordnet lexical resource method with the supervised machine learning method to improve the accuracy of this system.

REFERENCES

Abulaish, M., Jahiruddin, Doja, N. M., & Ahmad, T. (2009). Feature and opinion mining for customer review summarization. In Pattern Recognition and Machine Intelligence (LNCS), (vol. 5909, pp. 219-224). Springer-Verlag Berlin Heidelberg.

Bhadane, C., Dalal, H., & Doshi, H. (2015). Sentiment analysis: Measuring opinions. *Procedia Computer Science, 45*, 808–814. doi:10.1016/j.procs.2015.03.159

Chinsha, T. C., & Shibily, J. (2014). Aspect based opinion mining from restaurant reviews. In *Proceedings of International Conference on Advanced Computing and Communication Techniques for High Performance Applications* (Vol. 1, pp. 1-4).

Gautam, G., & Yadav, D. (2014). Sentiment analysis of twitter data using machine learning approaches and semantic analysis. In *Proceedings of IEEE Seventh International Conference on Contemporary Computing* (pp. 437-442). doi:10.1109/IC3.2014.6897213

Ghosh, M., & Kar, A. (2013). Unsupervised linguistic approach for sentiment classification from online reviews using sentiwordnet 3.0. *International Journal of Engineering Research & Technology, 2*(9), 55–60.

Jo, Y., & Oh, A. H. (2011). Aspect and sentiment unification model for online review analysis. In *Proceedings of the fourth ACM international conference on Web search and data mining* (pp. 815-824). doi:10.1145/1935826.1935932

Medhat, W., Hassan, A., & Korashy, H. (2014). Sentiment analysis algorithms and applications: A survey. *Ain Shams Engineering Journal., 5*(4), 1093–1113. doi:10.1016/j.asej.2014.04.011

Nithya, R., & Maheswari, D. (2014). Sentiment analysis on unstructured review. In *Proceeding of IEEE International Conference on Intelligent Computing Applications* (pp.367-371).

Popescu, A.-M., & Etzioni, O. (n.d.). Extracting product features and opinions from reviews. In *Proceedings of Conference on Empirical Methods in Natural Language Processing* (pp. 339-346). doi:10.3115/1220575.1220618

Singh, V. K., Piryani, R., Uddin, A., & Waila, P. (2013). Sentiment analysis of textual reviews. In *Proceedings of IEEE 5th International Conference on Knowledge and Smart Technology* (pp. 122-127).

Suchdev, R., Kotkar, P., Ravindran, R., & Swamy, S. (2014). Twitter sentiment analysis using machine learning and knowledge-based approach. *International Journal of Computers and Applications, 103*(4), 36–40. doi:10.5120/18066-9006

Taylor, M. E., & Velásquez, J. D. (2014). A novel deterministic approach for aspect-based opinion mining in tourism products reviews. *Expert Systems with Applications, 41*(17), 7764–7775. doi:10.1016/j.eswa.2014.05.045

Varghese, R., & Jayasree, M. (2013). Aspect based sentiment analysis using support vector machine classifier. In *Proceedings of IEEE International Conference on Advances in Computing, Communications and Informatics* (pp.1581-1586). doi:10.1109/ICACCI.2013.6637416

Yang, H., Si, L., & Callan, J. (2006). Knowledge transfer and opinion detection in the TREC2006 blog track. In *Proceedings of TREC*.

Yi, J., Nasukawa, T., Bunescu, R., & Niblack, W. (2003). Sentiment analyzer: Extracting sentiments about a given topic using natural language processing techniques. In *Proceedings of IEEE International Conference on Data Mining* (pp. 427-434).

ADDITIONAL READING

Liu, B. (2012). *Sentiment analysis and opinion mining, Synthesis Lectures on Human Language Technologies*. Morgan and Claypool Publishers.

KEY TERMS AND DEFINITIONS

Bayesian Network (BN): Bayesian network iis the directed acyclic graph in which the nodes represent the random variable and the edge represent the conditional dependencies. it specified the joint probability distribution over all the variable.

Decision Tree Classifiers: In decision tree classifiers we provides the training data in the hierarchical form and for dividing the data we used the conditions on attributes and to perform the spilt we use the similarity based multi-attribute split.

Maximum Entropy Classifier: This classifier determine the most likely class for a document set it convert the labelled document set into a vector using encoding and with the help of encoded vector we calculate the weight of a document and combine to get the result.

Naive Bayes Classifier: It is a simple probability based classifier based on bayes theorem with strong independence assumption it compute the posterior probability of a class based on the distribution of the word in the document it ignore the position of the word in the document.

Neural Network (NN): Neural network is combination of neuron. Neural network is used for both classification and prediction. Neural network contain three layers for computation first is input layer second is hidden layer and last is output layer.

Rule-Based Classifiers: Rule based classifier is a sets of rule for classification and uses term absence and presence for the classification. In this classifier we define some criteria to generate the rule and theses rule are generates at the training time.

Support Vector Machine (SVM): It determine the linear separator by constructing hyperlanes that separates the cases that belong to different categories. Hyperlanes provide best separation between the class and it takes the maximum margin for separation because the normal distance between any data point is largest.

Chapter 11

Sentiment Analysis with Social Media Analytics, Methods, Process, and Applications

Karteek Ramalinga Ponnuru
BML Munjal University, India

Rashik Gupta
BML Munjal University, India

Shrawan Kumar Trivedi
BML Munjal University, India

ABSTRACT

Firms are turning their eye towards social media analytics to get to know what people are really talking about their firm or their product. With the huge amount of buzz being created online about anything and everything social media has become 'the' platform of the day to understand what public on a whole are talking about a particular product and the process of converting all the talking into valuable information is called Sentiment Analysis. Sentiment Analysis is a process of identifying and categorizing a piece of text into positive or negative so as to understand the sentiment of the users. This chapter would take the reader through basic sentiment classifiers like building word clouds, commonality clouds, dendrograms and comparison clouds to advanced algorithms like K Nearest Neighbour, Naïve Biased Algorithm and Support Vector Machine.

INTRODUCTION

Web 2.0 model lets the free flow of content, allowing the user to communicate with each other, expressing their ideas and opinions with each other on the platform of Internet, the classic example being Facebook. There are hundreds of communities/groups/pages online set up by the experts. These communities can include groups set up by physical training experts, cooking experts, and any other. They also have a huge following, where the followers follow the topics shared by the experts. Other examples include

DOI: 10.4018/978-1-5225-2031-3.ch011

the IMDB, where the critics share the review of the movie online. Twitter has been a great platform for people to share their opinions in limited words, these are called tweets. Right from celebrities to politicians everyone has been pretty active on twitter in terms of sharing their opinions and this makes twitter a great place to analyse sentiments.

Sentiment Analysis is basically analysing a piece of text and understand what that text really means for a company. We all have the habit of reading movie reviews before we actually go and watch a movie, movie reviews sometimes form the basis of our perception towards our attitude towards a movie. In this case, sentiment analysis can be used to understand if a user is having a positive inclination towards a movie or a negative on and accordingly the fate of the movie can be decided. Such is the power of Sentiment Analysis. This is why marketers are investing a lot in assessing the sentiment of the customers towards their products, and the results from these analyses can be used to make strategies for the further marketing plans.

As there are various mediums to express the sentiments of the users, there are also different ways in which the sentiments can be analysed. The basic technique involves text analytics to analyse the words on the basis of their occurrence, for now let us assume that the sentiment of the user is directly proportional to the number of good words or bad words used in a sentence. This will actually make the work of the analyst easy but there is a problem of ambiguity with this technique. Consider the following tweets posted online "Hillary is not good", "Hillary might not be a good candidate for President Elections", "Hillary is good", and so on. Now we can see that the word 'good' is the most frequent, which means that the overall sentiment of the people must be positive towards Hillary (according to the technique), but it is not actually so. As we can see the first tweet is negative, second tweet is neutral and the third tweet is positive, making the overall sentiment neutral. Hence the problem of ambiguity occurs, because the technique works on the frequency of words, and does not consider other factors. To resolve this, there are advanced algorithms for classification, which work on different criteria, hence making the overall task of classification more efficient.

This chapter covers two basic applications of Social Media Analytics, the first being using Text Analytics to determine the sentiments of the people of US for the presidential elections between Trump and Hillary. The second application is a part of advanced analytics, i.e. by using the advanced algorithms like k-nearest neighbour, Support Vector Machine, Naïve Bayes to classify the sentiments of the students towards the services provided in the education Institution into positive, negative and neutral, and then using the best classification method to build a model using logistic Regression.

APPLICATION 1: SENTIMENT ANALYSIS OF US CITIZENS FOR PRESIDENTIAL ELECTIONS USING TEXT ANALYTICS IN R

Model and Analysis

Performing sentiment analysis on Twitter is not as complicated. The whole process can be divided into the following phases in Figure 1.

The above illustration (Figure 1) helps in understanding how we can perform a simple sentiment analysis on Twitter with the help of R programming language. Firstly, the user who would like to perform sentiment analysis would have to create access token and id on twitter. There is a lot of information online on how to create an API key and Id on Twitter. The reader is advised to read the same and

Figure 1. Performing a simple sentiment analysis on Twitter

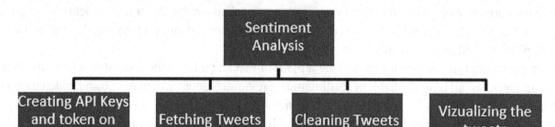

get familiarized on the same. The next step is to fetch tweets into our R consol. Remember that we are working on real time data. R has a specialized package to retrieve real time tweets called twitteR. The reader can use this package to retrieve tweets being tweeted using a particular hashtag. The function searchTwitter can be used. Remember that we are looking for tweets specially on Donald Trump and Hillary Clinton and are using #Trump for Donald Trump and #HillaryClinton for Hillary Clinton. Let us assume we would want to retrieve 1000 tweets in English language (H Wang, 2012). So, the code for searching the tweets for Hillary Clinton would be

searchTwitter("#HillaryClinton", n=1000, lang="en")

The function returns us with 1000 tweets each for both the hashtags we have put into use. Therefore, now we have all the tweets with us the next step which comes in the series of our sentiment analysis is cleaning these tweets. We would be required first to convert all the tweets to lower case, we can use the function *tolower* for the same. After converting them into the lowercase, the next step is to remove all the punctuation marks the function *removePunctuation* in the *tm* package can be used for the same. Removing the stop words would be the next thing to do, remember that we would be required to specify the stopwords on a beforehand for the same.

Once we have removed all the stopwords, punctuation marks and converted all the text into lower case, we would now prepare a wordcloud out of the text we have gathered. R has a package named *wordcloud* for the same. We can use the function *wordcloud* for preparing a wordcloud out of our data. We would then go ahead preparing a dendrogram. A dendrogram is a tree like structure showing relationships of words. In our case it would show us how the most frequently used word has been formed.

We would then proceed by creating a comparison word cloud. A comparison word cloud is one which compares frequently used words of two or more entities by displaying them side by side. For creating a comparison word cloud on R, the function *comparison.cloud()* can be used. We are sure that there some words which people tweet for both Hillary Clinton and Trump and for the same we can use a function called commonality word cloud. A commonality word cloud is one which is generally used to display the common words used by Twitter users for both Trump and Hillary. The function to prepare a commonality word cloud is *commonality.cloud()*

Analysis

Once, we run the code on R we get a series of images of wordclouds, dendrograms, commonality and comparison word clouds (W Cui, 2010).

The Figure 2 is a word cloud for Hillary Clinton. One might be surprised by the names likes Donald and Trump, it clear that once a candidate is standing in the presidential election he or she would be compared to their peers and so it is in this case as well. Hillary Clinton is being compared to Donald Trump on a level, other words like president, election, women etc can also be seen in this word cloud.

The Figure 3 is the word cloud of Donald Trump, one can see words like Thank, will, crooked, great, make America great again, sanders associated with Trump. But, can we actually figure anything out of these word clouds. To some extent we can understand the people's feelings towards these two candidates but on a whole it is very difficult to assess the sentiments.

The Figure 4 is an illustration of how different words have been associated together to form the word of Hillary Clinton. Words like specific, reference, grave, Regan have been associated together. These words have been clustered using hierarchical clustering using Ward's method by calculating the Euclidean distance.

The Figure 5 is a commonality word cloud. As explained earlier this cloud is used to find out the common words which were used for both Trump and Hillary. We can see words like people, Hillary, trump seem to be tweeted the most. This is for sure that when people tweet against the names, these

Figure 2. Word cloud for Hillary Clinton

Figure 3. Word cloud for Donald Trump

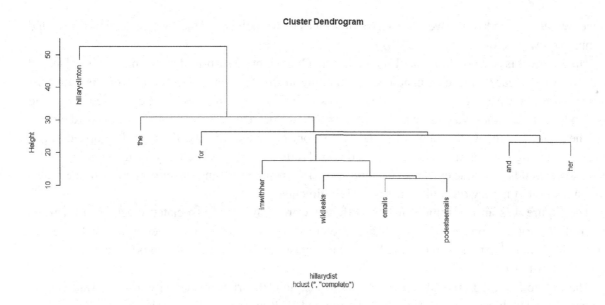

Figure 4. Dendrogram from the words of Hillary Clinton

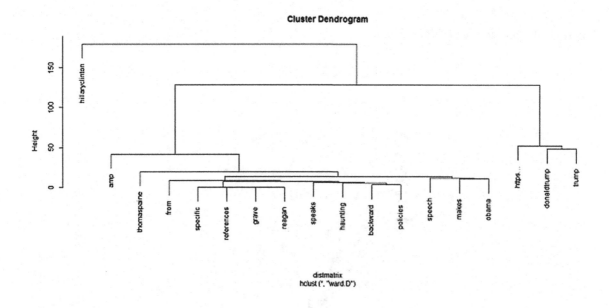

would surely appear. We can also see words like ISIS, election, war, chance, president, support etc are also seen in the commonality word cloud (F Heirmerl, 2014).

The best way to assess the sentiment of the US voters towards Trump and Hillary (Figure 6) is through using a comparison word cloud. In a comparison word cloud we can see the most frequently used words against the two candidates. Words like Crooked, Worse, Great, Make America Great Again, worst etc. have been used to classify Trump while words like Economy, Trump, Women, Tax, Campaign etc. were used to describe Hillary.

Figure 5. Commonality word cloud

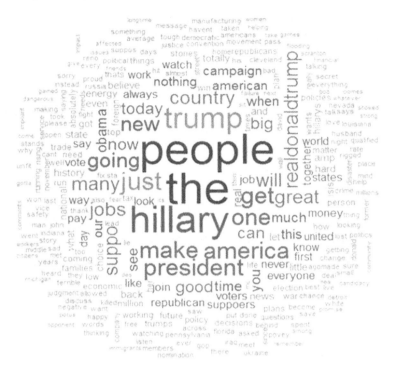

Figure 6. Word cloud US voters towards Trump and Hillary

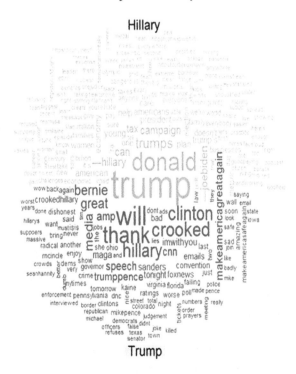

APPLICATION 2: ADVANCED ANALYTICS FOR SENTIMENT ANALYSIS TO ACCESS THE SATISFACTION OF STUDENTS FOR SERVICES PROVIDED IN THEIR CAMPUS USING R

None of the system is perfect, so is the Institution, which is the part of our research. Even with the best try, there are certain areas in which the gap is left. This gap is larger when the system is new. It is observed that when the system is in its Initial phase, there are certain areas in which it is left behind in providing the satisfactory services. Due to this difference, the students face certain challenges. Hence the topic of our Research is a recently established Educational Institution, which is accommodating the students across the Nation, imparting them with the work class Education facility. However being located in remote area, it has been facing challenges in meeting certain needs of the students. As per the students, there are numerous problems, like network problem, connectivity problem, and access to any near/far place is the biggest challenge. The campus has been doing hard in terms of meeting the needs of the customers by having tie-ups with various Vendors, but still some of dis-satisfaction pertains among students. This dis-satisfaction is a problem and needs to be captured for improvement. In the research this has been done through collection of reviews using free text, which in other terms would mean the sentiments of the students, towards the services offered by the campus administration. The effectiveness of the administration has been measured across six different parameters, namely

- Quality of Drinking Water
- Quality of Education
- Variety of Eateries
- Ease of Commuting
- Ease access to grocery sites
- The Quality of food offered

The sentiments were captured by asking the students to express themselves on the questions based on the above variables. Since the data collected has been in the form of free text, it is necessary to classify the data into positive and negative using classification algorithms, which include k-nearest neighbour, support vector machines, decision trees, and naïve bayes algorithm. The basis of each of the algorithm is different, hence the efficiency output would also be different. A brief on these algorithms is as follows.

K-Nearest Neighbor

k-nn or k-Nearest Neighbour is a simple classification technique (Figure 7), which is the used to classify on the basis of nearness. It is a supervised learning technique, which means the model is trained by using both outputs and inputs i.e. the inputs learn or train from the outputs.

In k-Nearest neighbour, the data collected is plotted on a 2 dimensional axis plot. Say the Class A data sets are placed using circles and the data sets of Class B are represented using crosses. Once the data sets are plotted, a model has been built.

This works on the principle that the test data is plotted in the same plot, and using k value its class is determined. The value of k is determined using the experience.

As we can see from the graph above, the k value is considered as 4 i.e. determination of the class depending on the 4 nearest neighbours. K – Nearest Neighbour is the simplest of the technique, but is

Figure 7. Process of Knn

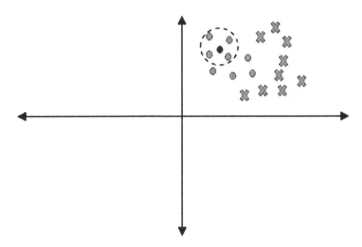

the not the most efficient in terms of classification, in that it lags in giving an accurate classification when the data is placed in the complex way, and determining the value of k for a particular project is difficult enough (G. Vinodhini, 2012).

Support Vector Machine

Support Vector Machine is the latest technique which is used for text classification. It works on the same principles of Neural Networks. However it is a supervised learning methodology. In Support Vector Machines, the complex data is converted into a higher dimensional image and the kernel function is used to classify the complexly placed data sets.

Here a hyper plane passes between the different classes of data sets. This hyper plane is generally in higher dimension, giving a more accurate classification. Using kernel function the Hyper plane is formed. The kernel function can be built in a variety of ways. In our case, we have used Poly kernel function, which means that the Hyperplane separating the data is built using Polynomial functions.

The function Support Vector Machine is immune to issues faced by noise addition and other changes. Also is associated the kernel gradient which is further used for the support in the classification. In SVM, only 2 classes are considered. This method works very accurate on smaller data sets and the problems of categorizing the text is also linearly separable (T Mullen, 2004).

Naïve Bayes Algorithm

Naïve Bayes algorithm is an advanced version of the Bayes algorithm. It is also categorized an unsupervised learning algorithm. The difference between the Bayes and Naïve Bayes algorithm is that, one is applicable for the quantitative data, while other is applicable for the qualitative data. This is a normal algorithm, in which the probability is assigned to the text words represented in the Document- Term Matrix. Depending on the probability of word being high for either positive, or negative, or neutral, the probability of the whole tweet is calculated.

Here in the algorithm, we use the concept of conditional probability:

$$P\left(A \mid B\right) = \frac{P(B \mid A)P(A)}{P(B)}$$

Here,

A = Class i.e. positive, negative or neutral

B = Tweets

Hence,

$$P(Pos\,or\,Neg \mid Tweets) = \frac{P(Tweet \mid Pos\,or\,Neg)P(Pos\,or\,Neg)}{P(Tweet)}$$

Now consider the above situation, where we know the probability of tweet if constant, and the probability of being positive, or negative, or neutral is 1/3 i.e. 0.33 or 33.34%. Also since it is a supervised learning method, hence we can also calculate the value oat the Probability of Tweet given the probability of class. Hence the overall equation comes out to be:

$$P(Pos\,or\,Neg) = P(Tweet \mid Pos\,or\,Neg)P(Pos\,or\,Neg)\,(\text{A Go,} \qquad\qquad 2009)$$

Decision Trees

Decision Trees is a very basic technique which is used for classification. This technique is used vastly in the field of marketing to segment the customers while targeting, and in Finance field to determine the fraud customers out of the total.

The Overall classification is done on the basis of Entropy Calculation and the Information Gain from each node and child node. The splitting criteria is so followed that the Entropy value calculated from by splitting on the basis of particular attribute should give the maximum entropy value and the information gain between the nodes and the sub nodes should be the maximum. The entropy calculation is done by the following algorithm:

$$Entropy = p_A \log p_A - p_B \log p_B$$

Here, pA and pb is the probability of being in A class or B class.

The Information Gain is the difference between Entropy before the split and the entropy after the split. This should give the maximum value in order to go for further splitting. If the value is less, then pruning is done to stop the splitting at that particular point (L Jia, 2009).

The overall objective of this study has been to collect the data, and then using various classification techniques to classify the data into positive and negative. Finally by using the data a model has been built with the help of Logistic Regression.

MODEL AND ANALYSIS

The overall process had been to capture the sentiments of the students across six different, and by applying the classification algorithm, classifying the data into positive and negative. Once the data is classified, model is built using Logistic Regression model. The model built would be in the form:

$$OverallSatisfaction = Coefficient + p_1\ Education +$$
$$p_2\ Food + p_3\ Water + p_4\ Eateries + p_5\ Commuting$$

where $p_1, p_2, p_3, p_{4,}$ and p_5 would be the estimated coefficients which would be determined after building the model.

Since the data which is collected is highly unstructured, in order to apply the basic classification algorithms on that data, the data needs to be converted into structured form. By building the Corpus and then building the TermDocumentMatrix out of it leads to the conversion of the categorical data into mathematical form, and hence algorithms can be easily implemented on the data for further classification. Below are the steps which are included in the Text Mining.

Text Mining

This unstructured data would contain a huge number of outliers, numbers, alphanumeric keywords, and various other words which might not be required during our analysis. Hence it is better to remove them before making any analysis. This will increase the efficiency of our analysis.

- **Corpus Building:** Since the data is available in the text files, in order to use the data in R, the following data needs to be converted in a format which is readable by R. For this, we have corpus, which compiles all the files in the same format i.e. a Corpus of documents, on which text mining can be applied.
- **Text Cleaning:** The text consists of various words, alphabets which are not required, and can create problem at the time of analysis, giving wrong outputs. Hence it is better to remove them by
  - RemoveStopWords(): For removing the frequently occurring words like "the", "a", etc. which do not play any role in the analysis.
  - RemoveNumbers(): The numeric figures are removed using this function.
  - RemoveAlphaNumeric(): All the alphanumeric words are removed using this function.
  - RemoveStemmedWords(): There are words like "go", "goes", "going" which in literal terms means the same. Hence this function removes the extra stemming in the words and bring them to the common root word like "go".

Once this is done, the data is free of unrequired text.

- **Sparsity Removal:** Now there are words which are found in one or two files out of thousand files. As most of the files are empty at that point, these generate empty spaces called as sparsity. These can be removed before making an analysis.

- **Document Term Matrix:** This step converts the categorical data into mathematical form. This is a two dimensional matrix, in which the columns represent the Terms and the rows represent the Documents. Hence if a Term1 is appearing in Doc 1 and Doc 3 only, the corresponding cell on the intersection of the two would be noted as 1, or else it would be 0.

The document term Matrix is a very important method, as it would be used as the input to almost all the functions for further analysis or classification. The documentTermMatrix may look like as follows, where the rows are represented by the terms, and columns is represented by Document (see Figure 8).

Now before going into detailed analysis of the data, a visual inspection to have an overview of the data can be done. This can be done by using wordcloud and Clustering Analysis. Wordcloud would determine the occurrence of a particular word, and cluster plot would tell which word is more related to which word. This is explained as follows.

Word Cloud

Word Cloud is the combination of words which appear in different color and sizes depicting the frequency of occurrence of each word. This means that the word appearing the biggest is the most frequently used one, followed by the next smaller word. This is nothing more than a visual analysis for the text data. It is a very good technique, as there is no need to go deep in depth of the document, and rather word cloud gives us a significant output which ca be accessed for further computation.

Food Quality

From the word Cloud, it can be seen that the most repeating word which has appeared is the word "Good" and Bad is used a little less frequent than the former one. This clearly states that the students are satisfied with the Quality of Food being offered in the campus. Going through the report, it is seen that with the introduction of a new vendor, the overall satisfaction has increased and the number of complaints has decreased, and this can be clearly seen in the wordcloud. Hence this makes it easy for analysis (see Figure 9).

Figure 8. Term to document matrix

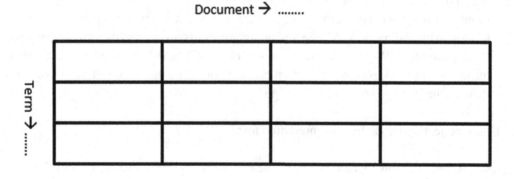

Figure 9. Word cloud for quality of food

Access to Eateries

The campus is in a far remote area, where it is really difficult to have an access to nearby eating hub spot. This makes the life of the students challenging who are always looking to explore something. But still students are capable enough to solve their problems on their own. If they do not get anything good to eat at one place, they manage to get it from anyother place. Hence we received an overall Good rating for this (see Figure 10).

Figure 10. Word cloud for access to eateries

Education Quality

As per the records, all the faculty which is coming in the campus is renowned faculty of big management institutions like IIM, MDI, and some of them are at eminent positions in big Multi National Corporations. And all the students are highly satisfied with the quality of education imparted in the college. The wordcloud shows us an overall rating of Good (see Figure 11).

Commuting Service

The campus is located in the remote location, from where it is very difficult to commute to any metropolitan city. The only way to commute to any hubspot location is either through Auto, Private Bus, or cab. But still there are problems, as traffic may be a major problem, and the cost factor which is related with the cab may be another prospect leading to dis-satisfaction (see Figure 12).

Figure 11. Word cloud for education quality

Figure 12. Word cloud for commuting service

Water Quality

There had been a number of complaints in the past one year regarding the quality of the water in the campus. Many complaints have been recorded in the past year for which the main cause was the poor water quality. Students not only face stomach related problems, but also throat related infections. As can be seen from the word cloud that the Bad appears in the biggest form. This might mean that there is an urgent need to replace some of the RO facilities inside the campus (see Figure 13).

The technique used above was just a visual analysis of the data collected. However to have a better and detailed analysis, classification techniques needs to applied to classify the data into different categories and hence build a model on it. The next section is Algorithm Selection. Since we have applied more than 1 algorithms, and each algorithm gives different efficiency, hence the best algorithm is selected and the data from this algorithm is fed to Regression for model building.

ALGORITHM SELECTION

The best method to calculate the efficiency of any classification technique is the Confusion Matrix. The Confusion Matrix (Table 1) is the matrix which the Total Number of Positive and Negative Tweets actual and predicted values are depicted. These are as shown in the table below.

Hence a maximum value of True Positive and True negative is expected for an efficient output.

The Table 2 shows the Confusion Matrix using all the 4 algorithms in all the cases. The value is in the range of {0,1}, which means that minimum could be 0 and maximum could be 1. From the Table 2, it can be seen that all the values satisfy this criteria.

Figure 13. Word cloud for water quality

Table 1. Confusion matrix

	0(Positive)	1(Negative)
0(positive)	True Positive	False Positive
1(negative)	False Negative	True Negative

Table 2. Machine learning classifiers comparison

Services/ ML Classifiers	SVM	K-nn	Naïve Bayes	Decision Tree
Food	.8712	.5677	.5847	.3314
Water	.7833	.6121	.3412	.5755
Eatery	.7144	.4188	.6256	.5174
Grocery	.5321	.3678	.2755	.4916
Commuting	.6812	.7413	.4645	.5617

Now, as we can see that the Confusion Matrix output for SVM i.e. Support Vector Machine is much-much better than the rest of the techniques. Hence it is preferred to select SVM as the base technique which would be used for classification of the test data. This means that the training model built using SVM would be used for further cases.

MODEL BUILDING

Once all the tweets are classified into positive and negative, Multiple Regression has been applied to the output to build a model identifying the degree of impact. To do this, the tweets with positive class are categorize as 1 and the tweets with negative class are categorized as 0.

Positive → 1, and Negative → 0

Hence, we have Independent variable with the categorical data of 0 or 1 and the dependent variable with continuous data from 1-10. A multiple Regression is applied on the above collected data and a strong model is built as follows:

$$Overall\ Satisfaction = 2.3 + 0.9\ Education + 0.04\ Food - 1.3\ Water - 0.051\ Eateries + 0.14\ Commuting$$

The output of the above Regression Equation can be seen in Table 3:

- R value tells us the coefficient of correlation which means the strength and the direction of the relationship between the dependent and the independent variables. It can vary from -1 t o+1, where something less than 0 would signify the negative correlation i.e. with the increase in one the other will increase and vice versa, and something more than 0 is positive correlation.
- R square defines the goodness fit of the model. i.e. If the model is good enough to explain the output. It can be seen from the above table that the model is 56% good fit.

Table 3. Output of regression equation

R Value	R Square Value	Adjusted R Square
0.75	0.56	0.52

- Adjusted R Square tells us if any additional variable is required to increase the explanatory power of the model. The difference between R Square and Adjusted R Square should not be more than 0.05 i.e. 5%. From the above output, it can be seen that the difference between R Square and Adjusted R Square is not more than 0.05, hence no additional variable Is required.
- The overall data is a little bit right skewed and the value of R-Square comes out to be a little less significant. The major reason behind the issue is the sample size. In order to mitigate these, the sample size needs to be increased.

Figure 14 is the model for Satisfaction of Students towards the services provided in the University (Name have not been shown for reason). The overall satisfaction lies on these five pillars, i.e. the Food, Education, Water, Commuting, and Variety if Eateries. Hence if any improvement is required, the management should first focus on improving these.

CONCLUSION

Two different applications of Sentiment Analysis have been discussed here. We can conclude the chapter with the help of both applications

Conclusion from First Application

Text Classification is one of the hardest things in the world because, every word comes with a context and it is that context which actually makes up the sentiment of the word. The same is in the case of Hillary and Trump. To understand what is the sentiment of the voters in the US towards Trump and Hillary polarity analysis can be done. As, of now we can see that the voters are a bit negative towards Trump and are neutral towards Hillary. No matter what the US elections have indeed become worth going through.

Figure 14. Conceptual model of application 2

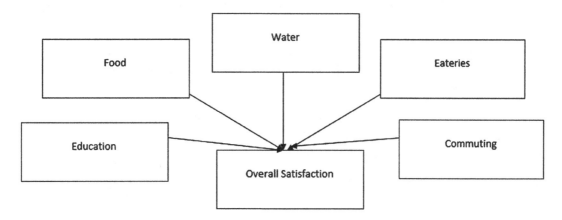

Conclusion from Second Application

The data collected from the respondents also comprised which zone in India they belong. The main reason for collection of this data was that, since the college is in the Northern Zone, and the students' strength is equally represented by all the zones. Hence it would be easier to find out which zone students are facing the challenges to adapt to the new environment. From the output, it was found that the 80% of students from South Zone unsatisfied with food. There could be a variety of reasons, like the taste of the food might not be that good, or they do not prepare appropriate South Indian food. Students in the age group 18-23 have most of the problems with food and other amenities. The selected campus is in the remote location and to have an access to the nearest facility for anything is very difficult. To suffice the needs there is a student Bazaar available in the campus, but the variety of items is too less. However the students are able to adjust with this. This means that the regression output showed that the Grocery variable was insignificant. Many students in the past year have been ill because of the quality of water. This can be easily seen from the degree of dissatisfaction with the Water and Commuting services. Hence it should the foremost priority of the management to resolve the water problem. It is interesting to the note that despite many complaints for the quality and taste of the food, the overall result comes out to be satisfactory. The reason could be that the sample is collected at the time when a new food Vendor came to the college and the students who responded to the survey majorly go to new food shop. Hence are more satisfied with the food. SOM rated education quality good

REFERENCES

Cui, W., Wu, Y., Liu, S., Wei, F., Zhou, M. X., & Qu, H. (2010, March). Context preserving dynamic word cloud visualization. In *2010 IEEE Pacific Visualization Symposium* (PacificVis) (pp. 121-128). IEEE.

Go, A., Bhayani, R., & Huang, L. (2009). Twitter sentiment classification using distant supervision. CS224N Project Report, Stanford, 1, 12.

Heimerl, F., Lohmann, S., Lange, S., & Ertl, T. (2014, January). Word cloud explorer: Text analytics based on word clouds. In *2014 47th Hawaii International Conference on System Sciences* (pp. 1833-1842). IEEE.

Jia, L., Yu, C., & Meng, W. (2009, November). The effect of negation on sentiment analysis and retrieval effectiveness. In *Proceedings of the 18th ACM conference on Information and knowledge management* (pp. 1827-1830). ACM. doi:10.1145/1645953.1646241

Mullen, T., & Collier, N. (2004, July). Sentiment Analysis using Support Vector Machines with Diverse Information Sources. In EMNLP (Vol. 4, pp. 412-418).

Vinodhini, G., & Chandrasekaran, R. M. (2012). Sentiment analysis and opinion mining: A survey. *International Journal (Toronto, Ont.)*, 2(6).

Wang, H., Can, D., Kazemzadeh, A., Bar, F., & Narayanan, S. (2012, July). A system for real-time twitter sentiment analysis of 2012 US presidential election cycle. In Proceedings of the ACL 2012 System *Demonstrations* (pp. 115-120). Association for Computational Linguistics.

Chapter 12
Organizational Issue for BI Success:
Critical Success Factors for BI Implementations within the Enterprise

Sanjiva Shankar Dubey
BIMTECH Greater Noida, India

Arunesh Sharan
AS Consulting, India

ABSTRACT

This chapter will focus on the transformative effect Business Intelligence (BI) brings to an organization decision making, enhancing its performance, reducing overall cost of operations and improving its competitive posture. This chapter will enunciate the key principles and practices to bridge the gap between organization requirements vs. capabilities of any BI tool(s) by proposing a framework of organizational factors such as user's role, their analytical needs, access preferences and technical /analytical literacy etc. Evaluation methodology to select best BI tools properly aligned to the organization infrastructure will also be discussed. Softer issues and organizational change for successful implementation of BI will be further explained.

INTRODUCTION

New technologies always fascinate organization leadership. They want to quickly adopt them and repeat the much-hyped success their first mover peers have already achieved. But emulating similar success by using similar technologies is hard to come by because all organizations are different and their needs are different. The key is to identify those organizational factors that help or impede implementation of a new technology and then take appropriate action while planning, selection, implementation, exploitation and cessation of any technology, in our case Business Intelligence(BI), Data analytics(DA) and data mining (DM) technology.

This chapter will focus on transformative impact BI, DA and DM can bring to an organization decision making, enhancing its performance, reducing costs and improving competitive posture. We will be

DOI: 10.4018/978-1-5225-2031-3.ch012

using Business Intelligence (BI) as a common word to depict all types of tools and technologies that are enabling organization use and exploit data to derive new meaning for enhancing their business performance and competitiveness. Since BI tools are usually self-service by users, proper selection of tool to meet various types of users within the organization is the key to success. This chapter enunciates key principles and practices which will help bridge organization requirements with what BI tool(s) offers. A framework of organizational factors such as user's role, their analytical needs, access preferences and technical /analytical literacy will be considered for BI success. This chapter will also cover evaluation methodology to select best BI tools based on these organizational factors and needs. This chapter will help its readers to identify the right BI solution which is properly aligned to the organization infrastructure and is able to meet its analysis needs to achieve anticipated business value. This chapter will outline the softer issues that need to be addressed so that its full potential can be realized during implementation of BI, DA and DM technologies. It will also outline how to bring about change in organization culture to ensure a successful implementation of BI, DA and DM technologies.

To summarize the objectives of this chapter would be:

- Examine the transformative impact of BI technologies.
- Selection and alignment of BI technologies with the organization needs and its long-term vision.
- Describe the framework for successful adoption of BI technologies for organizational success.

BACKGROUND

BI is used to derive insights from vast amount of Data for better and faster decisions. For this it needs the following four:

1. Algorithms
2. Technology building blocks
3. IT infrastructure
4. Skills for
    a. Business insight
    b. Data Science
    c. Information Technology

Analytics is no longer part of IT function and is being practiced currently by business users who want faster actions with better speed-to-insight response. Business function users can justify higher cost of IT and may like to go independently for quick results by acquiring tools and infrastructure against the wishes of their IT peers who try to trade off speed with lower cost by attempting to implement common platforms for BI. However, the later approach by IT would normally take time but would have better architecture. The former approach will yield quicker results but will lead to integration problems besides increased cost, duplicate investments and redundancy. The choice between these two is also about who takes decision for the technology, such as the choice of BI tools and IT Infrastructure. Such conflicts have been faced regularly by most organization and the successful group is the one who is able to get more support from top management in decision making. No wonder while cloud-as-a-analytics alternative is increasingly getting popular with business functional users who can pay as they use and have no dependency on IT control, it is not much welcomed by IT leaders of the organization.

It is also a fact that while a quick and simple BI solution used by a small department may produce some results but it may not scale up to the enterprise analytics needs. By allowing disorganized and disjoined initiatves by many departments, the organization may ultimately be self-limiting its capability to for wider exploitation. Such disjoint data bases, data marts and plethora of BI tools and solution will lead to islands of data which will prevent from doing enterprise wide analysis. Such disjointed implementation of BI will be operationally inefficient and will fail to present a common view of enterprise wide data because it is residing on platforms of various vendors such as SAS, SAP Business Objects, Cognos, Hyperion, Oracle etc. Further such implementation will be a maintenance nightmare.

It is common knowledge that business doesn't take enough ownership of BI projects especially on the technology selection process and IT departments are not fully equipped to understand Business challenges and have not developed enough empathy to business problems to be able to partners effectively. If not resolved early this lack of partnership between business and IT leads to issues such as ownership of data preparation, poor response to user training and finally not enough interest for exploitation of the BI solution. Ironically the organization is confronted with these issues when the project reaches implementation stage and much investment has already been committed. In order to address the business and IT divide especially for BI projects many companies have adopted various combination of assigning responsibilities between business and IT but no one approach has been found useful for all types of organization. Best BI organizational structure is neither clinically centralized so that decision making is limited to few and the speed of execution slow nor chaotically decentralized so that left arm does not know what the right arm is doing leading to enormous waste of organization efforts and resources.

What is a Right BI Structure?

The test of right BI Organization structure is that it should be agile, flexible and reactive to competition and market. Generally, a good BI organizational structure separates data preparation and data usage task. It is recommended that Business users should not invest their time for running ETL (extraction, transformation, and loading) task which is usually done as batch jobs and putting the data into a data warehouse or data mart. This task should be ideally done by IT department. After which IT should leave the action in the hands of business Functional users.

It may be noted that data needs would be different for front and back office functions and hence the type of data, its frequency and accuracy would vary from function to function. While accuracy is more important than speed to CFO, those dealing with customers or competitive situations prefer speed of response and are likely to accept approximate answers within a reasonable time frame usually in next few minutes! BI structure must address to meet these differing requirements and ensure balance between maintaining accuracy and risk tolerance arising out of the delay.

BI Follows a Maturity Curve

In fact, BI usage also follows a maturity curve. Initially, organizations start using BI for business performance reporting. This is normally initiated by CFO or sales leadership. This type of BI depends on fetching data from transactional system such as ERP, CRM, Core banking etc. This type of BI is simpler to implement. Many organizations have successfully implemented this type of BI as a departmental initiative. Choice of BI technology for such need is also simple. For example, if you have SAP as ERP solution used in the organization, and if SAP's BI tool has been selected for this purpose then the integration is simpler. Similarly, for any organization using Oracle data base, the obvious choice is Hyperion which would be easier to integrate. Any choice of tools coming from different product vendors on different platform would make enterprise BI initiatives difficult to maintain and sustain. Precisely this is reason why IT specialist inputs are needed for the choice of tool which can allow scalability and ease of maintainability when organization wide BI initiatives are taken.

BI Evolves with Organization Needs

Organizations normally do not need deep Data Science skills to start with for BI projects. Standard business performance reporting cubes are easy to build by IT departments with some data analytics expertise. However, competitive advantage by the firm on a sustained basis can only be achieved when analytics is used for proactive and predictive analysis. For example, if organization want to explore how much customers will buy when they intend to launch a new product or services, the answer is much more complex than finding out the pattern of purchase for the existing products by the existing customers! Such complex requirements for BI also forces a more centralized initiative along with building of a Centre of Excellence (COE) structure for BI. On technical front, the data required to answer complex questions such as the one given above, may need the analysis to go beyond structured transactional data from ERP or from within the organization. It would need an integration of information from transaction system, interaction systems (CRM, email, web interaction, exchanges taking place at retail shop and contact center) as well as social media inputs. The insight about customer buying behaviour and predicting about their wants and needs demands amalgamation of structured and unstructured data.

Data Warehouse Approach for BI

Most enterprise wide BI initiative when driven by IT function follow Data warehouse approach. By understanding the existing data already available on enterprise servers which are captured through the transaction processing systems, a data warehouse or data mart(s) are created. Typically, Data warehouse is initially created for analytics involving routine analysis such as to identify target customer segment for running promotional campaigns for sales and marketing. Other popular Data warehouse application examples are churn analysis for identifying customers who are likely to discontinue services of a credit card or mobile phone connection. Banks use data warehouse for detecting target customer segments for personal or consumer durable loans. Such data warehouse analytics is built over a three-tiered architecture:

1. **Data Warehouse:** Storage of data from large number of diverse sources.
2. **Data Mart:** Smaller subset of data store of summarized and analyzed data suitable for a departmental use.
3. **Visualization Engine:** Visualization Engine is the interface through which business user interacts with large amount of stored data in data warehouse or data mart. The insight is presented in visual manner such as graphs or charts to support decision making. It also provides capability for limited analysis.

BI Needs Joint Working of Business and IT

A successful BI approach for an organization which is aiming to adopt BI analytics in a big way, must involve joint working of people having the three skill sets described earlier, which are, business insight, data science and Information Technology Skills. Based on a vision of end objectives outlined by the organization, the first step is performed by IT and Data scientists who together design and build the right data warehouse architecture, select the right technology and provision requisite IT infrastructure. The decision on what data sources to use and what target information pattern for decision making to be used will have to be advised by the business users. Such business users must have a deep functional understanding and have foresight to visualize the type of insights business would need in the future. Once the initial structure of data warehouse is ready, the task is handed over to IT professionals who set up and maintain the IT environments, tools, populate the data warehouse, take regular back up of data, run batch jobs to update data warehouse on day to day basis. Summarization and population of data warehouse also needs joint working between all the three-skilled people. One the data warehouse (or data mart) is up and running, all business users who are trained in the access of data using BI tools are allowed use the BI environment and seek necessary reports.

But it is not fair to assume that from day one all business users would be proficient in using BI tools and would be able to get all reports required by them easily. There will be a learning process involved here. Let us take an example of building a behavior model of a customer with an objective of offering him a suitable product. The process starts with Business analyst making a hypothesis. Hypothesis will involve linking a behavior to a profile (Age, economic status, location…etc). This needs to be tested using analytics tools. If the test shows positive correlation, then the analysis will be implemented across larger set of data and sales team will reach out to such identified customers to drive sale based on these inputs on a regular basis.

In many cases, such as credit card fraud or suggesting product in online buying etc. BI tools must react very fast. Such analysis and pattern recognition has to happen on a real-time basis for quick action to prevent a financial fraud as in the case of bank. Similarly, a suggested product based on the customer profile must pop up on the customer screen before he/she leave the e commerce site. In both cases the BI system must have a sub second response and automated action must take place without any manual intervention. The technology platform required for such analysis needs to be very different.

BI and Organization

It is important at this stage to understand the impact of BI tools and technology on any organization. In the fiercely competitive globalized business environment of current times, management functions at any level of the organization cannot run based on 'gut' feeling or just the past data. BI technology is one such lever that can help organization to transform from being hunch oriented in its decision making to one based on deep insight based on hard data.

Many organization claim that they have vast amount of data but are not able to derive suitable information that can help them become better as compared to their competitors. Data overload is a major concern in many organization and at times overwhelming to many managers. It is well known that vast amount of data gets generated from many sources, both structured and unstructured in modern corporations. It is not only the transaction details from sales or customer orders, purchase transactions or from supply chain but also from sensors such as RFID, smart tags and data pertaining to social media and emails. The data quantity is multiplying at a faster pace which can drown the unprepared organization unless a proper enterprise data management structure is put in place to follow well designed processes by empowered and motivated people using suitable technology platform.

If you think deeper it would be clearer that while organization desperately needs mechanism to figure out new meaning from the vast amount data for its operations and strategic reasons, it must also embrace the transformative opportunities BI and related technologies bring in. BI implementation will require setting up new organization units to plan and orchestrate BI management and educate the older ones to adopt the newer behaviors' or approach to problem solving using BI as shown in Figure 1.

BI COE will facilitate organization move along quickly the information value chain (Figure 2) by eliminating duplication and streamlining processes.

Departmental vs. Enterprise BI COE

Often the decision to go for a departmental BI vs. Enterprise BI is a not technical but based on enterprise internal power structure. Ideally and if aligned properly, BI implementation ensures that two contradictory extremes of objectives are met through a well-crafted implementation. A well-orchestrated and well federated BI implementation will have speed and flexibility that is needed for departmental needs and standards, consistency and optimization at the enterprise level. A well-crafted BI implementation will have business and IT whether they are departmental or enterprise levels speaking the same language. This ideal scenario is difficult though not impossible but when achieved helps organization catapult to greater heights of operational effectiveness and enhanced competitive postures using power of BI.

Figure 1. Organization and BI interrelationship

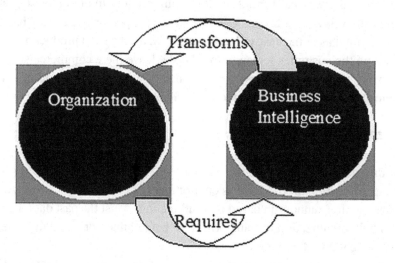

Figure 2. Information value chain

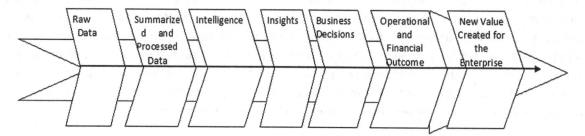

Different Approaches of BI Implementation

Typically, the implementation of BI starts with small implementation at a functional level and then it is extended to the rest of the enterprise. The initial small scale implementation at functional level may be due to some exigencies faced by the functional unit. In such implementation, the BI tools use data analysis using simple spreadsheets or perational data base management systems. This stage is an example of decentralized BI implementation. This stage of BI implementation is also needed or has to be crossed as most organization may not have established a formal BI set up driven by organization vision or strategy. This decentralized implementation of BI solves immediate needs and provides quick answers to the functional managers and builds organization awareness for BI tools. However, for the senior management level of the organization these independent efforts neither present a cohesive and integrated view nor is fast enough for enterprise wide analysis based on all sets of data at one place. Data and processing redundancy forces the senior management to consolidate all such efforts and create the next stage of BI systems called centralized implementation.

Centralized implementation of BI brings in order to the chaotic situation. It helps consolidation of IT resources and economy of scale. Standards tools are selected, regular reports are generated based on well planned data structures. But in this process the speed of service gets sacrificed and process bureaucracy sets in.

The middle path between the two extremes of BI implementation viz clinically slow and centralized against chaotic but faster decentralized is found in Federated BI implementation. Here the central team dictates the architecture and implementation but the day to day usage is left to the functional people who no longer are required to send a request to the centralized team but take analysis themselves. This is achieved through cross-training of analysts responsible for functional area and at times through co-location. The reporting structure of the team also is dual or matrix. Functional analysts report to the functional managers but the central business and data architects report to the CIO (IT) organization. Extensive use of self-service tools are advocated though the task of data preparation is retained with the central team, a task that is done at a regular batch intervals. The Figure 3, Figure 4 and Figure 5 show the three types of BI COE implementations.

Figure 3. Decentralized

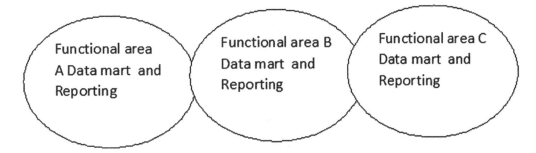

Figure 4. Centralized

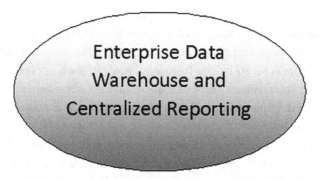

Figure 5. Federated

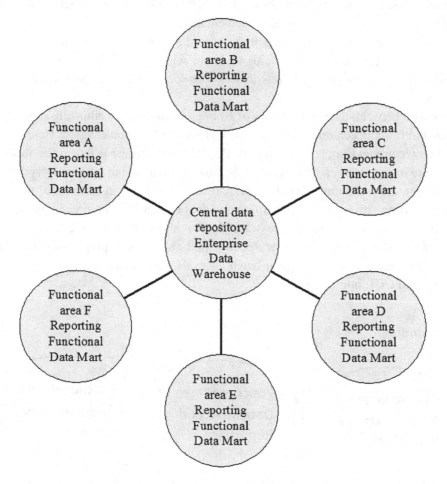

VARIOUS TYPES OF BI COE ORGANIZATION

Organizations Responsibility of BI

It is evident from the figure above that the responsibility of planning, implementation and usage of the BI systems will differ in all these three types of BI COE Organization structures. While the responsibility of doing, everything lies either with functional or central team in the case of decentralized or centralized organization respectively, this reasonability is shared in the case of federated organization. In the case of federated structure the prime role of corporate BI team is to manage all architecture, planning and setting up standards for tools and data structure across all functions as they are the one responsible for the enterprise data warehouse (EDW). The central BI team will also create and load functional data marts at the pre-specified intervals. However, the reporting responsibilities is divided between the corporate and functional units.

These shared responsibilities are described as follows:

- Corporate level re-posting for data consolidated across all (more than one) function, especially those of regular nature will be done by the corporate BI team. This includes generation of performance dashboards and reports that are presented to the CEO, CFO and board of directors.
- The functional users do most of the ad-hoc reporting and perform in depth exploration and analysis for specific one time use.
- Data Scientist design the structure of the data warehouse and help in selecting the right tool for analysis.

BI Implementation Models

There are multiple implementation models for BI implementation that an organization can chose from the following:

- **In-House Functional Departmental Driven Initiative**: Usually, finance and sales organizations take initiative to solve their day to day issues using BI tools as the first mover in any organization. They become frustrated due to IT function's lack of quick response for their needs and therefore try to use BI tools of their own. With more and more IT savvy business users joining the workforce, such initiatives are also encouraged by the leadership as well. In some cases, such initiative is one off in nature. For example, a FMCG company analyzed it account receivable data over past 2-3 years to recover money from distributors. This model is usually low cost option and may not take the organization to best in class level but serves their immediate needs. Such initiatives are definitely better than waiting for IT department which promises to implement a multi-million Dollar sleek BI project after 3 years!
- Large transformational initiative with large budgets and supported by BI Centre of Excellence (COE) set up specifically for taking enterprise wide BI initiatives within the organization. Such initiatives can only be sustained by a critical strategic objective approved at the highest level.
- **Outsourced Initiative**: Many services organizations are offering end to end analytics supported by execution under Business Process Outsourcing model. The latest trend is sharing profits/money saved arising out of BI based decision making. This model is successfully implemented by sev-

eral telecom companies for upselling or cross-selling value added services along with their basic voice and data services. Banking and insurance companies are also experimenting with this model to upsell, improve insurance continuity and generate new business from new financial products. Success of such outsources model depends on the establishing a right governance model, sharing risk and reward with the outsourcing vendor and by establishing an effective joint BI COE which has business functional representatives, vendor technology and business function specialist and in house IT team, if available.

BI CoE Best Practices Approach

Like any other technology adoption BI and analytics also face similar challenges to align organization objectives with available technology by enabling people so that their functioning can improve. But here the challenge is somewhat more intense because of the need of increased participation of users in the planning and use of BI technology and data not being available at one place or available in different silos. The chances are that owners of these data silos would not easily loosen their control and may at times contest the outcome just because the analysis of result is based on the data they don't hold. In order to address these and many more organization challenges would need the following best practices approaches:

- BI COE must have a strong senior level sponsor from amongst the decision makers.
- BI COE team must have expertise in IT, Data management, Functional domain and BI tools for BI analysis and reporting.
- BI COE must be given a clear mandate of its role responsibilities.
- BI COE will have to have the ability to work with multiple stakeholders, users group and decision makers. They will have to negotiate their work around their egos and focus on end results.
- BI COE should be able to train the users to use the BI tools and make them independent rather than holding all expertise and in the process become a report producing department.

In order to achieve the above, BI COE should:

- Decide its offerings and support processes
- Define turnaround time for request and SLAs
- Establish overall governance framework
- Ensure appropriate IT tools and infrastructures are made available
- Work with project mind set and report its progress, achievements and challenges to seek support as and when necessary from higher management
- Manage issues and risk of its projects properly and in timely manner
- Drive change within the organization through proper communications and appropriate training of IT personnel and business user community
- Ensure quality of its deliverables

Hybrid Model of BI Implementation

Many organizations for the reasons of lack of adequate resources or in depth understanding may toy with the idea of outsourcing the BI function. They may want to get away from the challenges of hiring and retaining high in demand BI analyst and other resources. The other advantage of outsourcing could come from the ability to scale and get expertise quickly from the outsourcing service provider. In addition, you pay only for the services sought and tap into the broad-based capabilities the vendor may offer.

However, doing in-house has several advantages especially when the organization wants to make BI COE as a permanent entity. Not only it will have more retained knowledge, low over all cost at the long run but will also ensure that the intellectual assets are retained within the organization. Internal BI COE will have greater visibility and accountability than an external agency at any time.

The better choice amongst the two is to a hybrid model where the organization usage some outsources activity led by a permanent in-house COE team. This combination is arrived at based on the parameters such as reducing overall cost, improved quality and productivity, rapid innovation and time-to-market which the organization is aiming at. The organization may decide to outsource functions such as data administration, routine reports development, data modeling from a vendor but should not outsource the roles such as Executive Sponsors, BI team leadership, Program and Project managers, Business analysts, key technology architects. Please note that this choice will have to be made by considering data privacy laws of the country (or countries in case of transnational firm). However, one time activity for data migration, consolidation, and synchronization can be outsourced.

SOLUTIONS AND RECOMMENDATIONS

If the organization plans to use analytics extensively to gain customer insight and competitive edge, then depending only on its internal resources may prove to be a constraining factor. Internal resources may not have wider experience on the use of BI tools and its business applications. In order to gain access to expertise the organization should explore outsourcing model as an alternative. Many leading BI technology vendors are ready to partners and offer risk and reward model. This model works best as the partner has skin in the game and will usually bring skills required to succeed.

Even in outsourced model, organization should build COE, manned by internal and partner resources. Risk reward model works well only when the performance indices are clearly defined and unequivocally measured. In many situation, performance is measured and compared with a similar business or customer segment of analysis where traditional means are used earlier. This method makes comparison relevant even if market and economic situation changes.

BI COE outsourcing needs to be initiated and driven by business leadership and not by IT. Even now, most of the CIOs consider outsourcing as loss of control for their authority and at times do not welcome such move. But in the case of BI COE business outcome can only be aimed and achieved by business leadership not by IT, hence the decision to seek outside help for BI COE must be owned by the Business leadership not IT.

On technology front, prevalent cloud model and Big data technologies should be considered both for data warehouse/data mart and for visualization. These technologies have matured enough for BI application and should be explored by starting small and then through rapid scaling up.

We need to realize that Analytics is a component of organizational decision making and not a standalone platform. Therefore, design and implementation should address its complete life cycle. For example, if business analytics is being used for customer micro-segmentation and upselling, then the BI platform needs to be integrated with a campaign engine so as to execute push model of customer engagement. BI platform should also have capability to measure effectiveness of campaign as well. One must realize that implementation of business analytics based solutions have a learning time and needs repeated fine tuning with exploration of various alternatives. Most BI technology is moving towards autonomous learning and would improve as it is being used. However, such maturity of BI solution has not reached its perfection. In such situation BI COE plays a key role. BI COE keeps fine-tuning the analytics solution and hands over its operations to business users for day to day decision making and application in business decision.

Representative Business Analytics Building blocks

Figure 6 shows a typical Business Analytics framework and various building blocks in an organization. This shows various sources of data, its consolidation in enterprise data warehouse and data marts. The access of analytics report is done through the Visualization engine that supports Execution and also provides tools for Decision Support.

On top of the framework is visualization engine, software tool that will help end users to access data in desired summarized form, in the form of graphs, charts or cube. The second layer is departmental data marts which focus on specific function supported by the third layer of enterprise wise data warehouse. Finally, the data sources are listed at the bottom where the data can be pulled and stored in the data warehouse and updated at a regular interval.

BI Road Map for Implementation

The road map to achieve this must go through various stages as shown in Figure 7.

Figure 6. Typical BI building blocks

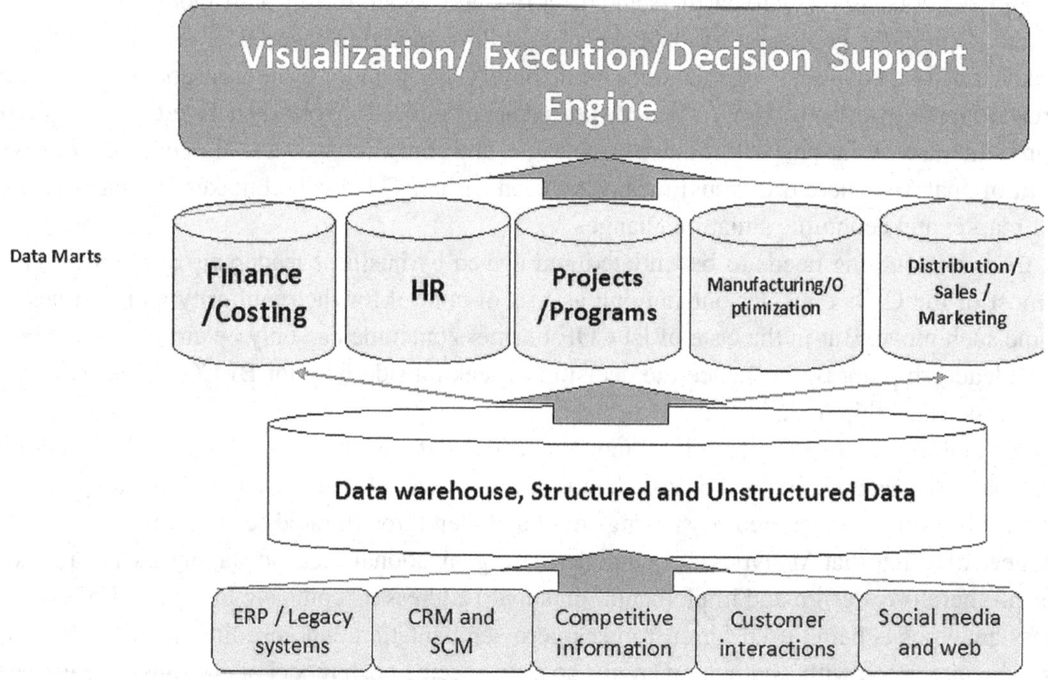

220

Figure 7. BI Road map for implementation

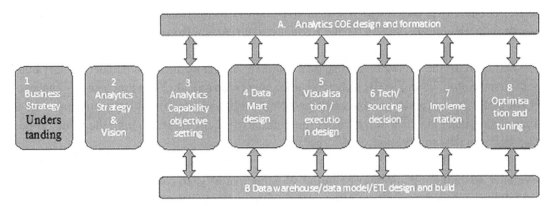

The steps are described as follows:

1. **Business Strategy Understanding:** At this stage the BI implementation team which usually comprises of the people having all the three skill sets described earlier, i.e. data science, business function and IT is led by an energetic leader who has top management mandate to drive the implementation.
2. **Analytics Strategy and Vision:** The team based on the Business strategy inputs carves out the strategy for Business Analytics and drives its vision for BI
3. **Analytics Capability and Objective Setting:** At this stage the team identifies what capabilities are needed to accomplish the task of Analytics and what are the precise objectives that will require to be achieved.
4. **Data Mart and Data Warehouse Design:** This step is led by the data scientist who based on the inputs so far, designs a suitable data warehouse and data mart strategy and structure.
5. **Visualization Execution Design:** Designing user interface is an important aspect of the BI implementation. At this stage the IT team designs the data visualization interface with support from business users.
6. **Technology Sourcing Decision:** Once the design phase is over the requisite technology is selected. This decision is influenced by the type of BI organization structure has been selected whether it is centralized, decentralized or federated.
7. **Implementation:** In this phase the BI project is implemented.
8. **Optimization and Tuning:** This is routine phase post implementation usually led by the IT professionals and Data scientists to improve BI systems performance.

All these steps are performed under the two governance initiatives as given below:

*   **Analytics COE Design and Formation:** In order to give BI implementation a permanence in the organization a center of excellence for BI is set up. This comprises of a permanent team that drives BI implementation and comes into existence after the Analytics vision and objectives are defined in step number 3.

- **Data Warehouse /Data Mart/ETL Design and Build:** This phase also starts alongside in a parallel, driven by IT professionals who have to plan of IT infrastructure, support team and process to create data warehouse, data marts and regular update of data from various sources.

The roadmap described above is an ideal one. However, if organization has decided to start small and wishes to first develop standalone BI initiatives in an area (such as Data Mart for customer analytics) led by CFO or CMO then it can be accepted as pilot before embarking the grand BI implementation. There is nothing wrong in taking such initiatives as these initiatives help in establishing the value proposition for BI adoption in the organization.

It is recommended that such standalone initiatives must be merged into the grand organizational initiative later when the organization BI initiative gains maturity. In case organizations continue with many standalone approach and allow mushrooming of many small departmental datamarts, then it would lead to issues such as:

- Limited analytics is done using only partial data available to a department
- Multiple data marts dependent on direct data loading leads to duplication of IT operations and becomes nightmarish
- May cost much more in the long run
- Organization loses in the long run as it becomes difficult to form a enterprise COE which looks at enterprise data and not departmental data

Case Study: A BI implementation Failed due to Poorly Designed Organization

A large multi-national telecom organization deployed BI for revenue assurance. The IT was outsourced to a leading IT Vendor and the initiative was purely CIO led. Business involvement and leadership in envisioning was minimal. Predictably the results after three years of massive investment in resources was suboptimal and has to be scrapped. In the process the BI vendor who has signed up with the telecom company a success based risk and reward sharing model, did not get any return and lost lots of money. Some key observations of this case were:

- The solution was one of the most expensive platform in the environment.
- Little effort was made for optimizing and prioritizing data summarization.
- Data loading and summarization was nightmarish.
- Reports where either too late for management decision or not suitable for management decision.
- Business decided to bypass the system and started doing most of the analysis on few small standalone systems.
- After spending millions of Dollars, the project was scaled down.

Measuring BI Performance

Measuring BI solution performance is a much needed yet not very easy. Not only the technology around BI science and the associated tools are evolving but the success depends largely upon how these tools are implemented and used. The success parameters are often application specific and hard to quantify. A simple and conventional way of measuring BI performance is to compare the goals vs. achievement in the form of KPI. This will also help to calculate return on investment on BI. However, there are technical performance measures as well which can be used to access the deployment capability. Some of them are:

- How much the BI implementation is scalable.
- Response time.
- How much BI interfaces are usable and reliable.
- How good is the quality of its results.

Most organizations take BI adoption/usage as a good primary indicator. The purpose of any measure is to help identify the corrective measures. For example, if usability of BI is poor then is it due to quality issue or performance issue? Quality is another measure that most organization use but the question to be asked is that is it due to poor input quality or processing quality using BI tools?

A balanced approach of measuring BI success would be to combine various measures such as:

- **Business and Financial Measure:** Return of investment, profits generated, Customer satisfaction increased, market share increase due to use of BI tools (before and after).
- **Internal Performance Improvement Measures:** Such as reduction in cost, speed to market and efficiency.
- **Increase in Employee Productivity and Capability Measures:** Has the BI tool helped employees to execute their task faster and more precisely than before and if yes then to what degree?
- **Usage Statistics:** This measures ascertains the active users increasing over the period. Taking feedback on performance and quality of output occasionally booth qualitative as well as quantitatively from users and senior management will be of help.

The BI performance measures relationship is shown in the Figure 8.

FUTURE RESEARCH DIRECTIONS

One of the future research area is to explore as to how Business analytics can become an integrated part of business strategy, processes and applications. While BI deployments take inputs from end user during design the subsequent interaction with business users on the effectiveness and efficiency of the BI system is not much. BI deployments demands that user change their traditional work style and adopt data driven approach. Business users are too busy on day to day and are not able to pause and think of data warehouse output. There is increasing role of Business Analytics in enhancing Value to Business Processes and organization redesign which the future research of BI should focus on.

CONCLUSION

It is evident from the discussion in this chapter that selecting the right organization structure and implementation approach governs the success of the BI initiatives in the organization. BI initiatives costs lot of many and time. If a careful planning and implementation supported by right organization design is not done, then there will be lot of wastage of efforts and loss of opportunity for the organization to reap the benefits from the data analytics.

Figure 8. BI implementation measure framework

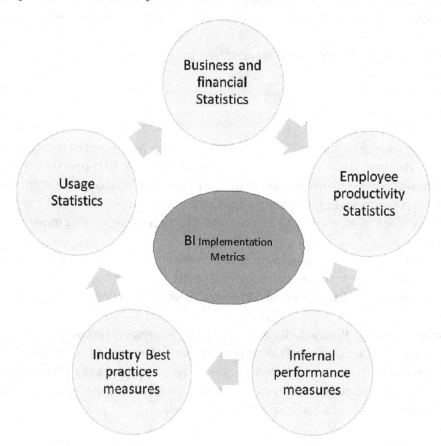

ADDITIONAL READING

Alex, B., Stephen, S., & Kurt, T. (2002). *Building Data Mining Applications for CRM*. McGraw Hill.

Davenport, T. H. (1993). *Process Innovation: Reengineering Work through Information Technology*. Boston: Harvard Business School Press.

KEY TERMS AND DEFINITIONS

Centralized BI Structure: Here the entire initiative for organization wide BI is done by a central team.
Decentralized BI Structure: All teams are free to take BI initiatives as they feel appropriate.
Federated: Here the architecture and strategy is designed by the central team but the implementation and management is left to the departmental units.
Organizational Change: BI brings about a change in organization in the way it operates, from purely 'hunch' based decision making it transforms the organization into data driven and fact based.

Chapter 13
Ethics of Social Media Research

Amir Manzoor
Bahria University, Pakistan

ABSTRACT

Over the last decade, social media platforms have become a very popular channel of communication. This popularity has sparked an increasing interest among researchers to investigate the social media communication. Many studies have been done that collected the publicly available social media communication data to unearth significant patterns. However, one significant concern raised over such practice is the privacy of the individual's social media communication data. As such it is important that specific ethical guidelines are in place for future researches on social media sites. This chapter explores various ethical issues related to researches related to social networking sites. The chapter also provides a set of ethical guidelines that future researches on social media sites can use to address various ethical issues.

1. INTRODUCTION

In a research on social media (Berkman Center for Internet & Society, Harvard University, 2008), the publicly released Facebook data of approximately 1700 students of an anonymous, northeastern American university was collected. The research team recognized the various privacy concerns of the individuals related to their personal information. Therefore, the research team took many steps to protect the privacy of the research participants such as removal of student identity information from the dataset. The dataset was also reviewed by the institutional review board and other researchers were given access to this data on the condition that they will agree to strict terms and conditions of data use. However, these steps were proved to insufficient to protect the privacy of the data as identity of the subjects was quickly discovered (Lewis, 2008).

On the business side, there are many stories of violation of ethical principles. Target Corporation initiated an analytics program that was somehow able to do data mining about the female customers' physique to determine whether customer is pregnant or not by calculating a pregnancy score. Target used this information to send coupons for baby items to customers according to their pregnancy scores. Target sent an email to a female customer who was a high school student. The email contained coupons for baby clothes and cribs. This email was read by the parents of the customers. Through Target apolo-

DOI: 10.4018/978-1-5225-2031-3.ch013

gized the parents for sending such an email, later it was discovered that this girl was indeed pregnant. However, this incident still highlighted how the large companies can secretly get access to customer private information and violate basic ethical principles (Hill, 2012). In another incident, travel company Orbitz used their data analytics program to find out that customers who owned Apple company products were willing to pay more for travel. Orbitz utilized this information to send higher price quotes for travel to customers who owned Apple phones (Riglian, 2012). In 2014, Facebook used the data of around 700,000 Facebook users in an experiment without their knowledge. Facebook manipulated these individuals' news feeds by reducing positive or negative content. The purpose of the study was to examine how the emotions of the individuals changes by looking at their subsequent posts (Klitzman, 2014). It appears that both academicians and companies are making innovative efforts to collect large datasets. However, the objectives of both are different. Academicians are using these large datasets to gain better understanding of certain phenomena. Companies are using these datasets to better understand customer needs and market their products. However, in their efforts, both academicians and companies are, intentionally or unintentionally, getting involved in violation of basic ethical principles related to privacy, data ownership and information ethics. Big data offers great opportunities to produce significant impact on social, cultural, political aspects of people lives. However, the use of big data also involves some unintended consequences such as violation of ethical principles. Some feel that such unintended consequences are part and parcel of the use of big data and. Whatever the case is, it is important that a set of ethical guidelines should be developed regarding the use of big data. It is important to recognize that these ethical guidelines for big data use shouldn't be based on individual moral standards because every individual differs with respect to their views about what constitutes an ethical action.

The Internet supports research in two quite different ways: as a tool for finding & accessing people and material and as a location for meeting & interacting with people & groups. However, this distinction is not so clear with social media because social media users no longer fit neatly into categories and the line between tool and location is blurring (Swatman, 2013). Research involving social media tends to fall under two categories: 1) research using social platforms and 2) research "into" social content. The example of first type of research is patient-led research, which might involve sites such as patientslikeme. The example of second type of research is research using online communities such as a "Cancer Survivors" Facebook page. Both categories of research have their own ethical implications. It is established that social media research should abide by ethical rules. However, there exist limited guidelines that researchers can use to interpret and apply well-established ethical principles on social media research.

Social media refers to websites and applications that enable users to create and share content or to participate in social networking (Oxford Dictionaries, 2013). In UK, over approximately 55 % of individuals aged 16 and over were users of social media site (Ofcom, 2013) and 72% of online American adults were users of social media sites (Duggan, 2015). The increasing amounts of big data about users, available publically and readily on the Internet, are becoming preferred choice for researchers to identify and recruit participants for studies. Researchers continue to use users' social media data (such as age, gender and occupation) more and more to gain deeper understanding of social media users and then recruit them to develop large sample for their research studies (Lohse, 2013; Brooks & Churchill, 2010; Bhutta, 2012). Online data can be collected using either 1) online using traditional methods (such as interviews) or 2) using existing data available online data. In first method, researchers use traditional methods (such as interviews) online to collect data. This method is cost effective, simple, and can attract a large number of participants (Woodfield et al, 2013). Existing online data, such as the data available on social media platforms, is another option that users can use to collect data that can be anonymous and provide more open and honest user opinion about a specific topic. Researchers can use data mining techniques to analyze the publicly shared information (such as tweet and posts) in social media space to better understand complex social issues. One good example is the use of Twitter data to analyze who was involved and what their motivations were during the riots that took place in UK in 2011 (The Guardian et al, 2011).

While social media platforms offer various potential opportunities and advantages for researchers there are associated number of methodological and ethical challenges related to inference of data that users collect from social media spaces. Preserving anonymity online is another challenge for researchers because online ethical behavior is an obligation for the researchers. However, available ethical guidelines are not flexible enough for their application on research using social media that is quickly changing, developing, and growing.

After introduction, section two explores various ethical issues related to social media research. Section three discusses users' views of social media research and their conflicting objectives in relation to social media research. Section four discusses various implications and provides a set of proposed ethical guidelines that social media researchers can use to not violate the subject's privacy while adhering to the ethical research standards. Section five provides some future research directions. Concluding remarks are provided in section six.

2. ETHICS IN SOCIAL MEDIA RESEARCH

2.1 Ethical Issues in Social Media Research

Following are some important ethical issues in social media research (Swatman, 2013):

- Recruitment.
- Privacy/Anonymity/Confidentiality.
- Consent.
- Data Sharing / Data Storage.
- Terms of Service / End-User License Agreements.

2.1.1 Recruitment

In traditional research studies, participant recruitment is generally "push" based where researchers know who they're targeting and participant groups are 'controlled'. In contrast, research using social media generally employs pull-based participant recruitment strategy. In this strategy, potential participants can discuss the invitation and tell others about it. The researcher has no control or influence over this. The response to participant invitation in traditional research studies is static. In social media research, response to participant invitation is interactive and can lead to unexpected outcomes e.g. subsequent posts may modify already-posted information.

2.1.2 Privacy/Anonymity/Confidentiality

Social media research has many associated issues of privacy, anonymity, and confidentiality. One important issue is whether the social media space being researched is seen as private by its users or not. Also it should also be determined that whether users know that they are being observed. Researchers need to carefully evaluate their role in the research study. One particular problem with social media is that it is difficult to establish the true identity of the participant due to anonymous nature of social media. So a researcher cannot easily determine whether a participant is really who he/she claim to be. Another related issue is the researcher's ability to ensure that his/her study participants really are anonymous. This is because IP addresses can generally be traced and tweets/posts may contain identifiers. Researchers also find it difficult to establish the frequency with which their study participants comment/contribute to the social media.

2.1.3 Consent

Obtaining consent from adults is relatively straightforward. Links from social networking sites to other, more reliable, sites can solve most problems. For example, researchers can use surveys (e.g. Survey Monkey, etc.) and portals. However, getting consent from children / young people is the most challenging task. This is because researchers have no way of ensuring participant's age / level of maturity. For example, how a researcher can ensure that all of the study participants recruited through Facebook are above the age of 18. Obtaining personal consent has many associated challenges. While obtaining personal consent is difficult, it is even harder ensure the truly identify who actually consented. Researchers should think carefully whether the form of research study they are doing is worth doing via social media.

2.1.4 Data Sharing / Data Storage

Every country has laws that protect the privacy of personal information. It is important for researchers to keep abreast of the applicable privacy laws. Since social media spaces allows data collection across boundaries, compliance with laws become more complex. Users need to ensure of the security of their data in the social networking spaces. They want to make sure that they can access their data as/when they need and no one else can access their personal information. They also need assurance that they can depend on privacy / reliability claims from a social media space (such as Facebook). Availability of the social media space is also important. Social networking platforms are mostly US-based, with real implications for users' data. US-based data are subject to the US Patriot Act & the US Foreign Intelligence and Surveillance Act. These laws allow that data can be accessed by US federal law enforcement agencies, irrespective of the ownership of the data. Foreign government access to users' data can severely hamper user participation in social media spaces and seriously limit the willingness of participation in any social media research (Hopewell, 2011). The nationals of other countries storing data on US sites cannot claim protection under the Fourth Amendment of the US Constitution (which protects against unlawful search and seizure of property and information) because their data is stored by a third party provider. Inter-governmental treaties and agreements (e.g. the European Convention on Cybercrime) allow data stored in the US to be requisitioned by European law enforcement agencies. This requisition by European law enforcement agencies can be made with information of the customer.

2.1.5 Terms of Service / End-User License Agreements

The ownership of the data created by the users on the social media is another important issue. Facebook claims the rights to any data collected from applications (including surveys) created within it. According to Jaquith (2009), Facebook's definition of data ownership does not include the right to export that data. According to Protalinski (2012), if there is content you don't want Facebook to own, don't upload it to Facebook. It is also important to understand that the terms of service vary greatly from one social media site to another.

3. USERS' VIEWS OF SOCIAL MEDIA RESEARCH

According to Beninger et al., (2014), users can have different views about the research using social media. Users form these views based on their individual knowledge and awareness of social media and research using social media. Following are the three general categories of users' views of social media research.

3.1 Skepticism

Skepticism about social media research refers to uncertainty users feel about the validity of the data collected through social media. Users may feel that the researcher is not transparent about the research objectives. They may also have concerns about the transparency of the social media itself. Users can feel unsure and confused about the use of their social media data and its utility as compared to the data collected using traditional face to face methods. Users may not have adequate understanding of the value of social media research. Therefore, it is important for researchers to educate participants how social media research is different from traditional research methods and why it is valuable. They should also educate them about the use of the user information in the research. These user concerns can pose serious concerns over legitimacy of researcher and transparency of the research purpose. That can not only discourage users to participate in research studies. Users must be satisfied that, if they participated, their information will not be used in a way unacceptable to users. The users' concerns about the legitimacy of researcher can be more if users are unsure about the way research using social media is to be conducted and the rules under which the researcher is going to work.

3.2 Acceptance

This refers to the participants' perception of value of methodological approach of the research and its benefits to society. Users with an acceptance view data collection methods used in social media research as beneficial in analyzing and understanding broad social trends. Such users view social media research valuable because they can respond more freely. User acceptance also means users view their participation in social media research to provide social benefit. These users think that the data they post on social media sites and regulating their behavior online is their own responsibility. As such these users have no issues if the social media researchers collect their data and analyze it in their research.

3.3 Ambivalence

Users having ambivalent view (i.e. neither concern nor acceptance), have neutral feelings towards social media research. For these users, social media research is something that has to happen and there is little that can be done to stop it. These users see use of social media data as inevitable.

4. IMPLICATIONS

Academicians and companies are feeling a lot of excitement about the value and potential of social media. Every day, conversations from social media are mined, collated, and displayed by various sources. It has become increasingly easier to find out who on social media is talking about what about any specific topic. Social media is now considered a huge source of immediate information capable of answering 'big' questions. It can be said that news, blogs, peer review platforms, and the like are usually produced with the expectation of publicity. As such, researchers may opt for not putting strong emphasis on ethical issues while mining those types of resources. However, researchers still need to understand the ethical boundaries of their research studies. It is important so that the design and approval of research studies involving social media can be made more realistic, reliable, and appropriate. There is a need to develop flexible ethical guidelines that can help researchers using social media for their research studies. It is still questionable whether consent of participants should be sought irrespective of the type of research involving online sources. While many participants may feel informed consent is not important in all situations, many held the view that choice of platform (Facebook or Twitter) or content to be used (such as tweets or posts) should not affect the requirement of mandatory informed consent. Given this, researchers should use reasonable measure to contact participants and obtain their consent. There involve many practical challenges in securing such informed consent. These challenges can be overcome, for example, by mass tweeting to the participants of your study, or sending Facebook messages to the participants, or emailing, or posting on the forum from where you got your participants. These methods may not ensure that all users were informed but at least researchers can show that he/she used reasonable measures to secure participant consent. Another issue is insecure communication over a digital platform. To mitigate this concern, a researcher can request a participant to provide his/her contact details. The researcher can then contact him/her to brief about the research study. Another option is that researcher can provide his/her contact details and invite the participant to discuss the research project.

Participants vary in their knowledge and understanding of social media and research using social media. This is important because when researchers cannot assume that their participants are knowledgeable about these things than they will dig deep to understand the participants' expectations and its impact on the design of the study.

Users may perceive many risks related to social media and its use. Researchers need to understand these risks to avoid undue harm to participants. A researcher should be transparent about his/her affiliation and aims/objectives of the research. Doing so, researcher can establish his/her credibility in the eyes of the participants. Providing early support to the participants is also important. This support can come in the form of web links or contact details that participants can use to gain better understanding of the research itself and the type of support they can avail. These steps can also make the research more attractive to participants.

Another important aspect is the quality and credibility of research using social media. Researchers should consider how they can enhance the nature, value, and rigor of their research study by possibly using a triangulation approach. Mixed method studies can provide large datasets and, coupled with other techniques, can help participants gain increased understanding of the research and its quality and credibility.

It is also important for researchers to understand that research using social media do not need developing new specific ethical guidelines. The global basic ethical practices apply on social media research but have different implications. Researchers need flexible ethical guidelines that are adaptable in different social media platforms and suitable for different methods/styles of data collection. British Psychological Society (2013) and (Beninger et al., 2014) provides one such ethics guidelines for Internet-mediated Research. Researchers should be cautious in applying these ethical guidelines on quickly evolving online platforms. Social media researchers should carefully consider how and when to apply ethical guidelines and principles in their research. Doing so will help them better deliver robust research results.

Research using social media is a nascent field that is still developing. As such, rigid, inflexible guidelines may not be appropriate. What is needed is a collaborative and supportive guidelines that researchers can use to learn plenty of lessons and build on them. To enable an effective learning environment, researchers should be open and honest in their discussion of the limitations and challenges of their research design. It would be better if a vigorous knowledge base about different types of social media research approaches is built. Such a knowledge base will help design and develop robust research using social media.

5. ETHICAL GUIDELINES FOR SOCIAL MEDIA RESEARCH

The research using social media can involve various stages such as recruitment, data collection/generation, and reporting results. Researchers need to be careful to not get involved in any violation of ethical principles. In this regard, following are some guidelines. At best, these guidelines are meant to provide ideas that social media researchers can consider to incorporate rigorous ethical principles in the design of their research studies. A researcher should be cautious when applying these guidelines because these guidelines may not be appropriate in all situations. As such, some changes in guidelines may be needed (Beninger et al., 2014).

The researcher use recruitment stage to establish his/her legitimacy and transparency of purpose and aims of the research to the participants. Doing so, researcher aims to recruit suitable participants for his/her social media research study. In the first step of recruitment, it is preferred that a researcher should determine the preferred method of communication of recruited participant. The use of email to contact users should not be preferred and rather researchers should approach possible participants over the social media platform they are going to use for their research. Researchers should develop recruitment materials that are transparent i.e. these materials should clearly indicate their affiliation, a web link to verify their idea and aims of research. For example, the researcher can provide his/her biography of the researcher on his/her organizational website. Whatever social media platform researcher is going to use the associated security and privacy terms should be clearly mentioned in the recruitment material. Researchers should also explain to users how they got their contact information (e.g. by searching the Facebook or Twitter public profiles). It is also a good idea to provide examples of previous researches done by the researcher. For example, the researcher can provide a web link to previous research reports on the organizational website. That will establish researcher's transparency about the research aims and also help to establish some reputation among the users.

The purpose of collecting or generating data is ensure findings are representative. Another objective is to understand the privacy risks of social media platform used in the research to uphold protection and trust of participants. Different participants may have different views about what may be considered an intellectual property and what is legally permitted to be collected. It is important that a researcher should be aware of these divergent views. Researchers should invest sufficient time to understand the openness of the social media platform they will be using in their research. They should discover whether there are any steps that they can take to gain participant trust. For example, it may be appropriate to approach participants using a closed chat room. In this initial conversation, the researcher can introduce himself and state the research objectives and ask participants to opt for research. The prospective participants may use different ways to engage online and to create and share content. A researcher should understand these ways and consider how his/her data collection effort may include specific views or types of participants.

The purpose of reporting results is to protect the identity and reputation of participants. It is important to maintain the trust of participants in the value of the research. It is also important to be open and honest in reporting so as to contribute to the advancement of the field. Researcher should take reasonable steps to test how a tweet or post can be traced and inform the users to protect their identity. To do so, researcher may consider paraphrasing the tweet or post and avoid using user names. However, the terms and conditions of specific social media platform may make such paraphrasing difficult. For example, Twitter's terms and conditions prohibit paraphrasing of users' tweet. Researcher should reasonably ensure to obtain informed consent to use verbatim quotes or images/videos provided by the users. Researcher may obtain the user consent by sending tweets, private messages or email to the users. When reporting the results of their study, researchers should acknowledge to the best of their knowledge all limitations of their research findings. These limitations can be related to of the representativeness and validity of the findings. It is also advised that researchers should clearly state the specific social media platform (such as Facebook) used in their study rather than stating they used social media.

Researchers engaging in social media research must recognize that they may not have complete understanding of the changing nature of privacy and challenges associated with making datasets anonymous. They can get help by interdisciplinary collaboration with other researchers. It is also important that the institutional review boards (IRBs) of the academic institutions are educated about the complexities of engaging in research using social media. Academic research institutions should also ensure that their offerings of research methods courses and research best practices/protocols recognize the unique challenges of social media research. Researchers should ensure that longstanding ethical practices are deeply rooted in research methods and processes.

6. CONCLUSION

There exist many emerging challenges of engaging in social media research including nature of consent, proper identification of user expectations of privacy, and data anonymization. Current knowledge base of ethical implications of social media research needs to be strengthened to fill significant knowledge gaps. These knowledge gaps can cause serious threats to the privacy of social media research participants even when researchers make good faith efforts for privacy protection. This chapter has attempted to fill this gap by exploring various ethical issues and providing ethical guidelines that researchers should consider while using social media in their research. While there are divergent users' views about the ethical issues, an advance assessment of these issues is very important for social media researchers. This assessment should continue throughout the research study and researchers should not make any assumptions about what is right or wrong. While overcoming ethical challenges in social media research is not easy, guidelines can be adopted to overcome these challenges.

7. FUTURE RESEARCH AREAS

While research using social media is gaining popularity, it is still far from being a well-known methodology amongst the masses. Since the masses are a major source for conducting research using social media, more research is needed to better to make masses understand the rationale of social media research. The research carried out to discover the users' perceptions of the research using social media is indecisive what exactly shapes these views i.e. choice of a specific social media platform, nature of the content, or a combination of both. More research is needed into the behavior of social media users to get a detailed understanding. This detailed understanding can help researchers better recruit the participants in their future research studies using social media. This understanding can also help fine-tune the support provided to the participants and build reputation of this field of research. Future research may also be done to distinguish whether the use of quantitative of qualitative methods of research into exploring users' views about ethics in social media research are different or not. Quantitative researches may also consider using large-scale datasets to enhance generalizability of the findings. Future research can be done to gain a better understanding of the contextual nature of privacy in social media spaces. This is because it cannot be assumed that by making their personal information available on a social network, users have granted an open license for everyone to capture and release this information to all. Similarly, further research is needed to understand the notion of ''consent'' within the context of disclosing personal information in social networking spaces (Stutzman 2006; Zimmer 2006; McGeveran 2007; Boyd 2008).

REFERENCES

Beninger, K., Fry, A., Jago, N., Lepps, H., Nass, L., & Silvester, H. (2014). *Research using social media; users' views*. Nat Cen Social Research.

Berkman Center for Internet & Society, Harvard University. (2008, September 25). *Tastes, Ties, and Time: Facebook data release*. Retrieved February 3, 2016, from https://cyber.law.harvard.edu/node/94446

Bhutta, C. B. (2012). Not by the Book: Facebook as a Sampling Frame. *Sociological Methods & Research, 41*(1), 57–88. doi:10.1177/0049124112440795

Boyd, D. (2008). *Putting privacy settings in the context of use (in Facebook and elsewhere)*. Retrieved from http://www.zephoria.org/thoughts/archives/2008/10/22/putting_privacy.html

British Psychological Society. (2013). *Ethics Guidelines for Internet-mediated Research. INF206/1.2013*. Author.

Duggan, M. (2015, August 19). *The demographics of social media users*. Retrieved from http://www.pewinternet.org/2015/08/19/the-demographics-of-social-media-users/

Hill, K. (2012, February 16). *How Target figured out a teen girl was pregnant before her father did*. Retrieved July 4, 2016, from http://www.forbes.com/sites/kashmirhill/2012/02/16/how-target-figured-out-a-teen-girl-was-pregnant-before-her-father-did/

Hopewell, L. (2011). *The Pitfalls of Offshore Cloud*. Available: http://www.zdnet.com/thepitfalls-of-offshore-cloud-1339308564/

Jaquith, W. (2009). Chris Anderson's Free contains apparent plagiarism. *The Virginia Quarterly Review*. Available at: www.vqronline.org/blog/2009/06/23/chris-anderson-free

Klitzman, R. (2014, July 2). *Did Facebook's experiment violate ethics?* Retrieved July 4, 2016, from http://www.cnn.com/2014/07/02/opinion/klitzman-facebook-experiment/index.html

Lewis, K. (2008). *Tastes, Ties, and Time: Cumulative codebook*. Retrieved from http://dvn.iq.harvard.edu/dvn/dv/t3

Lohse, B. (2013). Facebook Is an Effective Strategy to Recruit Low-income Women to Online Nutrition Education. *Journal of Nutrition Education and Behavior*, *45*(1), 69–76. doi:10.1016/j.jneb.2012.06.006 PMID:23305805

McGeveran, W. (2007). *Facebook, context, and privacy*. Retrieved from http://blogs.law.harvard.edu/infolaw/2007/09/17/facebook-context/

Ofcom. (2013). *Internet use and attitudes: 2013 Metrics Bulletin*. Ofcom.

Oxford Dictionaries. (2013a). *Definition of data mining*. Available from: http://www.oxforddictionaries.com/definition/english/data-mining

Oxford Dictionaries. (2013b). *Definition of social media*. Available from: http://www.oxforddictionaries.com/definition/english/social-media

Protalinski, E. (2012). *Facebook Launches Native App for iPhone and iPad, Rebuilt From Ground Up*. Retrieved from http://www.thenextweb.com

Riglian, A. (2012, November). *"Big data" collection efforts spark an information ethics debate*. Retrieved February 3, 2016, from http://searchcloudapplications.techtarget.com/feature/Big-data-collection-efforts-spark-an-information-ethics-debate

Stutzman, F. (2006). *How Facebook broke its culture*. Retrieved from http://chimprawk.blogspot.com/2006/09/how-facebook-broke-its-culture.html

Swatman, P. (2013). *Ethical issues in social networking research*. Retrieved from http://www.deakin.edu.au/__data/assets/pdf_file/0007/269701/Swatman-Ethics-and-Social-Media-Research.pdf

Woodfield, K., Morrell, G., Metzler, K., Blank, G., Salmons, J., Finnegan, J., & Lucraft, M. (2013). *Blurring the Boundaries? New Social Media, New Social Research: Developing a network to explore the issues faced by researchers negotiating the new research landscape of online social media platforms: A methodological review paper*. Southampton, UK: National Centre for Research Methods.

Zimmer, M. (2006). *More on Facebook and the contextual integrity of personal information flows.* Retrieved from http://michaelzimmer.org/2006/09/08/more-onfacebook-and-the-contextual-integrity-of-personal-informationflows/

ADDITIONAL READING

Albrechtslund, A. (2008). Online social networking as participatory surveillance. First Monday Retrieved 2008, March 3, from http://www.uic.edu/htbin/cgiwrap/bin/ojs/index.php/fm/articlc/view/2142/1949

Barnes, S. (2006). A privacy paradox: Social networking in the United States. First Monday Retrieved October 12, 2007, from http://www.firstmonday.org/ISSUES/issue11_9/barnes/

Barratt, M. J., & Lenton, S. (2010). Beyond recruitment? Participatory online research with people who use drugs. *International Journal of Internet Research Ethics, 3*(12), 69–86.

Benfield, J., & Szlemko, W. (2006). Internet-Based Data Collection: Promises and Realities. *Journal of Research Practice, 2*(2), 1–15.

Boyd, D. (2008b). Taken out of context: American teen sociality in networked publics. Unpublished Dissertation, University of California-Berkeley.

Boyd, D., & Ellison, N. (2008). Social network sites: Definition, history, and scholarship. *Journal of Computer-Mediated Communication, 13*(1), 210–230. doi:10.1111/j.1083-6101.2007.00393.x

British Psychological Society. (2007). *Report of the Working Party on Conducting Research on the Internet: Guidelines for ethical practice in psychological research online.* Leicester: The British Psychological Society.

Brooks, A., & Churchill, E. F. (2010). Knowing Me, Knowing You: A Case Study of Social Networking Sites and Participant Recruitment, CSCW 2010, 02/06/2010. Savannah, GA.

Buchanan, E. (2012) *Social Media, Research, and Ethics: Challenges and Strategies.* The Rockefeller University Center for Clinical and Translational Science Webinar Series, New York, NY, Available: http://www.uwstout.edu/faculty/buchanane/

Bull, S., Breslin, L., Wright, E., Black, S., Levine, D., & Santelli, J. (2010). Case Study: An Ethics Case Study of HIV Prevention Research on Facebook: The Just/Us Study. *Journal of Pediatric Psychology, 36*(10), 1082–1092. doi:10.1093/jpepsy/jsq126 PMID:21292724

Cheezburger (2012). *On the Internet, no-one knows you're a cat.* Available: http://cheezburger.com/5830762496

Crawford, K., Gray, M. L., & Miltner, K. (2014). Big Data| Critiquing Big Data: Politics, Ethics, Epistemology| Special Section Introduction. *International Journal of Communication, 8*, 10.

Dove, E. S., & Özdemir, V. (2015). What role for law, human rights, and bioethics in an age of Big Data, consortia science, and consortia ethics? The importance of trustworthiness. *Laws, 4*(3), 515–540. doi:10.3390/laws4030515 PMID:26345196

Economic and Social Research Council. (2012). *ESRC Framework for Research Ethics*. Swindon: Economic and Social Research Council.

Government Social Research Unit. (2006). *GSR Professional Guidance: Ethical Assurance for Social Research in Government*. London: HM Treasury.

Grimmelmann, J. (2009). Facebook and the social dynamics of privacy. *Iowa Law Review, 95*, 4.

Gross, R., & Acquisti, A. (2005). Information revelation and privacy in online social networks. Paper presented at the 2005 ACM workshop on Privacy in the electronic society, Alexandria, VA. doi:10.1145/1102199.1102214

Jacquith, M. (2009) 'Facebook's bizarre definition of data ownership', Tempus Fugit blog, 26 February 2009, Avaialble: http://txfx.net/2009/02/26/facebooks-bizarre-definition-of-data-ownership/

Lang, D. (2011) 'Where should you post your status?', Breaking Copy blog, Available: http://www.breakingcopy.com/socialmedia-flowchart-status

Law, P. (2015). Legal Problems in Data Management: Ethics of Big Data Analytics and the Importance of Disclosure, 31 J. *Marshall J. Info. Tech. & Privacy, L*, 641.

Lenhart, A., & Madden, M. (2007). Teens, privacy & online social networks. Pew internet & American life project Retrieved from http://www.pewinternet.org/pdfs/PIP_Teens_Privacy_SNS_Report_Final.pdf

Lewis, K., Kaufman, J., Gonzalez, M., Wimmer, A., & Christakis, N. (2008). Tastes, Ties, and time: A new social network dataset using Facebook. com. *Social Networks, 30*(4), 330–342. doi:10.1016/j.socnet.2008.07.002

Lewis, P., Newburn, T., Taylor, M., Mcgillivray, C., Greenhill, A., Frayman, H., & Proctor, R. (2011) 'Reading the riots: investigating England's summer of disorder', Report – The Guardian and The London School of Economics. <http://eprints.lse.ac.uk/46297/1/Reading%20the%20riots%28published%29.pdf>

Liu, S. B. (2010). The Emerging Ethics of Studying Social Media Use with a Heritage Twist. "Revisiting Research Ethics in the Facebook Era: Challenges in Emerging CSCW Research." Workshop at ACM Conference on Computer-Supported Cooperative Work (CSCW 2010), Savannah, GA.

Market Research Society. (2012). *MRS Guidelines for Online Research*. London: MRS Evidence Matters.

Mittelstadt, B. D., & Floridi, L. (2015). The ethics of big data: Current and foreseeable issues in biomedical contexts. *Science and Engineering Ethics*, 1–39. PMID:26002496

MRS Market Research Standards Board. (2012). 'Online Data Collection and Privacy Discussion Paper.' http://www.mrs.org.uk/pdf/2012-04-04%20Online%20data%20collection%20and%20privacy.pdf

Narayanan, A., & Shmatikov, V. (2008). Robust de-anonymization of large sparse datasets. Paper presented at the IEEE Symposium on Security and Privacy, 2008.

Narayanan, A., & Shmatikov, V. (2009). De-anonymizing social networks. Paper presented at the 30th IEEE Symposium on Security and Privacy.

Nissenbaum, H. (2009). *Privacy in context: Technology, policy, and the integrity of social life*. Stanford, CA: Stanford University Press.

Protalinksi, E. (2012) 'It's yours – until you upload it', In Dignan, L. 'The Social Web: who owns your data?' ZDNet Online Debate, Avaiable: http://www.zdnet.com/debate/the-socialweb-who-owns-your-data/10087130/

Richards, N. M., & King, J. H. (2014). Big data ethics. *Wake Forest Law Review*, *49*, 393.

Roberts, L. (2012) Ethical Issues in Conducting Qualitative Research in Online Communities, published on the NSMNSS blog, available at: http://nsmnss.blogspot.co.uk/2012/07/ethical-issues-in-conducting.html

Solove, D. (2007). *The future of reputation: Gossip, rumor, and privacy on the internet*. New Haven, CT: Yale University Press.

Stutzman, F. (2008). Facebook datasets and private chrome. Unit Structures Retrieved from http://fs-tutzman.com/2008/09/29/facebook-datasets-and-private-chrome/

Sweeney, L. (2002). k-anonymity: A model for protecting privacy. *International Journal of Uncertainty, Fuzziness and Knowledge-based Systems*, *10*(5), 557–570. doi:10.1142/S0218488502001648

Thelwall, M. (2010).Researching the public web 12 July. eResearch Ethics. Available from: http://eresearchethics.org/position/researching-the-public-web/

Vayena, E., Salathé, M., Madoff, L. C., & Brownstein, J. S. (2015). Ethical challenges of big data in public health. *PLoS Computational Biology*, *11*(2), e1003904. doi:10.1371/journal.pcbi.1003904 PMID:25664461

Webster, S., Lewis, J., & Brown, A. (2013). Ethical Considerations in Qualitative Research. In *Qualitative Research Practice: A guide for Social Science Students and Researchers* (pp. 77–107). London: Sage Publications.

Zimmer, M. (2008). More on the ''Anonymity'' of the Facebook dataset—It's Harvard College. michaelzimmer.org Retrieved from http://michaelzimmer.org/2008/10/03/moreon-the-anonymity-of-the-facebook-dataset-its-harvard-college/

Zwitter, A. (2014). Big data ethics. *Big Data & Society*, *1*(2), 2053951714559253. doi:10.1177/2053951714559253

KEY TERMS AND DEFINITIONS

Ambivalence: The state of having mixed feelings or contradictory ideas about something or someone.

Data Anonymization: A type of information sanitization whose intent is privacy protection. It is the process of either encrypting or removing personally identifiable information from data sets, so that the people whom the data describe remain anonymous.

End User License Agreement (EULA): Refers to a legal contract between a software application author or publisher and the user of that application.

Ethical Guidelines: Also called ethical codes, these are used by groups and organizations to define what actions are morally right and wrong.

Ethics: Refers to moral principles that govern a person's behavior or the conducting of an activity.

Privacy: Refers to the right to be let alone, or freedom from interference or intrusion.

Skepticism: Refers to any questioning attitude or doubt towards one or more items of putative knowledge or belief.

Social Media: Social media refers to websites and applications that enable users to create and share content or to participate in social networking.

Section 3
Big Data Analytics:
Its Methods and Applications

Chapter 14
Big Data Analytics in Health Care

Keerthi Suneetha
SVEC, India

ABSTRACT

With the arrival of technology and rising amount of data (Big Data) there is a need towards implementation of effective analytical techniques (Big Data Analytics) in health sector which provides stakeholders with new insights that have the potential to advance personalized care to improve patient outcomes and avoid unnecessary costs. This chapter covers how to evaluate this big volume of data for unknown and useful facts, associations, patterns, trends which can give birth to new line of handling of diseases and provide high quality healthcare at lower cost to all citizens. This chapter gives a wide insight of introduction to Big Data Analytics in health domain, processing steps of BDA, Challenges and Future scope of research in healthcare.

INTRODUCTION OF BIG DATA ANALYTICS

Big data analytics refers to the process of collecting, organizing and analyzing large sets of data to discover patterns and other useful information. An enormous amount of data often referred to as Big Data is getting generated everyday by diverse segments of industries like business, finance, manufacturing, healthcare, education, research and development etc. Big data analytics will help organizations to better understand the information contained within the data and will also help identify the data that is most important to the business and future business decisions. Big data analysts basically want the knowledge that comes from analyzing the data. The healthcare industry historically has generated large amounts of data, driven by record keeping, compliance & regulatory requirements, and patient care. While most data is stored in hard copy form, the current trend is toward rapid digitization of these large amounts of data. Big Data includes huge volume, high velocity, and extensible variety of data. The data in it will be of three types. Structured data: Relational data. Semi Structured data: XML data and Unstructured data: Word, PDF, Text, Media Logs.

DOI: 10.4018/978-1-5225-2031-3.ch014

Big data is critical to our life and its emerging as one of the most important technologies in modern world. Follow are just few benefits which are very much known to all of us:

- Using the information kept in the social network like Facebook, the marketing agencies are learning about the response for their campaigns, promotions, and other advertising mediums.
- Using the information in the social media like preferences and product perception of their consumers, product companies and retail organizations are planning their production.
- Using the data regarding the previous medical history of patients, hospitals are providing better and quick service.

Big data technologies are important in providing more accurate analysis, which may lead to more concrete decision-making resulting in greater operational efficiencies, cost reductions, and reduced risks for the business. To harness the power of big data, you would require an infrastructure that can manage and process huge volumes of structured and unstructured data in real-time and can protect data privacy and security.

There are various technologies in the market from different vendors including Amazon, IBM, Microsoft, etc., to handle big data. While looking into the technologies that handle big data, we examine the following two classes of technology:

1. **Operational Big Data**
   This includes systems like MongoDB that provide operational capabilities for real-time, interactive workloads where data is primarily captured and stored. NoSQL Big Data systems are designed to take advantage of new cloud computing architectures that have emerged over the past decade to allow massive computations to be run inexpensively and efficiently. This makes operational big data workloads much easier to manage, cheaper, and faster to implement. Some NoSQL systems can provide insights into patterns and trends based on real-time data with minimal coding and without the need for data scientists and additional infrastructure.

2. **Analytical Big Data**
   This includes systems like Massively Parallel Processing (MPP) database systems and Map Reduce that provide analytical capabilities for retrospective and complex analysis that may touch most or all the data. Map Reduce provides a new method of analyzing data that is complementary to the capabilities provided by SQL, and a system based on MapReduce that can be scaled up from single servers to thousands of high and low end machines.

OBJECTIVE OF BDA

- Analyze disease patterns and tracking disease outbreaks and transmission to improve public health surveillance and speed response
- Patients must be encouraged to play an active role in their own health by making the right choices about diet, exercise, preventive care, and other lifestyle factors.
- Detect diseases at earlier stages and can be treated more easily and effectively
- Patients must receive the most timely, appropriate treatment available

- Providers and payers continually look for ways to improve value while preserving or improving health-care quality.
- Stakeholders focuses on identifying new therapies and approaches to health-care delivery
- Faster development of more accurately targeted vaccines, e.g., choosing the annual influenza strain.
- Turning large amounts of data into actionable information can be used to identify needs, provide services, and predict and prevent crises, especially for the benefit of populations
- Provide right intervention to the right patient at the right time from massive amount of data

BIG DATA ANALYTICS IN HEALTHCARE

With the world's population increasing and everyone living longer, models of treatment delivery are rapidly changing, and many of the decisions behind those changes are being driven by data. The drive now is to understand as much about a patient as possible, as early in their life as possible – hopefully picking up warning signs of serious illness at an early enough stage that treatment is far more simple (and less expensive) than if it had not been spotted until later. The healthcare industry has generated enormous amount of data till date which is measured in petabyte /exabyte scale. The goal of healthcare industry is to analyse this big volume of data for unknown and useful facts, patterns, associations and trends with help of machine learning algorithms, which can give birth to new line of treatment of diseases. The aim is to provide high quality healthcare at lower cost to all. This will benefit the community and nation as a whole. The 5 V's of Big Data relevant to healthcare are:

- **Volume:** As mentioned earlier, healthcare industry generates prodigious data at staggering rate. The report from EMC and the research firm IDC anticipates an overall increase in health data of 48 percent annually. According to the report, the volume of healthcare data in 2013 was 153 exabytes and it may increase to 2,314 exabytes by 2020 (Dormehl, 2015).
- **Variety:** In the past, the emphasis had been on generating clinical data for patients with similar symptoms, storing and analyzing it to derive the most effective course of treatment for the admitted patient. Now the healthcare industry is focusing on complete healthcare, by providing an effective treatment through analysis of a patient's data from various other sources too. This refers to variety.
- **Variety:** The varied health care data generally falls into one of the three categories i.e. structured, semi structured and unstructured. Generally the following data is gathered: clinical data from Clinical Decision Support systems (CDSS) (physician's notes, genomic data, behavioural data, data in Electronic Health Records (EHR), Electronic Medical Records (EMR)), machine generated sensor data, data from wearable devices, Medical Image data (from CT scan, MRI, X Ray's etc), medical claim related data, hospital's administrative data, national health register data, medicine and surgical instruments expiry date identification based on RFID data (McNulty, 2014), social media data like twitter feeds, Face book status, web pages, blogs, articles (Raghupathi and Raghupathi, 2014).
- **Velocity:** It refers to the speed at which new data is generated and moves around. The sensor devices and wearable collect real time physiological data of patients at a rapid pace or velocity. This new data being generated every second poses a big challenge for data analysts. Social media data

also adds to velocity as the users views, posts, feeds scale up in seconds to enormous amount in case of epidemics/national disasters.

- **Veracity:** It refers to trustworthiness of data. Analyzing such a voluminous, variable and fast paced data is a hurricane task. There is no scope for error especially in critical healthcare solutions where patient's life is at stake. The primary aim is to ensure the data is reliable. It is quite difficult to ensure the reliability of unstructured data for e.g. usage of different terms/abbreviations for disease/symptoms, misinterpreted prescriptions due to bad handwriting, false/fake comments on social portals, improper readings from faulty machines/sensors, incomplete/inaccurate data filled by patients etc.

BENEFITS OF USING BIG DATA ANALYTICS IN HEALTHCARE

Patients today are more empowered to take control of their health and are becoming an increasingly important part of the care team. Data analytics can help make use of fast-changing information that comes from many different sources. By discovering associations and understanding patterns and trends within vast amount of data, data analytics has the potential to improve accurate diagnoses, better management of chronic conditions and better overall patient care which should always be the central focus of healthcare provision. Thus, data analytics in healthcare taken an advantage of the explosion of data to extract insights for making better informed decisions.

By digitizing, combining and effective usage of data analytics in health care provides potential benefits include detecting diseases at earlier stages when they can be treated more easily and effectively, able to detect health care fraud more quickly and efficiently, makes it easier for doctors to follow up with patients and track continuing care, both under their supervision and that of the patient's other doctors. Also in case of any emergency, these records can provide critical, life-saving information to emergency care providers such as patient's medical history, blood type and allergy information, when the patient is unable to communicate. For more successful capture, storage and manipulation of large volumes of data, many development platforms are provided with advances in data management system mainly virtualization and cloud computing concepts.

Data is accumulated in real-time with a rapid pace, or velocity. The constant flow of new data accumulating at unprecedented rates presents new challenges. Just as the volume and variety of data that is collected and stored has changed, so too has the velocity at which it is generated and is essential for retrieving, analyzing, comparing and making decisions based on the output. Now-a-days most of the healthcare data has been traditionally static such as paper files, x-ray films, and scripts. Velocity of mounting data increases with data that represents regular monitoring, such as multiple daily diabetic glucose measurements or more continuous control by insulin pumps and blood pressure readings etc., Many applications of real-time data, such as detecting infections at the early stage, identifying them quickly and applying the right treatments could reduce patient morbidity and mortality and even prevent hospital outbreaks.

As the nature of health data has evolved, so too have analytics techniques scaled up to the complex and sophisticated analytics necessary to accommodate volume, velocity and variety. The data collected in earlier days are in electronic health records which are in almost structured format. Currently almost every data is in multimedia and unstructured format. As the voluminous amount of data is structured, unstructured and semi-structured nature which makes healthcare data both interesting and challenging.

Structured data is data that can be easily stored, queried, recalled, analyzed and manipulated by machine. Traditionally, in healthcare, structured and semi-structured data includes instrument readings and data generated by the ongoing conversion of paper records to electronic health and medical records. Historically, the point of care generated unstructured data: office medical records, handwritten nurse and doctor notes, hospital admission and discharge records, paper prescriptions, radiograph films, MRI, CT and other images. The structured data include input record fields such as patient name, data of birth, address, physician's name, hospital name and address, treatment reimbursement codes, and other information easily coded into and handled by automated databases. The need to field-code data at the point of care for electronic handling is a major obstacle to recognition of EMRs by physicians and nurses, who lose the natural language ease of entry and understanding that handwritten notes provide. On the other hand, most providers concur that an easy way to decrease prescription errors is to use digital entries rather than handwritten scripts.

With the rapid growth in the number of healthcare organizations as well as the number of patients has resulted in the better use of computer-aided medical diagnostics and decision support systems in clinical settings. Several areas in health care such as diagnosis, prognosis, and screening can be enhanced by utilizing computational intelligence. The integration of computer analysis with appropriate care has potential to help clinicians improve diagnostic accuracy. The integration of medical images with other types of electronic health record (EHR) data and genomic data can also improve the accuracy and reduce the time taken for a diagnosis.

METHODOLOGY AND PROCESSING STEPS OF BDA

Methodology

The following are the list of methodological steps to be followed while processing the BDA:

1. **Data Collection from Various Sources:** Electronic health records (EHRs) are one way of collecting patient information.
2. **Selection of Variables:** Independent and dependent variables are identified.
3. **ETL and Data Transformation for Data Analytics:** Lots of unnecessary information, incorrect entries, and even duplicate information needs to be cleansed before it can be used successfully.
4. **Platform/Tool Selection:** A large number of open source and proprietary platforms and tools are available in market. Some of them are Hadoop, MapReduce, Storm, GridGrain. Big data databases like Cassanadra, HBase, MongoDB, CouchDB, OrientDB, Terrastore, Hive etc. Also various Data Mining tools like RapidMiner,Mahout, Orange, Weka, Rattle, KEEL etc and File systems like HDFS and Gluster. Programming languages like Pig/PigLatin, R, ECL.
5. **Analytical Techniques:** Applying various big data analytics techniques to the data.
6. **Applying Machine-Learning Algorithms:** Association, clustering, classification, etc.
7. **Results & Insight**

We can map steps taken up while performing BDA Process to the data mining knowledge discovery steps as follows:

1. **Data Acquisition and Storage:** Efficient, systematic data collection, storage and management drive automation is essential for high-quality patient care. Initially the data is fed to the system through many external sources like clinical data from Clinical Decision Support systems (CDSS), EMR, EHR, machine generated sensor data, data from wearable devices, national health register data, drug related data from Pharmaceutical companies, social media data like twitter feeds, Facebook status, web pages, blogs, articles and many more (Raghupathi and Raghupathi, 2014). This data is either stored in databases or data warehouse. With advent of cloud computing, it is convenient to store such voluminous data on the cloud rather than on physical disks. This is more cost effective and manageable way to store data.

2. **Data Cleaning:** The data which has been collected should be complete and should be in a structured format to perform effective analysis. But generally, the healthcare data contains flaws like, many patients don't share their data completely like data about their dietary habits, weight and lifestyle. In such cases the empty fields need to be handled appropriately. Another example can be for e.g.: for field like Gender of person, there can be at most one of two values i.e. male or female. In case any other value or no value is present then such entries need to marked and handled accordingly. The data from sensors, prescriptions, medical image data and social media data need to be articulated in a structured form suitable for analysis (Agrawal et al., 2012).

3. **Data Integration:** The BDA process uses data accumulated across various platforms. This data can differ in metadata (the number of fields, type, and format). The entire data has to be aggregated properly and consistently into a dataset which can be successfully used for data analysis purpose. This is a very challenging task, considering the big volume and variety of big data.

4. **Data Querying, Analysis and Interpretation:** Once the data is cleaned and integrated, the next step is to query the data. A query can be simple query like for eg: What is mortality rate in a particular region? Or a complex query as, how many patients with diabetes are likely to develop heart related problems in next 5 years? Depending on the complexity of the query, the data analyst must choose appropriate platform and analysis tools. Big data search tools like Lucene, Solr etc.Data Aggregation and transfer tools like Sqoop, Flume, Chukwa. Other tools like Oozie, Zookeeper, Avro, Terracotta. Some open source platforms are also available like Lumify, IKANOW (Harvey, 2012).

The criteria for platform assessment can differ for different organizations. Generally, the ease of use, availability, the capability to handle huge amount of data, support for visualization, high quality assurance, cost, and security can be some of the variables to decide upon the platform and tool to be used.

BIG DATA CHALLENGES IN HEALTH CARE

The healthcare industry has become extremely efficient at collecting data. The adoption of electronic claims systems, laboratory information systems, radiology information systems, electronic health records, and more have created massive stores of clinical and financial data that have the potential to drive significant healthcare performance improvement. However, healthcare data challenges persist. According to a survey of the Health Leaders Media Council in July 2014, 89% of healthcare leaders agree that they need to be able to analyze this data across the care continuum in order to ensure their organizations' clinical and financial success.

While there is agreement on the importance of using these information resources, healthcare lags other industries in putting in place the healthcare data analytics and business intelligence solutions that will help them meet these healthcare big data challenges.

- Amassed data is so large that is difficult to find the most valuable pieces of information
- Segregating the sheer volume and variety of data to identify the areas that are vital from an analytics point of view is of grave importance
- Finding the right ways to infuse analytics into everyday operations.
- Managing specific individual and population health and detecting health care fraud more quickly and efficiently

Big Data allows healthcare providers to meaningfully evaluate their practices and compare them within and across organizations. Physicians often rely on their intuition and past experience to treat patients. Big Data pools thousands of patient experiences, indicating which treatments worked best. Establishing evidence-based practices at the organizational level creates opportunities to place the right patient with the right provider, eliminating some of the burden and cost of unnecessary specialization. Of course, the personal physician-patient connection will always be crucial, but analysis of Big Data makes it clear where organizations can foster that connection most effectively.

HOW TO SUPPORT PATIENTS WITH MULTIPLE COMORBIDITIES

Patients battling several health problems access healthcare most frequently and cause the highest costs. Providers who utilize Big Data will see the most significant results through having the relevant information directly in a patient's EHR. Data systems can alert providers of problematic trends or a lack of data. It provides an opportunity to get involved early rather than waiting for an emergent and costly episode. By linking data to shopping histories, social media, and geographical information through third-party data vendors, healthcare providers can achieve a window onto their customers' daily health behaviors, which are thought to determine up to 50 percent of overall health status.

- Leveraging the patient/data correlations in longitudinal records.
- Understanding unstructured clinical notes in the right context.
- Efficiently handling large volumes of medical imaging data and extracting potentially useful information and biomarkers.
- Analyzing genomic data is a computationally intensive task and combining with standard clinical data adds additional layers of complexity.
- Capturing the patient's behavioral data through several sensors; their various social interactions and communications.

CHALLENGES TO HEALTHCARE PROVIDERS

Big Data is deemed "big" for three reasons: Volume, Velocity and Variety. The volume of stored healthcare data has quadrupled since 2010, and much of that data is stored unstructured and multimedia data such as image and video formats. This leads to several challenges in terms of cost, expertise, and security.

FUTURE RESEARCH DIRECTIONS

Today, Big Data is influencing IT industry like few technologies have done before. The enormous amount of data generated from sensor-enabled machines, mobile devices, cloud computing, social media and satellites help different organizations to improve their decision making and take their business to an additional level.

Every day data is generated in such a rapid manner that, traditional database and other data storing system will gradually give up in storing, retrieving, and finding relationships among data. Big data technologies have addressed the problems related to this new big data revolution through the use of commodity hardware and distribution. Companies like Google, Yahoo!, General Electric, Cornerstone, Microsoft, Kaggle, Facebook, Amazon that are investing a lot in Big Data research and projects. IDC estimated the value of Big Data market to be about $ 6.8 billion in 2012 growing almost 40 percent every year to $17 billion by 2015. By 2017, Wikibon's Jeff Kelly predicts the Big Data market will top $50 billion (Furrier, 2012). Demand is so hot for solutions that all companies are exploring big data strategies.

The problem is that the companies lack internal expertise and best practices. The side effect is that there are services and consulting boom in big data. It's a perfect storm of product and services‖ says Wikibon's Jeff Kelly. Recently it was announced that, Indian Prime Minister's office is using Big Data analytics to understand Indian citizen's sentiments and ideas through crowd sourcing platform www. mygov.in and social media to get a picture of common people's thought and opinion on government actions (McNulty, 2014).

Google is launching the Google Cloud Platform, which provides developers to develop a range of products from simple websites to complex applications. It enables users to launch virtual machines, store huge amount of data online, and plenty of other things. Basically, it will be a one stop platform for cloud based applications, online gaming, mobile applications, etc. All these require huge amounts of data processing where Big Data plays an immense role in data processing.

The predictions from the IDC Future Scope for Big Data and Analytics are:

1. Visual data discovery tools will be growing 2.5 times faster than rest of the Business Intelligence (BI) market. By 2018, investing in this enabler of end-user self-service will become a requirement for all enterprises.
2. Over the next five years spending on cloud-based Big Data and analytics (BDA) solutions will grow three times faster than spending for on-premise solutions. Hybrid on/off premise deployments will become a requirement.
3. Shortage of skilled staff will persist. In the U.S. alone there will be 181,000 deep analytics roles in 2018 and five times that many positions requiring related skills in data management and interpretation.

4. By 2017 unified data platform architecture will become the foundation of BDA strategy. The unification will occur across information management, analysis, and search technology.
5. Growth in applications incorporating advanced and predictive analytics, including machine learning, will accelerate in 2015. These apps will grow 65% faster than apps without predictive functionality.
6. 70% of large organizations already purchase external data and 100% will do so by 2019. In parallel more organizations will begin to monetize their data by selling them or providing value-added content.
7. Adoption of technology to continuously analyze streams of events will accelerate in 2015 as it is applied to Internet of Things (IoT) analytics, which is expected to grow at a five-year compound annual growth rate (CAGR) of 30%.
8. Decision management platforms will expand at a CAGR of 60% through 2019 in response to the need for greater consistency in decision making and decision making process knowledge retention.
9. Rich media (video, audio, image) analytics will at least triple in 2015 and emerge as the key driver for BDA technology investment.
10. By 2018 half of all consumers will interact with services based on cognitive computing on a regular basis (Vesset et al., 2014).

Big data isn't new, but now has reached critical mass as people digitize their lives. "People are walking sensors," said Nicholas Skytland, project manager at NASA within the Human Adaptation and Countermeasures Division of the Space Life Sciences Directorate (Dignan, 2012).

Taking an average of all the figures suggested by leading big data market analyst and research firms, it can be concluded that approximately 15 percent of all IT organizations will move to cloud-based service platforms, and between 2015 and 2021, this service market is expected to grow about 35 percent.

CONCLUSION

Big Data in healthcare is being used to predict epidemics, cure disease, improve quality of life and avoid preventable deaths. With the world's population increasing and everyone living longer, models of treatment delivery are rapidly changing, and many of the decisions behind those changes are being driven by data. The drive now is to understand as much about a patient as possible, as early in their life as possible – hopefully picking up warning signs of serious illness at an early enough stage that treatment is far more simple (and less expensive) than if it had not been spotted until later.

Patients today are more empowered to take control of their health and are becoming an increasingly important part of the care team. Big Data analytics can help make use of fast-changing information that comes from many different sources. By discovering associations and understanding patterns and trends within vast amount of data, big data analytics has the potential to improve care, save lives and lower costs. Thus, big data analytics in healthcare taken advantage of the explosion in data to extract insights for making better informed decisions.

REFERENCES

Agrawal, D., Bernstein, P., Bertino, E., Davidson, S., Dayal, U., Franklin, M., & Widom, J. (2012). *Challenges and Opportunities with Big Data: A white paper prepared for the Computing Community Consortium committee of the Computing Research Association*. Retrieved from http://cra.org/ccc/resources/ccc-led-whitepapers/

Dignan, L. (2012). *30 Big Data Project Takeaways*. ZDNet. Retrieved from http://www.zdnet.com/article/30-big-data-project-takeaways/

Dormehl, L. (2015). *President Obama's New Health Care Initiative Will Harness the Power of Big Data*. Fast Company & Inc. Retrieved from http://www.fastcompany.com/3041775/fast-feed/president-obamas-new-healthcare-initiative-willharness-the-power-of-big-data

Furrier, J. (2012). Big Data is Creating the Future - It's A $50 Billion Market. *Forbes*. Retrieved from http://www.forbes.com/sites/siliconangle/2012/02/29/big-data-is-creating-the-future-its-a-50-billion-market/

Harvey, C. (2012). *50 Top Open Source Tools for Big Data*. Datamation: IT Business Edge. QuinStreet Enterprise. Retrieved from http://www.datamation.com/datacenter/50-top-open-source-tools-for-big-data-1.html

McNulty, E. (2014). *Indian Government Using Big Data to Revolutionise Democracy*. Dataconomy. Retrieved from http://dataconomy.com/indian-government-using-big-data-to-revolutionise-democracy/

Raghupathi, W., & Raghupathi, V. (2014). Big data analytics in healthcare: promise and potential. *Health Information Science and Systems*, *2*, 3. Retrieved from http://www.hissjournal.com/content/2/1/3

Vesset, D., Olofson, C. W., Schubmehl, D., McDonough, B., Woodward, A., Stires, C., ... Dialani, M. (2014). *IDC FutureScape: Worldwide Big Data and Analytics 2015 Predictions*. IDC Research, Inc. Retrieved from http://www.idc.com/getdoc.jsp?containerId=prUS25329114

Chapter 15
Mining Big Data for Marketing Intelligence

Khadija Ali Vakeel
Indian Institute of Management Indore, India

ABSTRACT

This chapter elaborates on mining techniques useful in big data analysis. Specifically, it will elaborate on how to use association rule mining, self organizing maps, word cloud, sentiment extraction, network analysis, classification, and clustering for marketing intelligence. The application of these would be on decisions related to market segmentation, targeting and positioning, trend analysis, sales, stock markets and word of mouth. The chapter is divided in two sections of data collection and cleaning where we elaborate on how twitter data can be extracted and mined for marketing decision making. Second part discusses various techniques that can be used in big data analysis for mining content and interaction network.

INTRODUCTION

Big data has transformed the way people interact with each other. It not only impacts the interaction between company and consumer but also between consumers. Big data can be analyzed to take effective decisions by the company for successful marketing strategy. In this chapter, we elaborate on techniques that could be effectively used in textual mining data for marketing intelligence. We explain the complete process of big data mining from data extraction, data cleaning, analysis, and visualization. Specifically, we would elaborate on how to use association rule mining, self-organizing maps, word cloud, sentiment extraction, network analysis, classification, and clustering for marketing intelligence. The application of these would be on decisions related to market segmentation, targeting and positioning, trend analysis, sales, stock markets and word of mouth.

Association rule mining on transactions help us show given X and Y item in the itemset, X leads to Y. Apriori algorithm is used to find frequent itemsets that occur together in transactions given minimum support and confidence.

DOI: 10.4018/978-1-5225-2031-3.ch015

Self-organizing maps or Kohonen maps are algorithms that embed the clusters in a low-dimensional space right from the beginning and proceed in a way that places related clusters close together in that space.

Word cloud is used to describe the importance of each word based on the frequency of the attributes occurring in the total corpus.

Sentiment analysis is performed to extract opinion and subjectivity knowledge from user generated content, formalize this knowledge discovery and analyze it for managerial implications. This type of knowledge discovery covers analyzing product user opinion, appraisals, attitudes, and emotions etc. related to entities, individuals, issues, events, topics, and their own attributes. Sentiment analysis involves techniques like machine learning, information retrieval, and natural language processing to process vast amounts of user generated content.

Topological models for community analysis help in detecting the structural properties of the social network. Average shortest path length, efficiency, clustering coefficient, degree distributions are used to derive the network characteristics. Different models such as random graph models, small-world model, and scale-free models are used for analysis.

Centrality analysis helps us in identifying key nodes of the network such that roles like leader, follower and bridge are discovered for efficient marketing strategy on a social media network. Three main centrality measurements named- degree, betweenness, and closeness are used.

Classification and clustering are a basic technique we explore Latent Dirichlet Allocation (LDA) for clustering. Topic models like LDA have previously been used for a variety of applications, including ad-hoc information retrieval, geographical information retrieval and the analysis of the development of ideas over time in the field of computational linguistics.

To conclude, all these techniques have extensively been used in mining, this chapter would deal with how BI tools can be used in the context of marketing. In the following sections, a framework for big data mining for marketing research is elaborated.

DATA COLLECTION AND CLEANING

Taking an example of twitter, following section shows how data collection and cleaning can be done. Once the communities on the twitter have been identified, user data and tweet information can be collected by the twitter APIs like rest or stream. Every user has unique id through which his profile details can be extracted. The usage pattern of a twitter user can be either personal, group, aggregator, satire or marketing related (Cheong & Lee, 2009). Users can also be categorized as tourist, minglers, devotees and insiders (Kozinets, 2002). Tweet search is generally based on time period or is a keyword search (Twitter Developer). Data about location, user mentions, friends, and followers can also be extracted with the help of these API. Example for pattern detection, retweet, replied and trend keyword can be used (Cheong & Lee, 2009). Re-tweet are special posts where one twitter user forwards the tweet of another user, this kind of tweets start with RT. Similarly, reply to a tweet can be detected as a reply starts with @username where username is the twitter user whom another user is replying too. Hashtags are another feature which starts with #keyword such that it creates an index for the keyword. This user information tweets and metadata can be stored in a relational database for further analysis. Further, not all the extracted tweets might to useful or related to the marketing research question. Classifying tweets as primarily on topic or off topic or primarily social or informational will help to get tweets related to the scope of the question (Kozinets, 2002).

Figure 1. Content and interaction analysis

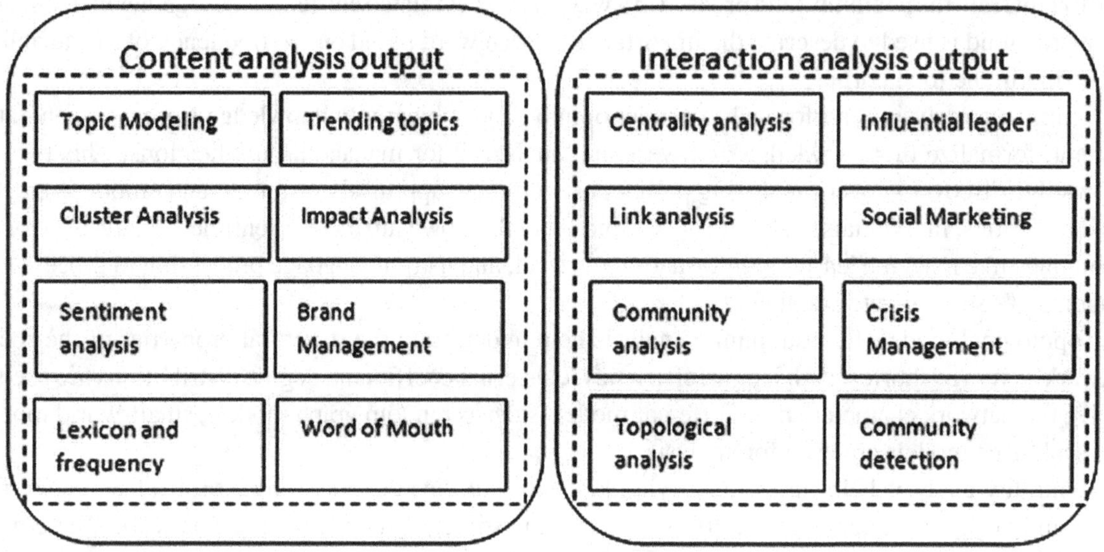

Content analysis output		Interaction analysis output	
Topic Modeling	Trending topics	Centrality analysis	Influential leader
Cluster Analysis	Impact Analysis	Link analysis	Social Marketing
Sentiment analysis	Brand Management	Community analysis	Crisis Management
Lexicon and frequency	Word of Mouth	Topological analysis	Community detection

CONTENT AND INTERACTION ANALYSIS

Figure 1 shows different techniques of analysis, where left part of content analysis output is the technique and the right part shows the marketing application where this technique can be utilized. We elaborate on these techniques in the subsequent paragraphs useful in analyzing content and interaction network of big data.

Association Rules Mining

Association rule mining on transactions help us show given X and Y item in an itemset, whether X leads to Y. Apriori algorithm is used to find frequent itemsets that occur together in transactions given minimum support and confidence. It is a data mining algorithm for generating association rules based on "if an itemset is not frequent, any of its supersets is never frequent". It is a three step algorithm where if rule X => Y is true then for a transaction set D the confidence c are those transactions in D where if X is there Y is also there. Similarly, support for a transaction set D is X U Y.

1. From frequent itemsets of size k, generate candidates C_{k+1}
2. Calculate the Support of each candidate itemset
3. Add items above minimum support to the class

The algorithm has two distinct functions join and prune where a union of candidates of frequent itemset of k+1 and size k is taken in join step. Then in the prune step, subsets of all non-frequent itemset are removed because a subset of a nonfrequent set cannot be frequent (Wu et al., 2008). Apriori algorithm can be used in market basket analysis like bread and butter are sold together or beer and diapers. For marketing purposes in supermarkets two different strategies can be used, bundling the products frequently sold together can increase the sales. On the other hand, if frequently sold group of products are kept separate apart such that the customer has to travel through the market, he can cruise through other products and thus increase sales of the products in the store.

Self-Organizing Maps

The process of grouping a set of abstract objects into classes of similar objects is called clustering (Han & Kamber, 2006). A cluster is a collection of objects such that objects in the same group are similar and objects in different groups are dissimilar (Han & Kamber, 2006). Clustering is unsupervised learning as no pre-defined class labels are there, for example, in classification. K-means algorithm is a top-down partitioning strategy which can make hard assignments or soft assignments to clusters. Hard assignments forcefully allocate 0/1 to the document but soft clustering does not make specific assignments (Chakrabarty, 2003).

Self-organizing maps (SOM) or Kohonen maps are algorithms that embed the clusters in a low-dimensional space right from the beginning and proceed in a way that places related clusters close together in that space (Chakrabarti, 2003). SOMs are unsupervised competitive Artificial neural network (ANN) based on the principle of winner takes all (Kohonen, 1995). It is made up of input and output layer with an array of interconnected matrix from input layer also called as Kohonen's Layer to output layer. A SOM learns through the weights associated with its neurons in each layer (Sharma & Dey, 2013). SOM essentially is a four-step algorithm:

1. Initialize weights of the neurons in the map.
2. Randomly select a training vector from the corpus.
3. Determine the Euclidean distance between input layer and the neuron's weight vector.
4. Update the weights according to the learning rate which controls the amount of learning in each iteration.

SOM is multi-pass algorithms where the first pass takes small training time and second pass fine tunes the SOM and takes longer time. Like soft k-means, SOM is an iterative process where representing vector is associated with a cluster. But unlike soft k-means, SOM also shows clusters in low dimensional space where representative vectors are graded according to the similarity (Chakrabarti, 2003). This visualization of gradient helps uniquely distinguish one cluster from another cluster (Cheong & Lee, 2010). Advantages of SOM include non-linear projection of the input space and cluster topology preservation (Sharma & Dey, 2013). In Emergent Self Organizing Maps (ESOM) the cluster boundaries are 'indistinct', the degree of separation between 'regions' of the map (i.e. clusters) being depicted by 'gradients' (Ultsch et al, 2005). SOM can be used for timely detection of hidden patterns on twitter messages using Cheong and Lee's "context" aware content analysis framework.

SOM can be used in the segmentation of customers while performing marketing analysis in the segmentation, targeting and positioning on the basis of different attributes. SOM will group customers with similar characteristics together and differentiate dissimilar customers through the color gradient. For example, Figure 2 shows SOM of customers clustered together such that blue boxes show one segment of customers and yellow boxes show different segment of customers.

Figure 2. Self-Organizing Maps (SOM) for segmentation

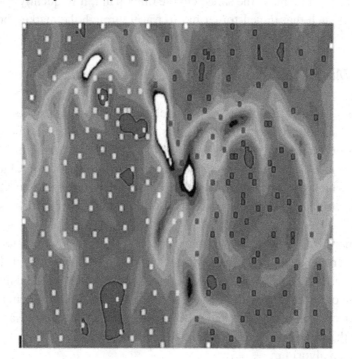

Word Cloud

To analyze the trends in which people were talking about, we can use a word cloud to describe the importance of each word based on the frequency of the attributes occurring in the textual data. To show how word cloud (Figure 3) can be useful, we use random 200 tweets from Amazon and after cleaning, we generate a word cloud. The most frequently appearing words in the tweets are higher in the area as presented by Amazon, Diwali, and Dhamaka; followed by attributes which occur less frequently like effect, safe. All the words occurring in the tweets more than 5 times were included in this word cloud. This could be helpful in knowing what people are talking about on the twitter and subsequently analyzing them to generate positive emotions about the company. In the case of Amazon, most of the people are talking about deals and moreover comparing Amazon to Flipkart which is another e-commerce giant in India.

Similarly, less frequent words like flops, fail, crash, disappointed show negative emotions of customers towards the Amazon sale whereas attributes like love shows positive experiences. There are other neutral words like morning, discount, and products etc which do not communicate any specific emotion but are useful in discovering the current topic of interest in the twitter community.

Sentiment Analysis

Sentiment refers to "an attitude, thought, or judgment prompted by feeling, specific view, or notion. Sentiment suggests a settled opinion reflective of one's feelings" (Pang & Lee, 2008). Sentiment is defined as a negative or positive opinion (Hu & Liu, 2004; Pang, Lee & Vaithyanathan, 2002). Sentiment analysis involves techniques like machine learning, information retrieval, and natural language process-

Figure 3. Word cloud for trend analysis

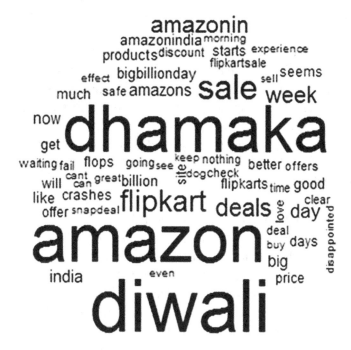

ing to process vast amounts of user generated content (Pang & Lee, 2008; Tsytsarau & Palpanas, 2011). Sentiment analysis is also related to appraisal extraction, with some association to affective computing that deals with computer recognition and expression of emotion (Picard, 2003). Social media monitoring is a nascent area of research, which is related to sentiment analysis and opinion mining (Colbaugh & Glass, 2010).

Sentiment analysis is performed to extract opinion and subjectivity knowledge from user generated content, formalize this knowledge discovery and analyze it for managerial implications. This type of knowledge discovery covers analyzing product user opinion, appraisals, attitudes, and emotions etc. related to entities, individuals, issues, events, topics, and their own attributes (Liu, 2010). Sentiment analysis can be performed at the document level (Chen, Ibekwe-SanJuan, SanJuan & Weaver, 2006; Pang et al., 2002; Turney, 2002), sentence level or feature level (Liu, Hu & Cheng, 2005). The dictionary based approach also known as sentiment lexicon contains opinion polarities of words example- Opinion Lexicons (Hu & Liu, 2004). Sentence level sentiment analysis is accomplished by taking an average or resultant sum score of polarities of words present.

Centrality Analysis

Social networks can have a positive or negative impact on brands (Jansen et al., 2009). Consumers use social networking services for opinions and information as trusted source for building brand perceptions (Jansen et al., 2009). "A tie is said to exist between communicators wherever they exchange or share resources such as goods, services, social support or information" (Haythornthwaite, 2002). Factors such as frequency of contact, duration of the association, intimacy of the tie, provision of reciprocal services, and kinship have been used as measures of tie strength (Haythornthwaite, 2002). The weak, strong and latent ties build into networks which can change the communication dynamics (Haythornthwaite, 2002). A networked audience is connected to each other such that an individual opinion might not make a difference but collective effort changes the dynamics. It has also been studied that social network reduces the cues available in face to face discussion but are used for advantages like mobility, brevity and pervasive access (Zhao & Rosson, 2009). The flow of information is mainly through weak ties rather than strong ties because of rapid mutual trust that develops in the community (Zhao & Rosson, 2009). The credibility of the source is another important characteristic that guides flow if the information in the network (Zhao & Rosson, 2009).

The following analysis of the social network can be done to mine insights for marketing:

Actors in the Network

According to the actor network theory; a network is formed of various actors in the group working in a synchronized pattern such that the outcome is achieved. It treats the social and technological aspects of a network in tandem and claims the people and artifacts are inseparable be it organization, human beings, computers, infrastructure, or technology hardware. Increasingly in IS research actor-network theory has been used for understanding human and non-human elements of a network.

In a social network positive, neutral and negative opinion propagate in tandem. Little effort has been made in past by researchers to study the negative opinion network separately from the other two. This is important in today's scenario when the trust on brand is made depending on the online reviews and sentiments generated from user post. It also helps managers understand what kind of different actors are available in network and design specific marketing strategies accordingly.

Topological Analysis, Community Analysis, and Centrality Analysis

Topological models help in detecting the structural properties of the social network. Average shortest path length, efficiency, clustering coefficient, degree distributions are used to derive the network characteristics. Different models such as random graph models, small-world model, and scale-free models are used for analysis.

Community analysis helps in tracing groups with denser links to the nodes as compared to other subgroups. In the case of twitter, these represent user mentions in the tweet by the twitter user. This sub-groups help in information dissemination, innovation diffusion, and knowledge sharing.

Centrality analysis helps us in identifying key nodes of the network such that roles like leader, follower and bridge are discovered for an efficient strategy to handle the service failure on a social media network. Three main centrality measurements named- degree, betweenness, and closeness are used. Popular bloggers are leaders, experts, or hubs which have a high degree. Betweenness is defined as a number of geodesics passing through a node. Actors with high betweenness are responsible for serving are bridges in the subgroups. Closeness is the sum of the length of geodesics between two pairs of actors in the network. Actors with low closeness are isolated and find it difficult to communicate in the network.

Latent Dirichlet Allocation

The Latent Dirichlet Allocation (Blei, Ng & Jordan, 2003) model is a Bayesian mixture model for discrete data where topics are assumed to be uncorrelated. Topic models have previously been used for a variety of applications, including ad-hoc information retrieval (Wei and Croft 2006), geographical information retrieval (Li, Wang, Xie, Wang & Ma 2008) and the analysis of the development of ideas over time in the field of computational linguistics (Hall, Jurafsky & Manning 2008). The method used for fitting the models is the Variational Expectation-Maximization (VEM) algorithm.

REFERENCES

Blei, D. M., Ng, A. Y., & Jordan, M. I. (2003). Latent dirichlet allocation. *Journal of Machine Learning Research, 3*(Jan), 993–1022.

Chakrabarti, S. (2003). *Mining the Web: Discovering knowledge from hypertext data.* Morgan Kaufmann.

Chen, C., Ibekwe-SanJuan, F., SanJuan, E., & Weaver, C. (2006, October). Visual analysis of conflicting opinions. In *2006 IEEE Symposium On Visual Analytics Science And Technology* (pp. 59-66). IEEE. doi:10.1109/VAST.2006.261431

Cheong, M., & Lee, V. (2009, November). Integrating web-based intelligence retrieval and decision-making from the twitter trends knowledge base. In *Proceedings of the 2nd ACM workshop on Social web search and mining*(pp. 1-8). ACM. doi:10.1145/1651437.1651439

Cheong, M., & Lee, V. 2010, August. A study on detecting patterns in twitter intra-topic user and message clustering. In *Pattern Recognition (ICPR), 2010 20th International Conference on* (pp. 3125-3128). IEEE. doi:10.1109/ICPR.2010.765

Colbaugh, R., & Glass, K. (2010, May). Estimating sentiment orientation in social media for intelligence monitoring and analysis. In *Intelligence and Security Informatics (ISI), 2010 IEEE International Conference on* (pp. 135-137). IEEE. doi:10.1109/ISI.2010.5484760

Hall, D., Jurafsky, D., & Manning, C. D. (2008, October). Studying the history of ideas using topic models. In *Proceedings of the conference on empirical methods in natural language processing* (pp. 363-371). Association for Computational Linguistics. doi:10.3115/1613715.1613763

Han, J., Kamber, M., & Pei, J. (2006). *Data mining, southeast asia edition: Concepts and techniques.* Morgan Kaufmann.

Haythornthwaite, C. (2002). Strong, weak, and latent ties and the impact of new media. *The Information Society, 18*(5), 385–401. doi:10.1080/01972240290108195

Hu, M., & Liu, B. (2004, August). Mining and summarizing customer reviews. In *Proceedings of the tenth ACM SIGKDD international conference on Knowledge discovery and data mining* (pp. 168-177). ACM.

Jansen, B. J., Zhang, M., Sobel, K., & Chowdury, A. (2009). Twitter power: Tweets as electronic word of mouth. *Journal of the American Society for Information Science and Technology, 60*(11), 2169–2188. doi:10.1002/asi.21149

Kohonen, T. (1995). *Self-organizing maps.* Springer-Verlag.

Kozinets, R. V. (2002). The field behind the screen: Using netnography for marketing research in online communities. *Journal of Marketing Research, 39*(1), 61–72. doi:10.1509/jmkr.39.1.61.18935

Liu, B. (2010). Sentiment Analysis and Subjectivity. Handbook of natural language processing, 2, 627-666.

Pang, B., & Lee, L. (2008). Opinion mining and sentiment analysis. *Foundations and Trends in Information Retrieval, 2*(1-2), 1-135.

Pang, B., Lee, L., & Vaithyanathan, S. (2002, July). Thumbs up?: sentiment classification using machine learning techniques. In *Proceedings of the ACL-02 conference on Empirical methods in natural language processing* (vol. 10, pp. 79-86). Association for Computational Linguistics. doi:10.3115/1118693.1118704

Picard, R. W. (2003). Affective computing: Challenges. *International Journal of Human-Computer Studies, 59*(1), 55–64. doi:10.1016/S1071-5819(03)00052-1

Sharma, A., & Dey, S. (2013). *Using Self-Organizing Maps for Sentiment Analysis.* arXiv preprint arXiv:1309.3946

Tsytsarau, M., & Palpanas, T. (2012). Survey on mining subjective data on the web. *Data Mining and Knowledge Discovery, 24*(3), 478–514. doi:10.1007/s10618-011-0238-6

Turney, P. D. (2002, July). Thumbs up or thumbs down?: semantic orientation applied to unsupervised classification of reviews. In *Proceedings of the 40th annual meeting on association for computational linguistics* (pp. 417-424). Association for Computational Linguistics.

Ultsch, A., & Mörchen, F. (2005). *ESOM-Maps: Tools for clustering, visualization, and classification with Emergent SOM.* Academic Press.

Wang, C., Wang, J., Xie, X., & Ma, W. Y. (2007, November). Mining geographic knowledge using location aware topic model. In *Proceedings of the 4th ACM workshop on Geographical information retrieval* (pp. 65-70). ACM. doi:10.1145/1316948.1316967

Wei, X., & Croft, W. B. (2006, August). LDA-based document models for ad-hoc retrieval. In *Proceedings of the 29th annual international ACM SIGIR conference on Research and development in information retrieval* (pp. 178-185). ACM.

Wu, X., Kumar, V., Quinlan, J. R., Ghosh, J., Yang, Q., Motoda, H., & Steinberg, D. et al. (2008). Top 10 algorithms in data mining. *Knowledge and Information Systems, 14*(1), 1–37. doi:10.1007/s10115-007-0114-2

Zhao, D., & Rosson, M. B. (2009, May). How and why people Twitter: the role that micro-blogging plays in informal communication at work. In *Proceedings of the ACM 2009 International Conference on Supporting Group Work* (pp. 243-252). ACM.

Chapter 16
Predictive Analysis for Digital Marketing Using Big Data:
Big Data for Predictive Analysis

Balamurugan Balusamy
VIT University, India

Tamizh Arasi
VIT University, India

Priya Jha
VIT University, India

Malathi Velu
VIT University, India

ABSTRACT

Big data analytics in recent years had developed lightning fast applications that deal with predictive analysis of huge volumes of data in domains of finance, health, weather, travel, marketing and more. Business analysts take their decisions using the statistical analysis of the available data pulled in from social media, user surveys, blogs and internet resources. Customer sentiment has to be taken into account for designing, launching and pricing a product to be inducted into the market and the emotions of the consumers changes and is influenced by several tangible and intangible factors. The possibility of using Big data analytics to present data in a quickly viewable format giving different perspectives of the same data is appreciated in the field of finance and health, where the advent of decision support system is possible in all aspects of their working. Cognitive computing and artificial intelligence are making big data analytical algorithms to think more on their own, leading to come out with Big data agents with their own functionalities.

DOI: 10.4018/978-1-5225-2031-3.ch016

INTRODUCTION

Due to the substantial scale evolution of structured, semi-structured, unstructured data, it has become a challenge for traditional storage systems and analytics tools. To unlock the great potential of the heterogeneous natured big data, advanced predictive analytics tools are the need of the era (Lohr, 2012) and (Waller, 2013). The data sources are highly scattered and are continuously generating huge data sets through transactions, clickstreams, surveillance, sensors and communication technologies (Tsai et.al, 2015). Predictive analytics for big data is an exponentially growing area of research today and the need of the hour for efficient analysis, management and faster real time utilization of both the stored data as well as real time data that are generated (Lohr, 2012). Predictive analysis is the advanced branch of data engineering that is concerned with predicting the outcome of events based on the analysis of historical data by applying sophisticated techniques of machine learning and regression (Ratner B., 2011) and (Mishra N., & Silakari S., 2012). Prediction is closely related to probability, the futuristic outcomes of certain events can be determined based on the analysis of historical and present data sets (Zaman and Mukhles, 2005). The current trends and patterns in the data sets are explored and after thorough analysis; the results are used to predict the outcomes of the future events.

Due to the vastness of the data sets, several important characteristics of information associated with the data, that could have been leveraged for productive applications often tend to remain unexplored and go to waste (Cao et.al, 2014), to prevent such loss, predictive analytics has a great role to play in the process. Analyzing data, discovering familiar patterns, deriving meaning from the patterns, formulating decisions and ultimately responding to the needs intelligently is the is the ideal goal of predictive analytics for big data. Today, businesses apply predictive analytics (forecasting, hypothesis testing, risk modeling, propensity modeling) in their working environment to increase involvement with their customers, reduce operational costs, and optimize processes involved and other numerous advantages that it offers (Tsai et.al, 2015). Figure 1 depicts the overall organization of the chapter.

Figure 1. Predictive analysis process overview

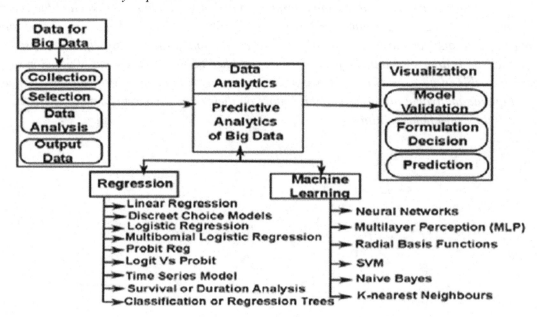

The predictor variable is the measurable variable for the entity. In other words, a predictor is a feature selected to be used as an input to a classification model (Jain et.al, 1999). A predictor can take four type of values-continuous, which consists of floating point or numerical magnitude values, categorical, for example Boolean values, word-like or text-like. Combining and integrating several predictor variables can result in a predictive model that can be used to make the required future forecasts within a certain level of reliability.

Predictive analytics has a heavy application in business environments (Banjade & Maharjan, 2011), (Chen et.al, 2012) and (Waller & Fawcett, 2013), as it associations commercial awareness with statistical and analytics techniques to better understand customers, products (Banjade & Maharjan, 2011), and partners and to identify potential opportunities and decrease the chances of risks for the company.

EVOLUTION OF PREDICTIVE ANALYTICS

Predictive analytics was not born yesterday; it has been in use since the time of WWII. A Kerrison predictor automated targeting of the anti-aircraft weapons against the enemy planes. Analytics also helped to decode German messages during the world war. Moreover, computer simulations were first used to predict the behavior of the nuclear chain reactions in 1944. During the decade of commercialization of analytics, in the 1950, ENIAC were known to generate the first weather forecast model (Zaman, M, 2005). In 1956, air travel and logistics were greatly improved by solving the shortest path problems through analytics. FICO, a leading analytics software company in 1958, FICO applied predictive modeling to credit risk decisions which has revolutionized entire industries. Also real time analytics to determine and fight credit card fraud was also developed in the 90's Black-Scholes model is the world's most well-known options pricing model. This model was first created in 1973 to predict stock prices. In 1980, the first commercial tools for building model-driven decision support systems were marketed which have greatly helped managers make efficient decisions over the years. In the late 90s, the e-commerce giants, Amazon, e-Bay competed to personalize online customer experience through relevant recommendations based on predictions. In 1998, Google implemented advanced algorithms to enhance web search experience of users. From 2000 onwards till date, predictive analytics has seen and contributed to numerous advancements across different industries. Structured and unstructured data are assessed and analyzed for generating results that are of significance to the analysts for driving decisions. Unlike earlier times, when advanced skills and expertise were required to use predictive analytics tools in business and understanding the outcomes was a complex procedure, the modern day predictive analytics tools are significantly user friendly and easy to use and implement in cross industry business environment. The key is in understanding the customer's "digital body language" (L. Sullivan, 2013). These tools are no longer restricted to advanced users but are well within the reach of naïve users and are marketed by proprietary software as well as freeware companies.

Predictive analytics is transforming the e-commerce industry in this era of data-driven market place (L. Sullivan, 2013; Waller et.al, 2013). Companies are using predictive analytics to anticipate the consumer's needs and behavior. Using this analysis and based on the customer's past behavior, these companies create recommendations for other products and services that the customer might me potentially interested in purchasing. Such services by these companies help consumers make educated decision as well as provide them with rich, customized experience as they now have the ability to take their brand experience in their own hands. With such personalization levels, enhancing customer retention and brand loyalty is a piece of cake.

DATA ANALYTICS

Data analytics is the initial step in the process of predictive analytics which involves gathering, selection, preprocessing, transformation, data mining (Ratner, 2011), evaluation and construal of raw data to get the useful data. Figure 2 depicts the steps involved in data analytics.

DATA INPUT

Data input comprises of gathering, selection, preprocessing, and transformation operators. After the data is gathered from various sources, relevant data is selected from the gathered pile. Preprocessing involves detection, cleaning, filtering of inconsistent data to get useful data. The data extraction, cleaning, integration, transformation, and data reduction processes are the preprocessing processes of data analysis (Han & Kamber, 2000). The secondary data thus acquired still might be in varied or scattered format which needs to be transformed into data-mining-capable format. Transformation involves dimensional reduction, sampling, coding etc to downsize data scale and reduce complexity. Complexity must be reduced in order to accelerate computation time and proliferation accuracy of the analytics results. Usually, the amount of data that is required or acquired from the various sources, for predictive analytics is very large. This big data needs to be extracted, transformed and loaded or stored into large storage systems. For this purpose cloud technology (Feng et.al, 2010; Alhamazani et.al, 2012) is used. Data is stored in cloud which might be distributed over various geographical locations or present in a local domain (Alhamazani et.al, 2012). Cloud computing is closely associated with big data as most of the data which forms big data comes from social media and other high valued databases, which form the big part of the cloud-client population. Cloud computing is revolutionizing the IT industry and providing high flexibility by enabling the organizations to pay only for the resources they use (Buyya et.al, 2009) and (Guazzelli, 2009). Although the value proposition of Clouds as a platform to carry out analytics is strong, there still are many challenges (Abadi, 2009) that need to be overcome to make Clouds an ideal platform for scalable analytics of data.

Figure 2. Data analytics process

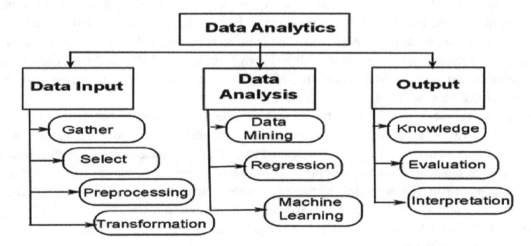

DATA ANALYSIS

Data analysis finds the hidden designs in the data sets. Data mining is the integral part of the analysis process. Data mining refers to the mining of the unexplored or hidden predictive familiarity (Weiss, & Indurkhya, 1998). and information from very huge Storage area or files, searching for patterns in stores of data using computational techniques from statistics and pattern recognition. Thus, pattern matching and data mining are closely related. Data mining tools and techniques are used to build predictive models, even though method definitions are simple, computation costs of data mining algorithms are high. To increase the response time of a data mining operator one can use machine learning, meta heuristic algorithms, and distributed computing. Also, these methods can be combined with the traditional data mining algorithms to provide more efficient ways. (Abbas, 2001) Thus the results from data mining techniques are often used to make prediction about future events, recommendations; however, the accuracy of the results largely depends on the data analysis levels and the quality and reliability of assumptions. The following is the generalized algorithm for data mining process:

1. Get Input data D
2. Candidate solutions r initialized
3. While the termination condition is equal to false
4. d =Scan(D)
5. v =Construct(d, r, o)
6. r= Update(v)
7. END
8. Output the rules r

The above algorithm starts with the initialization of data input and output, Scan () function performs data scan, Construct () performs rules construction, and Update () updates rules. D represents the raw data, d represents the data from the scan operator, r represents the rules, o represents the predefined measurement, and v represents the candidate rules. The scan, construct, and update operations are performed repeatedly until termination condition is met.

Classification and clustering are well known data mining problems (Weiss, & Indurkhya, 1998). The basic idea behind classification (Jain et.al, 1999) problem is to divide a set of unlabeled input data into k different groups, e.g., such as k-means (MacQueen, 1967). Classification (Han & Kamber, 2000) is the opposite of clustering because it depends on a set of labeled input data to construct a set of classifiers which are then used to classify the unlabeled input data to the groups to which they belong. In order to solve the classification problem, the decision tree-based algorithm (Safavian & Landgrebe, 1990) naïve Bayesian classification (McCallum and Nigam, 1998; Gelmen et.al, 2014), support vector machine (SVM) (Boser et. al, 1992) are used very often. Also, association rules (Agrawal et.al, 1993) and sequential patterns are focused on finding out the relationships between the input data which attempt to classify the input data into groups. Association rules (Agrawal et.al, 1993) find out all the co-occurrence relationships between the input data. The apriori algorithm (Agrawal et.al, 1993) is one of the most popular methods for the association rules problem but since it is computationally very expensive, different approaches have been discovered (Kaya & Alhajj, 2005) to reduce the cost, such as applying the genetic algorithm. The sequence or time series of the input data are also considered in addition to considering the relationships between the input data this is called the sequential pattern mining (Srikant & Agrawal, 1996). Statistical or machine learning technologies have also been used to analyze the data for several years. Figure 3 explains the data mining process.

Figure 3. Data mining standard process

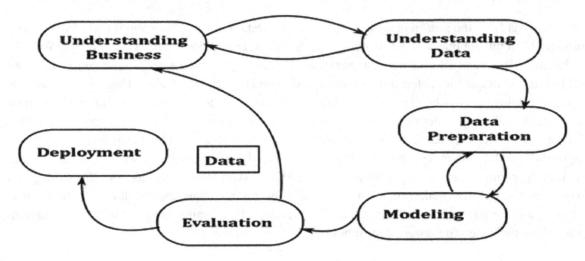

DATA OUTPUT

Output comprises of two main steps; evaluation and interpretation. The precision (n), recall (l), and C-measure can be used to estimate the ordering results, TP and TN indicate the numbers of positive examples and the number of negative examples that are correctly classified, respectively.

n= PE

PE+NE

And the meaning of recall l, is defined as:

l= PE

PE+NA

Finally, c-measure is computed as:

C= 2nl

n+l

Table 1. Confusion matrix of a classifier

	Classified Positive	Classified Negative
Actual positive	PE	NA
Actual negative	FP	TN

In addition to the above, response time and computation cost are other measurement criteria for data mining results. After the evaluation process, the meaningful interpretation (d'Aquin, M. & Jay, 2013) of the data mining results needs to be done. A simplified summarization (Mani & Bloedorn, 1997) of the results is the next step in line, so that the user is capable of understanding the results obtained and formulate right decisions based on the obtained results.

PREDICTIVE ANALYTICS TECHNIQUES

The data profiling and transformation, sequential pattern analysis and time series tracking (Bei-bei, & Xue-bo, 2015) are the three basic techniques for predictive analysis. Data profiling is basically examining the properties of the available data variable from an existing data source, to check whether it can be used for other purposes. Sequential pattern matching identifies frequently observed sequential occurrence of data in the given data sets. This method is a special case of structured data mining.

Predictive analytics can be approached using either regression techniques or machine learning technique. Machine learning belongs to the subfields of computer science and artificial intelligence which uses algorithms that help the system to learn from the data instead of explicitly programmed instructions while regression comes under the category of statistical modeling approach, which is the subfield of mathematics and the main concern there is finding relationships among the variables to predict an outcome using mathematical equations. Linear regression, probit regression, discreet choice models etc. are a few statistical regression models that will be discussed further in the later parts of the chapter.

REGRESSION TECHNIQUES

Linear Regression

Modeling and analyzing a given set of data can help us establish a meaningful relationship between various given sets of dependent and independent data, one such common statistical approach is linear regression. The main objective of regression analysis being "to know the unknown" i.e we try to estimate the unknown parameters in the given hypothetical regression model. The available data is scanned and parameters that most appropriately fit the needs of available data are filtered out after proper computation.

Big Data, Prediction and Linear Regression

There is an evolving necessary for information stream organization due to the introduction and growth of network, sensor technology and an exponential increase in transactional data (Kaisler et.al, 2013). Regression or Linear regression to be specific can be used as a tool to predict the behavior of voluminous streams of data so that it can further help in proper data stream management. Real-time data querying, analysis and collection of data has led to the introduction of several predictive analytics for the characteristics of data we encounter today, which is more than ever voluminous currently (Demirkan & Delen, 2013). Classification and regression are the main objectives of such analytics in harnessing the best out of large data sets. From statistical point of view it is easier for the big data sets to fit a model if there is a linearly dependent relationship with the unknown parameters when compared to the non-linearly dependent counterparts because the statistical properties of the resulting estimators in case of former are comparatively easier to determine. In addition to the above, this model is a good choice because of its simplicity, interpretability, widespread availability, scientific acceptance which aids in proper big data analytics. But, many real-time scenario of events and data sets do not correspond to the assumptions (linearity, independence of errors, assumptions of predictor variables etc) of this model.

APPLICATIONS OF LINEAR REGRESSION

Linear regression can be of vast implication in business. Some popular applications are as follows:

Linear regressions find great deal of applicability in business such as evaluating trends and making forecasts. Several other applications in various fields of work are also being implemented using this method. These applications thus make it possible to use large data sets and find out the hidden relationship in them in order to harness the most of every resource data that we are provided with, which is the ultimate goal of analytics in big data.

LOGISTIC REGRESSION

Logistic regression is known to measure the association among categorical dependent data and one or more independent data by estimating probabilities. It is closely related to the methods used in machine learning (Samli, 1996) (Perceptron and Support vector machine). The outcomes of this category of regression are discreet and are coded as 0 or 1, thus making the interpretation simple, straightforward and convenient. The predictor or independent data can be either continuous or categorical, depending on the given situation.

LOGISTIC REGRESSION IN BIG DATA

Big data analytics can be made interactive and real-time with the aid of logistic regression. Classification problems are common to many real-world objects and systems that come up with a strict classification Several fields including telecom, biomedicine and internet among others face such classification problem (Chambers, and Dinsmore, 2014). Logistic regression can be of help in framing algorithms for solving such issues catering to the fact that its outcomes are binary, each binary value can be transformed in to distinct and meaningful sets. Once we have a clear perception of the sets, further logistics and analysis can help us determine the more important facts and observations. Furthermore, we precisely determine the threshold of possibility of event/outcomes. This way one can predict the possibility of a certain outcome by analyzing a large data set using proper mathematical tools. The logistic regression function can be written as:

$$P = \frac{e^{a+bx}}{1+e^{a+bx}}$$

where P represents the probability, e is the base of the natural logarithm (about 2.718), a and b are the parameters of the model. The value of a gives P when x is zero, and b indicates how the probability changes when x changes by a single unit. Because the relation between x and P is nonlinear, b does not have a straightforward interpretation in this model unlike linear regression.

MULTINOMIAL LOGISTIC REGRESSIONS

Multinomial logistic regression is an addition of the logistic regression for modeling variables in the dependent data sets that are not binary. It is based on the concept of probability of membership (Ankalikar and Pande, 2007) of each category of dependent variable in the given data sets thus, it is a logistic regression which analyses binary dependents. However, the independent variable may be either of binary nature or take up interval based continuous values.

The formula for multinomial logistic regression is shown in Figure 4.

$\Pr\left(yi = j\right)$ is the probability of belonging to group j, Xi represents a vector of explanatory variables and is the coefficient, which is estimated using maximum likelihood estimation. Multinomial logistic regression uses the maximum likelihood estimation method to evaluate the probability of categorical membership. It requires careful consideration of sample size and thorough examination of outlying cases. Sparse multinomial logistic regression (Huh et.al, 2013) has emerged out as an important tool in carrying out research regarding the development of methodologies for formulating faster algorithms and generalization bounds. MLR is considered an attractive choice for analyzing large data sets with the help of regression techniques.

DISCREET CHOICE MODELS

Large data sets are largely infamous for creating several computational difficulties. The task of choosing from a large variety of alternative data sets is a difficult choice to make (Keane & Wasi, 2012) discreet choice models come handy in such situation. Through this approach, the user has to make choices depending on a number of alternative data sets that they are provided with. On the basis of the available number of data sets, different types of discreet choice modelling methods can be used. When one is provided with two alternatives only, the method used is binomial choice models otherwise, when we need to select goals from more than two alternative data sets, we go for multinomial choice models. The decision maker can choose from n potential targets and the benefit of each target is computed and the goal with maximum benefit qualifies as the choice. The utility or benefit is decided using the observable

Figure 4. Multinomial logistic regression

$$\Pr(y_i = j) = \frac{\exp(X_i \beta_j)}{1 + \sum_{j=1}^{J} \exp(X_i \beta_j)}$$

and unobservable components of the goals thus the utility to the decision maker d, of potential goal I can be denoted as:

$$U(i,d) = O(i,d) + \overline{O(i,d)}$$

where $\overline{O(i,d)}$ = Unobservable component and $O(i,d)$ = Observable component.

The DCM creates choice probabilities associated with the data sets, which take the form of integrals whose dimension is comparable to the size of choice sets of data, with no closed form.

DCM IN BIG DATA

The data sets from business and marketing fields, mainly the transactional data, have grown to a great extent (Pota et.al, 2013). Moulding a proper choice among the large number of alternative data sets or choice modeling is an important step in the workflow designed to handle such big data. Discreet choice models help the decision maker responsible for the big data, in molding such crucial decisions. Using discreet choice approach, the strategic pricing of the products and product development schedules can be planned by analysis and study of the business big data (Krishnapuram et.al, 2015).

PROBIT REGRESSION

Probit regression is used to model the data sets with the binary outcome or response data. Basically, this model works with binomial response variable i.e, a response variable with only two outcomes. For example, yes or no, true or false, heart attack or no heart-attack and similar situations. Probit regression transforms the generated sigmoid curves generated with the analysis of data set relationships, to straight lines (Keane and Wasi, 2012). In probit regression the inverse standard normal distribution is modeled as the linear combination of predictors indicates the C.D.F of standard normal distribution.

$$\Pr(y = 1 \mid x) = \phi(x\beta)$$

$$\phi(x\beta) = \int_{-\infty}^{x\beta} \phi(z)dz = \pi$$

$$\phi(z) = \frac{1}{\sqrt{2\pi}} e^{\frac{z^2}{2}}$$

$$x\beta = \beta_0 + \beta_1 x_1 + \cdots\cdots \beta_n x_n = \phi^{-1}(\pi)$$

IMPLEMENTATION OF PROBIT IN PREDICTIVE ANALYTICS OF BIG DATA

Probit regression approach can be used to predict the results of an individual candidate in a political campaign. Suppose we are interested in knowing whether a particular candidate wins or loses in the campaign, we will need to accumulate all possible data (which can be vast and possibly fall in the category of big data) corresponding to the campaign led by the candidate and then we can assess the factors that could possibly influence the whole campaign. The predictor sets can be formed by the individual candidate's expense on the campaign, time spent on campaigning etc. The outcome variable or response data in our case being binary natured; the candidate will either win the campaign or lose. Thus we can make use of probit approach to predict the results. The dose-response relationships (Train Kenneth, 2003) with binomial response data have long been known to be studied using probit regression to obtain interesting results. The reaction of the chemicals for the exact concentration can be determined using this method. Also, a vast are of research in the field of medicine is being carried out using probit regression.

LOGIT VS. PROBIT

Both the logit and probit regression techniques for implementing regressions is used for probabilistic prediction related to huge information groups. The expected values is limited between 0 and 1. But the preference of one model over the other tends to vary by discipline. The difference between the two is mainly observed in the assumption for the distribution of errors in the analyzed data sets. Probit model has been there since before the use of logit models, but, due to the high computational difficulties in case of probit, mainly because of the requirement of numerically calculating the integrals, the logit model was formulated.

TIME SERIES MODEL

To measure the attributes of the relationship among very large data sets which belong to varied domains with great heterogeneity, time series models are used. This approach helps in the successive measurements associated with big data and prediction of the futuristic outcomes evolving from the same. A vast ocean of information can be unveiled with the proper digging of knowledge using this approach. The focus of time series approach is to discover all possible patterns in the given huge data sets and analyze them by transforming the observed patterns into meaningful relationships among the attributes of the data set provided. Big data, due to its vastness and the huge amount of effort in addition with the high computational resource requirement, tends to hide a large extent of valuable information within it. In today's modern technical era of internet and world-wide web, the data generation is at an ever-high peak, time series model is finding numerous applications in the field of transactional big data analysis in addition to other areas. It has also found its root in the generation of several real-time applications in the field of sensor data automation (Curriero et.al, 2001) Smart sensors and smart devices form the category of major contributors to growing amount of data, for which, such models prove to be of great importance. Time series model greatly reduces the dimensionality and complexity of large data sets therefore they are very suitable for subtle prediction of meaningful outcomes with respect to the big data. In addition to the above, time series approach is widely used in data mining (Thomson, 1947).

SURVIVAL AND DURATION ANALYSIS

For analyzing large sets of data where the consequence adjustable is measured by the time taken for the occurrence of a certain event of interest, we use survival and duration analysis method. For example, if the event of interest is a divorce, then the survival time will be the time taken (in years, months, days) until the couple gets separated officially. The dependent variable in this method is composed of event status; which tells whether or not the event occurred. The other component is time that the event took to occur. An observation is said to be censored if the information about its survival time is incomplete. Censoring is an important part of survival analysis as it gives information about a certain type of missing data. Survival analysis unlike other ordinary regression models has the ability to interpret the information from both censored and uncensored observations, which is further used for appropriate model parameter estimations.

Survival function which estimates the probability of surviving till a certain time can be estimated by several parametric, non-parametric and semi-parametric methods. Cox proportional hazard regression (Chipman et.al, 2001) is an important and widely used model for the same.

The examples for the same can be predicting the lifetime of an electronic device, home appliance. In medical science, this method can be used for the prediction of the estimated number of years the patient will be likely to survive after being diagnosed with a certain chronic disease (Jirkovsky et.al, 2014).

CLASSIFICATION AND REGRESSION TREES

Prediction trees belong to the category of non-linear predictive models. Prediction models can be formulated from large data sets by the machine learning [60] methods, which include classification and regression trees. The large data sets are recursively partitioned in a logical fashion into smaller chunks of data sets, over each of these smaller chunks, a prediction model is implemented for further analysis of the provided data. These smaller partitions should be capable enough to be implemented into meaningful decision trees.

CLASSIFICATION TREES

Point prediction and distributional prediction (Li, 2002) are the two categories of predictions which the classification trees are capable of making. Point prediction makes a particular guess about the category or class to which the given data set belongs. Distributional prediction provides the possibility for each class of data and is better than the former because one can always extract point prediction from probability forecasts.

Precisely, if we have n observations for a data variable Y, which takes up values 1,23,4,5...k and p predictor variables $x1, x2, x3....xp$. Classification trees method will help us to formulate a model which is capable of predicting the values of Y from the new X values.

X is partitioned into k disjoint sets:

A1, A2, A3…..Ak, such that the predicted value of Y is j if X belongs to Aj, for j=1,2,3….k. These yield rectangular sets Aj. Classification trees make data sets easier to interpret. These are easy to understand and prioritize the variables to make accurate predictions (Chen et.al, 2012). Also, these models come in handy when the true regression surface, with the associated data sets is not smooth.

REGRESSION TREES

Regression trees are very alike to the grouping trees except for the fact that the dependent variable takes ordered values from the finite data sets. Classification trees try to predict the class or discreet category rather than a numerical value, which is done by regression trees. Linear regression is considered as a global model (Sadeghzadeh & Fard, 2015). There we have single predictive formula that holds over the entire data space. This global model is classified in to two parts one is recursive partitioning wherein the data space is repeatedly subdivided into smaller chunks to make the interactions between data variables more manageable, the other is a guileless model for each cell of the panel (Gopinath et.al, 2006). The target variable determines the type of the decision tree i.e classification tree or regression tree needed. Regression trees lack the ability to handle highly non-linear parameters, so in such cases we use classification trees.

MULTIVARIATE ADAPTIVE REGRESSION SPLINES

Multivariate adaptive regression splines technique is generally used when a large number of explanatory variable candidates have to be considered. MARS is a non-parametric regression (Quinlan, 2014) approach which has grown widely in the recent years for various applications such as data mining and forecasting (Breiman et.al, 1984). It is a piece-wise regression approach to efficiently approximate the relationship between a set of variables and a dependent variable.

MARS builds models of form:

$$f(x) = c_0 + \sum c_i B_i(x)$$

where f(x) is the basis function which can be anything among a constant, a hinge function or a product of two or more hinge functions. The global parametric modeling techniques like linear regression are relatively easy in interpretation. Recursive partitioning regression is one of the non-parametric modeling approaches which approximates functions and is capable of handling large sets of explanatory variables in the data sets. MARS is an extension or generalized version of RPR, and it successfully overcomes the limitations of RPR in the modeling approaches. MARS has been successively used in recent years for developing several prediction and data mining applications like- Modeling data for time series analysis, speech modeling (Cover & Hart, 1967), mobile radio channel predictions, intrusion detection (Segal, 1988) in information system security etc. It has also been used to describe the transport of pesticides in soils (Friedman, 1991), to predict average monthly foreign exchange rates (Hong & Hsiao, 2002), to model credit scoring (Zareipour et.al, 2006) and data mining on breast cancer patterns (Haas & Kubin, 1998).

MACHINE LEARNING TECHNIQUES

Machine learning came into existence only recently (in the 90s), with the advancements in computation and digitization. Machine learning, (Alpaydin, 2014) as the name suggests, requires a lot less human effort than statistical methods, hence making it more convenient for processing big data. It holds great potential for future computations associated with large data-sets. Also, the extent of assumptions involved with machine learning algorithms and methods are comparatively fewer than those with statistical methods. Statistical methods are good for smaller data-sets while machine learning techniques work effectively for data with a wide variety of attributes and large number of observations.

K-NEAREST NEIGHBORS

K-nearest neighbors is one amongst the best sorts of classification algorithms that return underneath the class of machine learning. (Cover & Hart, 1967), so as to perform classification, a distance metric is chosen and any new information that's encountered is compared against all-ready noted information things. The new information item is then assigned to the category that is has the most similarity amongst its k nearest neighbors. IBk is Associate in Nursing implementation of the k-nearest-neighbors classifier (Aha, 1992) wherever, predictions square measure supported a majority vote that's forged by neighboring samples, as high k may result in over fitting and model instability, thus, applicable values should be selected for a given application. the quantity of nearest neighbors (k) are often set manually, or it are often determined mechanically exploitation cross-validation.

NEURAL NETWORKS

The Neural Network is Associate in Nursing accommodative system that changes its structure and moulds itself supported external or internal data that flows through the network (Song et.al, 2012) and (Ripley, 2007). Neural networks belong to the class of non-linear applied mathematics information modeling tools that square measure accustomed model advanced relationships between inputs and outputs or for locating patterns in information (Ripley, 2007). Artificial Neural Networks (ANN) are wide employed in modeling the power of the biological nervous systems therefore on train machines to acknowledge patterns and objects. Their basic design includes of networks of primitive functions that square measure capable of receiving multiple weighted inputs. the rear propagation rule Multi-Layer Perceptron (MLP) is employed for categorizing a choice victimization 2 input nodes particularly affirmative and no wherever (no=0 and yes=1).

NAÏVE BAYES

Naïve Thomas Bayes classifier produces probabilistic rules used for classification functions. Whenever a brand new information item is given, the Naïve Thomas Bayes model presents it with a likelihood proportion that is employed to categorize it into doable category classes (Langley et.al, 1992). Naïve Thomas Bayes estimates {the category| the category} conditional possibilities by presumptuous that for any given class the inputs ar freelance of every alternative. This yields a discrimination operate that is indicated by the merchandise of the joint possibilities that the categories ar true, supported the given inputs. This reduces the matter of discriminating categories for finding category conditional marginal densities, that represent the likelihood that a given sample could be one among the doable target categories. The well-known Thomas Bayes rule is applied to every attribute of the model and also the likelihood over associate degree freelance category variable (label) C is computed to perform the classification. it's a illustration of the theorem classifier and provides terribly promising results on many world datasets. This model performs well against alternative alternatives however doesn't work all right if the info contains correlative inputs.

SUPPORT VECTOR MACHINE

Support Vector Machines (SVM) ar wont to define non-linear call boundaries in high-dimensional variable house. this is often done by resolution a quadratic optimization downside (Foody & Mathur, 2004). the fundamental theory says that for a given non-linearly severable dataset containing points from 2 completely different categories there ar AN infinite variety of doable hyperplanes that divide categories. the choice of a hyperplane that's capable of optimally separating 2 categories is meted out victimization solely a set of coaching samples that is noted as support vectors. To represent the optimum call boundary, the peak margin M (distance) between the support vectors (Oommen et.al, 2008) and (Kovačević et.al, 2009) is taken. In non-separable linear cases, SVM computes M whereas incorporating a value parameter C, that defines a penalty for misclassifying support vectors. High values of C will generate complicated call boundaries to misclassify minimum variety of support vectors. For issues wherever categories don't seem to be linearly severable, SVM uses AN implicit transformation of input variables employing a kernel operate that permits SVM to separate non-linearly severable support vectors employing a linear hyperplane. choice of AN applicable kernel operates and kernel breadth, s, is needed to optimize the performance for many applications. SVM will be extended to multi-class issues by constructing c(c-1)/2 binary classification models that generate predictions supported a majority vote.

GENERALIZED WORKFLOW OF PREDICTIVE ANALYTICS PROCESS

There is no general technique followed for predictive analytics modeling, instead, the steps or process are decided in accordance with the specific type of problem domain. The following steps are incorporated for creating predictive models by various cross industry processes:

Project Definition

This involves defining corporate objectives and desired aftermaths from the project and translating these purposes into the goals and tasks for predictive analytics. The model is doomed to fail if the objectives are unclear and ambiguous, thus this is an important aspect to be considered while preparing the predictive model.

Data Exploration

This caters to finding and deciding the most appropriate source of data as the model is only as good as the data that constitutes it. A good data source is one that has a large number of records, history, and variables. The larger is the sum of variables, the greater are the chances of finding relevant patterns and relationship among the data sets. fortuitously, most of the information to make prognosticative model, is hold on within the knowledge warehouses, so minimizing the time to seem for relevant knowledge across multiple systems and domains There are basic tools available for analysts to compile some of the descriptive statistical characteristics (max, min, standard deviation etc) of the fields involved in the model. Data profiling tools are also used in data feature tasks to analyze the characteristics of data fields and determine the relationship. Advanced visualization tools are used to explore characteristics of source data or visually analyze the models.

Data Preparation

This is the most time-consuming process in the workflow of predictive modeling it takes 25% of the total time. This process converts the data in various from to a regular for that is identifiable or attuned with the analytical tools and the machine learning predictive model. The process begins with fishing out or selecting appropriate data sets according to their relevance with the project. Later the data cleansing is done to rectify errors, the analysts reconstitute the data fields (if required), and further additional transformations are done to optimize data sets for specific types of algorithms. The analyst must know the data and its limitations thoroughly so that it qualifies to be used for and applied to the problem at hand. The issue of low quality and low quantity of data usually arise at this point, which needs to be eliminated for effective processing.

Model Building

This is the next step in the process of predictive modeling. This phase involves running procedures beside the data sets with the well-known principles for the reliant on variables that is the variable whose value we are interested in predicting. Later the data set is divided into training data set and testing data set. Model is finally validated by testing it with live data in real time scenarios. The process of training, testing and validating is of iterative nature. Numerous mixtures of variables are tested to see which has the record influence. Also, OLAP and statistical tools are found to be of great use to analyst to identify significant trends in data and determine the important variables that must be included in the model. Model accuracy can be improved by recombining existing data fields in different ways. Modeling is a highly labor-intensive work. Time taken to create a good analytical model depends on the range of problem, availability and worth of information.

Model Deployment

This is a crucial part of the predictive modeling process prophetic models will fail if their predictions fail to supply positive outcome for business or if the business users ignore their results. Thus, it is crucial to implement proper methods for deployment of predictive model. Model insights can be shared with business users through presentation paper reports, conversation. This will help to minimize the cost risk of the client. The predictive model can be scored that is, most organizations transform the predictive models into programming code or database and the results are kept in the database, in the form of a variable that ranges from 0 to 1, which gives the score. The model can be embedded into a business intelligence report so as to overawed the difficulty of limited distribution. The model can also be deployed by embedding it into some operational applications. This can be done by embedding the model results into a set of rules which create a set of if-else statements.

MANAGING MODELS

This is the last step within the method of prognosticative analytics modeling. A majority of organizations (61%) still notable to use an advertisement hoc or project-based approach for developing analytical models, in keeping with a recent survey Model management helps to minimize overhead, access control, improve performance etc. The increase in demand for model management is expected in near future due to the increasing demands for proper analytics techniques.

VALIDATION OF PREDICTIVE MODEL

Predictive modeling comprises of finding good subsets of predictors or explanatory variables and models that fit the data. Predictive modeling involves 3 types of validations; apparent validation which includes performance on a sample that is used to develop the model. The second type is internal validation which checks for performance on population underlying the sample and the last type is external validation which deals with performance on related but slightly different population.

Furthermore, there are 3 internal validation techniques namely:

- Split sample
- Cross validation
- Bootstrap

Split-sample involves creating of a random split, leading to e.g. a five hundredth development and a five hundredth validation sample. Cross-validation uses constant principle as split sample; however, the event and validation samples are alternated during this case (e.g. 50:50 split suggests that two development and take a look at rounds; a 90:10 split ten rounds). The bootstrap technique is but the typically most well-liked technique.

The performance of a prophetic model might lead to overestimation if it's merely determined supported the sample of subjects that was accustomed construct the model therefore we want to travel for internal validation ways that aim at providing a a lot of correct estimate of the model performance in new subjects. Internal validity of a prophetic supplying regression model will best be calculable with bootstrapping because of the very fact that it provides stable estimates with low bias. during a bootstrap procedure, we tend to take many random samples with replacement from the sample, and for every of those resamples, data point of interest is computed. This data point distribution approximates the sampling distribution of that data point. This methodology is free from creating assumptions concerning the character of population distribution. we will estimate the quality errors to form chance statements work from the sample information alone. The bootstrap is usually best-known to be used to enhance estimates of prediction error inside a leave-one-out cross-validation method. Multi-fold cross-validation is another variation on the training-and-test theme, wherever sample information is divided into M folds of roughly equal size and a series of tests ar conducted to validate the model. the worth of a model lies within the quality of its predictions. Akaike data criterion (AIC) or the mathematician data criterion (BIC)are indices that facilitate to match and choose one model against another, providing a balance between goodness-of-fit and parsimony

External validation of prophetic model is another validation technique that is moderately straight-forward to calculate given the condition that acceptable information needed for the method ar out there, e.g. containing the predictor and outcome variables needed for the prediction model. The construct of external validation is that predictions ar calculated from a antecedently developed model, and tested on a brand new information that's totally different from the event population. many external validation techniques will be used like temporal, spacial and totally external validation. The strength of the proof for validity is sometimes thought of to be stronger with a totally external validation. Apparent validation is found to be restricted in price owing to optimism within the performance estimates. Internal valida-tion, that is ideally done by bootstrapping, ought to be tried. External validation may be a stronger take a look at of model performance, and will be determined in alternative populations, that ar (subjectively) thought of 'plausibly related'.

APPLICATIONS/CASE STUDY

Several domains make use of big data predictive analytics to solve complex problems in their specific environment. These problems can be solved by data driven predictive analytics algorithms. One such domain is the health industry. The health care industry is huge and evolving with new techniques and practices at a great pace along with an exponential growth in the health-related data records (Ser et.al, 2014). The industry could save $300 billion annually by leveraging big data. Electronic health records can greatly eliminate the chances of dangerous medical mistakes and reduce costs. The hospitalization risks for an individual can be predicted through patient risk calculators. Through proper analysis of patient data, the doctors can predict the time for which the patient would need to stay in the intensive care unit and accordingly allocate resources for the service. Similarly, there are several other domains that make use of predictive analytics to offer efficient functionality.

SOFTWARE FAULT PREDICTION USING PREDICTIVE ANALYTICS APPROACH:

Software fault prediction refers to a discipline that involves prediction of fault disposition of the long run modules exploitation essential prediction metrics and historical fault knowledge (Zhou & Leung, 2006). it's vital to see whether or not a package module is vulnerable to fault because it assists in distinguishing modules that need elaborate testing. this can be studied through the appliance of adaptive Neuro Fuzzy abstract thought System (ANFIS) (Jang, 1993) or artificial neural networks (ANN). Reliable package is one wherever minimum variety of failures occur once the program runs. the advantages of package fault prediction ar varied.

The check method are often refined to extend system quality. it's doable to specify modules that need refactoring throughout the upkeep section. Applying package fault prediction exploitation class-level metrics throughout the look section helps in choosing the simplest of the look alternatives. package fault prediction (Alsmadi & Najadat, 2011) provides stability and high assurance. It can even greatly cut back the time and energy spent within the code review method.

Machine learning ways, are often used to predict package imperfection because of their ability to find out from hidden relationships embedded within the knowledge. once the information changes, the model will lose its performance dramatically therefore in package fault prediction, modification of information suggests that modification in project size, domain, package design. adaptive Neuro Fuzzy abstract thought System (ANFIS) becomes exceptional once it involves build a model that is a smaller amount sensitive to vary in knowledge, because of its hybrid approach. The distinction between ANFIS and also the different knowledge driven ways (ANN, SVM, and call tree (DT)) is that adaptive Neuro Fuzzy abstract thought System (ANFIS) uses professional information to make the model and more uses knowledge to optimize it. adaptive Neuro Fuzzy abstract thought System may be a supervised technique that mixes the benefits of a fuzzy abstract thought system (FIS) and Artificial Neural Network (ANN) ways. package fault prediction systems have to be compelled to be created additional sensible, as a result of value of correcting faults within the later phases of the package development life cycle will increase more, thus, there's a requirement for a classifier which might are available handy within the early stages of the project development time to classify whether or not or not the module is faulty. The earliest time of the package development cycle that the model are often used as classifier depends on the generalization ability of the model. Thus, the additional generalizable models are often helpful within the earlier phases of the event and ANFIS (Daoming & Jie, 2006) has additional advantage to be general thanks to the professional information equipped to that. However, similar researches have to be compelled to be finished massive sized knowledge and completely different kind of package comes to get generalized results

CONCLUSION

Big data analytics is a burning issue in today's world of enormously growing data. Approximately 5 Exabyte of data has been created, from the beginning of time till 2003. The same amount is now generated every 2 days. This reflects upon the issue of management of this huge amount of data through proper analytics. Big data is playing a major role in all the fields across all domains and effectively revolutionizing the era of technology by harnessing and extracting the in-depth, potentially useful data from beneath the layers of the voluminous data sets. The harnessed data can reveal astonishing facts and lead to significant discoveries. Predictive analysis using big data will help to see the future using existing and historical data analysis. The emotions of the consumer's change on a regular basis and is influenced by several tangible and intangible factors. Measuring these factors yields a lot of directional projections that can be used for futuristic decision making. Statistical modeling and analysis of data to get different perspectives of decision making can be achieved by means of big data analytics by making use of open source and proprietary tools available .The development of these tools are on a high rise and enables each of the companies to tailor design their own tools for their specific purpose like suggestion, recommendation and optimization .The possibility of connecting data to find their relationship leads to a lot of observations for decision making and forecasting and it is a challenge to do over very large amount of data, growing exponentially and dynamically. For the purpose, cognitive computing and artificial intelligence are making big data analytical algorithms to think more on their own and learning from previous human interactions, leading to come out with big data agents with their own functionalities.

REFERENCES

Abadi, D. J. (2009). Data management in the cloud: Limitations and opportunities. *IEEE Data Eng. Bull.*, *32*(1), 3–12.

Abbass, H. A. (Ed.). (2001). *Data Mining: A Heuristic Approach*. IGI Global.

Ag, B. (2004, May). *Introduction of the Radial Basis Function (RBF) Networks*. Online Symposium for Electronics Engineers, DSP Algorithms: Multimedia. Retrieved from http://www. osee. net

Agrawal, R., Imieliński, T., & Swami, A. (1993). Mining association rules between sets of items in large databases. *SIGMOD Record*, *22*(2), 207–216. doi:10.1145/170036.170072

Aha, D. W. (1992). Tolerating noisy, irrelevant and novel attributes in instance-based learning algorithms. *International Journal of Man-Machine Studies*, *36*(2), 267–287. doi:10.1016/0020-7373(92)90018-G

Alhamazani, K., Ranjan, R., Rabhi, F., Wang, L., & Mitra, K. (2012, December). Cloud monitoring for optimizing the QoS of hosted applications. In *Cloud Computing Technology and Science (CloudCom), 2012 IEEE 4th International Conference on* (pp. 765-770). IEEE. doi:10.1109/CloudCom.2012.6427532

Alpaydin, E. (2014). *Introduction to machine learning*. MIT Press.

Alsmadi, I., & Najadat, H. (2011). Evaluating the change of software fault behavior with dataset attributes based on categorical correlation. *Advances in Engineering Software*, *42*(8), 535–546. doi:10.1016/j.advengsoft.2011.03.010

Analysis_Regression and Correlation_Probit Analysis. (n.d.). Retrieved from http://www.statsdirect.com/help/Default.htm#regression_and_correlation/probit_analysis.htm

Ankalikar, A., & Pande, R. (n.d.). *JD Edwards Upgrades Made Easy*. Academic Press.

Association for Computing Machinery. (2007). *ACM transactions on knowledge discovery from data*. ACM.

Banjade, R., & Maharjan, S. (2011, November). Product recommendations using linear predictive modeling. In *Internet (AH-ICI), 2011 Second Asian Himalayas International Conference on* (pp. 1-4). IEEE. doi:10.1109/AHICI.2011.6113930

Bei-bei, M., & Xue-bo, J. (2015, May). Compression processing estimation method for time series big data. In *Control and Decision Conference (CCDC), 2015 27th Chinese* (pp. 1807-1811). IEEE. doi:10.1109/CCDC.2015.7162212

Boser, B. E., Guyon, I. M., & Vapnik, V. N. (1992, July). A training algorithm for optimal margin classifiers. In *Proceedings of the fifth annual workshop on Computational learning theory* (pp. 144-152). ACM. doi:10.1145/130385.130401

Breiman, L., Friedman, J., Stone, C. J., & Olshen, R. A. (1984). *Classification and regression trees.* CRC Press.

Buyya, R., Yeo, C. S., Venugopal, S., Broberg, J., & Brandic, I. (2009). Cloud computing and emerging IT platforms: Vision, hype, and reality for delivering computing as the 5th utility. *Future Generation Computer Systems*, *25*(6), 599–616. doi:10.1016/j.future.2008.12.001

Cao, J., Zeng, K., Wang, H., Cheng, J., Qiao, F., Wen, D., & Gao, Y. (2014). Web-based traffic sentiment analysis: Methods and applications. Intelligent Transportation Systems. *IEEE Transactions on*, *15*(2), 844–853.

Chambers, M., & Dinsmore, T. W. (2014). *Advanced analytics methodologies: Driving business value with analytics*. Pearson Education.

Chen, H., Chiang, R. H., & Storey, V. C. (2012). Business Intelligence and Analytics: From Big Data to Big Impact. *Management Information Systems Quarterly*, *36*(4), 1165–1188.

Chipman, H., George, E. I., McCulloch, R. E., Clyde, M., Foster, D. P., & Stine, R. A. (2001). The practical implementation of Bayesian model selection. *Lecture Notes-Monograph Series*, 65-134.

Classification and Regression Trees. (2009). Retrieved from http://www.stat.cmu.edu/~cshalizi/350/lectures/22/lecture-22.pdf

Cover, T. M., & Hart, P. E. (1967). Nearest neighbor pattern classification. *Information Theory. IEEE Transactions on*, *13*(1), 21–27.

Curriero, F. C., Patz, J. A., Rose, J. B., & Lele, S. (2001). The association between extreme precipitation and waterborne disease outbreaks in the United States, 1948-1994. *American Journal of Public Health*, *91*(8), 1194–1199. doi:10.2105/AJPH.91.8.1194 PMID:11499103

d'Aquin, M., & Jay, N. (2013, April). Interpreting data mining results with linked data for learning analytics: motivation, case study and directions. In *Proceedings of the Third International Conference on Learning Analytics and Knowledge* (pp. 155-164). ACM. doi:10.1145/2460296.2460327

Daoming, G., & Jie, C. (2006). ANFIS for high-pressure waterjet cleaning prediction. *Surface and Coatings Technology*, *201*(3), 1629–1634. doi:10.1016/j.surfcoat.2006.02.034

Decision Boundaries. (n.d.). Retrieved from http://www.cs.princeton.edu/courses/archive/fall08/cos436/Duda/PR_simp/bndrys.htm

Demirkan, H., & Delen, D. (2013). Leveraging the capabilities of service-oriented decision support systems: Putting analytics and big data in cloud. *Decision Support Systems*, *55*(1), 412–421. doi:10.1016/j.dss.2012.05.048

Electronic Health Records, Ophthalmic EHR Central, American Academy of Ophthalmic Executives. (n.d.). *The practice management division of the American Academy of Ophthalmology*. Available: http://www.aao.org/aaoe/ehr-central/index.cfm

Feng, J., Wen, P., Liu, J., & Li, H. (2010, June). Elastic stream cloud (ESC): A stream-oriented cloud computing platform for Rich Internet Application. In *High Performance Computing and Simulation (HPCS), 2010 International Conference on* (pp. 203-208). IEEE.

Foody, G. M., & Mathur, A. (2004). A relative evaluation of multiclass image classification by support vector machines. *Geoscience and Remote Sensing. IEEE Transactions on, 42*(6), 1335–1343.

Friedman, J. H. (1991). Multivariate adaptive regression splines. *Annals of Statistics, 19*(1), 1–67. doi:10.1214/aos/1176347963

Gelman, A., Carlin, J. B., Stern, H. S., & Rubin, D. B. (2014). *Bayesian data analysis* (Vol. 2). Boca Raton, FL, USA: Chapman & Hall/CRC.

Girardin, F., Calabrese, F., Fiore, F. D., Ratti, C., & Blat, J. (2008). Digital footprinting: Uncovering tourists with user-generated content. *Pervasive Computing, IEEE, 7*(4), 36–43. doi:10.1109/MPRV.2008.71

Gopinath, D. P., Divya Sree, J., Mathew, R., Rekhila, S. J., & Nair, A. S. (2006, December). Duration Analysis for Malayalam Text-To-Speech Systems. In *Information Technology, 2006. ICIT'06. 9th International Conference on* (pp. 129-132). IEEE. doi:10.1109/ICIT.2006.48

Guazzelli, A., Stathatos, K., & Zeller, M. (2009). Efficient deployment of predictive analytics through open standards and cloud computing. *ACM SIGKDD Explorations Newsletter, 11*(1), 32–38. doi:10.1145/1656274.1656281

Haas, H., & Kubin, G. (1998, November). A multi-band nonlinear oscillator model for speech. In *Signals, Systems & Computers, 1998.Conference Record of the Thirty-Second Asilomar Conference on* (*Vol. 1*, pp. 338-342). IEEE. doi:10.1109/ACSSC.1998.750882

Han, J., & Kamber, M. (2000). *Data mining: Concepts and techniques*. Morgan Kaufmann.

Hong, Y. Y., & Hsiao, C. Y. (2002, September). Locational marginal price forecasting in deregulated electricity markets using artificial intelligence. In *Generation, Transmission and Distribution, IEE Proceedings* (Vol. 149, No. 5, pp. 621-626). IET. doi:10.1049/ip-gtd:20020371

Huh, J., Yetisgen-Yildiz, M., & Pratt, W. (2013). Text classification for assisting moderators in online health communities. *Journal of Biomedical Informatics, 46*(6), 998–1005. doi:10.1016/j.jbi.2013.08.011 PMID:24025513

Jain, A. K., Murty, M. N., & Flynn, P. J. (1999). Data clustering: A review. *ACM Computing Surveys, 31*(3), 264-323.

Jang, J. S. R. (1993). ANFIS: Adaptive-network-based fuzzy inference system. *Systems, Man and Cybernetics. IEEE Transactions on, 23*(3), 665–685.

Jirkovsky, V., Obitko, M., Novak, P., & Kadera, P. (2014, September). Big Data analysis for sensor time-series in automation. In Emerging Technology and Factory Automation (ETFA), 2014 IEEE (pp. 1-8). IEEE. doi:10.1109/ETFA.2014.7005183

Kaisler, S., Armour, F., Espinosa, J. A., & Money, W. (2013, January). Big data: Issues and challenges moving forward. In *System Sciences (HICSS), 2013 46th Hawaii International Conference on* (pp. 995-1004). IEEE.

Kaya, M., & Alhajj, R. (2005). Genetic algorithm based framework for mining fuzzy association rules. *Fuzzy Sets and Systems*, *152*(3), 587–601. doi:10.1016/j.fss.2004.09.014

Keane, M. P., & Wasi, N. (2012). *Estimation of Discrete Choice Models with Many Alternatives Using Random Subsets of the Full Choice Set: With an Application to Demand for Frozen Pizza* (No. 2012-W13). Academic Press.

Kovačević, M., Bajat, B., Trivić, B., & Pavlović, R. (2009, November). Geological units classification of multispectral images by using support vector machines. In *Intelligent Networking and Collaborative Systems, 2009. INCOS'09. International Conference on* (pp. 267-272). IEEE. doi:10.1109/INCOS.2009.44

Krishnapuram, B., Carin, L., Figueiredo, M. A., & Hartemink, A. J. (2005). Sparse multinomial logistic regression: Fast algorithms and generalization bounds. *Pattern Analysis and Machine Intelligence. IEEE Transactions on*, *27*(6), 957–968.

Kumar, S. A. (2006). *Production and operations management*. New Age International.

Langley, P., Iba, W., & Thompson, K. (1992, July). An analysis of Bayesian classifiers. In AAAI (Vol. 90, pp. 223-228).

Li, H., & Luan, Y. (2002, December). Kernel Cox regression models for linking gene expression profiles to censored survival data. In *Pacific Symposium on Biocomputing* (Vol. 8, p. 65). doi:10.1142/9789812776303_0007

Liu, B. (2007). *Web data mining: exploring hyperlinks, contents, and usage data*. Springer Science & Business Media.

Lohr, S. (2012). The age of big data. *New York Times*, 11.

MacQueen, J. (1967, June). Some methods for classification and analysis of multivariate observations. In *Proceedings of the fifth Berkeley symposium on mathematical statistics and probability* (Vol. 1, No. 14, pp. 281-297).

Mani, I., & Bloedorn, E. (1997). *Multi-document summarization by graph search and matching*. arXiv preprint cmp-lg/9712004

McCallum, A., & Nigam, K. (1998, July). A comparison of event models for naive bayes text classification. In AAAI-98 workshop on learning for text categorization (Vol. 752, pp. 41-48).

Mishra, N., & Silakari, S. (2012). Predictive Analytics: A Survey, Trends, Applications, Oppurtunities & Challenges. *International Journal of Computer Science and Information Technologies*, *3*(3), 4434–4438.

Oommen, T., Misra, D., Twarakavi, N. K., Prakash, A., Sahoo, B., & Bandopadhyay, S. (2008). An objective analysis of support vector machine based classification for remote sensing. *Mathematical Geosciences, 40*(4), 409-424.

Pota, M., Esposito, M., & De Pietro, G. (2013). Transforming probability distributions into membership functions of fuzzy classes: A hypothesis test approach. *Fuzzy Sets and Systems, 233,* 52–73. doi:10.1016/j.fss.2013.03.013

Quinlan, J. R. (2014). *C4. 5: programs for machine learning.* Elsevier.

Ratner, B. (2011). *Statistical and machine-learning data mining: Techniques for better predictive modeling and analysis of big data.* CRC Press. doi:10.1201/b11508

Ripley, B. D. (2007). *Pattern recognition and neural networks.* Cambridge University Press.

Sadeghzadeh, K., & Fard, N. (2015, January). Nonparametric data reduction approach for large-scale survival data analysis. In *Reliability and Maintainability Symposium (RAMS), 2015 Annual* (pp. 1-6). IEEE. doi:10.1109/RAMS.2015.7105128

Safavian, S. R., & Landgrebe, D. (1990). *A survey of decision tree classifier methodology.* Academic Press.

Samli, A. C. (1996). *Information-Driven Marketing Decisions: Development of Strategic Information Systems.* Greenwood Publishing Group.

Schneeweiss, S. (2014). Learning from big health care data. *The New England Journal of Medicine, 370*(23), 2161–2163. doi:10.1056/NEJMp1401111 PMID:24897079

Segal, M. R. (1988). Regression trees for censored data. *Biometrics, 44*(1), 35–47. doi:10.2307/2531894

Sensing as a Service and Big Data, ICT Centre, CSIRO, ACT, 2601. (n.d.). Research School of Computer Science, The Australian National University, Canberra, Australia. Retrieved from http://arxiv.org/ftp/arxiv/papers/1301/1301.0159.pdf

Ser, G., Robertson, A., & Sheikh, A. (2014). A qualitative exploration of workarounds related to the implementation of national electronic health records in early adopter mental health hospitals. *PLoS ONE, 9*(1), e77669. doi:10.1371/journal.pone.0077669 PMID:24454678

Song, X., Duan, Z., & Jiang, X. (2012). Comparison of artificial neural networks and support vector machine classifiers for land cover classification in Northern China using a SPOT-5 HRG image. *International Journal of Remote Sensing, 33*(10), 3301–3320. doi:10.1080/01431161.2011.568531

Srikant, R., & Agrawal, R. (1996). *Mining sequential patterns: Generalizations and performance improvements.* Springer Berlin Heidelberg.

Sullivan, L. (2013). *Data Overload Stifling Customer Service Improvements.* Retrieved from www.mediapost.com/publications/article/214310/data-overload-stifling-customerservice-improvemen.html

Thomson, G. (1947). *Probit Analysis: A statistical treatment of the sigmoid response curve.* Academic Press.

Train Kenneth, E. (2003). *Discrete choice methods with simulation.* Academic Press.

Tsai, C. W., Lai, C. F., Chao, H. C., & Vasilakos, A. V. (2015). Big data analytics: A survey. *Journal of Big Data, 2*(1), 1–32. doi:10.1186/s40537-015-0030-3 PMID:26191487

Waller, M. A., & Fawcett, S. E. (2013). Data science, predictive analytics, and big data: A revolution that will transform supply chain design and management. *Journal of Business Logistics, 34*(2), 77–84. doi:10.1111/jbl.12010

Weiss, S. M., & Indurkhya, N. (1998). *Predictive data mining: a practical guide*. Morgan Kaufmann.

Witten, I. H., & Frank, E. (2005). *Data Mining: Practical machine learning tools and techniques*. Morgan Kaufmann.

Zaman, M. (2005). *Predictive Analytics: the Future of Business Intelligence*. Technology Evaluation Centers.

Zareipour, H., Bhattacharya, K., & Canizares, C. A. (2006, June). Forecasting the hourly Ontario energy price by multivariate adaptive regression splines. In *Power Engineering Society General Meeting*. IEEE. doi:10.1109/PES.2006.1709474

Zhou, Y., & Leung, H. (2006). Empirical analysis of object-oriented design metrics for predicting high and low severity faults. *Software Engineering. IEEE Transactions on, 32*(10), 771–789.

Chapter 17
Strategic Best-in-Class Performance for Voice to Customer:
Is Big Data in Logistics a Perfect Match?

Supriyo Roy
Birla Institute of Technology, India

Kaushik Kumar
Birla Institute of Technology, India

ABSTRACT

For any forward-looking perspective, organizational information which is typically historical, incomplete and most of the time inaccurate, needs to be enriched with external information. However, traditional systems and approaches are slow, inflexible and cannot handle new volume and complexity of information. Big data, an evolving term, basically refers to voluminous amount of structured, semi-structured or unstructured information in the form of data with a potential to be mined for 'best in class information'. Primarily, big data can be categorized by 3V's: volume, variety and velocity. Recent hype around big data concepts predicts that it will help companies to improve operations and makes faster and intelligent decisions. Considering the complexities in realms of supply chain, in this study, an attempt has been made to highlight the problems in storing data in any business, especially under Indian scenario where logistics arena is most unstructured and complicated. Conclusion may be significant to any strategic decision maker / manager working with distribution and logistics.

INTRODUCTION

Data never dies! ....Nowadays, business world is awash with a 'flood of data'. Big data as it name suggested, refers to very huge and disparate volumes of data being generated every moment by use of man – machine interaction. In the arena of globalization, any management decision requires innovative, new and scalable technology to assemble, host and processing analytically the large amount of data collected

DOI: 10.4018/978-1-5225-2031-3.ch017

in order to predict real-time business insights that directly relate to suppliers and end users; and also concerning risk, profit, performance, and productivity in order to enhance shareholder value (Antai & Olson, 2013).

In today's extended supply chain, Big data is generating intense quantity of attention amongst suppliers, shop floor managers, logistic managers and even end users / consumers. Together with advanced analytics like digital channels, cloud-based technologies and data visualization, all these are thought of as all part of current diverse ecosystem generated by technology megatrends. Some even proclaim the potential transformative authority of current trends as countering that of internet. Keeping researchers view in the line of business perspective, concepts of big data is typically designated by four 'V's (Sanders, 2014; Manyika et. al. 2011):

- **Volume**: Date created is more voluminous than that using traditional data sources.
- **Variety**: Sources of Data are diverse and are created by both people and machines.
- **Velocity**: Data generation is extremely fast—a process that never ends.
- **Veracity**: Testing of veracity/quality of the data is essential, and Big data is sourced from many different places.

In the business parlance, application of Big data analysis poses both opportunities and challenges starting from strategic sourcing. Extract value for big data, data must be processed and analyzed in a real-time manner, and the results need to be available in such a way as to make effective business decisions. Effectiveness of using Big data analysis in any organisation demand proper collaboration / right combination of people, process and technology. Traditional restraints are overcome by Big data in cost-effective sense and opens opportunities to store, ingest and process data from any sources from the market. Basic capability of Big data allows organizations to 'integrate multiple data sources' in a seamless manner with effectively less effort within a stipulated time frame. Equipped with a lower cost of storage, this blend of technology allows organizations to create a federated vision of customers by transforming customer data from different interdisciplinary business areas into a single way (Sahay & Jayanti Ranjan, 2008; Pearson, 2011b). In particular, users of Big data find three thrust areas that appears to make a sea difference in the decision making process to any complex problem: Thrust on developing a strong enterprise-wide analytics strategy (Strategic); Ensuring Big data analytics to be embedded in supply chain operations in order to make improve decision making across the organization (Operational); and finally, Hiring a blend of interdisciplinary people with an unique mix of analytical skills and knowledge in the business in order to produce actionable insights from big data (Human Resource) (Edwards et al., 2001).

ALIGNING BIG DATA WITH LOGISTICS MANAGEMENT

Today's business scenario is changing real time basis - accelerated economic development across the world has created global business networks that need seamless flows of good (Grimes, 2000). With this global competition, companies focus on core competencies and try to minimize as much as possible in their own vertical integration. In addition to that, variations of a particular product are ramped up to satisfy any time demand while at the same time the product lifecycle shortens. As a result, complexity and dynamics of global supply chains are taken to a higher level of importance (Smith, 2000). Customers expect real time at par services like dynamic shipment routing, just-in-time supplies and same-day delivery....all at a time. Considering all complexities in multiple vertical segments through the supply chain, importance and value for logistics management becomes a key element of competitiveness in the market place.

In order to seamless adaption to changing demand with regards to quantity as well as quality excellence, logistics providers have to enhance their strategic and operational capabilities (Barratt, & Oke, 2007). At par forecast of market demand, radical customization of services offered with introduction to business growth models are lighthouse examples for exploit of untapped data sources. Companies are investigating huge amount to transform large-scale data amounts into 'competitive decision'. Current research on logistics trends shows that market players are increasingly concerned about satisfying their customers' expectations. Across different categories of firms, managers have ranked 'meeting customer requirements' as their top priority. All the above complexity comes under obvious question: why do customer expectations finally become of importance in logistics?

Effect originates basically at both ends of the supply chain. In downstream direction, end users / consumers have a heightened demand for flexible shipment options like self-collection, follow-me routing or same-day delivery. In contrast, coming in the upstream direction, manufacturers and retailers are also increasingly demanding with regards to performance and agility of services as provided in logistics. Driven by the development of a global economy, company's domain of expertise ranging from strategic multiple sourcing to serving 'extended to ultimate' customers. Consequently, complexity of supply chain systems is growing while requirements for tight delivery windows stay unchanged. In addition industry-specific features like real-time tracking in global positioning system platform, cold chain management and shelf stocking are stretching capabilities of logistics providers to the limit. In contrast, globalization forces many logistics providers to expand complexity of their operational model as part of their efforts to serve more markets with more product variations through different sales channels. Due to this, many logistics domains like road freight and supply chain solutions are seems to be highly fragmented markets. The majority of market participants owns a comparatively small market share and is limited to either geographical boundaries or vertical segments. Though concepts like sub-contracting and collaboration exists in the supply chain but the level of standardization and business interoperability is low. In fact, many providers operate in a niche of industry. Subsequently, requirements for logistics services with regards to adaptability, scalability and localization are also increasing. Complexity becomes even higher as management of sustainability; governmental regulation and risk on a global scale are demanding more and more. Current best practice touches many vertical markets; it is quite obvious that Big data will play as backbone of the disruptive trend for the logistics industry. However, implementation of Big data and its synchronization with the specific sector is not so easy...specifically in logistics domain, it is too complex; requires many parameters to 'make fit' before implementation.

BIG DATA APPROACH IN LOGISTICS: VALUE DRIVEN STRATEGIES

Ability to manage, access and analyze large volumes of generated data while fast growing information architecture has long been critical to logistics management as they improve business performance and efficiency (Oracle white paper, 2015). While operational potency and favourable client experience and differentiation are the essential requirements to success, anticipating demand and optimizing routing of products and services conjointly leads to maximization of overall profitability (Marabotti, 2003). With growing end users demand, transportation networks and logistics management become larger, more complicated and driven by client for more exacting service levels, volume and type of data that has to manage also tend to be more complicated.

Companies while going to adopt Big data as part of their business strategy, start-up question that arises is about the type of value Big data are driving.... does it contribute to upper or lower levels only, or is it merely treated as a non-financial driver? From the above value point, any application of Big data analytics fits into one of three dimensions. The first and most obvious is 'operational efficiency' (O'Dwyer, & Renner, 2011). Here, data is used in order to improve process quality and performance, to optimize resource consumption and to make better decisions. Automated data processing has always provided this, but with an enhanced set of capabilities. 'Customer experience' being second dimension aims at increasing customer loyalty, at performing precise customer segmentation and at optimizing customer service. Finally, Big data explores 'new business models' to harmonize revenue streams from current products or to create additional revenue from adsolutely new (data) products (Manyika et al., 2011). Considering all, strategies in relate to Value Dimension Matrix can be represented in the following way (Table 1):

VALUE DRIVEN BIG DATA TO LOGISTICS: A ROAD MAP FOR VIABLE COMPETITION IN MARKET

For a start up discussion on how to utilize Big data to logistics is to fresh look at its characteristics with regard to creating and consuming information. Basic question starts with the following: Which area(s) are heavily dependent on data? Which area(s) are there where there is an opportunities to generate data? Answer to the above questions highlights sector-specific areas where smart usage of data unleashes a new order of efficiency / unique asset for monetization. For any logistics industry, five distinct properties make Big Data Analytics a viable instrument for competitive advantage. Properties 1 and 2 is meant for 'customers'; while properties 3 and 4 'integrates business functions', and last one is meant to companies 'ultimate objective to profit'.

Table 1. Value dimension matrix

Operational Efficiency	Customer Experience	Models for New Business
Data Usage in order to:	*Exploit data for:*	*Capitalize on data by:*
Increase Level of Transparency	Increase customer loyalty	Expanding revenue streams from existing products
Optimize Resource Allocation	Performing customer segmentation	Creating new revenue streams by introducing new products
Improve Process Quality	Optimize *'quick-in-response'* towards customer value driven services	Significant improvement in process quality and performance

Ref.: White paper (2013) on Value dimensions for Big Data use cases; Source: DPDHL / Detecon - Modified

Tangible Goods: Tangible Customers

A number of vertical industries has sacrificed direct customer interaction in favor of standardization and cost efficiency. Travel, banking and all kinds of commerce are increasingly using indirect channels for customer interaction, above all internet and mobile portals. Although this move has inarguably driven down the cost of core sales and customer service processes it has at the same time abandoned a number of opportunities that result from a personal customer touch point. In contrast to flight booking or transfer of funds, transportation of tangible goods needs direct communication at pickup and delivery. Apart from some automation efforts mainly for parcel delivery, logistics providers largely stay in touch directly with their customer base. Millions of customer touch points a day, on a global scale, create a bi-directional communication link for services like consumer feedback or even for market dynamics. Big Data theory provides diversified analytic means as well as complementary data points from public internet sources in order to create valuable insight on quality of product. Common strategies in relate to Value Dimension Matrix for the above dimension may be represented in the following way (Table 2):

Synergizing with Customer Business

Expansion of markets is demanding with the existing one; and to be sustainable in this growing market, relevance of logistics services may be treated as a critical factor to any company's operational procedures. Modern logistics solutions tailored to customer specific requirements seamlessly in order to integrate distribution and production processes in different industries. On the whole, right level of amalgamation with customer operations let logistics providers realize the heartbeat of individual businesses, vertical segments as well as customized markets. Leveraging this comprehensive knowledge puts logistics providers in a unique position to become valuable advisors for business customers. Common strategies in relate to Value Dimension Matrix for the above dimension may be represented in the following manner (Table 3):

Network of Information

A distinct asset of logistics provider is the real-time maintenance of transport system and delivery network. Highly optimized infrastructure that constantly forwards goods around the globe are on the other side is the source of generation of data. Apart from utilizing data for further optimization of the network itself it should also provide valuable insights to external parties. On an aggregated, macroscopic level

Table 2. Value dimension matrix (tangible goods - tangible customers)

Big Data Sources	Big Data Techniques	Big Data Usage
Customer data e.g., shipping volumes inCRM systems	Data mining for pattern detection	Customer value assessment for business analytics
Data bases of financial analyst firms	Semantic analytics	Anticipation of customer attrition
Transport management systems for shipment records	Natural language processing	Improvement of Continuous service operations
Customer emails and feedback forms	Data mining for pattern detection	Identification of new product innovation requirement

Ref.: White paper (2013) on Value dimensions for Big Data use cases; Source: DPDHL / Detecon - Modified

Table 3. Value dimension matrix (synergizing with customer business)

Big Data Sources	Big Data Techniques	Big Data Usage
Model of customer supply chain topology	Text Mining	Report on upcoming risks for supply chain disruption
Operational supply chain data	Social Media Analytics	Recommendations for counter measures for sustained operations
External data on economy, or health from social media / other public sources, etc.	Complex Event Processing	Recommended sustainability in adhere to operational effectiveness

Ref.: White paper (2013) on Value dimensions for Big Data use cases; Source: DPDHL / Detecon - Modified

logistics data has been used as an economic indicator already in the past; treated as the secondary source. Analysis and segmentation of global flow of goods is not only a powerful tool to every business functions but also to detect developing trends and changing environment in any customized market. Applying diversity and power of Big data analytics significantly changes the level of co-ordination in the supply chain down to a micro-economic viewpoint. Common strategies in relate to Value Dimension Matrix for the above dimension may be represented in the following manner (Table 4):

Global Footage: Local Presence

The fourth distinct property that separates logistics from many other industries is the 'requirement of decentralized operation'. Local presence is nowadays required in order to serve customers both at starting and endpoint of far-flung supply chains. In this sequel, logistics providers engage a fleet of vehicles that moves across countries with blanket coverage in order to pick up, forward and deliver various types of shipments. To give better service in future, companies follow the basic thumb rule: 'when picking up shipments, why not picking up data instantly?' Collecting local information in an automated way along with transport routes may create a valuable insight for demographic, environmental and traffic statistics. For global logistics providers, ability to collect and monetize local data virtually comes in a systematize manner. Common strategies in relate to Value Dimension Matrix for the above dimension may be represented in the following way (Table 5):

Table 4. Value dimension matrix (network of information)

Big Data Sources	Big Data Techniques	Big Data Usage
Shipment data from logistics production	Regression analysis / Predictive Modeling	Demand and supply forecast figures for different industries
External market intelligence sources	Time Series Analysis	Data analytics platform for financial analytics
Segmental data for different tier(s)	Cluster Analysis	Decision making
Sub assembling data	Data fusion and integration	Market Intelligence

Ref.: White paper (2013) on Value dimensions for Big Data use cases; Source: DPDHL / Detecon - Modified

Table 5. Value dimension matrix (global footage - local presence)

Big Data Sources	Big Data Techniques	Big Data Usage
Sensors and cameras attached with fleets / vehicles	Image / video recognition	Micro studies for urban development, marketing, and demographic statistics
Driver-collected data	Image processing	Road condition screening
Sensor data from mobile devices	Cluster Analysis	Environmental Monitoring
GPS based location data	Geo-correlation Analysis	Address Identification / Source Verification

Ref.: White paper (2013) on Value dimensions for Big Data use cases; Source: DPDHL / Detecon - Modified

Optimization to the Core

Logistics services appear to be simple in individual norms. Functional point of view, items is moving as parcel(s) from origin to destination; does not require a much of planning. Complexity arises from vast number of diversified shipments and destinations, deterministic lead time and finite amount of available resources. As a consequence, optimization of pertinent factors like resource utilization, delivery time and geographical coverage is an inherent threat to large-scale logistics operations. Obvious question arises in this consequence: 'how good can optimization be without data?' Information on payload, quantity, size, location, destination and many more are fundamentally required to control efficiency and service quality in any logistic network. Availability of more earlier and more precise information is the key benefit towards 'optimization to the core results'. So, strong dependency of logistics operations on timely and accurate information is a key opportunity for Big data towards 'better address and more success'. Advanced prognosticative techniques and real-time operation of events promise to produce a new quality in capability forecasts and resource control. Matrix for value dimension for this aspect may be shown by the following customized manner (Table 6):

ALIGNING LOGISTICS MATURITY MODEL IN BIG DATA ANALYSIS

Big data movement is fueling business transformation in logistics operations. Companies that are adopting big data as business transformational are advancing from a retrospective, rear view mirror of business insight that utilizes partial slices of aggregated or sampled data in group to monitor the busi-

Table 6. Matrix for value dimension (optimization)

Big Data Sources	Big Data Techniques	Big Data Usage
Telemetric and traffic information services	Complex Event Processing	Real-time Sequencing and driving directions for delivery
RFID tags attached to delivery items	Geo-Correlation	Scheduling of assignments for crowd-based delivery
Location data of Recipients	Combinatorial Optimization	Real-time prediction of Estimated Time of Arrival
Data from order management and shipment tracking	Transition Techniques	Real-time Scheduling approach for better tracking

Ref.: White paper (2013) on Value dimensions for Big Data use cases; Source: DPDHL / Detecon - Modified

Figure 1. Changing decision making scenario with big data evolution

ness to a predictive, forward-looking view of logistic operations that utilizes all available data in a real time manner to optimize business performance. Big data decision making in logistic operation is more penetrative; be depicted by the following way (Figure 1):

Keeping the entire above, Logistics Maturity model within the Organization may be well represented in the following way:

1. Initialize, in Business Monitoring phase (stage 1), we deploy traditional Data warehouse capabilities and Business Intelligence to report on, or monitor, on-going business performance. This phase utilizes the basic analytics to identify areas in relate to logistics like: Trending, Benchmarking, Performance indices like brand development, customer satisfaction, financial benefits etc.
2. Business Insight phase (stage 2), introduces business monitoring to the next level by utilizing new unstructured data sources with sophisticated statistical techniques like data mining, predictive analytics etc., augmented with real-time data feeds, in order to get a actionable, significant business insight towards business optimization of logistic parameters (towards stage 3).
3. Business Optimization phase (stage 3) establish the business maturity where organization employs embedded analytics to optimize business performance in specific areas.
4. Data Monetization phase (stage 4) refers to the situation where organizations tries to introduce usage of Big data for new revenue opportunities. For this phase, focus is on identification of target customers with their desired solution. Services like same day delivery, good packaging, real time monitoring of delivery, etc. should be there. With these, advanced analytics (models and algorithms), transformation processes and data augmentation are necessary to create resultants that address business decisions.

Figure 2. Changing decision making scenario with big data evolution

Decision making without Big data	EVOLUTION	Decision making without Big data
Use only a part of available data based on different sectors.	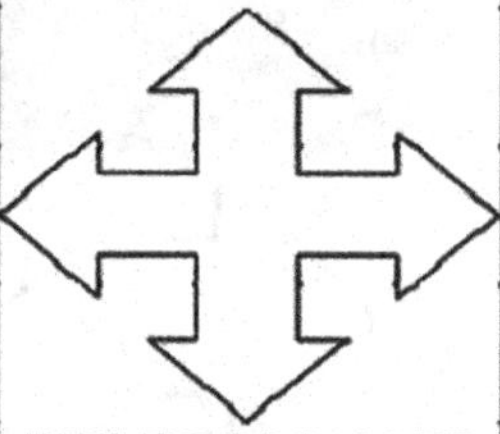	Exploit all data collected from diverse sources
Discrete and Incomplete; most of the time governed by Batch wise		Rely on Continuous, Real-time, and Correlated manner
'Rear view Mirror' hindsight		'Forward looking' recommendations
'Monitoring' business	PERFORMANCE	business 'Optimization'

5. Last phase (stage 5), Business Metamorphosis confers the ultimate vision for organizations that need to leverage the insights they are capturing concerning their performance behaviors, customers' usage patterns and overall market trends to remodel business models into new and innovative markets. All the stages are inter-connected; depicted in Figure 2.

BIG DATA ANALYSIS IN LOGISTICS: CRITICAL RISK FACTORS

Surfeit of data can gum up the decision-making process and make it more difficult to pinpoint the root causes of problems that are undermining the efficiency in logistics network. Causes of data proliferation, which seems to be very relevant in applying Big data in the logistics space.

1. **Functional Misalignment**: These refer to the problem when data is not aligned with specific needs of the functional group. It's easy to get bogged down in streams of data generated by inappropriate metrics. The same is true for secondary metrics that support the primary set of performance measures. To get out of it, we have to monitor in creating role-based metrics that help to create clarity and alignment with business strategy.
2. **Off-Target Targets**: Setting unrealistic or unsuitable performance targets can easily put on the road to analysis paralysis.... we must make our strategic planning in the line of objectives.
3. **Too Many Variations on the Theme**: These days, the number of ways in which data can be sliced and diced seems limitless. On the one hand, this provides huge analytical benefits; on the other hand, being spoiled for choice can tempt the user into ordering reports that are largely redundant or duplicative....is a serious treat in applying Big data concepts.
4. **Organizational Fragmentation**: When implementing a Big data concepts, it is routine for the system provider to sit down with the people involved and work out what types of data are needed by the enterprise.
5. **Lack of Understanding**: Logistics business intelligence tools have grown immensely in both scope and sophistication, providing users with analytical capabilities that did not exist recent past. But it can be a struggle to keep up with these developments, and some tools might not be used properly or not to their full potential....so it is essential to monitor all the above issues before going to implement Big data analysis.

LOGISTICS AND BIG DATA: IS THIS A PERFECT MATCH?

It is obvious that neither bigger trucks nor faster trains are the solution for today's challenging world. Instead, transparency, foresight and responsiveness are the key controls to successfully navigate the transition of the entire industry. In this respect, logistics segment is ideally suited to benefit from methodological and technological advancements towards fitment of Big data analytics. Logistics means 'practical arithmetic' in its ancient Greek roots, which gives a strong hint that mastering data was a key factor in this discipline from the beginning. Today logistics providers create a massive datasets while managing a massive flow of goods (White paper, 2015). For huge number of shipments every day size, location, origin and destination, weight and content are tracked in order to efficiently operate the provider's global delivery network. The obvious question is: 'does that fully exploit the value within this inexhaustible stream of data?'.. probably not. Most probably there remains a huge untapped potential for improving customer experience, optimizing resources or creating new business models. Moreover, integration of supply chain data streams from multiple logistics providers may overcome current market fragmentation and enable powerful cooperative services (Smith, 2000; Smith et al., 2007). Many market players become aware of the fact that Big data is a game changing trend for the logistics industry. In a recent servey on supply chain trends, 60% of the respondent announced that they are thinking to invest in Big data analytics within the next five years (White paper 2013-Logistics Trend radar). Considering the functional area, challenge in business, and more likely the opportunity to explore may be represented in the following tabular forms (Table 7):

Table 7. Future big data analysis

Functional Area	Business Challenge	Opportunity to Excel
Environment friendly Distribution Centre(s) with 'best optimal' Warehousing	Optimal size and location distribution centres with 'green' warehousing	Increased inventory turnover/ Decreased inventory write-downs/ Right time inventory / Same day delivery/ Reduced movement stock(s)
Strategic Planning for Network Resource	Ability to tune network upwards or downwards depending on demand functioning	Best optimal demand forecasting/ Optimal fleet utilization / Proper Scheduling
Strategic Line Route Optimization	Ability to perform best optimal pick-up and delivery system	Best optimal delivery scheduling/ Accidental hazard optimization /Maximize fuel efficiency in terms of tonnage of goods
Anytime Service to customers with loyalty	Service innovation and differentiation with competitors leading to sustainability in business	Improved client satisfaction index / Extended collaborative network / Improved service level satisfaction index / Reduced cost of service
Introduction to Promotional Marketing	Strategic planning for market coverage / Proper segmentation / innovative strategies to profit	Generate customers with value base service / Cross and up-sell to existing customers / Measurement of impact of sales/ New location based services
Predicting Risk analysis	Ability to establish as reliable firms to the end users	Understand potential liability/ Accomplishment as 'most respected and reliable' firm to the customers
Proper Maintenance	Cost containment and Optimal scheduling for prompt and on-time delivery	Optimize work breakdowns structures / Initiative proper Quality Policy / Waste Minimization / Improve service quality levels

Ref: white paper of ORACLE (2015). Improving Logistics & Transportation Performance with Big Data-Modified

CONCLUSION

Today's business world has entered an era of Big Data. Big data is recent concept in information driven business world- it is like a 'tsunami' that has transformed firms towards a new direction. A usually popular axiom is that 'small data is for people; big data is for machines'. Through better analysis of enormous volumes of data that are getting offered, there is the potential for quicker advances in several disciplines and raising profit and success. Challenges embody not simply the apparent problems with scale, however, additionally error-handling, heterogeneity, privacy, timeliness, lack of structure, visualization and provenance at all stages of the analysis pipeline from data collection to result interpretation. These technical challenges are common across a large variance of application domains, and thus are not cost-efficient to handle within the context of a single specific domain. Transformative solutions would be needed for such challenges, and will not be addressed naturally by the next generation of industrial products. We must adhere, encourage and continue basic research towards addressing these technical challenges if we are to acquire the speculated benefits of Big data techniques. The very fact that Big Data analysis usually involves multiple stages highlights a challenge that arises routinely in practice. New data must be accounted for in a stepwise manner, taking into account the results of previous analysis and pre-existing information. Current systems offer meagre or no assistance for such Big Data pipelines, and this itself is a challenging objective (Nada R. Sanders, 2014). A key success issue for corporations is that the handiness of seamless information at right time. Businesses require to know what decisions should be taken, when they are supposed to be taken and how these decisions would affect operational performance and financial results (Zeng et al., 2011). Such typical demand fuels the growth of big data to equip them to make better, real-time, smarter and data-driven outcomes that will modify the way they tackle their operations and compete in the marketplace.

Organizations cannot ignore the benefits of big data as the field is evolving very rapidly (Kevin, 2015). At the same time, they have to look methodically at the way they utilize the data to ensure that the new opportunities are under control where as the new expected risks are manageable. Organizations in successfully executing a big data has also to take the challenge for developing strategy to develop sound basics that are accommodative enough to cater to the organization's data requirements of present and future. Looking ahead Big Data has to admittedly overcome numerous obstacles before it has a pervasive influence on the logistics industry - technical feasibility, data quality and privacy being only a few. In future, these are all lesser importance as Big data is primarily and foremost driven by entrepreneurial spirit (Waller, and Fawcett, 2013). Thus, affectivity of any Big data implementation solely depends on relevance and accuracy of data points that have been obtained. These data points should be further augmented with existing internal data to derive analytics that ensures meaningful and precise business decision making. Finally, it may be concluded that these theories may be considered as comparatively untapped asset that organizations may exploit once they decide a shift of mindset and apply right applications in right time at right position.

REFERENCES

Antai, I., & Olson, H. (2013). Interaction: A new focus for supply chain vs. supply chain competition. *International Journal of Physical Distribution & Logistics Management*, *43*(7), 511–528. doi:10.1108/IJPDLM-06-2012-0195

Barratt, M., & Oke, A. (2007). Antecedents of supply chain visibility in retail supply chains: A resource-based theory perspective. *Journal of Operations Management, 25*(6), 1217–1233. doi:10.1016/j.jom.2007.01.003

Chae, B., Sheu, C., Yang, C., & Olson, D. (2014). The impact of advanced analytics and data accuracy on operational performance: A contingent resource based theory (RBT) perspective. *Decision Support Systems, 59*(1), 119–126. doi:10.1016/j.dss.2013.10.012

Christopher, M. (2011). *Logistics & supply chain management* (4th ed.). Prentice Hall.

Edwards, P., Peters, M., & Sharman, G. (2001). The Effectiveness of Information Systems in Supporting the Extended Supply Chain. *Journal of Business Logistics, 22*(1), 11–27.

Gartner Lustig, I., Dietrich, B., Johnson, C., & Dziekan, C. (2010). *The Analytics Journey*. Institute for Operations Research and the Management Sciences.

Grimes, S. (2000). Here today, gone tomorrow. *Intelligent Enterprise, 3*(9), 42–48.

Kevin, L. (2015). *A roadmap to green supply chain: Using supply chain Archaeology and Big data analysis*. Industrial Press.

Manyika, J., Chui, M., Brown, B., Bughin, J., Dobbs, R., Roxburgh, C., & Byers, A. H. (2011). *Big data: The next frontier for innovation, competition, and productivity*. Competition & Productivity.

Marabotti, D. (2003). Build supplier metrics, build better product. *Quality, 42*(2), 40–43.

Nada, R. S. (2014). Big data driven supply chain management - A framework for implementing analysis and turning information into intelligence, Pearson Education Inc.

O'Dwyer, J., & Renner, R. (2011). The Promise of Advanced Supply Chain Analytics, *Supply Chain. Management Review, 15*(1), 32–37.

Pearson, M. (2011b). Predictive Analytics: Looking forward to better supply chain decisions. *Logistics Management, 50*(9), 22–26.

Sahay, B. S., & Ranjan, J. (2008). Real time business intelligence in supply chain analytics. *Information Management & Computer Security, 16*(1), 28–48. doi:10.1108/09685220810862733

Siegel, E. (2013). *Predictive Analytics: The Power to Predict Who Will Click, Buy, Lie, or Die*. Wiley Publishing.

Smith, G. E., Watson, K. J., Baker, W. H., & Pokorski, J. A. II. (2007). A critical balance: Collaboration and security in the IT-enabled supply chain. *International Journal of Production Research, 45*(11), 2595–2613. doi:10.1080/00207540601020544

Smith, M. (2000). The visible supply chain. *Intelligent Enterprise, 3*(16), 44–50.

Waller, M. A., & Fawcett, S. E. (2013). Data Science, Predictive Analytics, and Big Data: A Revolution That Will Transform Supply Chain Design and Management. *The Journal of Business, 34*(2), 77–84.

White Paper of DHL. (2011). *Are you ready for anything?* DHL Supply Chain Matters.

White Paper of DHL. (2013a). *Big Data in Logistics-A DHL Perspective on how to move beyond the hype*. DHL Customer Solutions & Innovation.

White Paper of DHL. (2013b). *Logistics Trend Radar- delivering insight today…creating value tomorrow*. DHL Customer Solutions & Innovation.

White Paper of ORACLE. (2015). *Improving Logistics & Transportation Performance with Big Data Architect's Guide and Reference - Architecture Introduction*. ORACLE Enterprise Architecture.

Zeng, X., Lin, D., & Xu, Q. (2011). Query Performance Tuning in Supply Chain Analytics. *4th International Conference on Computational Sciences and Optimization*, (pp. 327-330).

Section 4
Advanced Data Analytics:
Decision Models and Business Applications

Chapter 18
First Look on Web Mining Techniques to Improve Business Intelligence of E-Commerce Applications

G. Sreedhar
Rashtriya Sanskrit Vidyapeetha (Deemed University), India

A. Anandaraja Chari
Rayalaseema University, India

ABSTRACT

Web Data Mining is the application of data mining techniques to extract useful knowledge from web data like contents of web, hyperlinks of documents and web usage logs. There is also a strong requirement of techniques to help in business decision in e-commerce. Web Data Mining can be broadly divided into three categories: Web content mining, Web structure mining and Web usage mining. Web content data are content availed to users to satisfy their required information. Web structure data represents linkage and relationship of web pages to others. Web usage data involves log data collected by web server and application server which is the main source of data. The growth of WWW and technologies has made business functions to be executed fast and easier. As large amount of transactions are performed through e-commerce sites and the huge amount of data is stored, valuable knowledge can be obtained by applying the Web Mining techniques.

INTRODUCTION

In the present day scenario the World Wide Web (WWW) is an important and popular information search tool. It provides convenient access to almost all kinds of information from education to entertainment. The World Wide Web is the key source of information and it is growing rapidly. The growth of World Wide Web and technologies has made business functions to be executed fast and easier. E-commerce has provided a cost efficient and effective way of doing business. As large amount of transactions are

DOI: 10.4018/978-1-5225-2031-3.ch018

performed through ecommerce sites and the huge amount of data is stored, valuable knowledge can be obtained by applying the Web Mining techniques. E-commerce websites have the advantage of reaching a large number of customers regardless of distance and time limitations. The advantage of e-commerce over traditional businesses is the faster speed and the lower expenses for both e-commerce website owners and customers in completing customer transactions and orders. The World Wide Web (WWW) has become an important channel for information retrieval, electronic commerce and entertainment (Nah, 2004). However, long Web page download times have remained a major cause of frustration among Web users (Selvidge 1999; 2003). According to the findings of the surveys conducted by Lightner, Bose and Salvendy (1996) and the GVU (Graphic, Visualization and Usability) Centre at Georgia Institute of Technology, long download times have always been a major problem experienced by Web users. The survey by Pitkow and Kehoe (1996) also indicates that the most widely cited problem using the WWW was that it took too long to download Web pages (i.e. 69% of respondents cited this problem). This problem is worsened by the exponential increase in the number of Web users over the years and the popularity of multimedia (e.g. video, voice) technology (Nah, 2004). This problem is so noticeable that Web users often equate the "WWW" acronym with "World Wide Wait"!

The long waiting time for downloading Web pages is often not tolerable even in the wired environment. Due to the increasing and excessive use of multimedia data (i.e. audio and video clips) on Web pages, this concern is continuously growing. The problem of 'long download time' is relevant not only to Web users but also to the authors and designers of websites, as websites that take a long time to download are rarely or less frequently visited (Reaux & Carroll 1997). Slow Loading pages affects the sales and longer negative effects. Akamai (2009) established that 40% of online shoppers feel comfortable to revisit if the website loads quickly.

MODEL AND ANALYSIS

The page load times of some of the popular E-commerce websites are considered for study to assess the performance and speed of the online business Websites. The study considers the analysis on page load time of the home page of E-commerce websites using statistical control chart analysis. The Home page download times of the websites are observed using GTmetrix developed by GT.net, a web performance hosting tool (GTmetrix, 2016). The study evolves the performance of 100 Popular E-commerce websites into five different categories:

1. Multiple Product websites
2. Electronic Product websites
3. Service websites
4. Fashion and Textile websites
5. Specific websites

The website download times are compiled using GTmetrix during March 2016 and are shown in Table 1, Table 2, Table 3, Table 4, and Table 5.

The page load times of the E-commerce websites are analyzed using Statistical Control Chart viz., Individual control chart with Moving range with three websites. The study evolves average page load times of E-commerce websites and variation pattern of page load times. The detailed analysis is carried

Table 1. The Dowload Times Of E-Commerce Website For Multiple Products

S.No.	Website	Down Load Time Of Home Page. (in Secs)
1	http://www.amazon.com	5.8
2	http://www.flipkart.com	4.7
3	http://ebay.com	4.2
4	http://www.infibeam.com	8.7
5	http://www.shopping.indiatimes.com	3.8
6	http://www.shopping.rediff.com	7.2
7	http://www.homeshop18.com	4
8	http://www.shopbychoice.com	4.9
9	http://www.zapstore.com	5.8
10	http://www.egully.com	5
11	http://www.snapdeal.com	1.1
12	http://www.jabong.com	0.5
13	http://www.paytm.com	8
14	http://www.grabmore.in	3.2
15	http://www.letsshop.in	20.4
16	http://www.rightshopping.in	7.7
17	http://www.bagittoday.com	4.4
18	http://www.shopclues.com	5.7
19	http://www.ezmaal.com	15.1
20	http://www.smartshoppers.com	1.7
21	http://www.bigadda.com	5.1

Table 2. The download times of E-commerce website for electronic products

S.No.	Website	Download Time Of * Home Page.(in Secs)
1	http://www.primeabgb.com	11.5
2	http://www.ezoneonline.in	30.3
3	http://www.univercell.in	8.4
4	http://www.themobilestore.in	5.7
5	http://www.bigcmobiles.in	8.8
6	http://www.hp.com	5.2
7	http://www.apple.com	1.8
8	http://www.gadgets.in	6.8
9	http://www.gadgetsguru.com	6.8
10	http://www.next.co.in	2.7
11	http://www.royalimages.in	4.4
12	http://www.smcinternational.in	15.6
13	http://www.theitdepot.com	9.2
14	http://www.vijaysales.com	5.7
15	http://www.jjmehta.com	4.4
16	http://www.dell.co.in	3
17	http://www.bitfang.com	19.9
18	http://www.lynx-india.com	6.6
19	http://www.deltapage.com	3.3
20	http://www.pristinenote.com	0.9
21	http://www.theitwares.com	3.9
22	http://www.cromaretail.com	2.3

by using Minitab software. The individual website page load time control chart of five categories of E- commerce websites are seen in Figure 1, Figure 2, Figure 3, Figure 4, and Figure 5.

The study reveals the fact that the websites page load time are observed to be not under random behavior as per statistical laws (Montgomery, 2009). This shows that web design process by the website designers are not operating under random process in all the five categories, because each of the category of websites download times are too high (i. e exceeding 3 sigma limit), or the Upper Control Limit (UCL) (see Figure 1 to 5 both individual and moving ranges of website page load times). This study identifies the fact that these websites have some assignable reasons in the design process and needs correction/ rectification of faults as per the World Wide Web Consortium (W3C) in order to improve the website design. This reduces page load time and to enable the E- Commerce websites to achieve the improved download time performance.

Table 3. The download times of E-commerce website for services

S.No.	Website	Download Time Of * Home Page. (in Secs)
1	http://www.irctc.co.in	7.9
2	http://www.apsrtconline.in	3.9
3	http://www.meeseva.gov.in	4.6
4	http://www.bsnl.gov.in	4.3
5	http://www.airtel.in	3.2
6	http://www.ideacellur.com	12.3
7	http://www.kesinenitravels.com	3.8
8	http://www.makemytrip.com	6.7
9	http://www.yatra.com	9.4
10	http://www.jetairways.com/en/IN/Home.aspx	6.4
11	http://www.airindia.in	5.3
12	http://www.goibibo.com	3.4
13	http://www.travelguru.com	5.8
14	http://www.travelchacha.com	2.3
15	http://goidirectory.nic.in/ministries_departments_view.php	18.3
16	http://goidirectory.nic.in/state_departments.php?ou=AP.	4.3
17	http://www.nearbuy.com	3.2
18	http://www.quickr.com	2.5
19	http://www.olx.in	3.2
20	http://www.click.in	5.6
21	http://commonfloor.com	9.1
22	http://www.mediahome.in	1

Table 4. The download times of E-commerce website for textiles, fashions etc.

S.No.	Website	Download Time Of * Home Page. (in Secs)
1	http://www.yebhi.com	4.9
2	http://www.shoppersstop.com	31.4
3	http://www.fashionara.com	5.3
4	http://www.firstcry.com	3.3
5	http://www.babyoye.com	5.5
6	http://www.koovs.com	3.5
7	http://www.fashionandyou.com	6.8
8	http://www.basicslife.com	4.2
9	http://www.biba.in	8.5
10	http://www.shopnineteen.com	5.3
11	http://www.ninecolours.com	3.9
12	http://www.dresshubb.com	21.5
13	http://www.sunglassesindia.com	1.6
14	http://www.brandsndeals.com	3.9
15	http://www.pantaloons.com	3.9
16	http://www.majorbrands.in	8.2
17	http://www.yepmeshopping.com	4
18	http://www.elitify.com	2.2
19	http://www.trendin.com	5.2
20	http://www.indiarush.com	3.6
21	http://www.yepme.com	6.5
22	http://www.spyder.com	5
23	http://www.shimply.com	9.7

Moreover, Web Technology studies have specification on the page load tolerance time, which states that users cannot tolerate to stay beyond 4 seconds of time and one third of the visitors leave the site if site does not load in 4 seconds of time (Nah, 2004; WebSiteOptimization, 2008). The present study identifies that many of the major online business websites are not capable to maintain the download tolerance time of 4 seconds. The categories wise the websites unable to meet the ideal page load time is detailed in the following Table 6, Table 7, Table 8, Table 9, and Table 10 (UsabilityNet, 2006).

Table 5. The download times of E-commerce website for specific category

S.No.	Website	Download Time Of * Home Page.(in Secs)
1	http://www.zoomin.com	3.4
2	http://www.vistaprint.in	1.7
3	http://www.bluestone.com	10.1
4	http://www.nyka.com	5.2
5	http://www.indiangiftsportal.com	3.5
6	http://www.bags109.com	5.8
7	http://www.bookchums.com	2.5
8	http://fitness.reebok.com/international	10.4
9	http://myspace.com	7.3
10	http://www.storeji.com	3.5
11	http://www.pepperfry.com	6.2
12	http://www.fabfurnish.com	3

Figure 1. Individual control chart for download time of E-commerce website home page - multiple products

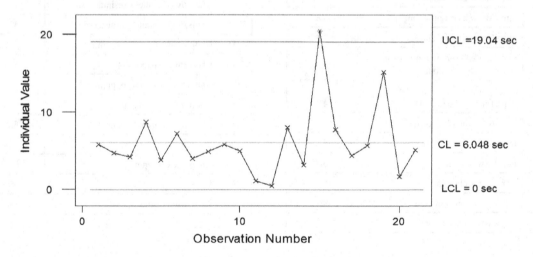

CATEGORY 1: MULTI PRODUCT WEBSITES

Chance (Percentage) of a website not capable to meet the required specified tolerance download time is 75.8%(i.e., approximately 76% of websites in this category does not meet the requirement of ideal page load time).

Figure 2. Individual control chart for download time of E-commerce website home page - electronic products

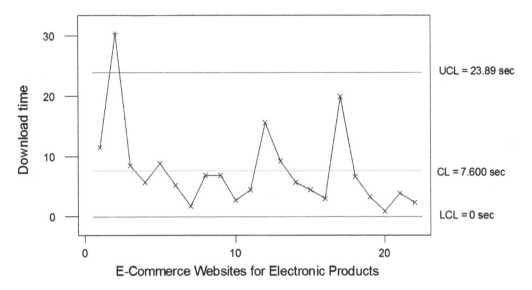

Figure 3. Individual control chart for download time of E-commerce website home page - services

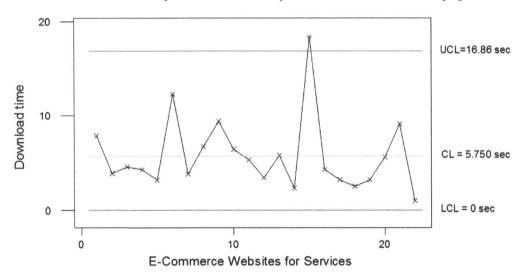

CATEGORY 2: ELECTRONIC PRODUCT WEBSITES

Chance (Percentage) of a website does not capable to the meet the required specified tolerance download time is 83.89% (i.e., approximately 84% of websites in this category does not meet the requirement of ideal page load time).

Figure 4. Individual control chart for download time of E-commerce website home page - fashions & textiles

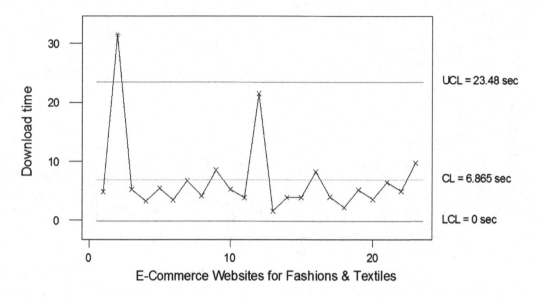

Figure 5. Individual control chart for download time of E-commerce website home page - specific products

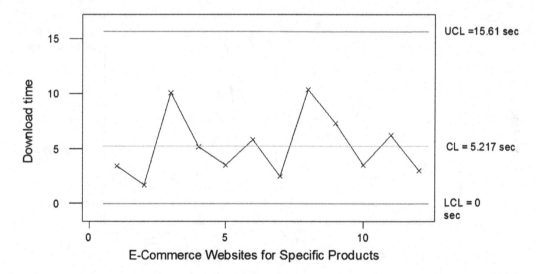

CATEGORY 3: SERVICES WEBSITES

Chance (Percentage) of a website not capable to meet the required specified tolerance of 4 seconds download time is 77.93% (approximately 78% of websites in this category does not meet the requirement of ideal page load time).

Table 6. The websites that are not capable to meet the required tolerance limit of PLT – multi product websites

S.NO	Websites are not capable to meet specified norm of 4 seconds
1	http://www.amazon.com
2	http://www.flipkart.com
3	http://ebay.com
4	http://www.infibeam.com
5	http://www.shopping.rediff.com
6	http://www.shopbychoice.com
7	http://www.zapstore.com
8	http://www.egully.com
9	http://www.paytm.com
10	http://www.letsshop.in
11	http://www.rightshopping.in
12	http://www.bagittoday.com
13	http://www.shopclues.com
14	http://www.ezmaal.com
15	http://www.bigadda.com

Table 7. The websites that are not capable to meet the required tolerance limit of PLT – electronic product websites

S.NO	Websites are not capable to meet specified norm of 4 seconds
1	http://www.primeabgb.com
2	http://www.ezoneonline.in
3	http://www.univercell.in
4	http://www.themobilestore.in
5	http://www.bigcmobiles.in
6	http://www.hp.com
7	http://www.gadgets.in
8	http://www.gadgetsguru.com
9	http://www.royalimages.in
10	http://www.smcinternational.in
11	http://www.theitdepot.com
12	http://www.vijaysales.com
13	http://www.jjmehta.com
14	http://www.bitfang.com
15	http://www.lynx-india.com

CATEGORY 4: FASHION AND TEXTILES WEBSITES

Chance (Percentage) of a website does not capable to the meet the required specified tolerance download time is 75.80%(i.e., approximately 76% of websites in this category does not meet the requirement of ideal page load time).

CATEGORY 5: SPECIFIC PRODUCTS WEBSITES

Chance (Percentage) of a website does not capable to the meet the required specified tolerance download time is 69.84%(approximately 70% of websites in this category does not meet the requirement of ideal page load time).

The research work also further investigated for Optimization of web design by the web tool RAGE Web Crusher (RAGE, 2016) to suggest the improvement needed in each of the websites. The details of savings and improvements by the tool was analyzed by the tool in the case of all categories of E- commerce website in the study. Thus, information of Optimized download time performance for all categories of E-commerce websites under study are compiled and presented in Table 11, Table 12, Table 13, Table 14 and Table 15. The Statistical Quality Control chart analysis was carried on these Optimized values of download times of the each of the E-commerce websites to find status of improvement achieved by the Optimization suggested by RAGE Web Crusher tool using again Mini Tab software (RAGE, 2016).

Table 8. The websites that are not capable to meet the required tolerance limit of PLT – services websites

S.NO	Websites are not capable to meet specified norm of 4 seconds
1	http://www.irctc.co.in
2	http://www.meeseva.gov.in
3	http://www.bsnl.gov.in
4	http://www.ideacellur.com
5	http://www.makemytrip.com
6	http://www.yatra.com
7	http://www.jetairways.com/en/IN/Home.aspx
8	http://www.airindia.in
9	http://www.travelguru.com
10	http://goidirectory.nic.in/ministries_departments_view.php
11	http://goidirectory.nic.in/state_departments.php?ou=AP.
12	http://www.click.in
13	http://commonfloor.com

Table 9. The websites that are not capable to meet the required tolerance limit of PLT – fashion and textiles websites

S.NO	Websites are not capable to meet specified norm of 4 seconds
1	http://www.yebhi.com
2	http://www.shoppersstop.com
3	http://www.fashionara.com
4	http://www.babyoye.com
5	http://www.fashionandyou.com
6	http://www.basicslife.com
7	http://www.biba.in
8	http://www.shopnineteen.com
9	http://www.dresshubb.com
10	http://www.majorbrands.in
11	http://www.trendin.com
12	http://www.yepme.com
13	http://www.spyder.com
14	http://www.shimply.com

Table 10. The websites that are not capable to meet the required tolerance limit of PLT – specific products websites

S.NO	Websites are not capable to meet specified norm of 4 seconds
1	http://www.bluestone.com
2	http://www.nyka.com
3	http://www.bags109.com
4	http://fitness.reebok.com/international
5	http://myspace.com
6	http://www.pepperfry.com

The Figure 6, Figure 7, Figure 8, Figure 9, and Figure 10 reveal the analysis of improvement of five categories of websites.

The improvements that are suggested by RAGE Web Crusher after optimization are shown in the following Table 16, Table 17, Table 18, Table 19 and Table 20 as comparing to the original performance analyzed previously.

Table 11. The optimized download times of home page of E-commerce website for multiple products

S.No.	Website	Optimized Download Time Of * Home Page. (in Secs)
1	http://www.amazon.com	4.06
2	http://www.flipkart.com	3.76
3	http://ebay.com	3.36
4	http://www.infibeam.com	6.09
5	http://www.shopping.indiatimes.com	2.28
6	http://www.shopping.rediff.com	5.76
7	http://www.homeshop18.com	3.2
8	http://www.shopbychoice.com	2.45
9	http://www.zapstore.com	2.32
10	http://www.egully.com	3.5
11	http://www.snapdeal.com	0.88
12	http://www.jabong.com	0.35
13	http://www.paytm.com	5.6
14	http://www.grabmore.in	2.56
15	http://www.letsshop.in	12.24
16	http://www.rightshopping.in	2.31
17	http://www.bagittoday.com	2.64
18	http://www.shopclues.com	3.99
19	http://www.ezmaal.com	13.59
20	http://www.smartshoppers.com	1.02
21	http://www.bigadda.com	4.08

Table 12. The optimized download times of home page of E-commerce website for electronic products

S.No.	Website	Optimized Download Time Of * Home Page. (in Secs)
1	http://www.primeabgb.com	8.05
2	http://www.ezoneonline.in	12.12
3	http://www.univercell.in	4.2
4	http://www.themobilestore.in	3.42
5	http://www.bigcmobiles.in	4.4
6	http://www.hp.com	4.68
7	http://www.apple.com	1.26
8	http://www.gadgets.in	2.04
9	http://www.gadgetsguru.com	4.76
10	http://www.next.co.in	1.08
11	http://www.royalimages.in	2.2
12	http://www.smcinternational.in	9.36
13	http://www.theitdepot.com	5.52
14	http://www.vijaysales.com	4.56
15	http://www.jjmehta.com	3.08
16	http://www.dell.co.in	2.4
17	http://www.bitfang.com	17.91
18	http://www.lynx-india.com	3.3
19	http://www.deltapage.com	2.64
20	http://www.pristinenote.com	0.72
21	http://www.theitwares.com	2.73
22	http://www.cromaretail.com	1.61

CATEGORY 1: MULTI PRODUCT WEBSITES (AFTER OPTIMIZATION)

Chance (Percentage) of a website does not capable to the meet the required specified tolerance download time is 51.59% (Approximately 52% of websites in this category does not meet the expected ideal Page load time). This indicates that at least 24% websites will enable to improve in this category with performance of ideal PLT.

Table 13. The optimized download times of home page of E-commerce website for services

S.No.	Website	Optimized Download Time Of * Home Page. (in Secs)
1	http://www.irctc.co.in	6.32
2	http://www.apsrtconline.in	3.51
3	http://www.meeseva.gov.in	3.68
4	http://www.bsnl.gov.in	3.44
5	http://www.airtel.in	2.24
6	http://www.ideacellur.com	4.92
7	http://www.kesinenitravels.com	1.9
8	http://www.makemytrip.com	5.36
9	http://www.yatra.com	7.52
10	http://www.jetairways.com/en/IN/Home.aspx	3.84
11	http://www.airindia.in	3.71
12	http://www.goibibo.com	2.72
13	http://www.travelguru.com	4.06
14	http://www.travelchacha.com	0.69
15	http://goidirectory.nic.in/ministries_departments_view.php	10.98
16	http://goidirectory.nic.in/state_departments.php?ou=AP.	2.58
17	http://www.nearbuy.com	0.96
18	http://www.quickr.com	2
19	http://www.olx.in	2.88
20	http://www.click.in	4.48
21	http://commonfloor.com	8.19
22	http://www.mediahome.in	0.2

Table 14. The optimized download times of home page of E-commerce website for textiles, fashions etc.

S.No.	Website	Optimized Download Time Of * Home Page. (in Secs)
1	http://www.yebhi.com	2.45
2	http://www.shoppersstop.com	28.26
3	http://www.fashionara.com	3.71
4	http://www.firstcry.com	1.98
5	http://www.babyoye.com	3.85
6	http://www.koovs.com	1.75
7	http://www.fashionandyou.com	4.76
8	http://www.basicslife.com	1.68
9	http://www.biba.in	5.1
10	http://www.shopnineteen.com	1.59
11	http://www.ninecolours.com	3.12
12	http://www.dresshubb.com	4.3
13	http://www.sunglassesindia.com	1.12
14	http://www.brandsndeals.com	2.34
15	http://www.pantaloons.com	1.17
16	http://www.majorbrands.in	2.46
17	http://www.yepmeshopping.com	2.4
18	http://www.elitify.com	1.76
19	http://www.trendin.com	2.08
20	http://www.indiarush.com	2.16
21	http://www.yepme.com	3.9
22	http://www.spyder.com	1.5
23	http://www.shimply.com	8.73

CATEGORY 2: ELECTRONIC PRODUCT WEBSITES (AFTER OPTIMIZATION)

Chance (Percentage) of a website does not capable to the meet the required specified tolerance download time is 61.40% (i.e., Approximately 61% of websites in this category does not meet the expected ideal page load time). This indicates that at least 23% websites will enable to improve in this category with performance of ideal PLT.

Table 15. The optimized download times of home page Of E-commerce website for specific category

S.No.	Website	Optimized Download Time Of * Home Page. (in Secs)
1	http://www.zoomin.com	1.02
2	http://www.vistaprint.in	1.02
3	http://www.bluestone.com	7.07
4	http://www.nyka.com	3.64
5	http://www.indiangiftsportal.com	1.75
6	http://www.bags109.com	2.32
7	http://www.bookchums.com	1.5
8	http://fitness.reebok.com/international	7.28
9	http://myspace.com	5.11
10	http://www.storeji.com	2.8
11	http://www.pepperfry.com	3.1
12	http://www.fabfurnish.com	2.1

Figure 6. Individual control chart for optimized download time of E-commerce website home page - multiple products

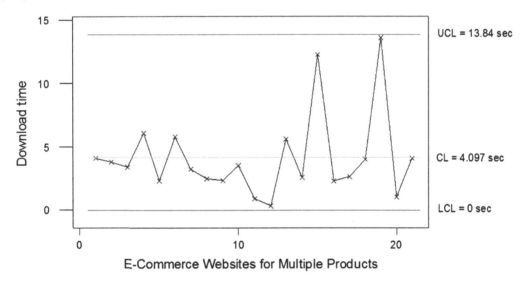

CATEGORY 3: SERVICES WEBSITES (AFTER OPTIMIZATION)

Chance (PERCENTAGE) of a website does not capable to the meet the required specified tolerance download time is 50% (50% of websites in this category does not meet the expected ideal page load time). This indicates that at least 28% websites will enable to improve in this category with performance of ideal PLT.

Figure 7. Individual control chart for optimized download time of E-commerce website home page - electronic products

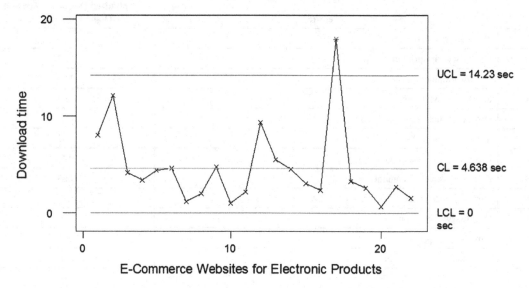

Figure 8. Individual control chart for optimized download time of E-commerce website home page - services

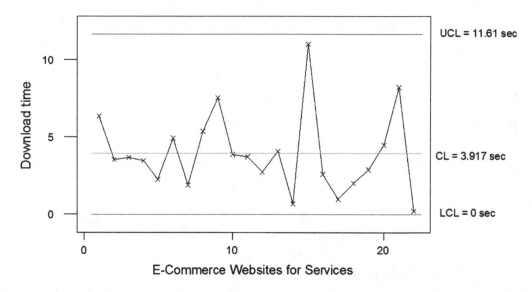

CATEGORY 4: FASHION AND TEXTILES WEBSITES (AFTER OPTIMIZATION)

Chance (Percentage) of a website does not capable to the meet the required specified tolerance download time is 15.95%. (i.e., approximately 16% of websites in this category do not meet the expected ideal page load time). This indicates that at least 60% websites will enable to improve in this category with performance of ideal PLT.

Figure 9. Individual Control chart for optimized download time of E-commerce website home page - fashion & textiles

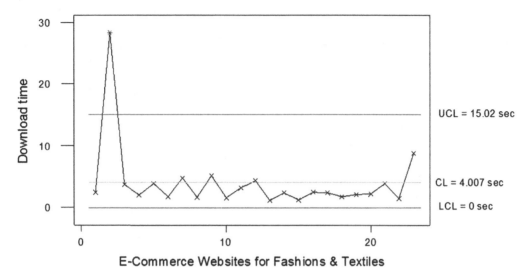

Figure 10. Individual control chart for optimized download time of E-commerce website home page - specific products

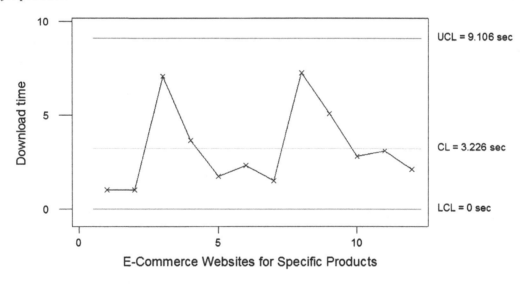

CATEGORY 5: SPECIFIC PRODUCTS WEBSITES (AFTER OPTIMIZATION)

Chance (Percentage) of a website does not capable to the meet the required specified tolerance download time is 22.24%. (i.e. Approximately 22% of websites in this category does not meet the expected ideal page load time). This indicates that at least 58% websites will enable to improve in this category with performance of ideal PLT.

Table 16. The websites that are not capable to meet the required tolerance limit of PLT after optimization – multi product websites

S.NO	Websites are not capable to meet specified norm of 4 seconds
1	http://www.amazon.com
2	http://www.infibeam.com
3	http://www.shopping.rediff.com
4	http://www.paytm.com
5	http://www.letsshop.in
6	http://www.ezmaal.com
7	http://www.bigadda.com

Table 17. The websites that are not capable to meet the required tolerance limit of PLT after optimization – electronic products websites

S.NO	Websites are not capable to meet specified norm of 4 seconds
1	http://www.primeabgb.com
2	http://www.ezoneonline.in
3	http://www.univercell.in
4	http://www.bigcmobiles.in
5	http://www.hp.com
6	http://www.gadgetsguru.com
7	http://www.smcinternational.in
8	http://www.theitdepot.com
9	http://www.vijaysales.com
10	http://www.bitfang.com

Table 18. The websites that are not capable to meet the required tolerance limit of PLT after optimization – services websites

S.NO	Websites are not capable to meet specified norm of 4 seconds
1	http://www.irctc.co.in
2	http://www.ideacellur.com
3	http://www.makemytrip.com
4	http://www.yatra.com
5	http://www.travelguru.com
6	http://goidirectory.nic.in/ministries_departments_view.php
7	http://www.click.in
8	http://commonfloor.com

Table 19. The websites that are not capable to meet the required tolerance limit of PLT after optimization – fashion & textiles websites

S.NO	Websites are not capable to meet specified norm of 4 seconds
1	http://www.shoppersstop.com
2	http://www.fashionandyou.com
3	http://www.biba.in
4	http://www.dresshubb.com
5	http://www.shimply.com

Table 20. The websites that are not capable to meet the required tolerance limit of PLT – specific products websites

S.NO	Websites are not capable to meet specified norm of 4 seconds
1	http://www.bluestone.com
2	http://fitness.reebok.com/international
3	http://myspace.com
4	http://www.pepperfry.com

CONCLUSION

The paper explores the recent status of performance in terms most important aspect of page load time of most popular Online Business websites. The study identifies that page load times of some most popular online Business websites are poor compared to expected ideal time specified as 3 to 4 seconds' time. The page load times of the websites of Online Business are not behaving under random operations but found to have some assignable faults contained in the web design. They can be further analyzed through attribute control charts to diagnose the average no of faults as well as quantum of faults to reduce them in order to improve the design.

The average download time performance in each category is much above the specified download tolerance time of 4 seconds. The percentage of websites exceeding Specified tolerance level of 4 seconds' time in each category is not less than 70%, which is very alarming and needs stern and immediate action to improve accessibility of on line business sites to improve the sales to the best of these organizations. The analysis also indicates the improvement that can be achieved if Optimization process of the website is attempted as per the RAGE Web crusher tool. Minimum of 25% websites can be improved to the expected level of tolerance limit of page load time by implementing the suggestion of RAGE web crusher web tool.

ACKNOWLEDGMENT

The authors are thankful to the University Grants Commission, New Delhi, Govt. of India for the support and funding the project during the financial years 2015-17.

REFERENCES

Akamai. (2009, September). *Akamai Reveals 2 Seconds as the New Threshold of Acceptability for E-Commerce Web Page Response Times*. Cambridge, MA: Akamai Technologies. Retrieved from https://www.akamai.com/us/en/about/news/press/2009-press/akamai-reveals-2-seconds-as-the-new-threshold-of-acceptability-for-ecommerce-web-page-response-times.jsp

GTmetrix. (2016). *Analyze Your Site's Speed and Make It Faster*. Retrieved from https://gtmetrix.com/

Lightner, N. J., Bose, I., & Salvendy, G. (1996). What is wrong with the world-wide web?: A diagnosis of some problems and prescription of some remedies. *Ergonomics*, *39*(8), 995–1004. doi:10.1080/00140139608964523

Nah, F. (2004). A Study on Tolerable Waiting Time: How long are Web Users Willing to Wait. *Behaviour & Information Technology*, *23*(3), 153–163. doi:10.1080/01449290410001669914

Pitkow, J. E., & Kehoe, C. M. (1996). Emerging trends in the WWW user population. *Communications of the ACM*, *39*(6), 106–108. doi:10.1145/228503.228525

RAGE. (2016). WebCrusher: Fast Loading Websites…Instantly! *RAGE Software*. Retrieved from http://www.ragesw.com/products/optimize-web-sites.html

Reaux, R. A., & Carroll, J. M. (1997). Human factors in information access of distributed systems. In G. Salvendy (Ed.), *Handbook of Human Factors & Ergonomics* (2nd ed.). New York: Wiley.

Selvidge, P. (1999). How long is too long for a website to load? *Usability News, 1*(2). Available at: http://psychology.wichita.edu/surl/usabilitynews/1s/time_delay.htm. 23

Selvidge, P. (2003). Examining tolerance for online delays. *Usability News, 5*(1). Available at: http://psychology.wichita.edu/surl/usabilitynews/51/delaytime.htm

UsabilityNet. (2006). *International Standards for HCI and Usability*. Retrieved from http://www.usabilitynet.org/tools/r_international.htm#18529

WebSiteOptimization. (2008). *The Psychology of Web Performance*. Retrieved from http://www.websiteoptimization.com/speed/tweak/psychology-web-performance/

Chapter 19
Artificial Intelligence in Stochastic Multiple Criteria Decision Making

Hanna Sawicka
Poznan University of Technology, Poland

ABSTRACT

This chapter presents the concept of stochastic multiple criteria decision making (MCDM) method to solve complex ranking decision problems. This approach is composed of three main areas of research, i.e. classical MCDM, probability theory and classification method. The most important steps of the idea are characterized and specific features of the applied methods are briefly presented. The application of Electre III combined with probability theory, and Promethee II combined with Bayes classifier are described in details. Two case studies of stochastic multiple criteria decision making are presented. The first one shows the distribution system of electrotechnical products, composed of 24 distribution centers (DC), while the core business of the second one is the production and warehousing of pharmaceutical products. Based on the application of presented stochastic MCDM method, different ways of improvements of these complex systems are proposed and the final i.e. the best paths of changes are recommended.

INTRODUCTION

Nowadays, an integral part of any organization is the application of practical tools and techniques that make changes to products, processes and services resulting in an introduction of something new in a market. Improving continuously operations is essential for a better performance of the organizations. Due to the growing impact of globalization, migration, technological and knowledge revolutions, it brings added value to customers and helps organizations to remain competitive. Many of them are forced to make changes in various areas, such as: technology, infrastructure, human resources etc. Moreover, to meet customers' expectations and needs, companies should also consider organization's manager interests, as well as the supplier's opinions, customers' point of view and the other stakeholders' preferences. It makes the decision situation very complex and the application of decision aiding methods seems crucial.

DOI: 10.4018/978-1-5225-2031-3.ch019

According to Vincke (1992) multiple criteria decision making (MCDM) is a field which aims at giving the decision maker (DM) some tools in order to enable him/her to solve a complex decision problem where several points of view must be taken into account. This methodology concentrates on suggesting "compromise solution", taking into consideration the trade-offs between criteria and the DM's preferences. The above mentioned compromise solution is selected from the family of variants. They are constructed in different ways. In some situations, it is assumed that the variants are exclusive and at least two of them cannot be implemented together. There are also real-world situations where two or more alternatives can be introduced conjointly.

The variants are evaluated by the set of criteria, which should be characterized by the following aspects (Roy, 1985):

- Completeness due to the decision-making aspects of the considered problem.
- Appropriate formation, taking into account the global preferences of the decision maker.
- Non-redundancy, i.e. a situation in which semantic ranges of criteria are not repeated.

Thanks to the criteria it is possible to compare variants, especially when the performances are expressed as deterministic values. However, in some cases the alternatives are modeled e.g. in a simulation tool and their performances are presented as stochastic values. In such circumstances the comparison process becomes complex. It is usually supported by stochastic MCDM methods, but most of them concentrate on decision maker's stochastic preferences. Based on the author's experience the methods dedicated to solve complex decision problems with stochastic criteria values are not efficient enough.

The procedure presented in this chapter shows that the combination of a classical group of MCDM methods aiming at ranking of variants, e.g. Electre III, Promethee II, with probability formula or a classical method of artificial intelligence aiming at classification of objects, e.g. Bayes classifier, could solve these complex problems.

Electre III method (Roy, 1985; Vincke, 1992) belongs to the European school of MCDM and it is based on the outranking relation. The method requires determination the model of DM's preferences by the indifference q, preference p, and veto v thresholds, as well as weights w for each criterion j. The aggregation procedure starts from the calculation of concordance and discordance indices. The first one measures the arguments in favor of the statement that alternative a outranks alternative b, while the second index represents the strengths of evidence against the above hypothesis. Based on these indices the outranking relation is calculated. The ranking of variants is based on two classification algorithms: descending and ascending distillations. Descending distillation procedure starts from choosing the best alternative i.e. the one with the highest value of qualification index $Q(a)$ and placing it at the top of the ranking. $Q(a)$ equals the difference between the number of alternatives, which are outranked by the alternative a and the number of alternatives that outrank a. In the consecutive steps, the best alternative from the remaining set of alternatives is selected and placed in the second position of the ranking. The procedure stops, when the set of alternatives is empty. Ascending distillation procedure starts from choosing the worst alternative and placing it at the bottom of the ranking. Then the worst alternative from the remaining set of alternatives is selected and placed in the second worst position of the ranking. The final graph corresponding to the outranking matrix is the intersection of the two distillations. It constitutes a graphical representation of indifference I, preference P and incomparability R relations between alternatives.

Promethee II method (Brans et al., 1986), similarly as Electre III method, represents the European school of MCDM based on the outranking relation. The method requires determination of the model of DM's preferences by the selection of a type of a generalized criteria function $p(x)$ for each criterion j and definition of this function characteristic parameters. There are distinguished six types of preference functions, widely described by Brans et al. (1986). They represent the level of preference intensity of alternative a compared with alternative b regarding each criterion j. The criteria function equals from 0 to 1 and its value increases when the difference between compared alternatives is getting higher. Next, the outranking relation is defined. It is calculated on the basis of the multicriteria preference index π of alternative a regarding alternative b. This index corresponds to concordance index in Electre III method. Finally, the positive $\Phi+$ and negative $\Phi-$ flows for each alternative are calculated. The positive value of $\Phi+$ represents the strength of this alternative over all the other alternatives, while the negative value of $\Phi-$ shows the strengths of all alternatives over considered alternative. The difference between $\Phi+$ and $\Phi-$ constitutes the net flow. The higher the net value, the better position in the ranking. Based on this information a graphical representation of indifference I and preference P relations between alternatives is obtained.

Classification theory (Smola & Vishwanatan, 2008; Demsar, 2006) is a quantitatively oriented methodology that helps the DM to classify and categorize objects into predefined classes. There is a wide variety of classification methods reported in the literature (Berger, 1985; Demsar, 2006; Mitchell, 1997), including:

- Classification by the induction of decision trees (Pisetta et al., 2010; Quinlan, 1986).
- K-NN – nearest-neighbor classification (Bremner et al., 2005; Hall et al., 2008).
- Bayesian classification (Berger, 1985; Mitchell, 1987; Smola & Vishwanatan, 2008).
- Rough sets theory (Pawlak, 1982; Yao, 2011).
- Neural networks (Cetiner, et al. 2010; Wei & Schonfeld, 1993).

Many authors (Berger, 1985; Mitchell, 1987) claim that one of the most efficient method to solve real-world classification problems is Bayesian classification. Its advantage is precision and effectiveness when solving problems associated with the manipulation on the large sets of data.

Mitchell (1997) states that Bayes classifier can predict class membership probabilities, such as the probability that an unknown target function f: $x(a) \rightarrow C(z)$, featured by the highest conditional a posteriori probability $P(C(z)|x(a))$ belongs to a particular class $C(z)$. This notation can be interpreted as follows: a certain object x described by the vector of description attributes a, has a chance (probability) $P(C(z)|x(a))$ to be assigned to a certain class $C(z)$.

The algorithm of Bayesian classification is composed of 3 phases, such as (Mitchell, 1997):

- The construction of learning model i.e. classifier.
- Testing of the learning model.
- Classification of the vector of observations to predefined classes.

In the proposed approach this machine learning method is utilized to classify the relations between variants and to generate the final stochastic ranking of variants.

In this chapter the combination of MCDM ranking method with Bayes classifier, and MCDM ranking method with classical probability formula are presented on real-world cases. The first one shows the distribution system composed of 24 distribution centers divided into 3 levels i.e. central, regional and local one. Different alternatives representing ways of changes are proposed. They are modeled in the simulation tool and evaluated by the consistent family of criteria. Their values are calculated on the basis of simulation experiments' results. They are presented as probability distributions. The decision problem is formulated as a multicriteria stochastic ranking problem. The above-described stochastic approach combining Promethee II method (Brans et al., 1986) and the probability formula is applied to solve it.

The second case presents pharmaceutical production company. Similarly, as in the previous case, the simulation model of the current state has been constructed and its redesign scenarios have been proposed and implemented in the simulation tool, as well. The set of evaluation criteria includes technical, organizational and social aspects. The values are presented as probability distributions. The decision problem is formulated as a multicriteria stochastic ranking problem. The stochastic approach combining Electre III method (Roy, 1985; Vincke, 1992) and Bayes classifier (Mitchell, 1997) is applied to solve it. In both cases, the computational results are completed by the sensitivity analysis.

BACKGROUND

Artificial intelligence (AI) is defined in two dimensions, i.e. the first one is a thought process and reasoning – an approach presented in the middle of 80's, while the second one is a behavior – many definitions were created at the beginning of 90's (Russel, & Norvig, 1995). Some of the researchers perceive this term as a field of study that seeks to explain and emulate intelligent behavior in terms of computational processes (Schalkoff, 1990).

Undoubtedly, since it beginning the goal of AI is to make machines do thing that would require intelligence if done by humans (Boden, 1977). In this context, intelligence can be defined as the ability to learn and understand, to solve problems and to make decisions (Negnevitsky, 2005). One of the topics of decision making widely described in the literature and applied in practice is multi criteria decision making (MCDM). Kahraman (2008) states that MCDM can be divided into two major approaches, i.e. multiple objective decision making (MODM) and multiple attribute decision making (MADM). In MODM problems the number of alternatives is usually large or sometimes it might be infinite. The alternatives are not given at the beginning of the decision process, but mathematical framework is provided for designing the set of them. Based on it the identified alternatives are evaluated and a level of multiple objective satisfactions is measured.

MADM problems, which are the most well-known within MCDM, are characterized by limited number of alternatives defined at the beginning of the decision process, by a number of decision criteria and additional information from decision maker or decision makers. The final solution of the MADM problem can be presented as a choice, sorting or ranking of alternatives. Based on this division, corresponding to the decision problem, MADM methods are classified into the following three groups:

- Choice methods, e.g. Genetic Algorithm (Goldberg, 1989), Pareto Simulated Annealing (Czyzak & Jaszkiewicz, 1998);
- Sorting methods, e.g. ELECTRE-TRI (Mousseau et al., 2000), UTADIS (Manshadi, 2015);

- Ranking methods, e.g. AHP (Saaty, 1980), Electre III (Roy, 1985; Vincke 1992), Promethee (Brans et al., 1986), UTA (Jacquet-Lagrèze & Siskos, 1982).

Many real-world problems, due to their complexity, are characterized by uncertainty. This phenomenon can be observed when the values of evaluation criteria are considered or the decision maker's preferences are collected. Thus, there are many modifications of the above-mentioned ranking methods, aiding the decision process. The examples of them are such as:

- SMAA-III (Tervonen & Figueira, 2008) – a modification of Electre III method.
- Stochastic PROMETHEE / GIS method (Marinoni, 2005) – a modification of Promethee method.
- Stochastic AHP method (Stam & Duarte Silva, 1997) – a modification of AHP method.
- Stochastic UTA method (Siskos, 1982) – a modification of UTA method.

SMAA-III

Stochastic Multicriteria Acceptability Analysis-III (Tervonen & Figueira, 2008) is a stochastic method of ranking alternatives based on outranking relation. It develops Electre III method by the non-deterministic components of the criteria values and decision maker's preferences. The values of criteria functions ξ_j corresponding to deterministic values $f_j(x)$ of density function $f\chi(\xi)$ in the space $\chi \subseteq R^{mxn}$, are presented as a probability distribution or expected value with its ranges of variations. Weights are also described by the probability distribution with the density function $f_w(w)$. Indifference q, preference p and veto v thresholds characteristic for Electre III method are defined by the decision maker and they are stochastic values represented by $\alpha_j(\cdot)$, $\beta(\cdot)$, $\gamma(\cdot)$ or by $\tau = (\alpha, \beta, \gamma)$. The issue of SMAA-III method is to aid the decision maker by computing the indices or paramters with the application of integrals of the area of stochastic values using Monte Carlo simulation method.

Based on the literature (Lahdelma et al., 1998; Tervonen & Figueira, 2008) there are presented three indices aiding the decisions, which are as follows: rank acceptability index, pair-wise winning index and incomparability index.

The computational procedure of SMAA-III method is composed of the three steps, presented below:

Step 1: Construction of the evaluation matrix and definition of the decision maker's preference model.
Step 2: Construction of the outranking relation based on the pair-wise winning index.
Step 3: Utilization of the outranking relation leading to the construction of the final ranking of alternatives based on the rank acceptability index and the incomparability index.

Stochastic Promethee

This method belongs to the group of MADM ranking methods (Marinoni, 2005). The values of criteria are presented as probability distributions. Marinoni (2005) suggests to use Monte Carlo simulation method to multiple sampling of the values of alternatives evaluated by each criterion, resulting in accumulated value ranging [0,1]. The number of iterations (samplings) should be as high as possible, i.e. at least 100 (Marinoni, 2005). The obtained results are the input data for further calculations carried out accordingly to Promethee method (Brans et al., 1986). They are presented as charts with alternatives' values related to each final rank or as rankings of each alternative. The values of alternatives may differ and the selection of the compromise solution might be a difficult task. Thus, Marinoni (2005) suggests the application of MSR index - mean stochastic rank index, calculated for each alternative i. Then, the stochastic ranking index SI is computed (Marinoni, 2005).

The computational procedure of stochastic Promethee method is composed of the three steps, which are as follows:

Step 1: Construction of the evaluation matrix and definition of the decision maker's preference model.
Step 2: Construction of the outranking relation based on the stochastic ranking index.
Step 3: Utilization of the outranking relation leading to the construction of the final ranking of alternatives.

The above presented MADM methods are applied in many areas to solve problems connected with environmental issues (Delhaye et al., 1991; Malczewski et al., 1997; Salminen et al., 1998), industrial problems (Anand & Kodali, 2008; de Boer et al., 1998; Hafeez et al., 2002), business issues (Buchanan & Sheppard 1998; Halouani et al., 2009; Ngai, 2003), logistics problems (Badri, 1999; Behzadian et al., 2010; Sawicka et al., 2010).

They have many advantages, such as: precise modeling of decision maker's preferences (e.g. Electre III method), modeling of preferential function of each criterion (e.g. Promethee method), hierarchical representation of the problem giving the possibility to formalize the structure of the considered problem, very useful while the complex problems are considered (e.g. AHP method), possibility to solve the problem with a large number of alternatives i.e. more than 10 (e.g. UTA method) possibility to model the stochastic criteria values (e.g. SMAA-III method), possibility to model uncertain preferences of the decision maker (e.g. stochastic Promethee method, stochastic AHP method, stochastic UTA method).

However, these methods are not devoid of disadvantages, e.g. adding or removing of one alternative could change the power of preferences between remaining variants, resulting from the distillation procedure in Electre III method; solving very complex decision problems is time consuming and many information must be collected (e.g. SMAA-III method, AHP mathod) or many iterations must be carried out (e.g. stochastic AHP method), some methods do not provide modeling of subcriteria (e.g. Promethee and stochastic Promethee methods), to construct reference set of alternatives, their number must be higher than 10 (e.g. UTA method) and finally to define values of criteria the probability distributions of each of them must be calculated, which is time consuming (e.g. stochastic UTA method).

THE METHODOLOGY OF SOLVING STOCHASTIC RANKING MADM PROBLEMS

Solving complex multiple criteria decision problems is often very difficult. On the one hand, some of the MADM methods are not suitable for the considered issues e.g. the solution of stochastic problems with an application of deterministic methods would fail or simplify the question. However, many analysts or decision makers are very used to one or a group of such methods. This subjective perspective is a result of their wide experience and knowledge.

On the other hand, the multiple criteria methods dedicated to solve particular class of problems could not always cope with them due to their specific characteristics.

The author of this chapter proposes the MADM method to solve complex ranking decision problems with stochastic information of criteria values and/or stochastic preferential information. The general idea is based on the transformation of the stochastic input information to deterministic values, which are then converted to stochastic final ranking of variants. The transformation encompasses the application of multiple criteria decision aiding methods and classification method or probability formula.

It is composed of 4 steps presented in Figure 1 and characterized below.

It is assumed that the character of the input information is fully stochastic or mixed - stochastic and deterministic. It usually happens when many aspects of the analyzed situation are considered and modeled in the simulation tool. As a result the evaluation of alternatives is stochastic and the decision maker expresses his/her hesitation of preferences. In such situations DM's preferences are defined as non-deterministic values.

The first step of the proposed procedure is the transformation of these values to deterministic information. If the analyzed problem is composed of stochastic evaluations of alternatives, then each of them is converted to at least 100 deterministic values using random number generator. One of the well-known is Monte Carlo method (Law & Kelton, 2000), which relies on repeated random sampling. The parallel operation can be done with stochastic preferential information, e.g. values of thresholds in Electre III method, pairwise comparisons between criteria, subcriteria and alternatives in AHP method. As a result, the set of many deterministic evaluations of alternatives and/or deterministic DM's preferences is obtained.

Based on them it is possible to calculate the relations between alternatives with an application of MADM ranking method – the second step. The number of rankings is at least 100. The type of relation between alternatives, i.e. quantitative or qualitative, depends on the applied method. Some of them, e.g. Promethee II, AHP methods provide precise distance between alternatives in the final rank, while other methods, e.g. Electre III, Promethee I present the qualitative relations, such as indifference, preference and incomparability.

Figure 1. Solution procedure of the stochastic multiple criteria decision problem
Source: Author's research based on Sawicka (2012)

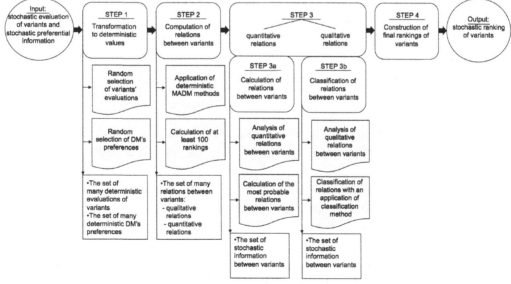

Thus, the third step is divided into two alternate parts *a* and *b*. In the step 3a the quantitative measures between alternatives are analyzed and the most probable relations are calculated. The step 3b is dedicated to qualitative relations between pairs of variants. Due to high number of results obtained in the previous step, the classification method is proposed. It helps to classify relations between alternatives to predefined classes (decision attributes). The result of both cases is the set of stochastic information between alternatives.

The fourth step is based on construction of the final ranking of variants. The probabilities of occurrence of particular relations between them are computed. The sensitivity analysis is advised. Finally, the stochastic ranking of alternatives is obtained.

SOLUTIONS AND RECOMMENDATIONS: APPLICATION OF STOCHASTIC MADM RANKING METHOD

Ranking of Distribution System Redesign Alternatives Using Promethee II Method and Probability Formula

Problem Definition

The first case study shows the distribution system of electrotechnical products. It is characterized by a high complexity. The system is composed of 24 distribution centers (DC) divided into 3 levels i.e. central with 1 DC, regional with 12 DC and a local one with 11 DC spread all over Poland. More than 75 suppliers supply these distribution centers and around 400 main customers are served. There are distributed various electrotechnical products, such as sockets, bulbs, extension cords, clusters, wires. There can be distinguished 38.000 assortments. The detailed analysis of the system reveals many strengths e.g. modern fleet and handling equipment, well developed promotion, highly qualified staff, as well as weaknesses i.e. high level of inventories, repetition of tasks in different organizational units, low utilization of the warehouse areas. Thus, different ways of changes based on system's redesign are proposed. Due to its complex character, the simulation model of a current state is constructed. It allows formalizing material and information flow in the system. Based on the simulation experiments the bottlenecks are recognized and quantitative analysis is carried out. The final information of the system is presented as a set of evaluation criteria. They represent various aspects i.e. technical, organizational, economical, social and environmental and the criteria are as follows:

C1: Time of delivery [days] – minimized criterion,
C2: Costs of distribution per month [m PLN] – minimized criterion,
C3: Utilization of in-company transportation means [%] – maximized criterion,
C4: Rotation level of inventory [days] – minimized criterion,
C5: Efficiency of system's employees (deviation from the optimum value) [%] – minimized criterion,
C6: Share of outsourced transportation orders [%] – maximized criterion,
C7: Difference between the levels of investments and divestments [m PLN] – minimized criterion.

Next, the distribution system's heuristically constructed 4 redesign scenarios are modeled in the simulation tool. They represent different changes resulting from the following aims:

Alternative A1: Reduction of distribution costs by eliminating the least effective distribution center; increasing the turnover, improving efficiency ratio;

Alternative A2: Reduction of the delivery time by shortening the distance between the distribution centers and customers, increasing the turnover, improving efficiency ratio connected with human and technical resources;

Alternative A3: Reduction of distribution costs by eliminating 11 local DC, reduction of the delivery time;

Alternative A4: Reduction of distribution costs by eliminating 11 local DC, reduction of inventory on regional level, reallocation of central DC, reduction of the delivery time.

The consistent family of criteria evaluates the alternatives, including the current state represented by alternative A0. The criteria values are calculated on the basis of simulation experiments' results. They are presented as probability distributions. See Table 1.

The graphical representation of the alternatives' distance to the ideal point (represented by the most desirable criteria values) and the nadir point (characterized by the most undesirable criteria values) (Vincke, 1992) is shown in Figure 2.

Based on the information presented in Table 1 and Figure 2, it is hard to decide which alternative is the compromise solution. The following aspects have the most important influence on this situation:

- Ambiguity of alternatives' evaluation i.e. some of them have the best values on one criterion while on the other they are close to the worst position, e.g. alternative A4 has the best value on criterion C6 and its position with respect to criterion C4 is the worst;

Table 1. Performance matrix of the distribution system of electrotechnical products and its redesign scenarios

Criteria			Alternatives				
Name	Direction of preferences	Value	A0	A1	A2	A3	A4
C1	Min	Expected value	4	3	2	1	1
		Range of variation	[3,87; 4,13]	[2,76; 3,20]	[1,78; 2,30]	[0,95; 1,25]	[0,95; 1,13]
C2	Min	Expected value	1,1	1,0	1,4	0,8	0,9
		Range of variation	[0,95; 1,17]	[0,87; 1,05]	[1,24; 1,60]	[0,65; 0,87]	[0,72; 1,04]
C3	Max	Expected value	0,52	0,43	0,50	0,80	0,80
		Range of variation	[0,51; 0,53]	[0,41; 0,45]	[0,44; 0,57]	[0,76; 0,85]	[0,77; 0,83]
C4	Min	Expected value	32	30	28	36	37
		Range of variation	[31,33; 32,67]	[29,84; 30,24]	[27,19; 29,49]	[34,96; 37,44]	[36,68; 37,24]
C5	Min	Expected value	50	50	30	15	10
		Range of variation	[48,80; 52,00]	[48,80; 52,00]	[28,09; 31,51]	[12,57; 17,43]	[8,80; 12,00]
C6	Max	Expected value	21,2	18,6	22,7	0	70
		Range of variation	[19,14; 23,34]	[17,95; 19,17]	[22,54; 22,90]	-	[68,37; 71,71]
C7	Min	Average value	0	-1,0	2,7	7,5	5,8

Figure 2. Alternatives' positions regarding evaluation criteria

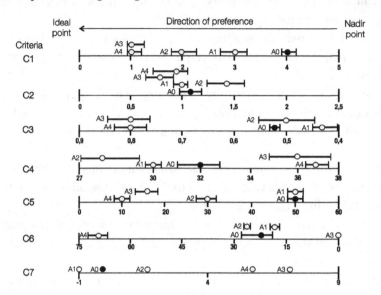

- Uncertainty of the alternatives' mutual position regarding each criterion i.e. in some criteria their ranges of variations are almost evenly distributed between the ideal and nadir point e.g. positions of variants regarding criterion C1, while on the other criteria part of the set of alternatives is cumulated around one value e.g. alternatives A0, A1, A2 regarding criterion C3 and distant from the other part of variants e.g. A3 and A4;
- Difficulty in evaluating such a large collection of information i.e. many criteria and alternatives, many data records, different levels of criteria importance expressed by the DM.

Based on these ambiguities, uncertainties and difficulties with interpretation of data the multicriteria stochastic ranking problem has been formulated. The above-described stochastic approach combining Promethee II method and the probability formula is applied to solve it.

Computational Experiments

In the first step of the computational procedure, decision maker's preferences are modeled according to the principles of Promethee II method. The type 5 of the generalized criteria function $\rho(x)$, which is characteristic for this method, is selected. The DM has assigned different weights to criteria, using the scale of 1 to 10 points, representing the least and the most important criteria, respectively. They are presented in Table 2. Based on the model of the DM's preferences one can conclude that the most important criterion is time of delivery – C1, while the least important one is the share of outsourced transportation orders – C6.

The definition of thresholds is a complex task. Thus, the analysis of difference between criteria values has been carried out based on the expected values and ranges of variation, too. The DM has decided to assign the values of q (indifference threshold) and p (preference threshold), using the information presented in Table 1.

Table 2. The model of DM's preferences for the distribution system

Criteria	Weights	Thresholds	
		Indifference q	Preference p
C1	10	0,60	1,10
C2	9	0,05	0,10
C3	5	0,10	0,20
C4	5	2,00	4,70
C5	6	6,00	14,00
C6	4	3,00	5,00
C7	7	0,50	1,00

The results indicate that the DM is highly sensitive to changes of some values of criteria e.g. C2 (one of the most important criterion), where the indifference threshold equals 0,05 and preference threshold equals 0,10; and his sensitivity to changes is rather low regarding other criteria e.g. C6 (the least important criterion), where the indifference threshold equals 3,00 and preference threshold equals 5,00.

Next, the random numbers of each criterion value have been generated. For this purpose, the Monte Carlo method has been applied. The number of iterations generating random numbers of criteria evaluating each alternative equals 150 and it provides large sample of random deterministic parameters. The example of results is presented in Table 3.

Table 3. Deterministic values of criteria randomly generated with an application of Monte Carlo method – the distribution system

Criteria	Alternatives				
	A0	A1	A2	A3	A4
Iteration 1					
C1	4,06	3,02	2,05	1,07	1,13
C2	0,95	0,89	1,55	0,87	0,81
C3	0,52	0,43	0,44	0,82	0,80
C4	31,79	30,16	29,00	36,16	36,91
C5	50,43	48,96	30,39	14,87	11,80
C6	19,81	18,72	22,82	0,00	69,02
C7	0,0	-1,0	2,7	7,5	5,8
Iteration 2					
C1	4,07	2,77	2,13	1,05	1,07
C2	1,09	0,89	1,57	0,67	0,83
C3	0,51	0,45	0,44	0,82	0,78
C4	32,63	30,07	28,18	37,14	37,05
C5	50,96	51,45	31,32	13,49	11,31
C6	23,12	19,12	22,60	0,00	68,41
C7	0,0	-1,0	2,7	7,5	5,8

Based on the data records presented in Table 3 one can conclude that the generated values are randomly dispersed in the ranges of variations and some values equal the minimum or maximum value of these ranges.

The results of iterations are the input data for the computational experiments (second step) with an application of MADM ranking method Promethee II. Thus, the total number of calculations equals 150.

The exemplary 3 results are presented in Figure 3.

The additional information to final rankings is the net flow value in Promethee II method. The relations between alternatives are very similar. However, the distances between them represented by the net flows vary e.g. the highest difference in the analyzed net flows is between alternatives A1 in the first and third ranking. The difference between net flow values of alternative A3 in these rankings is very low. Thus, the distance between A1 and A3 in the first ranking is small, while in the third one is very high.

In most of the rankings the best position is occupied by A4, the second location has A3 and the third one – A1. The next position has the alternative A1 and the last one – A0. In the last ranking the locations of alternatives A1 and A2 are switched.

Analyzing the total set of data composed of 150 rankings with the distance between alternatives (quantitative information), the author of this paper has decided to calculate the expected value of the relations between these variants. These computations constitute the third step of the presented stochastic MCDM method and the result is presented in Figure 4. Finally, in the fourth step the final ranking of alternatives is shown. See Figure 4.

The best scenario is the alternative A4. It represents the most radical changes in the analyzed distribution system. Next position in the ranking is occupied by the alternative A3. The changes modeled in

Figure 3. Three selected final rankings of alternatives resulting from calculations with an application of Promethee II method

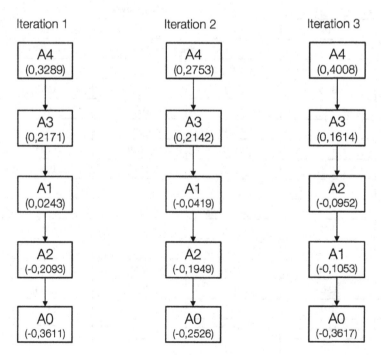

Figure 4. Final ranking of alternatives with the expected values of net flows

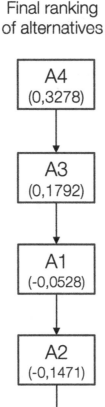

this variant are significant, too. On the third position is the alternative A1, which is featured by slight changes in the existing distribution system of electrotechnical products. On the fourth location is the alternative A2 and the worst position is occupied by the current state of the system represented by the alternative A0.

The computational experiments are finished by the sensitivity analysis. It is carried out for the minimum (Figure 5a), maximum (Figure 5b) and expected values (Figure 5c) of ranges of variations of each alternative evaluated by the set of criteria.

The results of the sensitivity analysis show that the rankings of alternatives are the same in terms of internal comparison and regarding the final ranking presented in Figure 4. The net flows are not the same. However, the difference between them is not significant. It is worth to mention that the expected value of the net flow (Figure 4) and the net value calculated for the expected values of the alternatives evaluated by the set of criteria (Figure 5c) are very close. The minimum difference between them equals 0,0056 - for the alternative A2 and the maximum difference is 0,0463 – for the alternative A0.

Based on the analysis of the final ranking of alternatives and the sensitivity analysis the author of this chapter recommends the most radical changes in the analyzed system represented by alternative A4. This step should radically improve the organization of the distribution system, while the current state is the worst scenario.

Ranking of Redesign Variants of Warehouse with Pharmaceutical Products Using Electre III Method and Bayes Classifier

Problem Definition

The second case presents company operating in Poland. Its core business is the production of pharmaceutical products. One of the important infrastructural objects of the company is a warehouse of finished goods. The composition of its rooms includes, among others: reception area, storage rooms, picking zone, edition zone and offices. In the area of admissions there is made an acceptance of the products and their control (qualitative and quantitative). Storage facilities are divided into three zones, i.e. high storage (inventories are stored in 5-levels' stacks), low storage (replenished by goods from high storage zone, picking takes place there) and the cold room (temperature is maintained at 2-6° C). Based on the detailed analysis of the system its major drawbacks are recognized, such as: zone admission is often full, and vehicles with finished goods have to wait for unloading (sometimes several days). There are numerous overtimes associated with the picking process. Similarly, as in the previous case, the simulation model of the current state has been constructed and its redesign scenarios have been implemented in the simulation tool, as well. The set of evaluation criteria includes technical, organizational, economical and social aspects. The values are presented as probability distributions and they are as follows:

Figure 5. (a) Rankings of alternatives with the values of net flows for the minimum; (b) maximum; (c) expected values of ranges of variations

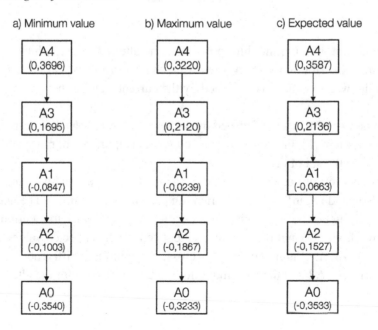

K1: Efficiency of warehouse employees (deviation from the optimum value) [-] – minimized criterion,
K2: Utilization of in-company transportation means [%] – maximized criterion,
K3: Efficiency of warehousing process [%] – maximized criterion,
K4: Difference between the levels of investments and divestments [PLN K] – minimized criterion.

The set of redesign scenarios is composed of 5 variants. They fulfill the following aims:

Variant V1: Increasing the employment in the warehouse leading to the improvement of employees efficiency ratio;
Variant V2: Reduction of the in-company transportation means, improving the efficiency ratio connected with technical resources;
Variant V3: Decreasing the queue of vehicles waiting for unloading, improving the efficiency ratio connected with human and technical resources;
Variant V4: Redesign of the warehouse area, improvement of the warehousing process;
Variant V5: Redesign of the warehouse area, reduction of the in-company transportation means, reallocation of tasks leading to the improvement of efficiency of human and technical resources and better organization of the warehouse.

The values of variants evaluated by different criteria are calculated on the basis of simulation experiments. They are presented in Table 4.

The decision problem is formulated as a multicriteria stochastic ranking problem.

As in the previous case study, it is hard to decide which alternative is the compromise solution while the information presented in Table 4 is considered. Some variants have the best performance on particular criteria, such as V1 on criterion K1, and V2 on criterion K4, and V4 on criterion K3, and V5 on criterion K2, while on the other criteria their values are the worst, such as V1 on criterion K2 and V4 on criterion K4. Variant V3 hasn't got the best nor the worst value of its performance. However, on some criteria its performance is very good, e.g. criteria K2 and K3, while on the others is very poor, e.g. K4.

Thus, the stochastic approach combining Electre III method and Bayes classifier is applied to solve it.

Table 4. Performance matrix of the warehouse with pharmaceutical products and its redesign scenarios

Criteria			Variants					
Name	**Direction of preferences**	**Value**	**V0**	**V1**	**V2**	**V3**	**V4**	**V5**
K1	Min	Expected value	15	1	4	5	8	5
		Range of variation	[14; 16]	[0; 2]	[0; 9]	[2; 13]	[6; 10]	[1; 11]
K2	Max	Expected value	43	39	84	82	78	88
		Range of variation	[25; 58]	[27; 58]	[73; 90]	[70; 87]	[68; 80]	[80; 92]
K3	Max	Expected value	89	91	90	97	100	98
		Range of variation	[80; 94]	[85; 96]	[84; 98]	[90; 99]	[99; 100]	[97; 100]
K4	Min	Expected value	0	0	-20	100	230	190
		Range of variation	-	-	[-35; -18]	[85; 120]	[200; 250]	[170; 210]

Computational Experiments

The first step of the computational procedure is based on modeling of decision maker's preferences according to the principles of Electre III method. At the beginning, the DM has assigned different weights to criteria. He has used the scale of 1 to 10 points, where 1 represents the least important criterion and 10 – the most significant one. Next, the thresholds values i.e. q (indifference), p (preference) and v (veto) have been specified. Weights and thresholds are presented in Table 5.

Model of the DM's preferences indicates that the economical issues are the most important. They are represented by criterion K4. Very significant meaning has the general operation of the warehouse, i.e. criterion K3. Criteria K1 and K2 representing social and technical aspects are important, too. However, the weights assigned to them are the lowest in the total set of evaluations.

The DM is sensitive to changes. Some aspects of redesign scenarios make them incomparable with the current state, which is emphasized by the veto threshold, e.g. V2 vs. V0 regarding the criterion K1. Carrying out pairwise comparison of variants, some of them are weakly preferred, e.g. V3 vs. V1 regarding the criterion K3 or strongly preferred to each other, e.g. V3 vs. V5 regarding the criterion K4.

Next, computations within this step are based on the random numbers of each criterion value generation. For this purpose, the Monte Carlo method has been applied. The number of iterations equals 150 providing sufficient sample of deterministic parameters for the next step of calculations. The exemplary sets of 3 iterations are presented in Table 6.

The values presented in Table 6 are randomly dispersed in the ranges of variations. Some of them are very close to the minimum or maximum values of these ranges.

In the second step, based on the results of all iterations the deterministic values are the input data for the computations with an application of MADM ranking method Electre III. Similarly, as in Promethee II method, the total number of calculations equals 150.The exemplary 2 results are presented in Figure 6.

These two matrices present the following relations: indifference I, preference P, reciprocal of preference P- and incomparability R. In both rankings, the indifference I relation is between V0 and V4 variants, the preference P relation is between V2 and V1, the reciprocal of preference P- relation is between variants V5 and V1, while the incomparability R relation can be observed between variants V2 and V3 in the first iteration.

The detailed analysis of the total set of data composed of 150 matrices, rankings and pairwise comparisons between variants' relations (qualitative information), led the author of this chapter to the conclusion that there are many differences between them. Based on that, it is hard to present the DM final recommendation regarding the changes in the analyzed warehouse. Thus, the classification of these relations and their allocation to predefined classes has been made. This allocation corresponds to

Table 5. The model of DM's preferences for the warehouse of pharmaceuticals

Criteria	Weights	Thresholds		
		Indifference q	Preference p	Veto v
K1	6	1	5	10
K2	5	10	20	40
K3	8	3	5	10
K4	9	20	50	100

Table 6. Deterministic values of criteria randomly generated with an application of Monte Carlo method – an example with the warehouse of pharmaceuticals

Criteria	Variants					
	V0	V1	V2	V3	V4	V5
Iteration 1						
K1	14,95	1,62	8,29	2,19	7,12	4,89
K2	47,75	39,92	84,16	83,41	72,08	81,85
K3	84,87	94,92	92,87	96,47	99,64	97,79
K4	0,00	0,00	-21,04	94,06	230,49	186,27
Iteration 2						
K1	15,95	1,42	4,63	6,92	8,13	6,80
K2	53,74	38,53	86,37	80,40	76,71	90,58
K3	86,59	91,57	93,61	94,11	99,38	99,41
K4	0,00	0,00	-24,50	93,70	237,61	183,71

Figure 6. Two selected final matrices of variants and their graphical representation resulting from calculations with an application of Electre III method

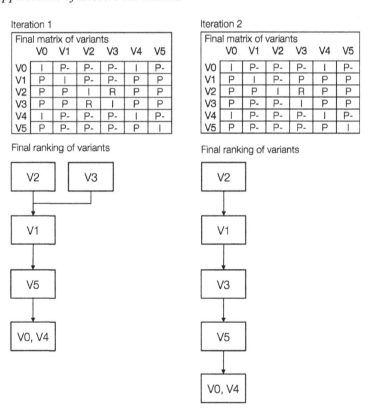

the definition of decision attributes. The classification is also the third step of the presented stochastic MCDM method. Bayes classifier has been applied to solve this problem.

Initially, 150 matrices have been split into 15 sets with 10 matrices in each of them. For each set the relations between variants represented by the description attributes (i.e. indifference I, preference P, reciprocal of preference P- and incomparability R relations) have been recognized and the probabilities of occurrence of particular relationships in the whole set have been calculated. See Table 7.

The values of description attributes are in the range [0,1]. Based on them the decision attributes with the following rules have been constructed:

- If the probability of the description attribute for a relation between variants has the value greater than 0,5 then the decision attribute is the same as the description attribute
- If the probabilities of the description attributes P- and R for a relation between variants have the same values lower than 0,5 then the decision attribute is the incomparability relation (R)
- If the probabilities of description attributes I and P for a relation between variants have values 0,5 then the decision attribute is a weak preference relation (Q)
- If the probabilities of description attributes I and P- for a relation between variants have values 0,5 then the decision attribute is a reciprocal of weak preference relation (Q-)

As a result, 6 decision classes (attributes) C(z) has been distinguished, such as:

C(I) = I: Indifference relation between variants
C(P) = P: Strong preference relation between variants
C(P-) = P-: Reciprocal of strong preference relation between variants
C(R) = R: Incomparability relation between variants
C(Q) = Q: Weak preference relation between variants
C(Q-) = Q-: Reciprocal of weak preference relation between variants

Table 7. The results of computational experiments of the share of relations I, P, P-, and R between pairs of variants for a part of testing set and their assignment to decision attributes

Relation between variants	Description attribute				Decision attribute (Class)
	I	P	P-	R	
V0-V0	1	0	0	0	I
V0-V1	0	0	1	0	P-
V0-V2	0	0	1	0	P-
V0-V3	0	0	1	0	P-
V0-V4	0,8	0,1	0,1	0	I
...					
V1-V3	0	0,2	0,4	0,4	R
...					
V2-V3	0	0,7	0	0,3	P
...					

Next, the training set T composed of 10 sets of matrices has been randomly selected and its testing has been carried out. Based on the information collected in this set, the a priori probabilities $P(C(z))$ of an event that the classes $C(z)$ occur as well as the conditional a priori probabilities $P(x(a)|C(z))$ have been calculated.

The remaining 5 sets of matrices (out of 15) have been utilized in the computational experiments. The conditional a posteriori probability has been calculated for each pair of variants. Based on it and based on the a priori probability of an event that the class $C(z)$ occur, the conditional a posteriori probability $P(C(z)|x(a))$ that a certain relation between variants occurs has been calculated.

For each pair of variants from the testing set the classification error β has been calculated. It equals 0,06, which means that the training model has been constructed correctly. The credibility of selected classification method in solving the presented problem is high.

The vector of observations with a priori unknown decision attributes has been selected. This vector has been composed of 30 relations between pairs of variants and has been characterized by the description attributes. They are the basis to assign 30 decision attributes concerning the relations between variants. 14 pairs of variants have been classified to class P, 14 pairs to class P- and remaining 2 pairs – to class I. No pair of variants have been classified to the decision attributes Q, Q- and R.

In the fourth step the final matrix and ranking of variants have been generated. The results are presented in Figure 7.

The final relations between variants are presented in the matrix (Figure 7a) as bold text. The information of probabilities of occurrence of particular relations between variants is also demonstrated. For example, the final relation between variants V0 and V4 is I (indifference) and the probability of its occurrence equals 0,720. This stochastic ranking matrix is transformed into the final ranking of variants and presented in Figure 7b. The best solution is at the top of the ranking, while the worst one - at the bottom. Dotted rectangular box is drawn for two variants for which the probability of occurrence of

Figure 7. (a) The stochastic ranking matrix representing the mutual relations between variants and (b) the final stochastic ranking of variants showing the positions of variants in the graphical form

a) Stochastic ranking matrix

	VO	V1	V2	V3	V4	V5
VO	I (1,000)	P- (0,993) I (0,007)	P- (1,000)	P- (1,000)	I (0,720) P (0,267) P- (0,013)	P- (0,993) I (0,007)
V1	P (0,993) I (0,007)	I (1,000)	P- (1,000)	P- (0,720) R (0,267) P(0,013)	P (1,000)	P (0,527) I (0,466) P- (0,007)
V2	P (1,000)	P (1,000)	I (1,000)	P (0,993) R (0,007)	P (1,000)	P (1,000)
V3	P (1,000)	P (0,720) R (0,267) P- (0,013)	P- (0,993) R (0,007)	I (1,000)	P (1,000)	P (0,993) P- (0,007)
V4	I (0,720) P- (0,267) P (0,013)	P- (1,000)	P- (1,000)	P- (1,000)	I (1,000)	P- (1,000)
V5	P (0,993) I (0,007)	P- (0,527) I (0,466) P (0,007)	P- (1,000)	P- (0,993) I (0,007)	P (1,000)	I (1,000)

b) Final ranking of variants

preference P and indifference I relations are close to 0,5. The analyst recognizes this pair of variants as almost indifferent.

Next, the ranking has been analyzed. The leader is variant V2. It is featured by slight changes i.e. reduction of in-company transportation means. The second position has the variant V3. It represents more radical changes in the organization of warehouse, leading to a higher level of internal fleet utilization, improvement of human resources efficiency ratio and radical reduction of vehicles waiting for unloading.

The strength of preference relation between V2 and V3 is high (0,993), which means that the distance between them is long with a high degree of certainty. Fourth and fifth location in the final rank have variants V1 and V5, representing evolutionary and revolutionary changes, respectively. The probability of preference and indifference relation between them is very close, i.e. 0,527 (P) and 0,466 (I). Thus, they are marked by the dotted line. The worst position in the ranking have variants V0 and V4. The relation between them is indifference I (0,720) and they are presented in one box.

Finally, the sensitivity analysis has been carried out. Similarly as in the previous case, the final rankings for minimum, maximum and expected values of criteria evaluating variants have been calculated. They are presented in Figure 8.

The results of the sensitivity analysis show that the rankings of variants are similar. All of them present variant V2 as the best scenario. Variants V0 and V4 are the worst redesign scenarios. However, their position is ambiguous – the following relations can be observed: I, P, P-. In two rankings the relation between variants V1 and V3 is R, while in one ranking it is P-. They are presented on the second or third location. In two rankings third position is occupied by the variant V5 and in one ranking this variant is on the second location.

Based on the analysis of the final stochastic ranking of variants and the sensitivity analysis the author of this chapter recommends evolutionary changes in the analyzed warehouse. They should be a good start for more radical transformation of the system.

Figure 8. (a) Ranking of alternatives for the minimum; (b) maximum; (c) expected values of ranges of variations calculated with an application of Electre III method

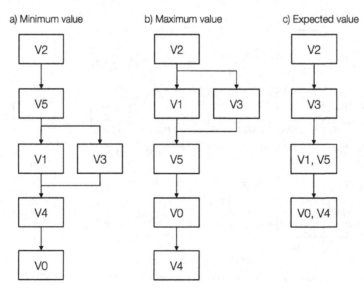

FUTURE RESEARCH DIRECTIONS

The consciousness of problems related to complex systems makes that the artificial intelligence becomes very eligible field of research. Intelligence combined with the application of selected MADM methods, probability theory and machine learning methods allows generating credible solutions, especially when dealing with uncertain and dynamically changing different systems' environments. They can be represented by the stochastic information bringing closer to the reality.

Thanks to the artificial intelligence it is possible to aid the decision process, i.e. to analyze and model unstructured decision situations, to take into account different points of view represented by the set of evaluation criteria, to collect preferential information, to generate reliable results and recommend satisfactory solutions. Based on these operations the general aim of systems operating on different markets, which is the improvement leading to the competitive advantage and constant development, can be achieved.

Considering systems presented in this chapter, it is worth mentioning about their complexity. This aspect has an influence on each step of their (and other systems) improvement. Systems' analysis and data collection has been the most time consuming process. At this stage, the artificial intelligence has been very helpful in finding, ordering the data and transforming them to the required form, as well. MADM methods have provided the bridge between the analytical part of the research and real-world information. They also have played an important role in coping with structuring process of the DM's preferences. The huge number of information the DM had to deal with during the analysis, raised doubts and sometimes disbelief of this process success. However, the step-wise procedure has helped to structure and clarify the situation. The probability analysis and Bayes classification method confirmed in the belief that the recommended solution is the best one taking into account the set of criteria and preferential information.

Undoubtedly, artificial intelligence plays an important role during the ordering of information, computational experiments, finding the best solutions. It also helps to cope with social problems, decision maker's doubts and uncertain information.

The next step in solving complex, stochastic decision problems would be concentrated on shortening the time of finding the best solution. Generally, the computational experiments with the application of stochastic MADM methods are time consuming and the algorithm of stochastic MADM method presented in this chapter, as well. Both cases proved that the computational procedure takes long hours and it is very laborious. One of the solutions is the implementation of this idea in computer – based decision support system developed to solve complex decision problems.

CONCLUSION

In this chapter, some deterministic ranking methods like Electre III (Roy, 1985; Vincke, 1990), Promethee II (Brans et al., 1986) and stochastic ranking methods like SMAA-III (Tervonen & Figueira, 2008), stochastic Promethee (Marinoni, 2005) have been presented. Based on them it is possible to solve decision problems with different types of data, i.e. stochastic values of criteria evaluating the set of alternatives, uncertain DM's preferences, his/her hesitations. However, some decision situations are very complex and the application of existing methods would not result in a desirable solution.

Thus, the concept of stochastic multiple criteria decision making method to solve such decision problems has been presented. The proposed approach can be implemented to solve complex decision problems aiming at ranking of variants. It is based on a composition of classical methodologies, i.e. MADM, probability theory and classification method. Depending on the considered situation, this stochastic method gives the opportunity to solve problems with deterministic, stochastic and mixed information about the alternatives evaluated by the set of criteria, and uncertain preferences of the decision maker.

After successful implementations of the proposed approach, results show the most desirable direction of changes leading to high improvements of both analyzed systems.

It is proved that the combination of classical methods and tools would result in a reasonable solution. Undoubtedly, it is time consuming and the final application would make it user friendly.

Artificial intelligence is still evolving. The recent subjects of research interests within its one area i.e. multiple criteria decision aiding, constitute future directions. They are, among others, as follows:

- The selection of the most suitable MADM method, which has been the subject of research of Guitouni and Martel (1998), Sawicka (2012)
- Robustness analysis, widely described by Dias and Climaco (1999) and recently presented by Zavadskas et al. (2013);
- Multiple decision makers, including group decision making process, public participation etc., with general issues presented by Keeney (1976), Belton and Stewart (2002) and recently presented by Yue (2011)

REFERENCES

Anand, G., & Kodali, R. (2008). Selection of Lean Manufacturing Systems Using the PROMETHEE. *Journal of Modeling in Management*, *3*(1), 40–70. doi:10.1108/17465660810860372

Badri, M. (1999). Combining the AHP and GP Model for Global Facility Location-Allocation Problem. *International Journal of Production Economics*, *62*(3), 237–248. doi:10.1016/S0925-5273(98)00249-7

Behzadian, M., Kazemzadeh, R., Albadvi, A., & Aghdasi, M. (2010). PROMETHEE: A Comprehensive Literature Review on Methodologies and Applications. *European Journal of Operational Research*, *200*(1), 198–215. doi:10.1016/j.ejor.2009.01.021

Belton, V., & Stewart, T. J. (2002). *Multiple Criteria Decision Analysis. An Integrated Approach*. Dordrecht: Kluwer Academic Publishers. doi:10.1007/978-1-4615-1495-4

Berger, J. (1985). *Statistical Decision Theory and Bayesian Analysis*. New York, NY: Springer-Verlag. doi:10.1007/978-1-4757-4286-2

Boden, M. A. (1977). *Artificial Intelligence and Natural Man*. New York, NY: Basic Books.

Brans, J. P., Vincke, P., & Mareschal, B. (1986). How to Select and How to Rank Projects: The PROMETHEE Method. *European Journal of Operational Research*, *24*(2), 228–238. doi:10.1016/0377-2217(86)90044-5

Bremner, D., Demaine, E., Erickson, J., Iacono, J., Langerman, S., Morin, P., & Toussaint, G. (2005). Output-Sensitive Algorithms for Computing Nearest-Neighbor Decision Boundaries. *Discrete & Computational Geometry*, *33*(4), 593–604. doi:10.1007/s00454-004-1152-0

Buchanan, J., & Sheppard, P. (1998). Ranking Projects Using the Electre Method. In *Proceedings of the 33rd Annual Conference of Operational Research Society of New Zealand*.

Cetiner, B., Sari, M., & Borat, O. (2010). Neural Network Based Traffic-Flow Prediction Model. *Mathematical and Computational Applications*, *15*(2), 269–278. doi:10.3390/mca15020269

Czyzak, P., & Jaszkiewicz, A. (1998). Pareto Simulated Annealing – a Metaheuristic Technique for Multiple-Objective Combinatorial Optimization. *Journal of Multi-Criteria Decision Analysis*, *7*(1), 34–47. doi:10.1002/(SICI)1099-1360(199801)7:1<34::AID-MCDA161>3.0.CO;2-6

de Boer, L., van der Wegen, L., & Telgen, J. (1998). Outranking Methods in Support of Supplier Selection. *European Journal of Purchasing and Supply Management*, *4*(2/3), 109–118. doi:10.1016/S0969-7012(97)00034-8

Delhaye, C., Teghem, J., & Kunsch, P. (1991). Application of the ORESTE Method to a Nuclear Waste Management Problem. *International Journal of Production Economics*, *24*(1-2), 29–39. doi:10.1016/0925-5273(91)90150-R

Demsar, J. (2006). Statistical Comparisons of Classifiers over Multiple Data Sets. *Journal of Machine Learning Research*, *7*(Jan), 1–30.

Dias, L., & Clímaco, J. (1999). On Computing ELECTREs Credibility Indices under Partial Information. *Journal of Multi-Criteria Decision Analysis*, *8*(2), 74–92. doi:10.1002/(SICI)1099-1360(199903)8:2<74::AID-MCDA234>3.0.CO;2-7

Goldberg, D. (1989). *Genetic Algorithms in Search, Optimization and Machine Learning*. Boston, MA: Addison-Wesley.

Guitouni, A., & Martel, J.-M. (1998). Tentative Guidelines to Help Choosing an Appropriate MCDA Method. *European Journal of Operational Research*, *109*(2), 501–521. doi:10.1016/S0377-2217(98)00073-3

Hafeez, K., Zhang, Y. B., & Malak, N. (2002). Determining Key Capabilities of a Firm Using Analytic Hierarchy Process. *International Journal of Production Economics*, *76*(1), 39–51. doi:10.1016/S0925-5273(01)00141-4

Hall, P., Park, B., & Samworth, R. (2008). Choice of Neighbor Order in Nearest-Neighbor Classification. *Annals of Statistics*, *36*(5), 2135–2152. doi:10.1214/07-AOS537

Halouani, N., Chabchoub, H., & Martel, J.-M. (2009). PROMETHEE-MD-2T Method for Project Selection. *European Journal of Operational Research*, *195*(3), 841–895. doi:10.1016/j.ejor.2007.11.016

Jacquet-Lagrèze, E., & Siskos, Y. (1982). Assessing a Set of Additive Utility Functions for Multicriteria Decision Making: The UTA Method. *European Journal of Operational Research*, *10*(2), 151–164. doi:10.1016/0377-2217(82)90155-2

Kahraman, C. (Ed.). (2008). *Fuzzy Multi-Criteria Decision-Making. Theory and Applications with Recent Developments*. New York, NY: Springer. doi:10.1007/978-0-387-76813-7

Keeney, R. L. (1976). A Group Preference Axiomatization with Cardinal Utility. *Management Science*, *23*(2), 140–145. doi:10.1287/mnsc.23.2.140

Lahdelma, R., Hokkanen, J., & Salminen, P. (1998). SMAA - Stochastic Multiobjective Acceptability Analysis. *European Journal of Operational Research, 106*(1), 137–143. doi:10.1016/S0377-2217(97)00163-X

Law, A. M., & Kelton, W. D. (2000). *Simulation, Modeling and Analysis*. New York, NY: McGraw Hill.

Malczewski, J., Moreno-Sanchez, R., Bojorquez-Tapia, L. A., & Ongay-Delhumeau, E. (1997). Multicriteria Group Decision-Making for Environmental Conflict Analysis in the Cape Region, Mexico. *Journal of Environmental Planning and Management, 40*(3), 349–374. doi:10.1080/09640569712137

Manshadi, E. D., Mehregan, M. R., & Safari, H. (2015). Supplier Classification Using UTADIS Method Based on Performance Criteria. *International Journal of Academic Research in Business and Social Sciences, 5*(2), 31–45. doi:10.6007/IJARBSS/v5-i2/1457

Marinoni, O. (2005). A Stochastic Spatial Decision Support System Based on PROMETHEE. *International Journal of Geographical Information Science, 19*(1), 51–68. doi:10.1080/13658810412331280176

Mitchell, T. (1997). *Machine Learning*. New York, NY: McGraw-Hill.

Mousseau, V., Slowinski, R., & Zielniewicz, P. (2000). A User-Oriented Implementation of the ELECTRE-TRI Method Integrating Preference Elicitation Support. *Computers & Operations Research, 27*(7-8), 757–777. doi:10.1016/S0305-0548(99)00117-3

Negnevitsky, M. (2005). *Artificial Intelligence. A Guide to Intelligent Systems*. Harlow: Addison-Wesley.

Ngai, E. W. T. (2003). Selection of Web Sites for Online Advertising Using AHP. *Information & Management, 40*(4), 233–242. doi:10.1016/S0378-7206(02)00004-6

Pawlak, Z. (1982). Rough Sets. *International Journal of Computer and Information Science, 11*(5), 341–356. doi:10.1007/BF01001956

Pisetta, V., Jouve, P.-E., & Zighed, D. (2010). Learning with Ensembles of Randomized Trees. In J. Balcazar, F. Bonchi, A. Gionis, & M. Sebag (Eds.), *Machine Learning and Knowledge Discovery in Databases* (pp. 67–82). Berlin: Springer-Verlag. doi:10.1007/978-3-642-15939-8_5

Quinlan, J. (1986). Induction of Decision Trees. *Machine Learning, 1*(1), 81–106. doi:10.1007/BF00116251

Roy, B. (1985). *Methodologie Multicritere d'Aide a la Decision*. Paris: Economica.

Russel, S. J., & Norvig, P. (1995). *Artificial Intelligence. A Modern Approach*. Englewood Cliffs, NJ: Prentice Hall.

Saaty, T. L. (1980). *The Analytic Hierarchy Process: Planning, Priority Setting, Resource Allocation*. New York, NY: Mc-Graw Hill.

Salminen, P., Hokkanen, J., & Lahdelma, R. (1998). Comparing Multicriteria Methods in the Context of Environmental Problems. *European Journal of Operational Research, 104*(3), 485–519. doi:10.1016/S0377-2217(96)00370-0

Sawicka, H. (2012). *The Method of Redesign the Distribution System* (Unpublished doctoral dissertation). Warsaw University of Technology, Warsaw, Poland.

Sawicka, H., Weglinski, S., & Witort, P. (2010). Application of Multiple Criteria Decision Aid Methods in Logistic Systems. *LogForum*, *6*(10), 99–110.

Schalkoff, R. I. (1990). *Artificial Intelligence: An Engineering Approach*. New York, NY: McGraw-Hill.

Siskos, J. (1982). A Way to Deal with Fuzzy Preferences in Multicriteria Decision Problems. *European Journal of Operational Research*, *10*(3), 314–324. doi:10.1016/0377-2217(82)90230-2

Smola, A., & Vishwanatan, S. (2008). *Introduction to Machine Learning*. Cambridge, UK: Cambridge University Press.

Stam, A., & Duarte Silva, A. P. (1997). Stochastic Judgments in the AHP: The Measurement of Rank Reversal Probabilities. *Decision Sciences*, *28*(3), 655–688. doi:10.1111/j.1540-5915.1997.tb01326.x

Tervonen, T., & Figueira, J. (2008). A Survey on Stochastic Multicriteria Acceptability Analysis Methods. *Journal of Multi-Criteria Decision Analysis*, *15*(1-2), 1–14. doi:10.1002/mcda.407

Vincke, P. (1992). *Multicriteria Decision-Aid*. Chichester, UK: John Wiley & Sons.

Wei, C., & Schonfeld, P. (1993). An Artificial Neural Network Approach for Evaluating Transportation Network Improvements. *Journal of Advanced Transportation*, *27*(2), 129–151. doi:10.1002/atr.5670270202

Yao, Y. (2011). Superiority of Three-Way Decisions in Probabilistic Rough Set Models. *Information Sciences*, *181*(6), 1080–1096. doi:10.1016/j.ins.2010.11.019

Yue, Z. (2011). A Method for Group Decision-Making Based on Determining Weights of Decision Makers using TOPSIS. *Applied Mathematical Modelling*, *35*(4), 1926–1936. doi:10.1016/j.apm.2010.11.001

Zavadskas, E. K., Antucheviciene, J., Saparauskas, J., & Turskis, Z. (2013). MCDM methods WASPAS and MULTIMOORA: Verification of Robustness of Methods when Assessing Alternative Solutions. *Economic Computation and Economic Cybernetics Studies and Research*, *47*(2), 5–20.

KEY TERMS AND DEFINITIONS

Classification Theory: The research field of artificial intelligence concentrated on categorization of objects to predefined classes. It is assumed that these objects are characterized by quantitative information.

Decision Maker: A person, who expresses his/her preferences, evaluates the decision situation and the results of the computational experiments. This person makes the final decision regarding the considered problem, e.g. selects the best redesign scenario.

Decision Problem: A situation where the decision maker has to face the problem of selecting one of at least two alternatives. The decision problem is composed of the description of the decision situation, definition of constraints and evaluation criteria, identification of the decision maker and his/her role in the decision process and definition of stakeholders, as well.

MADM: An abbreviation of Multiple Attribute Decision Making. It is one of the Multiple Criteria Decision Making approaches referring to the situation of finite set of alternatives evaluated by the set of attributes leading to the selection of the best solution.

MCDM: An abbreviation of Multiple Criteria Decision Making. It is composed of two approaches, i.e. MADM (Multiple Attribute Decision Making) and MODM (Multiple Objective Decision Making). In MADM problems the number of alternatives is finite and the evaluation attributes are usually conflicting, while in MODM problems the set of alternatives is infinite and the evaluation criteria are described by continuous function.

Ranking Methods: A group of MCDM methods concentrated on finding the final hierarchy of alternatives, i.e. the rank. Generally, ranking methods are divided into two sets referring to different methodological backgrounds. The first one originates from European school and it is based on outranking relation, e.g. Electre III, Promethee II methods. The second one, belongs to American school and it is based on multiattribute utility theory, e.g. AHP, UTA methods.

Stochastic Information: Information represented by a random number, usually by a random probability distribution. It is connected with uncertainty about the values of parameters, expected input or output information. In the real-world systems the stochastic information is the result of unexpected disturbances, demand fluctuations etc.

Chapter 20
Joint Decision for Price Competitive Inventory Model with Time–Price and Credit Period Dependent Demand

Nita H. Shah
Gujarat University, India

ABSTRACT

The problem analyzes a supply chain comprised of two front-runner retailers and one supplier. The retailers' offer customers delay in payments to settle the accounts against the purchases which is received by the supplier. The market demand of the retailer depends on time, retail price and a credit period offered to the customers with that of the other retailer. The supplier gives items with same wholesale price and credit period to the retailers. The joint and independent decisions are analyzed and validated numerically.

INTRODUCTION

For a firm, price of the product and change of behavior of customers with time for the product are very important issues to formulate marketing strategies. The firm uses delay in payments as a promotional tool to boost customer's demand which depends on the retail price of the product. Choi (1991) studied channel competition with two competing manufactures and one retailer. He studied effect of cost differences on equilibrium prices and profits using Stackelberg and Nash games. Ingene and Parry (1995) worked out policy under which a manufacturer does a business with heterogeneous retailers and non-identical competing retailers. They advocated a manufacturer to offer two-part payment policies against quantity discount. Yao and Liu (2005) analyzed the pricing equilibrium between a manufacturer with an e-tail channel and a manufacturer with a retail channel for Bertrand and Stackelberg price competition models. Xie and Wei (2009) considered price dependent demand with advertisement. They concluded that the coordinated decision is beneficial. Li et al. (2010) discussed a model when supply disrupts for a single-retailer and two suppliers. Sinha and Sarmah (2010) studied the problem of price competition

DOI: 10.4018/978-1-5225-2031-3.ch020

without channel coordination, and global coordination in a two-stage distribution channel where two retailers deal with two differentiated products using a common distributor. For more studies on inventory models with pricing policy models read Pal et al. (2012), Sana (2011), Sona and Choudhuri (2008), Wei and Chen (2011), Wu et al. (2012) and their cited references.

Now-a-days, trade credit is considered to be a bridge between two players where one player supplies order but receives payment after/on pre-specified date. This tool helps both the players to boost their demands. Goyal (1985) formulated economic order quantity model when a player offers delay period to settle the accounts due against the purchases. Refer to review article by Shah et al. (2011) on inventory modeling and trade credit. Huang (2003) formulated inventory policies with two-level trade credit scheme. Chung et al. (2005) discussed model when order quantity depends on the credit period. Ho (2011) studied integrated decision for supplier-retailer supply chain by assuming that the credit period offered by the supplier is longer than that of the retailer who passes it to the customer when demand is price and customer's credit period sensitive. Zhou et al. (2012) studied decision rules for a supply chain comprising of supplier-retailer when floor space is constraint for the retailer. Shah and Shah (2012) extended above problem for constant rate of deterioration of items and fuzzy demand. Pal et al. (2014) studied two-echelon competitive integrated supply chain with price and credit period dependent demand. They assumed that the wholesale price and credit periods offers by the supplier to the two retailers are same and demand of one retailer depends on the selling price of the other retailer.

In this chapter, a competitive supply chain comprising of two antagonist retailers dealing with one common supplier is analyzed. The retailers compete with each other in terms of time, price and credit period to increase their profits. The demand decreases with time and sensitive to retail price and length of credit periods offered to the customers by both the antagonist retailers. The coordinated objective function of supply chain is maximized. The independent decision is maximized using vertical Nash equilibrium. The rest of the chapter is organized as follows. The notations and assumptions are given in section 2, the mathematical model is formulated in section 3. Section 4 validates mathematical development using numerical data and a conclusion is given in section 5.

ASSUMPTIONS AND NOTATIONS

Notations

The problem stated uses the following notations:

$i = 1, 2$

C : Purchase cost / item of the supplier (in $)

w : Wholesale price / item set by the supplier (in $)

P_i : Retail price for the ith retailer (in $)

$R_{r_i}(t, N_i, P_i)$: Demand rate for the ith retailer

N_i : Credit period offered by the ith retailer to the customer (in years)

M : Credit period offered by the supplier to the retailer (in years)

I_c : Interest payable per $/unit time

I_e : Interest earned per $ per unit time; ($I_e < I_c$)

T_i : Replenishment time for the ith retailer (in years)

Assumptions

- The model is developed using following assumptions (as given in Pal *et al.* (2014)).
- The supply chain under consideration deals with one common supplier and two antagonist retailers for a single item.
- Each retailer competes with the other bases on retail price and credit period.
- Demand is decreasing function of time and depends on each retailer's retail price, credit period, antagonist's retail price and credit period.
- Lead-time is zero and shortages are not allowed.

MATHEMATICAL MODEL

Basic Model

The competitive business world depends on the time, retail price, and promotional tool used to enhance the customers. In the problem, we consider a competitive supply chain consists of two retailers and a common supplier. The demand of the ith retailer is time dependent. It is also assumed that the ith retailer's credit period N_i compete with the jth retailer's credit period N_j. Thus, the market demand is

$$R_{r_i}(t, N_i, P_i) = (a_i(1 + b_i t - c_i t^2) - d_i P_i + e P_j) N_i^\alpha N_j^\beta,$$

$$i, j = 1, 2, i \neq j, \ a_i > 0, \ d_i > e > 0, \ \alpha, \beta > 0. \ d_i > e$$

is required to establish that sales are more sensitive to price at that retailer compared to the price for antagonist retailer. The difference $(d_i - e)$ is inversely related to the interchangeability between the two retailers. Each retailer increases their market demand by offering credit period. To study the competition in retailer's offer for credit period assume $\alpha > \beta$. It is in accordance with the market observation that the active retailer is more effective than the competing retailer to boost the demand. The supplier offers same credit period of M - time to each of retailers. This results to incur interest charges during $[0, M]$ for the cases either $M \leq T_i$ or $M > T_i$. The interest incurred by the supplier per unit time is

$$IC(M \leq T_i) = \frac{CIc}{T_i} \int_0^M R_{r_i}(t, N_i, P_i) t dt \ \text{ and}$$

$$IC(M > T_i) = \frac{CIc}{T_i} \left[\int_0^{T_i} R_{r_i}(t, N_i, P_i) dt + R_{r_i}(T_i, N_i, P_i)(M - T_i) \right].$$

Under the assumption that the ith retailer passes credit period of N_i - time units, three cases arise.

Case 1: $N_i \leq M$ i.e. the credit period M offered by the supplier to each of the retailers is greater than the credit period offered by the ith retailer to the customer. The retailers will generate revenue during $[N_i, T_i]$ on which interest can be earned at the rate I_e during $[N_i, M]$. Depending on the lengths of N_i, M and T_i, we need to compute interest earned and interest charged for three possible scenarios viz. $N_i \leq M \leq T_i$, $N_i \leq T_i \leq M$ and $T_i \leq N_i \leq M$. The interests earned per unit time in each case are:

$$IE(N_i \leq M \leq T_i) = \frac{PI_e}{T_i} \int_0^{M-N_i} R_{r_i}(t, N_i, P_i) t\, dt$$

$$IE(N_i \leq T_i \leq M) = \frac{PI_e}{T_i} \left[\int_0^{T_i-N_i} R_{r_i}(t, N_i, P_i) t\, dt + \int_0^{T_i} R_{r_i}(t, N_i, P_i) t\, dt (M - T_i) \right], \text{ and}$$

$$IE(T_i \leq N_i \leq M) = \frac{PI_e}{T_i} \left[\int_0^{T_i} R_{r_i}(t, N_i, P_i) t\, dt (M - N_i) \right], \text{ respectively.}$$

The interests paid per unit time in each case are:

$$IC(N_i \leq M \leq T_i) = \frac{wI_c}{T_i} \left[\int_0^M R_{r_i}(t, N_i, P_i)\, dt + \int_0^{M-N} R_{r_i}(t, N_i, P_i)\, dt \right] (T_i - M), \text{ and}$$

$$IC(N_i \leq T_i \leq M) = 0 = IC(T_i \leq N_i \leq M), \text{ respectively.}$$

Case 2: $N_i \geq M$. Here, no interest is earned by the retailers as the credit period offered to customer by retailer is longer than that of the supplier to the retailer. The ith retailer incurs revenue during $[N_i, T_i]$ if $N_i \leq T_i$ or at a time N_i if $N_i \geq T_i$. The possible scenarios depending on the lengths of T_i, M and N_i are $M \leq N_i \leq T_i$, $M \leq T_i \leq N_i$ and $T_i \leq M \leq N_i$. The interests paid per unit time by the ith retailer are:

$$IC(M \leq N_i \leq T_i) = \frac{wI_c}{T_i} \left[\int_M^{N_i} R_{r_i}(t, N_i, P_i) t\, dt + \int_0^{N_i} R_{r_i}(t, N_i, P_i)\, dt (T_i - N_i) \right]$$

$$IC(M \leq T_i \leq N_i) = \frac{wI_c}{T_i} \left[\int_M^{T_i} R_{r_i}(t, N_i, P_i) t\, dt + \int_0^{T_i} R_{r_i}(t, N_i, P_i)\, dt (N_i - T_i) \right], \text{ and}$$

$$IC(T_i \leq M \leq N_i) = \frac{wI_c}{T_i} \left[\int_0^{T_i} R_{r_i}(t, N_i, P_i)dt(N_i - M) \right], \text{respectively.}$$

Hence, the total profit per unit time for the supplier is:

$$TPS(M \leq T_i) = \sum_{i=1}^{2} \left(\frac{(w - C)}{T_i} \int_0^{T_i} R_{r_i}(t, N_i, P_i)dt - IC(M \leq T_i) \right) \tag{1}$$

$$TPS(M > T_i) = \sum_{i=1}^{2} \left(\frac{(w - C)}{T_i} \int_0^{T_i} R_{r_i}(t, N_i, P_i)dt - IC(M > T_i) \right) \tag{2}$$

The total profit per unit time of ith retailer is:

$$TPR_1^i(N_i \leq M \leq T_i) = \frac{(P_i - w)}{T_i} \int_0^{T_i} R_{r_i}(t, N_i, P_i)dt + IE(N_i \leq M \leq T_i) - IC(N_i \leq M \leq T_i) \tag{3}$$

$$TPR_2^i(N_i \leq T_i \leq M) = \frac{(P_i - w)}{T_i} \int_0^{T_i} R_{r_i}(t, N_i, P_i)dt + IE(N_i \leq T_i \leq M) \tag{4}$$

$$TPR_3^i(T_i \leq N_i \leq M) = \frac{(P_i - w)}{T_i} \int_0^{T_i} R_{r_i}(t, N_i, P_i)dt + IE(T_i \leq N_i \leq M) \tag{5}$$

$$TPR_4^i(M \leq N_i \leq T_i) = \frac{(P_i - w)}{T_i} \int_0^{T_i} R_{r_i}(t, N_i, P_i)dt - IC(M \leq N_i \leq T_i) \tag{6}$$

$$TPR_5^i(M \leq T_i \leq N_i) = \frac{(P_i - w)}{T_i} \int_0^{T_i} R_{r_i}(t, N_i, P_i)dt - IC(M \leq T_i \leq N_i) \tag{7}$$

$$TPR_6^i(T_i \leq M \leq N_i) = \frac{(P_i - w)}{T_i} \int_0^{T_i} R_{r_i}(t, N_i, P_i)dt - IC(T_i \leq M \leq N_i) \tag{8}$$

Total Profit of the Supply Chain

Under coordination, a supplier and two retailers act as one entity. The total profit per unit time; ITP of a supply chain is:

$$
ITP = \begin{cases}
\pi_1 = \sum_{i=1}^{2} \left[TPS(M \leq T_i) + TPR_1^i(N_i \leq M \leq T_i) \right] \\
\pi_2 = \sum_{i=1}^{2} \left[TPS(M \leq T_i) + TPR_2^i(N_i \leq T_i \leq M) \right] \\
\pi_3 = \sum_{i=1}^{2} \left[TPS(M \leq T_i) + TPR_3^i(T_i \leq N_i \leq M) \right] \\
\pi_4 = \sum_{i=1}^{2} \left[TPS(M \geq T_i) + TPR_4^i(M \leq N_i \leq T_i) \right] \\
\pi_5 = \sum_{i=1}^{2} \left[TPS(M \geq T_i) + TPR_5^i(M \leq T_i \leq N_i) \right] \\
\pi_6 = \sum_{i=1}^{2} \left[TPS(M \geq T_i) + TPR_6^i(T_i \leq M \leq N_i) \right]
\end{cases}
\tag{9}
$$

For fixed N_i, $\pi_1(T_i = M) = \pi_2(T_i = M)$, $\pi_2(T_i = N_i) = \pi_3(T_i = N_i)$, $\pi_4(T_i = N_i) = \pi_5(T_i = N_i)$ and $\pi_5(T_i = M) = \pi_6(T_i = M)$. Hence, π_k is well-defined and continuous function for $k = 1, 2, ..., 6$. For fixed N_i, $i = 1, 2$, the selling price of the retailers can be computed by the first order conditions $\dfrac{\partial \pi_k}{\partial P_1} = 0$ and $\dfrac{\partial \pi_k}{\partial P_2} = 0$ for $k = 1, 2, ..., 6$. The obtained values of P_1 and P_2 maximizes the integrated

profit per unit time provided the Hessian matrix $\begin{vmatrix} \dfrac{\partial^2 \pi_k}{\partial P_1^2} & \dfrac{\partial^2 \pi_k}{\partial P_1 \partial P_2} \\ \dfrac{\partial^2 \pi_k}{\partial P_2 \partial P_1} & \dfrac{\partial^2 \pi_k}{\partial P_2^2} \end{vmatrix}$ is negative definite. The non-linearity of the objective function π_k hinders to get the closed form of solutions. We will establish solution and negative definiteness using numerical data.

Vertical Nash Equilibria

If the supplier and two retailers prefer to take decision independently, then the supplier maximizes the profit by setting suitable wholesale price. The retailer will decide retail price, irrespective of the decision of the supplier and competing retailer. Assume that the ith retailer's sales margin to be $f_i = P_i - w, i = 1, 2$. Then the demand function of the ith retailer will be

$$
R_{r_i}^{vn}(f_i, t, N_i, P_i) = (a_i(1 + b_i t - c_i t^2) - d_i(w + f_i) + e(w + f_j))N_i^\alpha N_j^\beta, \quad i, j = 1, 2, i \neq j.
$$

Substitute this in eqs. (1) – (8), gives profit functions of the supplier and retailers. Denote it by π_s^{vn} and $\pi_{kr_i}^{vn}$ respectively. The corresponding first-order conditions are $\dfrac{\partial \pi_s^{vn}}{\partial w} = 0, \dfrac{\partial \pi_{kr_i}^{vn}}{\partial P_1} = 0$ and $\dfrac{\partial \pi_{kr_i}^{vn}}{\partial P_2} - 0$, $i = 1, 2$ for maximizing individual profits with respect to wholesale price and retail prices of the supplier and two retailers' respectively.

Numerical Examples

In this section, we will illustrate the results previously discussed.

Example 1

Consider supply chain with following data (Pal *et al.* (2016)). The purchase cost of the supplier is \$ 15 per unit, the wholesale price is \$ 40 per unit. The demand parameters of the retailers are $a_2 = 4800$ units, $b_1 = 25\%$, $b_2 = 15\%$, $c_1 = 20\%$, $c_2 = 14\%$, $d_1 = 85$, $d_2 = 80$ and $e = 20$. The credit mark-ups of the retailers are $\alpha = 1.5$ and $\beta = 1$. Interest payable per \$ per unit time is $I_c = 8\%$ and interest earned per \$ per unit time is $I_e = 7\%$. The cycle time for retailer 1 and retailer 2 are $T_1 = T_2 = 30$ days. The optimum values of the decision variables, profits of the supplier, the retailers, and the supply chain are shown in Table 1.

The observations for $N_i \leq M$ and $N_i \leq M \leq T_i$ from Table 1 are:

- The joint decision is more advantageous compared to independent decision.
- Offering longer credit period by the retailer 1 than that of the retailer 2 may not give more profit to retailer 1 than retailer 2.
- When players take independent decisions, the retailers' profit is higher but the supplier's profit is less than from the joint decision.

The observations for $N_i \leq M$ and $N_i \leq T_i \leq M$ from Table 1 are:

- The supply chain profit in this scenario also increases.
- The retailer 2 has more profit than that of retailer 1 when retailer 1 offers longer credit period than that of the retailer 2.
- When $M = 21, N_1 = 30$ and $N_2 = 35$ days, total profit of the supply chain and the retailer 2 are maximum and when $N_1 = 25$ and $N_2 = 20$ days, the retailer 1's profit is maximum in joint decision.
- In both the policies, the retailers profit is less but the supplier's profit is higher.

The observations for $N_i \leq M$ and $T_i \leq N_i \leq M$ from Table 1 are:

- The outputs are almost similar to above two scenarios. The maximum profit of the supply chain is obtained when credit periods offered by the players are almost equal.

Table 1. Optimum solution

Case	M Days	N₁ Days	P₁ $	R_r1 Units	TRP_r1 $	N₂ Days	P₂ $	R_r2 Units	TRP_r2 $	w $	TSP $	ITP $	Strategy
$N_i \leq M \leq T_i$	20	5	46.61	121.92	790.29	10	47.48	116.39	856.78	40	5845.30	7492.37	I
			42.64	148.74	132.51		53.51	83.47	962.59	41.75	6091.61	7186.71	D
		10	46.62	229.82	1484.63	15	47.48	219.42	1611.45	40	11018.64	14114.72	I
			49.25	218.35	2330.18		53.46	172.43	2562.15	38.31	8911.79	13804.12	D
		15	46.63	351.71	2266.61	18	47.49	335.88	2464.35	40	16865.03	21595.99	I
			50.52	334.28	3879.21		52.32	263.98	4174.04	37.33	13069.21	21122.46	D
		10	46.63	689.26	4453.90	5	47.46	658.83	4863.27	40	33065.54	42382.71	I
			51.50	582.61	5932.66		52.05	569.51	6198.44	41.02	29321.20	41452.30	D
		15	46.63	632.97	4079.71	10	47.47	604.96	4452.09	40	30363.43	38895.23	I
			50.56	554.38	5003.07		51.25	536.91	5277.28	41.26	28047.44	38327.79	D
		18	46.64	554.66	3571.00	15	47.48	529.98	3891.82	40	26603.41	34066.23	I
			51.47	467.21	6393.42		51.60	467.89	6546.25	37.36	20451.25	33390.92	D
$N_i \leq T_i \leq M$	31	15	46.62	316.68	2062.01	20	47.47	302.41	2237.43	40	15166.13	19465.57	I
			51.47	272.31	696.25		53.49	243.94	1111.15	48.89	17090.56	18897.96	D
		20	46.63	389.99	2533.66	25	47.48	372.48	2752.08	40	18678.38	23964.12	I
			52.26	336.85	130.91		57.26	247.08	1302.84	51.89	21003.80	22437.55	D
		25	46.62	454.15	2946.60	30	47.48	433.80	3203.62	40	21752.34	27902.56	I
			51.58	332.82	332.82		53.61	348.48	992.47	50.72	25730.63	27055.92	D
		30	46.63	596.98	3871.62	30	47.48	570.26	4211.21	40	28593.89	36676.72	I
			53.04	474.20	901.22		53.30	473.30	1036.52	51.09	33386.46	35324.20	D
		30	46.63	716.36	4646.03	25	47.47	684.34	5055.59	40	34312.98	44014.60	I
			51.44	628.20	1037.99		55.10	507.44	2675.67	49.75	38526.71	42240.37	D
		25	46.63	681.18	4420.21	20	47.47	650.80	4813.61	40	32629.68	41863.50	I
			51.75	570.87	3294.24		52.37	556.06	3595.69	45.83	33944.16	40834.09	D
		20	46.62	649.90	4223.38	15	47.47	620.98	4602.48	40	31132.86	39958.72	I
			52.31	540.96	379.48		54.20	488.46	1261.88	51.62	36804.49	38445.85	D

continued on following page

Table 1. Continued

Case	M Days	N_1 Days	P_1 $	R_{r1} Units	TRP_{r1} $	N_2 Days	P_2 $	R_{r2} Units	TRP_{r2} $	w $	TSP $	ITP $	Strategy
$T_i \le N_i \le M$	35	30	46.67	559.69	3649.53	32	47.48	534.50	3959.66	40	26788.53	34397.72	I
			55.61	423.83	1031.92		60.37	305.61	2165.69	53.15	27026.83	30224.44	D
		32	46.63	580.26	3775.14	34	47.48	554.15	4096.82	40	27773.07	35645.03	I
			56.36	384.28	1203.25		53.67	470.38	247.38	53.15	31767.79	33218.42	D
		33	46.63	590.28	3836.01	35	47.49	563.72	4163.32	40	28252.77	36252.10	I
			54.86	426.21	714.93		53.53	473.39	174.92	53.15	33465.84	34355.69	D
		35	46.63	644.64	4180.50	35	47.48	615.79	4547.16	40	30858.26	39585.92	I
			53.74	499.36	312.44		54.24	492.36	553.97	53.10	36852.19	37718.60	D
		35	46.64	683.65	4434.26	33	47.48	653.23	4832.70	40	32729.85	41996.81	I
			53.75	529.56	331.95		54.24	522.31	596.25	53.10	39087.78	40015.98	D
		34	46.64	675.04	4383.41	32	47.48	645.00	4776.75	40	32317.96	41478.12	I
			53.45	545.04	304.34		56.42	457.31	1597.88	52.89	37010.15	38912.37	D
		32	46.63	657.51	4279.24	30	47.48	628.25	4662.21	40	31478.82	40420.27	I
			46.63	511.14	686.17		56.65	444.63	1662.17	52.89	35271.97	37620.31	D
$M \le N_i \le T_i$	5	5	46.44	149.90	1690.28	8	47.34	144.12	1759.95	40	5856.33	9306.56	I
			51.26	128.69	1187.49		53.33	116.12	1313.40	41.87	6504.22	9005.11	D
		8	46.45	202.21	2278.77	12	47.34	194.43	2373.24	40	7859.66	12511.67	I
			51.13	174.33	1832.56		53.15	157.81	1981.33	40.43	8352.08	12165.97	D
		12	46.45	297.12	3346.85	15	47.34	285.75	3487.59	40	11550.13	18384.57	I
			51.84	246.27	2728.83		52.72	238.96	2872.52	40.54	12253.58	17854.93	D
		15	46.45	519.01	5845.64	12	47.34	499.21	6093.57	40	20177.22	32116.43	I
			52.26	429.60	5323.05		54.39	385.74	5620.95	39.63	19847.60	30791.60	D
		15	46.45	415.22	4676.56	15	47.34	399.35	4874.11	40	16141.50	25692.17	I
			50.34	375.60	3862.73		54.10	305.49	4293.18	39.86	16742.83	24898.74	D
		12	46.45	557.07	6274.95	8	47.34	535.92	6544.38	40	21658.54	34477.87	I
			51.34	478.89	5191.25		53.75	423.05	5623.27	40.29	22551.63	33366.15	D
		8	46.44	485.24	5468.42	5	47.33	466.85	5703.95	40	18866.50	30038.87	I
			52.65	382.56	4343.78		52.05	406.82	4414.78	41.08	20355.10	29113.66	D

continued on following page

Table 1. Continued

Case	M Days	N₁ Days	P₁ $	R_r1 Units	TRP_r1 $	N₂ Days	P₂ $	R_r2 Units	TRP_r2 $	w $	TSP $	TTP $	Strategy
$M \leq T_i \leq N_i$	5	15	46.45	415.22	4676.56	15	47.34	399.35	4676.56	40	16141.50	25494.62	I
			50.72	362.52	4066.41		52.49	333.14	4342.20	39.29	16713.23	25121.84	D
		15	46.45	346.05	3897.58	18	47.36	332.64	4056.05	40	13448.91	21402.54	I
			50.30	303.24	3449.72		51.05	295.78	3595.16	38.71	14052.86	21097.74	D
		18	46.46	409.25	4604.62	20	47.36	393.46	4794.69	40	15906.32	25305.63	I
			49.73	369.00	4432.04		51.19	345.29	4663.69	37.48	15889.73	24985.46	D
		20	46.47	479.16	5387.62	20	47.36	460.86	5616.05	40	18627.37	29631.04	I
			48.36	449.42	5567.44		49.04	438.25	5755.28	35.72	18212.51	29535.23	D
		20	46.47	532.36	5985.80	18	47.36	512.23	6245.92	40	20599.47	32831.19	I
			49.04	494.22	6365.26		50.95	450.90	6094.96	35.90	19550.78	32611.00	D
		18	46.46	545.56	6138.33	15	47.34	525.02	6407.94	40	21214.56	33760.83	I
			51.09	453.42	6275.86		49.73	498.75	6291.42	36.97	20700.86	33268.14	D
$T_i \leq M \leq N_i$	20	20	46.45	479.47	5424.11	20	47.34	461.15	5651.37	40	18593.19	29668.67	I
			54.26	359.04	2250.52		54.81	357.82	2454.46	47.89	23251.36	27956.34	D
		20	46.45	383.65	4340.11	25	47.36	368.63	4510.53	40	14870.25	23720.90	I
			52.12	321.03	2578.97		54.74	279.30	2967.06	43.97	17157.91	22703.94	D
		25	46.47	446.53	5043.00	30	47.38	429.06	5241.79	40	17307.74	27592.53	I
			50.36	395.00	4557.69		52.10	363.68	4831.07	38.62	17690.32	27079.08	D
		30	46.49	586.51	6612.75	30	47.38	564.13	6891.86	40	22744.48	36249.09	I
			51.31	491.82	7460.64		51.35	500.71	7665.26	35.84	20413.20	35539.10	D
		30	46.49	703.68	7933.79	25	47.36	677.48	8289.63	40	27301.28	43524.70	I
			49.96	624.29	7566.32		50.57	613.01	7870.44	37.59	27600.29	43037.05	D
		25	46.47	669.54	7561.64	20	47.34	644.60	7899.58	40	25976.63	41437.85	I
			53.30	505.20	5236.41		51.25	586.95	4969.20	42.72	29880.11	40085.72	D

I: Integrated decision, D: Independent decision

Example 2

Consider the data as given in example 1 with $w = \$35$ and $T_1 = T_2 = 15$ days. The optimum values of the decision variables and maximum profits are exhibited in Table 1 for different scenarios.

The observations for $N_i \geq M$ and $M \leq N_i \leq T_i$ from Table 1 are:

- The joint decision results more profit compared to independent decision.
- From data, when $M = 5, N_1 = 12$ and $N_2 = 8$ days, the supply chain and all the players have maximum profit.
- In the *VN*-model, the retailer's profit is less but supplier's profit is higher than that from the joint decision.

The observations for $N_i \geq M$, $M \leq T_i \leq N_i$ and $T_i \leq M \leq N_i$ are almost similar to that of $M \leq N_i \leq T_i$.

CONCLUSION

The coordinated competitive supply chain model when demand is decreasing with time under two-level trade credit policy is analyzed. The supplier distributes a product to two antagonist retailers who compete with each other in terms of the selling price and offering credit periods to the customers. The model is analyzed for different scenarios for centralized and vertical Nash decentralized decisions. It is established that the players should take favorable decisions according to market behavior and competitor.

ACKNOWLEDGMENT

The author thanks DST-FIST for technical support with file # MSI-097.

REFERENCES

Choi, S. C. (1991). Price competition in a channel structure with a common retailer. *Marketing Science*, *10*(4), 271–296. doi:10.1287/mksc.10.4.271

Chung, K. J., Goyal, S. K., & Huang, Y. F. (2005). The optimal inventory policies under permissible delay in payments depending on the order quantity. *International Journal of Production Economics*, *95*(2), 203–213. doi:10.1016/j.ijpe.2003.12.006

Goyal, S. K. (1985). Economic order quantity under conditions of permissible delay in payments. *The Journal of the Operational Research Society*, *36*(4), 335–338. doi:10.1057/jors.1985.56

Ho, C. H. (2011). The optimal integrated inventory policy with price-and- credit-linked demand under two-level trade credit. *Computers & Industrial Engineering*, *60*(1), 117–126. doi:10.1016/j.cie.2010.10.009

Huang, Y. F. (2003). Optimal retailers ordering policies in the EOQ model under trade credit financing. *The Journal of the Operational Research Society, 54*(9), 1011–1015. doi:10.1057/palgrave.jors.2601588

Ingene, C. A., & Parry, M. E. (1995). Channel coordination when retailers compete. *Marketing Science, 14*(4), 360–377. doi:10.1287/mksc.14.4.360

Li, J., Wang, S., & Chang, T. C. E. (2010). Competition and cooperation in a single-retailer two- supplier supply chain with supply disruption. *International Journal of Production Economics, 124*(1), 137–150. doi:10.1016/j.ijpe.2009.10.017

Pal, B., Sana, S. S., & Chaudhuri, K. S. (2012). Multi-item EOQ model while demand is sales price and price break sensitive. *Economic Modelling, 29*(6), 2283–2288. doi:10.1016/j.econmod.2012.06.039

Pal, B., Sana, S. S., & Chaudhuri, K. S. (2016). Two-echelon competitive integrated supply chain model with price and credit period dependent demand. *International Journal of Systems Science, 47*(5), 995–1007. doi:10.1080/00207721.2014.911383

Sana, S. S. (2011). Price-sensitive demand for perishable items: An EOQ model. *Applied Mathematics and Computation, 217*(13), 6248–6259. doi:10.1016/j.amc.2010.12.113

Sana, S. S., & Chaudhuri, K. S. (2008). A deterministic EOQ model with delay in payments and price-discount offers. *European Journal of Operational Research, 184*(2), 509–533. doi:10.1016/j.ejor.2006.11.023

Shah, N. H., Soni, H., & Jaggi, C. K. (2010). Inventory models and trade credit: A review. *Control and Cybernetics, 39*(3), 867–882.

Shah, N. H., & Shah, A. D. (2012). Optimal ordering- Transfer policy for deteriorating inventory items with fuzzy-stock dependent demand. *Mexican Journal of Operations Research, 1*(1), 29–44.

Sinha, S., & Sarmah, S. P. (2010). Coordination and price competition in a duopoly common retailer supply chain. *Computers & Industrial Engineering, 59*(2), 280–295. doi:10.1016/j.cie.2010.04.010

Wei, Y., & Chen, Y. F. (2011). Joint determination of inventory replenishment and sales effort with uncertain market responses. *International Journal of Production Economics, 134*(2), 368–374. doi:10.1016/j.ijpe.2009.11.011

Wu, C. H., Chen, C. W., & Hsieh, C. C. (2012). Competitive pricing decisions in a two-echelon supply chain with horizontal and vertical competition. *International Journal of Production Economics, 135*(1), 265–274. doi:10.1016/j.ijpe.2011.07.020

Xie, J., & Wei, J. C. (2009). Coordinating advertising and pricing in a manufacturer retailer channel. *European Journal of Operational Research, 197*(2), 785–791. doi:10.1016/j.ejor.2008.07.014

Yao, D. Q., & Liu, J. J. (2005). Competitive pricing of mixed retail and e-tail distribution channels. *Omega, 33*(3), 235–247. doi:10.1016/j.omega.2004.04.007

Zhou, Y. W., Zhong, Y., & Li, J. (2012). An uncooperative order model for items with trade credit, inventory-dependent demand, and limited displayed-shelf space. *European Journal of Operational Research, 223*(1), 76–85. doi:10.1016/j.ejor.2012.06.012

Chapter 21

On Development of a Fuzzy Stochastic Programming Model with Its Application to Business Management

Animesh Biswas
University of Kalyani, India

Arnab Kumar De
Government College of Engineering and Textile Technology, India

ABSTRACT

This chapter expresses efficiency of fuzzy goal programming for multiobjective aggregate production planning in fuzzy stochastic environment. The parameters of the objectives are taken as normally distributed fuzzy random variables and the chance constraints involve joint Cauchy distributed fuzzy random variables. In model formulation process the fuzzy chance constrained programming model is converted into its equivalent fuzzy programming using probabilistic technique, α-cut of fuzzy numbers and taking expectation of parameters of the objectives. Defuzzification technique of fuzzy numbers is used to find multiobjective linear programming model. Membership function of each objective is constructed depending on their optimal values. Afterwards a weighted fuzzy goal programming model is developed to achieve the highest degree of each of the membership goals to the extent possible by minimizing group regrets in a multiobjective decision making context. To explore the potentiality of the proposed approach, production planning of a health drinks manufacturing company has been considered.

INTRODUCTION

In today's highly competitive, fluctuating complex organizational situation, organizations around the world have increasingly emphasized on aggregate production planning (APP) for determining a best way to achieve the highest possible extent of a set of objectives in an environment of conflicting interests, incomplete information and limited resources as studied by Simon (1977). APP deals with matching supply and demand of forecasted and fluctuated customer's orders over the period of medium time range.

DOI: 10.4018/978-1-5225-2031-3.ch021

The problem of APP is concerned with management's response to fluctuations in the demand pattern. Specifically, how can the productive, man power, goods resources and other controllable factors can be utilized effectively in the face of changing demands in order to minimize the total cost of operations over a given planning horizon (Nam & Logendran, 1992; Buxey, 1995).

The APP problems have been extensively investigated and much effort has been expended in developing decision models (Saad, 1982). Thereafter, many researchers studied APP problems and developed different optimization models (Jain & Palekar, 2005; Gomes da Silva et al., 2006; Leung et al., 2006; Leung & Chan, 2009). Most of the above models were developed under crisp environments, and can be categorized as deterministic optimization models. However, it is frequently observed that the APP problems contain many uncertain factors, viz., customer demand, production fluctuation, and their associated costs (Mula et al. 2006). In particular, in many practical applications, the imprecise information embedded in APP can be obtained subjectively (Wang & Liang, 2004; Jamalnia & Soukhakian, 2009). Zadeh (1965), and Bellman and Zadeh (1970) introduced fuzzy set theory to handle uncertainties of this type. After the pioneering work on fuzzy linear programming (FLP) by Tanaka et al. (1973) and Zimmermann (1978), several kinds of FLP models appeared in the literature and different methods have been proposed to solve such problems. Some methods are based on the concepts of the penalty method (Jamison & Lodwick, 2001), the satisfaction degree of the constraints (Liu, 2001), the statistical confidence interval (Chiang, 2001), and the multiobjective optimization method (Zhang et al, 2003). Other kinds of methods are semi-infinite programming method (Leon & Vercher, 2004), the superiority and inferiority of fuzzy numbers (FNs) (Hop, 2007), and the degrees of feasibility (Jimenez et al, 2007). Ganesan and Veeramani (2006) discussed a method for solving FLP problems without converting them to crisp linear programming problems. There have been relatively few studies of fuzzy APP problems (Lai & Hwang 1992). Since the APP problem in crisp environments can be modelled as a linear program, on the basis of FLP (Zimmermann 1976) several fuzzy optimization methods for solving fuzzy APP problems have been developed (Rommelfanger 1996). Rinks (1982) investigated APP problems based on fuzzy logic and fuzzy linguistics and developed the fuzzy APP model and algorithm, and examined the robustness of this model under varying cost structures. Lee (1990) discussed the APP problems for a single product type with a fuzzy objective, fuzzy workforce levels, and fuzzy demands. Gen et al. (1992) proposed a method for solving the APP problem with multiple objectives and fuzzy parameters, and provided interactive solutions that suggest the best compromise aggregate production plan. Tang et al. (2000) developed an approach to multi-product APP problems with fuzzy demands and capacities. Afterwards, Tang et al. (2003) focused on the simulation analysis of the APP problems of this kind. There are several other related studies, including the approaches developed by Wang and Fang (2001), and Wang and Liang (2005).

To convert fuzzy programming (FP) problems into its equivalent deterministic problems different defuzzification techniques of FNs are applied. Defuzzification of FNs is a mapping from the set of FNs to the set of real numbers. Thus for each FN there is a unique real number called the defuzzified value of that FN. Thus defuzzification method of FNs is an important topic in the field of fuzzy optimization. Different defuzzification techniques have been studied and were applied to fuzzy control and fuzzy expert system (Filev & Yager, 1991; Yager & Filev, 1993) by several researchers in the past. The major idea behind these methods was to obtain a typical value from a given fuzzy set according to some specified characters, such as central gravity, median etc. A probabilistic approach to rank complex FNs was developed by Yoon (1996). Delgado et al. (1998) described a defuzzification method using the α-cut of the FNs. A new defuzzification method of FNs using the distance between two FNs was developed by Ma et al. (2000). Another defuzzification method of FNs by centroid method was presented by Wang et al. (2006). Abbasbandy and Asady (2006) developed a method of ranking FN based on sign distance between FNs. A new approach for ranking of trapezoidal FNs based on the left and the right spreads at some α - levels of trapezoidal FNs was described by Abbasbandy and Hajjari (2009). A ranking of L-R type generalized FNs were proposed by Kumar et al. (2011). Different defuzzification techniques were further developed by Asady (2010), Brandas (2011), Barik and Biswal (2012) and others.

In many practical situations, it is seen that the probabilistic uncertainties are also included in APP problems. Chance constrained programming (CCP) introduced by Charnes and Cooper (1959) are used to handle optimization problems with probabilistic uncertainties. Thereafter different methodological aspects of CCP technique were discussed by Kataoka (1963), Panne and Pop (1963), Miller and Wagner (1965), Pre'kopa (1973) and other researchers. Contini (1978) developed an algorithm for stochastic programming problems where the random variables are normally distributed with known means and variances. An interval-parameter dynamic CCP approach for capacity planning under uncertainty was developed by Dai et al. (2012). In 2004, Sharafali *et al.* (2004) considered a model for production scheduling in a flexible manufacturing system with stochastic demand. In a recent paper, Wu and Ierapetritou (2007) presented a production planning and scheduling model through a hierarchical framework. Multiobjective production planning problem with probabilistic constraints was developed by Sahoo and Biswal (2009). To the best of authors' knowledge, an efficient solution technique for solving fuzzy multiobjective stochastic APP (FMOSAPP) problem following normal distribution and joint Cauchy distribution from the viewpoint of its potential use in different planning problems involving fuzzy parameters is yet to appear in the literature.

In this chapter, a fuzzy goal programming (FGP) methodology has been developed for multiobjective APP problems involved with chance constraints and have joint Cauchy distributed fuzzy random variable (FRV) in right side parameters of the system constraints. The parameters of the objectives are taken as normally distributed FRVs and the left sided parameters of the constraints are considered as triangular FNs (TFNs). Taking the expectation of all the parameters of the objectives the expectation model of the objectives is formed. The fuzzy multiobjective CCP problem is first converted into FP model by applying chance constrained methodology developed for fuzzy Cauchy distribution with the help of α-cuts of FNs. Then a defuzzification method of FNs is applied to construct a deterministic multiobjective linear programming model. Each objective is then solved independently under the modified system constraints to find the best and worst values of the objectives. The membership function of each objective is then developed on the basis of best and worst solutions. After that FGP technique is applied to find the most suitable compromise solution of all the objectives. Lastly the proposed methodology is applied to multiobjective APP model for health drinks manufacturing industry and the solution obtained by the proposed methodology indicates the acceptance of the proposed approach to the decision makers.

BACKGROUND

In this section the basic concepts of FN, TFN, defuzzification of TFN, normal distribution, joint probability distribution following Cauchy distribution that are necessary requirements for developing the fuzzy multiobjective CCP (FMOCCP) model which expressed multiobjective APP model under FGP framework are described briefly.

Fuzzy Numbers (Dubois and Prade, 1978)

A FN $\tilde{A}$ is a fuzzy subset on $\mathbb{R}$ which is convex and its membership function $\mu_{\tilde{A}}(x)$ is written in the form

$$\mu_{\tilde{A}}(x) = \begin{cases} f_{\tilde{A}}^{L}(x) & \text{if } \quad a \leq x \leq b \\ 1 & \text{if } \quad b \leq x \leq c \\ f_{\tilde{A}}^{R}(x) & \text{if } \quad c \leq x \leq d \\ 0 & \text{otherwise} \end{cases}$$

where $f_{\tilde{A}}^{L} : [a,b] \to [0,1]$ is monotonic increasing and continuous function on $[a,b]$ and $f_{\tilde{A}}^{R} : [c,d] \to [0,1]$ is monotonic decreasing and continuous function on $[c,d]$.

Geometrically a FN $\tilde{A}$ is expressed as in Figure 1.

2.2 Triangular Fuzzy Number (Kaufmann And Gupta, 1985)

A TFN $\tilde{A} = (a,b,c)$ is a FN with its membership function $\mu_{\tilde{A}}(x)$ is given by

$$\mu_{\tilde{A}}(x) = \begin{cases} 0 & if \quad x < a \; or \; x > c \\ \dfrac{x-a}{b-a} & if \quad a \leq x \leq b \\ \dfrac{c-x}{c-b} & if \quad b \leq x \leq c \end{cases}$$

Figure 1. Fuzzy number

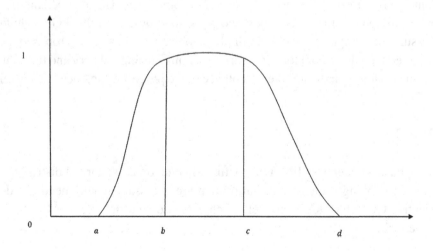

Figure 2. Triangular fuzzy number

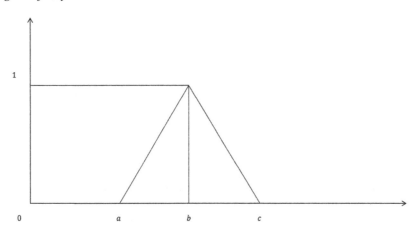

2.3 Defuzzification of Triangular Fuzzy Number (Wang et al., 2006)

Let $\tilde{A}$ be a FN, whose membership function $\mu_{\tilde{A}}(x)$ can generally be defined as

$$\mu_{\tilde{A}}(x) = \begin{cases} f_{\tilde{A}}^{L}(x) & \text{if} \quad a \leq x \leq b \\ 1 & \text{if} \quad b \leq x \leq c \\ f_{\tilde{A}}^{R}(x) & \text{if} \quad c \leq x \leq d \\ 0 & \text{otherwise} \end{cases}$$

where $f_{\tilde{A}}^{L} : [a,b] \to [0,1]$ is monotonic increasing and continuous function on $[a,b]$ and $f_{\tilde{A}}^{R} : [c,d] \to [0,1]$ is monotonic decreasing and continuous function on $[c,d]$.

Since $f_{\tilde{A}}^{L}$ and $f_{\tilde{A}}^{R}$ are both strictly monotonic and continuous functions, their inverse functions exist and should also be continuous and strictly monotonic. Let $g_{\tilde{A}}^{L} : [0,1] \to [a,b]$ and $g_{\tilde{A}}^{R} : [0,1] \to [c,d]$ be the inverse functions of $f_{\tilde{A}}^{L}$ and $f_{\tilde{A}}^{R}$ respectively. Then $g_{\tilde{A}}^{L}(y)$ and $g_{\tilde{A}}^{R}(y)$ should be integral on the closed interval $[0,1]$. In other words, both the integrals $\int_{0}^{1} g_{\tilde{A}}^{L}(y)\,dy$ and $\int_{0}^{1} g_{\tilde{A}}^{R}(y)\,dy$ should exist.

The centroid point of the FN is defined as

$$x_{0}(\tilde{A}) = \frac{\int_{-\infty}^{\infty} x\mu_{\tilde{A}}(x)\,dx}{\int_{-\infty}^{\infty} \mu_{\tilde{A}}(x)\,dx} = \frac{\int_{a}^{b} xf_{\tilde{A}}^{L}(x)\,dx + \int_{b}^{c} x\,dx + \int_{c}^{d} xf_{\tilde{A}}^{R}(x)\,dx}{\int_{a}^{b} f_{\tilde{A}}^{L}(x)\,dx + \int_{b}^{c} dx + \int_{c}^{d} f_{\tilde{A}}^{R}(x)\,dx}$$

$$y_0\left(\tilde{A}\right) = \frac{\int_0^1 y\left(g_{\tilde{A}}^R\left(y\right) - g_{\tilde{A}}^L\left(y\right)\right)dy}{\int_0^1 \left(g_{\tilde{A}}^R\left(y\right) - g_{\tilde{A}}^L\left(y\right)\right)dy}$$

Hence the defuzzified value of the FN $\tilde{A}$ in terms of its centroid point is

$$DV\left(\tilde{A}\right) = \sqrt{x_0\left(\tilde{A}\right)^2 + y_0\left(\tilde{A}\right)^2}.$$

In this chapter all the FNs are taken as TFNs. If $\tilde{A}$ be a TFN of the form $\tilde{A} = \left(a, b, c\right)$, then its membership function is given by

$$\mu_{\tilde{A}}\left(x\right) = \begin{cases} 0 & if \quad x < a \ or \ x > c \\ \dfrac{x-a}{b-a} & if \quad a \leq x \leq b \\ \dfrac{c-x}{c-b} & if \quad b \leq x \leq c \end{cases}$$

Thus $f_{\tilde{A}}^L\left(x\right) = \dfrac{x-a}{b-a}$ and $f_{\tilde{A}}^R\left(x\right) = \dfrac{c-x}{c-b}$. The inverse functions of $f_{\tilde{A}}^L$ and $f_{\tilde{A}}^R$ are given by $g_{\tilde{A}}^L\left(y\right) = \left[a + \left(b-a\right)y\right]$ and $g_{\tilde{A}}^R\left(y\right) = \left[c - \left(c-b\right)y\right]$ respectively.

Using the membership function the centroid point of the TFN is evaluated as

$$x_0\left(\tilde{A}\right) = \frac{\int_{-\infty}^{\infty} x\mu_{\tilde{A}}\left(x\right)dx}{\int_{-\infty}^{\infty}\mu_{\tilde{A}}\left(x\right)dx} = \frac{\int_a^b x\dfrac{x-a}{b-a}dx + \int_b^c x\dfrac{c-x}{c-b}dx}{\int_a^b \dfrac{x-a}{b-a}dx + \int_b^c \dfrac{c-x}{c-b}dx} = \frac{a+b+c}{3} \text{ and }$$

$$y_0\left(\tilde{A}\right) = \frac{\int_0^1 y\left[c - \left(c-b\right)y\right]dy - \int_0^1 y\left[a + \left(b-a\right)y\right]dy}{\int_0^1\left[c - \left(c-b\right)y\right]dy - \int_0^1\left[a + \left(b-a\right)y\right]dy} = \frac{1}{3}.$$

Thus the defuzzified value of the TFN $\tilde{A}$ is

$$DV\left(\tilde{A}\right) = \sqrt{x_0\left(\tilde{A}\right)^2 + y_0\left(\tilde{A}\right)^2} = \frac{1}{3}\sqrt{\left(a+b+c\right)^2 + 1}.$$

Fuzzy Random Variable

Let X be a continuous random variable with probability density function $f(x, v)$, where v is a parameter describing the density function. If v is considered as FN $\tilde{v}$, then X becomes a fuzzily described random variable $\tilde{X}$ with density function $f(x, \tilde{v})$. A FRV $\tilde{X}$ on a probability space $(\mathbb{C}, \mid, P)$ is a fuzzy valued function $\tilde{X}: \Omega \to \Phi_0(\mathbb{R})$, $\omega \to X_\omega$ such that for every Borel set B of $\mathbb{R}$ and for every $\pm \in (0,1]$, $(\tilde{X}[\alpha])^{-1}(B) \in \Phi$, where $\Phi_0(\mathbb{R})$ and $\tilde{X}[\alpha]$ are the set of FNs and the set valued function, respectively. The set valued function, $\tilde{X}[\alpha]$, has the form $X[\alpha]: \mathbb{C} \to 2^\mathbb{R}$, $\omega \to X_\omega[\alpha] = \{x \in \mathbb{R} : X_\omega(x) \geq \alpha\}$. FRVs are found by using decomposition theorem on FNs as $X = \bigcup_{\alpha \in (0,1]} \alpha \cdot \tilde{X}[\alpha]$.

Fuzzy Random Variable Following Normal Distribution

Let X be a random variable following normal distribution. Then the density function of the random variable X is given by

$$f(x\ ; m, \sigma) = \frac{1}{\sqrt{2\pi}\sigma} e^{-\frac{(x-m)^2}{2\sigma^2}}, -\infty \leq x \leq \infty$$

where the parameters m is the mean and σ is the standard deviation of the normally distributed random variable X.

In real life situation, the parameters of the normally distributed random variable X may not be found accurately. So these parameters of the random variable X are represented by FNs. Then the random variable becomes a FRV $\tilde{X}$ with parameters $\tilde{m}$ and $\tilde{\sigma}$. Thus the normal density function $f(x\ ; \tilde{m}, \tilde{\sigma})$ for fuzzily described random variable $\tilde{X}$ is given as:

$$f(x\ ; \tilde{m}, \tilde{\sigma}) = \frac{1}{\sqrt{2\pi}t} e^{-\frac{(x-s)^2}{2t^2}},$$

where the support of $\tilde{X}$ is defined on the set of real numbers; $s \in \tilde{m}[\alpha]$ and $t \in \tilde{\sigma}[\alpha]$; $\tilde{m}[\alpha]$ and $\tilde{\sigma}[\alpha]$ are the α –cut of the FN $\tilde{m}$ and $\tilde{\sigma}$ respectively. The fuzzy parameter $\tilde{m}$ is the mean and $\tilde{\sigma}^2$ is the variance of the FRV $\tilde{X}$.

Joint Probability Distribution Following Cauchy Distribution

It is already clarified that in almost every real-life decision making problems, the parameters of the random variable X are not found precisely. Hence the parameters of the random variable X are considered as FNs. Now let $\tilde{\lambda}$ and $\tilde{\beta}$ be considered as two FNs representing the respective median and the scale parameters of the Cauchy distributed random variable $\tilde{X}$. Then the Cauchy density function $f\left(x \; ; \tilde{\beta} \; , \tilde{\lambda}\right)$ for fuzzily described random variable $\tilde{X}$ with fuzzy parameters $\tilde{\beta}$ and $\tilde{\lambda}$ is expressed as

$$f\left(x; \; \tilde{\beta}, \tilde{\lambda}\right) = \frac{t}{\pi\left[t^2 + \left(x - s\right)^2\right]},$$

where the support of $\tilde{X}$ is defined on the set of real numbers ; $t \in \tilde{\beta}\left[\alpha\right], s \in \tilde{\lambda}\left[\alpha\right]$; $\tilde{\beta}\left[\alpha\right], \tilde{\lambda}\left[\alpha\right]$ being the α –cut of the FNs $\tilde{\beta} \; , \tilde{\lambda}$, respectively.

Also, in practical situation it is often seen that more than one random variable are required simultaneously. Thus if $\tilde{X}$ and $\tilde{Y}$ be two independent continuous Cauchy distributed FRVs with joint probability distribution, then the probability density function of the FRV $\left(\tilde{X}, \tilde{Y}\right)$ is

$$f\left(x, y; \tilde{\beta}_1, \tilde{\lambda}_1, \tilde{\beta}_2, \tilde{\lambda}_2\right) = f\left(x; \tilde{\beta}_1, \tilde{\lambda}_1\right) \times f\left(y; \tilde{\beta}_2, \tilde{\lambda}_2\right) = \frac{t}{\pi\left[t^2 + \left(x - s\right)^2\right]} \times \frac{v}{\pi\left[v^2 + \left(x - u\right)^2\right]}$$

wherethesupportof $\tilde{X}$ and $\tilde{Y}$ aredefinedonthesetofrealnumbers; $t \in \tilde{\beta}_1\left[\alpha\right], s \in \tilde{\lambda}_1\left[\alpha\right], v \in \tilde{\beta}_2\left[\alpha\right], u \in \tilde{\lambda}_2\left[\alpha\right]$; $\tilde{\beta}_i\left[\alpha\right], \tilde{\lambda}_i\left[\alpha\right]$ being the α –cut of the FNs $\tilde{\beta}_i \; , \tilde{\lambda}_i$; $\left(i = 1, 2\right)$ respectively.

MAIN FOCUS OF THE CHAPTER

The main focus of this chapter is to develop FGP methodology for solving MOSLP problems in hybrid fuzzy environment and to apply the developed methodology in the field of business intelligence so as to achieve a solution which is most acceptable to all the decision makers in a production planning environment. Depending on the nature of different parameters associated with the APP problems, some of them are considered as FRVs following different types of probability distributions and others are considered as different types of FNs. The CCP technique is applied to convert the fuzzy stochastic problem into a fuzzy multiobjective programming problem. Defuzzification of FNs is then used to find the equivalent multiobjective model in deterministic form. Finally, FGP technique is used to achieve the most acceptable solution in the decision making contexts. Thus the methodology presented in this chapter can efficiently achieve most satisfactory compromise solution of the objectives so that this developed methodology can be implemented effectively to different organizational fields.

With the consideration of the above ideas the fuzzy probabilistic multiobjective linear programming model which articulate multiobjective APP model is derived in the following section.

FUZZY PROBABILISTIC MULTIOBJECTIVE LINEAR PROGRAMMING MODEL FORMULATION

A FMOLSP problem having multiple objectives with parameters as normally distributed FRVs and the chance constraints, involved with joint Cauchy distributed FRVs as right sided parameters is presented as

$$\text{Max / Min } \tilde{Z}_k \cong \sum_{j=1}^{n} \tilde{c}_{kj} x_j; \ k = 1, 2, \dots, K$$

subject to

$$\Pr\left(\sum_{j=1}^{n} \tilde{a}_{1j} x_j \le \tilde{b}_1, \sum_{j=1}^{n} \tilde{a}_{2j} x_j \le \tilde{b}_2, \dots, \sum_{j=1}^{n} \tilde{a}_{mj} x_j \le \tilde{b}_m \right) \ge 1 - \gamma$$

$$x_j \ge 0; \ j = 1, 2, \dots, n \tag{1}$$

where $\tilde{a}_{ij} \left(i = 1, 2, \dots, m \ ; j = 1, 2, \dots, n \right)$ are TFNs, $\tilde{c}_{kj} \left(k = 1, 2, \dots, K \ ; j = 1, 2, \dots, n \right)$ are normally distributed FRVs and $\tilde{b}_i \left(i = 1, 2, \dots, m \right)$ are independent Cauchy distributed FRVs. The parameters $\tilde{\lambda}_i, \tilde{\beta}_i \left(i = 1, 2, \dots, m \right)$ of the Cauchy FRVs $\tilde{b}_i \left(i = 1, 2, \dots, m \right)$ and the mean $E\left(\tilde{c}_{kj} \right) = m_{\tilde{c}_{kj}} \left(k = 1, 2, \dots, K \ ; j = 1, 2, \dots, n \right)$ of the normally distributed FRVs $\tilde{c}_{kj} \left(k = 1, 2, \dots, K \ ; j = 1, 2, \dots, n \right)$ are taken as FNs. The probabilistic constraints in (1) is a joint probabilistic constraint with a specified probability level $\gamma \in \mathbb{R}$ with $0 \le \gamma \le 1$.

Construction of Fuzzy E: Model of Objectives

The parameters $\tilde{c}_{kj} \left(k = 1, 2, \dots, K \ ; j = 1, 2, \dots, n \right)$ of all the objectives are considered as normally distributed FRVs. Let the mean $E\left(\tilde{c}_{kj} \right) = m_{\tilde{c}_{kj}} \left(k = 1, 2, \dots, K \ ; j = 1, 2, \dots, n \right)$ associated with FRVs $\tilde{c}_{kj} \left(k = 1, 2, \dots, K \ ; j = 1, 2, \dots, n \right)$ be considered as TFNs. Considering the expectation of all the parameters of the objectives, the fuzzy E - model of the objectives can be presented as

$$\text{Max / Min } E(\tilde{Z}_k) \cong \sum_{j=1}^{n} E\left(\tilde{c}_{kj} \right) x_j; \ k = 1, 2, \dots, K \tag{2}$$

FP Model Derivation

Now the joint probability constraints in (1) is expressed as

$$\Pr\left(\sum_{j=1}^{n}\tilde{a}_{1j}x_j \leq \tilde{b}_1 ,\sum_{j=1}^{n}\tilde{a}_{2j}x_j \leq \tilde{b}_2 ,....,\sum_{j=1}^{n}\tilde{a}_{mj}x_j \leq \tilde{b}_m\right) \geq 1 - \gamma$$

i.e. $\prod_{i=1}^{m}\Pr\left(\sum_{j=1}^{n}\tilde{a}_{ij}x_j \leq \tilde{b}_i\right) \geq 1 - \gamma$

i.e. $\prod_{i=1}^{m}\Pr\left(\tilde{A}_i \leq \tilde{b}_i\right) \geq 1 - \gamma$, where $\tilde{A}_i = \sum_{j=1}^{n}\tilde{a}_{ij}x_j$

i.e. $\prod_{i=1}^{m}\left\{\frac{1}{\pi}\int_{u_i}^{\infty}\frac{t}{t^2 + (b_i - s)^2}\,db_i \;:t \in \tilde{\beta}_i[\alpha], s \in \tilde{\lambda}_i[\alpha], u_i \in \tilde{A}_i[\alpha]\right\} \geq 1 - \gamma$

i.e. $\prod_{i=1}^{m}\left(\frac{\pi}{2} - \tan^{-1}\frac{(u_i - s)}{t}\right) \geq \pi^m(1 - \gamma)$

Since the above inequality is valid for all $\alpha \in (0,1]$, the expression can be written in terms of $\alpha - cut$ as

$$\prod_{i=1}^{m}\left(\frac{\pi}{2} - \tan^{-1}\frac{\left(\tilde{A}_i[\alpha] - \tilde{\lambda}_i[\alpha]\right)}{\tilde{\beta}_i[\alpha]}\right) \geq \pi^m(1 - \gamma) \tag{3}$$

Now using first decomposition theorem, the above expression reduced to the following form as

$$\text{i.e.}\prod_{i=1}^{m}\left(\frac{\pi}{2} - \tan^{-1}\frac{\left(\sum_{j=1}^{n}\tilde{a}_{ij}x_j - \tilde{\lambda}_i\right)}{\tilde{\beta}_i}\right) \geq \pi^m(1 - \gamma) \tag{4}$$

Hence the FMOLSP model (1), is converted into its equivalent FP model by using the derived methodology as

$$\text{Max / Min } E(\tilde{Z}_k) \cong \sum_{j=1}^{n}E\left(\tilde{c}_{kj}\right)x_j; \; k = 1,2,...,K$$

subject to

$$\prod_{i=1}^{m}\left[\frac{\pi}{2}-\tan^{-1}\frac{\left(\sum_{j=1}^{n}\tilde{a}_{ij}x_{j}-\tilde{\lambda}_{i}\right)}{\tilde{\beta}_{i}}\right]\geq\pi^{m}\left(1-\gamma\right)$$

$$x_{j}\geq 0;\ j=1,2,...,n\ . \tag{5}$$

where $E\left(\tilde{c}_{kj}\right)$, $\tilde{a}_{ij}$, $\tilde{\lambda}_{i}$, $\tilde{\beta}_{i}$ ($k=1,2,...,K$; $i=1,2,...,m$; $j=1,2,...,n$) are all TFNs.

Development of Deterministic Model

In this subsection, the deterministic model of the above defined FP model (5) is developed by applying the method of defuzzification of FNs. Since $E\left(\tilde{c}_{kj}\right)$, $\tilde{a}_{ij}$, $\tilde{\lambda}_{i}$, $\tilde{\beta}_{i}$ ($k=1,2,...,K$; $i=1,2,...,m$; $j=1,2,...,n$) are taken as TFNs, thus these FNs are expressed as

$$E\left(\tilde{c}_{kj}\right)=\left(E\left(c_{kj}^{L}\right),E\left(c_{kj}\right),E\left(c_{kj}^{R}\right)\right),\ \tilde{a}_{ij}=\left(a_{ij}^{L},a_{ij},a_{ij}^{R}\right),\ \tilde{\lambda}_{i}=\left(\lambda_{i}^{L},\lambda_{i},\lambda_{i}^{R}\right),\ \tilde{\beta}_{i}=\left(\beta_{i}^{L},\beta_{i},\beta_{i}^{R}\right)$$

where the superscript $"R"$ denotes the right tolerance and the superscript $"L"$ denotes the left tolerance of the TFNs.

The crisp values of these FNs are obtained as described by

$$DV\left(E\left(\tilde{c}_{kj}\right)\right)=\frac{1}{3}\sqrt{\left(E\left(c_{kj}^{L}\right)+E\left(c_{kj}\right)+E\left(c_{kj}^{R}\right)\right)^{2}+1}\ ;\ k=1,2,...,K\ ;\ j=1,2,...,n$$

$$DV\left(\tilde{a}_{ij}\right)=\frac{1}{3}\sqrt{\left(a_{ij}^{L}+a_{ij}+a_{ij}^{R}\right)^{2}+1}\ ;\ i=1,2,...,m\ ;\ j=1,2,...,n$$

$$DV\left(\tilde{\lambda}_{i}\right)=\frac{1}{3}\sqrt{\left(\lambda_{i}^{L}+\lambda_{i}+\lambda_{i}^{R}\right)^{2}+1}\ ;\ i=1,2,...,m$$

$$DV\left(\tilde{\beta}_{i}\right)=\frac{1}{3}\sqrt{\left(\beta_{i}^{L}+\beta_{i}+\beta_{i}^{R}\right)^{2}+1}\ ;\ i=1,2,...,m$$

Thus, the equivalent deterministic model of the FP problem (5) can be stated as

$$\text{Max / Min}\ DV\left(E(\tilde{Z}_{k})\right)=\sum_{j=1}^{n}DV\left(E\left(\tilde{c}_{kj}\right)\right)x_{j}\ ;\ k=1,2,...,K$$

subject to

$$\prod_{i=1}^{m}\left(\frac{\pi}{2}-\tan^{-1}\frac{\left(\sum_{j=1}^{n}DV\left(\tilde{a}_{ij}\right)x_{j}-DV\left(\tilde{\lambda}_{i}\right)\right)}{DV\left(\tilde{\beta}_{i}\right)}\right)\geq\pi^{m}\left(1-\gamma\right)$$

$$x_{j}\geq0;\ j=1,2,...,n\,.\tag{6}$$

The deterministic equivalence model can be expressed as

$$\text{Max / Min }DV\left(E(\tilde{Z}_{k})\right)=\sum_{j=1}^{n}\frac{1}{3}\sqrt{\left(E\left(c_{kj}^{L}\right)+E\left(c_{kj}\right)+E\left(c_{kj}^{R}\right)\right)^{2}+1}x_{j};\ k=1,2,...,K$$

subject to

$$\prod_{i=1}^{m}\left(\frac{\pi}{2}-\tan^{-1}\frac{\left(\sum_{j=1}^{n}\frac{1}{3}\sqrt{\left(a_{ij}^{L}+a_{ij}+a_{ij}^{R}\right)^{2}+1}x_{j}-\frac{1}{3}\sqrt{\left(\lambda_{i}^{L}+\lambda_{i}+\lambda_{i}^{R}\right)^{2}+1}\right)}{\frac{1}{3}\sqrt{\left(\beta_{i}^{L}+\beta_{i}+\beta_{i}^{R}\right)^{2}+1}}\right)\geq\pi^{m}\left(1-\gamma\right)$$

$$x_{j}\geq0;\ j=1,2,...,n\,.\tag{7}$$

In an optimization problem, the DMs specify the fuzzy goals of each objective on the basis of their aspiration level which is obtained when each objective is solved individually under the system constraints defined in Model (7). The aspiration or target level of the objectives are depends on the maximization or minimization types of objectives.

Fuzzy Goals for Maximization Type of Objectives

In a maximization type problem, the DMs specify the fuzzy goals in such a manner that the value of objectives should be substantially greater than or equal to some assigned value. To obtain the aspiration level to the fuzzy goals, each objective is solved independently under the modified set of system constraints. Let $DV\left(E(\tilde{Z}_{k})\right)^{b}$ (maximum) and $DV\left(E(\tilde{Z}_{k})\right)^{w}$ (minimum) ; $k=1,2,...,K$ be the best and worst values obtained by solving each objective independently. Hence the fuzzy objective goal for each of the objectives can be expressed as:

$$DV\left(E(\tilde{Z}_{k})\right)\gtrsim DV\left(E(\tilde{Z}_{k})\right)^{b}\text{ (maximum) for }k=1,2,...,K\tag{8}$$

Fuzzy Goals for Minimization Type of Objectives

In the case of minimization type problem, the DMs specify the fuzzy goals such that the value of the objectives should be substantially less than or equal to some assigned value. Each objective is now solved separately under the customized set of system constraints to achieve the desired target level to the fuzzy goals. Let $DV\left(E(\tilde{Z}_k)\right)^b$ (minimum) and $DV\left(E(\tilde{Z}_k)\right)^w$ (maximum); $k = 1, 2, ..., K$ be the best and worst values of the $k-$th objective obtained as described above. Hence the fuzzy objective goal for each of the objectives can be expressed as:

$$DV\left(E(\tilde{Z}_k)\right) \precsim DV\left(E(\tilde{Z}_k)\right)^b \text{ (minimum) for } k = 1, 2, ..., K \tag{9}$$

Construction of Membership Functions

The above defined fuzzy goals can be quantified by eliciting the corresponding membership functions of each objective on the basis of its best and worst values obtained by solving each objective independently under the modified set of system constraints. Thus, the membership function for each of the objectives can be written as:

$$\mu_{DV\left(E(\tilde{Z}_k)\right)}\left(x\right) = \begin{cases} 0 & DV\left(E(\tilde{Z}_k)\right) \leq DV\left(E(\tilde{Z}_k)\right)^w \\ \dfrac{DV\left(E(\tilde{Z}_k)\right) - DV\left(E(\tilde{Z}_k)\right)^w}{DV\left(E(\tilde{Z}_k)\right)^b - DV\left(E(\tilde{Z}_k)\right)^w} & DV\left(E(\tilde{Z}_k)\right)^w \leq DV\left(E(\tilde{Z}_k)\right) \leq DV\left(E(\tilde{Z}_k)\right)^b \; ; \\ 1 & DV\left(E(\tilde{Z}_k)\right) \geq DV\left(E(\tilde{Z}_k)\right)^b \end{cases}$$

$k = 1, 2, .., K$ (for maximizing type of objectives) $\tag{10}$

Or

$$\mu_{DV\left(E(\tilde{Z}_k)\right)}\left(x\right) = \begin{cases} 0 & DV\left(E(\tilde{Z}_k)\right) \geq DV\left(E(\tilde{Z}_k)\right)^w \\ \dfrac{DV\left(E(\tilde{Z}_k)\right)^w - DV\left(E(\tilde{Z}_k)\right)}{DV\left(E(\tilde{Z}_k)\right)^w - DV\left(E(\tilde{Z}_k)\right)^b} & DV\left(E(\tilde{Z}_k)\right)^b \leq DV\left(E(\tilde{Z}_k)\right) \leq DV\left(E(\tilde{Z}_k)\right)^w \; ; \\ 1 & DV\left(E(\tilde{Z}_k)\right) \leq DV\left(E(\tilde{Z}_k)\right)^b \end{cases}$$

$k = 1, 2, .., K$ (for minimizing type of objectives) $\tag{11}$

Considering the above membership functions, the FGP model is derived in the following subsection.

FGP MODEL FORMULATION

In FGP model, achievement of above defined fuzzy goal to its aspired level means achievement of the associated membership function to its highest degree (unity). This is done by introducing under- and over- deviational variables to each of them. It may be mentioned here that in the case of a crisp goal either under- or over deviational variables or both of them are minimized to achieving the aspired level of the goal and that depends on the decision-making situation. But in case of achieving the aspired level of a fuzzy membership goal, any over-deviation from it means full achievement of the associated fuzzy goal (Dyson, 1981). As such, only under deviational variables are required to minimize for achieving the aspired levels of the membership goals to the extent possible in a fuzzy stochastic decision- making environment. Thus, the FGP model can be formulated as:

$$\text{Min D} = \sum_{k=1}^{K} w_k d_k^-$$

subject to

$$\mu_{DV\left(E(\tilde{Z}_k)\right)} + d_k^- - d_k^+ = 1 \,; \, \left(k = 1, 2, ..., K\right)$$

$$\prod_{i=1}^{m} \left(\frac{\pi}{2} - \tan^{-1} \frac{\left[\sum_{j=1}^{n} \frac{1}{3}\sqrt{\left(a_{ij}^L + a_{ij} + a_{ij}^R\right)^2 + 1} x_j - \frac{1}{3}\sqrt{\left(\lambda_i^L + \lambda_i + \lambda_i^R\right)^2 + 1} \right]}{\frac{1}{3}\sqrt{\left(\beta_i^L + \beta_i + \beta_i^R\right)^2 + 1}} \right) \geq \pi^m \left(1 - \gamma\right)$$

$$x_j \geq 0 \,; \, j = 1, 2, ..., n \,. \tag{12}$$

where $d_k^-, d_k^+ \geq 0$ and $d_k^- . d_k^+ = 0$ and $w_k, \left(k=1,2, ..K\right)$ are the fuzzy weights representing the relative importance of achieving the aspired levels of the goals in the decision making context with the values

$$w_k = \frac{1}{DV\left(E(\tilde{Z}_k)\right)^b - DV\left(E(\tilde{Z}_k)\right)^w} \,; \text{(for maximizing objectives) or}$$

$$w_k = \frac{1}{DV\left(E(\tilde{Z}_k)\right)^w - DV\left(E(\tilde{Z}_k)\right)^b} \,; \text{(for minimizing objectives) } k = 1, 2, ...K \tag{13}$$

The developed model (12) is solved to find the most satisfactory solution in a fuzzy stochastic decision making environment.

SOLUTION ALGORITHM

The methodology for describing the fuzzy multiobjective probabilistic programming model is summarized in the form of an algorithm as follows:

Step 1: Considering the expectation of all the parameters of the objectives following normal distribution the E-model of the objectives is generated.

Step 2: The CCP technique is applied to convert the probabilistic constraints into constraints involving only fuzzy parameters.

Step 3: On the basis of nature of the FNs, the multiobjective FP model are translated into multiobjective linear programming model.

Step 4: The individual best and worst values of each of the objectives is found in isolation under the modified set of system constraints.

Step 5: The fuzzy membership goals of each of the objectives are constructed on the basis of the aspiration level.

Step 6: The membership function for each type of objectives are developed depending on their best and worst values.

Step 7: FGP approach is used to achieve maximum degree of each of the membership goals.

Step 8: Stop.

AN ILLUSTRATIVE EXAMPLE

To demonstrate the efficiency and acceptability of the proposed approach, the following problem of a hypothetical health drinks manufacturing company is considered as a part of APP problems and solved.

A hypothetical health drinks manufacturing company produces three types of health drinks, viz., HD1, HD2 and HD3, say. Those health drinks are characterized according to the proportion of minerals contain in it. HD1 contains about 2 gms of potassium and about 1 gm of calcium, HD2 contains about 1 gm of potassium and about 2 gms of calcium, and HD3 contains about 2 gms of potassium and about 4 gms of calcium per 100 gms, respectively. It is assumed that the cost of making HD1, HD2 and HD3 are uncertain. It depends on the price of different minerals. Also the selling price of the health drinks is uncertain. It depends on demands of the markets and production of other health drink manufacturing companies. Again, the times for producing health drinks are not certain. It depends on the number of labours and different machineries of the factory. So the parameters representing production cost, selling price of the health drinks and time for manufacturing health drinks are considered as normally distributed FRVs with known mean and variances. Further it is assumed that the daily requirements of potassium and calcium are represented using FRVs $\tilde{b}_1$ and $\tilde{b}_2$ following joint Cauchy distribution with known fuzzy parameters $\tilde{\lambda}_1 = \widetilde{15}$, $\tilde{\beta}_1 = \tilde{8}$ and $\tilde{\lambda}_2 = \widetilde{18}$, $\tilde{\beta}_2 = \tilde{9}$ for FRVs $\tilde{b}_1$ and $\tilde{b}_2$ respectively. Also depending on the previous statistical data the managing director of the company ensure that about 11 kgs of HD1, about 11 kgs of HD2 and about 10 kgs of HD3 are needed in a week on the different markets. Considering all these assumptions the company wants to:

1.   Minimize the total manufacturing cost

2. Minimize the total production time
3. Maximize the total profit of the organization

The following terms are used to convert the production planning problem into the proposed FMOLSP model.

Index Set

$i = $ types of health drinks HDi; $i = 1, 2, 3$

Objectives

Three objectives of this study are to minimize total manufacturing cost, total production time and to maximize total profit which are presented below:

$\tilde{Z}_1 = $ total manufacturing cost (in Rs.)

$\tilde{Z}_2 = $ total production time (in hrs.)

$\tilde{Z}_3 = $ total selling price (in Rs.)

Decision Variable

$x_i = $ amount of $i-$th health drinks to be produced by the health drinks manufacturing companies; (in kg.)

Fuzzy Random Variable

It is already mentioned that in APP the manufacturing costs of health drinks are uncertain due to the fluctuating price of minerals and price of health drinks specified by other manufacturing companies. Also, the production time of each health drinks are uncertain as it depends on the number of labours and different machineries. Again, the selling price of the health drinks depends on the demands of the products on the markets and the selling price of the health drinks of the other manufacturers. Thus, the parameters representing production cost, selling price of the health drinks and time for manufacturing health drinks are considered as normally distributed FRVs. Finally, as the daily requirement of potassium and calcium are not fixed so these are considered as Cauchy distributed FRVs.

$\widetilde{PC}_i = $ production cost of the $i-$th health drink produced by the hypothetical manufacturing company which is normally distributed; $(i = 1, 2, 3)$ (in Rs./ gm)

$\widetilde{SP}_i = $ selling price of the $i-$th health drink produced by the hypothetical manufacturing company which also follows normal distribution; $(i = 1, 2, 3)$ (in Rs./ gm)

$\widetilde{TMH}_i$ = time required for manufacturing i – th health drink produced by the companies which is normally distributed; $(i = 1, 2, 3)$ (in hrs./ kg.)

$\widetilde{PR}$ = daily requirement of potassium which is Cauchy distributed; (in gm.)

$\widetilde{CP}$ = daily requirement of calcium which also follows Cauchy distribution; (in gm.)

Fuzzy Parameters

The amounts of ingredients required in the health drinks are considered as FNs. It may be fluctuating i.e. some amounts of vagueness may exist in the quantities of the ingredients in APP problem. Therefore some kinds of possibilistic uncertainty may occur. Thus for more acceptability in real life the parameters representing the amounts of minerals in health drinks are considered as FNs.

$\widetilde{AP}_i$ = amount of potassium in the i – th health drink; $(i = 1, 2, 3)$ (in gm.)

$\widetilde{AC}_i$ = amount of calcium in the i – th health drink; $(i = 1, 2, 3)$ (in gm.)

Thus the FMOLSP model for the health drinks manufacturing industry is formulated as follows:

$$\text{Min } \tilde{Z}_1 \cong \sum_{i=1}^{3} \widetilde{PC}_i x_i$$

$$\text{Min } \tilde{Z}_2 \cong \sum_{i=1}^{3} \widetilde{TMH}_i x_i$$

$$\text{Max } \tilde{Z}_3 \cong \sum_{i=1}^{3} \widetilde{SP}_i x_i$$

subject to

$$\Pr\left(\sum_{i=1}^{3} \widetilde{AP}_i x_i \leq \widetilde{PR}, \sum_{i=1}^{3} \widetilde{AC}_i x_i \leq \widetilde{CP}\right) \geq 1 - \gamma$$

$$x_i \geq 0 \, ; \, i = 1, 2, 3 \tag{14}$$

Here $\widetilde{PC}_i, \widetilde{TMH}_i, \widetilde{SP}_i \, (i = 1, 2, 3)$ are normally distributed FRVs, $\widetilde{PR}, \widetilde{CP}$ are Cauchy distributed FRVs, and $\widetilde{AP}_i, \widetilde{AC}_i \, (i = 1, 2, 3)$ are TFNs.

Taking the expectation of all the parameters of the objectives and applying the CCP technique, the FP model is evaluated as

$$\text{Min } E\left(\tilde{Z}_1\right) \cong \sum_{i=1}^{3} E\left(\widetilde{PC}_i\right) x_i$$

$$\text{Min } E\left(\tilde{Z}_2\right) \cong \sum_{i=1}^{3} E\left(\widetilde{TMH}_i\right) x_i$$

$$\text{Max } E\left(\tilde{Z}_3\right) \cong \sum_{i=1}^{3} E\left(\widetilde{SP}_i\right) x_i$$

Subject to

$$\left[\frac{\pi}{2} - \tan^{-1} \frac{\left(\sum_{i=1}^{3} \widetilde{AP}_i x_i - \tilde{\lambda}_1\right)}{\tilde{\beta}_1}\right]\left[\frac{\pi}{2} - \tan^{-1} \frac{\left(\sum_{i=1}^{3} \widetilde{AC}_i x_i - \tilde{\lambda}_2\right)}{\tilde{\beta}_2}\right] \geq \pi^2 \left(1 - \gamma\right)$$

$$x_i \geq 0 \,;\, i = 1, 2, 3 \tag{15}$$

The expectation $E\left(\widetilde{PC}_i\right)$, $E\left(\widetilde{TMH}_i\right)$, $E\left(\widetilde{SP}_i\right)$ of the normally distributed FRVs $\widetilde{PC}_i, \widetilde{TMH}_i, \widetilde{SP}_i$ $(i = 1, 2, 3)$, the parameters $\tilde{\lambda}_1$, $\tilde{\beta}_1$ of the Cauchy distributed FRV $\widetilde{PR}$ and the parameters $\tilde{\lambda}_2$, $\tilde{\beta}_2$ of the Cauchy distributed FRV $\widetilde{CP}$ are taken as TFNs.

The values of the parameters are given in the following Table 1, Table 2, and Table 3.

Applying the defuzzification technique of FNs the deterministic equivalent of FP model (15) is formulated. As described in the solution algorithm the objectives of the deterministic model are solved under the system constraints to find the best and worst values of the objectives.

The best and worst values of the objectives are shown in the following Table 4.

Table 1. Values of the expectation of normally distributed FRVs

$E\left(\widetilde{PC}_i\right)$ (Rs./gm)	$E\left(\widetilde{TMH}_i\right)$ (hrs./gm)	$E\left(\widetilde{SP}_i\right)$ (Rs./gm)
$E\left(\widetilde{PC}_1\right) = \tilde{4} = \left(3.95, 4, 4.05\right)$	$E\left(\widetilde{TMH}_1\right) = \tilde{3} = \left(2.95, 3, 3.05\right)$	$E\left(\widetilde{SP}_1\right) = \tilde{5} = \left(4.5, 5, 5.5\right)$
$E\left(\widetilde{PC}_2\right) = \tilde{3} = \left(2.5, 3, 3.5\right)$	$E\left(\widetilde{TMH}_2\right) = \tilde{2} = \left(1.55, 2, 2.45\right)$	$E\left(\widetilde{SP}_2\right) = \tilde{4} = \left(3.95, 4, 4.05\right)$
$E\left(\widetilde{PC}_3\right) = \tilde{6} = \left(5.8, 6, 6.2\right)$	$E\left(\widetilde{TMH}_3\right) = \tilde{4} = \left(3, 4, 5\right)$	$E\left(\widetilde{SP}_3\right) = \widetilde{6.5} = \left(6, 6.5, 7\right)$

Table 2. Values of median and scale parameters of Cauchy distributed FRVs

Random variable	Scale parameter $\tilde{\beta}_i$	Median $\tilde{\lambda}_i$
$\widetilde{PR}$	$\tilde{\beta}_1 = \left(7.95, 8, 8.05\right)$	$\tilde{\lambda}_1 = \left(14.5, 15, 15.5\right)$
$\widetilde{CP}$	$\tilde{\beta}_2 = \left(8.9, 9, 9.1\right)$	$\tilde{\lambda}_2 = \left(16, 18, 20\right)$

Table 3. Values of the parameters of the constraints

Constraints	Amounts of potassium and calcium in health drinks (gm)
1st constraint	*Amounts of potassium (gm)* $\widetilde{AP}_1 = \tilde{2} = \left(1.95, 2, 2.05\right),\ \widetilde{AP}_2 = \tilde{1} = \left(0.95, 1, 1.05\right)$ $\widetilde{AP}_3 = \tilde{2} = \left(1.5, 2, 2.5\right)$
2nd constraint	*Amounts of calcium (gm)* $\widetilde{AC}_1 = \tilde{1} = \left(0.5, 1, 1.5\right),\ \widetilde{AC}_2 = \tilde{2} = \left(1.95, 2, 2.05\right)$ $\widetilde{AC}_3 = \tilde{4} = \left(3.85, 4, 4.15\right)$

Table 4. Best and worst solution of the objectives

Objectives	Best Solution	Worst Solution
$\tilde{Z}_1$ (total manufacturing cost in Rs.)	$DV\left(E(\tilde{Z}_1)\right)^b = 111060$	$DV\left(E(\tilde{Z}_1)\right)^w = 131510$
$\tilde{Z}_2$ (total production time in hrs.)	$DV\left(E(\tilde{Z}_2)\right)^b = 74.62$	$DV\left(E(\tilde{Z}_2)\right)^w = 95.70$
$\tilde{Z}_3$ (total selling price in Rs.)	$DV\left(E(\tilde{Z}_3)\right)^b = 144930$	$DV\left(E(\tilde{Z}_3)\right)^w = 132780$

Finally, FGP technique is used to find the most compromise and acceptable solution of all the objectives. The compromise solution obtained by applying the proposed methodology are shown in the following Table 5.

The Comparison between the compromise solution and best solution are shown in the following diagram.

From this diagram, it is very much clear that the compromise solution of all the objectives is very close to their best solution values. Thus, solution obtained by applying the proposed methodology is acceptable to the organizations. Also from the solution obtained it is clear that the total production cost

Table 5. Compromise solution of the objectives

Objectives	Solution Point	Compromise Solution	Membership Value
total manufacturing cost (in Rs.)	$x_1 = 8.71$ $x_2 = 11.00$ $x_3 = 8.14$	$DV\left(E(\tilde{Z}_1)\right) = 116680$	$\mu_{DV\left(E(\tilde{Z}_1)\right)} = 0.72$
total production time (in hrs.)		$DV\left(E(\tilde{Z}_2)\right) = 80.66$	$\mu_{DV\left(E(\tilde{Z}_2)\right)} = 0.71$
total selling price (in Rs.)		$DV\left(E(\tilde{Z}_3)\right) = 140460$	$\mu_{DV\left(E(\tilde{Z}_3)\right)} = 0.64$

Figure 3. Comparison between the best, worst and compromise solutions

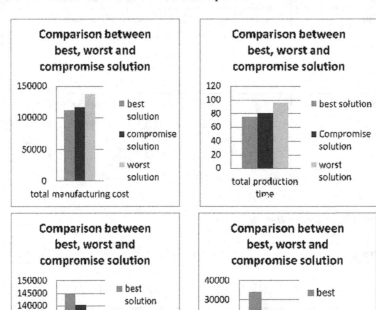

of the organization is Rs.1,16,680. The total time for manufacturing the health drinks is 80.66 hrs. and the total selling price of the products is Rs.1,40,460. Thus, the profit of the organization is Rs.23,780. This result indicates that the organization will make a good amount of profit in a very competitive market situation which is one of the most important goals of organization.

In this chapter, it is assumed that the FRVs involved with the right sided parameters of the constraints of the fuzzy stochastic model are jointly distributed, as in real life almost every constraint is occurred simultaneously.

Now, the proposed APP model is solved using FGP technique considering all the constraints appeared separately instead of considering joint distribution to establish the efficiency of the proposed model.

It is observed that with joint probability distribution the achieved solutions are more acceptable to the DMs than the model with constraints occurred separately.

The compromise solution obtained are shown in the following Table 6.

From Table 6, it is clear that the total production cost of the organization is Rs. 1,21,656. The total time for manufacturing the health drinks is 84.25 hrs. and the total selling price of the products is Rs. 1,38,560. Thus, the total profit of the organization is calculated as Rs.16904.

From this comparison, it is seen that if the APP problem be solved by taking the FRVs jointly then the total production cost increases, total time for manufacturing the health drinks increases and the total selling price decreases.

The compromise solution obtained is compared to the compromise solution obtained by the methodology developed in this chapter. The comparison is shown by the following bar diagram.

From this result, it is clear that the solution obtained by the methodology described in this chapter provides better result than the solution obtained by considering the constraints separately. This result is more realistic as it agrees with the situation that happens in real life complex decision making situation.

Table 6. Compromise solution of the objectives

Objectives	Solution Point	Compromise Solution	Membership Value
total manufacturing cost (in Rs.)	$x_1 = 8.5$ $x_2 = 10.09$ $x_3 = 9.5$	$DV\left(E(\tilde{Z}_1)\right) = 121656$	$\mu_{DV\left(E(\tilde{Z}_1)\right)} = 0.70$
total production time (in hrs.)		$DV\left(E(\tilde{Z}_2)\right) = 84.25$	$\mu_{DV\left(E(\tilde{Z}_2)\right)} = 0.65$
total selling price (in Rs.)		$DV\left(E(\tilde{Z}_3)\right) = 138560$	$\mu_{DV\left(E(\tilde{Z}_3)\right)} = 0.61$

Figure 4. Comparison between the solutions

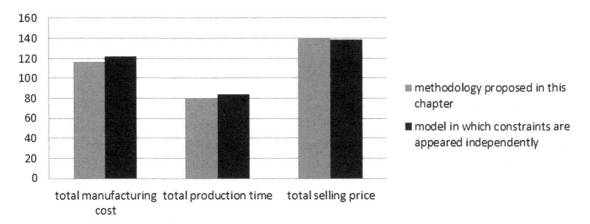

FUTURE RESEARCH DIRECTIONS

The model developed in this chapter may be extended in the following directions for the future research work:

- In this chapter the model is developed with parameters taken as TFNs. Researchers can extend the developed model by taking the parameters as other form of FNs such as trapezoidal FNs, one sided FNs, Gaussian FNs, etc. Also in this chapter defuzzification method of FN using centroid point of the FNs is used. Therefore, in future, researchers can apply other defuzzified methods instead of centroid method of FNs.
- In this chapter the expectation of all the parameters of the objectives are considered as these are all FRVs. Instead of taking the expectation, the variance of the FRVs can also be considered. In that case the minimization of the variance model should be taken. Thus, it is an alternative direction in which further research work may be continued.
- In this chapter the parameters of the objectives are taken as normally distributed FRVs and the right sided parameters of the constraints are taken as Cauchy distributed FRVs. Therefore, in future the developed methodology can be extended by taking FRV with other probability distributions.
- Methodological development of mathematical model with intuitionistic FNs was at an early stage. Therefore, implementation of intuitionistic FNs in this methodology is very interesting topic for further research.
- Fuzzy stochastic multiobjective programming problem with parameters as type-II FNs are yet to be widely circulated in the literature. Methodological developments in hybrid fuzzy environment fields with type-II FNs are necessary due to its massive applicability in the real life decision making problems.
- In this chapter the compromising solution of the objectives are obtained in applying weighted FGP technique. In further research study the researchers can apply priority based FGP technique, genetic algorithm technique as an alternative way of finding compromise solution of all the objectives.
- The methodologies developed in this chapter can be extended by implementing hesitant fuzzy set in this field. Mathematical programming problem with hesitant FN is yet to appear in the literature. Therefore, in future researchers can give their attention in this field.

CONCLUSION

In this chapter, an efficient solution technique for solving fuzzy multiobjective probabilistic APP problem with Cauchy distributed and normally distributed FRVs have been presented. The main advantage of this methodology is that is includes both uncertainties fuzziness and randomness simultaneously. Defuzzification technique of FNs has been used to develop an equivalent deterministic model from the fuzzy APP model. Based on FGP a compromise decision of the multiobjective APP problem is achieved. The proposed procedure can be extended to solve quadratic fuzzy multiobjective programming problems, fractional programming problems, bilevel / multilevel programming problems. Furthermore, the proposed methodology has been applied to a hypothetical case of health drinks manufacturing industry which is also an APP problem. The proposed mathematical model focused on total production cost, total selling price of the health drinks and total time for manufacturing health drinks of the organization. A result of the case study indicates that useful compromise solutions for production planning management have been generated and it emphasizes the validity and applicability of the proposed methodology. Finally, it is hoped that the methodological development of stochastic multiobjective programming in hybrid fuzzy environment and its application to APP problems may open new vistas in near future in stochastic fuzzy complex decision making environment.

REFERENCES

Abbasbandy, S., & Asady, B. (2006). Ranking of fuzzy numbers by sign distance. *Information Sciences*, *176*(16), 2405–2416. doi:10.1016/j.ins.2005.03.013

Abbasbandy, S., & Hajjari, T. (2009). A new approach for ranking of trapezoidal fuzzy numbers. *Computers & Mathematics with Applications (Oxford, England)*, *57*(3), 413–419. doi:10.1016/j.camwa.2008.10.090

Asady, B. (2010). *The revised method of ranking LR fuzzy number based on deviation degree*. Academic Press.

Barik, S. K., & Biswal, M. P. (2012). Probabilistic Quadratic Programming Problems with Some Fuzzy Parameters. *Advances in Operations Research*, *2012*, 1–13. doi:10.1155/2012/635282

Bellman, R. E., & Zadeh, L. A. (1970). Decision making in a fuzzy environment. *Management Science*, *17*(4), 141–164. doi:10.1287/mnsc.17.4.B141

Brandas, A. (2011). Approximation of fuzzy numbers by trapezoidal fuzzy numbers preserving the core the ambiguity and the value. *Advanced Studies in Contemporary Mathematics, 21*, 247-259.

Buxey, G. (1995). A managerial perspective on aggregate planning. *International Journal of Production Economics*, *41*(1-3), 127–133. doi:10.1016/0925-5273(94)00070-0

Charnes, A., & Cooper, W. W. (1959). Chance-constrained programming. *Management Science*, *6*(1), 73–79. doi:10.1287/mnsc.6.1.73

Chiang, J. (2001). Fuzzy linear programming based on statistical confidence interval and interval-valued fuzzy set. *European Journal of Operational Research*, *129*(1), 65–86. doi:10.1016/S0377-2217(99)00404-X

Contini, B. (1978). A stochastic approach to goal programming. *Operations Research*, *16*(3), 576–586. doi:10.1287/opre.16.3.576

Dai, C., Li, Y. P., & Huang, G. H. (2012). An interval-parameter chance-constrained dynamic programming approach for capacity planning under uncertainty. *Resources, Conservation and Recycling*, *62*, 37–50. doi:10.1016/j.resconrec.2012.02.010

Delgado, M., Vila, M. A., & Voxman, W. (1998). On a canonical representation of fuzzy number. *Fuzzy Sets and Systems*, *93*(1), 125–135. doi:10.1016/S0165-0114(96)00144-3

Filev, D. P., & Yager, R. R. (1991). A generalized defuzzification method via Bad Distribution. *International Journal of Intelligent Systems*, *6*(7), 687–697. doi:10.1002/int.4550060702

Ganesan, K., & Veeramani, P. (2006). Fuzzy linear programs with trapezoidal fuzzy numbers. *Annals of Operations Research, 143*(1), 305–315. doi:10.1007/s10479-006-7390-1

Gen, M., Tsujimura, Y., & Ida, K. (1992). Method for solving multi objective aggregate production planning problem with fuzzy parameters. *Computers & Industrial Engineering, 23*(1-4), 117–120. doi:10.1016/0360-8352(92)90077-W

Gomes da Silva, C., Figueira, J., Lisboa, J., & Barman, S. (2006). An interactive decision support system for an aggregate production planning model based on multiple criteria mixed integer linear programming. *Omega, 34*(2), 167–177. doi:10.1016/j.omega.2004.08.007

Hop, N. V. (2007). Solving fuzzy (stochastic) linear programming problems using superiority and inferiority measures. *Information Sciences, 177*(9), 1977–1991. doi:10.1016/j.ins.2006.12.001

Jain, A., & Palekar, U. S. (2005). Aggregate production planning for a continuous reconfigurable manufacturing process. *Computers & Operations Research, 32*(5), 1213–1236. doi:10.1016/j.cor.2003.11.001

Jamalnia, A., & Soukhakian, M. A. (2009). A hybrid fuzzy goal programming approach with different goal priorities to aggregate production planning. *Computers & Industrial Engineering, 56*(4), 1474–1486. doi:10.1016/j.cie.2008.09.010

Jamison, K. D., & Lodwick, W. A. (2001). Fuzzy linear programming using a penalty method. *Fuzzy Sets and Systems, 119*(1), 97–110. doi:10.1016/S0165-0114(99)00082-2

Jimenez, M., Arenas, M., Bilbao, A., & Rodrıguez, M. V. (2007). Linear programming with fuzzy parameters: An interactive method resolution. *European Journal of Operational Research, 177*(3), 1599–1609. doi:10.1016/j.ejor.2005.10.002

Kataoka, S. (1963). A stochastic programming model. *Econometrica, 31*(1/2), 181–196. doi:10.2307/1910956

Kumar, A., Singh, P., Kaur, P., & Kaur, A. (2011). A new approach for ranking of L-R type generalized fuzzy numbers. *Expert Systems with Applications, 38*(9), 10906–10910. doi:10.1016/j.eswa.2011.02.131

Lai, Y. J., & Hwang, C. L. (1992). *Fuzzy mathematical programming: methods and applications*. Berlin: Springer. doi:10.1007/978-3-642-48753-8

Lee, Y. Y. (1990). *Fuzzy set theory approach to aggregate production planning and inventory control* (Unpublished doctoral dissertation). Kansas State University.

Leon, T., & Vercher, E. (2004). Solving a class of fuzzy linear programs by using semi-infinite programming techniques. *Fuzzy Sets and Systems, 146*(2), 235–252. doi:10.1016/j.fss.2003.09.010

Leung, S. C. H., & Chan, S. S. W. (2009). A goal programming model for aggregate production planning with resource utilization constraint. *Computers & Industrial Engineering, 56*(3), 1053–1064. doi:10.1016/j.cie.2008.09.017

Leung, S. C. H., Wu, Y., & Lai, K. K. (2006). A stochastic programming approach for multi-site aggregate production planning. *The Journal of the Operational Research Society, 57*(2), 123–132. doi:10.1057/palgrave.jors.2601988

Liu, X. (2001). Measuring the satisfaction of constraints in fuzzy linear programming. *Fuzzy Sets and Systems, 122*(2), 263–275. doi:10.1016/S0165-0114(00)00114-7

Ma, M., Kandel, A., & Friedman, M. (2000). A new approach for defuzzification. *Fuzzy Sets and Systems, 111*(3), 351–356. doi:10.1016/S0165-0114(98)00176-6

Miller, L. B., & Wagner, H. (1965). Chance-Constrained Programming with Joint Constraints. *Operations Research, 13*(6), 930–945. doi:10.1287/opre.13.6.930

Mula, J., Poler, R., Garcia-Sabater, J. P., & Lario, F. C. (2006). Models for production planning under uncertainty: A review. *International Journal of Production Economics, 103*(1), 271–285. doi:10.1016/j.ijpe.2005.09.001

Nam, S. J., & Logendran, R. (1992). Aggregate production planning – a survey of models and methodologies. *European Journal of Operational Research, 61*(3), 255–272. doi:10.1016/0377-2217(92)90356-E

Panne, V. D., & Popp, W. (1963). Minimum Cost Cattle Feed under Probabilistic Protein Constraints. *Management Science, 9*(3), 405–430. doi:10.1287/mnsc.9.3.405

Prekopa, A. (1973). Contribution to the Theory of Stochastic Programming. *Management Science, 4*, 202–221.

Rinks, D. B. (1982). The performance of fuzzy algorithm models for aggregate planning and different cost structure. In M.M. Gupta & M.M. Sachez (Eds.), Approximate reasoning in decision analysis (pp.-267-278). Amsterdam: North-Holland.

Rommelfanger, H. (1996). Fuzzy linear programming and applications. *European Journal of Operational Research, 92*(3), 512–527. doi:10.1016/0377-2217(95)00008-9

Saad, G. (1982). An overview of production planning model: Structure classification and empirical assessment. *International Journal of Production Research, 20*(1), 105–114. doi:10.1080/00207548208947752

Sahoo, N. P., & Biswal, M. P. (2009). Computation of a multi-objective production planning model with probabilistic constraints. *International Journal of Computer Mathematics, 86*(1), 185–198. doi:10.1080/00207160701734207

Sharafali, M., Co, H. C., & Goh, M. (2004). Production scheduling in a flexible manufacturing system under random demand. *European Journal of Operational Research, 158*(1), 89–102. doi:10.1016/S0377-2217(03)00300-X

Simon, H. A. (1977). *The new science of management decision*. Prentice-Hall, Inc.

Tanaka, H., Okuda, T., & Asai, K. (1973). On fuzzy mathematical programming. *Journal of Cybernetics and Systems, 3*(4), 37–46. doi:10.1080/01969727308545912

Tang, J., Fung, R. Y. K., & Yung, K. L. (2003). Fuzzy modeling and simulation for aggregate production planning. *International Journal of Systems Science, 34*(12-13), 661–673. doi:10.1080/00207720310001624113

Tang, J., Wang, D., & Fang, R. Y. K. (2000). Fuzzy formulation for multi-product aggregate production planning. *Production Planning and Control, 11*(7), 670–676. doi:10.1080/095372800432133

Wang, R. C., & Fang, H. H. (2001). Aggregate production planning with multiple objectives in a fuzzy environment. *European Journal of Operational Research, 133*(3), 521–536. doi:10.1016/S0377-2217(00)00196-X

Wang, R. C., & Liang, T. F. (2004). Application of multi-objective linear programming to aggregate production planning. *Computers & Industrial Engineering, 46*(1), 17–41. doi:10.1016/j.cie.2003.09.009

Wang, R. C., & Liang, T. F. (2005). Applying possibilistic linear programming to aggregate production planning. *International Journal of Production Economics, 98*(3), 328–341. doi:10.1016/j.ijpe.2004.09.011

Wu, D., & Ierapetritou, M. (2007). Hierarchical approach for production planning and scheduling under uncertainty. *Chemical Engineering and Processing: Process Intensification, 46*(11), 1129–1140. doi:10.1016/j.cep.2007.02.021

Yager, R. R., & Filev, D. P. (1993). A simple adaptive defuzzification method. *IEEE Transactions on Fuzzy Systems, 1*(1), 69–78. doi:10.1109/TFUZZ.1993.390286

Yoon, K. P. (1996). A probabilistic approach to rank complex fuzzy numbers. *Fuzzy Sets and Systems, 80*(2), 167–176. doi:10.1016/0165-0114(95)00193-X

Zadeh, L. A. (1965). Fuzzy sets. *Information and Control, 8*(3), 338–353. doi:10.1016/S0019-9958(65)90241-X

Zhang, G., Wu, Y. H., Remias, M., & Lu, J. (2003). Formulation of fuzzy linear programming problems as four objective constrained optimization problems. *Applied Mathematics and Computation, 139*(2-3), 383–399. doi:10.1016/S0096-3003(02)00202-3

Zimmerman, H. J. (1978). Fuzzy programming and linear programming with several objective functions. *Fuzzy Sets and Systems, 1*(1), 45–55. doi:10.1016/0165-0114(78)90031-3

Zimmermann, H. J. (1976). Description and optimization of fuzzy systems. *International Journal of General Systems, 2*(4), 209–216. doi:10.1080/03081077608547470

Chapter 22
Ranking of Cloud Services Using Opinion Mining and Multi-Attribute Decision Making:
Ranking of Cloud Services Using Opinion Mining and MADM

Srimanyu Timmaraju
Institute for Development and Research in Banking Technology, India

Vadlamani Ravi
Institute for Development and Research in Banking Technology, India

G. R. Gangadharan
Institute for Development and Research in Banking Technology, India

ABSTRACT

Cloud computing has been a major focus of business organizations around the world. Many applications are getting migrated to the cloud and many new applications are being developed to run on the cloud. There are already more than 100 cloud service providers in the market offering various cloud services. As the number of cloud services and providers is increasing in the market, it is very important to select the right provider and service for deploying an application. This paper focuses on recommendation of cloud services by ranking them with the help of opinion mining of users' reviews and multi-attribute decision making models (TOPSIS and FMADM were applied separately) in tandem on both quantitative and qualitative data. Surprisingly, both TOPSIS and FMADM yielded the same rankings for the cloud services.

DOI: 10.4018/978-1-5225-2031-3.ch022

INTRODUCTION

Cloud computing is a new paradigm of computing that is often referred to computing on demand. Cloud computing is suitable for small and medium enterprises that cannot invest in huge datacenters to deliver their services/products. Cloud computing is a model for enabling usable and accessible virtualized resources that are dynamically reconfigured to adjust to a variable load, allowing for an optimum resource utilization, typically exploited by a pay-per-use model (Vaquero et al. 2009). The basic service delivery models in cloud computing are:

- Infrastructure as a Service (IaaS)
- Platform as a Service (PaaS)
- Software as a Service (SaaS)

With the increasing number of cloud services, the selection of best services for a user becomes a very challenging problem. One of the reasons for the difficulty in selection are varying quality of service (QoS) attributes including performance, security and compliance, vendor lock-in, and cost. It is also observed that the above mentioned attributes are fuzzy in nature because an ideal service provider is expected to have high desirability levels of these attribute values. Even though these values are measured on a numerical scale, their treatment by users is inherently subjective, thereby making them fuzzy.

As there are several cloud services offering infrastructure as a service in today's market, the obvious question is to select a particular cloud service in order to deploy our applications. Once the applications are deployed they have to work with robustness and help in improving the businesses using the particular cloud service(s). The selection of a cloud service becomes crucial so that the service itself should not become a hindrance. Therefore, in order to select a cloud service, generally, we analyze the quantitative metrics representing quality of service attributes of a cloud service that can be found from cloud service providers and cloud benchmarking providers. In today's social media dominated world, there exists a vast amount of users' reviews (as free text) that are provided by the real users of cloud service(s) in a timely and democratized way to understand the experience of the users using the particular service(s). So we developed a novel approach that employs text mining (Aggarwal & Zhai, 2012) of users' reviews to understand the real experience of the users and applied multi-attribute decision making models (Shurjen & Ching 1992) using various quantitative QoS attributes to rank the cloud services.

The proposed ranking procedure has two stages as follows:

1. Mining the unstructured data of users' reviews to gain insights from the real users or the current users of different cloud services.
2. Applying Multi Attribute Decision Making (MADM) models (Technique for Order Preference by Similarity to Ideal Solution (TOPSIS) and Fuzzy MADM (FMADM)) on quantitative (QoS attributes) as well as qualitative (users' reviews) data on different cloud services.

To the best of our knowledge, this is the first study that combines opinion mining of users' reviews of various cloud services and their quantitative QoS attributes for ranking cloud services within the framework of multi-attribute decision making.

BACKGROUND

In this section, we discuss some of the methods that were developed for ranking of various services and mining of various user reviews.

Shivakumar et al. (2013) proposed a ranking mechanism for various cloud services using fuzzy multi-attribute decision making with respect to some standard quality of service attributes. The contribution made by them is the recognition of the quality of service attributes as fuzzy sets and formulating the problem as a fuzzy multi attribute decision making problem. The present work is different from that of (Shivakumar et al. 2013) as follows:

1. Users' reviews/sentiments/opinions are considered as an important input to the ranking of cloud services here, whereas they did not consider them at all. This required full-fledged text mining.
2. The dataset considered by them was not taken from authentic source, whereas we collected the quantitative data from cloud service providers and cloud benchmarking providers.

Garg et al. (2013) defined a framework for ranking cloud services using analytical hierarchy process which evaluates the cloud services based on the different applications depending on the QoS requirements. As some QoS attributes are qualitative in nature and could not be easily measured (although they can be quantified), we adopted the FMADM method over Cloud QoS, which could be seen as a distinctive approach to (Garg et al. 2013). Further, Garg et al. (2013) have not considered opinion mining of reviews of users of cloud services.

Yan et al. (2012) proposes a systematic framework on top of a hybrid cloud management platform for enterprises to automatically recommend and select cloud services according to business requirements, company policies and standards, and the specifications of cloud offering, leveraging multiple criteria decision making (MCDM) techniques. However, the said paper does not propose any evaluations on cloud service recommendation using proposed techniques. Thurow et al. (2010) proposes a method that utilizes opinion mining techniques to extract information about the QoS attributes of web services based on user reviews. However, the method proposed by (Thurow et al. 2010) lacks generalizability for efficiency.

An analytic hierarchy process based ranking algorithm for web services, considering the various quality of service attributes of web services is proposed in (Tran et al. 2009). The proposed ranking algorithm considers the roles and views of users and domain experts specifying their requirements on QoS demand in Web service requests. However, the algorithm does not cope with certain imprecise QoS constraints by adopting fuzzy sets. Qu et al. (2013) proposes an approach for cloud service selection by combining an objective performance assessment from a third party with a subjective assessment from cloud users. Considering the real world situations, the authors apply a fuzzy simple additive weighting system to normalize and aggregate all types of objective and subjective attributes of a cloud service so that some specific performance aspects of a cloud service can be taken into account according to potential cloud user's requirements. Although the said approach performs effective ranking by using benchmarks and users' feedback of cloud services, the limitation of the said approach is comparing and ranking of services with limited qualitative measures.

A singular value decomposition (SVD) technique for cloud service ranking is proposed in (Chan et al. 2010). This approach performs better in situations where the service providers are few and comparison measures are limited and clear. However, the method results in the selection of only one service based on users' requirement. It fails to rank all of the services considered for the experiment. Furthermore, value decomposition technique on large matrices is time consuming and infeasible in some cases.

Zheng et al. (2013) proposes a QoS-driven component ranking methodology for cloud applications by using the past component usage experiences of different component users, considering different received qualitative values for users. The important limitation of this approach is its dependency on trained data set. Also, this approach does not consider all of the qualitative values for comparing services.

In this chapter, we propose a novel method that leverages both the quantitative data and the qualitative data to rank the cloud services. To the best of our knowledge, it is the first research work that proposes a way to recommend/rank cloud services combing subjective (reviews of users) and objective (QoS attribute measures) information that comes from real sources. We apply text mining on the qualitative data to convert the textual data to numeric data. Then, we apply the MADM models on both the data to get the ranking of cloud services.

DATA COLLECTION METHODOLOGY AND DATASET

We have collected two kinds of datasets. The first dataset collected consists of users' reviews on the services. We collected users' reviews since the user experience is the most realistic one, considering the fact that the reviews are true and are not written by the provider himself or by any competitor. The users' reviews have been collected from various websites, blogs, forum and social networks including www.datacenterknowledge.com, www.quora.com, www.zdnet.com, etc. The reviews that are collected mostly focus on the following QoS attributes of cloud services.

1. **Price:** Including virtual machine cost (VM cost), storage cost, and network data outbound cost.
2. **Configurations:** Including:
    a. **CPU Speed:** Instructions per second as a measure of a computer's processor speed.
    b. **Cache:** The cache is a memory component that stores data from the main memory locations that are frequently accessed so that the future requests for that data can be served in a faster manner.
3. **Assurance:** Cloud assurance is the level of confidence that the cloud service is free from all possible failures, measured in terms of the following sub-attributes,
    a. **Upload Bandwidth:** This refers to the amount of data that can be uploaded to a server in the cloud in a fixed amount of time.
    b. **Download Bandwidth:** This refers to the amount of data that can be downloaded in a fixed amount of time. Generally, the download bandwidth is more than the upload bandwidth.
    c. **Object Push Bandwidth:** This refers to the speed at which the data can be transferred to a persistent storage or speed at which the data can be written to a persistent storage,
    d. **Object Pull Bandwidth:** This refers to the speed at which the data can be pulled or retrieved from a persistent storage.
    e. **Availability:** High availability must be ensured before adopting cloud services in terms of the number of replication of the resources. Availability can be measured in terms of application, middleware and infrastructure.
    f. **Response Time:** It is the average time taken by the service for handling user requests measuring the expected delay between the moment when the service request is sent and the moment when the service is rendered.
4. **Performance:** A task or operation seen in terms of how successfully it is performed, performance is measured in terms of CPU performance, Disk performance and Memory performance.

We collected user reviews for four different cloud services as mentioned previously, for each provider containing up to 50 to 60 reviews, totaling to 200 or above. A sample of the user reviews is presented in Table 1. The second dataset collected contains the quantitative values for the 13 different QoS attributes (VM Cost, Storage Cost and Network Data Outbound Cost, CPU Speed, Cache, Upload Bandwidth, Download Bandwidth, Object Push Bandwidth, Object Pull Bandwidth, Availability, Response Time, CPU Performance, Disk Performance, Memory Performance) as discussed earlier. The data is collected from the cloud service provider websites, and some cloud benchmarking providers including Cloud-Harmony (www.cloudharmony.com) and CloudSleuth (www.cloudsleuth.net). The collected data are illustrated in Table 2.

MINING OF USERS' REVIEWS OF CLOUD SERVICES USING TEXT MINING

In this study, we employed text mining to convert the users' reviews into some meaningful numerical values that measure the positive and negative sentiments. The process of converting the user reviews into

Table 1. Sample user reviews on four different cloud services

Provider Name	User Reviews
S2	*"S2 has wide variety of options to choose in terms of number of cores, ram size, and storage size. All the VM's are connected together with S2's advances networking technologies and topologies" (Source: extremetech.com)*
S4	*"With the current Microsoft license, it's illegal to install any version other than SQL Express on S4 cloud. Which I think makes S4's Windows servers essentially useless. This is a details few catch – S4 should make this more clear" (Source: quora.com)*

Table 2. Quantitative dataset which includes 13 QoS attributes

	QoS Attribute	Units	S1	S2	S3	S4
Price	VM Cost	$	0.45	0.42	0.24	0.16
	Storage Cost and Network Data Outbound Cost	$	0.165	0.147	0.195	0.12
Configurations	CPU Speed	GHz	2.4	2.6	2.1	3
	Cache(L3)	MB	12	20	6	8
Assurance	Upload Bandwidth	Mbps	83.21	55.12	16.83	37.02
	Download Bandwidth	Mbps	86.16	46.32	72.73	48.57
	Object Push Bandwidth	Mbps	91.6	128.91	100.34	78.81
	Object Pull Bandwidth	Mbps	132.9	205.6	150.25	93.7
	Availability	%	98.85	99.6	99.68	98.63
	Response Time	seconds	13.926	12.74	12.51	11.77
Performance Benchmarks	CPU	-	25.86	23.66	17.53	7.21
	Disk	-	77.19	100.55	78.49	125.48
	Memory	-	129.03	131.81	70.8	47.83

numerical values is depicted in Figure 1. At first, the collected users' reviews are grouped provider-wise and extracted to a text file. This is achieved by using an Application Programming Interface like JxL API or Apache POI API. After extraction to text files, these text files are fed as input to a data mining tool, RapidMiner (http://rapidminer.com/products/rapidminer-studio/). The output of the RapidMiner is the Term-Document Matrix which is a matrix that describes the frequency of word occurrences in the collection of text files/users' reviews. Now we extract the terms and their frequency from this matrix and store them. The Parts Of Speech (POS) of the terms extracted have to be known so as to get the adjectives, since the adjectives indeed describe the quality of services.

Then, we present the terms as input to another tool viz., Stanford POS Tagger (http://nlp.stanford.edu/software/tagger.shtml) and later filter the adjectives. All the selected adjective terms are fed as input to SentiWordNet 3.0 (Baccinella & Danielo, 2010), which is a lexical resource used for supporting applications on opinion mining and sentiment classification, having a database of around 120,000 words to obtain their respective term scores. SentiWordNet 3.0 assigns three sentiment scores: objectivity, positivity, negativity for each synset of WordNet. Each synset is associated to three numerical scores Pos(s), Neg(s), and Obj(s) which indicate how positive, negative, and objective the terms contained in the synset are. Same terms with different senses may have different opinion-related properties.

The scores obtained for the terms are multiplied with their respective term frequencies stored earlier in order to get weighted scores. Then we aggregate separately all the positive term scores and negative term scores. Thereafter, we compute the ratio of aggregated positive term scores to that of the aggregated negative term scores, to get a unique number. We call this ratio as '*Sentiment Ratio*' (in a similar way to Thurow & Delano, 2010) that will be used as a proxy for the users' reviews, a qualitative attribute.

Figure 1. Process of mining of users' reviews

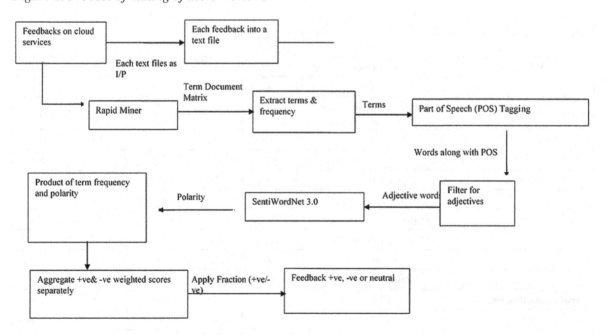

Methodology for Ranking Cloud Services using MADM

Multiple-attribute decision making (MADM) is concerned with structuring and solving decision and planning problems involving multiple attributes. In this paper, we adopt the following two methods of MADM techniques:

1. TOPSIS
2. Fuzzy MADM

Methodology for Ranking Cloud Services using TOPSIS

Technique for Order Preference by Similarity to Ideal Solution (TOPSIS) approach (TOPSIS) is a multiple criteria method to identify solutions from a finite set of alternatives (Jahanshahloo et al., 2006; Hwang & Yoon, 1981). The basic principle is that the chosen alternative should have the shortest distance from the positive ideal solution and the farthest distance from the negative ideal solution (Chen & Hwang, 1992). The procedure of TOPSIS can be expressed in a series of steps as follows:

1. Identify the relevant evaluation criteria for the given decision problem and Develop the preference for the criteria by assigning them weight.

2. Calculate the normalized decision matrix. The normalized value n_{ij} is calculated as, $n_{ij} = x_{ij} \Big/ \sqrt{\sum_{i=1}^{m} x_{ij}^2}$,

   $i = 1,\ldots, m, j = 1,\ldots.n,$

3. Calculate the weighted normalized decision matrix. The weighted normalized value v_{ij} is calculated as $v_{ij} = w_j n_{ij}$ $i = 1,\ldots,m, j = 1,\ldots,n,$

where w_j is the weight of the ith attribute or criterion, and $\sum_{j=1}^{n} w_j = 1.$

4. Determine the positive ideal and negative ideal solution

$$A^+ = \{v_1^+,\ldots,v_n^+\} = \{(\max_j v_{ij} \mid i \in I),(\min_j v_{ij} \mid i \in J)\}$$

$$A^- = \{v_1^-,\ldots,v_n^-\} = \{(\min_j v_{ij} \mid i \in I),(\max_j v_{ij} \mid i \in J)\}$$

where I is associated with benefit criteria, and J is association with cost criteria.

5. Compute separation of each criteria value for each alternative from both ideal and negative ideal solution, using the n-dimensional Euclidean distance. The separation of each alternative from the ideal solution is given as

$$d_i^+ = \{\sum_{j=1}^{n} (v_{ij} - v_{ij}^+)^2\}^{1/2}, i = 1,\ldots,m,$$

Similarly, the separation from the negative ideal solution is given as

$$d_i^- = \left\{ \sum_{j=1}^{n} (v_{ij} - v_{ij}^-)^2 \right\}^{1/2}, i = 1,\dots,m,$$

6.   Determine the relative closeness to ideal solution. The relative closeness of the alternative A_i with respect to A^+ is defined as

$$R_i = d_i^- / (d_i^+ + d_i^-), i = 1, \dots, m.$$

Since $d_i^- \geq 0$ and $d_i^+ \geq 0$, then, clearly, $R_i \in [0,1]$.

7.   Rank the preference order. For ranking alternatives using this index, we can rank alternatives in decreasing order.

Methodology for Ranking Cloud Services using Fuzzy MADM

Fuzzy multi attribute decision making (FMADM) models are justified by the argument that goals/criteria gj are attained by the alternatives xi which cannot be defined crisply but only as fuzzy sets. FMADM model is described as follows. Let X = {xi, i = 1, 2 ... n} be a set of alternatives i.e. the cloud service providers. Let the attributes be considered as fuzzy sets and represented by Gj j = 1, 2 ...m. Let the priority or weight of the jth attribute or jth goal be represented by wj. The attainment of goal Gj by alternative xi is expressed by the degree of membership $\mu_{G_j(x_i)}$. The decision is the intersection of all the fuzzy goals raised to the power of wi (summation of all weights is equal to one) and is given as follows:

$$D = G_1^{w_1} \cap G_2^{w_2} \dots \dots \cap G_m^{w_m}$$

Ranking of cloud services involves consideration of several quality of service attributes whose values change across providers and also subjectivity creeps in their treatment. So to evaluate the overall performance of cloud services and rank them with respect to all the attributes together with the users' reviews, we formulate this problem as an FMADM problem. The FMADM has the following phases (Shurjen, 1992):

- Determining pairwise comparison matrix and the weights of attributes using Analytical Hierarchy Process (AHP).
- Eliciting the fuzzy membership functions for the fuzzy sets which define the attributes from a domain expert.
- Applying Yager's model to obtain ranks for different service providers (Yager, 1978).

Determining Pairwise Comparison Matrix and the Weights of Attributes using AHP

Analytical Hierarchy Process (AHP) is a structured technique for organizing and analyzing complex decisions, based on mathematics and psychology (Saaty, 1990). AHP consists of subphases which include pairwise comparison matrix and calculation of weights or priorities of the attributes. We evaluate the importance of each attribute on the overall QoS attributes of cloud services; the pairwise comparison matrix is first constructed. The scale we use ranges from 1 to 9 (Saaty, 1990).

The judgments are described by the pairwise comparisons. One of the best uses of hierarchy is that it allows us to judge separately on each of several attributes for making decisions. The most effective way to judge is to take a pair of attributes and compare them without the other attributes in picture. This process is repeated to cover all possible cases of pairs of attributes and a pairwise matrix is formed. All these comparisons are elicited from a domain expert. Since we capture the pairwise comparisons of all attributes on a scale of 1 to 9, the consistency of the comparisons of attributes is very important. The allowed consistency ratio is less than or equal to 10%, which indicates that a domain expert is allowed to be inconsistent up to 10% level in making pairwise comparisons. By subjecting the pairwise comparison matrix to Eigen analysis, we compute the weights of QoS attributes of the Cloud services.

After obtaining the weights for the 13 QoS attributes, we scale down the weights to 80% of its obtained value, so that the remaining 20% is allocated for the sentiment ratio. In other words, we assign a weightage of 80% to the numerical QoS attributes and 20% to the users' reviews. This reflects the priority that we assign quantitative and qualitative attributes.

Eliciting the Membership Functions

The membership functions for the fuzzy sets defining the attributes of the cloud services are of two types:

1. An increasing function
2. A decreasing function as presented in Table 3

The parameters a and b in the functions denote the lower and upper bound values and specified by a domain expert in cloud computing.

Table 3. Fuzzy membership functions

Function Type	Function
Increasing membership function	$$\mu(x) = \begin{cases} 0 & if x \leq a \\ \dfrac{x-a}{b-a} & if a < x < b \\ 1 & if x \geq b \end{cases}$$
Decreasing membership function	$$\mu(x) = \begin{cases} 1 & if x \leq a \\ \dfrac{x-a}{b-a} & if a < x < b \\ 0 & if x \geq b \end{cases}$$

Applying Yager's Model

This phase evaluates the overall performance of the cloud service providers and ranks them using the FMADM model. We weigh the membership values exponentially by their respective attribute weights or priorities. The resulting fuzzy sets are $(G_j(x_i))^{w_i}$. Then determine the intersection of all $(G_j(x_i))^{w_i}$ as $\tilde{D}$. The final decision turns out to be a fuzzy set given as $\{\tilde{D}, (G_j(x_i))^{w_i}\}$. The fuzzy '*and*' operator is defined as:

$$\mu_{G_j(x)} = {}_{i=1}^{n}Min(\mu_i(x)) + \frac{1}{n}\sum_{i=1}^{n}\mu_i(x)$$

The results are then sorted to get the membership values of the cloud services in descending order. Then the cloud service with the largest degree of membership value is ranked first and so others follow in the same order of the larger membership value. This in turn indicates that the first ranked cloud service provider is the closest to the ideal provider with respect to all the attributes and users' reviews; second ranked provider is the second closest and so on.

EXPERIMENTAL RESULTS AND DISCUSSION

In this section, we apply TOPSIS and FMADM methods on the dataset comprising users' reviews and QoS attributes of cloud services. We compute the weights or priorities of the attributes of the cloud services using AHP. The pairwise comparison matrix, obtained from a domain expert and used for calculating the weights of the attributes, is presented in Table 4. The table headers 1 to 13 represent the 13 QoS attributes (listed as in Table 2).

The weights of the attributes are obtained by calculating the Eigen vectors of the pairwise comparison matrix. The weights obtained for the QoS attributes are presented in the Table 5.

Now we analyze the users' reviews using the method depicted in Figure 1. The sentiment ratio of cloud services after applying text mining is presented in Table 6.

As the qualitative data (users' reviews) have been quantified as sentiment ratio, we include it as one of the new attributes to the QoS attributes set. Therefore, we now have 14 QoS attributes to help us in ranking the cloud services. The priorities of the attributes are adjusted to give appropriate priority to sentiment ratio. We assigned 20% priority to sentiment ratio and the remaining 80% priority to other QoS attributes. Thus, the previous priorities presented in Table 5 have been scaled down to 80% of the value. The new priorities of the 14 QoS attributes are presented in Table 7.

Ranking of Cloud Services using TOPSIS on QoS Attributes and Mining Users' Reviews

The weights of the 14 QoS attributes (in Table 7) are used in the process of evaluation of the decision matrix (Table 8). The Normalized Decision Matrix is shown in Table 9. The weighted normalized decision matrix is shown in Table 10. The positive ideal solutions (PIS) and negative ideal solutions (NIS) are shown in the Table 11. The separation measures using the n-dimensional Euclidean distance are

Table 4. Pairwise comparison matrix for the 13 QoS attributes.

	1	2	3	4	5	6	7	8	9	10	11	12	13
1	1	1	0.17	4	0.25	0.25	3	3	0.11	0.12	0.14	0.2	0.17
2	1	1	0.14	3	0.2	0.2	3	3	0.11	0.11	0.14	0.2	0.14
3	6	7	1	5	3	3	3	3	0.14	0.17	1	5	3
4	0.25	0.33	0.2	1	0.17	0.17	2	2	0.11	0.12	0.14	0.33	0.17
5	4	5	0.33	6	1	0.5	3	3	0.12	0.14	0.25	3	0.25
6	4	5	0.33	6	2	1	5	5	0.14	0.17	0.33	3	1
7	0.33	0.33	0.33	0.5	0.33	0.2	1	1	0.11	0.11	0.17	0.33	0.17
8	0.33	0.33	0.33	0.5	0.33	0.2	1	1	0.11	0.11	0.17	0.25	0.17
9	9	9	7	9	8	7	9	9	1	2	4	6	4
10	8	9	6	8	7	6	9	9	0.5	1	2	4	3
11	7	7	1	7	4	3	6	6	0.25	0.5	1	4	2
12	5	5	0.2	3	0.33	0.33	3	4	0.17	0.25	0.25	1	0.33
13	6	7	0.33	6	4	1	6	6	0.25	0.33	0.5	3	1

Table 5. Priorities of the QoS attributes

Attribute	Priority/ Weight
VM Cost	0.022
Storage Cost and Network Data Outbound Cost	0.02
CPU Speed	0.101
Cache	0.015
Upload Bandwidth	0.048
Download Bandwidth	0.062
Object push bandwidth	0.014
Object pull bandwidth	0.014
Availability	0.268
Response Time	0.203
CPU Performance	0.111
Disk Performance	0.04
Memory Performance	0.082

Table 6. Sentiment ratios of cloud services

Cloud Services	Sentiment Ratio
S1	0.2965
S2	0.849
S3	0.968
S4	0.1675

Table 7. Priorities of attributes after including sentiment ratio

Attribute	Priority/ Weight
VM Cost	0.0176
Storage Cost and Network Data Outbound cost	0.016
CPU Speed	0.0808
Cache	0.012
Upload Bandwidth	0.0384
Download Bandwidth	0.0496
Object push bandwidth	0.0112
Object pull bandwidth	0.0112
Availability	0.2144
Response Time	0.1624
CPU Performance	0.0888
Disk Performance	0.032
Memory Performance	0.0656
Sentiment Ratio	0.2

shown in the Table 12. The separation of each alternative from the positive ideal solution is shown in the second column of Table 12 and the separation of each alternative from the negative ideal solution is shown in the third column of Table 12.

Now after calculating the relative closeness to the ideal solution we get the values as shown in the third column of Table 13. Rearranging these values in the decreasing order of their magnitude we get the ranks of the cloud services as shown in Table 14. The order is S2, S3, S1, S4, with S2 in the first position and S4 in the last position.

Ranking of Cloud Services using FMADM on QoS Attributes and Mining Users' Reviews

The membership functions of the fuzzy sets defining the attributes used for ranking the cloud services are presented in Table 15. The FMADM model is applied on the dataset shown in Table 2 along with the sentiment ratio. The FMADM model is implemented in Java. The resulting ranks of the cloud services are presented in Table 16 along with the values obtained after applying FMADM model on the dataset.

Table 8. Decision matrix

	1	2	3	4	5	6	7	8	9	10	11	12	13	14
S1	0.45	0.17	2.4	12	83.21	86.16	91.6	132.9	98.85	13.93	25.86	77.19	129.03	1.59
S2	0.42	0.15	2.6	20	55.12	46.32	128.91	205.6	99.6	12.74	23.66	100.55	131.81	2.7
S3	0.24	0.2	2.1	6	16.83	72.73	100.34	150.25	99.68	12.51	17.53	78.49	70.8	2.94
S4	0.16	0.12	3	8	37.02	48.57	78.81	93.7	98.63	11.77	7.21	125.48	47.83	1.33

Table 9. Normalized decision matrix

	1	2	3	4	5	6	7	8	9	10	11	12	13	14
S1	0.66	0.52	0.47	0.47	0.77	0.66	0.45	0.44	0.50	0.55	0.65	0.40	0.63	0.35
S2	0.62	0.46	0.51	0.79	0.51	0.35	0.63	0.68	0.50	0.50	0.59	0.52	0.65	0.60
S3	0.35	0.61	0.41	0.24	0.16	0.55	0.49	0.50	0.50	0.49	0.44	0.40	0.35	0.65
S4	0.24	0.37	0.59	0.32	0.34	0.37	0.39	0.31	0.50	0.46	0.18	0.64	0.24	0.30

Table 10. Weighted normalized decision matrix

	1	2	3	4	5	6	7	8	9	10	11	12	13	14
S1	0.0117	0.0084	0.0381	0.0057	0.0296	0.0326	0.0050	0.0049	0.1068	0.0886	0.0576	0.0127	0.0416	0.0707
S2	0.0109	0.0074	0.0413	0.0095	0.0196	0.0175	0.0071	0.0076	0.1076	0.0811	0.0527	0.0165	0.0425	0.1201
S3	0.0062	0.0098	0.0333	0.0028	0.0060	0.0275	0.0055	0.0056	0.1077	0.0796	0.0391	0.0129	0.0228	0.1307
S4	0.0041	0.0059	0.0476	0.0038	0.0132	0.0184	0.0043	0.0035	0.1066	0.0749	0.0161	0.0206	0.0154	0.0591

Table 11. +ve and –ve ideal solutions

	1	2	3	4	5	6	7	8	9	10	11	12	13	14
IS	0.0041	0.0059	0.0476	0.0095	0.0296	0.0326	0.0071	0.0076	0.1077	0.0749	0.0576	0.0206	0.0425	0.1307
NIS	0.0117	0.0098	0.0333	0.0028	0.0060	0.0175	0.0043	0.0035	0.1066	0.0886	0.0161	0.0127	0.0154	0.0591

Table 12. Separation measures

	d_i^+	d_i^-
S1	0.0635	0.0580
S2	0.0246	0.0787
S3	0.0409	0.0770
S4	0.0901	0.0241

Table 13. Relative closeness to ideal solution

d_i^+	d_i^-	$d_i^- / (d_i^+ + d_i^-)$
0.0635	0.0580	0.477457
0.0246	0.0787	0.761406
0.0409	0.0770	0.653024
0.0901	0.0241	0.211054

Table 14. Ranks of cloud services using TOPSIS

Rank	Cloud Service	Value
1	S2	0.761406
2	S3	0.653024
3	S1	0.477457
4	S4	0.211054

Table 15. Fuzzy membership function

Attribute	Fuzzy Membership Function
VM Cost	$\mu(x) = \begin{cases} 1 & if\, x \leq 0.3 \\ \dfrac{0.4 - x}{0.4 - 0.3} & if\, 0.3 < x < 0.4 \\ 0 & if\, x \geq 0.4 \end{cases}$
Storage Cost and Network Data Outbound Cost	$\mu(x) = \begin{cases} 1 & if\, x \leq 0.15 \\ \dfrac{0.2 - x}{0.2 - 0.15} & if\, 0.15 < x < 0.2 \\ 0 & if\, x \geq 0.2 \end{cases}$
CPU Speed	$\mu(x) = \begin{cases} 0 & if\, x \leq 2 \\ \dfrac{x - 2}{2.5 - 2} & if\, 2 < x < 2.5 \\ 1 & if\, x \geq 2.5 \end{cases}$
Cache	$\mu(x) = \begin{cases} 0 & if\, x \leq 5 \\ \dfrac{x - 5}{15 - 5} & if\, 5 < x < 15 \\ 1 & if\, x \geq 15 \end{cases}$
Upload Bandwidth	$\mu(x) = \begin{cases} 0 & if\, x \leq 30 \\ \dfrac{x - 30}{60 - 30} & if\, 30 < x < 60 \\ 1 & if\, x \geq 60 \end{cases}$
Download Bandwidth	$\mu(x) = \begin{cases} 0 & if\, x \leq 45 \\ \dfrac{x - 45}{70 - 45} & if\, 45 < x < 70 \\ 1 & if\, x \geq 70 \end{cases}$
Object Push Bandwidth	$\mu(x) = \begin{cases} 0 & if\, x \leq 80 \\ \dfrac{x - 80}{90 - 80} & if\, 80 < x < 90 \\ 1 & if\, x \geq 90 \end{cases}$

continued on following page

Table 15. Continued

Attribute	Fuzzy Membership Function
Object Pull Bandwidth	$$\mu(x) = \begin{cases} 0 & if\, x \leq 125 \\ \dfrac{x - 125}{200 - 125} & if\, 125 < x < 200 \\ 1 & if\, x \geq 200 \end{cases}$$
Availability	$$\mu(x) = \begin{cases} 0 & if\, x \leq 98 \\ \dfrac{x - 98}{99.5 - 98} & if\, 98 < x < 99.5 \\ 1 & if\, x \geq 99.5 \end{cases}$$
Response Time	$$\mu(x) = \begin{cases} 1 & if\, x \leq 12 \\ \dfrac{14 - x}{14 - 12} & if\, 12 < x < 14 \\ 0 & if\, x \geq 14 \end{cases}$$
CPU Performance	$$\mu(x) = \begin{cases} 0 & if\, x \leq 10 \\ \dfrac{x - 10}{20 - 10} & if\, 10 < x < 20 \\ 1 & if\, x \geq 20 \end{cases}$$
Disk Performance	$$\mu(x) = \begin{cases} 0 & if\, x \leq 75 \\ \dfrac{x - 75}{100 - 75} & if\, 75 < x < 100 \\ 1 & if\, x \geq 100 \end{cases}$$
Memory Performance	$$\mu(x) = \begin{cases} 0 & if\, x \leq 50 \\ \dfrac{x - 50}{100 - 50} & if\, 50 < x < 100 \\ 1 & if\, x \geq 100 \end{cases}$$
Sentiment Ratio	$$\mu(x) = \begin{cases} 0 & if\, x \leq 1 \\ \dfrac{x - 1}{3 - 1} & if\, 1 < x < 3 \\ 1 & if\, x \geq 3 \end{cases}$$

Table 16. Ranks of cloud services using FMADM

Rank	Cloud Services	Values
1	S2	0.911
2	S3	0.901
3	S1	0.866
4	S4	0.669

Thus, the quantified values after applying TOPSIS are 0.477457, 0.761406, 0.653024, and 0.211054 for S1, S2, S3, and S4. The quantified values after applying FMADM model are 0.866, 0.911, 0.901, and 0.699 for S1, S2, S3, and S4. Arranging these values in the descending order of their magnitude gives the ranks for the services as S2, S3, S1 and S4. Thus, both TOPSIS and FMADM yielded the same ranking, which is interesting and unexpected.

CONCLUSION

As there are several cloud services with different quality of service attributes, the selection of suitable service(s) becomes challenging for users. To select the best cloud service appropriately from among different cloud services, users look for quality of service attributes and users' reviews regarding the cloud services. This paper presents a novel method that combines opinion mining of users' reviews of various cloud services and their quantitative QoS attributes for ranking cloud services within the framework of crisp and fuzzy multiple attributes decision making. We have evaluated our proposed method on a dataset consisting of more than 200 free text reviews and 13 different quantitative QoS attributes related to four different services. One may argue that the number of user reviews and different quantitative QoS attributes service providers considered in this study are rather limited. However, collecting the real world data set regarding user reviews and quantitative QoS attributes was extremely challenging. We aim to publish our collected dataset so that researchers could validate the experiments and further use for their research purposes. Interestingly, both TOPSIS and FMADM produced the same ranking as S2, S3, S1 and S4. This is a significant result of the study. In our future work, we further refine our text mining approach by analyzing review quality and employ nonlinear membership functions for the QoS attributes of the cloud services.

REFERENCES

Aggarwal, C., & Zhai, C. (2012). *Mining Text Data*. Springer. doi:10.1007/978-1-4614-3223-4

Baccinella, S., & Danielo, J. D. (2010). SentiWordNet 3.0: An enhanced lexical resource for sentiment analysis and opinion mining. In *Proceedings of the 7th Language Resources and Evaluation Conference (LREC)*.

Chan, H., & Chieu, T. (2010). Ranking and mapping of applications to cloud computing services by SVD. In *Proceedings of the Network Operations and Management Symposium Workshops*, (pp. 362-369). doi:10.1109/NOMSW.2010.5486550

Chen, S. J., & Hwang, C. L. (1992). *Fuzzy Multiple Attribute Decision Making: Methods and Applications*. Berlin: Springer. doi:10.1007/978-3-642-46768-4

Garg, S. K., Versteeg, S., & Buyya, R. (2013). A framework for ranking of cloud computing services. *Future Generation Computer Systems*, *29*(4), 1012–1023. doi:10.1016/j.future.2012.06.006

Hwang, C. L., & Yoon, K. (1981). *Multiple Attribute Decision Making Methods and Applications*. Berlin: Springer. doi:10.1007/978-3-642-48318-9

Jahanshahloo, G. R., Lotfi, F., & Izadikhah, M. (2006). Extension of the TOPSIS method for decision-making problems with fuzzy data. *Applied Mathematics and Computation*, *181*(2), 1544–1551. doi:10.1016/j.amc.2006.02.057

Qu, L., Wang, Y., & Orgun, M. A. (2013). Cloud service selection based on the aggregation of user feedback and quantitative performance assessment. In *Proceedings of the IEEE International Conference on Service Computing*, (pp. 152-159). doi:10.1109/SCC.2013.92

Saaty, T. L. (1990). How to make a decision: The analytic hierarchy process. *European Journal of Operational Research*, *48*(1), 9–26. doi:10.1016/0377-2217(90)90057-I

Shivakumar, U., Ravi, V., & Gangadharan, G. R. (2013). Ranking cloud services using fuzzy multi-attribute decision making. In *Proceedings of the IEEE International Conference on Computational Fuzzy Systems (FUZZIEEE)*. doi:10.1109/FUZZ-IEEE.2013.6622319

Shurjen, C., & Ching, H. (1992). *Fuzzy Multiple Attribute Decision Making: Methods and Applications*. Springer.

Thurow, N. A., & Delano, J. D. (2010). Selection of web services based on opinion mining of free-text user reviews. In *Proceedings of the International Conference on Information Systems*.

Tran, V. X., Tsuji, H., & Masuda, R. (2009). A new QoS ontology and its QoS based ranking algorithms for Web services. *Simulation Modelling Practice and Theory*, *17*(8), 1378–1398. doi:10.1016/j.simpat.2009.06.010

Vaquero, L. M., Rodero-Merino, L., & Cáceres, J. (2009). Lindner, M., A break in the Clouds: towards a Cloud definition. *ACM Computer Communication Reviews*, *39*(1), 50-55.

Wen, M., Yang, D., & Rose, C. P. (2014). Sentiment analysis in MOOC discussion forums: what does it tell us. In Proceedings of Educational Data Mining.

Yager, R. R. (1978). Fuzzy decision making including unequal objectives. *Fuzzy Sets and Systems*, *1*(2), 87–95. doi:10.1016/0165-0114(78)90010-6

Yan, S., Chen, C., Zhao, G., & Lee, B. S. (2012). Cloud service recommendation and selection for enterprises. In *Proceedings of the 8th IEEE International Conference on Network and Service Management and Workshop on Systems Virtualization Management*, (pp. 430-434).

Zheng, Z., Wu, H., Zhang, Y., Lyu, M. R., & Wang, J. (2013). QoS ranking prediction for Cloud services. *IEEE Transactions on Parallel and Distributed Systems*, *24*(6), 1213–1222. doi:10.1109/TPDS.2012.285

KEY TERMS AND DEFINITIONS

Cloud Computing: A way of delivering IT enabled capabilities to users in the form of 'services' with elasticity and scalability.

Opinion Mining: A type of natural language processing for tracking the mood of the public about a particular product.

Multiple-Attribute Decision Making (MADM): A sub-discipline of operations research that is concerned with structuring and solving decision and planning problems involving multiple attributes.

SentiWordNet 3.0: A lexical resource for supporting applications on opinion mining and sentiment classification.

Compilation of References

Abadi, D. J. (2009). Data management in the cloud: Limitations and opportunities. *IEEE Data Eng. Bull., 32*(1), 3–12.

Abbasbandy, S., & Asady, B. (2006). Ranking of fuzzy numbers by sign distance. *Information Sciences, 176*(16), 2405–2416. doi:10.1016/j.ins.2005.03.013

Abbasbandy, S., & Hajjari, T. (2009). A new approach for ranking of trapezoidal fuzzy numbers. *Computers & Mathematics with Applications (Oxford, England), 57*(3), 413–419. doi:10.1016/j.camwa.2008.10.090

Abbasi, A., Chen, H. & Salem, A. (2008). Sentiment Analysis in Multiple Languages: Feature Selection for Opinion Classification in Web Forums. *ACM Transactions on Information Systems, 26*(3), 12:1- 12:34.

Abbass, H. A. (Ed.). (2001). *Data Mining: A Heuristic Approach*. IGI Global.

Abdelhalim & Traore. (2009). Identity Application Fraud Detection using Web. *International Journal of Computer and Network Security*, 31-44.

Abulaish, M., Jahiruddin, Doja, N. M., & Ahmad, T. (2009). Feature and opinion mining for customer review summarization. In Pattern Recognition and Machine Intelligence (LNCS), (vol. 5909, pp. 219-224). Springer-Verlag Berlin Heidelberg.

Acquisti, A., & Gross, R. (2006). Imagined communities: Awareness, information sharing, and privacy on the Facebook. In *International workshop on privacy enhancing technologies* (pp. 36–58). Springer. doi:10.1007/11957454_3

Adejuwon, A., & Mosavi, A. (2010). Domain Driven Data Mining-Application to Business. *International Journal of Computer Science, 7*(4), 41-44.

Ag, B. (2004, May). *Introduction of the Radial Basis Function (RBF) Networks*. Online Symposium for Electronics Engineers, DSP Algorithms: Multimedia. Retrieved from http://www. osee. net

Agarwal, R. (1993). Mining association rules between sets of items in large database. In *Proc. of ACM SIGMOD'93*. ACM Press. doi:10.1145/170035.170072

Aggarwal, C., & Zhai, C. (2012). *Mining Text Data*. Springer. doi:10.1007/978-1-4614-3223-4

Agrawal, D., Bernstein, P., Bertino, E., Davidson, S., Dayal, U., Franklin, M., & Widom, J. (2012). *Challenges and Opportunities with Big Data: A white paper prepared for the Computing Community Consortium committee of the Computing Research Association*. Retrieved from http://cra.org/ccc/resources/ccc-led-whitepapers/

Agrawal, R., & Srikant, R. (1994). Fast algorithm for mining association rules in large databases. IBM Almaden Research Center.

Agrawal, R., & Srikant, R. (2000). Privacy-Preserving Data Mining. In Proceedings of the 2000 ACM SIGMOD on Management of Data, (pp. 439-450). doi:10.1145/342009.335438

Agrawal, R., Imieliński, T., & Swami, A. (1993). Mining association rules between sets of items in large databases. *SIGMOD Record, 22*(2), 207–216. doi:10.1145/170036.170072

Aha, D. W. (1992). Tolerating noisy, irrelevant and novel attributes in instance-based learning algorithms. *International Journal of Man-Machine Studies, 36*(2), 267–287. doi:10.1016/0020-7373(92)90018-G

Ahmad Haris Abdul Halim. (2008). Integration between Location Based Service (LBS) and Online Analytical Processing (OLAP): Semantic Approach. *Journal of Information Systems, Research & Practices, 1*(1).

Akamai. (2009, September). *Akamai Reveals 2 Seconds as the New Threshold of Acceptability for E-Commerce Web Page Response Times*. Cambridge, MA: Akamai Technologies. Retrieved from https://www.akamai.com/us/en/about/news/press/2009-press/akamai-reveals-2-seconds-as-the-new-threshold-of-acceptability-for-ecommerce-web-page-response-times.jsp

Aleskerov, E., & Freisleben, B. (1997). CARD WATCH: a neural network based database mining system for credit card fraud detection. In *Proceedings of the computational intelligence for financial Engineering*.

Alex, B., Stephen, S., & Kurt, T. (2002). *Building Data Mining Applications for CRM*. McGraw Hill.

Alhamazani, K., Ranjan, R., Rabhi, F., Wang, L., & Mitra, K. (2012, December). Cloud monitoring for optimizing the QoS of hosted applications. In *Cloud Computing Technology and Science (CloudCom), 2012 IEEE 4th International Conference on* (pp. 765-770). IEEE. doi:10.1109/CloudCom.2012.6427532

Alpaydin, E. (2014). *Introduction to machine learning*. MIT Press.

Alsmadi, I., & Najadat, H. (2011). Evaluating the change of software fault behavior with dataset attributes based on categorical correlation. *Advances in Engineering Software, 42*(8), 535–546. doi:10.1016/j.advengsoft.2011.03.010

Analysis_Regression and Correlation_Probit Analysis. (n.d.). Retrieved from http://www.statsdirect.com/help/Default.htm#regression_and_correlation/probit_analysis.htm

Anand, G., & Kodali, R. (2008). Selection of Lean Manufacturing Systems Using the PROMETHEE. *Journal of Modeling in Management, 3*(1), 40–70. doi:10.1108/17465660810860372

Anders & Kochen. (2001). *Data mining for Automated GIS data Collection*. Wichmann Verlag Heidelberg.

Ankalikar, A., & Pande, R. (n.d.). *JD Edwards Upgrades Made Easy*. Academic Press.

Anselin, L. (1998). Interactive techniques and exploratory spatial data analysis. Academic Press.

Antai, I., & Olson, H. (2013). Interaction: A new focus for supply chain vs. supply chain competition. *International Journal of Physical Distribution & Logistics Management, 43*(7), 511–528. doi:10.1108/IJPDLM-06-2012-0195

Armstrong, K. (2014). Big data: A revolution that will transform how we live, work, and think. *Information Communication and Society, 17*(10), 1300–1302. doi:10.1080/1369118X.2014.923482

Asady, B. (2010). *The revised method of ranking LR fuzzy number based on deviation degree*. Academic Press.

Association for Computing Machinery. (2007). *ACM transactions on knowledge discovery from data*. ACM.

Baccinella, S., & Danielo, J. D. (2010). SentiWordNet 3.0: An enhanced lexical resource for sentiment analysis and opinion mining. In *Proceedings of the 7th Language Resources and Evaluation Conference (LREC)*.

Badri, M. (1999). Combining the AHP and GP Model for Global Facility Location-Allocation Problem. *International Journal of Production Economics, 62*(3), 237–248. doi:10.1016/S0925-5273(98)00249-7

Baesens, B. (2014). *Analytics in a big data world: The essential guide to data science and its applications.* Wiley.

Bailey-Kellogg, C., Ramakrishnan, N., & Marathe, M. V. (2006). Spatial Data Mining to Support Pandemic preparedness. *SIGKDD Explorations, 8*(1), 80–82. doi:10.1145/1147234.1147246

Banjade, R., & Maharjan, S. (2011, November). Product recommendations using linear predictive modeling. In *Internet (AH-ICI), 2011 Second Asian Himalayas International Conference on* (pp. 1-4). IEEE. doi:10.1109/AHICI.2011.6113930

Barik, S. K., & Biswal, M. P. (2012). Probabilistic Quadratic Programming Problems with Some Fuzzy Parameters. *Advances in Operations Research, 2012,* 1–13. doi:10.1155/2012/635282

Barratt, M., & Oke, A. (2007). Antecedents of supply chain visibility in retail supply chains: A resource-based theory perspective. *Journal of Operations Management, 25*(6), 1217–1233. doi:10.1016/j.jom.2007.01.003

Bartlett, J., Birdwell, J., & Littler, M. (2011). The new face of digital populism. *Demos (Mexico City, Mexico).*

Batista, L., & Ratt, S. (2012). A Multi-Classifier System for Sentiment Analysis and Opinion Mining. In *Proceedings of the IEEE/ACM International Conference on Advances in Social Networks Analysis and Mining*(pp. 96-100).

Beaubouef & Petry. (2010). Methods for handling imperfect spatial info. In R. Jeansoulin, . . . (Eds.), Fuzzy and Rough Set Approaches for Uncertainty in Spatial Data (pp. 103–129). Springer.

Behzadian, M., Kazemzadeh, R., Albadvi, A., & Aghdasi, M. (2010). PROMETHEE: A Comprehensive Literature Review on Methodologies and Applications. *European Journal of Operational Research, 200*(1), 198–215. doi:10.1016/j.ejor.2009.01.021

Bei-bei, M., & Xue-bo, J. (2015, May). Compression processing estimation method for time series big data. In *Control and Decision Conference (CCDC), 2015 27th Chinese* (pp. 1807-1811). IEEE. doi:10.1109/CCDC.2015.7162212

Bellman, R. E., & Zadeh, L. A. (1970). Decision making in a fuzzy environment. *Management Science, 17*(4), 141–164. doi:10.1287/mnsc.17.4.B141

Belton, V., & Stewart, T. J. (2002). *Multiple Criteria Decision Analysis. An Integrated Approach.* Dordrecht: Kluwer Academic Publishers. doi:10.1007/978-1-4615-1495-4

Beninger, K., Fry, A., Jago, N., Lepps, H., Nass, L., & Silvester, H. (2014). *Research using social media; users' views.* Nat Cen Social Research.

Berger, J. (1985). *Statistical Decision Theory and Bayesian Analysis.* New York, NY: Springer-Verlag. doi:10.1007/978-1-4757-4286-2

Berkman Center for Internet & Society, Harvard University. (2008, September 25). *Tastes, Ties, and Time: Facebook data release.* Retrieved February 3, 2016, from https://cyber.law.harvard.edu/node/94446

Bhadane, C., Dalal, H., & Doshi, H. (2015). Sentiment analysis: Measuring opinions. *Procedia Computer Science, 45,* 808–814. doi:10.1016/j.procs.2015.03.159

Bhutta, C. B. (2012). Not by the Book: Facebook as a Sampling Frame. *Sociological Methods & Research, 41*(1), 57–88. doi:10.1177/0049124112440795

Bifet, A., & Frank, E. (2010). Sentiment knowledge discovery in Twitter streaming data. In *Proceedings of the 13th International Conference on Discovery Science* (pp. 1–15), Canberra, Australia. Springer. doi:10.1007/978-3-642-16184-1_1

Blank, G. (2013). Who creates content? Stratification and content creation on the Internet. *Information Communication and Society, 16*(4), 590–612. doi:10.1080/1369118X.2013.777758

Blei, D. M., Ng, A. Y., & Jordan, M. I. (2003). Latent dirichlet allocation. *Journal of Machine Learning Research*, *3*(Jan), 993–1022.

Bloomberg. (2015). *How ATT Could Keep Crooks from Using Your Credit Card*. Retrieved from http://www.bloomberg.com/news/2015-06-26/how-at-t-could-keep-crooks-from-using-your- credit-card.html

Boden, M. A. (1977). *Artificial Intelligence and Natural Man*. New York, NY: Basic Books.

Bolton, R. J., Hand, D. J., Provost, F., Breiman, L., Bolton, R. J., & Hand, D. J. (2002). Statistical fraud detection: A review. *Statistical Science*, *17*(3), 235–255. doi:10.1214/ss/1042727940

Boser, B. E., Guyon, I. M., & Vapnik, V. N. (1992, July). A training algorithm for optimal margin classifiers. In *Proceedings of the fifth annual workshop on Computational learning theory* (pp. 144-152). ACM. doi:10.1145/130385.130401

Boyd, D. (2008). *Putting privacy settings in the context of use (in Facebook and elsewhere)*. Retrieved from http://www.zephoria.org/thoughts/archives/2008/10/22/putting_privacy.html

Brandas, A. (2011). Approximation of fuzzy numbers by trapezoidal fuzzy numbers preserving the core the ambiguity and the value. *Advanced Studies in Contemporary Mathematics, 21,* 247-259.

Brans, J. P., Vincke, P., & Mareschal, B. (1986). How to Select and How to Rank Projects: The PROMETHEE Method. *European Journal of Operational Research*, *24*(2), 228–238. doi:10.1016/0377-2217(86)90044-5

Breiman, L., Friedman, J., Olshen, R., & Stone, P. (1992). *Classification and regression trees*. Belmont, CA: Wadsworth International Group.

Bremner, D., Demaine, E., Erickson, J., Iacono, J., Langerman, S., Morin, P., & Toussaint, G. (2005). Output-Sensitive Algorithms for Computing Nearest-Neighbor Decision Boundaries. *Discrete & Computational Geometry*, *33*(4), 593–604. doi:10.1007/s00454-004-1152-0

British Psychological Society. (2013). *Ethics Guidelines for Internet-mediated Research. INF206/1.2013*. Author.

Brodley, C.E., & Utgoff, P.E. (n.d.). *Multivariate decision trees*. Academic Press.

Bruns, A. (2008). *3.1. The Active Audience: Transforming Journalism from Gatekeeping to Gatewatching*. Academic Press.

Buchanan, J., & Sheppard, P. (1998). Ranking Projects Using the Electre Method. In *Proceedings of the 33rd Annual Conference of Operational Research Society of New Zealand*.

Buxey, G. (1995). A managerial perspective on aggregate planning. *International Journal of Production Economics*, *41*(1-3), 127–133. doi:10.1016/0925-5273(94)00070-0

Buyya, R., Yeo, C. S., Venugopal, S., Broberg, J., & Brandic, I. (2009). Cloud computing and emerging IT platforms: Vision, hype, and reality for delivering computing as the 5th utility. *Future Generation Computer Systems*, *25*(6), 599–616. doi:10.1016/j.future.2008.12.001

Cao, J., Zeng, K., Wang, H., Cheng, J., Qiao, F., Wen, D., & Gao, Y. (2014). Web-based traffic sentiment analysis: Methods and applications. Intelligent Transportation Systems. *IEEE Transactions on*, *15*(2), 844–853.

Cetiner, B., Sari, M., & Borat, O. (2010). Neural Network Based Traffic-Flow Prediction Model. *Mathematical and Computational Applications*, *15*(2), 269–278. doi:10.3390/mca15020269

Chae, B., Sheu, C., Yang, C., & Olson, D. (2014). The impact of advanced analytics and data accuracy on operational performance: A contingent resource based theory (RBT) perspective. *Decision Support Systems*, *59*(1), 119–126. doi:10.1016/j.dss.2013.10.012

Chakrabarti, S. (2003). *Mining the Web: Discovering knowledge from hypertext data*. Morgan Kaufmann.

Chambers, M., & Dinsmore, T. W. (2014). *Advanced analytics methodologies: Driving business value with analytics*. Pearson Education.

Chan, H., & Chieu, T. (2010). Ranking and mapping of applications to cloud computing services by SVD. In *Proceedings of the Network Operations and Management Symposium Workshops*, (pp. 362-369). doi:10.1109/NOMSW.2010.5486550

Charnes, A., & Cooper, W. W. (1959). Chance-constrained programming. *Management Science, 6*(1), 73–79. doi:10.1287/mnsc.6.1.73

Charniak, E. (1991). Bayesians networks without tears. *Artificial Intelligence Magazine, 12*(4), 49–63.

Chawla, et al. (2001). Modeling Spatial Dependencies for Mining Geospatial Data. *Proceedings of the 2001 SIAM International Conference on Data Mining*.

Chen, P., & Liu, S. (2008). Rough set-based SVM classifier for text categorization. In *Proceedings of the Fourth IEEE International Conference of Natural Computation*, (Vol. 2, pp. 153–157).

Chen, C., Ibekwe-SanJuan, F., SanJuan, E., & Weaver, C. (2006, October). Visual analysis of conflicting opinions. In *2006 IEEE Symposium On Visual Analytics Science And Technology* (pp. 59-66). IEEE. doi:10.1109/VAST.2006.261431

Chen, H., Chiang, R. H., & Storey, V. C. (2012). Business Intelligence and Analytics: From Big Data to Big Impact. *Management Information Systems Quarterly, 36*(4), 1165–1188.

Chen, S. J., & Hwang, C. L. (1992). *Fuzzy Multiple Attribute Decision Making: Methods and Applications*. Berlin: Springer. doi:10.1007/978-3-642-46768-4

Chen, T.-H., & Chen, C.-W. (2010). Application of data mining to the spatial heterogeneity of foreclosed mortgages. *Expert Systems with Applications, 37*(2), 993–997. doi:10.1016/j.eswa.2009.05.076

Cheong, M., & Lee, V. 2010, August. A study on detecting patterns in twitter intra-topic user and message clustering. In *Pattern Recognition (ICPR), 2010 20th International Conference on* (pp. 3125-3128). IEEE. doi:10.1109/ICPR.2010.765

Cheong, M., & Lee, V. (2009, November). Integrating web-based intelligence retrieval and decision-making from the twitter trends knowledge base. In *Proceedings of the 2nd ACM workshop on Social web search and mining*(pp. 1-8). ACM. doi:10.1145/1651437.1651439

Chiang, J. (2001). Fuzzy linear programming based on statistical confidence interval and interval-valued fuzzy set. *European Journal of Operational Research, 129*(1), 65–86. doi:10.1016/S0377-2217(99)00404-X

Chinsha, T. C., & Shibily, J. (2014). Aspect based opinion mining from restaurant reviews. In *Proceedings of International Conference on Advanced Computing and Communication Techniques for High Performance Applications* (Vol. 1, pp. 1-4).

Chipman, H., George, E. I., McCulloch, R. E., Clyde, M., Foster, D. P., & Stine, R. A. (2001). The practical implementation of Bayesian model selection. *Lecture Notes-Monograph Series*, 65-134.

Chiu, C. C., & Tsai, C. Y. (2004). A Web services-based collaborative scheme for credit card fraud detection. In *e-Technology, E-Commerce and e-Service; IEEE International Conference on*.

Choi, H., & Varian, H. (2012). Predicting the present with Google Trends. *The Economic Record, 88*(s1), 2–9. doi:10.1111/j.1475-4932.2012.00809.x

Choi, S. C. (1991). Price competition in a channel structure with a common retailer. *Marketing Science, 10*(4), 271–296. doi:10.1287/mksc.10.4.271

Christopher, M. (2011). *Logistics & supply chain management* (4th ed.). Prentice Hall.

Chung, K. J., Goyal, S. K., & Huang, Y. F. (2005). The optimal inventory policies under permissible delay in payments depending on the order quantity. *International Journal of Production Economics, 95*(2), 203–213. doi:10.1016/j.ijpe.2003.12.006

Chung, W., Chen, H., & Nunamaker, J. F. (2005). A visual framework for knowledge discovery on the web: An empirical study on business intelligence exploration. *Journal of Management Information Systems, 21*(4), 57–84.

Chung, W., & Tseng, T. L. (2012). Discovering business intelligence from online product reviews: A rule-induction framework. *Expert Systems with Applications, 39*(15), 11870–11879. doi:10.1016/j.eswa.2012.02.059

Cios, K. J., Pedrycz, W., Swiniarski, R. W., & Kurgan, L. (2010). *Data Mining: A Knowledge Discovery Approach.* Springer Limited.

Clark, P., & Niblett, T. (1989). The CN2 induction algorithm. *Machine Learning, 3*(4), 261–283. doi:10.1007/BF00116835

Classification and Regression Trees. (2009). Retrieved from http://www.stat.cmu.edu/~cshalizi/350/lectures/22/lecture-22.pdf

Cohen, R., & Ruths, D. (2013). Classifying Political Orientation on Twitter: It's Not Easy! In *Seventh International AAAI Conference on Weblogs and Social Media.* Retrieved from http://www.aaai.org/ocs/index.php/ICWSM/ICWSM13/paper/view/6128

Cohen, W. (1995). Fast effective rule induction. In *Proceedings of the twelfth international conference on machine learning*(pp. 115–123). Lake Tahoe, CA: Morgan Kaufmann.

Colbaugh, R., & Glass, K. (2010, May). Estimating sentiment orientation in social media for intelligence monitoring and analysis. In *Intelligence and Security Informatics (ISI), 2010 IEEE International Conference on* (pp. 135-137). IEEE. doi:10.1109/ISI.2010.5484760

Contini, B. (1978). A stochastic approach to goal programming. *Operations Research, 16*(3), 576–586. doi:10.1287/opre.16.3.576

Cover, T. M., & Hart, P. E. (1967). Nearest neighbor pattern classification. *Information Theory. IEEE Transactions on, 13*(1), 21–27.

Cover, T., & Hart, P. E. (1967). Nearest neighbour pattern classification. *IEEE Transactions on Information Theory, 13*(1), 21–27. doi:10.1109/TIT.1967.1053964

Cui, W., Wu, Y., Liu, S., Wei, F., Zhou, M. X., & Qu, H. (2010, March). Context preserving dynamic word cloud visualization. In *2010 IEEE Pacific Visualization Symposium* (PacificVis) (pp. 121-128). IEEE.

Curriero, F. C., Patz, J. A., Rose, J. B., & Lele, S. (2001). The association between extreme precipitation and waterborne disease outbreaks in the United States, 1948-1994. *American Journal of Public Health, 91*(8), 1194–1199. doi:10.2105/AJPH.91.8.1194 PMID:11499103

Czyzak, P., & Jaszkiewicz, A. (1998). Pareto Simulated Annealing – a Metaheuristic Technique for Multiple-Objective Combinatorial Optimization. *Journal of Multi-Criteria Decision Analysis, 7*(1), 34–47. doi:10.1002/(SICI)1099-1360(199801)7:1<34::AID-MCDA161>3.0.CO;2-6

Dai, C., Li, Y. P., & Huang, G. H. (2012). An interval-parameter chance-constrained dynamic programming approach for capacity planning under uncertainty. *Resources, Conservation and Recycling, 62*, 37–50. doi:10.1016/j.resconrec.2012.02.010

Dang, Y., Zhang, Y., & Chen, H. (2010). A lexicon-enhanced method for sentiment Classification: An experiment on online product reviews. *IEEE Intelligent Systems*, *25*(4), 46–53. doi:10.1109/MIS.2009.105

Daniel, A. K., et al. (2003). PixelMaps: A New Visual Data Mining Approach for Analyzing Large Spatial Data Sets. *IEEE International Conference on Data Mining*.

Daniel, A., et al. (2008). Visual Data Mining in Large Geospatial Point Sets. *IEEE Computer Society*, 36-44.

Daoming, G., & Jie, C. (2006). ANFIS for high-pressure waterjet cleaning prediction. *Surface and Coatings Technology*, *201*(3), 1629–1634. doi:10.1016/j.surfcoat.2006.02.034

d'Aquin, M., & Jay, N. (2013, April). Interpreting data mining results with linked data for learning analytics: motivation, case study and directions. In *Proceedings of the Third International Conference on Learning Analytics and Knowledge* (pp. 155-164). ACM. doi:10.1145/2460296.2460327

Das, T. K., Acharjya, D. P., & Patra, M. R. (2014). Business Intelligence from Online Product Review - A Rough Set Based Rule Induction Approach. In *Proceedings of the 2014 International Conference on Contemporary Computing and Informatics* (pp.800-803). Mysore, India: IEEE Xplore.

Das, T. K., Acharjya, D. P., & Patra, M. R. (2014). Opinion Mining about a Product by Analyzing Public Tweets in Twitter. In Proceedings of the 2014 International Conference on Computer Communication and Informatics (pp. 1- 4), Coimbatore, India: IEEE Xplore.

Das, T. K. (2016). Intelligent Techniques in Decision Making: A Survey. *Indian Journal of Science and Technology*, *9*(12), 1–6. doi:10.17485/ijst/2016/v9i12/86063

Das, T. K., & Kumar, P. M. (2013). BIG Data Analytics: A Framework for Unstructured Data Analysis. *IACSIT International Journal of Engineering and Technology*, *5*(1), 153–156.

Dave, K., Lawrence, S., & Pennock, D. M. (2003). Mining the peanut gallery: opinion extraction and semantic classification of product reviews. In *Proceedings of the International World Wide Web Conference* (pp. 519–528). doi:10.1109/ICCCI.2014.6921727

Davenport, T. H. (1993). *Process Innovation: Reengineering Work through Information Technology*. Boston: Harvard Business School Press.

de Boer, L., van der Wegen, L., & Telgen, J. (1998). Outranking Methods in Support of Supplier Selection. *European Journal of Purchasing and Supply Management*, *4*(2/3), 109–118. doi:10.1016/S0969-7012(97)00034-8

Decision Boundaries. (n.d.). Retrieved from http://www.cs.princeton.edu/courses/archive/fall08/cos436/Duda/PR_simp/bndrys.htm

Deepali Kishor Jadhav. (2013). Big Data: The New Challenges in Data Mining. *International Journal of Innovative Research in Computer Science & Technology, 1*(2), 39-42.

Delgado, M., Vila, M. A., & Voxman, W. (1998). On a canonical representation of fuzzy number. *Fuzzy Sets and Systems*, *93*(1), 125–135. doi:10.1016/S0165-0114(96)00144-3

Delhaye, C., Teghem, J., & Kunsch, P. (1991). Application of the ORESTE Method to a Nuclear Waste Management Problem. *International Journal of Production Economics*, *24*(1-2), 29–39. doi:10.1016/0925-5273(91)90150-R

Demirkan, H., & Delen, D. (2013). Leveraging the capabilities of service-oriented decision support systems: Putting analytics and big data in cloud. *Decision Support Systems*, *55*(1), 412–421. doi:10.1016/j.dss.2012.05.048

Demsar, J. (2006). Statistical Comparisons of Classifiers over Multiple Data Sets. *Journal of Machine Learning Research, 7*(Jan), 1–30.

Department for Work and Pensions. (2014, December 18). *Use of social media for research and analysis.* Retrieved July 5, 2016, from https://www.gov.uk/government/publications/use-of-social-media-for-research-and-analysis

Dias, L., & Clímaco, J. (1999). On Computing ELECTREs Credibility Indices under Partial Information. *Journal of Multi-Criteria Decision Analysis, 8*(2), 74–92. doi:10.1002/(SICI)1099-1360(199903)8:2<74::AID-MCDA234>3.0.CO;2-7

Dignan, L. (2012). *30 Big Data Project Takeaways.* ZDNet. Retrieved from http://www.zdnet.com/article/30-big-data-project-takeaways/

Ding & Liu. (2007). The Utility of Linguistic Rules in Opinion Mining.*Proceedings of the 30th Annual International ACM SIGIR Conference on Research and Development on Information Retrieval.*

Ding, X., Liu, B., & Yu, P. S. (2008). A holistic lexicon-based approach to opinion mining. In*Proc. of the Intl. Conf. on Web search and web data mining, WSDM '08,* (pp. 231–240). doi:10.1145/1341531.1341561

Dormehl, L. (2015). *President Obama's New Health Care Initiative Will Harness the Power of Big Data.* Fast Company & Inc. Retrieved from http://www.fastcompany.com/3041775/fast-feed/president-obamas-new-healthcare-initiative-willharness-the-power-of-big-data

Dorronsoro, Ginel, Sgnchez, & Cruz. (1997). Neural fraud detection in credit card operations. *IEEE Transactions on Neural Networks,* (8), 827-834.

Duggan, M. (2015, August 19). *The demographics of social media users.* Retrieved from http://www.pewinternet.org/2015/08/19/the-demographics-of-social-media-users/

Duggan, M., & Brenner, J. (2013, February 14). *The Demographics of Social Media Users — 2012.* Retrieved from http://www.pewinternet.org/2013/02/14/the-demographics-of-social-media-users-2012/

Duman, E., & Ozcelik, M. H. (2011). Detecting credit card fraud by genetic algorithm and scatter search. *Expert Systems with Applications, 38*(10), 13057–13063. doi:10.1016/j.eswa.2011.04.110

Dutton, W. H., Blank, G., & Groselj, D. (2013). *OxIS 2013 Report: Cultures of the Internet.* Oxford, UK: Oxford Internet Institute, University of Oxford.

Edwards, P., Peters, M., & Sharman, G. (2001). The Effectiveness of Information Systems in Supporting the Extended Supply Chain. *Journal of Business Logistics, 22*(1), 11–27.

Electronic Health Records, Ophthalmic EHR Central, American Academy of Ophthalmic Executives. (n.d.). *The practice management division of the American Academy of Ophthalmology.* Available: http://www.aao.org/aaoe/ehr-central/index.cfm

Ellison, N. B. (2007). Social network sites: Definition, history, and scholarship. *Journal of Computer-Mediated Communication, 13*(1), 210–230. doi:10.1111/j.1083-6101.2007.00393.x

Excell D. (2012). Bayesian inference-the future of online fraud protection. *Computer Fraud & Security,* (2), 8-11.

Farvaresh, H., & Sepehri, M. (2011). A data mining framework for detecting subscription fraud in telecommunication. *Engineering Applications of Artificial Intelligence, 24*(1), 182–194. doi:10.1016/j.engappai.2010.05.009

Fayyad, U., Shapiro, G. P., & Smyth, P. (1996). From data mining to knowledge discovery: An overview. Advances in Knowledge Discovery and Data Mining, 1–34.

Feldman, R. (2013). Techniques and applications for sentiment analysis. *Communications of the ACM, 56*(4), 82–89. doi:10.1145/2436256.2436274

Feng, J., Wen, P., Liu, J., & Li, H. (2010, June). Elastic stream cloud (ESC): A stream-oriented cloud computing platform for Rich Internet Application. In *High Performance Computing and Simulation (HPCS), 2010 International Conference on* (pp. 203-208). IEEE.

Filev, D. P., & Yager, R. R. (1991). A generalized defuzzification method via Bad Distribution. *International Journal of Intelligent Systems, 6*(7), 687–697. doi:10.1002/int.4550060702

Foody, G. M., & Mathur, A. (2004). A relative evaluation of multiclass image classification by support vector machines. *Geoscience and Remote Sensing. IEEE Transactions on, 42*(6), 1335–1343.

Friedman, J. H. (1991). Multivariate adaptive regression splines. *Annals of Statistics, 19*(1), 1–67. doi:10.1214/aos/1176347963

Furnas, A., & Gaffney, D. (2012, July 31). *Statistical Probability That Mitt Romney's New Twitter Followers Are Just Normal Users: 0%*. Retrieved July 6, 2016, from http://www.theatlantic.com/technology/archive/2012/07/statistical-probability-that-mitt-romneys-new-twitter-followers-are-just-normal-users-0/260539/

Furrier, J. (2012). Big Data is Creating the Future - It's A $50 Billion Market. *Forbes*. Retrieved from http://www.forbes.com/sites/siliconangle/2012/02/29/big-data-is-creating-the-future-its-a-50-billion-market/

Ganesan, K., & Veeramani, P. (2006). Fuzzy linear programs with trapezoidal fuzzy numbers. *Annals of Operations Research, 143*(1), 305–315. doi:10.1007/s10479-006-7390-1

Garg, S. K., Versteeg, S., & Buyya, R. (2013). A framework for ranking of cloud computing services. *Future Generation Computer Systems, 29*(4), 1012–1023. doi:10.1016/j.future.2012.06.006

Gartner Lustig, I., Dietrich, B., Johnson, C., & Dziekan, C. (2010). *The Analytics Journey*. Institute for Operations Research and the Management Sciences.

Gautam, G., & Yadav, D. (2014). Sentiment analysis of twitter data using machine learning approaches and semantic analysis. In *Proceedings of IEEE Seventh International Conference on Contemporary Computing* (pp. 437-442). doi:10.1109/IC3.2014.6897213

Gebremeskel, G. B. (2013). Data Mining Prospects in Mobile Social Networks. IGI Global.

Gelman, A., Carlin, J. B., Stern, H. S., & Rubin, D. B. (2014). *Bayesian data analysis* (Vol. 2). Boca Raton, FL, USA: Chapman & Hall/CRC.

Gen, M., Tsujimura, Y., & Ida, K. (1992). Method for solving multi objective aggregate production planning problem with fuzzy parameters. *Computers & Industrial Engineering, 23*(1-4), 117–120. doi:10.1016/0360-8352(92)90077-W

Gennady Andrienko, et al. (2006). Mining spatiotemporal data. *J Intell Inf Syst., 27*, 187-190. doi: 10.1007/s10844-006-9949-3

Ghag & Shah. (2014). SentiTFIDF – Sentiment Classification using Relative Term Frequency Inverse Document Frequency. *International Journal of Advanced Computer Science and Applications, 5*(2).

Ghosh, M., & Kar, A. (2013). Unsupervised linguistic approach for sentiment classification from online reviews using sentiwordnet 3.0. *International Journal of Engineering Research & Technology, 2*(9), 55–60.

Ghosh, S., & Reilly, D. L. (1994). Credit Card Fraud Detection with a Neural- Network.*Proceedings of the Twenty-Seventh Hawaii International Conference on System Science* (pp. 621-630). doi:10.1109/HICSS.1994.323314

Girardin, F., Calabrese, F., Fiore, F. D., Ratti, C., & Blat, J. (2008). Digital footprinting: Uncovering tourists with user-generated content. *Pervasive Computing, IEEE, 7*(4), 36–43. doi:10.1109/MPRV.2008.71

Go, A., Bhayani, R., & Huang, L. (2009). Twitter sentiment classification using distant supervision. CS224N Project Report, Stanford, 1, 12.

Gokulakrishnan, B., Priyanthan, P., Ragavan, T., Prasath, N., & Perera, A. (2012). Opinion mining and sentiment analysis on a twitter data stream. In *Proceedings of the International Conference on Advances in ICT for Emerging Regions* (pp. 182-188). doi:10.1109/ICTer.2012.6423033

Golbeck, J., & Hansen, D. (2014). A method for computing political preference among Twitter followers. *Social Networks, 36*, 177–184. doi:10.1016/j.socnet.2013.07.004

Goldberg, D. (1989). *Genetic Algorithms in Search, Optimization and Machine Learning*. Boston, MA: Addison-Wesley.

Gomes da Silva, C., Figueira, J., Lisboa, J., & Barman, S. (2006). An interactive decision support system for an aggregate production planning model based on multiple criteria mixed integer linear programming. *Omega, 34*(2), 167–177. doi:10.1016/j.omega.2004.08.007

Gonzalez-Bailon, S., & Wang, N. (2013). The bridges and brokers of global campaigns in the context of social media. *SSRN Work. Pap.*

Goodwin, M. (2013, May 25). London attack: generations divided on feelings about Muslims after killing. *The Guardian*. Retrieved from https://www.theguardian.com/uk/2013/may/26/public-attitude-muslims-complex-positive

Gopinath, D. P., Divya Sree, J., Mathew, R., Rekhila, S. J., & Nair, A. S. (2006, December). Duration Analysis for Malayalam Text-To-Speech Systems. In *Information Technology, 2006. ICIT'06. 9th International Conference on* (pp. 129-132). IEEE. doi:10.1109/ICIT.2006.48

Goyal, M. & Rajan, V. (2012). Applications of Data Mining in Higher Education. *International Journal of Computer Science, 9*(2), 113-120.

Goyal, S. K. (1985). Economic order quantity under conditions of permissible delay in payments. *The Journal of the Operational Research Society, 36*(4), 335–338. doi:10.1057/jors.1985.56

Graham, M., Hale, S. A., & Gaffney, D. (2014). Where in the world are you? Geolocation and language identification in Twitter. *The Professional Geographer, 66*(4), 568–578. doi:10.1080/00330124.2014.907699

Grimes, S. (2000). Here today, gone tomorrow. *Intelligent Enterprise, 3*(9), 42–48.

Grivan, M., & Newman, M. E. J. (2002). Community structure in social and biological network. In *Proceedings of the National Academy of Sciences*.

GTmetrix. (2016). *Analyze Your Site's Speed and Make It Faster*. Retrieved from https://gtmetrix.com/

Guazzelli, A., Stathatos, K., & Zeller, M. (2009). Efficient deployment of predictive analytics through open standards and cloud computing. *ACM SIGKDD Explorations Newsletter, 11*(1), 32–38. doi:10.1145/1656274.1656281

Guitouni, A., & Martel, J.-M. (1998). Tentative Guidelines to Help Choosing an Appropriate MCDA Method. *European Journal of Operational Research, 109*(2), 501–521. doi:10.1016/S0377-2217(98)00073-3

Guo, D., & Cui, W. (2008). Mining moving objects trajectories in Location-based services for spatiotemporal database update, Geoinformatics and Joint Conference on GIS and Built Environment: Geo-Simulation and Virtual, GIS Environments. *Proceedings of the Society for Photo-Instrumentation Engineers, 7143*, 71432M. doi:10.1117/12.812625

Guo, D., & Mennis, J. (2009). Spatial data mining and geographic knowledge discovery—An introduction, Elsevier, Computers. *Environment and Urban Systems*, *33*(6), 403–408. doi:10.1016/j.compenvurbsys.2009.11.001

Haas, H., & Kubin, G. (1998, November). A multi-band nonlinear oscillator model for speech. In *Signals, Systems & Computers, 1998.Conference Record of the Thirty-Second Asilomar Conference on* (Vol. 1, pp. 338-342). IEEE. doi:10.1109/ACSSC.1998.750882

Ha, Back, & Ahn. (2015). MapReduce Functions to Analyze Sentiment Information from Social Big Data. *International Journal of Distributed Sensor Networks*.

Hafeez, K., Zhang, Y. B., & Malak, N. (2002). Determining Key Capabilities of a Firm Using Analytic Hierarchy Process. *International Journal of Production Economics*, *76*(1), 39–51. doi:10.1016/S0925-5273(01)00141-4

Hair, J., Black, W., Tatham, R. L., & Anderson, R. (2011). *Multivariate Data Analysis*. Pearson Education.

Hall, D., Jurafsky, D., & Manning, C. D. (2008, October). Studying the history of ideas using topic models. In *Proceedings of the conference on empirical methods in natural language processing* (pp. 363-371). Association for Computational Linguistics. doi:10.3115/1613715.1613763

Hall, P., Park, B., & Samworth, R. (2008). Choice of Neighbor Order in Nearest-Neighbor Classification. *Annals of Statistics*, *36*(5), 2135–2152. doi:10.1214/07-AOS537

Halouani, N., Chabchoub, H., & Martel, J.-M. (2009). PROMETHEE-MD-2T Method for Project Selection. *European Journal of Operational Research*, *195*(3), 841–895. doi:10.1016/j.ejor.2007.11.016

Han, J., & Kamber, M. (2000). *Data mining: Concepts and techniques*. Morgan Kaufmann.

Han, J., Kamber, M., & Pei, J. (2011). *Data Mining: Concepts and Techniques*. Morgan Kaufmann Publishers.

Han, J., Kamber, M., & Pei, J. (2012). Data Mining Concepts and Techniques (3rd ed.). Elsevier Inc.

Hanagandi, V., Dhar, A., & Buescher, K. (1996). Density-based clustering and radial basis function modeling togenerate credit card fraud scores. *Computational Intelligence for Financial Engineering, Proceedings of the IEEE/IAFE Conference on.*

Hand D. J. (2007). *Statistical techniques for fraud detection, prevention, and evaluation*. NATO advanced study institute on mining massive data sets for security.

Hand, D. J., & Blunt, G. (2001). *Prospecting for gems in credit card data. IMA Journal of Management Mathematics.*

Hand, D., Mannila, H., & Smyth, P. (2001). *Principles of Data Mining*. Cambridge, MA: The MIT Press.

Han, J. (2006). *Data mining concepts and techniques*. San Francisco: Morgan Kaufmann.

Han, J., Kamber, M., & Pei, J. (2006). *Data mining, southeast asia edition: Concepts and techniques*. Morgan Kaufmann.

Han, J., & Pei, M. K. A. J. (2011). Data Mining: Concepts and Techniques. In *Data Management Systems*. Morgan Kaufmann Publishers.

Hargittai, E., & Walejko, G. (2008). The Participation Divide: Content creation and sharing in the digital age 1. *Information Communication and Society*, *11*(2), 239–256. doi:10.1080/13691180801946150

Harvey, C. (2012). *50 Top Open Source Tools for Big Data*. Datamation: IT Business Edge. QuinStreet Enterprise. Retrieved from http://www.datamation.com/datacenter/50-top-open-source-tools-for-big-data-1.html

Hassibi, K. (2000). Detecting payment card fraud with neural networks. Business Applications of Neural Networks, 141-157. doi:10.1142/9789812813312_0009

Hastie, Tibshirani, & Friedman. (2001). *Elements of Statistical learning: Data mining, inference, and prediction.* Springer-Verlag.

Hastie, T., Tibshirani, R., & Friedman, J. (2001). *Elements of Statistical learning: Datamining, Inference, and Prediction.* Springer. doi:10.1007/978-0-387-21606-5

Haythornthwaite, C. (2002). Strong, weak, and latent ties and the impact of new media. *The Information Society, 18*(5), 385–401. doi:10.1080/01972240290108195

Heimerl, F., Lohmann, S., Lange, S., & Ertl, T. (2014, January). Word cloud explorer: Text analytics based on word clouds. In *2014 47th Hawaii International Conference on System Sciences* (pp. 1833-1842). IEEE.

Hill, K. (2012, February 16). *How Target figured out a teen girl was pregnant before her father did.* Retrieved July 4, 2016, from http://www.forbes.com/sites/kashmirhill/2012/02/16/how-target-figured-out-a-teen-girl-was-pregnant-before-her-father-did/

Ho, C. H. (2011). The optimal integrated inventory policy with price-and- credit-linked demand under two-level trade credit. *Computers & Industrial Engineering, 60*(1), 117–126. doi:10.1016/j.cie.2010.10.009

Hong, Y. Y., & Hsiao, C. Y. (2002, September). Locational marginal price forecasting in deregulated electricity markets using artificial intelligence. In *Generation, Transmission and Distribution, IEE Proceedings* (Vol. 149, No. 5, pp. 621-626). IET. doi:10.1049/ip-gtd:20020371

Hopewell, L. (2011). *The Pitfalls of Offshore Cloud.* Available: http://www.zdnet.com/thepitfalls-of-offshore-cloud-1339308564/

Hop, N. V. (2007). Solving fuzzy (stochastic) linear programming problems using superiority and inferiority measures. *Information Sciences, 177*(9), 1977–1991. doi:10.1016/j.ins.2006.12.001

Hoque, S. (2013). A Clustering Method for Seismic Zone Identification and Spatial Data Mining. *International Journal of Enhanced Research in Management and Computer Applications, 2*(9), 5–13.

Hormozi, A. M., & Giles, S. (2004). Data Mining: A Competitive Weapon for Banking and Retail Industries.Information Systems Management, 62-71.

Hu, Z. (2012). *Decision Rule Induction for Service Sector Using Data Mining - A Rough Set Theory Approach* (M. S. Thesis). The University of Texas at El Paso.

Huang, Y. F. (2003). Optimal retailers ordering policies in the EOQ model under trade credit financing. *The Journal of the Operational Research Society, 54*(9), 1011–1015. doi:10.1057/palgrave.jors.2601588

Huh, J., Yetisgen-Yildiz, M., & Pratt, W. (2013). Text classification for assisting moderators in online health communities. *Journal of Biomedical Informatics, 46*(6), 998–1005. doi:10.1016/j.jbi.2013.08.011 PMID:24025513

Hu, M., & Liu, B. (2004). Mining opinion features in customer reviews.*Proceedings of the 19th International Conference on Artificial Intelligence*, (pp. 755-760).

Hu, M., & Liu, B. (2004, August). Mining and summarizing customer reviews. In *Proceedings of the tenth ACM SIGKDD international conference on Knowledge discovery and data mining* (pp. 168-177). ACM.

Hunt, J., Timmis, J., Cooke, D., Neal, M., & King, C. (1998). Development of an artificial immune system for real-world applications.Artificial Immune Systems and their Applications, 157–186.

Hwang, C. L., & Yoon, K. (1981). *Multiple Attribute Decision Making Methods and Applications*. Berlin: Springer. doi:10.1007/978-3-642-48318-9

Ingene, C. A., & Parry, M. E. (1995). Channel coordination when retailers compete. *Marketing Science, 14*(4), 360–377. doi:10.1287/mksc.14.4.360

Ioannidis, J. P. (2005). Why most published research findings are false. *PLoS Medicine, 2*(8), e124. doi:10.1371/journal.pmed.0020124 PMID:16060722

Jacobsen, , Jacobsen, & Munar. (2014). Motivations for sharing tourism experiences through social media. *Tourism Management*.

Jacquet-Lagrèze, E., & Siskos, Y. (1982). Assessing a Set of Additive Utility Functions for Multicriteria Decision Making: The UTA Method. *European Journal of Operational Research, 10*(2), 151–164. doi:10.1016/0377-2217(82)90155-2

Jagadeesh Kumar, M. (2014). Expanding the boundaries of your research using social media: Stand-up and be counted. *IETE Technical Review, 31*(4), 255–257. doi:10.1080/02564602.2014.944442

Jahanshahloo, G. R., Lotfi, F., & Izadikhah, M. (2006). Extension of the TOPSIS method for decision-making problems with fuzzy data. *Applied Mathematics and Computation, 181*(2), 1544–1551. doi:10.1016/j.amc.2006.02.057

Jain, A. K., Murty, M. N., & Flynn, P. J. (1999). Data clustering: A review. *ACM Computing Surveys, 31*(3), 264-323.

Jain, A., & Palekar, U. S. (2005). Aggregate production planning for a continuous reconfigurable manufacturing process. *Computers & Operations Research, 32*(5), 1213–1236. doi:10.1016/j.cor.2003.11.001

Jamalnia, A., & Soukhakian, M. A. (2009). A hybrid fuzzy goal programming approach with different goal priorities to aggregate production planning. *Computers & Industrial Engineering, 56*(4), 1474–1486. doi:10.1016/j.cie.2008.09.010

Jamison, K. D., & Lodwick, W. A. (2001). Fuzzy linear programming using a penalty method. *Fuzzy Sets and Systems, 119*(1), 97–110. doi:10.1016/S0165-0114(99)00082-2

Jangde, P., Chandel, G. S., & Mishra, D. K. (2011). Hybrid Technique for Secure Sum Protocol. *World of Computer Science and Information Technology Journal, 1*(5), 198-201.

Jang, J. S. R. (1993). ANFIS: Adaptive-network-based fuzzy inference system. *Systems, Man and Cybernetics. IEEE Transactions on, 23*(3), 665–685.

Jansen, B. J., Zhang, M., Sobel, K., & Chowdury, A. (2009). Twitter power: Tweets as electronic word of mouth. *Journal of the American Society for Information Science and Technology, 60*(11), 2169–2188. doi:10.1002/asi.21149

Jaquith, W. (2009). Chris Anderson's Free contains apparent plagiarism. *The Virginia Quarterly Review*. Available at: www.vqronline.org/blog/2009/06/23/chris-anderson-free

Jia, L., Yu, C., & Meng, W. (2009, November). The effect of negation on sentiment analysis and retrieval effectiveness. In *Proceedings of the 18th ACM conference on Information and knowledge management* (pp. 1827-1830). ACM. doi:10.1145/1645953.1646241

Jimenez, M., Arenas, M., Bilbao, A., & Rodrıguez, M. V. (2007). Linear programming with fuzzy parameters: An interactive method resolution. *European Journal of Operational Research, 177*(3), 1599–1609. doi:10.1016/j.ejor.2005.10.002

Jirkovsky, V., Obitko, M., Novak, P., & Kadera, P. (2014, September). Big Data analysis for sensor time-series in automation. In Emerging Technology and Factory Automation (ETFA), 2014 IEEE (pp. 1-8). IEEE. doi:10.1109/ETFA.2014.7005183

Jithendra Dara Laxman Gundemoni. (2006). *Credit card security and E-payment Enquiry into credit card fraud in e-payment* (Master thesis). Lulea University of Technology.

Jo, Y., & Oh, A. H. (2011). Aspect and sentiment unification model for online review analysis. In *Proceedings of the fourth ACM international conference on Web search and data mining* (pp. 815-824). doi:10.1145/1935826.1935932

Kahraman, C. (Ed.). (2008). *Fuzzy Multi-Criteria Decision-Making. Theory and Applications with Recent Developments.* New York, NY: Springer. doi:10.1007/978-0-387-76813-7

Kaisler, S., Armour, F., Espinosa, J. A., & Money, W. (2013, January). Big data: Issues and challenges moving forward. In *System Sciences (HICSS), 2013 46th Hawaii International Conference on* (pp. 995-1004). IEEE.

Kantarcioglu, M., & Clifto, C. (2004). Privacy-Preserving distributed mining of association rules on horizontally partitioned data. *IEEE Transactions on Knowledge and Data Engineering Journal, 16*(9), 1026-1037.

Kataoka, S. (1963). A stochastic programming model. *Econometrica, 31*(1/2), 181–196. doi:10.2307/1910956

Kaundinya, D. P., Balachandra, P., Ravindranath, N. H., & Ashok, V. (2013). A GIS (geographical information system)-based spatial data mining approach for optimal location and capacity planning of distributed biomass power generation facilities: A case study of Tumkur district, India. *Energy, 52*, 77–88. doi:10.1016/j.energy.2013.02.011

Kaya, M., & Alhajj, R. (2005). Genetic algorithm based framework for mining fuzzy association rules. *Fuzzy Sets and Systems, 152*(3), 587–601. doi:10.1016/j.fss.2004.09.014

Keane, M. P., & Wasi, N. (2012). *Estimation of Discrete Choice Models with Many Alternatives Using Random Subsets of the Full Choice Set: With an Application to Demand for Frozen Pizza* (No. 2012-W13). Academic Press.

Keeney, R. L. (1976). A Group Preference Axiomatization with Cardinal Utility. *Management Science, 23*(2), 140–145. doi:10.1287/mnsc.23.2.140

Kevin, L. (2015). *A roadmap to green supply chain: Using supply chain Archaeology and Big data analysis.* Industrial Press.

Kim, M. J., & Kim, T. S. (2002). A Neural Classifier with Fraud Density Map for Effective Credit Card Fraud Detection. *Proceedings of the Third International Conference on Intelligent Data Engineering and Automated Learning.* doi:10.1007/3-540-45675-9_56

Klitzman, R. (2014, July 2). *Did Facebook's experiment violate ethics?* Retrieved July 4, 2016, from http://www.cnn.com/2014/07/02/opinion/klitzman-facebook-experiment/index.html

Kohonen, T. (1995). *Self-organizing maps.* Springer-Verlag.

Koperski, et al.. (1996). Spatial Data Mining: Progress and Challenge, Survey Paper. *SIGMOD Workshop on Research Issues on data Mining and Knowledge Discovery* (DMKD).

Kovačević, M., Bajat, B., Trivić, B., & Pavlović, R. (2009, November). Geological units classification of multispectral images by using support vector machines. In *Intelligent Networking and Collaborative Systems, 2009. INCOS'09. International Conference on* (pp. 267-272). IEEE. doi:10.1109/INCOS.2009.44

Kozinets, R. V. (2002). The field behind the screen: Using netnography for marketing research in online communities. *Journal of Marketing Research, 39*(1), 61–72. doi:10.1509/jmkr.39.1.61.18935

Krause-Traudes, M. (2008). Spatial data mining for retail sales forecasting. *11th AGILE International Conference on Geographic Information Science*, (pp. 1-11).

Krishnapuram, B., Carin, L., Figueiredo, M. A., & Hartemink, A. J. (2005). Sparse multinomial logistic regression: Fast algorithms and generalization bounds. *Pattern Analysis and Machine Intelligence. IEEE Transactions on, 27*(6), 957–968.

Kumar, A., Singh, P., Kaur, P., & Kaur, A. (2011). A new approach for ranking of L-R type generalized fuzzy numbers. *Expert Systems with Applications, 38*(9), 10906–10910. doi:10.1016/j.eswa.2011.02.131

Kumar, S. A. (2006). *Production and operations management*. New Age International.

Lahdelma, R., Hokkanen, J., & Salminen, P. (1998). SMAA - Stochastic Multiobjective Acceptability Analysis. *European Journal of Operational Research, 106*(1), 137–143. doi:10.1016/S0377-2217(97)00163-X

Lai, Y. J., & Hwang, C. L. (1992). *Fuzzy mathematical programming: methods and applications*. Berlin: Springer. doi:10.1007/978-3-642-48753-8

Lakshmanan, V., & Smith, T. (2009). Data Mining Storm Attributes from Spatial Grids. *American Metrological Society, 26*, 2353–2365.

Langley, P., Iba, W., & Thompson, K. (1992, July). An analysis of Bayesian classifiers. In AAAI (Vol. 90, pp. 223-228).

Lavrac, N. (2008). Mining Spatio-temporal Data of Traffic Accidents and Spatial Pattern Visualization. *Metodološki Zvezda, 5*(1), 45–63.

Law, A. M., & Kelton, W. D. (2000). *Simulation, Modeling and Analysis*. New York, NY: McGraw Hill.

Lazer, D., Kennedy, R., King, G., & Vespignani, A. (2014). The parable of Google flu: Traps in big data analysis. *Science, 343*(6176), 1203–1205. doi:10.1126/science.1248506 PMID:24626916

Lee, Y. Y. (1990). *Fuzzy set theory approach to aggregate production planning and inventory control* (Unpublished doctoral dissertation). Kansas State University.

Lee, A. J. T., Chen, Y.-A., & Ip, W.-C. (2009). Mining frequent trajectory patterns in spatial–temporal databases. *Information Sciences, 179*(13), 2218–2231. doi:10.1016/j.ins.2009.02.016

Leon, T., & Vercher, E. (2004). Solving a class of fuzzy linear programs by using semi-infinite programming techniques. *Fuzzy Sets and Systems, 146*(2), 235–252. doi:10.1016/j.fss.2003.09.010

Leung, S. C. H., & Chan, S. S. W. (2009). A goal programming model for aggregate production planning with resource utilization constraint. *Computers & Industrial Engineering, 56*(3), 1053–1064. doi:10.1016/j.cie.2008.09.017

Leung, S. C. H., Wu, Y., & Lai, K. K. (2006). A stochastic programming approach for multi-site aggregate production planning. *The Journal of the Operational Research Society, 57*(2), 123–132. doi:10.1057/palgrave.jors.2601988

Lewis, K. (2008). *Tastes, Ties, and Time: Cumulative codebook*. Retrieved from http://dvn.iq.harvard.edu/dvn/dv/t3

Lightner, N. J., Bose, I., & Salvendy, G. (1996). What is wrong with the world-wide web?: A diagnosis of some problems and prescription of some remedies. *Ergonomics, 39*(8), 995–1004. doi:10.1080/00140139608964523

Li, H., & Luan, Y. (2002, December). Kernel Cox regression models for linking gene expression profiles to censored survival data. In *Pacific Symposium on Biocomputing* (Vol. 8, p. 65). doi:10.1142/9789812776303_0007

Li, J., Wang, S., & Chang, T. C. E. (2010). Competition and cooperation in a single-retailer two- supplier supply chain with supply disruption. *International Journal of Production Economics, 124*(1), 137–150. doi:10.1016/j.ijpe.2009.10.017

Lindell, Y., & Pinkas, B. (2000). Privacy preserving data mining. In *Proceedings of 20th Annual International Cryptology Conference (CRYPTO)*.

Linoff, G., & Michael, B. (2014). *Data Mining Techniques*. Wiley Publishing Inc.

Little, R. J. A., & Rubin, D. B. (2002). *Statistical analysis with missing data*. Wiley. doi:10.1002/9781119013563

Liu & Yang. (2012). An improvement of TFIDF weighting in text categorization. International Proceedings of Computer Science and Information Technology, 47(9).

Liu, B. (2007). *Web data mining: Exploring hyperlinks, contents, and usage data*. Berlin: Springer-Verlag.

Liu, B. (2010). Sentiment Analysis and Subjectivity. Handbook of natural language processing, 2, 627-666.

Liu, B. (2007). *Web data mining: exploring hyperlinks, contents, and usage data*. Springer Science & Business Media.

Liu, B. (2010). *Sentiment Analysis and Opinion Mining*. Morgan & Claypool Publishers.

Liu, H., Wang, X., He, J., Han, J., Xin, D., & Shao, Z. (2009). Top-down mining of frequent closed patterns from very high dimensional data, Elsevier. *Information Sciences*, *179*(7), 899–924. doi:10.1016/j.ins.2008.11.033

Liu, X. (2001). Measuring the satisfaction of constraints in fuzzy linear programming. *Fuzzy Sets and Systems*, *122*(2), 263–275. doi:10.1016/S0165-0114(00)00114-7

Lohr, S. (2012). The age of big data. *New York Times*, 11.

Lohse, B. (2013). Facebook Is an Effective Strategy to Recruit Low-income Women to Online Nutrition Education. *Journal of Nutrition Education and Behavior*, *45*(1), 69–76. doi:10.1016/j.jneb.2012.06.006 PMID:23305805

MacQueen, J. (1967, June). Some methods for classification and analysis of multivariate observations. In *Proceedings of the fifth Berkeley symposium on mathematical statistics and probability* (Vol. 1, No. 14, pp. 281-297).

Maes, S., Tuyls, K., Vanschoenwinkel, B., & Manderick, B. (1993). Credit card fraud detection using Bayesian and neural networks. In *Proceedings of the First International NAISO Congress on Neuro Fuzzy Technologies*.

Malczewski, J., Moreno-Sanchez, R., Bojorquez-Tapia, L. A., & Ongay-Delhumeau, E. (1997). Multicriteria Group Decision-Making for Environmental Conflict Analysis in the Cape Region, Mexico. *Journal of Environmental Planning and Management*, *40*(3), 349–374. doi:10.1080/09640569712137

Ma, M., Kandel, A., & Friedman, M. (2000). A new approach for defuzzification. *Fuzzy Sets and Systems*, *111*(3), 351–356. doi:10.1016/S0165-0114(98)00176-6

Mani, I., & Bloedorn, E. (1997). *Multi-document summarization by graph search and matching*. arXiv preprint cmp-lg/9712004

Manikandan, G., & Srinivasan, S. (2013). An Efficient Algorithm for Mining Spatially Co-located Moving Objects. *American Journal of Applied Sciences*, *10*(3), 195–208. doi:10.3844/ajassp.2013.195.208

Manikas, K. (2008). *Outlier Detection in Online Gambling* (Master thesis). Department of Computer Science. University of Goteborg, Sweden.

Manshadi, E. D., Mehregan, M. R., & Safari, H. (2015). Supplier Classification Using UTADIS Method Based on Performance Criteria. *International Journal of Academic Research in Business and Social Sciences*, *5*(2), 31–45. doi:10.6007/IJARBSS/v5-i2/1457

Manyika, J., Chui, M., Brown, B., Bughin, J., Dobbs, R., Roxburgh, C., & Byers, A. H. (2011). *Big data: The next frontier for innovation, competition, and productivity*. Competition & Productivity.

Marabotti, D. (2003). Build supplier metrics, build better product. *Quality*, *42*(2), 40–43.

Marinoni, O. (2005). A Stochastic Spatial Decision Support System Based on PROMETHEE. *International Journal of Geographical Information Science, 19*(1), 51–68. doi:10.1080/13658810412331280176

Marlene, D. (2010). Privacy Issues of Spatial Data Mining in Web Services. *International Journal of Engineering Science and Technology, 2*(10), 5626–5636.

Martin Ester et al. (2001). *Algorithms and Applications for Spatial Data Mining, Geographic Data Mining, and Knowledge Discovery, Research Monographs in GIS*. Taylor and Francis.

Martineau, J., & Finin, T. (2009). Delta TFIDF - an Improved Feature Space for Sentiment Analysis.*Third AAAI International Conference on Weblogs and Social Media*.

McCallum, A., & Nigam, K. (1998, July). A comparison of event models for naive bayes text classification. In AAAI-98 workshop on learning for text categorization (Vol. 752, pp. 41-48).

McGeveran, W. (2007). *Facebook, context, and privacy*. Retrieved from http://blogs.law.harvard.edu/infolaw/2007/09/17/facebook-context/

McNulty, E. (2014). *Indian Government Using Big Data to Revolutionise Democracy*. Dataconomy. Retrieved from http://dataconomy.com/indian-government-using-big-data-to-revolutionise-democracy/

McPherson, M., Smith-Lovin, L., & Cook, J. M. (2001). Birds of a Feather: Homophily in Social Networks. *Annual Review of Sociology, 27*(1), 415–444. doi:10.1146/annurev.soc.27.1.415

Medhat, W., Hassan, A., & Korashy, H. (2014). Sentiment analysis algorithms and applications: A survey. *Ain Shams Engineering Journal., 5*(4), 1093–1113. doi:10.1016/j.asej.2014.04.011

Meena & Prabhakar, T.V. (2007). Sentence Level Sentiment Analysis in the Presence of Conjuncts Using Linguistic Analysis. *29th European Conference on Information Retrieval Research ECIR 2007*, (LNCS) (vol. 4425, pp. 573 – 580). Springer.

Mestyán, M., Yasseri, T., & Kertész, J. (2013). Early prediction of movie box office success based on Wikipedia activity big data. *PLoS ONE, 8*(8), e71226. doi:10.1371/journal.pone.0071226 PMID:23990938

Miller, L. B., & Wagner, H. (1965). Chance-Constrained Programming with Joint Constraints. *Operations Research, 13*(6), 930–945. doi:10.1287/opre.13.6.930

Mishra, N., & Silakari, S. (2012). Predictive Analytics: A Survey, Trends, Applications, Oppurtunities & Challenges. *International Journal of Computer Science and Information Technologies, 3*(3), 4434–4438.

Mislove, A., Lehmann, S., Ahn, Y.-Y., Onnela, J.-P., & Rosenquist, J. N. (2011). Understanding the Demographics of Twitter Users. In *Fifth International AAAI Conference on Weblogs and Social Media*. Retrieved from http://www.aaai.org/ocs/index.php/ICWSM/ICWSM11/paper/view/2816

Mitchell, T. (1997). *Machine Learning*. New York, NY: McGraw-Hill.

Mohammad & Zitar. (2011). Application of genetic optimized artificial immune system and neural networks in spam detection. *Applied Soft Computing*, (11), 3827–3845.

Mosteller, F., & Doob, L. W. (1949). *The pre-election polls of 1948*. Social Science Research Council.

Mousseau, V., Slowinski, R., & Zielniewicz, P. (2000). A User-Oriented Implementation of the ELECTRE-TRI Method Integrating Preference Elicitation Support. *Computers & Operations Research, 27*(7-8), 757–777. doi:10.1016/S0305-0548(99)00117-3

Mukhanov, L. E. (2008). Using Bayesian belief networks for credit card fraud detection.*Proceeding of the IASTED International Conference on Artificial Intelligence and Applications.*

Mula, J., Poler, R., Garcia-Sabater, J. P., & Lario, F. C. (2006). Models for production planning under uncertainty: A review. *International Journal of Production Economics, 103*(1), 271–285. doi:10.1016/j.ijpe.2005.09.001

Mullen, T., & Collier, N. (2004, July). Sentiment Analysis using Support Vector Machines with Diverse Information Sources. In EMNLP (Vol. 4, pp. 412-418).

Muthu Lakshmi, N. V. (2012). Privacy Preserving Association Rule Mining without Trusted Site for Horizontal Partitioned database. *International Journal of Data Mining & Knowledge Management Process, 2*, 17–29. doi:10.5121/ijdkp.2012.2202

Muthulakshmi, N. V., & Rani, S. K. (2012). Privacy Preserving Association Rule Mining in Horizontally Partitioned Databases Using Cryptography Techniques. *International Journal of Computer Science and Information Technologies, 3*(1), 3176 – 3182.

Nada, R. S. (2014). Big data driven supply chain management - A framework for implementing analysis and turning information into intelligence, Pearson Education Inc.

Nagaprasad, S. (2010). Spatial Data Mining Using Novel Neural Networks for Soil Image Classification and Processing. *International Journal of Engineering Science and Technology, 2*(10), 5621–5625.

Nah, F. (2004). A Study on Tolerable Waiting Time: How long are Web Users Willing to Wait. *Behaviour & Information Technology, 23*(3), 153–163. doi:10.1080/01449290410001669914

Nam, S. J., & Logendran, R. (1992). Aggregate production planning – a survey of models and methodologies. *European Journal of Operational Research, 61*(3), 255–272. doi:10.1016/0377-2217(92)90356-E

Negnevitsky, M. (2005). *Artificial Intelligence. A Guide to Intelligent Systems.* Harlow: Addison-Wesley.

Newman, M. L., Groom, C. J., Handelman, L. D., & Pennebaker, J. W. (2008). Gender differences in language use: An analysis of 14,000 text samples. *Discourse Processes, 45*(3), 211–236. doi:10.1080/01638530802073712

Ngai, E. W. T. (2003). Selection of Web Sites for Online Advertising Using AHP. *Information & Management, 40*(4), 233–242. doi:10.1016/S0378-7206(02)00004-6

Ngai, E. W. T., Hu, Y., Wong, Y. H., Chen, Y., & Sun, X. (2011). The application of data mining techniques in financial fraud detection: A classification framework and an academic review of literature. *Decision Support Systems, 50*(3), 559–569. doi:10.1016/j.dss.2010.08.006

Ng, R. T., & Han, J. (1994). Efficient and Effective Clustering Methods for Spatial Data Mining. *Proceedings of the 20th VLDB Conference.*

Nithya, R., & Maheswari, D. (2014). Sentiment analysis on unstructured review. In *Proceeding of IEEE International Conference on Intelligent Computing Applications* (pp.367-371).

O'Dwyer, J., & Renner, R. (2011). The Promise of Advanced Supply Chain Analytics, *Supply Chain. Management Review, 15*(1), 32–37.

Ofcom. (2013). *Internet use and attitudes: 2013 Metrics Bulletin.* Ofcom.

Office for National Statistics. (2012). *Internet Access - Households and Individuals - Office for National Statistics.* Retrieved July 5, 2016, from http://www.ons.gov.uk/peoplepopulationandcommunity/householdcharacteristics/homeinternetandsocialmediausage/bulletins/internetaccesshouseholdsandindividuals/2013-02-28

Oommen, T., Misra, D., Twarakavi, N. K., Prakash, A., Sahoo, B., & Bandopadhyay, S. (2008). An objective analysis of support vector machine based classification for remote sensing. *Mathematical Geosciences, 40*(4), 409-424.

Ortega, F., Gonzalez-Barahona, J. M., & Robles, G. (2008). On the inequality of contributions to Wikipedia. In *Hawaii International Conference on System Sciences, Proceedings of the 41st Annual* (pp. 304–304). IEEE. doi:10.1109/HICSS.2008.333

Oxford Dictionaries. (2013a). *Definition of data mining.* Available from: http://www.oxforddictionaries.com/definition/english/data-mining

Oxford Dictionaries. (2013b). *Definition of social media.* Available from: http://www.oxforddictionaries.com/definition/english/social-media

Pal, B., Sana, S. S., & Chaudhuri, K. S. (2012). Multi-item EOQ model while demand is sales price and price break sensitive. *Economic Modelling, 29*(6), 2283–2288. doi:10.1016/j.econmod.2012.06.039

Pal, B., Sana, S. S., & Chaudhuri, K. S. (2016). Two-echelon competitive integrated supply chain model with price and credit period dependent demand. *International Journal of Systems Science, 47*(5), 995–1007. doi:10.1080/00207721.2014.911383

Paltoglou, G., & Thelwall, M. (2012). Twitter, MySpace, Digg: Unsupervised Sentiment Analysis in Social Media. *ACM Transactions on Intelligent Systems and Technology, 3*(4), 66:1-66:19.

Pang, B., & Lee, L. (2004). A sentimental education: sentiment analysis using subjectivity summarization based on minimum cuts. In *Proceedings of the Association for Computational Linguistics* (pp. 271–278).

Pang, B., & Lee, L. (2008). Opinion mining and sentiment analysis. *Foundations and Trends in Information Retrieval, 2*(1-2), 1-135.

Pang, B., & Lee, L. (2008). Opinion mining and sentiment analysis. *Foundations and Trends in Information Retrieval, 2*(1-2), 1–135. doi:10.1561/1500000011

Pang, B., Lee, L., & Vaithyanathan, S. (2002). Thumbs up: Sentiment classification using machine learning techniques. In *Proceedings of the International Conference on Empirical Methods in Natural Language Processing* (pp. 79–86). doi:10.3115/1118693.1118704

Panne, V. D., & Popp, W. (1963). Minimum Cost Cattle Feed under Probabilistic Protein Constraints. *Management Science, 9*(3), 405–430. doi:10.1287/mnsc.9.3.405

Parimala, M. (2011). A Survey on Density Based Clustering Algorithms for Mining Large Spatial Databases. *International Journal of Advanced Science and Technology, 31*, 59–66.

Pawlak, Z. (1982). Rough Sets. *International Journal of Computer and Information Science, 11*(5), 341–356. doi:10.1007/BF01001956

Pawlak, Z. (1991). *Rough sets: Theoretical aspects of reasoning about data.* Dordrecht, The Netherlands: Kluwer Academic Publishers. doi:10.1007/978-94-011-3534-4

Pearson, M. (2011b). Predictive Analytics: Looking forward to better supply chain decisions. *Logistics Management, 50*(9), 22–26.

Pérez-Ortega, et al. (2010). Spatial Data Mining of a Population-Based Data Warehouse of Cancer in Mexico. *International Journal of Combinatorial Optimization Problems and Informatics, 1*(1), 61-67.

Perrin, A. (2015, October 8). *Social Media Usage: 2005-2015*. Retrieved from http://www.pewinternet.org/2015/10/08/social-networking-usage-2005-2015/

Phua, C. W. C. (2007). *Data Mining in Resilient Identity Crime Detection* (Doctoral thesis). Clayton School of Information Technology, Monash University.

Phua, C., Lee, V., Smith, K., & Gayler, R. (2005). A comprehensive survey of data mining based fraud detection research. *Artificial Intelligence Review*.

Picard, R. W. (2003). Affective computing: Challenges. *International Journal of Human-Computer Studies, 59*(1), 55–64. doi:10.1016/S1071-5819(03)00052-1

Pinterest. (2013). *13 "Pinteresting" Facts About Pinterest Users* [INFOGRAPHIC]. Retrieved July 5, 2016, from https://www.pinterest.com/pin/234257618087475827/

Pisetta, V., Jouve, P.-E., & Zighed, D. (2010). Learning with Ensembles of Randomized Trees. In J. Balcazar, F. Bonchi, A. Gionis, & M. Sebag (Eds.), *Machine Learning and Knowledge Discovery in Databases* (pp. 67–82). Berlin: Springer-Verlag. doi:10.1007/978-3-642-15939-8_5

Pitkow, J. E., & Kehoe, C. M. (1996). Emerging trends in the WWW user population. *Communications of the ACM, 39*(6), 106–108. doi:10.1145/228503.228525

Poirier, D., & C'ecile, B. (2008). Automating Opinion analysis in Film reviews: The case of statistic versus Linguistic approach. *Language Resources and Evaluation Conference*.

Popescu & Etzioni, O. (2005). Extracting product features and opinions from reviews.*Proceedings of the Conference on Human Language Technology and Empirical Methods in Natural Language Processing*.

Popescu, A.-M., & Etzioni, O. (n.d.). Extracting product features and opinions from reviews. In *Proceedings of Conference on Empirical Methods in Natural Language Processing* (pp. 339-346). doi:10.3115/1220575.1220618

Pota, M., Esposito, M., & De Pietro, G. (2013). Transforming probability distributions into membership functions of fuzzy classes: A hypothesis test approach. *Fuzzy Sets and Systems, 233*, 52–73. doi:10.1016/j.fss.2013.03.013

Potamitis, G. (2013). *Design and Implementation of a Fraud Detection Expert System using Ontology-Based Techniques* (Masters Dissertation). Faculty of Engineering and Physical Sciences, Monash University.

Prekopa, A. (1973). Contribution to the Theory of Stochastic Programming. *Management Science, 4*, 202–221.

Protalinski, E. (2012). *Facebook Launches Native App for iPhone and iPad, Rebuilt From Ground Up*. Retrieved from http://www.thenextweb.com

Provost, F. (2002). Comment on: Statistical Fraud Detection—A review. *Statistical Science, (17)*, 249-251.

Qian & Zhang. (2004). *GraphZip: A Fast and Automatic Compression Method for Spatial Data Clustering*. ACM.

Qian & Zhang. (2005). *The Role of Visualization in Effective Data Cleaning*. ACM.

Qibei, L., & Chunhua, J. (2011). Research on Credit Card Fraud Detection Model Based on Class Weighted Support Vector Machine. *Journal of Convergence Information Technology, 6*(1), 62–68. doi:10.4156/jcit.vol6.issue1.8

Quah, J. T. S., & Sriganesh, M. (2008). Real-time credit card fraud detection using computational intelligence. *Expert Systems with Applications, 35*(4), 1721–1732. doi:10.1016/j.eswa.2007.08.093

Quinlan, J. (1986). Induction of Decision Trees. *Machine Learning, 1*(1), 81–106. doi:10.1007/BF00116251

Quinlan, J. R. (2014). *C4. 5: programs for machine learning*. Elsevier.

Qu, L., Wang, Y., & Orgun, M. A. (2013). Cloud service selection based on the aggregation of user feedback and quantitative performance assessment. In *Proceedings of the IEEE International Conference on Service Computing*, (pp. 152-159). doi:10.1109/SCC.2013.92

RAGE. (2016). WebCrusher: Fast Loading Websites…Instantly! *RAGE Software*. Retrieved from http://www.ragesw.com/products/optimize-web-sites.html

Raghupathi, W., & Raghupathi, V. (2014). Big data analytics in healthcare: promise and potential. *Health Information Science and Systems, 2*, 3. Retrieved from http://www.hissjournal.com/content/2/1/3

Rajan, et al. (2012). Efficient Utilization of DBMS Potential in Spatial Data Mining Applications – Neighborhood Relation Modeling Approach. *International Journal of Information and Communication Technology Research, 2*(5), 465-470.

Ramanathan, V. (2012). *Adversarial face recognition and phishing detection using multi-layer data fusion* (Doctoral Dissertation). George Mason University.

Ratner, B. (2011). *Statistical and machine-learning data mining: Techniques for better predictive modeling and analysis of big data*. CRC Press. doi:10.1201/b11508

Ravikumar, K., & Gnanabaskaran, A. (2010). ACO based spatial data mining for risk traffic analysis. *International Journal of Computational Intelligence Techniques, 1*(1), 6-13.

Reaux, R. A., & Carroll, J. M. (1997). Human factors in information access of distributed systems. In G. Salvendy (Ed.), *Handbook of Human Factors & Ergonomics* (2nd ed.). New York: Wiley.

Riglian, A. (2012, November). *"Big data" collection efforts spark an information ethics debate*. Retrieved February 3, 2016, from http://searchcloudapplications.techtarget.com/feature/Big-data-collection-efforts-spark-an-information-ethics-debate

Rinks, D. B. (1982). The performance of fuzzy algorithm models for aggregate planning and different cost structure. In M.M. Gupta & M.M. Sachez (Eds.), Approximate reasoning in decision analysis (pp.-267-278). Amsterdam: North-Holland.

Ripberger, J. T. (2011). Capturing curiosity: Using Internet search trends to measure public attentiveness. *Policy Studies Journal: The Journal of the Policy Studies Organization, 39*(2), 239–259. doi:10.1111/j.1541-0072.2011.00406.x

Ripley, B. D. (2007). *Pattern recognition and neural networks*. Cambridge University Press.

Rommelfanger, H. (1996). Fuzzy linear programming and applications. *European Journal of Operational Research, 92*(3), 512–527. doi:10.1016/0377-2217(95)00008-9

Roy, B. (1985). *Methodologie Multicritere d'Aide a la Decision*. Paris: Economica.

Roy, S. S., Gupta, A., Sinha, A., & Ramesh, R. (2012). Cancer data investigation using variable precision Rough set with flexible classification. In *Proceedings of the Second International Conference on Computational Science, Engineering and Information Technology* (pp. 472-475). ACM. doi:10.1145/2393216.2393295

Roy, S. S., Viswanatham, V. M., & Krishna, P. V. (2016). Spam detection using hybrid model of rough set and decorate ensemble. *International Journal of Computational Systems Engineering, 2*(3), 139–147. doi:10.1504/IJCSYSE.2016.079000

Russel, S. J., & Norvig, P. (1995). *Artificial Intelligence. A Modern Approach*. Englewood Cliffs, NJ: Prentice Hall.

Ruths, D., & Pfeffer, J. (2014). Social media for large studies of behavior. *Science, 346*(6213), 1063–1064. doi:10.1126/science.346.6213.1063 PMID:25430759

Saad, G. (1982). An overview of production planning model: Structure classification and empirical assessment. *International Journal of Production Research, 20*(1), 105–114. doi:10.1080/00207548208947752

Saaty, T. L. (1980). *The Analytic Hierarchy Process: Planning, Priority Setting, Resource Allocation.* New York, NY: Mc-Graw Hill.

Saaty, T. L. (1990). How to make a decision: The analytic hierarchy process. *European Journal of Operational Research, 48*(1), 9–26. doi:10.1016/0377-2217(90)90057-I

Sadeghzadeh, K., & Fard, N. (2015, January). Nonparametric data reduction approach for large-scale survival data analysis. In *Reliability and Maintainability Symposium (RAMS), 2015 Annual* (pp. 1-6). IEEE. doi:10.1109/RAMS.2015.7105128

Safavian, S. R., & Landgrebe, D. (1990). *A survey of decision tree classifier methodology.* Academic Press.

Sahay, B. S., & Ranjan, J. (2008). Real time business intelligence in supply chain analytics. *Information Management & Computer Security, 16*(1), 28–48. doi:10.1108/09685220810862733

Sahoo, N. P., & Biswal, M. P. (2009). Computation of a multi-objective production planning model with probabilistic constraints. *International Journal of Computer Mathematics, 86*(1), 185–198. doi:10.1080/00207160701734207

Salminen, P., Hokkanen, J., & Lahdelma, R. (1998). Comparing Multicriteria Methods in the Context of Environmental Problems. *European Journal of Operational Research, 104*(3), 485–519. doi:10.1016/S0377-2217(96)00370-0

Samet, H. (1995). *Spatial Data Structures.* Reading, MA: ACM Press.

Samli, A. C. (1996). *Information-Driven Marketing Decisions: Development of Strategic Information Systems.* Greenwood Publishing Group.

Sana, S. S. (2011). Price-sensitive demand for perishable items: An EOQ model. *Applied Mathematics and Computation, 217*(13), 6248–6259. doi:10.1016/j.amc.2010.12.113

Sana, S. S., & Chaudhuri, K. S. (2008). A deterministic EOQ model with delay in payments and price-discount offers. *European Journal of Operational Research, 184*(2), 509–533. doi:10.1016/j.ejor.2006.11.023

Sawicka, H. (2012). *The Method of Redesign the Distribution System* (Unpublished doctoral dissertation). Warsaw University of Technology, Warsaw, Poland.

Sawicka, H., Weglinski, S., & Witort, P. (2010). Application of Multiple Criteria Decision Aid Methods in Logistic Systems. *LogForum, 6*(10), 99–110.

Schalkoff, R. I. (1990). *Artificial Intelligence: An Engineering Approach.* New York, NY: McGraw-Hill.

Schneeweiss, S. (2014). Learning from big health care data. *The New England Journal of Medicine, 370*(23), 2161–2163. doi:10.1056/NEJMp1401111 PMID:24897079

Schoen, H., Gayo-Avello, D., Takis Metaxas, P., Mustafaraj, E., Strohmaier, M., & Gloor, P. (2013). The power of prediction with social media. *Internet Research, 23*(5), 528–543. doi:10.1108/IntR-06-2013-0115

Scholz, T., & Conrad, S. (2013). Opinion Mining in Newspaper Articles by Entropy-based Word Connections. In *Proc. of the 2013 Conference on Empirical Methods in Natural Language Processing* (pp. 1828–1839).

Segal, M. R. (1988). Regression trees for censored data. *Biometrics, 44*(1), 35–47. doi:10.2307/2531894

Selvidge, P. (1999). How long is too long for a website to load? *Usability News, 1*(2). Available at: http://psychology.wichita.edu/surl/usabilitynews/1s/time_delay.htm. 23

Selvidge, P. (2003). Examining tolerance for online delays. *Usability News, 5*(1). Available at: http://psychology.wichita.edu/surl/usabilitynews/51/delaytime.htm

Sensing as a Service and Big Data, ICT Centre, CSIRO, ACT, 2601. (n.d.). Research School of Computer Science, The Australian National University, Canberra, Australia. Retrieved from http://arxiv.org/ftp/arxiv/papers/1301/1301.0159.pdf

Ser, G., Robertson, A., & Sheikh, A. (2014). A qualitative exploration of workarounds related to the implementation of national electronic health records in early adopter mental health hospitals. *PLoS ONE, 9*(1), e77669. doi:10.1371/journal.pone.0077669 PMID:24454678

Shah, N. H., & Shah, A. D. (2012). Optimal ordering- Transfer policy for deteriorating inventory items with fuzzy-stock dependent demand. *Mexican Journal of Operations Research, 1*(1), 29–44.

Shah, N. H., Soni, H., & Jaggi, C. K. (2010). Inventory models and trade credit: A review. *Control and Cybernetics, 39*(3), 867–882.

Sharafali, M., Co, H. C., & Goh, M. (2004). Production scheduling in a flexible manufacturing system under random demand. *European Journal of Operational Research, 158*(1), 89–102. doi:10.1016/S0377-2217(03)00300-X

Sharma, A., & Dey, S. (2013). *Using Self-Organizing Maps for Sentiment Analysis.* arXiv preprint arXiv:1309.3946

Sheikh, R., Kumar, B., & Mishra, D. (2010a). A Distributed k- Secure sum Protocol for Secure Multi Site Computations. *Journal of Computing, 2*, 239–243.

Sheikh, R., Kumar, B., & Mishra, D. (2010b). A modified Ck Secure sum protocol for multi party computataion. *Journal of Computing, 2*, 62–66.

Shinde-Pawar. (2015). Formation of smart sentiment analysis technique for big data. *International Journal of Innovative Research in Computer and Communication Engineering.*

Shivakumar, U., Ravi, V., & Gangadharan, G. R. (2013). Ranking cloud services using fuzzy multi-attribute decision making. In *Proceedings of the IEEE International Conference on Computational Fuzzy Systems (FUZZIEEE).* doi:10.1109/FUZZ-IEEE.2013.6622319

Siegel, E. (2013). *Predictive Analytics: The Power to Predict Who Will Click, Buy, Lie, or Die.* Wiley Publishing.

Simon, H. A. (1977). *The new science of management decision.* Prentice-Hall, Inc.

Singh, V. K., Piryani, R., Uddin, A., & Waila, P. (2013). Sentiment analysis of textual reviews. In *Proceedings of IEEE 5th International Conference on Knowledge and Smart Technology* (pp. 122-127).

Sinha, S., & Sarmah, S. P. (2010). Coordination and price competition in a duopoly common retailer supply chain. *Computers & Industrial Engineering, 59*(2), 280–295. doi:10.1016/j.cie.2010.04.010

Siskos, J. (1982). A Way to Deal with Fuzzy Preferences in Multicriteria Decision Problems. *European Journal of Operational Research, 10*(3), 314–324. doi:10.1016/0377-2217(82)90230-2

Smith, G. E., Watson, K. J., Baker, W. H., & Pokorski, J. A. II. (2007). A critical balance: Collaboration and security in the IT-enabled supply chain. *International Journal of Production Research, 45*(11), 2595–2613. doi:10.1080/00207540601020544

Smith, M. (2000). The visible supply chain. *Intelligent Enterprise, 3*(16), 44–50.

Smola, A., & Vishwanatan, S. (2008). *Introduction to Machine Learning.* Cambridge, UK: Cambridge University Press.

Song, X., Duan, Z., & Jiang, X. (2012). Comparison of artificial neural networks and support vector machine classifiers for land cover classification in Northern China using a SPOT-5 HRG image. *International Journal of Remote Sensing*, *33*(10), 3301–3320. doi:10.1080/01431161.2011.568531

Srikant, R., & Agarwal, R. (1994). Mining generalized association rules. In VLDB'95, (pp. 479-488).

Srikant, R., & Agarwal, R. (1995). Mining generalized association rules. In *Proceedings of the International Conference on Very Large Databases*.

Srikant, R., & Agrawal, R. (1996). *Mining sequential patterns: Generalizations and performance improvements*. Springer Berlin Heidelberg.

Stam, A., & Duarte Silva, A. P. (1997). Stochastic Judgments in the AHP: The Measurement of Rank Reversal Probabilities. *Decision Sciences*, *28*(3), 655–688. doi:10.1111/j.1540-5915.1997.tb01326.x

Stutzman, F. (2006). *How Facebook broke its culture*. Retrieved from http://chimprawk.blogspot.com/2006/09/how-facebook-broke-its-culture.html

Su, et al. (2013). Uncertainty-aware visualization and proximity monitoring in urban excavation: a geospatial augmented reality approach. *Visualization in Engineering*, 1-13. Retrieved from http://www.viejournal.com/content/1/1/2

Suchdev, R., Kotkar, P., Ravindran, R., & Swamy, S. (2014). Twitter sentiment analysis using machine learning and knowledge-based approach. *International Journal of Computers and Applications*, *103*(4), 36–40. doi:10.5120/18066-9006

Sugumar, Jayakumar, R., & Rengarajan, C. (2012). Design a Secure Multi Site Computation System for Privacy Preserving Data Mining. *International Journal of Computer Science and Telecommunications*, *3*, 101–105.

Sullivan, L. (2013). *Data Overload Stifling Customer Service Improvements*. Retrieved from www.mediapost.com/publications/article/214310/data-overload-stifling-customerservice-improvemen.html

Sumuthi, S. (2008). Spatial Data Mining: Techniques and its Applications. *Journal of Computer Applications*, *1*(4), 28–30.

Swatman, P. (2013). *Ethical issues in social networking research*. Retrieved from http://www.deakin.edu.au/__data/assets/pdf_file/0007/269701/Swatman-Ethics-and-Social-Media-Research.pdf

Sweeney, L. (2002). k-anonymity: A model for protecting privacy. *International Journal of Uncertainty, Fuzziness and Knowledge-based Systems*, *10*(5), 557–570. doi:10.1142/S0218488502001648

Syeda, M., Zhang, Y. Q., & Pan, Y. (2002). Parallel Granular Neural Networks for Fast Credit Card Fraud Detection. *Proceedings of the IEEE International Conference*, (1), 572–577 doi:10.1109/FUZZ.2002.1005055

Tanaka, H., Okuda, T., & Asai, K. (1973). On fuzzy mathematical programming. *Journal of Cybernetics and Systems*, *3*(4), 37–46. doi:10.1080/01969727308545912

Tang, J., Fung, R. Y. K., & Yung, K. L. (2003). Fuzzy modeling and simulation for aggregate production planning. *International Journal of Systems Science*, *34*(12-13), 661–673. doi:10.1080/00207720310001624113

Tang, J., Wang, D., & Fang, R. Y. K. (2000). Fuzzy formulation for multi-product aggregate production planning. *Production Planning and Control*, *11*(7), 670–676. doi:10.1080/095372800432133

Taylor, M. E., & Velásquez, J. D. (2014). A novel deterministic approach for aspect-based opinion mining in tourism products reviews. *Expert Systems with Applications*, *41*(17), 7764–7775. doi:10.1016/j.eswa.2014.05.045

Teixeira, et al.. (2005). Online data mining services for dynamic spatial databases II: quality air location based services and sonification. *II International Conference and Exhibition on Geographic Information*.

Teng, Z., Ren, F., & Kuriowa, S. (2007). Emotion recognition from text based on the rough set theory and the support vector machines. In *Proceedings of 2007 international conference of the natural language processing and knowledge engineering* (pp. 36– 41). Beijing, China: IEEE Computer Society. doi:10.1109/NLPKE.2007.4368008

Tervonen, T., & Figueira, J. (2008). A Survey on Stochastic Multicriteria Acceptability Analysis Methods. *Journal of Multi-Criteria Decision Analysis*, *15*(1-2), 1–14. doi:10.1002/mcda.407

Thangavel, K., Jaganathan, P., Pethalakshmi, A., & Karnan, M. (2005). Effective classification with improved quick reduct for medical database using rough system. *Bioinformatics and Medical Engineering*, *5*(1), 7–14.

Thomson, G. (1947). *Probit Analysis: A statistical treatment of the sigmoid response curve*. Academic Press.

Thurow, N. A., & Delano, J. D. (2010). Selection of web services based on opinion mining of free-text user reviews. In *Proceedings of the International Conference on Information Systems*.

Ting, K.-C. T., Ting, P.-H., & Hsiao, P.-W. (2014). Why are bloggers willing to share their thoughts via travel blogs? *International Journal of Technology Management*, *64*(1), 89. doi:10.1504/IJTM.2014.059237

Top Credit Card Processors. (2015). *Rankings of Best Fraud Detection Companies*. Retrieved from http://www.topcreditcardprocessorsguide.com/rankings-of-best-fraud-detection-companies

Train Kenneth, E. (2003). *Discrete choice methods with simulation*. Academic Press.

Tran, V. X., Tsuji, H., & Masuda, R. (2009). A new QoS ontology and its QoS based ranking algorithms for Web services. *Simulation Modelling Practice and Theory*, *17*(8), 1378–1398. doi:10.1016/j.simpat.2009.06.010

Tsai, C. W., Lai, C. F., Chao, H. C., & Vasilakos, A. V. (2015). Big data analytics: A survey. *Journal of Big Data*, *2*(1), 1–32. doi:10.1186/s40537-015-0030-3 PMID:26191487

Tsytsarau, M., & Palpanas, T. (2012). Survey on mining subjective data on the web. *Data Mining and Knowledge Discovery*, *24*(3), 478–514. doi:10.1007/s10618-011-0238-6

Tufekci, Z. (2014). Big Questions for Social Media Big Data: Representativeness, Validity and Other Methodological Pitfalls. In *Eighth International AAAI Conference on Weblogs and Social Media*. Retrieved from http://www.aaai.org/ocs/index.php/ICWSM/ICWSM14/paper/view/8062

Tumasjan, A., Sprenger, T., Sandner, P., & Welpe, I. (2010). Predicting elections with twitter: What 140 characters reveal about political sentiment. *Word Journal Of The International Linguistic Association*, *280*(39), 178–185.

Tuo, J., Ren, S., Liu, W., Li, X., Li, B., & Lei, L. (2004). Artificial immune system for fraud detection. *IEEE International Conference on Systems, Man and Cybernetics*, (2), 1407-1411. doi:10.1109/ICSMC.2004.1399827

Turney, P. D. (2002, July). Thumbs up or thumbs down?: semantic orientation applied to unsupervised classification of reviews. In *Proceedings of the 40th annual meeting on association for computational linguistics* (pp. 417-424). Association for Computational Linguistics.

Ultsch, A., & Mörchen, F. (2005). *ESOM-Maps: Tools for clustering, visualization, and classification with Emergent SOM*. Academic Press.

UsabilityNet. (2006). *International Standards for HCI and Usability*. Retrieved from http://www.usabilitynet.org/tools/r_international.htm#18529

Vaidya, Clifton, Kantarcioglu, & Patterson. (2008). Privacy preserving decision trees over vertically partitioned data. *ACM Transactions on Knowledge Discovery from Data*, *2*(3), 14–41.

Vaidya, J. (2004). *Privacy preserving data mining over vertically partitioned data* (Ph.D. dissertation). Purdue University.

Valêncio et al. (2013). 3D Geovisualisation Techniques Applied to Spatial Data Mining. Springer-Verlag.

Vaquero, L. M., Rodero-Merino, L., & Cáceres, J. (2009). Lindner, M., A break in the Clouds: towards a Cloud definition. *ACM Computer Communication Reviews, 39*(1), 50-55.

Varghese, R., & Jayasree, M. (2013). Aspect based sentiment analysis using support vector machine classifier. In *Proceedings of IEEE International Conference on Advances in Computing, Communications and Informatics* (pp.1581-1586). doi:10.1109/ICACCI.2013.6637416

Vatsavai, et al. (2012). *Spatiotemporal Data Mining in the Era of Big Spatial Data: Algorithms and Applications.* ACM.

Vesset, D., Olofson, C. W., Schubmehl, D., McDonough, B., Woodward, A., Stires, C., ... Dialani, M. (2014). *IDC FutureScape: Worldwide Big Data and Analytics 2015 Predictions.* IDC Research, Inc. Retrieved from http://www.idc.com/getdoc.jsp?containerId=prUS25329114

Vincke, P. (1992). *Multicriteria Decision-Aid.* Chichester, UK: John Wiley & Sons.

Vinodhini & Chandrasekaran. (2012). Sentiment Analysis and Opinion Mining: A survey. *International Journal of Advanced Research in Computer Science and Software Engineering, 2*(6).

Vinodhini, G., & Chandrasekaran, R. M. (2012). Sentiment analysis and opinion mining: A survey. *International Journal (Toronto, Ont.), 2*(6).

Waller, M. A., & Fawcett, S. E. (2013). Data Science, Predictive Analytics, and Big Data: A Revolution That Will Transform Supply Chain Design and Management. *The Journal of Business, 34*(2), 77–84.

Waller, M. A., & Fawcett, S. E. (2013). Data science, predictive analytics, and big data: A revolution that will transform supply chain design and management. *Journal of Business Logistics, 34*(2), 77–84. doi:10.1111/jbl.12010

Wang, et al. (2009). Cloud Model-Based Spatial Data Mining. *Geographic Information Sciences, 9*(1-2), 60-70. DOI: 10.1080/10824000309480589

Wang, H., Can, D., Kazemzadeh, A., Bar, F., & Narayanan, S. (2012, July). A system for real-time twitter sentiment analysis of 2012 US presidential election cycle. In Proceedings of the ACL 2012 System *Demonstrations* (pp. 115-120). Association for Computational Linguistics.

Wang, C., Wang, J., Xie, X., & Ma, W. Y. (2007, November). Mining geographic knowledge using location aware topic model. In *Proceedings of the 4th ACM workshop on Geographical information retrieval* (pp. 65-70). ACM. doi:10.1145/1316948.1316967

Wang, R. C., & Fang, H. H. (2001). Aggregate production planning with multiple objectives in a fuzzy environment. *European Journal of Operational Research, 133*(3), 521–536. doi:10.1016/S0377-2217(00)00196-X

Wang, R. C., & Liang, T. F. (2004). Application of multi-objective linear programming to aggregate production planning. *Computers & Industrial Engineering, 46*(1), 17–41. doi:10.1016/j.cie.2003.09.009

Wang, R. C., & Liang, T. F. (2005). Applying possibilistic linear programming to aggregate production planning. *International Journal of Production Economics, 98*(3), 328–341. doi:10.1016/j.ijpe.2004.09.011

Warden, P. (2011). *Big Data Glossary.* O'Reilly.

WebSiteOptimization. (2008). *The Psychology of Web Performance.* Retrieved from http://www.websiteoptimization.com/speed/tweak/psychology-web-pcrformance/

Wei, C., & Schonfeld, P. (1993). An Artificial Neural Network Approach for Evaluating Transportation Network Improvements. *Journal of Advanced Transportation*, *27*(2), 129–151. doi:10.1002/atr.5670270202

Weiss, S. M., & Indurkhya, N. (1998). *Predictive data mining: a practical guide.* Morgan Kaufmann.

Wei, X., & Croft, W. B. (2006, August). LDA-based document models for ad-hoc retrieval. In *Proceedings of the 29th annual international ACM SIGIR conference on Research and development in information retrieval* (pp. 178-185). ACM.

Wei, Y., & Chen, Y. F. (2011). Joint determination of inventory replenishment and sales effort with uncertain market responses. *International Journal of Production Economics*, *134*(2), 368–374. doi:10.1016/j.ijpe.2009.11.011

Wen, M., Yang, D., & Rose, C. P. (2014). Sentiment analysis in MOOC discussion forums: what does it tell us. In Proceedings of Educational Data Mining.

White Paper of DHL. (2011). *Are you ready for anything?* DHL Supply Chain Matters.

White Paper of DHL. (2013a). *Big Data in Logistics-A DHL Perspective on how to move beyond the hype.* DHL Customer Solutions & Innovation.

White Paper of DHL. (2013b). *Logistics Trend Radar- delivering insight today...creating value tomorrow.* DHL Customer Solutions & Innovation.

White Paper of ORACLE. (2015). *Improving Logistics & Transportation Performance with Big Data Architect's Guide and Reference - Architecture Introduction.* ORACLE Enterprise Architecture.

White, D. S., & Le Cornu, A. (2011). Visitors and Residents: A new typology for online engagement. *First Monday*, *16*(9). doi:10.5210/fm.v16i9.3171

Witten, I. H., & Frank, E. (2005). *Data Mining: Practical machine learning tools and techniques.* Morgan Kaufmann.

Woodfield, K., Morrell, G., Metzler, K., Blank, G., Salmons, J., Finnegan, J., & Lucraft, M. (2013). *Blurring the Boundaries? New Social Media, New Social Research: Developing a network to explore the issues faced by researchers negotiating the new research landscape of online social media platforms: A methodological review paper.* Southampton, UK: National Centre for Research Methods.

Wu, C. H., Chen, C. W., & Hsieh, C. C. (2012). Competitive pricing decisions in a two-echelon supply chain with horizontal and vertical competition. *International Journal of Production Economics*, *135*(1), 265–274. doi:10.1016/j.ijpe.2011.07.020

Wu, D., & Ierapetritou, M. (2007). Hierarchical approach for production planning and scheduling under uncertainty. *Chemical Engineering and Processing: Process Intensification*, *46*(11), 1129–1140. doi:10.1016/j.cep.2007.02.021

Wu, X., Kumar, V., Quinlan, J. R., Ghosh, J., Yang, Q., Motoda, H., & Steinberg, D. et al. (2008). Top 10 algorithms in data mining. *Knowledge and Information Systems*, *14*(1), 1–37. doi:10.1007/s10115-007-0114-2

Xie, J., & Wei, J. C. (2009). Coordinating advertising and pricing in a manufacturer retailer channel. *European Journal of Operational Research*, *197*(2), 785–791. doi:10.1016/j.ejor.2008.07.014

Yaakub, M. R., Li, Y., & Feng, Y. (2011). Integration of Opinion into Customer Analysis Model. In *Proceedings of the Eighth IEEE International Conference on e-Business Engineering* (pp. 90-95). doi:10.1109/ICEBE.2011.53

Yager, R. R. (1978). Fuzzy decision making including unequal objectives. *Fuzzy Sets and Systems*, *1*(2), 87–95. doi:10.1016/0165-0114(78)90010-6

Yager, R. R., & Filev, D. P. (1993). A simple adaptive defuzzification method. *IEEE Transactions on Fuzzy Systems*, *1*(1), 69–78. doi:10.1109/TFUZZ.1993.390286

Yahia, M. E., & El-Mukashfi El-Taher, M. (2010). A New Approach for Evaluation of Data Mining Techniques. *IJCSI*, *7*(5), 181–186.

Yang, H., Si, L., & Callan, J. (2006). Knowledge transfer and opinion detection in the TREC2006 blog track. In *Proceedings of TREC*.

Yan, S., Chen, C., Zhao, G., & Lee, B. S. (2012). Cloud service recommendation and selection for enterprises. In *Proceedings of the 8th IEEE International Conference on Network and Service Management and Workshop on Systems Virtualization Management*, (pp. 430-434).

Yao, D. Q., & Liu, J. J. (2005). Competitive pricing of mixed retail and e-tail distribution channels. *Omega*, *33*(3), 235–247. doi:10.1016/j.omega.2004.04.007

Yao, Y. (2011). Superiority of Three-Way Decisions in Probabilistic Rough Set Models. *Information Sciences*, *181*(6), 1080–1096. doi:10.1016/j.ins.2010.11.019

Yap, B. W., Rani, K. A., Rahman, H. A. A., Fong, S., Khairudin, Z., & Abdullah, N. N. (2013). An application of oversampling, undersampling, bagging and boosting in handling imbalanced datasets. In *Proceedings of International Conference on Advanced Data and Information-Lecture Notes in Electrical Engineering*, (pp. 13-22).

Yasseri, T., Sumi, R., & Kertész, J. (2012). Circadian patterns of wikipedia editorial activity: A demographic analysis. *PLoS ONE*, *7*(1), e30091. doi:10.1371/journal.pone.0030091 PMID:22272279

Yi, J., Nasukawa, T., Bunescu, R., & Niblack, W. (2003). Sentiment analyzer: Extracting sentiments about a given topic using natural language processing techniques. In *Proceedings of IEEE International Conference on Data Mining* (pp. 427-434).

Yoon, K. P. (1996). A probabilistic approach to rank complex fuzzy numbers. *Fuzzy Sets and Systems*, *80*(2), 167–176. doi:10.1016/0165-0114(95)00193-X

Yue, Z. (2011). A Method for Group Decision-Making Based on Determining Weights of Decision Makers using TOPSIS. *Applied Mathematical Modelling*, *35*(4), 1926–1936. doi:10.1016/j.apm.2010.11.001

Yu, L., Yue, W., Wang, S., & Lai, K. K. (2010). Support vector machine based multi agent ensemble learning for credit risk evaluation. *Expert Systems with Applications*, *37*(2), 1351–1360. doi:10.1016/j.eswa.2009.06.083

Zadeh, L. A. (1965). Fuzzy sets. *Information and Control*, *8*(3), 338–353. doi:10.1016/S0019-9958(65)90241-X

Zaman, M. (2005). *Predictive Analytics: the Future of Business Intelligence*. Technology Evaluation Centers.

Zaragozi, B., Rabasa, A., Rodríguez-Sala, J. J., Navarro, J. T., Belda, A., & Ramón, A. (2012). Modeling farmland abandonment: A study combining GIS and data mining techniques. *Agriculture, Ecosystems & Environment*, *155*, 124–132. doi:10.1016/j.agee.2012.03.019

Zareipour, H., Bhattacharya, K., & Canizares, C. A. (2006, June). Forecasting the hourly Ontario energy price by multivariate adaptive regression splines. In *Power Engineering Society General Meeting*. IEEE. doi:10.1109/PES.2006.1709474

Zaslavsky V., A. Strizhak. (2006). Credit card fraud detection using self organizing maps. *Information & Security: An International Journal*, (18), 48-63.

Zavadskas, E. K., Antucheviciene, J., Saparauskas, J., & Turskis, Z. (2013). MCDM methods WASPAS and MULTI-MOORA: Verification of Robustness of Methods when Assessing Alternative Solutions. *Economic Computation and Economic Cybernetics Studies and Research*, *47*(2), 5–20.

Zeng, X., Lin, D., & Xu, Q. (2011). Query Performance Tuning in Supply Chain Analytics. *4th International Conference on Computational Sciences and Optimization*, (pp. 327-330).

Zeng, B. Z., & Gerritsen, R. (2014). *What do we know about social media in tourism? A review*. Tourism Management Perspectives.

Zeng, L., Li, L., & Duan, L. (2012). Business intelligence in enterprise computing environment. *Information Technology and Management, Springer*, *13*(4), 297–310. doi:10.1007/s10799-012-0123-z

Zghal, B. (2007). A Framework for Data Mining Based Multi-Agent: An Application to Spatial Data, World Academy of Science. *Engineering and Technology International Journal of Computer Information Science and Engineering*, *1*(5), 202–206.

Zhang, L., Ghosh, R., Dekhil, M., Hsu, M., & Liu, B. (2011). *Combining lexicon based and learning-based methods for twitter sentiment analysis*. Technical Report HPL-2011-89.

Zhang, F. (2011). A GIS-based method for identifying the optimal location for a facility to convert forest biomass to biofuel, Elsevier. *Biomass and Bioenergy*, *35*, 3951–3961.

Zhang, G., Wu, Y. H., Remias, M., & Lu, J. (2003). Formulation of fuzzy linear programming problems as four objective constrained optimization problems. *Applied Mathematics and Computation*, *139*(2-3), 383–399. doi:10.1016/S0096-3003(02)00202-3

Zhang, Z. (2008). Weighing stars: Aggregating online product reviews for intelligent e-commerce applications. *IEEE Intelligent Systems*, *23*(5), 42–49. doi:10.1109/MIS.2008.95

Zhao, D., & Rosson, M. B. (2009, May). How and why people Twitter: the role that micro-blogging plays in informal communication at work. In *Proceedings of the ACM 2009 International Conference on Supporting Group Work* (pp. 243-252). ACM.

Zheng, Z., Wu, H., Zhang, Y., Lyu, M. R., & Wang, J. (2013). QoS ranking prediction for Cloud services. *IEEE Transactions on Parallel and Distributed Systems*, *24*(6), 1213–1222. doi:10.1109/TPDS.2012.285

Zhou, Y. W., Zhong, Y., & Li, J. (2012). An uncooperative order model for items with trade credit, inventory-dependent demand, and limited displayed-shelf space. *European Journal of Operational Research*, *223*(1), 76–85. doi:10.1016/j.ejor.2012.06.012

Zhou, Y., & Leung, H. (2006). Empirical analysis of object-oriented design metrics for predicting high and low severity faults. *Software Engineering. IEEE Transactions on*, *32*(10), 771–789.

Zhu, F., & Zhang, X. M. (2010). Impact of online consumer reviews on sales: The moderating role of product and consumer characteristics. *Journal of Marketing*, *74*(2), 133–148. doi:10.1509/jmkg.74.2.133

Zicari, R. (2012). *Big Data: Challenges and Opportunities*. Academic Press.

Zikopoulos, P., deRoos, D., Parasuraman, K., Deutsch, T., Corrigan, D., & Giles, J. (2013). *Harness the Power of Big Data*. McGraw-Hill.

Zikopoulos, P., Eaton, C., deRoos, D., Deutsch, T., & Lapis, G. (2012). *Understanding Big Data – Analytics for Enterprise Class Hadoop and Streaming Data*. McGraw-Hill.

Zimmer, M. (2006). *More on Facebook and the contextual integrity of personal information flows*. Retrieved from http://michaelzimmer.org/2006/09/08/more-onfacebook-and-the-contextual-integrity-of-personal-informationflows/

Zimmerman, H. J. (1978). Fuzzy programming and linear programming with several objective functions. *Fuzzy Sets and Systems*, *1*(1), 45–55. doi:10.1016/0165-0114(78)90031-3

Zimmermann, H. J. (1976). Description and optimization of fuzzy systems. *International Journal of General Systems*, *2*(4), 209–216. doi:10.1080/03081077608547470

About the Contributors

Shrawan Kumar Trivedi is an assistant professor of Information Systems in the School of Management at BML Munjal University. He has completed his Fellow (FPM) from Indian Institute of Management Indore. Prior to this, he did his M.Tech (IT) from Indian Institute of Information Technology Allahabad, M.Sc. (Electronics) from University Institute of Technology, C.S.J.M. University Kanpur and B.Sc (PCM) from C.S.J.M. University Kanpur. He has his expertise in Data Mining, Text Mining and Big Data. His area of interest includes Business Intelligence and Analytics, Management Information Systems, Enterprise Resource Planning, Knowledge Management, IT Strategy etc. He also has expertise in several software tools like SPSS, SAS, Matlab, Clementine and some other business analytics tools. In addition to this, he has published his research papers in reputed international journals and presented his research in many international conferences. His papers can be viewed in IEEE Xplore, ACM portals and many peer reviewed journals. In his academics, he has done many projects like Wireless Transmitter, PC Remote, Power Amplifier, E10 B switching Systems, GSM etc. During his M.Tech (IT), he has worked on Wireless Sensor Network where he has designed a new protocol for routing. In his FPM, he has worked on Text mining and developed some new algorithms for classification. His research interest includes Text Mining, Data Mining, Big Data, Inter Organisation Systems and applications like Spam Classification, Sentiment Analysis etc.

Shubhamoy Dey is a professor of information systems at Indian Institute of Management Indore, India. He completed his Ph. D from the School of Computing, University of Leeds, UK, and Master of Technology from Indian Institute of Technology (IITKharagpur). He specializes in Data Mining and has 25 years of research, consulting and teaching experience in UK, USA and India.

Anil Kumar is a faculty of Operation Management and Quantitative Techniques in the School of Management at BML Munjal University, Gurgaon India. He completed his Ph.D in Management Science from Indian Institute of Information Technology and Management, Gwalior. He earned his MBA, MSc (Mathematics) from Department of Mathematics (Kurukshetra University, Kurukshetra) and Graduation in Mathematics-Hons from the same University. He also qualified UGC-NET. He published more than 27 research papers/book chapters and also four books in his credit. His research interest includes marketing analytics, multi-criteria decision making, fuzzy multi-criteria decision making, fuzzy optimisation, application of soft-computing and econometrics modelling in marketing, multi-criteria decision making and fuzzy applications in e-commerce and M-commerce.

Tapan Panda is an alumnus of University of Houston, USA, where he completed an MBA in Global Energy. He holds a PhD in Business Administration. He has worked as a full-time faculty member at 3 IIMs – Lucknow, Kozhikode and Indore. He has also officiated as Director, Indian Institute of Management, Indore before joining Everonn Education Limited (a BSE and NSE listed company) as its president -marketing & corporate affairs. He has more than twenty years of academic experience in marketing, branding and customer relationship management. He was also Director at Great Lakes Institute of Management, Chennai. He has visited C.T. Bauer College, University of Houston, Texas, USA; University of Cincinnati, Ohio, USA; Fudan University, Shanghai, China; on visiting academic assignments. He has trained people from reputed organizations like ONGC, GAIL, SAIL, EIL, HUL, LG, AXIS Bank, and TVS Motors. He is a member of American Marketing Association (AMA), National Board of Accreditation (NBA), and AIMA. He has published extensively in reputed national and international journals and presented in international conferences across the world. He has more than 50 research papers and 16 books to his credit. His books include: Sales and Distribution Management (Oxford University Press), Marketing Management (Excel Books), Tourism Management (Orient Longman). He is a regular contributor to business newspapers and magazines; and has participated in CNBC and Zee Business programmes.

* * *

Askarunisa A. works as a Professor in the Department of Computer science & Engineering, Recognised Supervisor in Anna University, chennai. Has published more than 20 papers in International Journals & Conferences.

Abirami A. M. completed B.E (CSE) degree in Government College of Technology, Coimbatore in the year 1999. Completed M.E (CSE) degree in the year 2010. Presently pursuing PhD in Information and Communication Engineering under Anna University Chennai in the domain of Text Analysis.

A. Sheik Abdullah works as Assistant Professor, Department of Information Technology, Thiagarajar College of Engineering, Madurai, Tamil Nadu, India. He completed his B.E (Computer Science and Engineering), at Bharath Niketan Engineering College, and M.E (Computer Science and Engineering) at Kongu Engineering College under Anna University, Chennai. He has been awarded as gold medalist for his excellence in the degree of Post Graduate. He is pursuing his Ph.D in the domain of Medical Data Analytics, and his research interests include Medical Data Research, E-Governance and Big Data. He has handled various E-Governance projects such as automation system for tracking community certificate, birth and death certificate, DRDA and income tax automation systems. He has published research articles in various reputed journals and International Conferences. He has been assigned as an reviewer in Various reputed journals such as European Heart Journal, Proceedings of the National Academy of Sciences, Physical Sciences (NASA) and so on. He has received the Honorable chief minister award for excellence in E-Governance for the best project in E-Governance. Currently he is working towards the significance of the medical data corresponding to various diseases and resolving its implications through the development of various algorithmic models.

Balamurugan Balusamy had completed his B.E(computer science) from Bharathidasan University and M.E(computer Science) from Anna University.He completed his Ph.D. in cloud security domain specifically on access control techniques.He has published papers and chapters in several renowned journals and conferences.

Animesh Biswas is rendering his service as an Assistant Professor in Department of Mathematics, University of Kalyani, India. Formerly, he served Sikkim Manipal University of Health, Medical and Technological Sciences, Sikkim, India and RCC Institute of Information Technology, Kolkata, India as a Lecturer in Mathematics. Being a visiting faculty, Dr. Biswas was associated with Indian Institute of Information Technology (IIIT), Kalyani, India, West Bengal State University, India and University of Gour Banga, India. He received M.Sc. and Ph.D. degree in Mathematics from University of Kalyani, India. The area of his research includes Fuzzy Programming, Fuzzy Stochastic Programming, Fuzzy Control, Multicriteria Decision Making, Artificial Intelligence and their applications to different real life problems. Dr. Biswas produced research articles in reputed international journals and conferences. He attended various international conferences within India and abroad, delivered invited talks, presented papers and chaired several technical sessions. He is one of the reviewers of leading International Journals and Conferences. Dr. Biswas is a member of Indian Statistical Institute, Kolkata, India, Operational Research Society of India, Soft Computing Research Society, India, Tripura Mathematical Society, India, Computational Intelligence Society, IEEE, World Academy of Science, Engineering and Technology (WASET), International Association of Engineers (IAENG), International Economics Development Research Center (IEDRC), Multicriteria Decision Making Society, Germany, etc.

A. Anandaraja Chari is working as Emeritus Professor in the Dept of OR & SQC, Rayalaseema University, Kurnool. He has over 30 years of teaching and research experience in the field of OR and SQC, Computer Science, Mathematics. He published number of research papers in these areas.

T. K. Das received Ph. D from VIT University, Vellore India in the year 2015 and M. Tech. from Utkal University, India in the year 2003. He is currently working as Associate Professor in VIT University, India. He has about 10 years' experience in academics, in addition to this he has worked in Industry in data warehousing domain for 3 years. He has authored many international journal and conference papers to his credit. His research interests include Artificial Intelligence, Data Analysis and Data Mining, Databases. He is associated with many professional bodies CSI, and ISCA.

Hirak Dasgupta has an experience of 16 years out of which 10 years in academics and 6 years in industry. He has supervised 6 MPhil students and one PhD student. He has presented papers in several national and international conferences and has published papers in quality journals. Currently he is Associate Professor, Symbiosis Institute of Management Studies, Symbiosis International University, Pune, Maharashtra.

Arnab Kumar De received B.Sc. in Mathematics from University of Burdwan in 2005 and M.Sc. in Mathematics from Jadavpur University in 2007. He stood 1st class 1st in B.Sc. and 1st class 3rd in M.Sc. examination. He is pursuing research work towards Ph. D. in Mathematics from University of Kalyani. Mr. De is now acting as an Assistant Professor in the Department of Mathematics, Govt. College of Engineering & Textile Technology, Serampore, INDIA. Formerly, he served Academy of Technology, India and Hooghly Engineering and Technology College, India as an Assistant Professor in the Department of Mathematics. He is a member of Indian Statistical Institute, Kolkata, India. IEEE,

Computational Intelligence Society. His research area includes Fuzzy Programming, Fuzzy Stochastic Programming, Fuzzy Sets, Fuzzy numbers, Decision Making, Operations Research, Soft Computing, Artificial Intelligence.

Sanjiva Dubey is a well known IT strategy and Innovation Expert with over 35 years of Industry and Academic experience. He was Asia Pacific Executive of IBM responsible for its IT operations across 17 countries till recently. His other career milestones include CEO of Raffles Solutions, Bhilwara Infotech, Country Head of IBM Consulting and Project executive of IBM Bharti Outsourcing project. He is a unique blend of Industry with academics who has been an Adjunct faculty with leading Indian B Schools like IIM Lucknow, Indore, Rohtak, FMS Delhi University, IIIT Delhi, IMT Gaziabad, BIMTECH and XLRI to name a few. He is Currently Professor at BIMTECH, Greater Noida India.

Sreedhar G. is working as a Associate Professor in the Department of Computer Science, Rashtiya Sanskrit Vidyapeetha (Deemed University), Tirupati, India since 2001. G. Sreedhar received his Ph.D in Computer Science and Technology from Sri Krishnadevaraya University, Anantapur, India in the year 2011. He has over 15 years of Experience in Teaching and Research in the field of Computer Science. He published more than 15 research papers related to web engineering in reputed international journals. He published 4 books from reputed international publications and he presented more than 15 research papers in various national and international conferences. He handled research projects in computer science funded by University Grants Commission, Government of India. He is a member in various professional bodies like academic council, board of studies and editorial board member in various international journals in the field of computer science, Information Technology and other related fields. He has proven knowledge in the field of Computer Science and allied research areas.

G. R. Gangadharan received the PhD degree in information and communication technology from the University of Trento, Italy, and the European University Association. He is currently working as an assistant professor at the Institute for Development and Research in Banking Technology, Hyderabad, India. His research interests include the interface between technological and business perspectives. He is a senior member of the IEEE and the ACM.

Gebeyehu Belay Gebremeskel is a postdoctoral research fellow in Chongqing University, China. He received his PhD from Chongqing University, since July 2013, Master's Degree from London South Bank University, UK and B. Sc. Degree from Alemaya University, Ethiopia. Dr. Gebeyehu gained solid experience in research and teaching in different positions and institutes. He also engaged and contributed fundamental professional skills in various IT projects and research activities. In his PhD and Master's studying program, he published more than 25 academic papers, which includes journals, conference papers, book chapters and other technical reports in his research area and computing field in general. His research interest includes Data Mining, Business Intelligence, Big Data, Machine Learning, Agent Technologies, Artificial Intelligence, Data cloud, and others in the field of Computer Science.

Rashik Gupta is taking his MBA in Business Analytics at BML Munjal University, Gurgaon India. His areas of research are consumer analytics, marketing optimisation, Social Media Analytics, Supply Chain Analytics, and big data analysis in the context of marketing analytics.

Zhongshi He is Professor and Vice Director of the College of Computer Science in Chongqing University. He is a distinguish scientist and lecturer in the college, and a Visiting Professor in few other high standard national and international universities. He received a B. Sc. and master's degree in Applied Mathematics and PhD degree in Computer Science from Chongqing University. He has been at Witwatersrand University in South Africa for Post-doctoral fellowship. His research and teaching activities have focused on Machine Learning and Artificial Intelligence. In his success, solid skills and interest to share his cumulative knowledge and experience, highly respected and honored professor in the college and in the University as a whole. His research themes include workstation design based research projects in Machine Learning and Artificial Intelligence. His research interests broad to the understanding, design, and performance of Machine Learning, Image processing, Artificial Intelligent, Data Mining and Bioinformatics. In these areas, he has worked on many practical and applicable researches, which has made numerous contributions to the field. Most of his publications and conference presentations deal with organizational issues on various real-world research issues. He has given numerous invited talks and tutorials in the other universities too. Professor He is published many high standard journals, conference papers, and other technical reports. Besides his administrative duties, Professor He is a faculty member at the College of Computer Science and responsible for many executive and academic tasks.

Ponnuru Karteek is taking his MBA in Business Analytics at BML Munjal University, Gurgaon India. His areas of research are consumer analytics, marketing optimisation, Social Media analytics, Supply Chain analytics and big data in the context of marketing analytics.

Kaushik Kumar, B.Tech (Mechanical Engineering, REC (Now NIT), Warangal), MBA (Marketing, IGNOU) and Ph.D (Engineering, Jadavpur University), is presently an Associate Professor in the Department of Mechanical Engineering, Birla Institute of Technology, Mesra, Ranchi, India. He has 14 years of Teaching & Research and over 11 years of industrial experience in a manufacturing unit of Global repute. His areas of teaching and research interest are Quality Management Systems, Optimization, Non-conventional machining, CAD / CAM, Rapid Prototyping and Composites. He has 9 Patents, 3 Book, 8 Book Chapters, 97 international Journal publications, 18 International and 8 National Conference publications to his credit. He is on the editorial board and review panel of 7 International and 1 National Journals of repute. He has been felicitated with many awards and honours.

Raghvendra Kumar has been working as Assistant Professor in the Department of Computer Science and Engineering at LNCT College, Jabalpur, MP, and as a PHD Research Scholar (Faculty of Engineering and Technology) at Jodhpur National University, Jodhpur, Rajasthan, India. He completed his Master of Technology from KIIT University, Bhubaneswar, Odisha, and his Bachelor of Technology from SRM University, Chennai, India. His research interests include Graph theory, Discrete mathematics, Robotics, Cloud computing and Algorithm. He also works as a reviewer, and an editorial and technical board member for many journals and conferences. He regularly publishes research papers in international journals and conferences and is supervising post graduate students in their research work.

Amir Manzoor is a senior faculty member in MIS/Finance Area at Bahria University, Karachi, Pakistan. He did MBA in General Management from Lahore University of Management Sciences (LUMS), Pakistan and an MBA in Finance from Bangor University, UK. He has about 10 years of corporate experience and more than six years of teaching experience. His research papers and book chapters have been published in reputed journals (such as SAGE Open) and by publishers (such as IGI Global). Amir has authored six books three of them adopted as reference texts in various reputable universities around the world. His research interests are in the areas of technology use for competitive advantage, quantitative analysis, management of academic institutions, and financial modeling.

Vinod Kumar Mishra is an Assistant Professor in the Department of Computer Science and Engineering at Bipin Tripathi Kumaon Institute of Technology, Dwarahat, Almora, India. He received his PhD in Mathematics in 2011 from Dr. Ram Manohar Lohia Avadh University, Faizabad, India. He completed his Master's degree in Mathematical Science in 2001 and another Master's degree in Computer Application in 2007. His research interests are in inventory system, queuing theory. Network Optimization, wireless network and mathematical modelling.

Priyanka Pandey is working as Assistant Professor in Computer Science and Engineering Department at L.N.C.T Group of College Jabalpur, M.P. India. She received B.E. in Information Technology from TIE Tech (RGPV University), Jabalpur, MP, India, in 2013, M. Tech. in Computer Science and Engineering from TIE Tech (RGPV University), Jabalpur, MP, India. She published many research papers in international journal and conferences including IEEE. She attends many national and international conferences, her researches areas are Computer Networks, Data Mining, wireless network and Design of Algorithms.

Prasant Kumar Pattnaik, Ph.D. (Computer Science), Fellow IETE, Senior Member IEEE is Professor at the School of Computer Engineering, KIIT University, Bhubaneswar. He has more than a decade of teaching research experience. Dr. Pattnaik has published numbers of Research papers in peer reviewed international journals and conferences. His researches areas are Computer Networks, Data Mining, cloud computing, Mobile Computing. He authored many computer science books in field of Data Mining, Robotics, Graph Theory, Turing Machine, Cryptography, Security Solutions in Cloud Computing, Mobile Computing and Privacy Preservation.

Vadlamani Ravi is a Professor in the Institute for Development and Research in Banking Technology (IDRBT), Hyderabad. He holds a PhD in Soft Computing from Osmania University, Hyderabad and RWTH Aachen, Germany (2001). Earlier, he worked as a Faculty at National University of Singapore. He visited RWTH Aachen under DAAD Long Term Research Fellowship during 1997–1999. In the last 28 years, he worked in soft computing, data mining, global/multi-criteria optimization, sentiment analysis, big data analytics. He published 168 papers in refereed international/national journals/conferences and invited chapters. He also edited a Book published by IGI Global, USA, 2007. Further, he is a referee and Editorial Board Member for several international journals of repute.

Supriyo Roy, M.Sc (Statistics), M.Tech (ORI&BM), Ph.D (Business Model Optimization), has been working as Associate Professor, Birla Institute of Technology - Mesra, Ranchi. A Post Doctoral Fellow from Airbus Group Endowed (Formerly EADS-SMI) Center for Sourcing and Management, IIM - Bangalore, Dr. Roy has a rich experience of more than 5 years in Industry and 15 years of Post Graduate Teaching. His teaching interest comprises interdisciplinary areas of Management Science, Production and Operations Management, Decision Science, Supply Chain Management, Soft Computing for Manufacturing, etc. He has to his credit published 1 Book, 10 International book chapters, 12

Conference papers and more than 45 research papers in leading International as well as National Journals. Dr. Supriyo is associated as impaneled reviewer of many International and National Journals of repute. He has been facilitated with award of 'Outstanding Contribution to Teaching' in Management Science.

Rajaram S. works as an Associate Professor, Department of Electronics and Communication Engineering, Thiagarajar College of Engineering, Madurai, India. He completed his B.E (Electronics and Communication Engineering), M.E., (Microwave & Optical Engineering) and Ph.D in Madurai Kamaraj University. He received Post Doctoral Fellowship from Georgia Institute of Technology. He has received the Young Scientist Fellowship award from TNSCST during 2001-2002 and BOYSCAST Fellowship from DST during 2010-2011.He has guided 10 PhD Scholars. He has published research articles more than 150 International conferences and 80 reputed journals. He is a reviewer for IEEE transaction and many reputed Journals. He is the co-coordinator of DST project on TIFAC Core in Wireless Technologies –Phase II, and Co-investigator for FIST, DST project and AICTE, New Delhi. In addition to, he did many Consultancy projects.

Selvakumar S. is a Professor in Computer Science & Engineering, G.K.M College of Engineering and Technology, Chennai. His research interests include in the domain of Knowledge & Data Engineering, Software Engineering, and Information Security. He has published more than 35 reputed journals and in various National and International conferences. He completed his research from Anna University, Chennai. He has 20 years of teaching experience with interests towards various fields such as software testing, data science and engineering, data warehousing and mining, and design methods.

Hanna Sawicka is an Assistant Professor in Division of Transport Systems at Poznan University of Technology, Poznan, Poland. She has an experience in academic and business practice. Her research interest is modeling of complex distribution/ logistic systems, the redesign process of real systems based on simulation techniques and multiple criteria decision aid methods – deterministic and stochastic. Hanna Sawicka graduated from Poznan University of Technology (2000). She had continued her educational program on doctoral studies, where in 2001 she was supported by the University of Porto, Faculty of Engineering, Porto, Portugal. In 2013 she received her Ph.D. from Warsaw University of Technology, Warsaw, Poland. Hanna Sawicka is the author of roughly 50 publications. She has also acted as a referee in the international journals, including International Journal of Multicriteria Decision Making. She is an active member of EURO Working Group on Transportation and International Society on Multiple Criteria Decision Making.

Nita H. Shah is a professor in the Department of Mathematics, Gujarat University, Ahmedabad, India. She received her Ph.D. in inventory control management, operations research. Currently, she is engaged in research in inventory control and management, supply chain management, forecasting and information technology and information systems, neural networks, sensors and image processing. She has more than 350+ papers published in international and national journals. She is author of nine books. She is serving as a member of the editorial board of Investigation Operational, Journal of Social Science and Management, International Journal of Industrial Engineering and Computations and Mathematics Today.

Pourya Shamsolmoali earned a PhD in Computer Science at Johns Hopkins University in New Delhi, India. Now, he works at the Euro-Mediterranean Center on Climate Change in the Advanced Scientific Computing Division.

Arunesh Sharan is a Consultant & Advisor, Former IBM Project Executive, Former CEO Iconnectiva. An alumnus of IIT Kanpur and XLRI Jameshdpur.

Timmaraju Srimanyu holds an M. Tech (IT) from University of Hyderabad. He is presently working in Dell International Services as a Software Dev Analyst. His research interests include cloud computing and opinion mining.

R. Suganya currently serves as an Assistant Professor at the Department of Information Technology at Thiagarajar College of Engineering, Madurai. Her areas of interest include Medical imaging, Big data Computing, Software Engineering, Video processing, Wireless Sensor Networks and Automation. Dr. R. Suganya completed her B. E. (Computer Science and Engineering) from R.V.S College of Engineering in 2003. She then completed her M.E (Computer Science and Engineering) from P.S.N.A College of Engineering. She completed her PhD in Information and Communication Engineering from Anna University, Chennai.She has published in 11 International Conference, 12 International Journal and One Edited Book Chapter. She has publication in eight Scopus indexed journals. He has published a Book on Classification of US liver images using Machine Learning techniques. She is a reviewer for many Journals. She is working with Thiagarajar College of Engineering, Madurai since 2006.

K. Suneetha obtained her Bachelor's Degree in Sciences from S.V.University Tirupathi. Then she obtained her Master's degree in Computer Applications from S.V.University, 2000. She is working in the Department of Master of Computer Applications at Sree Vidyanikethan Engineering College, A.Rangampet, Tirupati since 2003. She presented many papers at National and Internal Conferences and published articles in National & International journals. Her domain areas are Data Warehousing and Data Mining, Web Mining, Data Analytics.

Himanshu Tiruwa has completed his M.Tech. in Computer Science and Engineering from Department of Computer Science and Engineering at Bipin Tripathi Kumaon Institute of Technology, Dwarahat, Almora, Uttarakhand, India

Khadija Ali Vakeel is a doctoral student in the area of Information Systems at Indian Institute of Management Indore, India. She is pursuing her thesis in the area of consumer behavior post online service failure with emphasis to emerging markets. Her current research interests include service failure, e-commerce, text mining and social media. Her work has been accepted for presentation at Annual meeting organized by Academy of Management (AOM) 2016. She has presented her research at various reputed international and national conferences such as China India Insights Program 2015, ACM Research in Adaptive and Convergent Systems 2015 among others. During the FPM program, she was one of the Indian delegate to visit China as part of cultural exchange in 2015.

Malathi Velu has completed a Master of Technology degree at VIT University in India.

Chai Yi is currently the Vis Director of College of Automation in Chongqing University. He holds a PhD degree major in Control theory and Engineering and Master's degree major in Industry Automation from Chongqing University, and his first degree from National University of Defense Technology major in Electronic Engineering, China. Professor Chai is a distinguished full professor in Chongqing University. He is a principal postgraduate courses' lecturer and PhD tutor, honorable academician and researcher in his field and in the college in general. Because of his deep academic scholastic, he innovated and running more than 40 national projects. Professor Chai is the famous and known academician, and in his successful achievement and patented work, he received more than 9 national awards.

Masoumeh Zareapoor works as a postdoctoral researcher in the institute of image processing and pattern recognition, Shanghai Jiao Tong University. She received her Ph.D. from Jamia Hamdard University, India in 2015. Her research interests include data mining, pattern recognition, and big data.

Index

A

Access preferences. Technical and analytical literacy 209

aggregate production planning 353, 376-378

Ambivalence 230, 237

analytics 1-7, 12-14, 50-51, 91, 98, 133, 143, 159, 162, 164-165, 169-170, 192-193, 198, 208-213, 217-223, 225-226, 236, 240, 242-244, 246-249, 257, 259-262, 265-266, 268, 273, 275-277, 279-283, 285, 287, 289, 291, 293-296

Anonymity 225, 227-228, 237

aspect based sentiment analysis 162, 166, 170-171, 173, 175, 177, 179, 182, 184-185, 189-190

association rule mining 4, 30, 52, 54, 59-61, 68, 104, 152, 250, 252

association rules 14-15, 30-33, 59-60, 86, 104, 252, 263, 278, 281

B

Bayes classifier 178, 191, 272, 315-318, 328-329, 332

Bayesian Network (BN) 191

big data 14-15, 34, 48, 50-51, 90-91, 98-99, 123, 126, 128, 138-141, 159, 162, 169, 171, 174, 219, 226, 234-237, 240-252, 259-260, 262, 265-266, 268-269, 272, 276-296

big data analysis 50, 139, 250, 269, 280, 284-285, 290, 292-295

business intelligence 7, 51, 142-143, 149-150, 156, 158-159, 161-162, 176, 209-210, 246-247, 275, 279, 283, 291-292, 295, 298, 360

C

Cauchy distribution 353, 355, 359, 367, 369

Centrality analysis 250-251, 255-256

Centralized BI Structure 224

Chance constrained programming 353, 355

Classification Theory 317, 339

cloud computing 22, 98, 241, 243, 245, 247, 262, 278-280, 379-380, 387, 395-396

clustering 4, 15, 18-20, 26-27, 30, 34, 37, 52-55, 60, 68-69, 87, 91-92, 99, 103-106, 112, 116-117, 124-126, 195, 202, 244, 250-251, 253, 256-258, 263, 280

Commonality Cloud 192

Comparision Cloud 192

complex decision problems 315-316, 320, 335

computational intelligence 86-88, 124, 142, 244

credit card fraud 29, 62-63, 65-66, 69-75, 78, 85-89, 213, 261

credit period 341-344, 347, 352

D

data analysis 16, 19-20, 30, 33-35, 50-52, 54, 59, 67, 91-92, 100, 106, 119, 121, 123, 131-132, 135, 137-139, 142, 152, 159, 169, 171, 215, 245, 250, 262-263, 269, 277, 280, 282, 284-285, 290, 292-295

Data Anonymization 232, 237

Data Classification 34, 37-38, 43, 51

data mining 14-17, 19-23, 27, 29-34, 36-38, 51-54, 59-64, 67-69, 71, 73, 76-77, 81, 85, 87-88, 90, 97, 99-100, 107, 112-113, 117, 120-121, 123-126, 160, 175-176, 190, 209, 224-225, 227, 234, 244-245, 250-252, 257-258, 262-265, 269, 271, 278-283, 291, 298, 384, 395

data prediction 1, 36

Data proximity 126

Decentralized BI Structure 224

decision maker 267-268, 284, 316, 318-321, 324, 330, 335-336, 339

decision making 6, 15, 19, 23-24, 30, 50, 159, 162-163, 165, 209-213, 217, 219-220, 224, 247-248, 250, 277, 285, 291-292, 294, 315-316, 318, 335-337, 339-340, 353, 359-360, 366, 373-375, 379-381, 385-386, 394-396

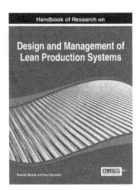
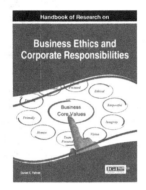

Stay Current on the Latest Emerging Research Developments

Become an IGI Global Reviewer for Authored Book Projects

The overall success of an authored book project is dependent on quality and timely reviews.

In this competitive age of scholarly publishing, constructive and timely feedback significantly decreases the turnaround time of manuscripts from submission to acceptance, allowing the publication and discovery of progressive research at a much more expeditious rate. Several IGI Global authored book projects are currently seeking highly qualified experts in the field to fill vacancies on their respective editorial review boards:

Applications may be sent to:
development@igi-global.com

Applicants must have a doctorate (or an equivalent degree) as well as publishing and reviewing experience. Reviewers are asked to write reviews in a timely, collegial, and constructive manner. All reviewers will begin their role on an ad-hoc basis for a period of one year, and upon successful completion of this term can be considered for full editorial review board status, with the potential for a subsequent promotion to Associate Editor.

If you have a colleague that may be interested in this opportunity, we encourage you to share this information with them.

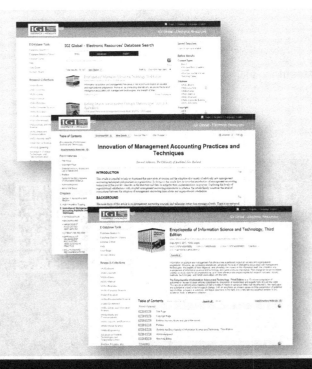

Become an IRMA Member

Members of the **Information Resources Management Association (IRMA)** understand the importance of community within their field of study. The Information Resources Management Association is an ideal venue through which professionals, students, and academicians can convene and share the latest industry innovations and scholarly research that is changing the field of information science and technology. Become a member today and enjoy the benefits of membership as well as the opportunity to collaborate and network with fellow experts in the field.

IRMA Membership Benefits:

- **One FREE Journal Subscription**

- **30% Off Additional Journal Subscriptions**

- **20% Off Book Purchases**

- Updates on the latest events and research on Information Resources Management through the IRMA-L listserv.

- Updates on new open access and downloadable content added to Research IRM.

- A copy of the Information Technology Management Newsletter twice a year.

- A certificate of membership.

IRMA Membership $195

Scan code or visit **irma-international.org** and begin by selecting your free journal subscription.

Membership is good for one full year.

Printed in the United States
By Bookmasters